1 MONTH OF FREE READING

at

www.ForgottenBooks.com

By purchasing this book you are eligible for one month membership to ForgottenBooks.com, giving you unlimited access to our entire collection of over 1,000,000 titles via our web site and mobile apps.

To claim your free month visit: www.forgottenbooks.com/free45442

* Offer is valid for 45 days from date of purchase. Terms and conditions apply.

ISBN 978-0-265-39678-0
PIBN 10045442

This book is a reproduction of an important historical work. Forgotten Books uses state-of-the-art technology to digitally reconstruct the work, preserving the original format whilst repairing imperfections present in the aged copy. In rare cases, an imperfection in the original, such as a blemish or missing page, may be replicated in our edition. We do, however, repair the vast majority of imperfections successfully; any imperfections that remain are intentionally left to preserve the state of such historical works.

Forgotten Books is a registered trademark of FB &c Ltd.
Copyright © 2018 FB &c Ltd.
FB &c Ltd, Dalton House, 60 Windsor Avenue, London, SW19 2RR.
Company number 08720141. Registered in England and Wales.

For support please visit www.forgottenbooks.com

THE ROMAN REPUBLIC
AND
THE FOUNDER OF THE EMPIRE

OXFORD UNIVERSITY PRESS
London   Edinburgh   Glasgow   Copenhagen
New York   Toronto   Melbourne   Cape Town
Bombay   Calcutta   Madras   Shanghai
HUMPHREY MILFORD
Publisher to the University

THE ROMAN REPUBLIC

AND

THE FOUNDER OF THE EMPIRE

BY

T. RICE HOLMES
[Thomas Edward]

HON. LITT.D. (DUBLIN.); HON. D.LITT. (OXON.);
HONORARY MEMBER OF THE ISTITVTO
PER LA STORIA DI ROMA ANTICA

VOLUME I

(FROM THE ORIGINS TO 58 B.C.)

OXFORD
AT THE CLARENDON PRESS
1923

DG
254
H6
v.1

Printed in England

PREFACE

IN this book, as in *Caesar's Conquest of Gaul* and *Ancient Britain*, I have discussed in Part II every problem that arose, and have provided readers who may wish to get behind my narrative with the means of forming their own opinion. Those who do not know Latin or Greek will have little or no difficulty in following the arguments; for where I have quoted extracts from ancient writers I have given their substance or translated them. I hope that those who read only for entertainment or to acquire a general knowledge of the subject will not be deterred by the sight of the Second Part (which some might not find tedious) from testing the staple of the book. In four chapters (VII, VIII, X, and XII), treating of events which I had described before, I have shortened the narrative as far as I could without impairing clearness or weakening force, omitting passages which, though they were required in works devoted to Gaul and Britain, could be dispensed with in a history of Rome.

  1 AKEHURST STREET,
     ROEHAMPTON, S.W. 15,
       November 16, 1922.

CONTENTS

OF THE FIRST VOLUME

	PAGE
PREFACE	v
LIST OF ILLUSTRATIONS	xvi

PART I

CHAPTER I

INTRODUCTION

Plan of the work	1
Prehistoric origins of the Roman People	1
Early struggles of the Republic	2
Achievement of supremacy in Italy	3
Sovereignty of the people	5
Status of Latins and Italian allies	5
The Punic wars	6
Their consequences in Italy	9
The provinces of Sicily and Spain	9
Formation of the province of Transalpine Gaul	9
Roman dominion extended to Greece and Asia	10
Influence of foreign wars upon the Roman constitution	11
Reaction, social and economic, of conquest upon Italy	12
Influence of Greek culture	13
Ruin of small landholders	13
Discontent of Italian allies	14
Tiberius Gracchus	15
The agrarian question and the movement for Italian enfranchisement after his death	19
Gaius Gracchus	21
The 'ultimate decree' and the fate of Gaius	29
The work of the Gracchi	30
Trial and acquittal of Opimius	31
A series of agrarian laws	31
Servilius Glaucia	32
The colony of Narbo	33
Effect of the Jugurthine war upon senatorial authority	33
Military innovations of Marius	37
Temporary reaction (?) in favour of the Senate	39

CONTENTS

	PAGE
Marius saves Italy from the Cimbri and Teutoni	39
Marius, Saturninus, and Glaucia	40
Law for excluding aliens	42
Condemnation of Rutilius Rufus	42
Livius Drusus	42
The Social War	45
Citizenship offered to Italians	46
Latin rights conferred upon Transpadane communities	47
Financial crisis	47
Sulpicius Rufus	47
He transfers the command against Mithradates from Sulla to Marius	48
Sulla marches on Rome : flight of Marius and execution of Sulpicius	49
Legislation of Sulla	50
Massacre of Italians in Asia	51
Sulla departs for the East	51
Cinna and Marius in power	51
The Marian proscription	52
Death of Marius	53
Tyranny of Cinna	53
Sulla victorious in Greece and Asia	54
Submission of Mithradates	54
Sulla's settlement of Asia	54
Hurried preparations of Cinna and Carbo to resist Sulla	55
Death of Cinna	55
Return of Sulla	56
He subdues his enemies	56
How he approached the work of reconstruction	58
His dictatorship	58
The Terror	59
How Sulla rewarded his partisans	60
His legislation	61
He abdicates	64
His epitaph	64

CHAPTER II

THE ROMAN WORLD IN THE CICERONIAN AGE

Rome and its environs	65
Religion	68
Stoicism	80
Education	83
Tenements and private houses	87
Decoration	89

CONTENTS

	PAGE
Slaves	90
Caution needed in generalizing from contemporary notices of Roman life	92
A dinner-party	94
Country houses of the rich	96
Travelling : inns and private lodges	97
Pleasure-seekers at Baiae	98
Horse-racing and gladiatorial shows	98
Plays and players	99
Music and dancing	100
Painting and sculpture	102
Neglect of science	102
Production and publication of books	103
Medicine, dentistry, and surgery	103
Water-supply	105
Drainage	105
Baths	105
Country life and agriculture	106
Ranches	108
Vineyards and olive-gardens	108
Exports and imports	109
Harbours	110
Italian men of business abroad	111
Handicrafts and guilds	111
Specialized industries	113
Roads	113
Postal messengers	114
Inadequate police	114
Conflagrations	115
— Military system	115
— Revenue	121
— Provincial administration	121

CHAPTER III

POMPEY THE GREAT

No prospect of permanence for the Sullan constitution	133
Attempted counter-revolution of Lepidus	134
Victorious career of Sertorius in Spain	138
The rise of Pompey	143
Pompey and Metellus oppose Sertorius	146
Democratic agitation against the Sullan constitution	149
Treaty of Sertorius with Mithradates	151
Failure and death of Sertorius	151

CONTENTS

	PAGE
Pompey settles affairs in Spain	153
Continued agitation for the restoration of the tribunician power	154
Spartacus	155
His revolt subdued by Crassus	160
Crucifixion of six thousand prisoners	161
Coalition of Crassus with Pompey	161
How Roman armies endangered the Republic	162
Pompey and Crassus consuls	163
Pompey backed by the populace and the knights	164
Restoration of the tribunician power	164
Reform of the juries	164
The remnant of the Sullan constitution	166
Sulla's surviving victims still dangerous	166
Disputes between Pompey and Crassus patched up by a hollow reconciliation	166
Prosecution of Cornelius	167
Pompey in retirement	167
The Mediterranean pirates	167
Extraordinary powers for their suppression conferred upon Pompey	169
Significance of the Gabinian law	172
Pompey suppresses piracy	174
Mithradates prepares to renew war with Rome	176
Alleged bequest of Bithynia to the Roman People	177
Lucullus and Cotta dispatched to the theatre of war	178
How Lucullus obtained his command	178
His character and antecedents	179
His army	179
His strategical plans	180
Disaster at Calchedon	180
Mithradates resolves to besiege Cyzicus	180
Caesar's *coup* in Asia	181
Lucullus outmanœuvres Mithradates	181
Mithradates, compelled to raise the siege, retreats to Nicomedia	183
While Lucullus destroys his fleet he escapes to Heraclea	183
Lucullus invades Pontus	184
Mithradates forced to take refuge in Armenia	187
Lucullus captures Cabira and Amisus and returns to the province of Asia	188
His brother supports him by a successful campaign in Thrace	188
Lucullus by checking Roman extortion incurs enmity in Rome	189
Tigranes refuses to surrender Mithradates	190
Fall of Heraclea	190
Lucullus captures Sinope	191
His humane treatment of Greek colonies	191
His campaign against Tigranes	192

CONTENTS

	PAGE
Siege of Tigranocerta	193
Victory of Lucullus near Tigranocerta	195
Tigranocerta captured	195
Intrigues in Rome against Lucullus	195
Mithradates constrains Tigranes to continue war	196
Lucullus marches against Artaxata	197
but is forced by mutiny to retreat	197
He captures Nisibis	197
but is superseded	198
P. Clodius stirs up the soldiery against him	198
Mithradates recovers Pontus	199
Humiliation of Lucullus	199
Why and how far he failed	200
Unlimited authority in the East granted to Pompey by the Manilian law	201
Cicero's speech in favour of the bill	202
Stormy interview of Pompey with Lucullus	204
Pompey's army	205
His treaty with Phraates	205
His successful campaign against Mithradates	206
Tigranes surrenders : terms imposed upon him by Pompey	207
His son made prisoner	208
Pompey declines to recognize the Euphrates as the Romano-Parthian frontier	208
He subdues the Albanians and Iberians	208
He breaks faith with Phraates	209
His settlement of Pontus	209
He annexes Syria	212
His treatment of Phraates	213
He invades Palestine and captures Jerusalem	214
Last efforts of Mithradates	215
His son Pharnaces plots against him : his death and character	216
Pompey's settlement of Syria	218
He returns to Pontus and makes final arrangements	218
The people of Italy in this period	219

CHAPTER IV

THE *ANNUS MIRABILIS* OF CICERO AND THE RISE OF CAESAR

Early life of Caesar	221
His quaestorship in Spain	224
He supports the agitation of the Transpadanes for Roman citizenship	225

CONTENTS

	PAGE
His aedileship	225
He fails to obtain a command in Egypt	227
His political standing in 65 B.C.	227
Marcus Cicero	227
His speech for Roscius of Ameria	228
He studies in the East	229
He tells a story against himself	229
His prosecution of Verres	230
Beginning of his correspondence with Atticus	231
Cicero in his environment	231
Catiline	232
The 'first conspiracy of Catiline'	234
Cicero's canvass for the consulship	235
Catiline acquitted of malversation	236
Candidates for the consulship	236
Caesar and Crassus fail to procure the enfranchisement of the Transpadanes	237
Q. Cicero advises Marcus about the conduct of his canvass	238
Dissolution of electioneering clubs	240
Cicero's invective against his fellow-candidate Catiline	240
Cicero elected	241
Catiline acquitted in Caesar's court of murder	241
The right of electing the Chief Pontiff restored through Caesar's influence to the people	242
Rullus proposes an agrarian law in the interest of Caesar and Crassus	242
Cicero's speeches against the bill	245
Cicero wins an oratorical triumph	249
The prosecution of Rabirius	249
Farcical termination of the trial	252
Caesar elected Chief Pontiff	253
Cicero defends Gaius Calpurnius Piso	253
opposes the rehabilitation of the sons of men proscribed by Sulla	253
and limits the duration of 'free embassies'	253
Catiline's designs and his supporters	253
His enterprise foredoomed to fail	256
His candidature for the consulship	256
Cicero challenges him to explain his seditious utterances: his defiant reply	258
His candidature fails	259
He purposes to resort to violence	259
Crassus furnishes Cicero with evidence against him	259
The Senate passes the ultimate decree	260
Cicero's precautionary measures	260
Financial crisis	261
Catiline instructs his accomplices in the house of Laeca	261

CONTENTS

	PAGE
Abortive plot to assassinate Cicero	262
Cicero's first oration against Catiline	262
Catiline joins his adherents in Etruria	263
Manlius appeals to Marcius Rex	263
Cicero informs the people of the state of affairs	264
Catiline proclaimed a public enemy	264
His accomplices plan an outbreak in Rome	265
Cicero defends the consul-elect Murena against a charge of bribery	266
He obtains evidence against the conspirators	267
who are arrested and brought before the Senate	269
They admit their guilt	270
and are committed to the custody of senators	271
An extraordinary honour conferred upon Cicero	272
He addresses the people	272
L. Tarquinius calumniates Crassus	272
The conspirators declared public enemies: attempts to release them	273
Debate in the Senate on their punishment	273
Their execution	277
Controversy on the conduct of Cicero reviewed	278
Sequel of the execution	282
Cicero attacked by Metellus Nepos	282

CHAPTER V

THE DISILLUSIONMENT OF POMPEY AND THE CONSEQUENT TRIUMVIRATE

Cicero's self-laudatory letter to Pompey	284
Caesar, as praetor, courts Pompey's favour	284
Metellus Nepos, in collusion with Caesar, proposes the recall of Pompey to save the State	285
Cato opposes Metellus: uproar in the Forum	285
The Senate suspends Caesar from office	286
but reinstates him	286
Defeat and death of Catiline	287
Adherents of Catiline condemned	287
L. Vettius fails to substantiate a charge against Caesar	288
Cicero disappointed by Pompey's answer to his letter	288
Pompey's homeward journey	289
He unexpectedly disbands his army	290
Clodius enters Caesar's house in female dress during a religious festival	292
Bill for the appointment of a commission to try him for sacrilege	292
Cicero's unfavourable opinion of Pompey	293
Pompey invited to speak on the bill	293

CONTENTS

	PAGE
Crassus eulogizes Cicero's consulship	294
The bill shelved : Clodius to be tried by a jury	295
The trial	296
Crassus bribes jurors to acquit Clodius	297
Acquittal by a small majority	297
Cicero denounces the corrupt jurors and inveighs against Clodius	298
Crassus enables Caesar to satisfy his creditors and assume the government of Further Spain	299
Pompey anxious for confirmation of his arrangements in the East	299
He celebrates his third triumph	300
Caesar's operations in Further Spain	301
Strained relations between the Senate and the knights	303
Pompey fails to obtain allotments for his veterans	305
Ariovistus and the Helvetii in Gaul	306
Caesar's candidature for the consulship alarms the Senate : attitude of Cicero	307
Coalition of Caesar, Crassus, and Pompey	308
Caesar and Bibulus elected consuls	309
Cicero disinclined to accept Caesar's overtures	311

CHAPTER VI
THE FIRST CONSULSHIP OF CAESAR AND THE EXILE OF CICERO

Caesar's agrarian laws	312
Clodius qualified by the aid of Caesar to become a tribune	317
Pompey marries Caesar's daughter	319
The ' Daily Gazette '	319
Amendment of the law relating to juries	319
Caesar's attempt to purify provincial administration	319
Cicero unwilling to accept office from Caesar	320
He describes the unpopularity of the triumvirs	320
Caesar conciliates the farmers of the taxes	322
Pompey's settlement of the East confirmed	323
The mysterious affair of L. Vettius	323
Caesar honours Ariovistus	325
He obtains the provinces of Gaul	325
His bargain with Ptolemy Auletes	326
He resolves to prevent Cicero from invalidating his laws	327
Futile attacks on Caesar after his consulship	327
Cicero fears the hostility of Clodius	328
but is reassured by Pompey	329
Legislation of Clodius	329
His bill directed against Cicero	331

xiv CONTENTS

	PAGE
General sympathy with Cicero	331
Pompey fails him	333
He goes into voluntary exile	333
Caesar then goes to encounter the Helvetii	336

PART II

THE AUTHORITIES OF OUR AUTHORITIES	337
THE UNREFORMED AND THE JULIAN CALENDAR	339
THE EQUIVALENTS IN OUR MONEY OF THE SESTERCE, THE DENARIUS, AND THE TALENT	344
THE LAWS OF THE PERIOD 133–81 B. C.—	
The alleged law of C. Gracchus for reforming the Senate	345
The date of the Gracchan colonial law	347
The attempts of C. Gracchus to extend the franchise	348
The law of Drusus exempting Latins from the punishment of flogging	350
The *lex Thoria*	351
The judiciary law of Q. Servilius Caepio	354
The laws of Saturninus	354
The judiciary law of the younger Drusus	355
The Julian law (90 B. C.)	356
Did Sulla absolutely deprive the tribunes of legislative power?	357
THE POPULATION OF ROME	360
THE ATTEMPTED REVOLUTION OF LEPIDUS.—	
Sallust's report of the speech of Lepidus	363
The corn laws of 78 and 73 B. C.	363
The rebellion of Lepidus	365
THE CHRONOLOGY OF THE SERTORIAN WAR	369
THE DATE OF POMPEY'S FIRST TRIUMPH	375
THE PASS BY WHICH POMPEY CROSSED THE ALPS	376
POMPEY'S LETTER TO THE SENATE	378
THE TREATY BETWEEN SERTORIUS AND MITHRADATES	378
THE WAR OF SERTORIUS	379
THE CORN LAW OF TERENTIUS AND CASSIUS AND THE DISTRIBUTION OF CORN IN 62–58 B. C.	384
THE *LEX PLOTIA* (OR *PLAUTIA*) *DE REDITU LEPIDANORUM*	385
SPARTACUS	386
THE FIRST CONSULSHIP OF POMPEY AND CRASSUS.—	
Did Pompey and Crassus retain their armies during their first consulship?	390
The *equites* and the *tribuni aerarii* mentioned in the Aurelian law	391
Did Sulla abolish the farming of taxes in Asia, and was it restored by Pompey?	395

CONTENTS

	PAGE
Were the 'Knights' opposed to the Gabinian law?	396
The debate on the Gabinian law	396

POMPEY AND THE MEDITERRANEAN PIRATES 397
WAS BITHYNIA BEQUEATHED TO ROME? 398
LUCULLUS IN THE THIRD MITHRADATIC WAR.—
    The chronology of the war 398
    The alleged invasion of the province Asia by Mithradates . 403
    The earlier operations of Lucullus 403
    The operations between Amisus and Cabira 404
    The numerical strength of the armies of Lucullus and Tigranes 408
    Tigranocerta 409
    The date of the siege of Nisibis 425
    The campaigns of Mithradates against Fabius and Triarius and
        the ultimate failure of Lucullus 425

POMPEY IN THE EAST.—
    Did Pompey and his army winter in Cilicia before he marched
        against Mithradates? 426
    The strength of Pompey's army in 66 B.C. 427
    Pompey's campaign against Mithradates 428
    Pompey's winter-quarters in 65–64 B.C. 433
    The date of the award made by Pompey to Deiotarus . . 434
    The 'eleven cities' of Pontus 434
    Some incredible statements in the original authorities . . 435

WAS CAESAR BORN IN 100 OR IN 102 B.C.? 436
EARLY EVENTS IN THE LIFE OF CAESAR 442
CICERO'S TUSCULAN VILLA 444
**CATILINE'S INTENDED CANDIDATURE FOR THE CONSULSHIP IN 688
(66 B.C.)** 445
THE SO-CALLED FIRST CONSPIRACY OF CATILINE . . . 446
CICERO'S ALLEGED DEFENCE OF CATILINE 449
THE *COMMENTARIOLUM PETITIONIS* 450
ON CASSIUS DIO, XXXVII, 37, 1 451
THE PROSECUTION OF RABIRIUS 452
THE CONSPIRACY OF CATILINE.—
    Some disputable statements of Sallust 455
    Cicero's relinquishment of his claim to the province of Macedonia 457
    The date of the consular election in 63 B.C. 458
    The dates of the attempt to murder Cicero and of his first
        oration against Catiline 461
    Catiline's pretended intention of going to Massilia . . 465
    The plan of Catiline for conflagration and massacre in Rome . 466
    The mission of Metellus Nepos 466
    The senatorial debate on December 5, 63 B.C. . . . 467
    The execution of the conspirators 470
    The alleged complicity of Caesar and Crassus in the conspiracy 470

CONTENTS

	PAGE
The Consular Provinces allotted by the Senate before the Elections of 60 B. C.	474
Caesar's Coalition with Pompey and Crassus	474
The First Consulship of Caesar.—	
The agrarian laws	476
The affair of L. Vettius	479
A complaint of Cicero against Torquatus	482
Cicero's Journey into Exile	482
ADDENDA	486
CORRIGENDA	486

LIST OF ILLUSTRATIONS

Italy	*to face page* 1
A ballistic engine	*page* 118
Spain	*to face page* 139
Asia Minor	,, ,, 177
The campaign of Cabira	*page* 186

[The dates in the narrative before January 1, 709 (45 B.C.) belong to the old calendar. From March 696 (58 B.C.) the corresponding Julian dates are given in the margin. The earlier events of the Roman year 705, for instance, are often loosely ascribed to 49 B.C.; but all dates in that year from January 1 to February 20 really belonged to 50.]

THE ROMAN REPUBLIC
AND
THE FOUNDER OF THE EMPIRE

CHAPTER I
INTRODUCTION

THIS book is intended to complete a trilogy, of which the former parts were devoted to the conquest of Gaul and to ancient Britain. Embracing the period that began with the reaction against the dictatorship of Sulla and ended with the death of Caesar, it coincides with the activity of the four representative men who were the chief actors in the dying Republic; and the events of the last twenty years, illustrated by original authorities, in particular by the correspondence of Cicero and the memoirs of Caesar and his continuators, are better attested than those of any other epoch of Roman history. But, just as, apart from its purely military aspects, the Civil War which occupied the closing years of Caesar's life and the reconstructive work which he performed in the last six months cannot be understood without knowledge of the developments that followed the death of Sulla, so, in order to grasp their meaning, one must discern the main lines of the revolution that began in the tribunate of Tiberius Gracchus. A brief sketch will suffice to remind the reader of the steps by which the Romans became supreme in Italy and extended their rule over the basin of the Mediterranean Sea.

Plan of the work

The origin of the Roman State must be sought in prehistoric times. Archaeology has shown that Italy, which Mommsen believed to have been uninhabited before metals were smelted and agriculture began, was occupied

Prehistoric Origins of the Roman People.

in the Old Stone Age by a people specimens of whose handiwork are to be seen in the Prehistoric Museum of Rome. When the Neolithic Age was far advanced and Italy, inhabited by tribes whose long narrow skulls show that they belonged to the so-called Mediterranean race, was already in communication with Central Europe, invaders from the region of the Danube, who introduced the use of bronze, began to settle in the valley of the Po, and built on platforms supported by piles villages, now known as *terremare*,[1] of which the precise orientation and the orderly arrangement, closely resembling that of a Roman camp, have led scholars to identify them with the ancestors of the primitive Roman people. At all events they were the earliest settlers of the Italic stock, which, at the dawn of history, overran Central Italy as well as Lombardy, and shared the peninsula with the Etruscans, who had come from the East, the Ligurians of the Alpine valleys and the north-western seaboard, and the Greek colonists of the south. By that time the Latins, probably descendants of the immigrants who had built the *terremare*, were mingled with the primitive population on the Alban hills and in Rome itself, while the Etruscans were about to become the leading power in Italy.[2] In the later period of the Roman monarchy they were masters not only of the Lombard plain and of Etruria, but also of Latium and even of Campania; and the king whose expulsion coincided with the foundation of the Republic was himself an Etruscan. The little state, which was constrained to pay for its liberation by loss of power, nevertheless entered upon the struggle for existence with advantages which it retained throughout its history. Standing on defensible hills on the southern bank of a navigable river, only fifteen miles from the sea and nearly equidistant from the northern and the southern

Early struggles of the Republic.

[1] L. Pigorini (*Bull. d. paletnol. ital.*, xxiii, 1897, pp. 56–65 and Tav. iv).
[2] See B. Modestov, *Intr^n à l'hist. rom.*, 1907, especially pp. 145–6, 151–2, 155, 159–60, 164, 167, 192, 196, 199, 207–8, 211, 213–4, 219, 224, 226–7, 229–31, 233–6, 239, 306–7, 311, 313, 339, 465; T. E. Peet, *The Stone and Bronze Ages in Italy*, 1909, pp. 331–71; and J. Déchelette, *Manuel d'arch.*, ii, 2, 1913, pp. 529–40.

extremity of the peninsula, Rome was well placed for trade; it formed an outpost against the Etruscans on the north; it was close to the kindred Latins, who served as a buffer against the Aequi and the Volsci; its central position enabled it to strike quickly in any direction; and the discipline which it had undergone at the hands of its Etruscan rulers had given it a citizen army which was from the first superior in quality to any of its enemies. Moreover, it was aided consistently by a good fortune which the virtues inherited from its ancestors and the diligence with which each successive step was secured before the next was made, deserved; it took advantage of dissensions among the powers that were alarmed by its growing strength; and it was not seriously weakened by the internal struggle, almost exactly contemporaneous with the contest for the supremacy of Italy, between the patricians and the plebeians [1]: for, notwithstanding occasional bitterness, that struggle was conducted in a spirit of compromise with moderation and good sense.

More than a century and a half elapsed before Rome became the mistress of Latium and of southern Etruria; and during the first fifty years it was all that she could do to hold her own. But, thanks to treaties of alliance which she concluded with the Latins and with the Hernici, she was able to repel the raids of the surrounding mountaineers, while the Etruscans, themselves menaced by Celts and Greeks and Samnites, suspended their hostility for a time, and after the Romans had captured the fortress of Veii, were gradually forced back to the Ciminian Forest. Even the Gallic victory of the Allia, followed by the capture of Rome, was not a real disaster, {Achievement of supremacy in Italy. Probably 387 B.C.[2]}

---

[1] Prof. T. Eric Peet (see *Class. Rev.*, xxviii, 1914, p. 71) makes the interesting conjecture that the plebeians represented the population of the Neolithic Age, whose amalgamation with the immigrants from the *terremare* formed the Roman people. But it is not necessary in this brief introduction to attempt to discuss the question of the origin of the plebeians.

[2] On the vexed question of the date see Th. Mommsen, *Röm. Forsch.*, ii, 1879, pp. 360–77; J. S. Reid (Sir J. Sandys, *Companion to Lat. Studies* ², 1913, §§ 145–6), and V. Kahrstedt (*Rhein. Mus.*, N.F., lxxii, 1918, pp. 267–74), whose conclusions *I* adopt.

for the Gauls departed with the ransom which they had exacted as suddenly as they had come ; and when, after the final subjection of the Aequi and the Volsci, the Latins and the Hernicans, who, fearing the loss of independence, had turned upon their former friends, were again admitted to alliance, they were reduced to virtual submission.

By the middle of the fourth century before our era Rome was the strongest power in Northern Italy, when, in answer to an appeal from the Samnites of Campania, who were menaced by their highland kinsmen, she entered upon the series of wars which were to decide the destiny of the peninsula. Her motive was the instinct of self-preservation, for the highlanders, if they could subdue the Campanian plain, would cross the river Liris to conquer Latium. Throughout the struggle, which lasted with intervals of peace for more than fifty years, the fortune of Rome was as constant as her tenacity. She took advantage of the long respite, due probably to enemies who threatened the southern frontier of the Samnites, that followed the first war, to crush a determined effort of her allies to throw off her yoke, and isolated from one another by stringent regulations all their communities whose territories she forbore to annex. In the most critical phase, when the Samnites renewed their offensive, the northern clans were half-hearted, while the Lucanians and Apulians, who sided with Rome, harassed her enemy from the south ; and though, before the end of the war, the Etruscans made a desperate attempt to recover their lost ground, they were defeated near Lake Vadimo. In the final period of the contest, when Samnites, Etruscans, and Celts united against Rome, the Samnites, who had pushed northward to join the Celts, were decisively beaten; the Etruscans, failing to support them, were fain to sue for peace ; and the Samnites, left to their own resources, were gradually overborne. The Romans followed up their success by separately defeating two aggressive Celtic tribes, the Senones and the Boi ; and then followed the war with King Pyrrhus of Epirus, who aimed at the conquest of the Western Mediterranean.

The Greek cities of Southern Italy, harassed by Samnite and Lucanian raids, appealed for aid to the Republic; but Tarentum, the most powerful of the group, was torn by dissension, the aristocracy desiring the protection of Rome, while the democrats accepted the championship of Pyrrhus. But the character of Pyrrhus was not equal to his ambition. When, despite his initial victories and the support which he received from Samnium and Lucania, he found that the Republic was too tough to yield, he allowed himself to be distracted by dreams of conquest in Sicily and Africa, but, failing to expel the Carthaginians from the island, recrossed the straits to suffer a decisive defeat. The supremacy of Rome in Italy was now secure.

Only a few years earlier the struggle between the patricians and the plebeians had come to an end. The plebeians achieved their aim; for they were indispensable. Since they had obtained the institution of the tribunate to protect them against consular tyranny, they had won successively the right of candidature for all the great offices of state and even for admission to the priestly colleges. The first plebeian consul entered office in the generation that followed the battle of the Allia: eighty years later the acts of the plebs in their assembly were recognized as binding upon the entire state, and the sovereignty of the people was thereby assured. *Sovereignty of the people.*

Meanwhile Rome had been taking steps for confirming her supremacy. She was far more powerful than any one of her allies. Her central position, the roads which she constructed to enable her armies to advance rapidly to any place where they might be needed, the colonies which she established to occupy strategic points, would enable her to subdue rebellion. Her own territory comprised the southern portion of Etruria, Latium, and Campania, the country of the Aequi and of the Sabines, and a part of Picenum, besides outlying districts which had been confiscated. Colonies of Roman citizens guarded the coast of Latium and the Adriatic; Latin colonies, so called because they retained certain rights which had *Status of Latins and Italian allies.*

been granted to the Latins under the original treaty of alliance, formed garrisons composed of Romans who, though they forfeited their citizenship, shared in booty and in grants of public land, while they helped to Romanize the people in whose country they were settled. The rights and obligations of the Italian allies differed according to the treaties which they had severally made with Rome ; but while all were bound to furnish contingents to the Roman army and had no voice in matters of foreign policy, they were left free to manage their own affairs. To guard against their combining to recover independence, the paramount power forbade them in many cases to trade or even to intermarry with each other, and favoured the local aristocracies, on whose support it could rely. Within the Roman state itself there were varieties of privilege. Besides the colonies of Roman citizens were certain Latin communities which had been enfranchised fully and others which, while they possessed every civil right, had no voice in electing to the great offices of state; but, subject to the authority of the Roman magistrates, all enjoyed local self-government, though justice was administered by prefects sent from Rome.

The Punic wars.

The strength of this constitution was tested when the consolidated Italian power found itself compelled either to submit to the domination of a rival or to hazard its existence in external war. The republic of Carthage, enriched by trade and established not only in Africa but also in Sardinia and Sicily, was a formidable rival. The incident that precipitated the inevitable struggle will be remembered by every reader of Roman history. When the Campanian mercenaries who had seized Messana, menaced by King Hiero of Syracuse, appealed for aid—one party to Carthage, which instantly responded, the other to Rome—the Senate anxiously deliberated before committing their country to a momentous and irrevocable decision. Wisely directed, their power was sufficient to ensure a speedy triumph. In Sicily the legions were at first successful, and Hiero soon joined what seemed the stronger side. But after the Romans, having created

INTRODUCTION 7

a fleet and defeated the Carthaginians on their own element, had utilized their victory by invading Africa, they nullified their own success by adhering to antiquated usage. One of the two consuls was recalled to preside at the elections, and with him half the army, because custom entitled citizen soldiers to return home after each campaign : the other consul, Regulus, replied to a request for peace by dictating intolerable terms. How the assistance of the Spartan *condottiere*, Xanthippus, restored the Carthaginian fortunes, is a familiar tale. For fourteen years the war dragged on. Repeated shipwrecks and naval disaster compelled the Romans to restrict the war to Sicily : but Hamilcar Barca defied all their efforts to dislodge him ; and it was not until the treasury was empty that a victory, gained by a fleet built by voluntary contributions, cut off the Carthaginians from the island and forced them to sue for peace. The loss of Western Sicily, which they were obliged to evacuate, and that of Sardinia and Corsica, which the Romans subsequently seized, were compensated by the conquest of Eastern Spain, which Hamilcar, Hasdrubal, and Hannibal successively wrought into a base for the contemplated war of revenge; but meanwhile the Romans by suppressing piracy in the Adriatic secured the friendship of the neighbouring states of Greece. When Hannibal, in order to disarm the friends of Rome in Spain, besieged Saguntum, thereby, as Roman historians insisted, violating a treaty by which its independence had been guaranteed,[1] a second Punic war became inevitable.

229–228 B. C.

219 B. C.

Hannibal invaded Italy by land because that way was not only more secure but would also enable him to open his campaign in conjunction with the Celts.[2] It may be doubted whether the Western Mediterranean was commanded by either side. Whenever Romans or Carthaginians were compelled to cross the sea, they did so

[1] See Professor Reid's article in *Journ. Rom. Studies*, iii, 1913, pp. 176–90. Livy (xxi, 2, 7) fancied that Saguntum was north of the Ebro ! beyond which Hasdrubal had agreed to make no conquest.

[2] It will be seen that *I* do not accept the well-known view of Mahan. Nor, *I* find, does Mr. David Hannay (*The Navy and Sea Power*, pp. 30–1).

unmolested. But even if the Romans had not possessed a single trireme, Hannibal would not have risked the transport of his entire army—sixty thousand men besides numerous camp-followers with nine thousand horses,[1] and thirty-seven elephants—on the long voyage from Spain to Italy over waters which had engulfed three Roman fleets. When, animated by a hatred in which there was nothing base, he essayed to humble Rome, he must have known that her resources were greater than his own ; but while he may have foreseen that the Senate, untaught by experience, would fail to make full use of them, he miscalculated when he expected that the Republic would be deserted by its Latin and Italian allies. Despite the inferiority of Roman generalship, despite the conservatism by which armies were entrusted to consuls without regard to their capacity, his enterprise was foredoomed to failure : not only superior numbers, but also close-knit political organization, and, above all, character, then consecrated in every citizen to the service of the State, assured ultimate success to Rome. Though the Celts supported the invader, though in the first three years he won four successive victories and was never beaten on Italian soil, though after Cannae all Southern Italy, except the Latin colonies and the Greek cities, joined him, and Syracuse, no longer ruled by Hiero, revolted, the communities of Northern and Central Italy stood firm ; Philip of Macedon, held in check by his Greek enemies, proved a useless ally. The

211 B. C. fall of Capua, on which the Romans would not let go their hold even when Hannibal threatened the capital, was the turning-point. Carthage, dreading the domination of the Barcine family, gave their general inadequate support ; and when the younger Hasdrubal, compelled by Scipio to evacuate Spain and prevented from joining his brother in

207 B. C. Southern Italy, was defeated on the Metaurus, the issue was no longer doubtful.

202 B. C Though, after Scipio defeated Hannibal in Africa, the Senate, always slow to accept the responsibilities of annexing territory, allowed the Carthaginians to retain

[1] Even if there were no remounts and not counting transport cattle.

their African possessions, they were forbidden to wage external war, or even, without Roman sanction, to repel attacks. The surrender of five hundred ships of war and the obligation of paying an indemnity did not prevent them from regaining strength by trade; but when, harassed beyond endurance by Masinissa, the Numidian King, who had been charged to watch them, they ventured to defend themselves, Rome took advantage of the breach of treaty. Carthage, after prolonged and desperate resistance, was destroyed, and her territory was organized as a Roman province, which the sons of Masinissa were to protect against native tribes. 149–146 B.C.

In Italy the Hannibalic War had wrought abiding changes. The Gauls paid dearly for having aided Hannibal, and on both sides of the Po those who survived defeat were gradually lost among Italian settlers. While Capua was punished by deprivation of civic rights, and its lands became Roman domain, the Apulians and Lucanians who revolted after Cannae forfeited territory likewise, and the Bruttii lost as well their status as allies. Syracuse had already been incorporated in the province of Sicily, and the two provinces of Nearer and Further Spain, in which Scipio had established Roman power, had been formed; but more than sixty years of intermittent warfare with unruly tribes elapsed before the insurrection of Viriathus, provoked by Roman extortion, was crushed by the capture of Numantia, and the peninsula, except the remoter regions, was tranquillized. A few years later communication by land with Italy was finally assured. The Romans had already invaded Transalpine Gaul to protect the Greek colony of Massilia, an old and faithful ally, against the Ligurian mountaineers. The Aedui, who inhabited the Nivernais and Western Burgundy, calculated that the support of the Republic would help them to secure ascendancy over their rivals; and by a treaty, fraught with unforeseen issues, they were recognized as Friends and Allies of the Roman People. The Allobroges, on the other hand, whose home was between the Lake of Geneva, the Rhône, and the Isère, refused to surrender a Ligurian chief who had claimed their protection; and Bituitus, King of the Arverni, with all the hosts of his dependent tribes, marched to support them. The battle in which Fabius Maximus defeated him was decisive. The Romans were now masters of the lower Rhône; and with unwonted promptitude, for they appreciated the importance of their victory, they formed the conquered territory into a province.

Meanwhile the motive of self-preservation had forced Rome to extend her dominion to the East. Philip of Macedon was a neighbour who, unchecked, would be as dangerous as Carthage, and when, in pursuance of an agreement which he had made with Antiochus of Syria for the partition of the outlying territories of Egypt, he attacked the Greek allies of Rome, the Senate induced the reluctant popular assembly to consent to war. The victory of Cynoscephalae left Philip helpless; but the Senate, as usual, avoided annexation, though Macedon, like Carthage, was rendered politically impotent. Antiochus, having conquered Coele Syria in accordance with his compact, attempted, although Rome had declared Greece free, to seize the Greek territories to which Philip had laid claim; but after his defeat at Thermopylae had compelled him to return to Asia, the victory of the Scipios at Magnesia reduced him to submission. While he was precluded under the ensuing treaty from crossing the river Halys and the Taurus, the states immediately westward of this boundary were enrolled among the Allies and Friends of Rome, and her existing allies—the King of Pergamum and the islanders of Rhodes—were rewarded by gifts of territory which would strengthen them as bulwarks of her power. But annexation was inevitable. Philip, who, though he had aided Rome against Antiochus, received no reward, intrigued with Greeks and barbarians against her: his successor by continuing this policy provoked the Senate to declare war. Even after the kingdom of Macedon had been extinguished in consequence of the victory at Pydna, the Senate, while they exacted tribute from the natives, shrank from the burden of administration; and it was not until more than twenty years had passed that the anarchy which of course resulted compelled them to create the Macedonian province. To say that the Romans did not pursue a policy of conquest is not to commend their political morality. In Greece, while they evaded the responsibilities of annexation, they encouraged intestine jealousies and feuds; for it was their interest that the communities, whose freedom they had proclaimed, should all continue weak. When at last the Achaean League, which had become strong enough to awaken their alarm, actually took up arms in vindication of their independence, the Senate felt that the time had come to end the farce. Corinth, Thebes, and Chalcis were utterly destroyed: the fortifications of every town which had joined the movement were demolished; no community was permitted to trade with any other; all were required to pay tribute; and although annexation was even now avoided, the Governor of Macedonia was charged to supervise affairs in Greece, while no Greek government that was not subservient to Rome was recognized. In Asia the course of events was not dissimilar. Pergamum and Rhodes became too prosperous: the former was weakened by attacks, encouraged by Rome, from the Galatians; the latter was deprived of the lands with which its services had been rewarded, and degraded to the status of a dependent ally. 148 B.C.

The struggle with Carthage had exerted an influence upon the Republican constitution which remained until Rome became dominant in the West and in the East. Although the sovereignty of the people was not disputed, circumstances had made the Senate virtually supreme. Since it was almost invariably recruited from those who had held great offices of state or from families which included such, these families—the nobility, as they were called, of Rome—became a separate order or a caste, which supported it from self-regarding as well as from patriotic motives, and into which no outsider could gain admission except in the rare cases in which ability or

Influence of foreign wars upon the Roman constitution.

fortune secured election to a magistracy, despite senatorial influence, for a 'new man'. The popular assembly could not act unless it was convened by a magistrate : its members had not the training nor the knowledge of affairs essential for deciding political or military questions ; and even if any of them had been so qualified, deliberate discussion in the Forum was impossible. Men therefore acquiesced in the supremacy of the experienced body which alone was competent to guide the State through a period of stress. Public opinion, hardened by custom, forbade magistrates to propose any measure to the assembly without senatorial approval ; even the granting of supply belonged not to the assembly but to the Senate ; and those magistrates who, being invested with that plenary authority which the Romans called *imperium*, had once, when the two consuls alone possessed it, treated the Senate as a merely consultative body, now, when their number had been increased by the addition of the praetors who administered justice and those who governed provinces, and some central power was needed to ensure their harmonious working, habitually deferred to them. But when the dangers that made it necessary to yield such deference had been removed and the city-state of Rome had to govern an empire, the predominance of the Senate would be challenged—especially if it governed in the interest of the class to which its members belonged.

Reaction, social and economic, of conquest upon Italy.

As the strain of the great wars became relaxed, the unrest by which such a period is always followed began to exercise reflective minds. The Roman temperament was being kneaded by new circumstances into new shapes. The Senate was confronted by problems, which in the stress of conflict had been ignored, arising from economic disturbance and social distress.

Since the downfall of the Carthaginian power riches had accrued to that community of farmers, not as the result of industrial production, but as the prize of conquest and with startling suddenness. Generals and their armies had appropriated the greater part of the booty which they had

INTRODUCTION

won ; objects of art had been plundered from Greek cities ; wagon-loads of silver had been taken from Spain. The fertile territory of Carthage, the mines of the Sierra Morena and of the Guadalquivir, the crown lands of the Macedonian kings belonged now to the Roman People. If some of the nobles who governed the newly acquired provinces were as upright as their ancestors in the time of Pyrrhus, there were others who exploited them for their own profit. The companies which contracted for the farming of the taxes, the financiers who advanced loans to embarrassed provincials amassed wealth which was making them a new power. The populace of Rome received gifts of corn and largesses of money, while spectacular entertainments were provided for their amusement. Sumptuary laws were passed in vain to curb the growing passion of Roman ladies for jewels, dress, and equipages and the growing appetite of men for the pleasures of the table. Slaves were imported in vast numbers to meet the increasing demands of a society which was becoming habituated to luxury. The high offices of state were no longer to be obtained except by the rich : one statute after another was directed against bribery ; and the Calpurnian law, 142 B. C. which established a permanent commission to try cases of extortion in the provinces, was a significant commentary on Roman administration.

Meanwhile Greek literature and Greek philosophy were fascinating the conquerors of Greece. Panaetius the Stoic and Polybius the historian became intimate with the Scipios ; and the minds of thoughtful Romans were at once expanded and unsettled by speculations of which they had not hitherto dreamed. Cato and others who suspected all innovations strove in vain to exclude strange religious rites and to expel the professors of the new learning ; indeed it was Greek influence that inspired the reformers who hoped to remedy the social evils of the State. *Influence of Greek culture.*

For while nobles and men of business were enriched, small landholders were threatened with extinction. Oppressed by prolonged military service in foreign lands, *Ruin of small landholders.*

they were being gradually ousted by their richer neighbours ; for they were compelled to sell or to abandon the plots which they could not cultivate, and a law [1] which forbade any individual to occupy more than five hundred *iugera* (three hundred and ten acres) of the public land or to keep more than a hundred horned cattle or five hundred sheep on the public pastures had not been enforced. Dispossessed husbandmen could seldom earn a livelihood as labourers, for it was more profitable to employ slaves, who were not liable to conscription. The highlanders of Central Italy, indeed, who could not be bought out by Roman citizens, still retained their little farms ; [2] but in Etruria and Apulia and in the Bruttian peninsula, where large tracts had been confiscated as a punishment for defection in the war with Hannibal, many of the inhabitants had been virtually reduced to serfdom. A vast area had been converted into cattle ranches and sheep walks tended by slaves. Rural slaves were frequently in revolt. Before Numantia fell the shepherds of Sicily, infuriated by ill usage, ravished women, murdered infants, and during ten years devastated the island until, driven into the stronghold of Tauromenium, where they were forced by famine to resort to cannibalism, the survivors, when the town was at last betrayed, were first tortured and then hurled headlong from the rocks. The Roman populace was swelled by the influx of ruined farmers, of manumitted slaves who with their descendants became citizens, and of vagrants who could find no employment. The Italians, who had fought side by side with Romans and had helped them to build up their empire, were beginning to press for admission· to the Roman citizenship because it alone gave adequate protection for person and property. Senators of liberal views admitted that reform was needed, and Gaius Laelius, whom Cicero regarded as his model statesman, contemplated a remedial

---

[1] For the purpose of this narrative it does not matter whether this (the so-called Licinian) law had really been passed in 367, as Soltau maintains (*Philol.*, lxiii, 1916, p. 529), or, as Niese tried to prove (*Hermes*, xxiii, 1888, pp. 410–28), in the earlier part of the second century B. C.

[2] See K. W. Nitzsch, *D. Gracchen*, 1847, p. 194.

INTRODUCTION

law; but he abandoned his intention when he realized the opposition which he must expect.[1] Nevertheless a young enthusiast, moved by sympathy with suffering, resolved to make the attempt.

Tiberius Sempronius Gracchus, whose mother Cornelia was a daughter of the great Scipio, and who had served with distinction in the last Punic War, was elected a tribune of the people in the year 134.[2] Passing through Etruria on his way to Numantia, he had observed that the labourers and the herdsmen were all alien slaves, and he had become inflamed with a desire, which was stimulated by Greek advisers, to restore the land to the poor;[3] but whether, if he succeeded, the slaves were to be emancipated without prospect of employment or turned loose to live on brigandage, he apparently did not reflect. His guiding motive was to increase the number of citizens whose means would qualify them for military service;[4] but we may doubt whether he considered how this end could be attained. If the small holder were sent on service, what would become of his farm? If his sons alone were of military age, how would he cultivate it without their aid? The bill which he introduced and which was not drafted until after he had taken counsel with three leading senators,[5] modified and strengthened the existing law. Five hundred *iugera* were still defined as the largest estate which any possessor of public land should be permitted to retain; but each of his sons was allowed to hold half this area as well, and compensation was to be granted in the shape of the freehold of that which the possessor occupied up to the specified limit.[6] Whatever land might remain was to be divided among needy citizens;[7] in

Tiberius Gracchus.

133 B. C.

---

[1] Plut., *T. Gr.*, 9, 3.
[2] *Ib.*, 1, 1; 4, 2; 8, 3; Vell., ii, 2, 2; App., *B. C.*, i, 9, 35.
[3] Plut., *T. Gr.*, 8, 3. 5.   [4] App., i, 9, 35; 11, 43–4.
[5] Plut., 9, 1; Cic., *Acad. Prior.*, ii, 5, 13.
[6] Cf. App., i, 11, 46 with Plut., 9, 1, and see Strachan-Davidson, *Appian : Book I*, p. 13. According to Plutarch (10, 2), Tiberius, provoked by opposition, withdrew this clause.
[7] It is not quite certain whether, as one might be inclined to infer from Appian, i, 9, 35 and 12, 53 (cf. *C. I. L.*, i, p. 90), the *I*talian allies were to benefit by the law. See G. Long, *Decline of the Rom. Republic*, i, 1864,

order to prevent the rich from encroaching upon thei holdings, no one was to be permitted to sell his allotment and, as a security for the observance of the law, thre commissioners, who were to vacate their places annually were to be charged with its administration.¹ Tiberiu perhaps realized that the agrarian question could neve be satisfactorily settled until the Italians were admitte to the citizenship, for it would appear that when h introduced his bill he hinted that he would propose measure with this aim.²

It is easy to imagine the opposition which the bil provoked. It was not only that men were required to vacate possessions which they and their fathers ha enjoyed without question for generations: those who ha increased their holdings by purchase asked indignantly whether they were to lose the money as well as the estate What was to become of the tombs of their ancestors, o the dowries which their wives had brought them anc which they had spent upon the land? How were creditors to recover loans which they had advanced upon landed security?³ Representatives of country towns whicl occupied public land,⁴ poor men who hoped to benefit by the bill flocked into Rome, swelled the rival factions, and abetted the rioters, who became more violent as the day on which the assembly were to decide its fate drew near. One of the tribunes, Marcus Octavius, was induced by the Conservatives to oppose it. When he refused to allow it to be submitted to the vote, Tiberius retaliated by using his tribunician power to suspend all administrative busi-ness; but, though he even went so far as to close the

p. 170; A. H. J. Greenidge, *Hist. of Rome*, i, 1904, p. 115, and J. Kromayer (*Neue Jahrb. f. d. klass. Altertum*, xxxiii, 1914, p. 158).

¹ Cic., *De lege agr.*, ii, 12, 31; Livy, *Epit.*, 58; App., i, 9–10, §§ 36–8. The Campanian region lay outside the scope of the law; for it was leased by the State to cultivators, who were therefore not possessors in the technical sense (*C. I. L.*, i, p. 79 (= C. G. Bruns, *Fontes iur. Rom.*⁶, 1893, p. 74); Cic., *De lege agr.*, i, 7, 21; ii, 29, 81).

² Vell., ii, 2, 3. Cf. *Eng. Hist. Rev.*, xx, 1905, p. 419
³ Plut., 9, 2; App., i, 10, 38–9.
⁴ See Greenidge, *op. cit.*, p. 118, n. 3, and *Journ. of Philol.*, xxxi, 1910, p. 269.

treasury, Octavius remained immovable. Failing to persuade him to withdraw his opposition, Tiberius, instead of awaiting the election of new tribunes, carried a motion for depriving him of office ; and, though some even of his own party were aghast at such violence, the bill was of course passed.[1]

The commission was immediately appointed, and when the names of the members—Tiberius himself, his younger brother Gaius, and his father-in-law Appius Claudius [2]— were published, it was evident that their work would be drastically performed. Attalus, the late King of Pergamum, had recently bequeathed his kingdom, which was to become the nucleus of the province Asia, to the Roman People ; and Tiberius announced his intention to propose a bill for distributing the money included in the legacy among the poor, to enable them to stock the allotments which they were to receive. Not content with this usurpation of authority, he declared that the Senate, to whom alone provincial administration belonged, had no right to determine how the cities of the Pergamene kingdom should be dealt with, and that he would refer the question to the people.[3] One of the censors charged him with aiming at monarchical power ; [4] and, finding that private citizens as well as senators were offended by his treatment of Octavius, he felt it necessary to address the people in his own defence. The gist of his apology, which ignored all constitutional practice, was that, just as Tarquin the Proud had been deposed for misrule, just as a Vestal virgin might be put to death for inchastity, so the Sovereign People might expel a tribune who opposed their will.[5] He knew that as soon as he lost the

[1] App., i, 10, § 41 ; 12-3, §§ 48-55 ; Cic., *Pro Mil.*, 27, 72 ; Diod. Sic., xxxiv, 6-7 ; Livy, *Epit.*, 58 ; Vell., ii, 2, 3 ; Plut., 10-3 ; Flor., ii, 2, 4-5 ; Dio, fr. 82, 4 ; Oros, v, 8, 3.
[2] Livy, *Epit.*, 58 ; Plut., 13, 1 ; App., i, 13, 55.
[3] Plut., 14, 1-2 ; Ps. Victor, *De vir. ill.*, 64, 5 ; Oros., v, 8, 4. According to Livy (*Epit.*, 58), the money received from the estate of Attalus was [? also] to be distributed among those for whom allotments, or sufficient allotments, of land were not available.
[4] Plut., 14, 2.
[5] *Ib.*, 15. Cf. von Stern (*Hermes*, lvi, 1921, pp. 248-50, 256), who exposes

immunity of office he would be exposed to prosecution, and in the hope of securing re-election, which was contrary to law, he promised further popular legislation. The period of military service should be shortened ; appeal to the people should be allowed from the verdicts of the courts ; and the juries should thenceforth be chosen not only from the Senate, but also, in equal proportion, from the knights [1]—so-called, although they were generally engaged in business, because they were qualified by income to serve as cavalry.[2] The wealthy landholders exerted all their influence to prevent his re-election, and he tried in vain to induce the rural voters, by whose aid he had passed the agrarian law, to leave the work of the harvest and support him. On the day of the election a band of senators and their partisans obeyed the summons of the Chief Pontiff, Scipio Nasica, to save the city from a tyrant; and Gracchus with three hundred of his followers was slain.[3] When Scipio Aemilianus heard the news he quoted the familiar line,

'So perish likewise all who work such deeds'.[4]

132 B.C. Although the Senate did not attempt to abrogate the agrarian law, which indeed was loyally administered at a later time by a staunch opponent of the Gracchan party,[5] they proceeded after the death of Tiberius to vindicate their authority by appointing a special commission to sit in judgement upon his adherents, of whom some were banished and others put to death.[6] The demagogues,
131 B.C. indeed, were by no means cowed, for a tribune, Papirius Carbo, introduced a bill for legalizing re-election to the tribunate, and Gaius Gracchus spoke strongly in its favour ;

the unsoundness of the attempts that have been made to justify Gracchus on constitutional grounds.

[1] So Plutarch says (16, 1) ; but see pp. 25, 345-7.
[2] Senators also were of course generally so qualified. The 'equestrian order' began to be recognized as such in the tribunate of C. Gracchus.
[3] Livy, *Epit.*, 58 ; Val. Max., iii, 2, 17 ; Vell., ii, 3, 1-2 ; Plut., 16-9 ; App., i, 14-6 ; Dio, fr. 82, 7-8 ; &c.
[4] Plut., 21, 3 ; Hom., *Od.*, i, 47. [5] Popilius Laenas (*C. I. L.*, i, 551).
[6] Plut., 20, 3-4 ; Cic., *De amic.*, 11, 37 ; Sall., *Iug.*, 31, 7 ; Vell., ii, 7, 3 ; Val. Max., iv, 7, 1. Cf. Strachan-Davidson, *Problems of the Rom. Crim. Law*, i, 1912, p. 239.

INTRODUCTION

but Scipio Aemilianus and Laelius opposed it, and, either through their arguments or the apathy of many of the voters, the measure was rejected.[1] Meanwhile the commissioners were struggling to fulfil their task. Appius Claudius and Publius Crassus, who had been elected as the successor of Tiberius, had died, and their places were filled by Carbo and Fulvius Flaccus, a senator of liberal views.[2] Landholders, who probably did not know how much of their possessions were public property, neglected or were unable to supply the information which the commissioners required; and any one who offered to give evidence was admitted as a witness. Men who had bought estates could not produce their title-deeds, or, when they did, found their titles, which were in many cases ambiguous, disputed. The surveyors whom the commissioners employed found it difficult to fix the boundaries between public and private land or to decide how far the rich had encroached upon the holdings of the poor.[3] The allied communities were particularly aggrieved; for, if they were not provided for by the agrarian law, they were required to prove that lands which they occupied were not part and parcel of public lands to which they were adjacent. Complaining that the decisions of the commissioners were hasty, they appealed to Scipio to protect their interests; and, feeling that their military services entitled them to sympathy, he persuaded the Senate that the commissioners should be deprived of their judicial powers.[4] One of the consuls, Sempronius Tuditanus, was entrusted instead with this invidious charge; but, finding that the difficulties of the office were too much for him, he devised a pretext for resignation. Meanwhile the commissioners were idle, and inveighed in the Forum against Scipio; the populace complained that he was favouring Italians at the expense of citizens; and his enemies

The agrarian question and the movement for Italian enfranchisement after his death.

130 B. C.

129 B. C.

---

[1] Cic., *De amic.*, 25, 96; Livy, *Epit.*, 59.
[2] Plut., 18, 2; App., i, 18, 73; *C. I. L.*, i, 554 (= H. Dessau, *Inscr. Lat.*, 25).   [3] App, i, 18, 73–7.
[4] *Ib.*, 19, 78–80. The concession was presumably sanctioned by the popular assembly, which alone had the right to amend the law of Gracchus.

C 2

insisted that his real object was to abrogate the agrarian law.[1] After Flaccus had denounced him from the Rostra he complained to the assembled people that his many services to the State were requited with ingratitude ; and that evening he was escorted from the Senate to his house by brother senators and Italian sympathizers. Next morning he was found in his bedroom, dead ; and various public men, including Flaccus, were suspected of having murdered him.[2]

The two years that followed the death of Scipio have left no trace : but it seems probable that there was already a movement, which soon afterwards came to a head, for inducing the Italian landholders, in return for the grant of citizenship, to desist from opposing the agrarian law ; and this agitation may have had some connexion with a step which was taken, perhaps at the instance of the Senate, in the ensuing year. Rome was crowded with aliens, of whom many must have been Italians ; and one of the tribunes, Marcus Pennus, proposed a law for their expulsion.[3] Gaius Gracchus, who perhaps expected that in the hands of a popular leader they would be serviceable tools, vainly argued that other states by banishing foreigners had brought ruin upon themselves.[4] The law may have been intended to facilitate a census which was taken in the following year, and according to which the number of citizens liable to military service is said to have increased within six years by seventy-seven thousand, or about twenty-five per cent.[5] If the figures are trustworthy, the agrarian law had apparently been so far successful that many of the proletariat had earned enough to qualify for service ;[6] but,

[1] Livy, *Epit.*, 59 ; Plut., *C. Gr.*, 10, 4 ; App., i, 19, 81.
[2] *Ib.*, 20, 83–5 ; Cic., *Fam.*, ix, 21, 3 ; *Q. fr.*, ii, 3, 3 : *De amic.*, 12, 41 ; Livy, *Epit.*, 59 ; Val. Max., iv, 1, 12 ; Vell., ii, 4, 5–6 ; Oros., v, 10, 9–10 ; *Schol. Bob. ad Milon.* 7, 16, ed. Stangl, p. 118 (ed. Orelli, p. 283). Cf. *Hermes*, 1921, p. 268, n. 1.   [3] Cic., *Brut.*, 28, 109 ; *De off.*, iii, 11, 47.
[4] Festus, ed. W. M. Lindsay, p. 362.
[5] Cf. Livy, *Epit.*, 59 and 60.
[6] G. Cardinali (*Studi Gracch.*, 1912, pp. 180–3) declines to draw any conclusion from this census ; but his arguments are refuted by Mr. Caspari (*Klio*, xiii, 1913, pp. 197–8).

however this may be, the opposition of the Italians was not relaxed, and in the same year Flaccus, now a consul, proposed a bill for their enfranchisement, with the proviso that individuals or communities who were unwilling to accept the suffrage should receive the right of appeal to the Roman People, and thus secure protection against tyranny. The Senate of course resisted the proposal, to which the people would have certainly refused to assent; and the bill was accordingly withdrawn.[1] The immediate consequence was that a Volscian town, Fregellae, one of the Latin colonies whose fidelity had saved the Republic in the war with Hannibal, rebelled. The premature outbreak was punished in the Roman way. The inhabitants of Fregellae were expelled; its lands were confiscated and its walls destroyed.[2] Such was the state of Italy when Gaius Gracchus entered upon his memorable tribunate.

Gaius was stronger than his elder brother. Equally enthusiastic, possessed by the same ideals, he was an astute politician who could look facts in the face, who knew how to purchase support by appealing to self-interest and was careful to secure his ground before he took each successive step. Young in years, he was habituated to the conflicts of the Forum; he had won distinction as a quaestor in the province of Sardinia and had gained experience as a member of the agrarian commission.[3] The extant fragments of his speeches reveal a vein of humour. 'Quirites,' he said, when he was introducing a bill, 'you will find that not one of us comes here without being paid. All we public speakers look for a reward, and no one presents himself before you except to get something from you. I myself . . . don't come for nothing; but I am not asking you for money, only for your appreciation and esteem.'[4] Cicero esteemed him as one of the greatest of Roman orators; and his powerful voice, his flashing eyes, his spirited gestures

Gaius Gracchus.

[1] Val. Max., ix, 5, 1; App., i, 21, 86–7.
[2] Ps.–Cic., *ad Herenn.*, iv, 15, 22; Livy, *Epit.*, 60; Vell., ii, 6, 4; Ascon., ed. Clark, p. 17, ll. 17–9 (ed. Stangl, p. 21); Plut., *C. Gr.*, 3, 1; Obseq.. 30 [90].
[3] Plut., *C. Gr.*, i, 3, 2; Gell., xv, 12, 3–4. [4] *Ib.*, vi, 10, 3.

could move even enemies to tears.¹ He started, moreover, with one great advantage which had been denied to Tiberius : since the abortive proposal of Papirius Carbo the re-election of tribunes had been legalized.² Nevertheless, Gaius entered office with the foreboding that he was doomed : his brother, he told his friends, had appeared to him in a dream and urged him to bestir himself, for they both had the same work to do, and their destiny was the same.³

123 B. C.

Gaius set before himself two great aims, which had both been foreshadowed by his brother—to extend the Roman citizenship [4] to the Italian allies, and to deprive the Senate of the control of the law courts, which it had used to shield its own members from the penalty of provincial misgovernment. He failed to see that to achieve the former by constitutional methods was impossible, for it was not less repugnant to the proletariat than to the aristocracy ; but he did realize that an indispensable condition was to have the middle classes and the populace on his side. He began by expounding his programme in the Forum. Expatiating on the grievances of the Italians, he told the assembly that a consul had scourged the quaestor of Teanum Sidicinum because the men's public baths, in which his wife chose to bathe, had not been properly or quickly prepared, and that a young officer, when a cowherd asked in jest whether the litter in which he was being carried contained a corpse, had had the man flogged to death.⁵ He reminded his hearers of his brother's murder and bade them remember how their ancestors, more upright than the Senate which had persecuted his brother's partisans, had never condemned a Roman without fair trial.⁶ The first measure which he proposed, disqualifying magistrates who had been deposed by the people for further office, and intended to punish Octavius for his

---

¹ Cic., *Pro Font.*, 17, 39 ; *Brut.*, 33, 125–6 ; *De or.*, iii, 56, 214 ; Plut., *T. Gr.*, 2, 2–4 ; Tac., *Dial.*, 18.
² App., i, 21, 90. Cf. Strachan-Davidson, *Appian : Book I*, p. 23.
³ Cic., *De div.*, i, 26, 56 ; Plut., *C. Gr.*, 1, 4.
⁴ Or at least the suffrage. See pp. 28–9, 348–50.
⁵ Gell., x, 3, 2–3. Cf. § 17.   ⁶ Plut., *C. Gr.*, 3, 3

opposition to Tiberius, was dropped in deference to the remonstrance of his mother.[1] The second, which was designed to prevent the renewal of commissions such as that by which the adherents of Tiberius had been condemned, declared it illegal for any magistrate to pronounce that a citizen had forfeited his civil rights : in other words, it laid down the principle that such forfeiture could only be ordained by a court authorized by popular decree. Substantially it was a re-enactment of old laws—the Valerian, which secured the right of appeal to the people from condemnation by a magistrate, and the Porcian, which, without prohibiting the punishment of death, gave additional sanction to such an appeal.[2] The law, which was either expressly declared or treated as being retrospective, was forthwith put in motion : Popillius Laenas, the consul who had punished the adherents of Tiberius, was on the motion of Gaius declared an outlaw, and retired into exile.[3] Having thus avenged his brother, Gaius brought forward a series of measures which were passed by the popular assembly without reference to, or in defiance of, the Senate. His brother's agrarian law, the working of which had been hampered by the enforced inactivity of the commission, was re-enacted or revised, and the judicial powers of the commissioners were probably restored.[4] He attempted to

[1] *Ib.*, 4, 1. In regard to the order of Gracchus's laws see E. Kornemann, *Klio*, Beih. i, 1903, pp. 42–51, and pp. 347–50, *infra*.

[2] *Ib.*; Cic., *Pro Rab.*, 4, 12 ; *In Cat.*, iv, 5, 10 ; *Schol. Ambros. in Cat.*, iv, § 10, ed. Stangl, p. 271 (ed. Orelli, p. 370). Cf. Greenidge, *Legal Procedure*, &c., pp. 318–24, and Strachan-Davidson, *Problems*, &c., i, 239. *I* doubt whether von Stern (*Hermes*, 1921, p. 272) is right in identifying this law with the law *NE QVIS IVDICIO CIRCVMVENIRETVR* (Cic., *Pro Cluent.*, 55, 151), which was intended to prevent the unjust conviction of innocent men and was re-enacted by Sulla in his law against murder (*de sicariis*).

[3] Cic., *De domo*, 31, 82 ; *De leg.*, iii, 11, 26 ; Diod. Sic., xxxv, 26 ; Vell., ii, 7, 4 ; Gell., xi, 13, 1. 5.

[4] Cic., *De lege agr.*, i, 7, 21 ; ii, 5, 10 ; Livy, *Epit.*, 60 ; Vell., ii, 6, 3 ; Plut., *C. Gr.*, 5, 1 ; Oros., v, 12, 4 ; C. G. Bruns, *Fontes*[6], &c., 1893, p. 74 (=*C. I. L.*, i, p. 79). Cf. *Hermes*, 1921, p. 276. Dr. Hardy (*Journ. of Philol.*, xxxi, 1910, pp. 274–5) infers, *I* think rightly, from the *lex agraria* (31) that 'little or no progress was yet made in the resumption of land in the occupation of colonies or Latin towns. Probably', he remarks, 'Gracchus recognized that to carry out this . . . without first dealing with the franchise question would be to provoke revolution ', &c.

lessen the odium of military service by clothing the troops at the public cost and forbidding the conscription of boys below the age of eighteen.[1] Far more important, however, was the famous bill for providing the people with cheap corn. From time to time, even during the Punic wars, when the regular supply was insufficient, the State had imported stocks which were retailed at a considerable loss.[2] Gaius enacted that grain should be sold to every citizen who applied for it at about half the average market price.[3] He must have foreseen that this innovation would not only entail a heavy charge upon the revenue,[4] but would also defeat the purpose of the agrarian law by tempting those who shrank from the toil of agriculture to come to Rome, and would fill the city with undesirable idlers and even with aliens who might hope under a lax system of registration to pass as citizens ; but he could not hope to carry the reforms on which his heart was set without support, and perhaps he satisfied his conscience with the reflexion that a mob is least dangerous

---

[1] Plut., 5, 1. Cf. Diod. Sic., xxxv, 25, 1.

[2] See J. Marquardt, *Röm. Staatsverw.*, ii², 1884, p. 114.

[3] Cic., *Pro Sest.*, 48, 103 and *Schol. Bob.* (ed. Stangl, p. 135 = Orelli, p. 303) ; *Brut.*, 62, 222 ;. *De off.*, ii, 21, 72 ; *Tusc.*, iii, 20, 48 ; Livy, *Epit.*, 60 ; Vell., ii, 6, 3 ; Plut., 5, 1 ; App., i, 21, 89. Cf. Th. Mommsen, *Röm. Gesch.*, i⁸, 1888, p. 841, note ; ii³, 1889, p. 105 (Eng. tr., iii, 1908, pp. 78 n. 1, 344).

[4] Gracchus of course maintained, as Cicero says, that his law would not burden the treasury ; but we may doubt whether he was a dupe of his own argument. Greenidge (*Hist. of Rome*, i, 206), unfamiliar perhaps with the special pleading of hard-driven politicians, suggests that he ' may have taken the view that a moderate, steady, and calculable loss . . . would be cheaper in the end than the cost entailed by the spasmodic attempts which the State had to make in times of crisis to put grain upon the market '. Warde Fowler (*Rom. Essays*, &c., 1920, pp. 103-4, 106) believes that he also intended ' to stimulate the production of corn in *I*taly . . . to keep the agricultural population on the land, and to facilitate the transport of their produce . . . [the small holder would be glad to sell to the Government what grain he had beyond the needs of his family or of the nearest town] '. Would small holders be encouraged by the prospect of getting half the market price for their surplus corn, and how were those who did not live close to Rome to defray the cost of transport ? Anyhow, as Cicero says, Gracchus exhausted the treasury. Von Stern affirms (*Hermes*, 1921, pp. 278-9), rashly *I* think, that he was guided by the corn law of Samos (*Sitzungsber. d. Königl. Preuss. Akad. d. Wiss.*, 1904, pp. 917-31).

INTRODUCTION

when it has enough to eat. At all events he achieved his immediate aim. When the time for the elections was approaching he had no need to canvass the electors or even to declare himself a candidate; and his mere recommendation secured one of the consulships for Gaius Fannius, a moderate politician, upon whose aid he believed that he could rely.[1]

Some four months had still to pass before his first tribunate would end; and during this period and the early months of the ensuing year his activity was at its height. If we may believe Livy and Plutarch, he attempted to reform the Senate by introducing fresh elements into the caste of which it was composed. The House comprised about three hundred members, almost all of whom belonged to the nobility. Six hundred members of the equestrian order—the men of business who formed the middle class—were now, so the epitomizer of Livy relates, to enter this corporation, from which the jurors in the permanent courts were exclusively chosen. But Gracchus could hardly have failed to see that the new members, once admitted, would inevitably become senatorial in sympathy, and that their admission would not ensure impartial verdicts. At all events, if the bill, of which Cicero and other authorities knew nothing, was introduced, it never took effect. We only know that Gaius carried the law by which he intended to gain the favour of the knights and probably also to remove the abuses which had arisen from the senatorial domination of the courts. Thenceforward the jurors were to be chosen from the knights,[2] who were also conciliated by a law which provided that the revenues of Asia should be farmed to syndicates like those which levied the taxes

---

[1] Plut., 8, 2. Kornemann (*Klio*, Beih. i, pp. 1–38, especially 20–1, 37–8) argues that Fannius was the primary source of our knowledge of the Gracchi. Readers familiar with the superabundant literature of *Quellenforschung* (investigation of primary authorities) will not be surprised that his conclusion has been questioned (for instance by E. Meyer [*Kl. Schr.*, 1910, p. 417, n. 2]), and that opinions are even divided as to whether Fannius the historian was identical with Fannius the consul (*Hermes*, 1921, p. 232, n. 1). [2] See pp. 28, 315–7.

of Sardinia and Sicily.¹ Thus a field for extortion was opened to the knights, while the judiciary law would enable them to intimidate provincial governors who might venture to restrain their greed. When Gaius was warned that it would lead to bloodshed, he replied that even if he were doomed to perish he would never withdraw the dagger which he had plunged into the body of the Senate.²

With the men of business and the populace behind him Gaius was all-powerful; and no reformer ever laboured with more indefatigable zeal. He enacted new duties upon imports,³ probably to make good the loss which the treasury would incur by the sale of corn. He constructed new roads, which, in view of the extension of the franchise, would facilitate access to the capital, besides improving regional communication; and though the control of public works had belonged hitherto to the censors, he appointed the contractors himself.⁴ He revolutionized the system by which provinces were assigned to consuls on the expiration of their term of office, enacting that they should be named before the election of the consuls who were to govern them, and, further, that the tribunician veto might not be exercised against the senatorial decision.⁵ His motive was evidently to prevent consuls from intriguing to secure the reversion of rich provinces and the Senate from favouring complaisant, or putting pressure upon independent consuls; while the suspension of the veto would make it impossible to rescind by collusion with any of the tribunes an arrangement which had once been made.⁶ A law was also passed for founding

---

[1] Cic., *Verr.*, iii, 6, 12; Diod. Sic., xxxv, 25, 1; *Schol.Bob.* on *Pro Planc.* § 31, ed. Stangl, p. 157 (ed. Orelli, p. 259).
[2] Diod. Sic., xxxvii, 9. Cf. Cic., *De leg.*, iii, 9, 20.
[3] Vell., ii, 6, 3; Gell., xi, 10, 3.   [4] Plut., 6, 2; App., i, 23, 98.
[5] Cic., *De prov. cons.*, 2, 3; 7, 17; *Pro Balbo*, 27, 61; *Fam.*, i, 7, 10; Sall., *Iug.*, 27, 3.
[6] Cf. Greenidge (*Hist. of Rome*, i, 222-3), whose explanation of the proviso seems more reasonable than that of Long (*Decline of the Roman Republic*, i, 1864, p. 271), that it may have been made 'for the purpose of reconciling the Senate to the change in the time of naming the consular provinces'.

colonies in Italy, two of which were immediately established;[1] and, as the colonists were to be taken only from approved citizens of good character,[2] it seems probable that the object was not to relieve Rome of its superfluous proletariat, but to encourage trade.[3] More contentious was a measure for granting full citizenship to the Latins,[4] which apparently brought to a head the growing resentment of the Senate. The consul Fannius, who could no longer conscientiously support Gracchus, harangued the people and, without wasting time in argument, made a more effective appeal. 'Do you suppose', he asked, 'that if you give citizenship to the Latins, there will be room for you in public meeting or that you will find a place at the games and festivals ? Don't you see that they will monopolize everything ? '[5] The Senate found a willing instrument among the tribunes, one of whom, Livius Drusus, endeavoured by outbidding Gracchus to capture the favour of the populace. Though he put his veto on the bill for enfranchising the Latins, he proposed another for exempting them from corporal punishment, even on military service,[6] and carried a bill for founding twelve colonies, each of which was to contain three thousand citizens, taken, not like the Gracchan colonists from the middle classes but from the poor, who were to pay no rent for their allotments.[7] Although many years elapsed before these colonies were established,[8] and the law for the benefit of the Latins either miscarried or was soon afterwards abrogated, the manœuvre of Drusus was successful. It was easy to persuade the mob in the Forum that the Gracchan colonial law was designed to benefit the rich. But Gracchus was quick to retaliate.[9]

[1] See pp. 347-8.   [2] Plut., *C. Gr.*, 9, 1.
[3] See K. W. Nitzsch, *D. Gracchen*, p. 404, Kornemann, *op. cit.*, p. 49, Greenidge, *op. cit.*, p. 224, and *Eng. Hist. Rev.*, xx, 1905, p. 226, n. 41.
[4] See pp. 348-50.
[5] Cic., *Brut.*, 26, 99 ; C. Halm, *Rhet. Lat. min.*, 1863, p. 402.
[6] See pp. 350-1.
[7] Cic., *Brut.*, 28, 109 ; *De fin.*, iv, 24, 66 ; Plut., 8, 3-4 ; 9, 1-2 ; Suet. *Tib.*, 3 ; App., i, 23, 101.   [8] *Ib.*, 35, 156.
[9] Cf. von Stern, *op. cit.*, p. 292.

He had conceived the novel plan of settling colonists beyond the sea. At his instance his colleague Rubrius carried a bill for establishing a colony at Carthage,[1] and immediately afterwards another tribune, Acilius, passed a law regulating trials for extortion, which fixed heavy penalties and expressly excluded senators from sitting on the juries.[2] Gracchus himself was one of the commissioners appointed to superintend the formation of the colony. While he was absent Drusus inflamed the populace against him, and when he returned he found that his power had been undermined. The colony at Carthage was unpopular. Scipio had pronounced a curse against any one who should attempt to rebuild a city upon the site,[3] and the story ran that its inauguration had been signalized by dire portents.[4] Fulvius Flaccus, the ex-consul, whom Gracchus had left to represent him, provoked hostility by acts of indiscretion,[5] and Opimius, the destroyer of Fregellae, who had been worsted by the influence of Gracchus in his candidature for the consulship, was preparing for revenge.[6]

Gracchus, who had hastened back on hearing of the mischief done by Flaccus, made a last effort to achieve his aim. He promulgated new laws, of which the purport is unknown.[7] But it has been argued, not wholly without reason, that, unwarned by the fate of his proposal in favour of the Latins, and feeling that he must fulfil a pledge which he had given in his programme, he brought forward another for granting the franchise to the Italians; for the consul Fannius was persuaded by the Senate to put in force the act of Pennus and expel all aliens from the city.[8] This much at least is certain: if Gracchus did

---

[1] Livy, *Epit.*, 60; Vell., i, 15, 4; ii, 7, 7; Plut., 10, 2; App., *Pun.*, 136; *B. C.*, i, 24, 102–4; Eutrop., iv, 21; Oros., v, 12, 1; *C. I. L.*, i, No. 198 (22).
[2] See pp. 346–7.   [3] App., *Pun.*, 135.   [4] Plut., 11, 1.
[5] *Ib.*, 10, 3–4.   [6] *Ib.*, 11, 2.
[7] *Ib.*, 11, 1; 12, 1. W. Judeich (*Hist. Zeitschr.*, cxi, 1913, p. 488) thinks that one of them was the law mentioned by Sallust (*De re p.*, ii, 8, 1–2) for the reform of the system of voting in the centuries. [E. Meyer and others, as *I* shall show in the third volume, hold that Sallust was really the author of the work just cited.]   [8] See pp. 348–50.

INTRODUCTION

not attempt to obtain full citizenship for the Italians, he proposed to give them equal rights of voting with Roman citizens. He announced that he would protect by his tribunician power any aliens who had the courage to remain : but he failed to redeem his promise ;[1] and his bill was either rejected or withdrawn. Opimius was successful in standing for the consulship. When Gracchus sought re-election he was beaten; and though it was alleged that the presiding officer had falsified the returns, it is certain that many of the electors disapproved the agrarian law,[2] while the universal resentment provoked by the attempt to extend the franchise was in itself enough to account for his defeat. A tribune, Minucius Rufus, who sided with the Senate, took advantage of his eclipse to propose the repeal of the law for the settlement of Carthage. Gracchus was at first inclined to acquiesce ; but if Minucius gained his object, he would lose his official standing as a commissioner, and prosecution would inevitably follow. Yielding to the exhortations of Flaccus, he assembled his adherents and occupied the Capitol, evidently intending to prevent the repeal by force.[3] When the assembly was about to vote an obscure individual was killed through some misunderstanding by the Gracchan faction, and Opimius, the only consul then in Rome, seized his opportunity. Gracchus, eager to explain to the people that he was innocent of the crime, had left the Capitol : Opimius promptly sent a force to take possession of it, and summoned the Senate to assemble. It was time to fulfil the first duty of every government. By an exercise of power which was apparently unprecedented, which set aside the first law of Gracchus, and which was destined to occasion bitter

The 'ultimate decree' and the fate of Gaius.

---

[1] Greenidge (*op. cit.*, p. 236 and n. 3), who gives a sound reason for questioning the view that ' the tribunician *auxilium* could be interposed solely for the assistance of ' Roman citizens, remarks that it was impossible for Gracchus to fulfil his promise, because ' the injured party could be aided only by the personal interposition of the magistrate ', and Gracchus could not be present everywhere.
[2] Plut., 12, 3–4 ; 13, 1 ; Oros., v, 12, 4.
[3] Plut., 13, 2. Cf. von Stern, *op. cit.*, pp. 295, 298.

controversies, the Senate passed what was afterwards known as the 'ultimate decree,'—'that the consul should see that the State took no harm': in other words, debarred from appointing a special commission, like that of Popillius, to sit in judgement upon Gracchus, they countered his law by administrative action.[1] Martial law was thus virtually declared, and Opimius called upon senators and knights to arm. Gracchus and Flaccus, summoned to appear before the Senate and explain their conduct, refused to obey, and took post upon the Aventine; but after Gracchus had attempted vainly to negotiate, Opimius stormed the hill, and the two democrats with many of their followers were slain.[2]

The dream of Gaius had been fulfilled—'the two noble brothers' had done their work and had reaped their reward. The absolute sovereignty of the People was conceived by youthful doctrinaires, who did not see that the conditions of a Greek city state were different from those of a world power.[3] The ideal of recreating the old Italian yeomanry, if it was not wholly unrealized, encountered not only economic forces but also the indolence of those whom it was designed to benefit; for it was counteracted by the offer of artificially cheap food combined with the gratuitous amusements of urban life. The reform of the law-courts substituted equestrian for senatorial corruption. The enfranchisement of Italy could not be accomplished by peaceful means. The project of transmarine colonization had to wait for its fulfilment. But if the Gracchi were not successful reformers, they were a great political force. The problems which they had set and had tried to solve were destined to agitate Roman parties for a generation and more.

Opimius, in virtue of the ultimate decree, proceeded to investigate the conduct of the partisans of Gracchus. The

---

[1] See Strachan-Davidson, *Problems*, &c., i, 243.
[2] Cic., *In Cat.*, i, 2, 4; iv, 5, 10; *Phil.*, viii, 4, 14; Diod. Sic., xxxiv, 28; Livy, *Epit.*, 61; Pliny, *Nat. Hist.*, xxxiii, 3 (14), 48; Vell., ii, 6, 5; Plut., 13–18, 1; Flor., ii, 3, 4–6; App., i, 24–6, §§ 105–120; Ps Victor, *De vir. ill.*, 65, 5; Oros, v, 12, 5–9.
[3] Cf. von Stern, *op. cit.*, pp. 299–300.

INTRODUCTION

property of those who were condemned, for the most part without trial, was confiscated; three thousand, it was said, were put to death; their wives were forbidden to wear mourning.[1] Opimius, however, was in turn impeached before the popular assembly, not merely in revenge, but also to test the legality of the ultimate decree. He was defended by the consul Papirius Carbo, who had abandoned the popular party; and, whether the influence of the Senate was too strong for the prosecution or a majority of the voters were convinced by the argument that the decree was required for the safety of the State, he was acquitted.[2] On the motion of a tribune, Calpurnius Bestia, who was devoted to the aristocracy, Popillius Laenas by a decree of the people was recalled from exile.[3] But Carbo was not allowed to go scot-free. Lucius Licinius Crassus, a youth of twenty-one, who was later celebrated as the first orator of his time,[4] brought him to trial, apparently on some charge of treason; and before the verdict could be given he committed suicide.[5]

Trial and acquittal of Opimius. 120 B.C.

119 B.C.

The next few years, which seem to have been comparatively calm, were marked by a series of enactments that settled the first phase of the agrarian question,—the struggle of the poor against the rich. The land commissioners, notwithstanding the temporary deprivation of their judicial powers, had been busy for so many years that their work may be supposed to have been virtually done; and now that food was to be obtained in the capital at half its cost, those who desired allotments on which they could only earn a living by incessant toil must have been very few: but the wealthy possessors and the Italian communities who occupied public land could not be sure that their holdings would never be resumed, and doubtless many petty cultivators who had

A series of agrarian laws.

---

[1] Sall., *Iug.*, 16, 2; 31, 7; Vell., ii, 7, 3; Plut., 17, 4; App., i, 26, 119–20; Oros, v, 12, 10.
[2] Cic., *Pro Sest.*, 67, 140; *De or.*, ii, 25, 106; 30, 132; 31, 133. 135; 40, 170; *De part. orat.*, 30, 104; Livy, *Epit.*, 61.
[3] Cic., *Brut.*, 34, 128.
[4] Cic., *Pro Caec.*, 18, 53.
[5] Cic., *Brut.*, 43, 159; *Verr.*, iii, 1, 3; *Fam.*, ix, 21, 3; Val. Max., vi, 5, 6.

no liking for their work would have exchanged their allotments for an idle life in Rome if they had not been forbidden by the Gracchan law to sell them. Soon after the death of Gaius a new statute, which must have been equally welcome to them and to the rich, permitted sale.[1]

114 B. C. ? A few years later a more important measure enacted that no more public land should be distributed, thus practically abolishing the commission, and at the same time guaranteed security of tenure to all the existing holders on condition of their paying rent, which was to be applied 112 B. C. to the benefit of the poor.[2] Soon afterwards Drusus, now a consul, confirmed this law by one which secured Latins and Italians who occupied public land against eviction.[3] 111 B. C. A fourth enactment, carried by a tribune named Spurius Thorius,[4] abolished rent, and thus made all the holders, rich and poor alike, absolute owners of their farms. Certain tracts, however, which had been assigned in usufruct not to individuals but to colonies and municipal towns, as well as commons on which the farmers had the right of pasturing their flocks, and the Campanian public land, which had been exempted from distribution by the Gracchi, remained the property of the State and continued to be subject to a rent, though, as a concession to small holders, a limited number of cattle were allowed free pasturage.[5] How far the smaller cultivators were encouraged by these measures is uncertain; but with the definitive restriction of the public land the struggle for possession between rich and poor was closed; the grievances of the Latins and the Italians were redressed; and the work of the Gracchi was so far justified.[6]

It is probable that about this time an attempt was made to repeal the Gracchan judiciary law; for in this very Servilius year Servilius Glaucia, a tribune whom Cicero denounced, Glaucia. carried a law relating to extortion, which while it con-

[1] App., i, 27, 121. [2] Ib., § 122.
[3] C. I. L., i, No. 200 (29).
[4] See pp. 351-4. This law dealt also with public land in Africa.
[5] C. I. L., i, No. 200 (5-8, 14-5, 29).
[6] Cf. Journ. of Philol., xxxi, 1910, pp. 283, 285.

INTRODUCTION 33

firmed the sole right of the knights to act as jurors, made certain alterations in procedure.[1] But in the course of the next few years the power of the Senate was still further weakened by attacks which their foreign policy provoked. When Rome became mistress of Southern Gaul, a proposal had been made to establish a colony at Narbo, the modern Narbonne. The Senate, which seems to have shrunk from an enterprise that might lead to further war, resisted the design ; but, warmly advocated by Licinius Crassus, it was carried, probably with the support of the equestrian order, who doubtless saw in it an opening for the trade which followed.[2] But it was the conflict with Jugurtha that gave the heaviest blow to the authority of the Senate. On the fall of Carthage Numidia had been declared a client kingdom under the protectorate of Rome. When Jugurtha, resolving to become master of the country, had murdered his co-heir Hiempsal, and Adherbal, the remaining heir, appealed to the Senate for redress, Jugurtha dispatched an embassy to Rome to state his own version of the case. He had served at Numantia under Scipio and had received from him a cordial testimonial ; he had many friends in the city ; and he trusted that his gold would procure more. His envoys represented that Hiempsal and Adherbal were in the wrong, and his friends endorsed their arguments. The majority of the Senate, who doubtless dreaded a long and costly war, were reluctant to interfere ; and, notwithstanding the opposition of a few, who insisted that the paramount power should do its duty, a compromise was effected : it was decided that the kingdom should be divided between Jugurtha and Adherbal.[3] As soon as the commissioners who were charged to define the frontier turned their backs, Jugurtha attacked Adherbal, whereupon the Senate sent a fresh commission to warn

The colony of Narbo.

118 B. C.

Effect of the Jugurthine war upon senatorial authority.

116 B. C.

[1] Cic., Verr., i, 9, 26 ; Pro Scauro, 1, 2 ; Pro Balbo, 24, 54 ; Pro Rab. Post., 4, 8 ; Brut., 62, 224 ; Ascon., ed. Clark, p. 21, ll. 18–20 (ed. Stangl, p. 24) ; C. I. L., i, p. 56. Cf. Greenidge, Legal Procedure, &c., p. 422.
[2] Cic., Pro Font., 5, 13 ; Pro Cluent., 51, 140 ; De or., ii, 55, 223 ; Diod. Sic., v, 38, 5 ; Vell., ii, 7, 8 ; Quint., Inst., vi, 3, 44 ; Eutrop., iv, 23.
[3] Sall., Iug., 12, 4–5 ; 13–6 ; Livy, Epit., 62 ; Flor., i, 36, 4–5.

the combatants to lay down their arms.¹ Jugurtha declined to let them see Adherbal, whom he accused of having plotted against his life ; and after this humiliation they had no choice but to return.² When messengers from Adherbal arrived in Rome with a despairing appeal for help, the advocates of Jugurtha protested against hasty action, and a compromise again ensued. A third commission, headed by Aemilius Scaurus, the leading member of the Senate, sailed for Africa, and summoned Jugurtha to their presence. He obeyed ; but the commissioners, after fulminating idle threats, returned, having accomplished nothing ; and not long afterwards the news reached Rome that Adherbal had been murdered by Jugurtha, and that the Italian brokers in the city of Cirta had been massacred.³ Even then a majority of the Senate wished to temporize ; but Gaius Memmius, one of the tribunes designate, insisted that Jugurtha had bribed his friends to get his crimes condoned. The populace were roused to fury : the eloquence of the tribune was doubtless seconded by the knights, whose representatives in Numidia had been butchered ; and the Senate was at length goaded into action. It was decided that Bestia, one of the consuls elect, should be dispatched with an army to Africa.⁴ Jugurtha, astonished at this display of energy, sent an embassy to Rome, which was forthwith expelled ; but when Bocchus, the King of Mauretania, offered his assistance to the Senate, he was rebuffed through the intrigues of Jugurtha's friends,⁵ while Bestia and Scaurus, who accompanied the army, were bribed, after a brief campaign, to accept a compromise. Jugurtha professed to surrender, and, to save appearances, delivered a few cattle and a small sum of money to the quaestor.⁶ The news caused a sensation

---

¹ Sall., 20, 1 ; 21 : Livy, *Epit.*, 64.
² Sall., 22.
³ *Ib.*, 23, 2 ; 25, 1–6, 10–1 ; 26 ; Livy, *Epit.*, 64 ; Diod. Sic., xxxiv, 31.
⁴ Sall., 27 ; Livy, *Epit.*, 64.
⁵ Sall, 80, 4–5.
⁶ *Ib.*, 28, 4–7, 29 ; Livy, *Epit.*, 64 ; Flor., i, 36, 7 ; Eutrop., iv, 26 ; Oros., v, 15, 4.

in the capital. The Senate could not decide whether they should confirm a disgraceful peace or disavow the action of the consul; but Memmius, who was now in office, took the decision from them. Arraigning their conduct of affairs during the past twenty years, he denounced them as traitors who had sold the safety of the empire, chided his hearers for having submitted to the tyrants who had persecuted the champions of the people, and induced them to decree that Jugurtha should be summoned instantly to Rome to give evidence against the men who had betrayed the State.[1] Meanwhile the officers whom Bestia had left behind were filling their pockets by restoring to Jugurtha the beasts which he had surrendered and the deserters who had come to the Roman camp. When Jugurtha appeared in Rome he took one of the tribunes into his pay and refused, despite the exhortations of Memmius and the clamour of the rabble, to give evidence. A few days later, having procured the assassination of a Numidian prince who was intriguing against him in the city, he was ordered by the Senate to depart. It was then that, according to the familiar story, he exclaimed, 'This city is for sale, and will soon perish when it finds a purchaser.'[2]

110 B.C.

Spurius Albinus, the consul to whose lot it fell to carry on the war, and who was confident of a speedy victory, failed to appreciate the difficulties of the country and the cleverness of his opponent. Returning to Rome, under suspicion of corruption, to preside at the consular elections, he left his brother, as propraetor, in command. Inveigled into a distant place, where he soon found himself surrounded, this officer made no resistance, but purchased safety on the condition that his army should pass under the yoke and quit Numidia within ten days.[3] The news caused shame and even panic in Italy. The Senate

[1] Sall., 30-1.
[2] Ib., 32-5; Diod. Sic., xxxiv, 35 A; Livy, Epit., 64; Flor., i, 36, 8; Oros., v, 15, 5.
[3] Sall., 36-8; Flor., i, 36, 9; Oros., v, 15, 6.

refused to ratify the convention, on the ground that no treaty could be made without its sanction and the consent of the Roman People. The consul hurried back to Africa, and found that the army was too demoralized to take the field.[1]

By this time the popular party were thoroughly roused. Mamilius Limetanus, one of the tribunes, borrowing from the Senate the weapon which it had used against the Gracchi, proposed a bill for appointing a commission to inquire into the conduct of those by whose counsel Jugurtha had flouted the authority of Rome, of those who had restored what he surrendered, and of those who were responsible for the late convention. Avowed opposition would have been tantamount to acknowledgement of guilt, and, though aliens were brought into the city to intimidate the assembly, the populace, in their hatred of the nobility, were resolute, and the bill was passed by acclamation. The knights who composed the jury had not forgotten the massacre at Cirta ; but Scaurus, who was pointed to as the arch-criminal, contrived to have himself nominated as one of the commissioners. The inquiry was conducted, according to the Roman historian of the war, himself a member of the popular party, with violence and harshness. Among those who were condemned were Albinus, Calpurnius Bestia, and one whose fate must have delighted every opponent of the Senate, Opimius, the slayer of Gaius Gracchus and the persecutor of his friends.[2]

The Senate had learned their lesson, and the war was now resumed in earnest. Quintus Caecilius Metellus, one of the new consuls, was sent to Numidia, while his colleague, Junius Silanus, went to Transalpine Gaul, to encounter an enemy more dangerous than Jugurtha. Metellus, whose integrity was above suspicion, restored order in the demoralized army, and gained successes which revived Roman confidence ; but the difficulties of the country were too much for him, and his enemy eluded

[1] Sall., 39.
[2] *Ib.*, 39–40 ; Cic., *Pro Sest.*, 67, 140 ; *Brut.*, 33–4, §§ 127–8.

INTRODUCTION

a decision.[1] Gaius Marius, a man of obscure origin [2] but an experienced soldier, who had won distinction on the general's staff, was ambitious to supplant him. When Metellus, wearied by his importunity, allowed him leave of absence to canvass for the consulship, he was supported by the men of business in Africa, whom he had persuaded that he could bring the struggle to an end, as well as by officers who admired his ability. The nobles were of course opposed to his election, but their influence was sapped by the recent verdict of the commission; and, backed by the equestrian order, by tribunes who harangued the people in his favour, and by yeomen who left their farms to vote for him, he was triumphantly returned. The Cimbri and the Teutoni, those fair-haired giants who had come down like an avalanche from the unknown lands that bordered on the northern sea, were already threatening the civilized world. The consul Silanus had been disastrously defeated; and the electors were convinced that the best soldier of the time should be charged to vindicate the Roman arms. Though the Senate had granted Metellus an extension of his command, the popular assembly, on the motion of a tribune, decided that he should be superseded by Marius.[3]

108 B.C.

The democratic consul inaugurated his office by an innovation which marked a turning-point in Roman history. Knowing that conscription was unpopular, he called for volunteers from the dregs of the population, whose property fell below the minimum of which account was taken in the census, and who would be glad to serve for the chance of booty as well as for their pay.[4] The significance of this step, which prolonged service in

Military innovations of Marius.

---

[1] Sall., 43–62; Livy, *Epit.*, 65; Val. Max., ii, 7, 2 : Frontin., *Strat.*, iv, 1, 2; Flor., i, 36, 10–2; App., *Num.*, 1–2; Eutrop., iv, 26; Oros., v, 15, 7.
[2] Vell., ii, 11, 1; 128, 2; Pliny, xxxiii, 11 (53), 150; Plut., *Mar.*, 3, 1; Dio, fr. 87, 2.
[3] Sall., 63–73; Diod. Sic., xxxv, 38; Livy, *Epit.*, 65; Vell., ii, 11, 1–2; Plut., *Mar.*, 7–8; 9, 1; Flor., i, 38, 4; Eutrop., iv, 27.
[4] Sall., 86, 1–2; Val. Max., ii, 3, 1; Plut., *Mar.*, 9, 1; Flor., i, 36, 13; Gell., xvi, 10, 10. We need not suppose that all the recruits belonged to the proletariat: probably Marius took men who were willing to serve from the classes liable to conscription. See p. 115.

foreign lands rendered inevitable, was that it transformed the national militia into a professional army, thereby entailing momentous consequences, which I shall hereafter describe. By the time when Marius arrived in Africa Jugurtha had been joined by Bocchus, whose proffered aid the Senate had declined. Marius conducted the war with vigour, but with no more success than the general whose authority he had undermined ; and only the diplomacy of his destined rival, Sulla, enabled him to achieve a semblance of making good his boast. The Roman army, with its weak cavalry and its stereotyped methods, was ill adapted to act in a country like North Africa against a foe like the elusive horsemen of Numidia. But Bocchus, who saw a prospect of coming to some arrangement which would be advantageous to himself, made overtures for negotiation ; and Sulla, who was serving under Marius, succeeded in inducing him to betray his ally.[1]

But if Marius had not proved himself a great commander, his soldiers and his countrymen believed in him ; and the Roman people chose him, despite senatorial opposition, to avert a danger more formidable than that of the Numidian War. It is true that there had been signs of a reaction in favour of the Senate. Metellus was respected because he was incorruptible. When he returned from Africa the passions awakened by the Mamilian commission had had time to cool ; he was welcomed by the populace as warmly as by his peers ; and he celebrated a triumph amid general rejoicing.[2] Servilius Caepio, one of the consuls elected in that year, was a supporter of the aristocracy,[3] and, backed by the eloquence of Licinius Crassus,

---

[1] Sall., 81–2 ; 86–113 ; Diod. Sic., xxxv, 39 ; xxxvi, 1 ; Livy, *Epit.*, 66 ; Vell., ii, 12, 1 ; Val. Max., vi, 9, 6 ; Plut., *Mar.*, 10 ; 12, 3–7 ; *Sulla*, 3 ; Flor., i, 36, 13–7 ; Eutrop., iv, 27 ; Oros., v, 15, 8–19.

[2] Sall., 88, 1 ; Vell., ii, 11, 2 ; Eutrop., iv, 27.

[3] Greenidge (*Hist. of Rome*, i, 476–7) infers that Atilius Serranus, the other consul designate, was also a supporter of the Senate from ' the resolution which he subsequently [100 B.C.] displayed in combating revolution ' (Cic., *Pro Rab.*, 7, 21) ; but in that year all classes rallied to the cause of order, and Hardy (*Journ. of Philol.*, xxxii, 1913, p. 102) remarks that the election of Serranus over Catulus [a staunch Conservative] ' is inconsistent with anything like a strong senatorial reaction '.

INTRODUCTION 39

he carried a law which was designed to restore to the Senate, enlarged by the admission of a number of knights, the control of the courts which Gaius Gracchus had withdrawn. But the law, if it ever took effect, was soon repealed;[1] and when the defeat of Silanus had been followed by a disaster in Transalpine Gaul, which was aggravated by a disgraceful surrender, and two consular armies had been destroyed by the Cimbri and Teutoni in the valley of the Rhône,[2] it was felt that the popular hero could alone save Italy from invasion. Marius, who had not yet returned from Africa, was re-elected consul, while those who protested against the dispensation which permitted his second candidature were driven from the Forum; and such was the distrust with which the nobility were regarded that their candidate, Lutatius Catulus, was beaten by a man whose family, like that of Marius, was new to public life.[3]

106 B. C. Temporary reaction (?) in favour of the Senate.

105 B. C.

After the victories of the Northmen on the Rhône, when Italy was at their mercy, and the panic-stricken inhabitants dreaded another Allia, fortune again befriended Rome. The Cimbri separated from the Teutoni to make raids in Spain and Gaul. Thus Marius had leisure to prepare for his life's work,—to save Italy from being submerged by barbarism before she could do her part for European civilization. He spent it in training his army, which had already profited by the system inaugurated by a former consul, Rutilius Rufus, of giving thorough instruction in the use of weapons to each recruit.[4] Again and again, as a matter of necessity, Marius was re-elected consul; and when, after three years' wandering, the Cimbri rejoined their allies and the two swarms headed for the south, Marius was waiting for them on the Rhône, and his brother consul, Catulus, in Cisalpine Gaul. Once more the host divided; and while the Teutoni encountered Marius in the neighbourhood of Aix, the Cimbri threaded

Marius saves Italy from the Cimbri and Teutoni.

102 B. C.

---
[1] See p. 354.
[2] See *Caesar's Conquest of Gaul*,[2] 1911, pp. 36, 548–9.
[3] Sall., 114, 3; Livy, *Epit.* 67 (cf. 56); Vell., ii, 12, 1; Plut., *Mar.*, 12, 1.
[4] *Ib.*, 14, 1–2; Val. Max., ii, 3, 2.

the Brenner Pass and descended into the valley of the Adige. The ghastly appellation of the Putrid Plain commemorated the slaughter of the Teutoni : the Cimbri were annihilated at Vercellae, near the confluence of the Sesia and the Po.[1]

After this crowning victory, which he won in conjunction with his colleague, Marius gained his sixth consulship, by dint of bribery :[2] but he was neither a statesman nor a politician ; and while he allied himself with two turbulent demagogues, Servilius Glaucia and Appuleius Saturninus, who counted upon his aid in harrying the Senate, his ambition was merely to provide for his old soldiers and to humiliate Metellus. While he was absent in Gaul the popular party had vented their spleen against the nobility by a series of prosecutions,[3] and it was a sign of the times when a tribune, Gnaeus Domitius, carried a bill for transferring the election of pontiffs and augurs, who had hitherto been chosen by the priestly colleges, to the popular assembly.[4] Saturninus had ingratiated himself in a former tribunate with Marius by passing a law for the distribution of allotments in Africa among his veterans.[5] In the following year Metellus, now a censor, attempted to exclude both Saturninus and Glaucia from the Senate ;[6] and when Saturninus, after murdering a rival, who had already been elected, had obtained his second tribuneship, he prepared to wreak his vengeance.[7] He began by proposing a law for assigning lands in Transalpine Gaul and apparently also in Sicily, Achaia, and Macedonia to the soldiers who had served under Marius. A clause, which was designed for the ruin of Metellus, required that within five days after the enactment of the law every senator should swear, on pain of a heavy fine and of

---

[1] See *Caesar's Conquest of Gaul, loc. cit.*
[2] Livy, *Epit.*, 69 ; Plut., *Mar.*, 28, 7.
[3] See Greenidge, *Sources for Rom. Hist.*, 1903, pp. 67-8.
[4] Cic., *De lege agr.*, ii, 7, 18 ; Vell., ii, 12, 3 ; Suet., *Nero*, 2, 1.
[5] For the legislation of Saturninus see pp. 354-5.
[6] Cic., *Pro Sest.*, 47, 101 ; App., i, 28, 126 ; Dio, *fr.* 93, 2.
[7] Livy, *Epit.*, 69 ; Flor., ii, 4, 1 ; App., i, 28, 127-9 ; Ps. Victor, *De vir ill.*, 73, 5.

INTRODUCTION 41

expulsion from the Senate, to observe it. The bill was welcomed by the Italians, many of whom would share in the intended distribution ; but for that very reason it was obnoxious to the urban populace ; and it was not carried until the hostile factions, armed with bludgeons, had fought a battle in the Forum. Marius, who assured the Senate that he would never take the oath, announced a few days later, to the consternation of the House, that he dreaded the anger of the populace, but would only swear to obey the law with the reservation, so far as it was legitimate. Metellus, alone among the senators, had the courage to refuse, and, being threatened with outlawry by Saturninus, retired into exile.[1] But the populace, although Saturninus had attempted to purchase their support by reducing the price which Gracchus had fixed for corn to a nominal amount, were indignant at the persecution of Metellus ; and when Saturninus and Glaucia hired a gang of ruffians, who murdered the ex-tribune Memmius, one of the candidates for the consulship and a resolute opponent of their measures, all classes turned against them. The Senate passed the ultimate decree, charging the consuls to save the commonwealth, and Marius reluctantly armed loyal citizens against his friends. Driven out of the Forum after a pitched battle, Saturninus and his followers fled for refuge to the Capitol, but, compelled by the cutting of the water-pipes to surrender under a pledge of safety, they were massacred by an infuriated mob.[2] The laws of Saturninus were annulled ; [3] Metellus was soon after-

[1] *Ib.*, Cic., *De domo*, 31, 82 ; *Pro Sest.*, 16, 37 ; Livy, *Epit.*, 69 ; Val. Max., iii, 8, 4 ; Plut., *Mar.*, 28, 5–6 ; 29, 2–9 ; Flor., ii, 4, 2–3 ; App., i, 29–31. Whether, as Plutarch and Appian assert, Marius deliberately deceived the Senate in order to entrap Metellus (how ?), or, as some modern writers imagine, was half-hearted and yielded to the demagogues, the reader, if he can, may decide.

[2] Cic., *Pro Rab.*, 7, 20 ; 10, 28 ; Livy, *Epit.*, 69 ; Vell., ii, 12, 6 ; Val. Max., iii, 2, 18 ; Plut., *Mar.*, 30, 2–5 ; Flor., ii, 4, 3–6 ; App., i, 32 (inaccurate) ; Ps. Victor, *De vir. ill.*, 73, 11–2 ; Oros., v, 17, 5–10 ; *C. I. L.*, i, p. 290 (=H. Dessau, *Inscr. Lat.*, 59). Cf. F. W. Robinson, *Marius, Saturninus u. Glaucia*, 1912, p. 122.

[3] Cic., *Pro Balbo*, 21, 48 ; *De leg.*, ii, 6, 14.

wards recalled amidst universal demonstrations of goodwill;[1] and the political career of Marius came to an end.

The next few years were uneventful, though a slave revolt, which had long devastated Sicily, was hardly ended when Saturninus fell,[2] and various signs must have led thoughtful men to fear that the question of Italian enfranchisement would soon come to a head. Italians who visited or were domiciled in Rome sometimes contrived, under lax scrutiny or defective registration, to pass as citizens; and five years after the death of Saturninus the consuls, Lucius Crassus and Mucius Scaevola, carried a law for inquiring into doubtful cases and banishing all residents who could not make good their claim. The law was bitterly resented, and turned the minds of Italians who brooded over it towards civil war.[3] Three years later an event occurred which, while it indirectly wrought upon this movement, illustrated the use which the equestrian order made of their judicial power and nearly occasioned revolution. Rutilius Rufus, the ex-consul whose reforms prepared the way for the victories of Marius, had served in Asia under Scaevola, one of the few upright Roman governors, and had protected the natives against the greed of the tax-collectors. In revenge he was prosecuted for extortion and, being condemned, retired into exile; but writers of all shades of opinion denounced the injustice of his trial and vindicated his integrity. It was this scandal as well as observation of the results of the late alien act that inspired the tribune Drusus to attempt the salvation of the State.[4]

Livius Drusus, a son of the tribune who had wrecked

---

[1] Cic., *Pro Planc.*, 28, 69; Diod. Sic., xxxvi, 16; Livy, *Epit.*, 69; Val. Max., iv, 1, 13; Plut., *Mar.*, 31, 1; Gell., xiii, 29, 1; App., i, 33, 147-9.
[2] Diod. Sic., xxxvi, 2-10; Flor., ii, 7, 9-12; &c.
[3] Cic., *Pro Sest.*, 13, 30; *Pro Balbo*, 21, 48; 24, 54; *De off.*, iii, 11, 47; Ascon., ed. Clark, p. 67, ll. 20-3, p. 68, ll. 1-6 (ed. Stangl, p. 54).
[4] Cic., *Pro Font.*, 13, 28 (17, 38); *In Pis.*, 39, 95; *Brut.*, 30, 114-5; Diod. Sic., xxxvii, 5, 1; Livy, *Epit.*. 70; Vell., ii, 13, 2; Val. Max., ii, 10, 5; Ascon., ed. Clark, p. 21, ll. 23-4 (ed. Stangl, p. 24); Dio, fr. 95; Oros., v, 17, 12-3.

the career of Gaius Gracchus, was a young man of serious demeanour who had frequented the Forum from his youth and lamented that even in boyhood he had never had a holiday.[1] His main objects were to restore the authority of the Senate, to purify the courts of law, and to enfranchise the Italians.[2] He hoped to promote harmonious working between the Senate, the equestrian order, and the people by securing the interests of each ; but he and the senators who supported him [3] failed to realize, notwithstanding the experience of fifty years, that the enfranchisement of the Italians was repugnant to every class, and he succeeded only in making enemies of all. To purchase popular support he re-enacted his father's law, which had never been executed, for establishing colonies in Italy and Sicily ; [4] provided for the distribution of grain, doubtless at a low price ; [5] and debased the coinage, either in order to meet the cost or to relieve embarrassed debtors.[6] But how was the Senate, which had been flouted by the condemnation of Rutilius, to be strengthened without offending the knights ? Merely to restore to it the control of the law courts was obviously impracticable. Drusus could think of nothing better than to revive the discredited plan of introducing three hundred knights into the Senate, from which, thus reconstituted, juries were thenceforth to be selected.[7] In truth it must be admitted that no other course was possible. There were only three hundred senators, and four hundred and fifty jurors were required under the Acilian law : it was therefore obviously necessary, if senators were again to engross judicial functions, to enlarge their number. A novel feature of

[1] Cic., *De off.*, i, 30, 108 ; Seneca, *De brev. vitae*, 6, 1.
[2] Cic., *De or.*, i, 7, 24 ; *Pro Mil.*, 7, 16 ; Diod. Sic., xxxvii, 10, 2 ; Livy, *Epit.*, 71 ; Vell., ii, 13, 2 ; Flor., ii, 5, 3–4.
[3] That a considerable number of senators favoured enfranchisement is proved by the records of the Varian commission (see p. 45) ; and of course Drusus would not have agitated for it without support.
[4] Livy, *Epit.*, 71 ; App., i, 35, 156.
[5] Livy, *Epit.*, 71.
[6] Pliny, xxxiii, 3 (13), 46. Cf. E. Babelon, *Traité des monn. grecques et rom.*, i, 1901, col. 637
[7] See pp. 355-6.

the bill, however, was a clause which gave the courts power to take cognizance of cases in which jurors might be accused of corruption.[1] The consequences might have been foreseen. The knights, who, as such, were no longer to be represented in the courts, resented a proviso which reflected on their honour; the majority, who would remain outside the Senate, were jealous of the preference to be given to a selected few. Many senators were indignant at the intrusion of those whom they regarded as inferiors; and thoughtful observers, who felt that neither order ought to monopolize judicial power, must have foreseen that the new members would become as exclusive in their sympathies as the nobles with whom they were to be associated. And, while senators and knights alike were thus exacerbated, the Italians who occupied public lands feared that they might be obliged to surrender them to the colonists, and that even their titles to their private holdings might be called in question. Nobody was satisfied except the urban populace and the Italians who clung to Drusus as the champion of enfranchisement.[2] It would seem indeed that it was with the aid of Italians who flocked into Rome and threatened or practised violence that he succeeded in passing his preliminary laws.[3] But although he was suspected of conspiring with the Italians to carry the contemplated enfranchisement by force,[4] his success was hopeless in the face of universal opposition, and his influence rapidly diminished. Philippus, one of the consuls, who had inveighed against the Senate so long as they allowed themselves to be guided by the tribune, persuaded them to combine against him;[5] and his

---

[1] Cic., *Pro Cluent.*, 56, 153; *Pro Rab. Post.*, 7, 16; App., i, 35, 158.

[2] Vell., ii, 13, 2; App., i, 35, 159-61; 36, 162; Ps. Victor, *De vir. ill.*, 66, 10. Cf. Strachan-Davidson, *Appian : Book I*, third note on p. 41.

[3] Livy, *Epit.*, 71; Flor., ii. 5, 7-8; Ps. Victor, 66, 8-9.

[4] Diod. Sic., xxxvii, 11; 13; Flor., ii, 5, 6-9; App., i, 35, 155; Ps. Victor, 66, 11-2. Cf. G. Long, *Decline of the Roman Republic*, ii, 1866, pp. 159-60, and W. Strehl, *M. Livius Drusus*, 1887, pp. 34-44. The statement of Velleius (ii, 14, 1), found in no other ancient writer, that Drusus determined to enfranchise the Italians because his other measures failed, is doubtless his own invention.

Cic., *De or.*, iii, 1, 2-4. See p. 356, n. 3.

INTRODUCTION

measures were invalidated on the ground that, contrary to an existing statute, they had been carried in violation of the essential religious rites and had been promulgated not separately but in a single bill.[1] Before his term of office ended Drusus was assassinated;[2] and if Tacitus[3] strained the truth in coupling him with Saturninus, his good intentions, for lack of statesmanship, led to the proverbial goal.

His death was speedily followed by the Social War, for which the disappointed Italians had prepared. They were not, however, all united. The Latins adhered to Rome throughout; the people of Etruria and Umbria were on her side at first; and even in some of the rebellious towns there were factions who tried to thwart their fellow-burgesses. The Romans, as in the days of their struggle for the mastery of Italy, had the advantage of interior lines : they were able to draw supplies from the provincials ; and when their treasury was depleted, the rents paid by the tenants of the Campanian land were a constant source of revenue.[4] The Senate conducted the war with resolution, and their authority was strengthened by a friendly tribune. Although the knights from motives of partisanship suborned a tribune, Quintus Varius, to propose the establishment of a commission to inquire into the conduct of those by whose machinations the Italians had rebelled, and various prominent nobles were in consequence prosecuted, Plautius Silvanus carried a law

The Social War.

---

[1] Cic., *De domo*, 16, 41 ; *De leg.*, ii, 6, 14 ; 12, 31 ; Diod. Sic., xxxvii, 10, 3 ; Ascon., ed. Clark, p. 68, l. 22 ; p. 69, ll. 1–7 (ed. Stangl, p. 55). Dr. Hardy (*Class. Rev.*, xxxii, 1913, p. 262), who gives good reasons for supposing that the *lex Caecilia et Didia*, which Drusus violated, did not merely forbid the passing of various measures under one law, but also violence and neglect of auspices, does not believe that 'laws so disparate as a judiciary and a corn law . . . could have been passed together, or that Drusus . . . representing the party which only seven years before had passed the lex Caecilia-Didia, would have violated it in so . . . barefaced a way '. The epitomizer of Livy [71], he adds, ' distinctly states that the judiciary law was passed later than the agrarian and corn laws '.
[2] Vell., ii, 14, 1–2 ; Seneca, *De brev. vit.*, 6, 2 ; App. i, 36, 164 ; *C. I. L.* i, p. 279, vii (=H. Dessau, *Inscr. Lat.*, 49).
[3] *Ann.*, iii, 27.
[4] Cic., *Verr.*, ii, 2, 2, 5 ; *De lege agr.*, ii, 29, 80 ; Oros., v, 18, 27.

by which the commission was transferred to freely elected jurors, including senators; and Varius was himself condemned and forced to go into exile.[1] When the difficulties of the Government were increased by war in Transalpine Gaul and by the news that the province of Asia was being threatened by Mithradates, they confirmed the goodwill of their faithful allies and weakened the coherence of their enemies by well-timed concession. In the course of the first campaign the consul Lucius Julius Caesar carried the famous law by which full citizenship was offered not only to the Latins, but also to the Italian communities which were not actually in arms. The consul, indeed, intended that the concession should detract nothing from those who already possessed the franchise, for the new citizens were enrolled not in the existing thirty-five, but in eight supernumerary tribes, and as the old ones voted first, they would probably have a permanent majority.[2] Still, the boon was accepted by the people of Etruria[3] and doubtless also by other states; and in the next year it was followed by a *plébiscite*, carried by two tribunes, Plautius Silvanus and Papirius Carbo, which enacted that all persons domiciled in Italy and enrolled as burgesses by allied communities might obtain Roman citizenship

90 B. C. Citizenship offered to Italians.

89 B. C.

---

[1] Cic., *Brut.*, 56, 205; 89, 304; Val. Max., viii, 6, 4; Ascon., ed. Clark, p. 22, ll. 5–8; p. 73, ll. 25–7; p. 74, ll. 1–4; p. 79, ll. 3–14 (ed. Stangl, pp. 24, 58, 61); App., i, 37.

[2] Cic., *Pro Balbo*, 8, 21; Vell., ii, 16, 4; Gell., iv, 4, 3; App., i, 49, 212. See p. 356. Lord Bryce (*Studies in Hist.*, &c., i, 1901, p. 32) remarks that the Government did not adopt 'what seems to us moderns the obvious expedient of allowing them [the *I*talians] to send delegates to an assembly which should meet in Rome'. Such representation was foreign to the ancient conception of a city state, which Rome in theory still remained. Just after the battle of Cannae, however, a senator, Spurius Carvilius, had made an abortive proposal that the depleted Senate should be recruited by two representatives from each Latin community (Livy, xxiii, 22, 4–5). We learn from an inscription (*Class. Rev.*, xxiii, 1909, pp. 158–9; *Journ. Rom. Studies*, ix, 1919, pp. 95–101. Cf. H. Dessau, *Inscr. Lat.*, 8888) that under the Julian law citizenship was conferred by Pompeius Strabo in 89 B. C. on certain men belonging to a troop of Spanish auxiliary cavalry in recognition of their valour.

[3] App., i, 49, 213. It was rejected by Naples, Heraclea, and Tarentum (Cic., *Verr.*, iv, 60, 135; *Pro Balbo*, 8, 21).

INTRODUCTION 47

by applying for it within sixty days.¹ Soon afterwards a third law authorized generals to confer the citizenship, as a reward for valour, upon Italian soldiers in Roman armies;² and these new citizens were enrolled in two new tribes.³ A further step was taken in the same year, when the consul Gnaeus Pompeius Strabo, the father of Pompey the Great, carried a law by which the urban communities north of the Po, where the population was still largely Celtic, received Latin rights, in virtue of which every one who had filled a local magistracy might become a Roman citizen.⁴ Nevertheless, although both Marius and Sulla were in command, the war dragged on; and a financial crisis increased the general distress. Creditors pressed for payment; debtors, relying upon an obsolete law which made usury penal, refused to pay, some even demanding that the creditors themselves should be mulcted in the fines to which, under this law, they were liable; and when the praetor Asellio appointed arbitrators to settle the disputes, he was murdered by the infuriated creditors, and the guilty parties were screened from punishment.⁵ While public feeling was thus excited a tribune was elected by whose action the struggle between Roman and Italian became merged in civil war.

Latin rights conferred upon Transpadane communities.

Financial crisis.

Publius Sulpicius Rufus, a patrician who had procured adoption into a plebeian family to make himself eligible for the tribunate,⁶ had hitherto been known as a friend of Drusus and a supporter of the conservative party.⁷ Cicero, who, as a boy of eighteen, listened daily when he was haranguing the assembly, recorded in later life the impression which he had received.—' He was of all the orators whom I have heard the most dignified and, I may

Sulpicius Rufus.

---

¹ Cic., *Pro Arch.*, 4, 7, and *Schol. Bob.* ed. Stangl, p. 175 (ed. Orelli, p. 353); App. i, 53, 231.
² H. Peter, *Hist. Rom. fr.*, p. 187. 120.—*Milites, ut lex Calpurnia concesserat, virtutis ergo civitate donari.* Cf. p. 46, n. 2, *supra*. Did this Calpurnian law extend the authority under which Pompeius Strabo acted?
³ See p. 356.
⁴ Ascon., ed. Clark, p. 3, ll. 5–12 (ed. Stangl, p. 12).
⁵ Livy, *Epit.*, 74; Val. Max., ix, 7, 4; App., i, 54.
⁶ The Sulpicii were patricians. See *Dig.*, i, 2, 2, 43.
⁷ Cic., *De or.*, i, 7, 25; iii, 3, 11.

say, the most tragical. His voice was powerful, mellifluous, and clear ; his gestures and movements were full of grace, though his action was that of one trained for the Forum, not for the stage ; his language was rapid and flowing without being redundant or diffuse.'[1] He now determined, as Cicero believed out of a personal grudge against the consul Pompeius Rufus, to abandon his former friends.[2] After carrying a law for the restoration of those who had gone into exile in fear of the Varian commission, on the ground that they had been expelled by violence,[3] and another, occasioned by scandals connected with the prevalence of debt, for the exclusion from the Senate of all members who owed more than eight thousand sesterces,[4] he proposed a yet more contentious measure : the new citizens, instead of being enrolled in the newly created tribes, were to be distributed among the old ones.[5] His motive was not merely to redress a grievance. The Senate had found itself obliged to declare war against Mithradates ; and Sulla, the colleague of Pompeius Rufus, had been appointed to lead the expeditionary force. Sulpicius, relying on the votes of the new citizens, proposed a bill for transferring the command to Marius, who, though he had long passed his prime, was still ambitious and had not forgotten how Sulla had deprived him of the glory of ending the Jugurthine war. The old voters assailed the Italians with stones and bludgeons, and after the riots had continued for some days, the consuls, in order to prevent the bill from being submitted to the vote, proclaimed a suspension of all public business. Sulpicius, who had armed ruffians in his pay and was attended by

[1] *Brut.*, 55, 203.
[2] Cic. (?), *De har. resp.*, 20, 43 ; *De or.*, iii, 3, 11 ; *Brut.*, 63, 226 ; *De amic.*, 1, 2 ; Vell., ii, 18, 5–6. It has been asserted by a modern writer that Sulpicius was bought by Marius.
[3] Ps. Cic., *Ad Herenn.*, ii, 28, 45 ; Livy, *Epit.*, 77. Cf. Greenidge, *Legal Procedure*, &c., p. 521. May one conjecture that the exiles whom Sulpicius was anxious to restore were those who, like Varius himself, had been condemned by the remodelled commission (see p. 46) ? *I* agree with Strachan-Davidson (*Appian : Bk. I*, p. 59) that ' the character and policy ' of Sulpicius ' must be left as a hopeless puzzle '.
[4] Plut., *Sulla*, 8, 4.
[5] Livy, *Epit.*, 77 ; App., i, 55, 242–3.

INTRODUCTION

a bodyguard of knights, declared that the act of the consuls was illegal and insisted that they should rescind it. They could only yield to force. Sulla, believing that his life was in danger, left the capital for Capua, where the legions destined for the Mithradatic war were quartered; the Sulpician law was passed; and by a decree of the popular assembly Marius was entrusted with the command.[1]

But the triumph of Sulpicius was short-lived. Sulla, appealing to the cupidity of his soldiers, who were in no mood to allow others to get the booty which they expected, marched direct on Rome, though the superior officers, for the most part, were too timid or too scrupulous to follow. Two praetors, who forbade him in the name of the Senate to advance, were chased away with insults by the troops; and, forcing his way, despite armed resistance, through the city, the first Roman general who had entered it by violence, he proceeded to re-establish order. Although no commander ever allowed his men such licence, none could maintain a stronger discipline; and those who ventured to plunder were punished in view of the inhabitants. In dealing with the Marian faction Sulla spared all except the ringleaders, who had precipitated civil war and had endeavoured to arm slaves against him. Twelve were outlawed by the Senate, of whom the majority doubtless sympathized with Sulla; among them Marius, who forthwith fled, and Sulpicius, who was caught and put to death. One of his slaves, who in return for the promise of freedom had betrayed him, was duly manumitted and immediately afterwards, by Sulla's order, hurled from the Tarpeian rock.[2]

Sulla marches on Rome: flight of Marius and execution of Sulpicius.

The Sulpician laws were of course instantly repealed; and Sulla, who probably foresaw that during his absence

---

[1] Diod. Sic., xxxvii, 29, 2; Livy, *Epit.*, 77; Vell., ii, 18, 5–6; Val. Max., ix, 7, *Mil. Rom.* 1; Plut., *Mar.*, 34, 1–2, 5–7; 35, 1–4; *Sulla*, 8, 3, 5–7; 9, 1; Flor., ii, 9, 6; App., i, 55–6, §§ 241–9.

[2] Cic., *In Cat.*, iii, 10, 24; Diod. Sic., xxxvii, 29, 3; Livy, *Epit.*, 77; Vell., ii, 19, 1; Val. Max., iii, 8, 5; vi, 5, 7; Plut., *Mar.*, 35, 4–7; *Sulla*, 8, 7; 9; 10, 1–2; App., i, 57–60; Eutrop., v, 4; Oros., v, 19, 4–7.

Legislation of Sulla.

there would be further troubles, proceeded, in conjunction with the Senate, to make such constitutional changes as might tend to keep the demagogues in check. The tribunes were forbidden to propose any measure to the assembly without the approval of the Senate; and as the number of the latter had been considerably reduced, it was to be doubled by the addition of three hundred selected knights. Thus it was intended that the project of Drusus should be realized; but we may doubt whether Sulla had then time to give effect to the reform.[1] A law was also passed for effecting a settlement between creditors and debtors, the object doubtless being to put an end to the disputes which had led to the murder of Asellio.[2] Though Sulla was now master of six legions, he sent them back to Capua and did not use his strength to place his partisans in office. One of his supporters, Gnaeus Octavius, was elected consul for the ensuing year; the other successful candidate, Cornelius Cinna, who had held a command in the Social War, belonged to the Marian party, but bound himself by a solemn oath to maintain the policy of Sulla. The friends of the exiles, however, among whom were wealthy ladies, encouraged by the withdrawal of Sulla's army, intrigued for their recall: designs were formed against the lives of Sulla and his brother consul; and the latter, who, in the hope of securing his safety during Sulla's absence, had obtained command of the force which was serving under Pompeius Strabo, was murdered by his soldiers at the instigation, as was generally believed, of their former chief. It was time for Sulla, whose enemies were encouraged secretly by Cinna, to depart. The most formidable adversary whom Rome had encountered since the time of Hannibal was master of the province of Asia, and the tragedy of

[1] Livy, *Epit.*, 77; App., i, 59, 265-8. Dr. Hardy (*Journ. Rom. Studies*, vi, 1916, p. 6), remarking that the selection of the new senators ' would require some time, and could hardly have been accomplished before Sulla left Italy ', and that afterwards ' there was a democratic reaction ', concludes that ' the three hundred were never actually added ' until Sulla became dictator.

[2] Festus, ed. W. M. Lindsay, p. 516, ll. 3-5.

INTRODUCTION

Cirta had been re-enacted on a greater scale : in obedience to Mithradates, his officers, aided by the Greek communities, on one day massacred the Italians—moneylenders, tax-gatherers, and speculators, whose greed had made them odious to the people.[1] When, early in the new year, Sulla sailed from Brundisium, he was committing himself to an enterprise unparalleled in history. The Samnites and the Lucanians were still fighting for independence with the resolution of despair. From the Roman Government he could expect no money and no aid : by some means he must make the war which he was about to wage self-supporting : his family, his friends, his property were at the mercy of his foes.[2]

Massacre of Italians in Asia.

87 B.C. Sulla departs for the East.

No sooner had Sulla turned his back than Cinna, determined to procure the recall of his exiled friends, revived the proposals of Sulpicius and instigated the Italians to demand registration in the existing tribes. His partisans assembled in the Forum, armed with daggers, and clamoured for the re-enactment of the Sulpician law ; but the old citizens, headed by Octavius and backed by a majority of the tribunes, overpowered them and drove them to the gates of the city. Cinna himself, after vainly endeavouring to purchase the aid of slaves, fled from Rome to rouse his adherents in the Latin towns, whereupon the Senate, following the example of Tiberius Gracchus, deposed him from his consulship. He responded by appealing to a corps at Capua, complaining that the Senate had robbed him of the dignity which the people had conferred, and, having gained their support and that of many Italian towns, marched for the capital, which Pompeius Strabo with his army had already been summoned to defend.[3] A few weeks later Marius, informed of the state of affairs and encouraged by Cinna to return,

Cinna and Marius in power.

[1] It would be futile to attempt to decide between the conflicting estimates —150,000 (Plut., *Sulla*, 24, 5) and 80,000 (Val. Max., ix, 2, *Ext.* 3, and others)—of the number of the victims.
[2] Livy, *Epit.*, 77–8 ; Vell., ii, 20, 1 ; Val. Max., ix, 7. *Mil. Rom.* 2 ; Plut., *Sulla*, 10, 5–8 ; App., i, 63–4, §§ 281–6 ; Dio, *fr.* 100, 2.
[3] Cic., *Pro Sest*, 36,77 ; *In Cat.*, iii, 10, 24, and *Schol. Gronov.* ed. Stangl,

after many adventures in Italy and Africa landed with a thousand Numidians in Etruria and, joined by other exiles, by slaves, to whom he promised freedom, and by Italians whom he attracted by the prospect of carrying the Sulpician law, made his way to the camp of Cinna. Strabo, who was suspected of treachery, remained inactive and suffered Rome to be invested by the rebels. Marius and Cinna, who intended to starve their opponents into submission, cut off all supplies by land and sea. The Senate, hoping to conciliate the Italians, promised the franchise in pursuance of the Papirian law, to all who laid down their arms; but comparatively few took advantage of the offer. At the same time they ordered Metellus, a son of the old opponent of Jugurtha, who was in arms against the Samnites, to make such terms with them as he could and hasten to protect the capital. The Samnites, seeing their opportunity, demanded not only the franchise but the restoration of all prisoners and the right of retaining all the booty which they had won. Metellus of course refused such humiliating conditions: Marius and Cinna eagerly accepted them. Octavius, though his troops were superior to their opponents in numbers and in discipline, was afraid to hazard a decisive battle; and the Senate were compelled by fear of famine to acknowledge Cinna as consul and to admit both him and Marius within the gates of Rome. How Marius satiated his lust for vengeance; how Octavius, whose life he had sworn to spare, Marcus Antonius the great orator, and other consulars were murdered and their gory heads suspended in the Forum; how Catulus committed suicide to avoid assassination; how during five days every one to whom Marius owed a grudge or whose wealth he coveted was butchered, and their headless trunks were devoured in the streets by dogs; how the laws of Sulla were annulled, his house destroyed, his property confiscated, his wife and children forced to flee—these things will be recalled by all upon whose memory in childhood was

The Marian proscription.

p. 286 (ed. Orelli, p. 410); *Phil.*, viii, 2, 7; Livy, *Epit.*, 79; Vell., ii, 20, 2–5; Plut., *Mar.*, 41, 1; *Sert.*, 4, 6–7; App., i, 64–6.

INTRODUCTION

impressed the tale of Marius. When all was over, the liberated slaves, who had been the instruments of his revenge, but now, turning upon their old masters, began to plunder and to murder on their own account, were surrounded and slaughtered to a man.[1]

Marius and Cinna declared themselves elected consuls, Marius for the seventh time. But the ferocious old soldier had only a few weeks to live. There were baseless rumours that Sulla had conquered Mithradates and was about to return; and Marius, dreading a contest with his enemy, broken by age and trouble, worn by sleeplessness, gave himself up to drinking and died delirious in his bed.[2]

Death of Marius. 86 B. C.

During the next three years Italy was quiescent under the successive consulships of Cinna. Financial conditions were so disorganized in consequence of the late disturbances that Valerius Flaccus, the consul who had succeeded Marius, passed a law by which creditors were obliged to accept one-fourth of what they had lent, in full discharge;[3] and the praetor, Marius Gratidianus, earned great popularity by restoring the debased coinage to its standard weight.[4] Cinna, though he was too supine or too improvident to prepare for impending civil war, exercised his power with such tyranny that most of the nobles fled the country and found an asylum in Sulla's camp.[5] Yet the stillness that prevailed throughout these years, even if it was the result of terror, is attested by Cicero, who adds,

Tyranny of Cinna.

[1] Cic., *De or.*, iii, 2-3, §§ 8-11; Diod. Sic., xxxviii, 2, 2; 4; Livy, *Epit.* 80; Vell., ii, 21, 6; 22; Val. Max, ii, 8, 7; Plut., *Mar.*, 41-4; *Sert.*, 5; Flor., ii, 9, 10-7; App., i, 67-74; Licinianus, ed. Flemisch, pp. 16, ll. 4-6; 17-9; 20, ll. 1-2; 21, ll. 9-11; Eutrop., v, 7; Oros., v, 19, 8-13. 24.

[2] Diod. Sic., xxxvii, 29, 4; Livy, *Epit.*, 80; Vell., ii, 23, 1; Plut., *Mar.*, 45, 3-11: App., i, 75; Oros., v, 19, 23.

[3] Sall., *Cat.*, 33, 2; Vell., ii, 23, 2.

[4] Cic., *De off.*, iii, 20, 80. Marius, says Babelon (*Traité des monn. grecques et rom.*, i, 638), had the coins tested, and gradually withdrew the plated ones from circulation (Pliny, xxxiii, 9 (45), 132; xxxiv, 6 (12), 27). Babelon adds that the forced circulation of plated coins was restored by Sulla, and cites [Julius] Paulus, *Sent.*, v, 25, 1, from whom we learn on the contrary that Sulla provided for the condign punishment of those who debased or defaced the coinage.

[5] Vell., ii, 23, 3; Plut., *Sulla*, 22, 1-2; Dio, *fr.* 102, 1; Oros., v. 20, 1.

'All this time I was busy night and day, meditating on every branch of study.'[1]

Sulla victorious in Greece and Asia.

Meanwhile Sulla, refusing to be distracted by the news from Italy, although Cinna dispatched Flaccus with an army to supersede him, had patiently achieved his aim. When, by the victories of Chaeronea and Orchomenus, he reconquered Greece and invaded Asia Minor, his supersession had turned to his advantage: Fimbria, the lieutenant of Flaccus, had murdered his chief, assumed command of the consular army, and expelled the troops of Mithradates from the province. Mithradates wanted peace, while Sulla, although he had defrayed the expenses of the war by selling his prisoners to the slave-dealers and plundering temples of their treasures, was near the end of his resources; Mithradates, if he were pressed too hard, might unite with Fimbria against him; and, above all, it was time for him to return to Italy. A peace was therefore made, which both parties equally desired, and which both doubtless recognized as temporary. Mithradates agreed to pay an indemnity of two thousand talents, to surrender seventy ships of war, and to restore the province of Asia to the Romans as well as Cappadocia and Bithynia, which he had conquered, to their native kings: in return, he was guaranteed possession of his own kingdom, Pontus, as a Friend and Ally of Rome.[2] Fimbria, deserted by his legions, which transferred their allegiance to Sulla, committed suicide,[3] and Sulla proceeded to settle the affairs of Asia. Those communities which had remained true to Rome were rewarded by the bestowal of self-government; but the rest of the provincials, who had already found that the tyranny of Mithradates was more intolerable than the exactions of their former rulers, were punished for the massacre which had inaugurated the war. They were required to pay arrears of taxes for the

85 B. C. *Submission of Mithradates.*

Sulla's settlement of Asia.

---

[1] *Brut.*, 90, 308.
[2] Livy, *Epit.*, 83; Plut., *Sulla*, 22, 7-8; 24; App., *Mithr.*, 54-8; *B. C.*, i, 76, 347; Licinianus, ed. M. Flemisch, p. 26, ll. 5-10, p. 27, ll. 1-7.
[3] Livy, *Epit.*., 83; Plut., *Sulla*, 25, 3.

INTRODUCTION

last five years and an indemnity of twenty thousand talents; while those who had been prominent as partisans of Mithradates were put to death. To raise the indemnity it was necessary to borrow from Italian usurers, with results which could be foreseen. The legions of Fimbria, which were left to garrison the province, were quartered on native householders, who were required not only to feed them and their invited guests, but also to give them pocket-money; for although Sulla had shown that he could enforce stern discipline, he was obliged to keep his soldiers in good humour. When he started on his homeward journey the province was a prey to pirates, while Ariobarzanes and Nicomedes, the kings of Cappadocia and Bithynia, were in no condition to defend themselves against renewed attack. Sulla doubtless recognized these evils, but he had neither the time nor the power to remove them: the state of Italy demanded that he should instantly return.[1]

84 B. C.

Alarmed by the prospect of imminent invasion, Cinna and his colleague, Carbo, set about the preparations which they ought to have begun three years before. Troops were hurriedly levied; agents were sent out to collect money; ships were fetched from Sicily to guard the coasts. But when a dispatch was received from Sulla, in which he declared that his services had been requited by outlawry and that, although he would respect the rights of inoffensive citizens, he intended to punish his enemies, the Senate was induced by its moderate members to send delegates to negotiate, and the consuls were ordered to suspend the levy. They pretended obedience, but, knowing that for them there was no hope of pardon, resolved to encounter Sulla, and made an attempt, which proved abortive, to cross the Adriatic; Cinna's recruits, who were half-hearted, mutinied; and when he endeavoured to coerce them he was murdered. Sulla's reply, in which he repeated that he would never forgive the

Hurried preparations of Cinna and Carbo to resist Sulla.

Death of Cinna.

[1] Cic., *Pro Flacc.*, 14, 32; *Q. fr.*, i, 1, 33; Plut., *Sulla*, 25, 3–4; *Luc.*, 4, 2; App., *Mithr.*, 61–3; Licinianus, ed. Flemisch, p. 28, ll. 4–7. See pp. 395–6.

crimes of his opponents and insisted that the refugees who had sought safety with him should be restored to their civic rights, made it evident that he would neither disband his army nor consent to compromise. A majority of the Senate recognized the fairness of his demand; but Carbo prevented its acceptance and in the hope of purchasing the support of the Italians induced the House to confirm [1] the law which promised them equality of suffrage. Early in the following year, thanks to the unskilful disposition of the consul's fleet, Sulla landed in Brundisium.[2]

His army, comprising five legions, six thousand horse, and a corps which he had raised in Greece and Macedonia,[3] was inferior in number to the force of his opponents, but far superior in quality. The legions, now seasoned veterans, were devoted to their leader; many of the troops arrayed against him were untrustworthy, the Samnites and Lucanians, who regarded him as their irreconcilable enemy, being alone formidable; and not one of the generals whom he encountered was his match. Advancing through Apulia, he restrained his soldiers from doing any damage to the land or injury to the inhabitants, and before a blow was struck he made overtures for peace, which were rejected; but men of standing soon declared for him—Marcus Crassus, the future millionaire, who recruited for him among the Marsi, the younger Metellus, who had raised a force in Africa, and Pompey, the son of Strabo, who enrolled three legions in Picenum. Crossing the Apennines, Sulla defeated the consul Norbanus in Campania, while the army of the other consul, Scipio, passed over to his side. Pompey meanwhile had gained successes in Picenum over enemies who quarrelled among themselves; and by the time when he joined Sulla the first campaign was won. In the following year the

---

[1] *I find that my view is supported by Mommsen (Röm. Staatsr., iii, 180, n. 1). Strachan-Davidson (Appian : Book I, p. 77) rejects Livy's statement (Epit., 84) on insufficient grounds.
[2] Livy, Epit., 83–4; Vell., ii, 24, 5; App., i, 76–9.
[3] Ib., 79, 363.

INTRODUCTION 57

conquest of Italy was completed. The seizure of Sardinia, one of the granaries of Italy, ensured supplies. The youthful consul Marius, a true son of his father, who rashly pitted himself against Sulla, was defeated, after several of his cohorts had deserted, near Praeneste, in which he was forced to stand a siege: Metellus and Pompey gained decisive victories in Cisalpine Gaul and Umbria; and on the 1st of November.[1] the Samnites and Lucanians, who had vainly attempted to relieve Praeneste, were overwhelmed by Sulla, after a desperate battle, near the Colline Gate of Rome. While Sulla was addressing the senators, whom he had summoned to assemble, they were startled by cries of anguish: with an unmoved countenance he bade them attend to him and give no heed to what was going on outside; some malefactors were being punished, that was all. The punishment was the massacre of three thousand Samnite prisoners, who had laid down their arms under a promise of their lives, and whose corpses were thrown into the Tiber.

Praeneste forthwith surrendered. The Roman citizens, save Marius, who perished in attempting to escape, were spared; the Samnites and the Praenestines were massacred to the last man. The Latin colony of Norba, which alone held out, was soon betrayed: the townsmen killed each other or committed suicide; and the town, which they had set on fire, was destroyed. It remained only to subdue the Marians in Sicily and Africa; and Pompey was entrusted with this charge.

What Italy had suffered since the death of Drusus it needs a sympathetic imagination to conceive.[2] Besides the thousands who had died in the Social and the Civil Wars, besides those who had been butchered to appease the hate of Marius, there were many who must have been hindered by the presence of the soldiery from tilling their fields or from practising their trades, and others, dependent upon them, who were threatened with starvation. The first need was to restore order, and that duty Sulla

[1] Vell., ii, 27, 1.   [2] See Pliny, ii, 83 (85), 199.

How he approached the work of reconstruction.

might be trusted to perform. But when he set about the task of reconstruction he was embittered by the provocation which he had received,—by the sentences of outlawry which had been pronounced upon himself and upon his friends, by the destruction of his property,[1] and by the savagery with which the younger Marius had gratified his lust for vengeance before he went to his own doom. It was not to be expected that he should forget how, with many victims of lesser note, Mucius Scaevola, the Chief pontiff and the most illustrious of Roman jurists, had been murdered and their bodies left unburied or pitched into the river.[2] A man of easy temper when he was not provoked, he was a whole-hearted partisan. He was obliged to make provision for his veterans on pain of losing their support; he intended to reward adherents no matter at whose cost; and if any one suggested that he should try to heal old feuds by conciliating his foes, he doubtless answered, with entire truth, that there was only one way to remove their enmity. Being no visionary, he did not believe that there was any panacea for the disease from which the State was suffering: he would put a stop to anarchy and do his best to reduce the demagogues to impotence; if the nobles failed to use the weapon which he put into their hands, they would have themselves to blame.

Sulla had the Roman respect for law; and he determined, for his own security, to act in legal form. As the consuls had both perished, he directed the Senate to nominate an interrex, whose function it was, in such circumstances, to hold the consular election: but, knowing that in that crisis he alone could govern, he intimated that the public safety required the appointment of a dictator, who should hold office until tranquillity was restored; and accordingly the interrex, Valerius Flaccus, carried a law in the popular assembly by which Sulla was made dictator for life and all his acts were ratified in advance.[3]

His dictatorship.

---

[1] App., i, 73, 340; 86, 390.   [2] *Ib.*, 88, 403-4.
[3] Cic., *De lege agr.*, iii, 2, 5; Att., ix, 15, 2; Livy, *Epit.*, 89; Vell., ii, 28, 2; Plut., *Sulla*, 33, 1-2.

The election of consuls, which he of course permitted, was only remarkable because one of his officers, Lucretius Ofella, who by a law which he had just enacted was ineligible, presumed nevertheless to come forward as a candidate, and was instantly killed by his order in the presence of the people. When they raised an outcry he declared that Ofella had been executed by his command, and went on to speak a parable : ' A yokel, tormented by lice when he was ploughing, stopped twice to purge his smock ; but as he was still bitten, he burned it to avoid being interrupted in his work. So I warn those who have been twice humbled not to bring upon themselves like punishment.' [1]

The Sullan reign of terror was never forgotten by the Romans and will be remembered by all who in boyhood learned the rudiments of Roman history ; but, except those who have witnessed the tyranny of Lenin, which of us can realize what it meant ? It was the purpose of Sulla to extirpate all who had supported his opponents and to inflict condign punishment upon the Samnites, those inveterate enemies of Rome ; but it was not these measures that provoked the detestation of posterity. He allowed his friends and followers to murder those whose wealth they coveted or against whom they bore a grudge. Even before the enactment of the Valerian law the massacre had begun.[2] Rewards were offered to any one who killed a man whose name appeared in the proscription lists, and all who harboured the victims shared their fate. Senators belonging to the minority which had supported Marius and Cinna were put to death, and likewise sixteen hundred knights, who, as they represented

The Terror.

---

[1] *Ib.*, §§ 5–6 ; Livy, *Epit.*, 89 ; App., i, 101, 471–2. It is a question whether Ofella was a candidate at the election of the consuls who were to hold office in 81 or in 80 (cf. W. Drumann, *Gesch. Roms*, ii², 1902, p. 409, n. 12). As the battle of the Colline Gate was fought on Nov. 1, it seems unlikely that Sulla enacted the law which Ofella violated before the end of the year : on the other hand, it is hardly credible that Ofella, after having been warned by Sulla, persisted in standing against Sulla himself, who held office in 80. Perhaps, as happened several times in later years, the consuls of 81 were elected in that, not in the preceding year.

[2] See Th. Mommsen, *Röm. Staatsr.*, ii³, 1887, p. 736, n. 5.

the order which had persistently opposed the nobles, were the objects of Sulla's especial hatred.[1] We, who are living in an age when class is embittered against class, can imagine how he felt. Cicero, if we may accept his evidence, saw the severed heads of senators displayed in the streets of Rome.[2] Cato, then a boy of thirteen, exclaimed indignantly to his tutor, who told him that the Dictator was more feared than hated, 'Why have you not given me a sword that I might kill him and set my country free from servitude?'[3] Marius Gratidianus, a son of Gaius Marius, was flogged through the city, then tortured till his death, to please a friend of Sulla whose father had been a victim of the Marian persecution.[4] Sulla himself stooped to gratify his rancour against Marius, whose remains he ordered to be disinterred and thrown into the river Anio, hard by his tomb.[5] The sons of the proscribed were deprived of all title to their father's property and permanently excluded from public life.[6] Rebellious communities were fined and the walls of their towns destroyed.[7] The people of Volaterrae and Arretium in Etruria, who had distinguished themselves by the pertinacity of their resistance, were disfranchised and reduced to the status of Latin colonies.[8] The territory of the Samnites was laid waste; prosperous towns were destroyed; and those who ventured to remonstrate with Sulla were cut short by the reply that Romans would never be at rest so long as the Samnites existed as a people.[9] Thousands of landowners were dispossessed and evicted from their homes to make room for soldiers, who would be bound by their own interest to uphold the government which Sulla purposed to create. Public lands which had not yet been

How Sulla rewarded his partisans.

---

[1] Cic., *De off.*, ii, 8, 27; Vell., ii, 28, 3; Plut., *Sulla*, 31, 1-6, 8-10; Flor., ii, 9, 24-5; App., i, 95, 441-4; &c., &c.
[2] *Pro Rosc. Amer.*, 32, 90.   [3] Plut., *Cato min.*, 3, 2.
[4] Q. Cic., *De pet. cons.*, § 10; Livy, *Epit.*, 88; Ascon., ed. Clark, p. 84, ll. 7-9 (ed. Stangl, p. 65); Val. Max., ix, 2, 1; Flor., ii, 9, 24-6; Oros., v, 21, 7-8.
[5] Cic., *De leg.*, ii, 22, 56-7.
[6] Livy, *Epit.*, 89; Vell., ii, 28, 4; Plut., *Sulla*, 31, 7.
[7] Cic., *Parad.*, vi, 2, 46; Flor., ii, 9, 27-8; App., i, 96, 447.
[8] Cic., *Pro Caec.*, 35, 102.   [9] Strabo, v, 4, 11.

INTRODUCTION

distributed, confiscated lands which belonged to rebellious cities or to individuals who had resisted Sulla were assigned to others, who were established as colonists in the towns and served as garrisons.[1] One centurion acquired an estate which was valued at ten million sesterces, the equivalent of a hundred thousand pounds;[2] and many became so rich that they could afford to live in princely state. The confiscations were so extensive that, while all the veterans were provided for, estates were available for purchasers who would uphold the new régime; and although many were sold to the Dictator's favourites at nominal prices, the whole amount realized was three hundred and fifty million sesterces, or three million five hundred thousand pounds.[3] Beautiful women, musicians, actors, even freedmen received lavish gifts from Sulla, who disposed of the money as he pleased.[4]

All this time Sulla was drafting laws by which he designed to restore to the Senate its old authority and to keep the knights and the commons in subjection. Above all, he determined to reduce the power of the tribunes, who, since the time of Tiberius Gracchus, had been a menace to the Senate, to insignificance.[5] They were forbidden to propose any law without the previous sanction of the Senate: all higher offices were to be closed to them, that able men might be discouraged from aspiring to the tribunate;[6] they might not convene meetings of the people—a prohibition tantamount to the suppression of free speech; and their right of veto, although it was not abolished, was restricted. In fine,

His legislation. 81 B.C.

---

[1] Cic., *De lege agr.*, i, 7, 21; ii, 29, 81; *Pro Mur.*, 24, 49; Livy, *Epit.*, 89; Pliny, xiv, 6 (8), 62; App., i, 96, 448; 100, 470; 104, 489; C. Lachmann, *D. Schr. d. röm. Feldmesser*, i, 1848, p. 237, l. 5; *C. I. L.*, x, p. 89. Sulla's allotments, like those of T. Gracchus, were inalienable (Cic., *De lege agr.*, ii, 28, 78).
[2] Ascon, ed. Clark, p. 90, ll. 25-6 (ed. Stangl, p. 70).
[3] Cic. *Pro Rosc. Amer.*, 2, 6; 43, 125-6; *Pro Quint.*, 24, 76; *De lege agr.*, i, 21, 56; 29, 81; Livy, *Epit.*, 89; Vell., ii, 28, 4; Plut., *Cic.*, 3, 2.
[4] Plut., *Sulla*, 33, 3; Athenaeus, vi, 261c.
[5] See pp. 357-60.
[6] Ascon., ed. Clark, p. 66, ll. 23-4; p. 67, ll. 1-4; p. 78, ll. 23-5 (ed. Stangl, pp. 53, 61); App., i, 100, 467.

their only privilege left unimpaired, apart from personal sacrosanctity, was that of aiding those citizens who appealed to their protection. The Senate, again greatly weakened, by losses in war and by proscription, was reinforced by three hundred knights and even by some private soldiers; but if, as we are told, the Dictator's choice was confirmed by the popular assembly, it is safe to conclude that their votes were given under the influence of fear.[1] Provision was made for maintaining the numbers of the Senate without the sanction of the censors, whose office was for a time disused, by increasing the number of the quaestors, who, as a matter of course, were to become senators.[2] The jurors were to be selected from the Senate alone, a provision which could not have been valid unless the number of senators had been increased;[3] and thus the knights were divested of the privilege which they had enjoyed for forty years and had frequently abused. Mindful of the repeated consulships of Marius and Cinna and the irregular appointment of the younger Marius, Sulla enacted further, in conformity with ancient usage, that no man might be elected praetor unless he had served as quaestor, or consul unless he had served as praetor, and that none might be re-elected to a curule magistracy until after an interval of ten years.[4] The populace were deprived of the doles of corn which Gaius Gracchus had bestowed [5] and of the right of electing candidates for the priestly colleges;[6] while, perhaps to gratify ambitious friends of the Dictator, the numbers of the pontiffs and the augurs were increased.[7] The law by which Gracchus had secured the impartial assignment

---

[1] App., i, 100, 468; Sall., *Cat.*, 37, 6; Dion. Hal., v, 77; Livy, *Epit.*, 89.
[2] *Schol. Gronov.* in Cic., *Div. in Caec.*, 3, 8, ed. Stangl, p. 326 (ed. Orelli, p. 384); Tac., *Ann.*, xi, 22; *C. I. L.*, i, No. 202 (=C. G. Bruns, *Fontes*⁶, &c., 1893, pp. 90–2).
[3] Tac., *Ann.*, xi, 22; Cic., *Verr.*, i, 13, 37; Vell., ii, 32, 3. Cf. Greenidge, *Legal Procedure*, &c., pp. 436–7, and *Class. Rev.*, xxvii, 1913, p. 263.
[4] App., i, 100, 466.
[5] Sall., *Hist.*, i, 55, 11; Licinianus, ed. Flemisch, p. 34, ll. 4–5. Cf. *Paulys Real-Ency.*, vii, 173.
[6] Dio, xxxvii, 37, 1.
[7] Livy, *Epit.*, 89; Ps. Victor, *De vir. ill.*, 75, 11.

INTRODUCTION

of the consular provinces remained in force; but the dictator supplemented it by regulations which were designed to ensure a constant succession of governors and to prevent, or at least to minimize, misgovernment. Outside Italy there were now ten provinces. The number of the praetors was therefore raised to eight, who, during their year of office, were to discharge their judicial duties in the capital, and afterwards to administer their respective provinces with proconsular authority : at the same time Sulla enacted that an outgoing governor must depart within thirty days after the arrival of his successor; restricted the expenditure which provincials might incur in sending deputations to return thanks for the benefits which he was alleged to have conferred; and forbade proconsuls to leave their provinces, to lead their troops beyond the frontiers, or to engage in war without the authority of the Senate and the Roman People.[1]

One benefit Sulla conferred upon the State, which his sternest critics gladly recognized. Although he took care to exempt his own agents from the penalty of murder, he established the criminal law upon a firm foundation. While he framed enactments against treason, extortion, peculation and bribery, assassination, poisoning, arson and assault, forgery, coining, and breach of trust, he brought all these offences under the jurisdiction of permanent courts, thus widening the procedure which had been established before the Gracchan era.[2] His sumptuary law and one by which he attempted to improve public morals are only noticeable because they were inevitably futile, and because, like other autocratic legislators, he flouted them himself.[3]

---

[1] Cic., *Fam.*, iii, 6, 3 ; viii, 8, 8 ; *In Pis.*, 21, 50 ; *Dig.*, i, 2, 2, 32. Cf. P. Willems, *Le sénat*, &c., ii, 1883, pp. 571-3, 575-6, 578.

[2] Cic., *Verr.*, ii, 1, 42, 108 ; *Pro Cluent.*, 54, 148 ; *Pro Mur.*, 20, 42 ; *Pro Sulla*, 5, 17, and *Schol. Bob.*, ed. Stangl, p. 78 (ed. Orelli, p. 361) ; *In Pis.*, 21, 50 ; *Pro Rab. Post.*, 4, 8-9 ; *Fam.*, iii, 11, 2 ; Ascon., ed. Clark, p. 60, l. 15 ; p. 62, l. 11 (ed. Stangl, pp. 49-50) ; *Dig.*, i, 2, 2, 32 ; xlviii, 1, 1 ; 8 ; 10 ; Justin., *Inst.*, iv. 4, 8 ; 18, 5-7. Cf. Greenidge, *Legal Procedure*, &c., p. 407, and Strachan-Davidson, *Problems*, &c., ii, 20-2.

[3] Plut., *Sulla*, 35, 3-4 ; *Comp. Lys. cum Sulla*, 3, 3 ; Gell., ii, 24, 11 ; Macrob., iii, 17, 11.

He abdicates
79 B.C

Sulla's work was done, and, since he loved pleasure more than power, he resigned his dictatorship after he had held it for two years,[1] and quitted Rome to spend the evening of his life on his estate near Cumae and to enjoy the society of the actors and actresses who were his boon companions.[2] No tyrant was ever absolute; but Sulla, though he knew that even he could not afford to defy public sentiment, was more nearly absolute than any other Roman; and those who have closely studied his career will probably conclude that in natural ability he was inferior to none. Although when he divested himself of power he doubtless trusted in the good fortune of which he often boasted and to which he ascribed the whole of his success,[3] he incurred little risk; for, besides the veterans who overawed his enemies, there were ten thousand emancipated slaves, whose masters he had put to death, and upon whom, when he set them free, he had bestowed the franchise, always prepared to do his bidding.[4]

His epitaph.

An inscription which he wrote and which he ordered to be engraved upon his tomb revealed his character: 'No friend has ever served, no enemy has ever wronged me whom I have not repaid in full.'[5]

[1] Plut., *Sulla*, 34, 6; App., i, 103, 480; 104, 484; Ps. Victor, *De vir. ill.*, 75, 11; Oros., v, 22, 1.
[2] Plut., 35, 5-8; 36, 1-2.
[3] Plut., 34, 3. 6. Cf. Vell., ii, 27, 5.
[4] App., i, 100, 469; *C. I. L.*, i, No. 585 (=H. Dessau, *Inscr. Lat.*, 871).
[5] Plut., 38, 5.

CHAPTER II

THE ROMAN WORLD IN THE CICERONIAN AGE

THE aim of this chapter is to give such a general view of life in Italy and the Roman provinces as may enable those who are not versed in Roman antiquities to picture the background of the events to be described in the succeeding narrative.

The reader who visits Rome must close his vision to its most imposing monuments if he would imagine the scene as it appeared in the time of Cicero and Caesar. The Colosseum, the Baths of Caracalla and of Diocletian, the Column of Trajan, the Arch of Severus, the Temple of Vespasian, the Arch of Titus must vanish from the picture. Let us suppose that a traveller from Gaul or from Illyricum is about to enter from the north. Standing on the Pincian hill, he sees on his right, as he passes through the gateway called Porta Salutaris, the villa, embowered in gardens, which Lucullus adorned with the wealth that he had amassed in Asia.[1] The city extending below, far more densely populated than the Rome of to-day, is thronged by a million souls;[2] but its aspect compares unfavourably with that of Athens or even Capua. After the destruction wrought by the Gauls the builders went to work with no considered plan, and a new town grew irregularly at haphazard.[3] But under Grecian influence improvements have been carried out : among the unsightly blocks of building in which the bulk of the population lodge princely mansions are descried on the Palatine, and above the Forum rise the temples of the Capitol. Descending the hill, the traveller makes his way over the Quirinal and

Rome and its environs.

[1] Plut., *Luc.*, 39, 2.   [2] See pp. 360–3.
[3] L. Friedlaender, *Darstell. aus d. Sittengesch. Roms*, i⁸, 1910, pp. 3–5 ;
F. Haverfield, *Anc. Town-Planning*, 1913, p. 83.

along the depression between it and the Viminal through streets so narrow that it will soon be necessary to prohibit vehicular traffic in the daytime.[1] Litters, borne by slaves, are conveying men of wealth,[2] while Jews, Greeks, Syrians, and other foreigners jostle on the narrow pavement with Roman citizens. Mountebanks, jugglers, fortune-tellers, stilt-walkers, mimes who earn odd coppers by mimicking the cries of animals, add to the animation of the scene.[3] Huge isolated tenements, some of which cover more than an acre of ground, rise to a height of four, five, or even six stories;[4] rows of shops on the ground-floor face the streets which enclose them.[5] Mingling with the crowd in the Forum, the traveller admires the halls closing its northern side, in which men of business congregate and trials are conducted;[6] and one day, if his visit is prolonged, he may hear Cicero addressing a jury in defence of some well-known client, or listen to Clodius haranguing a popular assembly from the Rostra, while aliens and slaves, elbowing the mob of citizens, yell in approval of the speaker's words.[7] Lining the longer sides of the oblong space are the offices of the bankers and money-changers who keep current accounts for their customers against which they draw cheques, pay interest on deposits, and negotiate bills of exchange.[8] Emerging from the eastern end, the visitor enters the Sacred Way, spanned by the triumphal arch which commemorates the victory that Fabius Maximus gained

[1] *Lex Iulia municipalis*, ll. 56 ff. (C. G. Bruns. *Fontes iur. Rom.*,[6] 1893, pp. 107-8). Cf. *Quart. Rev.*, ccix, 1908, p. 109, n.*.
[2] Cic., *Pro Rosc. Amer.*, 46, 134; Daremberg and Saglio, *Dict. des ant. grecques et rom.*, iii, 1004.
[3] Plaut., *Poen.*, iii, 1, 27; Hor., *Sat.*, i, 6, 114; Daremberg and Saglio, iii, 1903.
[4] Cic., *De off.*, iii, 16, 66; Vitruv., ii, 8, 17. Cf. Strabo, v, 3, 7; *Notizie d. Scavi*, 1901, p. 391; H. Stuart Jones, *Companion to Rom. Hist.*, 1912, p. 35; F. Haverfield, *op. cit.*, pp. 78-9.
[5] Daremberg and Saglio, iii, 546.
[6] A. H. J. Greenidge, *Legal Procedure*, &c., 1901, p. 133.
[7] Cic., *Pro Flac.*, 28, 66-7. Cf. vol. ii, *passim*.
[8] Cic., *Fam.*, iii, 5, 4; *Q. fr.*, i, 3, 7; *Att.*, v, 15, 2; xi, 1, 2; 24, 3; xii, 24, 1; 27, 2. Cf. Daremberg and Saglio, i, 407-8; *Paulys Real-Ency.*, ii, 707-9.

over the Allobroges.¹ On his right is the Palatine, the most fashionable quarter of the city, where, among other imposing edifices, he may gaze at the palatial mansion for which, with its surrounding gardens, Clodius paid fourteen million eight hundred thousand sesterces, the equivalent of one hundred and forty-eight thousand pounds.² Standing upon the summit of the hill, one looked down upon the Great Circus, which filled the depression between the Palatine and the Aventine, and on the opening day of the games that were there celebrated might watch the procession defiling through the Forum on its way to the arena.³ Retracing his steps and again traversing the Forum, our traveller would ascend the Capitol, observing at its foot the Temple of Saturn, which contained the Treasury, then the Tabularium, or Public Record Office, and, dominating all, the great temple of Jupiter, lately erected in place of that which was destroyed by fire just before Sulla returned from the Mithradatic War.⁴ Below, extending to the left bank of the Tiber, lay the Field of Mars, where youths might be seen engaged in manly exercises—running, leaping, hurling the discus, playing games of ball, or plunging into the swift stream.⁵ Conspicuous on the broad expanse were colonnades, which, like all the public buildings of the period, had been designed under Greek influence, and of which other examples might be descried lining the course of the river, below the Palatine and the Aventine.⁶ Within the Field, hard by the western slope of the Capitol, was the Flaminian Circus; and one who visited the city in the second consulship of Pompey would have noticed, a little farther to the west, close to the Triumphal Gate, the great stone theatre which he had just erected—the first permanent structure of its kind in Rome.

55 B.C

¹ Cic., *Pro Planc.*, 7, 17; *De or.*, ii, 66, 267.
² Pliny, *Nat. Hist.*, xxxvi, 15 (24), 103. In regard to houses on the Palatine and the Caelian see Sall., *Cat.*, 12, 3; Val. Max., ix, 1, 4; Pliny, xvii, 1 (1), 2; xxxvi, 3 (3), 7; 6 (7), 48. ³ Dion. Hal., vii, 72.
⁴ See p. 78. For an account of the remains of the temple of Jupiter see *The Times*, Lit. Suppl., Dec. 15, 1921, p. 842.
⁵ Cic., *Pro Cael.*, 15, 36; Hor., *Carm.*, i, 8, 8–12; iii, 12, 7–9.
⁶ Daremberg and Saglio, iv, 586; Stuart Jones, *op. cit.*, pp. 108, 110.

After a stranger had observed all that appealed to him within the walls he might wish to see something of the suburbs and the surrounding country. Rich men owned villas along the river and near the roads that traversed the Campagna, to which they betook themselves in the early spring, and from which they could drive daily to the capital to attend to official duties or private business.[1] Passing through the Porta Capena and driving in a hired carriage down the Appian Way, the visitor would gaze at the line of monuments that marked the sepulchres of the rich, and of which a somewhat later specimen, commemorating Caecilia Metella, the daughter of the conqueror of Crete, is familiar to the tourists of our day.

Religion. Sepulchral usage was of course associated with religion. Roman religion is a vast subject, the elucidation of which has made great progress during the last few years ; but we are concerned only with the connexion between religion and politics and the reciprocal influence of religion and national character : ignoring controversies and details which have no interest except for those who study religious history for its own sake, we may confine ourselves to a few main facts which are definitely known. But to understand what Cicero and his contemporaries thought about religion is impossible unless one has followed from the outset what has been called the religious experience of the Roman People.[2]

Roman religion, like almost every other, retained in its late development traces of taboos and magical practices which had prevailed in prehistoric times, but had of course lost their pristine meaning. Infants were still subjected on the eighth or the ninth day to the rite of purification ;[3] a sacrifice was part of the ceremonial that marked the investiture of boys after the age of puberty with the dress

[1] R. Lanciani, *Anc. Rome*, 1888, p. 268.
[2] The brief sketch which *I* am about to give may serve to encourage some readers to pursue the study. They would do well to begin with Dr. Warde Fowler's *Religious Experience of the Roman People*, not omitting to consult the authorities whom he cites at the end of each chapter.
[3] Macrob., i, 16, 36.

of manhood;[1] the ceremony called *aquaelicium*, or the drawing down of water, in which magistrates, lictors, and pontiffs alike took part, survived from a time when husbandmen whose crops were suffering from drought endeavoured by magical arts to procure rain;[2] and another relic, which the priests who directed the religion of the State may have felt obliged to sanction because the populace clung to a time-honoured superstition, remained in the festival of the Lupercalia, which Shakespeare[3] has made familiar, and in which the leaders of the priestly colleges, running round the Palatine hill, struck with strips of hide cut from sacrificial victims at the women who came close to them, in order to promote fecundity.[4] An amulet, which has its parallels in the charms, the 'lucky pigs', and the mascots of our own day, was worn by every Roman child—an emblem, enclosed in a case, of man's generative power, which was hung round their necks for luck.[5]

But what helped to fortify the Roman character was the religion of the family, which, amid all vicissitudes, remained, especially in rustic households, essentially the same,[6] and which is traceable to the time when the primitive Romans, no longer nomadic, settled down to cultivate the land. Their religion, like every other—I repeat what I have written of the Gauls—was rooted in animism, that habit of mind, common to savages and children, which peoples the universe with spirits, which ascribes to sun, moon, and stars, to earth and sea, to fire and water and everything that moves—even to many things that are inert—the life and will which they feel within themselves. The husbandman believed himself surrounded by a host of spirits, some friendly, others hostile, and he felt that he

[1] Ovid *Fasti*, iii, 783. Cf. J. Marquardt, *D. Privatleben d. Römer*,[2] 1886, pp. 124–6.
[2] S. P. Festi, *De verb. signif.*, p. 2; Tertull., *De ieiun.*, 16; Servius *in Aen.*, iii, 175. Cf. W. Warde Fowler, *Religious Experience*, &c., 1911, p. 50.
[3] *Julius Caesar*, Act. *I*, sc. I, l. 68.
[4] Plut., *Caes.*, 61, 1. Cf. Warde Fowler, *Roman Festivals*, 1899, p. 320 and n. 6.
[5] Pliny, xxviii, 4 (7), 39. Cf. Warde Fowler, *Religious Experience*, p. 60.
[6] *Ib.*, p. 69.

must keep himself and his belongings on good terms with them—retain their friendship or appease their enmity by prayer and sacrifice.[1] The countryside swarmed with wolves,[2] which might prey upon his flocks and herds. Flood or drought, tempest or lightning might injure his growing crops or wreck his harvest. In the single room with a hole in its roof, which admitted light and through which the rain fell into a hollow on the floor, were the hearth which served as his altar and the fire by which his wife cooked his food. After the midday meal a portion of what remained was thrown into the embers as an offering to Vesta, the spirit of the fire.[3] The cupboard behind the hearth was the abode of the Penates, who would guard its contents while they were duly worshipped; and no impure hand might touch that store.[4] The door, through which evil spirits or the ghosts of dead members of the family might enter if they were not excluded by proper ceremonies, was the haunt of Janus.[5] Peculiar to the master of the house was the guardian spirit, his Genius, which gave its name to his nuptial bed and, as he believed, gave him the power to propagate his race.[6] When his wife, whom he had married by due sacramental rites, bore him a child, he was anxious lest evil spirits from the woods should come through the doorway to torment the babe; and a rite, symbolical of agriculture, was enacted to keep them off.[7] When one of the family died, the body was carried out to burial by night feet foremost, to prevent its spirit from finding a way to return.[8]

It was in the time of the kings, while urban life was beginning, but before the Etruscans conquered the infant city, that a lawgiver, whom later writers identified with Numa Pompilius, framed the calendar of festivals which

---

[1] J. Marquardt, *Röm. Staatsverw.*, iii², 1885, p. 126.
[2] Virg., *Aen.*, ix, 59–64; Ovid, *Ars amat.*, ii, 147.
[3] Servius *in Aen.*, i, 730.   [4] *Ib.*, 270; Hor., *Carm.*, iii, 23, 17–20.
[5] Plut., *Quaest. Rom.*, 5. Cf. Warde Fowler, *Religious Experience*, p. 76.
[6] W. H. Roscher, *Lex. d. griech. u. röm. Mythol.*, i, 2, col. 1614–5; *Paulys Real-Ency.*, vii, 1156–60.
[7] Augustine, *De civ. Dei.*, vi, 9. Cf. Warde Fowler, *op. cit.*, pp. 83, 274.
[8] *Ib.*, pp. 76, 84–5.

was to organize the religion of the State.¹ Among the deities then worshipped we recognize, besides Janus and Vesta, Jupiter, Juno, Mars, Tellus or Mother Earth, and others, such as Saturn, Neptune, and Vulcan, whose names were mere adjectives, denoting the functions that were attibuted to them.² Jupiter, the god of the sky, if he was not thought of as the sky itself, the deity common to all Aryan peoples, was far older than the Roman State, though he was not yet the supreme god which he was later to become.³ Mars was not merely the god of war, but also of vegetation, which began to appear in the month that derived its name from him; and his aid was regularly invoked in the lustration of the farm.⁴ But these deities were not invested, like the gods of the imaginative Greeks, with human attributes : they were impersonal powers, vaguely conceived, and as yet they had no temples and no images.⁵ Familiarity with the names, which were given by authority, may, however, have led, especially when priests were attached to their worship, and when they came to be identified with Grecian deities, to their being conceived of as personal gods.⁶ The ritual with which they were worshipped was formulated by regulations as precise as those of which we read in *Leviticus*. The priests wore a distinctive dress of red or purple,⁷ while the Vestal virgins, who took no part in the sacrifice of victims, were habited in white.⁸ Lay worshippers as well as priests, sacred utensils and implements must be purged of all uncleanness ; ⁹ the victims, oxen, sheep, or swine, were selected according to rules which prescribed their sex, their age, their colour ; and when they had been duly garlanded and decked with

---

[1] *Ib.*, pp. 94–7, 108.   [2] *Ib.*, pp. 118–22, 135–6.
[3] *Ib.*, pp. 128–9.   [4] Cato, *De agri cult.*, 141.
[5] Tertull., *Apol.*, 25 ; Augustine, *De civ. Dei.* iv, 31 ; Servius *ad Aen.*, iii, 351. Cf. J. B. Carter, *The Religious Life of Anc. Rome*, 1911, pp. 10–1.
[6] Warde Fowler, *op. cit.*, pp. 119–20, 124.
[7] H. Diels, *Sibyl. Blätter*, 1890, p. 70, note ; Mrs. Arthur Strong, *Roman Sculpture*, 1907, pl. xi (p. 47) ; pl. xv (p. 54).
[8] Marquardt, *Röm. Staatsverw.*, iii², 340.
[9] Livy, xlv, 5, 4. Cf. Cic., *De leg.*, ii, 10, 24 and Marquardt, *op. cit.*, pp. 174–5.

fillets, they must be rejected unless they followed without resistance the attendants who led them to the slaughter.[1] It was essential that every detail should be performed in exact obedience to prescription, that every word should be spoken as it was set down in the liturgy, lest the deity invoked should take offence and refuse to grant the boon which his votaries desired : if the least mistake had been involuntarily made, the vitiated ceremony must be begun anew,[2] and an instance is recorded in which the repetition was prolonged to thirty times.[3]

No wonder that historians have condemned such religion as mere formalism, imbued with the spirit of the attorney, which could have no effect in ennobling character, and of which the essence was to bargain with the powers who were the object of the cult. Certainly the Romans felt little interest in their deities except as beings who might help them, and cared only for the process by which they hoped to secure that help. Undoubtedly those who vowed to dedicate an offering in return for the preservation of life or of the State or for some other benefit did make the covenant as men of business intent upon a bargain. But, while we need not insist upon the fact that the vow was occasionally fulfilled before the hoped-for blessing could be received,[4] it is evident that formalism and self-seeking were common to the Roman religion and to many others, and that the Romans have been singled out for blame because their bent for law made them lay special stress upon the punctilios of liturgy and of ritual. 'Pure religion and undefiled before God and the Father is this, to visit the fatherless and widows in their affliction and to keep himself unspotted from the world'—that is an ideal to which very few under any creed attain ; and if any Roman ever dreamed of it, he was not inspired by the religion of his fathers, but by Stoicism. But was the ritual prescribed by Roman priests more formal than that

[1] Marquardt, *op. cit.*, pp. 170–4, 180.
[2] Fr. Buecheler, *Umbrica*, 1883, vi, B. 48 (p 21) ; Cato, *De agri cult.*, 141.
[3] Plut., *Coriol.*, 25, 5.
[4] Livy, viii, 9, 5–8.

of *Leviticus* ?[1] Did not Jacob,[2] Jephthah,[3] and Hannah[4] make vows of which the fulfilment was conditional upon the bestowal of the benefits which they sought ? If the Romans had no prophets who bade them consider that mercy is better than sacrifice, is it certain that those who practised mercy were fewer than among the Jews, and when the most sympathetic expounder of Roman religion affirms that the Roman had never been conscious of individual duty except in relation to the State or to his family,[5] does he remember his habitual caution ? It is true that the recorded Italian prayers show no desire in the worshipper to conform his will with that of the deity except in ritual, no desire for righteousness, but only for earthly benefits.[6] But while Roman religion, before it felt Etruscan influence, made no appeal to hope or fear by the prospect of a future life, the habits of exact obedience and of ordered worship may well have had as bracing an effect upon Roman character as military discipline upon a raw recruit. Religion born of fear may not ennoble, but it tends to keep its votaries from breaches of duty which may displease the imaginary gods. The religion of the family tended to make it play its part in the service of the State, for it has been truly said that in the life of the family must have originated the word *pius*, which denoted 'the sense of duty towards family, state, and gods'.[7] 'The fear of the Lord' was with the Roman 'the beginning of wisdom '—not of that wisdom which the Psalmist[8] had in mind, but of that which made his country great. Cicero[9] was as sure as Polybius[10] and Posidonius[11] that the power of Rome was rooted in its religion.

---

[1] The following verse in *Leviticus* (xiv, 25) is noteworthy : ' the priest shall take some of the blood of the trespass offering, and put it upon the tip of the right ear of him that is to be cleansed, and upon the thumb of his right hand, and upon the great toe of his right foot '. Cf. the remark of Tertullian, *De praescr.*, i, 40.   [2] *Gen.*, xxviii, 20–2 ; *Numbers*, xxi, 2.
[3] *Judges*, xi, 30–1.   [4] 1 *Sam.*, i, 11.
[5] Warde Fowler, *Social Life at Rome*, &c., 1908, p. 341.
[6] See Fr. Buecheler, *Umbrica*, pp. 16 (vi. A. 50–5), 57 (vi. A. 27–8).
[7] Warde Fowler, *Religious Experience*, p. 63. Cf. p. 174.   [8] cxi, 10.
[9] *De nat. deor.*, ii, 3, 8. Cf. *De harusp. resp.*, 9, 19.
[10] vi, 56, 6–15.   [11] Athenaeus, vi, p. 274 A.

But influences were already working to impair its force. That organization of religion which was in one sense its strength contained the germs of its decay. The worship of the farmer at seed-time,[1] at harvest,[2] and when he sent his cattle from their stalls to pasture in the hills,[3] was alive; but when the rural festivals were fixed for stated days, while the calendar was not always kept in due relation to the solar year, they were liable to lose connexion with the events to which they properly belonged.[4] Again when the duty of the layman towards the religion of the State was merely to abstain from work (unless he could plead that it was necessary)[5] on holy days and to leave the conduct of worship to the priests, he must have tended to lapse into indifference.[6] Gradually, as the State expanded, strange deities were introduced. As early as the siege of Veii the dictator Camillus vowed to build a temple in honour of Juno Regina, the protectress of that city, if she would deign to come and take up her abode in Rome,[7] and the precedent was often followed in later times, notably during the siege of Carthage.[8] But new gods also made their way into Rome in the course of trade or with enlarged dominion. Minerva, herself an old Italian deity, had been introduced not long after the framing of the calendar from Etruria, where, under Greek influence, she had become, like Athene, the patroness of handicrafts;[9] Hercules (the Greek Heracles), Castor and Pollux from Campania and Magna Graecia, Diana from Aricia, her arrival coinciding with the assumption by Rome of the headship of the Latin league.[10] The famous Capitoline temple, sacred to Jupiter, Juno, and Minerva, was of Etruscan origin. It was there that for the first time an

---

[1] Warde Fowler, *Roman Festivals*, p. 252.
[2] *Ib.*, pp. 189-90, 195-6, 207-9.   [3] Calpurnius, *Ecl.*, v, 24-5.
[4] See Warde Fowler, *Religious Experience*, p. 102.
[5] Macrob., i, 16, 11.   [6] See Warde Fowler, *op. cit.*, pp. 250, 254.
[7] Livy, v, 21, 3.   [8] *Macrob.*, iii, 9, 6.
[9] Ovid, *Fasti*, iii, 843; Statius, *Silv.*, ii, 2, 2; iii, 2, 24; v, 3, 165; K. O. Müller and W. Deecke, *Die Etrusker*, ii, 1877, p. 47; G. Wissowa, *Religion*, &c., 1902, pp. 204-5.
[10] Macrob., iii, 6, 11. 17. Cf. Wissowa, *op. cit.*, p. 217, and Warde Fowler, *op. cit.*, pp. 230-4, 237, 244.

image of a god was set up in Rome;[1] and it was then that Jupiter 'the Best and the Greatest', the first of the trinity, became, as he remained for centuries, the guardian of the Roman State, now liberated from Etruscan rule.[2] But in obedience to utterances, believed to emanate from Cumae, like those which were later embodied in the famous Sibylline 'books',[3] cults of another kind were introduced. In the infancy of the Republic and in consequence of famine the three deities of corn, Demeter, Dionysus, and Persephone, who were worshipped in the Greek cities of Italy and in Sicily, were housed in another temple, built for their reception, where they were known as Ceres, Liber, and Libera.[4] During the long siege of Veii, when a pestilence broke out and the people in their distress were looking for some religious remedy, the Senate ordered that the oracles should be consulted, and a strange Greek rite was for the first time adopted: for eight successive days images of Apollo and Latona, Hercules and Diana, Mercury and Neptune—the first three Greek, the others transformed under Greek influence —were laid reclining on couches with offerings of food and drink placed before them.[5] Soon afterwards fresh ceremonies were adopted, which in later ages took the form of thanksgiving services decreed in honour of a victorious general: men, women, and children, carrying branches of laurel, marched in procession, halting by the couches, to the temples, where before the altars they prostrated themselves after the manner of the Greeks.[6] These innovations doubtless served the purpose of diverting a population now largely adulterated by foreign elements; but they and the new gods in whose honour they were held were to the Romans as the golden calf and Baal to the Jews.[7]

[1] Pliny, xxxv, 12 (45), 157: Augustine, *De civ. Dei*, iv, 23.
[2] See Warde Fowler, *op. cit.*, pp. 238–41.
[3] Ovid, *Fasti*, iv, 158; H. Diels, *Sibyl. Blätter*, p. 81.
[4] Warde Fowler, *Roman Festivals*, pp. 74–5; *Religious Experience*, pp. 255–8.   [5] Livy, v, 13, 4–6. Cf. vii, 2, 1–2.
[6] Marquardt, *Röm. Staatsverw.*, iii², pp. 48–51, 188–9; Wissowa, *op. cit.*, pp. 358–9.   [7] See Warde Fowler, *Religious Experience*, p. 266.

Meanwhile an institution of native growth, although it accomplished much useful work, was tending to deaden the religious instinct of the people. The college of pontiffs, which had probably originated in the time of the kings, and, after the abolition of monarchy, remained the sole exponent of religious law, was continually acquiring greater power, because it was called upon to frame rules for adoption and other ceremonies, and thus became the author of the civil law,[1] which, with the increasing complexity of life, gradually detached itself from that of religion.[2] Moreover, it was a self-elected body; and though, after the praetorship was established, it could no longer monopolize the civil law,[3] though the Senate and the magistrates settled the relations between Rome and the conquered peoples of Italy, except in so far as they were connected with religion, and though the magistrates from first to last were alone responsible, under priestly advice, for maintaining harmony between the State and its divinities, and therefore Rome never became subject to a hierarchy, the pontiffs by their excessive formalizing as well as by introducing foreign cults and foreign rites, which could not be really engrafted in the old religion, helped to paralyse its growth.[4]

The college of augurs, whose business it was to ascertain by divination whether a battle or any other contemplated act would be favoured by the gods, contributed to this decadence; for the rules which they formulated tended more and more to be used for merely political purposes. It was in their power to declare the election of a magistrate irregular or to impede the passage of a law;[5] and, as we shall see in later chapters, the way in which they used this power brought augury into general contempt.[6]

[1] Warde Fowler, op. cit., pp. 272–3, 275, 278.   [2] Dig., i, 2. 2, 6.
[3] Livy, ix, 46, 5; Val. Max., ii, 5, 2. Cf. Warde Fowler, op. cit., pp. 278–9.
[4] Ib., pp. 288, 292. Cf. J. B. Carter, op. cit., p. 44
[5] Cic., De leg., ii, 8, 21; 12, 31; iii, 4, 11; Phil., ii, 32, 80–1; Ascon., ed. Clark, p. 69, ll. 4–7 (ed. Stangl, p. 55). The augurs, as such, could only give an opinion, not, unless they were also magistrates, annul an election or prevent the passage of a law. See Wissowa's criticism (Paulys Real-Ency., ii, 2334–5) of Cicero's statement.
[6] See Cicero, De nat. deor., ii, 3, 7–8; Dion Hal., ii, 6.

Fortunately the augurs, like the pontiffs, were prevented from acquiring excessive influence by the rule that the magistrate alone could take the auspices, the augurs merely interpreting their meaning; and the process gradually became a formality, maintained by custom alone and occasionally treated with neglect.[1] Thus when the Romans entered upon the struggle with Hannibal, their religion proved inadequate.[2] Again and again, after the successive defeats and the reports of prodigies that followed them, the populace were seized by superstitious dread; and to reassure them the Senate had recourse to the Sibylline oracles. Images of deities were again displayed on couches; gifts of gold and silver were offered to the trinity of the Capitoline temple. After the disaster of the Trasimene Lake the fruits of the earth for an entire season and all male infants born in the spring were dedicated to Jupiter; extraordinary games were promised in honour of various gods; twelve deities in pairs, Greek as well as Roman, were placed on couches for all to see.[3] After the calamity of Cannae a Greek and a Gaul, each with a woman of his own race, were buried alive in the cattle market—a sacrifice to Mother Earth and to the spirits of the dead.[4] As the war dragged on Etruscan soothsayers were consulted;[5] women, whose husbands or sons had fallen, abandoned the worship of their country's gods and resorted to rites introduced by foreign priests;[6] and when a Sibylline oracle was said to have foretold that Hannibal would be forced to depart if the Great Mother were brought from Pessinus, the king of Pergamum permitted a black stone which symbolized the goddess to be removed. The populace flocked to welcome it and burned incense as it passed; and for the

[1] Cic., *De div.*, i, 15, 28; Livy, xxi, 63, 5. Cf. Th. Mommsen, *Röm. Staatsr.*, i³, 1887, pp. 76–116.
[2] Remember the growth of 'spiritism' and kindred phenomena in the World War.
[3] Livy, xxi, 62; xxii, 1; 9, 7–10; 10. Cf. Wissowa, *op. cit.*, p. 356.
[4] Livy, xxii, 57–6. Compare the comments of Warde Fowler (*op. cit.*, p. 320) with those of Prof. Reid (*Journ. Rom. Studies*, ii, 1912, pp. 37–40).
[5] Livy, xxiv, 10, 12.
[6] *Ib.*, xxv, 1, 6–12. Cf. Warde Fowler, *op. cit.*, pp. 324–5.

first time an Oriental deity with eunuch priests and outlandish rites was received in Rome.[1]

A few years later the worship of Dionysus, accompanied, according to the questionable narrative of Livy, by scandalous immoralities, began to be practised, first in Etruria and then in Rome ; and though the Government, clutching at doubtful evidence, punished the worshippers as conspirators who were attempting to overthrow the religion of the State, they were compelled by popular sentiment to permit, under certain restrictions, the continuance of the rites.[2] Plautus[3] amused his audiences by making the gods ridiculous ; Ennius taught that[4] they cared nothing for mankind ; and the chief pontiff, Scaevola, could only affirm that religion, true or false, was essential to the existence of the State.[5] One may consider how far the decadence which Polybius[6] observed in some of his contemporaries was due to cessation of that fear of divine displeasure to which he ascribed the integrity of their ancestors.[7] It was in accordance with the view of Scaevola that envoys were dispatched to Sicily, Greece, and Asia to collect new oracles for a restoration of the Sibylline Books, which had been destroyed in the fire that consumed the temple of Jupiter ;[9] for although Cicero,[10] who knew how the oracles were manipulated, openly derided them, they were too useful to the Senate to be dispensed with.

83 B.C.[8]

---

[1] Livy, xxix, 10, 4–11, 8 ; 14, 8–14 ; Dion. Hal., ii, 19.

[2] Livy, xxxix, 8–18. Cf. xxxix, 41, 6–7, xl, 19, 9–10. Salomon Reinach (*Cultes, mythes et religions*, iii, 1908, pp. 266–70) shows that the evidence which Livy adduces for the alleged villanies of the worshippers is inconclusive. He points out, further, that the Senate dreaded a Hellenistic coalition, supported by Macedonia and Syria, which would find allies in Southern *I*taly, and argues that their action was directed against a secret society which, under the cloak of religion, might conceal revolutionary aims.

[3] *Cistellaria*, ii, 1, 36–9. Cf. *Asin.*, ii, 1, 11–5 and *Persa*, ii, 3, 1–6.

[4] O. Ribbeck, *Scaen. Romanorum poesis*, i², 1871, p. 54, ll. 269–70. Cf. Cic., *De div.*, ii, 50, 104.

[5] Augustine, *De civ. Dei.*, iv, 27. Cf. Cic., *De nat. deor.*, i, 22, 61 ; iii, 17, 43 ; *De div.*, ii, 12, 28.

[6] xviii, 35, 1–2. Cf. xxxii, 11, 3.   [7] vi, 56, 6–15.

[8] Cassiod., *Chron.* (*Mon. Germ. hist.*, t. xi, vol. ii, 1894, p. 132).

[9] Daremberg and Saglio, iv, 1296–7.   [10] *De div.*, ii, 54, 110.

It must not, indeed, be supposed that even in the last century of the Republic unbelief was general. Women continued scrupulously to discharge their religious duties.[1] Though the temples were so neglected that Augustus was obliged to restore more than eighty which had fallen into decay,[2] Cicero could still appeal to a popular gathering by glorifying the Best and the Greatest Jupiter,[3] who even to his sceptical intellect was in one sense not unreal.[4] Tiberius Gracchus, if not Cicero himself, invoked the gods before he addressed the Senate or the People;[5] and when Pompey entered upon his first consulship, Varro reminded him that the business of the House must always begin with sacrifice and prayer.[6] Domestic worship, if it was often perfunctory, still survived;[7] the soldier still respected the oath which bound him to be faithful to his commander;[8] the peasant still believed in the gods of the countryside and prayed them to be propitious to his flocks;[9] and, though there were Roman citizens who emasculated themselves that they might become priests of Cybele,[10] repeated attempts, which, to be sure, encountered obstinate resistance, were made to eradicate the worship of Isis and other Egyptian deities.[11] Superstition was of course ineradicable. In the lifetime of Cicero and Caesar the Senate was obliged to pass a decree forbidding human sacrifice.[12] Etruscan soothsayers, who, as Pacuvius said, found more intelligence in the livers of animals than in their own,[13] were consulted not only in streets and villages, but by statesmen like Sulla and Pompey.[14] Appius Claudius, unlike

---

[1] Cic., *Att.*, i, 3, 1; *Fam.*, xiv, 4, 1; 7, 1.
[2] *Res gestae div. Aug.*, ed. Th. Mommsen, 1883, p. lviii (4, 17-8). Cf. Hor., *Carm.*, iii, 6, 1-4.
[3] *In Cat.*, iii, 9, 22. Cf. Warde Fowler, *op. cit.*, p. 240.
[4] See Warde Fowler, *Roman Ideas of Deity*, 1914, pp. 5-6, 51-2.
[5] Ps. Cic., *ad Herenn.*, iv, 55, 68.   [6] Gell., xiv, 7, 9.
[7] Marquardt, *Röm. Staatsverw.*, iii², 126.
[8] Caes., *B. C.*, i, 86, 3; ii, 28, 2; 32, 9.   [9] Hor., *Carm.*, iii, 18, 1-4.
[10] Val. Max., vii, 7, 6.
[11] *Ib.*, i, 3, 4; Apul., *Met.*, xi, 30; Dio, xl, 47, 3; xlii, 26, 2; *C. I. L.*, vi, pars 1, 2247; Tertull., *ad Nat.*, i, 10. Cf. *Paulys Real-Ency.*, ix, 2103.   [12] Pliny, xxx, 1 (3), 12.
[13] Cic., *De div.*, i, 57, 131.   [14] *Ib.*, 33, 72; 58, 132; ii, 24, 53.

his brother augur Cicero, believed in the efficacy of the sacred chickens [1] and, like some eminent men of our generation, fancied that he could call up the spirits of the dead.[2] Sulla carried about an image of Apollo, to which he prayed when he was in peril ;[3] and even Caesar, after he had once had an accident, never entered his carriage without thrice repeating a spell, a practice which, as the elder Pliny said,[4] was in his time general. Nevertheless thoughtful Romans, for the most part, were without religion,[5] when, in the closing years of the Republic, a new influence came from Greece to quicken their moral sense.

The philosophy of Epicurus, though, containing the germs of scientific discovery,[6] it appealed to the powerful mind of Lucretius and made converts,[7] who were attracted more by its easily perverted doctrine that the aim of life is pleasure [8] than by the solution which it offered of the riddle of the universe, had little or no regenerative influence. The effect of its rival was very different. Panaetius, the friend of Scipio Aemilianus,[9] who was the founder of Roman Stoicism, and whose teaching was popularized by Cicero,[10] understood the people with whom he had to deal and, having himself discarded or modified its more rigid dogmas, presented it to them in a form which they could understand.[11] Few Romans would care for the divergent Stoic theories about the nature of the universe—whether it was to be ultimately destroyed by fire [12] or, as Panaetius himself believed, was everlasting.[13] Controversies about free will and necessity would be barren.[14] Practical men would listen with indifference or

---

[1] Cic., *De leg.*, ii, 13, 32. Cf. *Fam.*, vi, 6, 3. [2] Cic., *Tusc.*, i, 16, 37.
[3] Plut., *Sulla*, 29, 10. [4] xxviii, 2 (4), 21.
[5] Augustine, *De civ. Dei.*, vi, 2 ; Cic., *De invent.*, i, 29, 46.
[6] See R. D. Hicks, *Stoic and Epicurean*, 1910, p. 205.
[7] Cic. *Tusc.*, iv, 3, 6-7. Cf. *Fam.*, xv, 16 ; 17, 5.
[8] Cf. Cic., *In Pis.*, 16, 37 with *Fam.*, xv, 19, 2.
[9] Cic., *De fin.*, iv, 9, 23. [10] *De off.*
[11] Cic., *De leg.*, iii, 6, 14 ; *De fin.*, iv, 28, 79 ; *Tusc.*, i, 32. Cf. E. V. Arnold, *Roman Stoicism*, 1911, pp. 100-2. [12] Cic., *De nat. deor.*, ii, 46, 118.
[13] H. Diels, *Doxogr. Graec.*, 1879, fr. 36 (p. 469), 41 (p. 593).
[14] Cic., *Acad.*, ii, 12, 39 ; Gell., vii, 2, 15.

irritation to the doctrine that pain was no evil;[1] nor need they be blamed if they indulged that grief for the dead which the straitest sect of Stoicism condemned.[2] The main point was, without attacking the religion of the State and while devising ingenious arguments to prove that it really harmonized with Stoic doctrine, to inculcate the belief that just as the human soul was the ruler of the body, divine power was the soul and the ruler of the universe, and that the whole duty of man was to order his life in unison with its will, in other words with nature.[3] Let him not trouble himself about future rewards or punishments : real or imaginary, they were no true motives for virtue.[4] Posidonius, whose inspiration Cicero acknowledged,[5] carried on the gospel of Panaetius, although on certain points he differed from him. Influenced himself by Plato, he taught his disciples to think of God as distinct from, yet pervading the world ;[6] and Varro, who imbibed his teaching, came to regard Jupiter as the supreme god and the other deities as powers immanent in him.[7]

It is easy to understand that the Academy, which taught that certainty was unattainable, failed, although it influenced Stoicism, to gain many adherents among a people whose genius was practical and positive. But why was Epicureanism overshadowed by its rival? Lucretius was animated by a truly religious zeal. Panaetius, like Epicurus, disbelieved in the immortality of the soul. But it was not only because Stoicism recognized an all-wise (though not all-powerful) Providence, but also because it was a potent moral stimulus, that it succeeded

---

[1] Cic., *De fin.*, iv, 9, 23. What would have been thought of this syllogism ? —' No evil is accompanied by glory ; but death is accompanied by glory ; therefore death is no evil ' (Seneca, *Ep.* 82, 9).

[2] *De fin.*, iii, 10, 35 ; *Tusc.*, iv, 28, 60.

[3] Cic., *De nat. deor.*, ii, 7, 19 ; 13, 36 ; *De off.*, iii, 3, 12–3.

[4] See E. V. Arnold, *op. cit.*, p. 325.   [5] *De nat. deor.*, ii, 28, 71 ; &c.

[6] Panaetius denied this (A. Schmekel, *D. Philos. d. mittl. Stoa*, 1892, p. 308) and also the immortality of the soul (Cic., *De nat. deor.*, iii, 13, 32 ; *Tusc.*, i, 32, 79).

[7] Augustine, *De civ. Dei*, iv, 7, 9, 11, 13 ; vii, 13 ; *De consensu evang.*, i, 23 (31, 34) ; Cornutus, 2.

where Epicurean quietism failed. The constructive work of Lucretius was purely scientific : his religious enthusiasm spent itself in a mere crusade against superstition. But the Stoic leader who said, ' So live with your fellow-men as believing that God sees you ; so hold converse with God as to be willing that all men should hear you,'[1] was a forerunner of à Kempis. The *vir pietate gravis* embodied the Stoic ideal ; and the best Romans were essentially Stoic before they heard the name of Zeno. The Stoic philosophers, as such, were sometimes wrong where their rivals were right : Posidonius, for example, clung on theological grounds to the old idea that the earth was the centre of the universe, though reason had long since vindicated the position of the sun.[2] But physics mattered less than ethics. The Stoics, with all their diversities, held fast to the principle that virtue was not merely its own but its only reward ; and therefore Stoicism, despite its errors, its paradoxes, its desperate efforts to reconcile the irreconcilable, was not merely a philosophy, but in some sort a religion.

For though, as the Epicurean Cassius said,[3] it is hard to convince men that goodness is desirable for its own sake, and proselytes were as yet comparatively few, Stoicism, if we may judge from the character of its principal adherents, was an inspiring creed. Laelius,[4] Mucius Scaevola,[5] Rutilius Rufus,[6] and Cato, who professed it in its most uncompromising form, were conspicuous among the Romans of the late Republic who governed their lives by principle. But it does not follow that their virtues were the fruit of Stoicism alone. Stoicism was the philosophy which in that period men who reflected upon ultimate questions and felt the need of guidance would be inclined to follow ; and we can only suppose that it helped them to pursue steadfastly ideals which they naturally approved. How far, if at all, the lower classes felt the stimulus, it is hard to say ;[7] but

---

[1] Seneca, *Ep.* 10, 5. [2] Schmekel, *op. cit.*, p. 465.
[3] Cic., *Fam.*, xv, 19, 2. [4] Cic., *De fin.*, ii, 8, 24.
[5] Cic., *De nat. deor.*, iii, 2, 5. [6] Cic., *Brut.*, 30, 114.
[7] Prof. E. V. Arnold (*Roman Stoicism*, 1911, p. 380), differing from

one may well believe that here and there some learned slave had read the ethical treatise of Panaetius, and felt himself thereby strengthened to live and not repine.

The beliefs of educated men about immortality varied of course as they do among ourselves. Catullus,[1] Lucretius, Caesar,[2] and doubtless many others[3] rejected absolutely the dream of a future life : Cicero, often sceptical,[4] was at times disposed, above all when he was grieving for his daughter's death, and allowed himself to be influenced by the faith of Posidonius, to believe.[5]

Polybius, who, himself a sceptic, admired Roman religion as a tonic influence, blamed the Romans, not without reason, for their neglect of education.[6] Still the majority of the Italian population could read and write,[7] and the education of the upper classes had been permeated for more than a century by the influence of Greece. Knowledge of Greek, which even the elder Cato had found it profitable to learn, was essential to every Italian who aspired to play a part in public life, even to many whose ambition was only to make money ; and Marius, who prided himself upon his ignorance,[8] was one of the rare exceptions that proved the rule. Cultured Romans could speak Greek more fluently and write it with greater accuracy than most Englishmen of the same class can write or speak French ; for it was the only foreign language which they were required in boyhood to learn, and they learned it in intercourse with Greeks. In the middle of the second century before our era the father of the Gracchan brothers addressed the Rhodians in their own tongue with a perfect command of idiom ; and a few

Education.

Warde Fowler (*Religious Experience*, p. 357), believes that Stoicism did appeal to the lower orders, and observes that ' the practice of street-preaching, as described by Horace . . . points this way '.

[1] 5, 5–6.   [2] Sall., *Cat.*, 51, 20 ; 52, 13 ; Cic., *In Cat.*, iv, 4, 7.
[3] For instance, Pliny, vii, 55 (56), 188.
[4] *Fam.*, v, 16, 4 ; 21, 4 ; vi, 3, 4 ; 4, 4 ; *Att.*, xii, 18, 1   *Pro Cluent.*, 61, 171 ; *Phil.*, ix, 6, 13 ; &c.
[5] *De rep.*, vi, 24.   For the belief of Posidonius that ' the air is full of immortal souls ' see Cic., *De div.*, i, 30, 64.   Cf. *Tusc.*, i, 12, 26–7 ; 16, 36.
[6] Cic., *De rep.*, iv, 3, 3.   [7] Marquardt, *Privatleben*², p. 96.
[8] Sall., *Iug.*, 85, 32.   Cf. Plut., *M3*.

years later Publius Crassus was able to converse in five Greek dialects.[1] Cicero wrote a history of his own consulship in Greek,[2] of which Posidonius avowed, presumably with the sincerity that became a Stoic, that its faultless execution deterred him from attempting the same theme;[3] and numerous quotations in Cicero's letters testify that he knew the poems of Homer and the works of the tragedians almost by heart. It is true that before a knowledge of the language became recognized as indispensable, much prejudice, due not only to conservatism, but also to the rascality of Greek adventurers who came to seek their fortunes in Rome, had to be overcome; and the paternal grandfather of Cicero was said to have observed that a man who knew Greek intimately was generally a knave.[4] In the year before the tribunate of the younger Drusus the censors issued an edict for the expulsion of Latin professors of rhetoric, on the ground that their lectures, far from strengthening the intellect, merely encouraged impudence.[5] But the effect of this measure was of course transitory. While Cicero was still a boy, one Lucius Plotius Gallus opened a school of rhetoric in Rome;[6] and before he entered public life the city abounded not only with Greek professors of rhetoric and philosophy, of music and the fine arts, but also with humbler scholars who came to earn a livelihood as schoolmasters or tutors. But no national system of education even then existed: any one was free to start a school who could hire a room for the accommodation of his pupils; and occasionally, as we may infer from a Pompeian picture, the teacher, accompanied by his class, went out of doors and taught in the open air.[7] Masters of elementary schools were commonly freedmen; in any case they were treated as inferiors; and since their pupils were rarely more than twelve years old, the curriculum was

---

[1] Quintil., *Inst.*, xi, 2, 50. [2] *Att.*, i, 19, 10.
[3] *Ib.*, ii, 1, 2.
[4] Cic., *De or.*, ii, 66, 265.
[5] *Ib.*, iii, 24, 93; Tac., *Dial.*, 35; Suet., *De rhet.*, 1; Gell., xv, 11, 1-2.
[6] Seneca, *Controv.*, ii, praef. 5. Cf. Suet., *De rhet.*, 2.
[7] Daremberg and Saglio, ii, 482.

limited to reading, writing, and arithmetic.[1] Children of the rich, however, often learned at home from a learned slave or a tutor, who was a regular inmate of wealthy houses, and who, when he did not give instruction, was responsible for instilling good manners into his charges and, if they went to school, accompanied them to keep them out of mischief.[2] The elder Cato, though he kept a tutor in his house, took pains to teach his son himself ; [3] but in the decline of the Republic such conscientious parents must have been very rare. Secondary schools, in which the age of the pupils ranged from twelve or thirteen to sixteen, were also generally kept by Greeks. The subjects taught were Greek and Latin : history, as we are told by Cicero,[4] was neglected ; but we may infer from many passages that patriotic Romans of the upper classes studied the records of their own country for themselves. Verbal and even textual criticism formed part of the course ; and the parents, indeed any one who took an interest in the boys, were free to enter the class-room and watch them taking notes at their desks. Disorderly or idle pupils, as we learn not only from the familiar instance of Orbilius,[5] but also from a picture which is to be seen in the Museum at Naples,[6] were beaten with a strap, and, as English schoolboys may be amused to learn, impositions were frequently set.[7] Young men were often sent after they had left school to attend the lectures of some eminent professor in Athens or Rhodes, Mytilene or Alexandria,[8] and occasionally, before they went abroad, studied at home under a private teacher ; [9] but their aim was always practical—to prepare for public speaking in the

[1] *Ib.* ; Hor., *Ep.* i, 20, 17–8 ; Ovid, Fasti, iii, 829 ; Marquardt, *Privatleben*[2], pp. 92–3.
[2] Cic., *Laelius*, 20, 74 ; Hor., *Sat.*, i, 6, 81–2 ; Suet., *Aug.*, 44, 2 ; *De gram.*, 23 ; App., *B. C.*, iv, 30, 128 ; Dio, xlvi, 5, 1 ; &c.
[3] Plut., *Cato mai.*, 20, 6–8. [4] *De leg.*, 1, 2, 5.
[5] Hor., *Ep.*, ii, 1, 70–1. Cf. Suet., *De gram.*, 9.
[6] Daremberg and Saglio, ii, 488, fig. 2613.
[7] *Ib.* ii, 488. For the schools of the *grammatici* in general see pp. 483–8.
[8] Cic., *De or.*, iii, 11, 43 ; *Brut.*, 97, 332 ; *Fam.*, xii, 16, 1.
[9] Cic., *Q. fr.*, iii, 1, 14.

Senate, on the Rostra, or at the bar. Sometimes a youth whose father desired that he should make a figure in the world was commended to the care of a well-known advocate or jurisconsult, for whom he devilled, and who in return initiated him into the secrets of forensic or political success.[1]

Art and science, despite Greek influence, still counted for little in education. Occasionally, indeed, a professor of music was hired by some wealthy noble to give lessons to his children;[2] but such science as was taught had a strictly utilitarian aim. Pure geometry was ignored: astronomy was neglected, except in so far as its rudiments were necessary—for navigation or to explain allusions in the works of poets.[3]

Of the education of women we know comparatively little.[4] Girls as well as boys of course went to school,[5] or studied at home under a tutor,[6] and one may reasonably suppose that many ladies could read and converse in Greek; but it may be doubted whether female instruction often went beyond reading, writing, and arithmetic, though daughters of wealthy parents took lessons in dancing and learned enough music to accompany themselves on the lyre when they sang.[7] Everybody has heard of the mother of the Gracchi, to whose fostering care her sons owed so much; but the attainments of Sempronia, the mother of Decimus Brutus, who added to graceful accomplishments a knowledge of Greek and Latin literature and amused herself by versification,[8] of Cornelia, the wife of Pompey, who was not only a musician and a scholar, but also studied mathematics and philosophy,[9] of Caerellia, the sympathetic friend of Cicero,[10] and of

[1] Cic., *De or.*, i, 45, 198 ; *De off.*, ii, 13, 46.
[2] Marquardt, *Privatleben*[2], p. 118 ; Daremberg and Saglio, ii, 481; iii, 2087.
[3] Cic., *Tusc.*, i, 2, 5 ; Seneca, *Ep.* 88, 14–7. Cf. Daremberg and Saglio, ii, 486–7.
[4] See Marquardt, *Privatleben*[2], pp. 65, 112. [5] Livy, iii, 44, 6.
[6] Cic., *Att.*, xii, 33, 2. Cf. Ovid, *Trist.*, ii, 369–70.
[7] Macrob., iii, 14, 4.
[8] Sall., *Cat.*, 25, 2. 5. [9] Plut., *Pomp.*, 55, 1.
[10] Cic., *Fam.*, xiii, 72, 1 ; *Att.*, xiii, 21, 5 ; Quintil., vi, 3, 112.

Hortensia, who actually appeared in public as a pleader,[1] were probably, as we may infer from the emphasis with which they were recorded, exceptional.

Opportunities for study and research were not yet provided by the State. While Pergamum and Alexandria were endowed with public libraries, there were none in Rome until after Caesar had projected them.

Let us now try to realize the life of the people who were moulded by these influences, and look into the interior of the dwellings upon which our traveller gazed when he was wandering through the streets of Rome. If he hired a carriage and extended his tour to some provincial town, he saw blocks of tenements and private houses of somewhat similar construction, though perhaps on a smaller scale.[2] As a rule, only the rich had houses of their own: as in the cities of the continent in our own time, the bulk of the population—not the poor only, but the bourgeoisie and even nobles whose purses were not deep—lived in flats or what are now called maisonettes.[3] Rents of course varied widely according to the locality, the nature of the building, and the quality of the accommodation. Labourers, artisans, or unemployed vagrants, who herded in single rooms at the top of a jerry-built block in the slums, paid accordingly, though they might find it hard to meet the demands of their landlord unless they had sold their votes for a sufficient sum. Sulla, whose early manhood was passed in poverty until his stepmother, who was as devoted to him as to her own son, and a courtesan, who had fallen in love with him, left him substantial legacies, could only afford to hire lodgings of the annual rental of three thousand sesterces: a freedman, who occupied [£30.] a room on the floor above, paid two thousand.[4] Caelius, on the other hand, whose bachelor's flat was in a mansion of which the landlord was the notorious Clodius, was charged thirty thousand sesterces a year, and afterwards, [£300.] in order to be near the Forum, took a house which, although it was on the fashionable Palatine, was leased

Tenements and private houses.

---

[1] Val. Max., viii, 3, 3.   [2] *Notiz. d. Scavi*, 1901, p. 391.
[3] Daremberg and Saglio, ii, 353.   [4] Plut., *Sulla*, 1, 6; 2, 6-7.

at a rate comparatively low.¹ The mansions of the rich, some of which have been revealed by excavation, were veritable palaces. The enormous prices charged for them were doubtless due not only to their size and elaborate decoration but also to the cost of land. When Caesar designed to enlarge and beautify the Forum, his agents were obliged to pay sixty million sesterces, or six hundred thousand pounds, as compensation to the owners who were disturbed.²

When a visitor called at one of these houses, he might, if the owner were a public man, meet a motley crowd of individuals who had been paying their respects to him or consulting him on business ; but unless he rose betimes, he would miss this characteristic spectacle, for Romans, as a rule, were early astir, and such levées were commonly held soon after sunrise.³ Making his way through the outgoing throng, he entered through the vestibule, adorned, let us suppose, like the famous house of Aemilius Lepidus,⁴ with a lintel of the finest marble, which led to a door some little distance from the street. Passing through it, he found himself in a large room, at the further end of which, in two recesses, one on the right, the other on the left, were ranged the waxen busts, discoloured by age or smoke, of the ancestors of the owner, with inscriptions recording their achievements in war and the honours which they had attained.⁵ In the modest dwellings that belonged to the Golden Age of the Republic such an apartment had served not only as the living room of the family and the bedroom of the owner and his wife, but also as the kitchen. Now it was the public room, in which callers who paid visits of ceremony were received. Curtained off at the back was the master's study, in which he kept his family archives, and which communicated by a door

---

¹ Cic., *Pro Cael.*, 7, 17–8.   ² Cic., *Att.*, iv, 16, 8.
³ Cic., *Q. fr.*, iii, 7, 2 ; Mart., iii, 36, 3 ; Juv., v, 19–24, 76–9. Readers of Cicero's letters will have noticed many passages which show that the Romans were early risers.
⁴ Pliny, xxxvi, 6 (8), 49 ; 15 (24), 109.
⁵ Cic., *In Pis.*, 1, 1 ; Corn. Nep., *Att.*, 18, 1 ; Livy, xlii. 31, 11 ; Val. Max., iv, 4, 1 ; v, 8, 3 ; Pliny, xxxv, 2 (2), 8.

with the garden. Flanking the study was a passage which led to an open court, surrounded by colonnades, in the centre of which, embowered in flowers and shrubs, a fountain was playing. Both the reception hall and the court were enclosed by rooms—salons, bedchambers, and others. The hall was lighted by openings in the ceiling, and the windows in the outer walls were few and small. If there was a second story, it was probably incomplete, for when additional rooms were wanted, they were built above those which surrounded the hall, and houses with three stories were extremely rare.[1]

The decoration, like the architecture, of the house owed much to that Grecian influence which had begun to make itself felt in the previous century. Mural paintings, which once adorned houses in Pompeii, fill several rooms in the Museum of Naples, while others still awaken the wonder of the tourists who visit the excavated city.[2] The subjects were generally landscape or derived from Greek mythology; but a fresco, found in a chamber tomb on the Esquiline hill, which represented victories won in the Samnite wars,[3] suggests, though it belonged to an earlier period, that the paintings of the Ciceronian Age, like those exhibited in the triumphs of Roman generals, generally appealed to national pride. A few houses were already embellished by mosaic pavements, which, however, did not become common until the Imperial period, though Caesar, when he was campaigning in Gaul, took with him slabs of such costly workmanship to serve as the floor of his tent.[4]

Decoration.

[1] Daremberg and Saglio, ii, 351–62 ; A. Mau, *Pompeii*², 1908, pp. 250–89, 300, 316, 318, 360–1 (Eng. tr., 245–79, 288, 302–3, 341–7) ; Stuart Jones, *op. cit.*, pp. 159–64. Dr. Ashby (*The Times*, Lit. Suppl., Jan. 15, 1920, p. 33, col. 1) remarks that 'recent excavations at Ostia and Pompeii have taught us to modify our previous ideas . . . At Ostia [under the Empire] the traditional plan with the atrium has only been found in one single instance '.

[2] Mau, *op. cit.*, pp. 472–83, 490 (Eng. tr., 456–64, 471) ; Stuart Jones, *op. cit.*, pp. 398–411.

[3] *Bull. d. Comm. arch. comun. di Roma*, 1889, p. 346 and Tav., xi, xii. Cf. Pliny, xxxv, 4 (7), 22.

[4] Cic., *De or.*, iii, 43, 171 ; *Brut.*, 79, 274 ; *Orat.*, 44, 149 ; Pliny, xxxvi, 25 (61), 185, (64) 189 ; Suet., *Div. Iul.*, 46 ; Mau, *op. cit.*, p. 300 (Eng. tr., p. 288).

Slaves.

But the change which had come over Roman customs with the inpouring of wealth was in nothing more conspicuous than in the multitude of slaves. In the infancy of the Republic even nobles had been contented with a man-servant and a maid :[1] the vast mansions of the Ciceronian Age as well as the ostentatious luxury of their owners demanded a multitude, each one of whom had his special duties to perform. The subdivision of labour exceeded that which caste requires in the household of an Anglo-Indian magnate. Besides the hall-porter and the door-keepers, the chef and his assistants, the bakers and confectioners, the butler and the cupbearers, the valets and the ladies' maids, the slaves who attended to the various rooms, the footmen, the palanquin-bearers, the running footmen, and the torch-bearers who lighted him home, the rich man had his steward, his cashier, his groom of the chambers, his children's tutor, or a menial who carried his children's books to school,[2] his family physician, his reader, his copying-clerks, his learned slaves (for whom he paid even more than for his cook),[3] and other domestics too numerous to name.[4] While a poor gentleman would require not less than ten slaves, a great establishment might have as many as two hundred.[5] Among them were occasionally to be seen unfortunate beings who had no tasks to perform, but merely served to amuse owners who were capable of deriving gratification from their infirmities—dwarfs, hermaphrodites, or even idiots.[6]

The treatment of slaves naturally varied according to the character of their masters ; for, though they often gained their freedom, sometimes in return for faithful service,[7] sometimes with earnings which they had been

---

[1] Pliny, xxxiii, 1 (6), 26.
[2] Hor., Sat., i, 6, 78 ; Suet., Nero, 36, 2.
[3] Pliny, vii, 39 (40), 128 ; Suet., De gram., 3 ; Marquardt, Privatleben², p. 174.
[4] In regard to household slaves in general, see Marquardt, pp. 135-53 (especially 144, 153), Daremberg and Saglio, iv, 1267-79.
[5] Hor., Sat., i, 3, 11-2 ; 6, 107-9.
[6] Pliny, vii, 3 (3), 34 ; 16 (16), 75.   [7] Cic., Phil., viii, 11, 32.

allowed to retain,[1] occasionally as a reward for devotion to the State,[2] the law, before manumission, granted them no protection.[3] Conditions had changed since the good old days when the patrician farmer and his servant, who was also his countryman, worked together on a friendly footing and dined in the same room :[4] now that slaves were counted by dozens—Asiatics, Greeks, Gauls, Spaniards, Numidians, Moors [5]—and differed not only in race, but also in religion and customs from their masters, there could rarely be sympathetic intercourse between them. The case of conscience, propounded by a pupil of Panaetius, which Cicero noticed in his work on Morals,[6] is significant—if it were necessary to lighten a ship in a gale, would one be justified in throwing overboard a worthless slave instead of a valuable horse ? But while every one who is versed in Latin literature will have noticed instances in which slaves were flogged, branded as thieves with a red-hot iron, transferred from the comparative comfort of the city to work in chains in the fields, or, for grave offences, even crucified,[7] and clumsy maids were pricked with needles on their bare breasts by capricious mistresses,[8] he may remember others which prove that mutual affection subsisted between humane masters and those who served them. One of the most dreaded evils to which slaves were liable resulted from a principle of Roman law : when they were summoned to give evidence in a court of justice, they were invariably examined under torture,[9] and if a master was murdered, no matter by whom, in his own house, all who were indoors at the time were put to death.[10] On the other hand,

[1] Tac., *Ann.*, xiv, 42.
[2] Livy., xxii, 57, 11-2 ; xxiv, 14, 3 ; xxv, 20, 4 ; &c.
[3] *Dig.*, l, 17, 32 ; iv, 5, 3.   [4] Pliny, xxxiii, 1 (6), 26.
[5] Cic., *Att.*, v, 20, 5 ; Caes., *B. G.*, ii, 33, 7 ; iii, 16 ; vii, 89, 5 ; Livy, xli, 11, 8 ; 28, 8 ; xlv, 34, 5 ; App., *Hisp.*, 99. Cf. Marquardt, *Privatleben*², pp. 169-70.
[6] *De off.*, iii, 23, 89.   [7] Cic., *Pro Cluent.*, 66, 187.
[8] Ovid, *Amor.*, i, 14, 15-8 ; *Ars amat.*, iii, 239-40 ; Juv., vi, 487-93.
[9] Cic., *Pro Cluent.*, 63, 176-7 ; *Pro Sulla*, 28, 78 ; *Pro Mil.*, 21, 57 ; *Part. or.*, 34, 117-8.
[10] Cf. Cic., *Fam.*, iv, 12, 3 with Tac., *Ann.*, xiii, 32 ; xiv, 42. See also Greenidge, *Legal Procedure*, &c., p. 372.

a case is recorded in which a slave, believing that his evidence would tell in his master's favour, requested permission to face the ordeal.[1] In the massacre perpetrated by Marius a certain Cornutus was saved by the fidelity of one of his slaves;[2] and Tiro was not the only one of Cicero's staff who earned his regard. 'My reader Sositheus, a dear fellow,' he writes to Atticus,[3] 'is dead, and his death has affected me more than that of a slave ought, I suppose, to do.'

<small>Caution needed in generalizing from contemporary notices of Roman life.</small>

Such utterances—indeed the whole body of Cicero's correspondence—may warn us to be careful in generalizing from the contemporary notices of Roman life. For what was striking and therefore exceptional was often singled out for notice; novels of manners, which might have portrayed more faithfully the life of the average man, were not yet written; and we have to search diligently for the positive evidence that may serve as a corrective. Excessive luxury was not universal even among the few who could afford to be self-indulgent. Though many public men, as we shall see hereafter, plunged into debt from ambition or from love of pleasure, we must not forget that usurers flourish at the expense of spendthrifts in our own time; and if the dinner-parties at which Atticus entertained his friends were unusually simple,[4] we need not imagine that the spectacle, to which Cicero[5] alluded with disgust, of debauchees who vomited at table and had to be carried home, was common. Every scholar has read the homily in which the censor Metellus (who practised what he preached) urged selfish bachelors to do their duty to the State, because Nature had ordained that although men could not live comfortably with wives, they could not live at all without them;[6] but who has not heard similar exhortations, without the censor's cynical humour, from English bishops? Though incest and sodomy were undoubtedly prevalent, men of the

---

[1] Val. Max., vi, 8, 1. [2] App., i, 73, 336. Cf. Val. Max., vi, 8, 2–7.
[3] i, 12, 4. [4] See *Brit. Review*, xii, 1915, pp. 218–9.
[5] *De fin.*, ii, 8, 23.
[6] Livy, *Epit.*, 59; Gell., i, 6, 1–2. Cf. Cic., *De leg.*, iii, 3, 7.

world will not infer from the charges which Cicero heaped upon his enemies and even upon former friends [1] that these vices were more rampant in ancient Italy than in modern England.[2] Much has been written about the immorality of Roman ladies,[3] and the emancipation of women, which began after the Second Punic War,[4] had certainly gone on apace. The most austere moralist will hardly blame them for having gained control of their dowries and the unfettered right of holding property,[5] perhaps not even for having become influential in public life ; but they could also divorce their husbands as easily as a Mohammedan can divorce his wife, and some of them did not scruple to exercise the right.[6] The time had passed when a man might with impunity flog his wife to death for having ventured to drink wine, or, like the Baluchis in the days when Napier governed Sind, kill her if she was taken in adultery.[7] But the Sempronias, the Clodias, and the Paullas were probably, even in fashionable circles, a minority ; Cornelia,[8] the wife of Lepidus, Cornelia, the wife of Pompey,[9] and Turia, the heroine of the Civil Wars,[10] were not the only virtuous Roman matrons ; besides the marbled palaces of Clodius and Mamurra, there were old-fashioned houses in which the mistress superintended her women at the loom ; [11] and Cicero's letters [12] are not wanting in notices of affectionate family intercourse. Though divorce had become frequent, and was sometimes practised for trivial reasons,[13] it does not follow that those

[1] *Cum senatui*, &c., 4, 10 ; *Pro Cael.*, 13, 32 ; *Phil.*, ii, 20, 50 ; and many other passages.
[2] See the remarks of Mr. Justice Darling (*Morning Post*, April 16, 1920, p. 8, col. 8).
[3] E. g. in *Athenaeum* (Pavia), viii, 1920, pp. 77-91. The writer relies upon fragments of Lucilius.
[4] Livy, xxxv, 2-7. [5] Marquardt, *Privatleben*², pp. 63-4.
[6] Cic., *Pro Cluent.*, 5, 14 ; *Fam.*, viii, 7, 2.
[7] Val. Max., vi, 3, 9 ; Pliny, xiv, 13, 89 ; Gell., x, 23, 4 ; Rice Holmes, *Four Famous Soldiers*, 1889, pp. 37, 104-5, 108.
[8] Ascon., ed. Clark, p. 43, ll. 12-4 (ed. Stangl, p. 38).
[9] Plut., *Pomp.*, 55, 1. [10] Val. Max., vi, 7, 2.
[11] *Laudatio Turiae*, i, 30 (C. G. Bruns, *Fontes*⁶, &c., 1893, p. 283 = H. Dessau, *Inscr. Lat.*, 8393). [12] E. g. *Att.*, vi, 1, 22.
[13] See e. g. Cic., *Fam.*, viii, 7, 2.

who *desired* it were less numerous when it was rare ; and historians who assume that its frequency is a proof of moral decadence might be impelled to reflect if they could watch the festering embitterment that often results from the reluctant cohabitation of an ill-mated couple. Though Horace,[1] holding up to scorn the wife who emulated Oriental dancers and made assignations with her lover at her husband's table, contrasted her with the stern mother of the countryside whose sons had vanquished Pyrrhus and Hannibal, the men who conquered Gaul, who fought at Pharsalia and on the Nile, at Thapsus and at Munda were as brave, as virile as they. The heart of the nation while its government was dying remained sound ; and all that one can safely say is that among the rich corruption, luxury, and moral laxity were sufficiently common to distinguish this period from earlier times. But for that reason they must not remain unnoticed.

A dinner-party.

Suppose that a distinguished provincial, anxious to study Roman customs, had been invited to dine by some wealthy noble of luxurious tastes. Ushered into a drawing-room,[2] the visitor found his host and hostess with his fellow-guests waiting until the banquet should be announced. The master of the house and the elder men were clean-shaven : the younger wore short carefully trimmed beards ;[3] the women, no longer irritated by sumptuary laws, were exquisitely dressed and covered with gems.[4] Among them, we may suppose, was one of those ladies who did not rely merely upon their beauty, their wardrobes, or their jewels, but who, by force of personality or charm, not only gave the law to society, but made their power felt in politics. Such were Servilia, the mother of Marcus Brutus, whose influence was sufficient to procure the alteration of a senatorial decree,[5]

[1] *Carm.*, iii, 6, 21-44.   [2] Cic., *Att.*, vi, 2, 5 ; Macrob., i, 7, 1.
[3] Cic., *Att.*, i, 14, 5 ; 16, 11 ; *In Cat.*, ii, 10, 22 ; Gell., iii, 4, 2-3.
[4] See p. 98. The presence of ladies at dinner-parties, where they now, like the men, reclined, though in old times they had been obliged to sit, is attested by Cicero (*Att.*, v, 1, 3-4 ; *Pro Cael.*, 8, 20), Nepos (praef. 6), Valerius Maximus (ii, 1, 2), Macrobius (iii, 13, 11), &c.
[5] Cic., *Att.*, xv, 11, 2 ; 12, 1. Cf. *Fam.*, v, 2, 6.

Sempronia, of whom we shall see more hereafter, and, most interesting of all, the notorious Clodia. In the dining-room, the walls of which were festooned with costly draperies,[1] three couches, each designed to accommodate three persons, were arranged round the sides of the table.[2] No piece of furniture in a rich man's house was so valuable as this;[3] and when he entertained it was covered with rich cloths[4] and loaded with silver plate. Pliny[5] assures us that the famous tribune Livius Drusus possessed silver weighing ten thousand Roman, or over seven thousand English, pounds : a sum equal to twelve thousand sterling was paid for two cups on which the Greek artist Zopyrus had wrought a representation of the court of the Areopagus and the trial of Orestes.[6] A bevy of slaves was ready to wait upon the party,—the carver, who performed his duties in their presence, the footman who brought in the dishes on a silver tray, the menial who arranged them in due order upon the table, the cup-bearers who handed round the choicest wines.[7] Sumptuary laws, one after another, had been set at naught;[8] and the prices paid for delicacies would be incredible if they were not vouched for by a contemporary who was the most learned and the most matter-of-fact of Roman writers. Readers of classical literature must have often noticed the contrast between the cheapness of necessaries and the dearness of luxuries. The mullets bred in the famous fish-ponds of Lucullus were sold after his death for forty thousand sesterces;[9] but the buyer must have secured a bargain, for in the reign of Tiberius three choice specimens cost thirty thousand.[10] Peacocks fetched two

[1] Livy, xxxix, 6, 7.
[2] Banquets are fully described by Daremberg and Saglio, i, 1277-82, and in *Paulys Real-Ency.*, iii, 1895-7, s. v. cena. For a menu see Macrob., iii, 13, 10-2, and cf. Varro, *R. R.*, iii, 2, 16.
[3] Cic., *Verr.*, iv, 17, 37 ; Pliny, xiii, 15 (29), 92.
[4] Cic., *Verr.*, ii, 2, 14, 35 ; iv, 15, 33 ; *Pro Mur.*, 36, 75 ; Pliny, viii, 48 (74), 196.
[5] xxxiii, 11 (50), 141.   [6] *Ib.*, 12 (55), 156.   [7] *Ib.*, xiv, 14, 96.
[8] Gell., ii, 24, 3. 12 ; Macrob., iii, 17, 3. Cf. Daremberg and Saglio, iv, 1563.   [9] Varro, *R. R.*, iii, 2, 17.
[10] Suet., *Tib.*, 34, 1. Cf. Pliny, ix, 17 (31), 67

hundred apiece ; peahen's eggs twenty, equal to about four shillings ;[1] Aufidius Lurco, a contemporary of Cicero, was said to make sixty thousand sesterces a year by breeding these much-prized birds.[2] The same amount was given for five thousand thrushes, the produce of a single aviary during one year.[3] Equally remarkable were the sums expended on the slaves who served these viands. A first-rate cook was worth as much as four talents [4]— nearly a thousand pounds ; and Mark Antony paid more than twice as much for a pair of those beautiful boys [5] who, daintily attired and effeminately adorned, served as cupbearers or pages and in less reputable ways ministered to the pleasure of their masters.[6]

After the banquet the guests were occasionally entertained by duels between gladiators [7] or by lascivious dancers whose limbs were revealed by their diaphanous silks.[8]

Country houses of the rich.

When the jaded politician or the successful man of business went out of town to recruit his energies at the seaside or on the Alban hills, he did not exchange luxury for the simple life. Every Roman who could afford it possessed at least one country house, and Cicero, who was not rich, had seven.[9] The shores of the Bay of Naples abounded with such villas, remains of which are still visible beneath the blue translucent waves.[10] Their colonnades and fountains, bath-rooms, courts for gymnastic exercise, gardens, fish-ponds, stocked with mullets and lampreys and communicating with the sea, their libraries, picture galleries, and works of art are familiar to the readers of Varro [11] and of Cicero,[12] who spent large sums,

[1] Varro, R. R., iii, 6, 6.   [2] Ib., § 1.   [3] Ib., 5, 8.
[4] Diod. Sic., xxxvii, 3, 4.   [5] Pliny, vii, 12, 56.
[6] Polyb., xxxii, 11, 5 ; Cic., De fin., ii, 8, 23 ; Phil., ii, 18, 45 ; Diod. Sic., xxxvii, 3, 4 ; Plut., Cato mai., 4, 5.   [7] Athenaeus, iv, p. 153 f.
[8] Mart., v, 78, 26-8 ; vi, 71, 2 ; Daremberg and Saglio, iv, 1054, 1252.
[9] See p. 444, infra. Cornelius Nepos (Att., 14, 3) records it as remarkable that Atticus had no seaside or suburban villa.
[10] R. T. Günther, Pausilypon, 1913, p. 145. Cf the same writer's Earth-Movements in the Bay of Naples.
[11] R. R., i, 13, 6-7 ; ii, 1, 2 ; iii, 2, 8 ; 3, 10 ; 17, 9.
[12] Q. fr., iii, 1, 1-5. Cf. Ch. Dubois, Pouzzoles, 1907, pp. 361-72.

which he could ill afford, in adorning his Tusculan retreat with Greek statues and Greek bronzes. The passion, which Cicero frequently derided,[1] of Roman nobles for their fish-ponds and for the fishes which would take food from their hands, is exemplified by a well-attested story : 92 B.C. when the censor Domitius Ahenobarbus reproached his colleague Crassus for having shed tears at the death of a lamprey, Crassus retorted, 'Yes, I wept for an animal, but you have buried three wives and wept for none of them.'[2]

The Bay of Naples was two days' journey from the capital, even for a letter-carrier or a dispatch-rider who travelled express,[3] and holiday-makers who did not like to be hurried would spend four or five days upon the road. Inns, most of which were wineshops frequented by the lower classes, criminals, and prostitutes, abounded in country towns as well as in Rome ; but though some few, situated in populous districts, may have been tolerably comfortable,[4] they were rarely patronized by the rich, who travelled with a suite of servants, took their provisions and wines with them, and stopped for the night in lodges which were their private property. Cicero possessed four of these little houses,[5] one of which could be bought for a sum equivalent to three hundred pounds. The carriage in which the journey was performed was generally drawn by mules or asses.[6] The prices paid for the latter, when they were of the best breed, almost exceed belief : Varro[7] mentions a case in which a team of four, probably stallions intended for the stud, fetched four hundred thousand sesterces, or four thousand pounds.

Travelling : inns and private lodges.

A statesman or a man of letters, if he was of a serious turn or only wished to escape from the bustle of Rome and to breathe fresh air, might be satisfied with the

[1] *Att.*, i, 18, 6 ; 19, 6.
[2] Aelian, *De nat. animal.*, viii. 4. Cf. Macrob., iii, 15, 3-5.
[3] *Att.*, xvi, 14, 2. Cf. xiv, 18, 1.
[4] Varro, *R. R.*, i, 2, 23 ; Cic., *Pro Cluent.*, 59, 163 ; *In Pis.*, 6, 13. Cf. Hor., *Sat.*, i, 5, 4 ; ii, 4, 62 ; Daremberg and Saglio, i, 973-4.
[5] *Att.*, viii, 3, 7 ; xii, 1, 1 ; xvi, 10, 1 ; *Fam.*, vii, 23, 3 ; xii, 20.
[6] Stuart Jones, *op. cit.*, p. 313. Jennets were occasionally driven (Lucr., iii, 1063). [7] *R. R.*, ii, 1, 14.

98 THE ROMAN WORLD CHAP.

Pleasure-seekers at Baiae.

comfort of his villa and the society of congenial friends ;[1] but young men would prefer the gaiety of Baiae, the most fashionable and the most dissolute of watering-places. Men of position and character, and doubtless also women who clung to the old-fashioned ideals, were rather shy of being seen in this notorious resort ;[2] but the tourist who has driven from Naples round the coast through Pozzuoli to the shores of Baia, and has looked across the delectable bay towards Posilipo and Vesuvius, Pompeii and the peninsula of Sorrento, will not wonder that it was the favourite haunt of pleasure-seekers, who lived in a round of banquets, concerts, yachting parties, garden parties, and amours.[3] There effeminate youths were not ashamed to flaunt in togas of transparent silk,[4] while leaders of society and ladies of the demi-monde could display their Greek costumes, their emeralds and the pearls which hung from their ears, encircled their necks, and gleamed in their tiaras, on their fingers, on their elaborately curled hair, on their dresses, and even on their shoes.[5] Conspicuous among the throng was Clodia, the widow of Metellus Celer, with her great lustrous eyes, who is made known to us by the gibes of Caelius, the invectives of Cicero, and the love-songs of Catullus—Clodia, of whom it has been finely said that of her personality ' none can read without feeling its power and intensity, though but one or two of the facts of her life are to be seen, and that fitfully, through the virulence of her foes, like a wild revel in the night revealed by flashes of lightning.'[6]

Horse-racing and gladiatorial shows.

The masses, who could not afford the delights of Puteoli or Baiae, had opportunities for amusement provided by

[1] See Cic., *Att.*, i, 6, 2 ; xii, 40, 3 ; &c.
[2] *Ib.*, i, 16, 10 ; *Fam.*, ix, 3, 1 ; 2, 5.
[3] Cic., *Pro Cael.*, ii, 27 ; 15, 35 ; 16, 38 ; 20, 49 ; Varro *apud* Nonius, p. 154.
[4] Varro *apud* Nonius, p. 448, 26 ; Diod. Sic., xxxvii, 3, 4.
[5] Pliny, viii, 48 (74), 196 ; ix, 35 (56), 114 ; (57), 116 ; (58) 117 ; Ovid, *Ars amat.*, iii, 165 ; Mart., v, 68 ; viii, 81, 4 ; xii, 23, ; Daremberg and Saglio, iii, 1596 ; *Numism. Chron.*, 4th ser., vi, 1906, pp. 42–4.
[6] R. Y. Tyrrell and L. C. Purser, *The Correspondence of Cicero*, iii, 1890, p. xliii.

the State. Many who read these pages will have seen the amphitheatre which has been revealed by excavation at Pompeii ; and Capua and Puteoli had theirs before the earliest was built in Rome.[1] But the populace of the capital were catered for in other ways. In the Great Circus, the rounded oblong of which was some seven hundred yards in length, chariot races were held, as they had been since the infancy of the Republic, on religious holidays.[2] Even more popular were the gladiatorial combats of Etruscan origin, which had been first held in Rome two centuries before in honour of a dead noble,[3] in which free men, who had hired themselves to the contractors, occasionally figured,[4] and which generally took place in the Forum on a temporary scaffolding.[5] There too lions and panthers and leopards, rhinoceroses and elephants, imported from Africa or Asia by magistrates who desired to ingratiate themselves with the people, fought with one another, or were baited by shikarees, or mangled and devoured criminals.[6] Cicero protested half-heartedly against the cruelty of such exhibitions, and even callous spectators were indignant when elephants were tormented[7] ; but St. Augustine[8] confessed that he had felt the spell of the arena. Forced in his youth by his fellow-pupils to accompany them to the amphitheatre, he closed his eyes to avoid seeing what his conscience condemned ; but, hearing a roar of applause, he could not resist the temptation to open them, and, intoxicated by the spectacle of blood, he returned again and again.

Compared with these violent delights, the drama in itself had little charm. The works of contemporary dramatists, if, indeed, they were intended for the stage, were not acceptable ; and managers were obliged to revive the tragedies of Naevius, Pacuvius, and Accius, or

Plays and players.

---

[1] Pliny, xxxvi, 15 (24), 117 ; *Paulys Real-Ency.*, i, 1961 ; iii, 1561.
[2] Pliny, vii, 53 (54), 186.
[3] Athenaeus, iv, p. 153 f.   [4] Cic., *De off.*, i, 42, 150.
[5] Cic., *Pro Sest.*, 58–9, 124–5 ; Plut., *C. Gr.*, 12, 3.
[6] Cic., *Fam.*, viii, 9, 3, &c. ; Strabo, vi, 2, 6
[7] *Fam.*, vii, 1, 3 ; *Tusc.*, ii, 17, 41. Cf. *Pro Mil.*, 34, 92.
[8] *Confess.*, vi, 8.

the comedies of Plautus—both alike adapted from the Greek.[1] Sensational shows, such as the introduction of a train of mules upon the stage during the performance of the *Clytemnestra*, were added to please the vulgar;[2] and mimes, or farcical sketches of the low life of the town, which, as written by Laberius or the Syrian actor Publilius, were raised to the rank of literature, attracted by their laughable immorality as much as by their wit.[3] These entertainments, like the races and the combats of gladiators and wild beasts, were open free of charge to all citizens as well as to their women folk and children; and even slaves, though they had no right to come, were not excluded. The temporary wooden buildings in which the performances took place before Pompey built his theatre were covered with awnings to screen the spectators from rain or sun, and the best seats were reserved for senators and knights, a privilege which was resented by the multitude.[4] Though actors and actresses were looked down upon, the inferior players indeed being generally slaves,[5] the profession was raised in public estimation by the genius of Roscius; and the friendship with which Sulla, Crassus, and Cicero honoured him, as well as the wealth which he and his colleagues gained, gradually overcame old-fashioned prejudices.[6] Roscius himself earned five hundred thousand sesterces a year:[7] Aesopus, notwithstanding his extravagance, left twenty millions, a fortune equal to two hundred thousand pounds.[8]

Music and dancing.

Musicians, who loved to deck themselves with jewels,[9]

[1] Cic., *Pro Sest.*, 56, 120; *Q. fr.*, iii, 5 and 6, 7; *Lael.*, 7, 24; W. S. Teuffel, *Gesch. d. röm. Lit.* 1890, §§ 13, 15, 163.
[2] Cic., *Fam.*, vii, 1, 2.
[3] Cic., *Fam.*, ix, 16, 7; Ovid, *Trist.*, ii, 497-506, 515. Cf. W. Smith, *Dict. Ant.*, ii³, 173.
[4] Plaut., *Poenulus*, prol. 23-7; Livy, xxxiv, 44, 5; 54, 4; Pliny, xix, 1 (6), 23; Daremberg and Saglio, v, 204, 677.
[5] Cic., *Pro Rosc. com.*, 10, 27-8; *Att.*, iv, 15, 6; Pliny, vii, 39 (40), 128.
[6] Nepos, praef., 5; Augustine, *De civ. Dei*, ii, 13; Daremberg and Saglio, iii, 229.
[7] Pliny, vii, 39 (40), 129.
[8] *Ib.*, x, 51 (72), 141; xxxv, 12 (46), 163.   [9] *Ib.*, xxxvii, 1 (3), 7.

and female dancers, one of whom earned an income of two hundred thousand sesterces,[1] performed at dinner-parties as well as in public entertainments: but while young men and maidens of gentle birth appeared in those dances which accompanied religious rites,[2] an amateur who displayed more than ordinary skill was liable to suspicion. Sallust[3] observed that Sempronia danced better than beseemed a modest woman; and when Cicero wished to convey a specially offensive innuendo against Gabinius, he denounced him as a *danseuse*.[4] The schools in which children of the upper classes learned to twirl the castanets were condemned by Scipio Aemilianus as hotbeds of abnormal vice;[5] and it may be doubted whether they were more strictly regulated in the time of Cicero. Pipers had from early days accompanied sacrifices, stage-plays, and processions;[6] but how the Romans appreciated music which was worthy of the name may be realized from the description of the first public performance, when the most illustrious flute-players of Greece, quickly understanding the taste of their audience, played different tunes simultaneously 'with inconceivable violence and discord', one of the chorus squared up to a musician who approached him, and four boxers, finally mounting the stage, fought in pairs, to the accompaniment of clarions and trumpets, amid shouts of applause.[7] 115 B.C. Soon after the death of Gaius Gracchus the censors, observing perhaps that dramatic and musical entertainments were liable to abuse, forbade their continuance and tabooed all instruments except the native pipe;[8] but the injunction, whatever its motive may have been, was unheeded or forgotten.

[1] Cic., *Pro Rosc. com.*, 8, 23; Gell., i, 5, 3.
[2] Hor., *Carm.*, iv, 6, 31–2; *Carm. saec.*, 5–8; Dion. Hal., vii, 72.
[3] *Cat.*, 25, 2.
[4] *In Pis.*, 8, 18. Cf. 10, 22; *In Cat.*, ii, 10, 22–3; *Pro Mur.*, 6, 13; *De off.*, iii, 19, 75; 24, 93; Nepos, *Epam.*, 1, 2.
[5] Macrob., iii, 14, 6–7. *In re* music and dancing see Marquardt, *Privatleben*[2], pp. 118–9, 835; Daremberg and Saglio, iv, 1050–4.
[6] App., *Pun.*, 66; Plut., *Aem. Paul.*, 33, 1.   [7] Polyb., xxx, 14, 2–11.
[8] Cassiodor., *Chron.* (*Mon. Germ. hist.*, xi, 1894, ed. Th. Mommsen, pp. 131–2).

Painting and sculpture.

Even in the last period of the Republic Romans who cultivated the arts derived from Greece were considered, notwithstanding the example of the patrician Fabius Pictor,[1] to be lacking in the grave dignity of the ideal national character;[2] and Cicero,[3] who fervently admired the creations of Greek genius, found it expedient, when he was denouncing the thefts of Verres, to pander to the prejudices of his countrymen. But even Romans who despised artists were eager, whether from love of display or from genuine admiration, to collect specimens of art. Sculpture, like painting, was generally confined to portraiture; and the busts were executed with uncompromising realism.[4] Probably, however, the sculptors were generally Greeks, who adapted their conceptions to the taste of their patrons.[5] Akin to sculpture was the engraving of gems, of which examples depicting Caesar,[6] Pompey,[7] and perhaps also Cicero,[8] have been preserved. Wealthy connoisseurs were not content with the productions of native or contemporary talent, and enormous prices were paid for real or reputed masterpieces. Lucullus, indeed, secured a work by the painter Pausias for two talents;[9] but Caesar was obliged to give eighty—as much as nineteen thousand two hundred pounds—for two pictures of Medea and Ajax by Timomachus of Byzantium, which he hung in a temple of his own foundation.[10]

Neglect of science.

For science, except in so far as it could be applied to

---

[1] Pliny, xxxv, 4 (7), 19. 23.
[2] Daremberg and Saglio, ii, 481-2. Cf. Cic., *De rep.*, i, 22, 36.
[3] *Verr.*, iv, 60, 134.
[4] Pliny, xxxvi, 15 (24), 110; Daremberg and Saglio, iv, 1155.
[5] Cf. Daremberg and Saglio, iv, 1154 with H. von Brunn, *Gesch. d. griech. Künstler*, i, 1857, p. 602 and Pliny, xxxiv, 7 (18), 44; xxxvi, 5 (4), 41. Though Pliny (xxxv, 4 [7], 20-1) mentions a few Roman painters I have searched in vain for evidence that more than two sculptors of Roman birth (Brunn mentions both) existed. Cf. Prof. P. Gardner's article in *Journ. Rom. Studies*, vii, 1917, pp. 3, 9, 14, 22.
[6] Brit. Mus., Dept. of Greek and Rom. Ant., Nos. 1557-8.
[7] Mrs. Strong, *Rom. Sculpture*, p. 91 and figs. 2, 3 (pl. xxx, p. 88). Mrs. Strong remarks that the engravers, 'as the inscriptions prove, were often Greeks'.
[8] A. Furtwängler, *D. ant. Gemmen*, i, 1900, Taf. xlvii, 13; ii, 225.
[9] Pliny, xxxv, 11 (40), 125. [10] *Ib.*, vii, 38 (39), 126; xxxv, 11 (40), 136.

practical life, the Romans had little enthusiasm : while Chaldaean astrologers flourished on popular superstition,[1] Archimedes and Hipparchus had no successors in Italy. Even Pliny never mentioned the momentous discovery of the precession of the equinoxes ; and it may be doubted whether any Roman had ever heard of it. On the other hand, this generation saw the beginning of the Golden Age of Latin literature. No law of copyright protected the interests of authors ; and when the works of Cicero, produced by experienced copyists whom Atticus had purchased, were circulated in Italy and Greece, there was nothing to prevent an enterprising tradesman from employing his own slaves to pirate, with gross blunders, the authorized edition.[2] The booksellers' shops were situated mainly in a street called the Argiletum, which abutted on the north of the Forum, not far from the Rostra.[3] The books were written on papyrus imported from Alexandria, and were mounted on wooden rollers.[4] The titles of new publications were posted upon pillars[5] outside the shops ; but their best advertisement, apart from the reputation of the writer, was the praise of his friends, when their judgement was known to be sound.[6] Their prices, considering that they were produced by hand, seem remarkably low : handsome copies of the first book of Martial's epigrams were sold for five denarii— about four shillings—a charge which the author thought excessive.[7]

Production and publication of books.

Just as the Romans were indebted to the Greeks for literature and art, though they developed what they borrowed in obedience to their own ideals, so they owed to them all that was then known of medicine and surgery.[8]

Medicine, dentistry, and surgery.

[1] Cato, *De agri cult.*, 5, 4 ; Plut., *Mar.*, 42, 6. Cf. Warde Fowler, *Religious Experience*, 397-8.
[2] Cic., *Att.*, ii, 1, 2 ; iv, 13, 2 ; xiii, 12, 2 ; 13, 1 ; 21, 4 ; *Q. fr.*, iii, 5-6, 6.
[3] Mart., i, 117, 9. Cf. Virg., *Aen.*, viii, 350.
[4] Pliny, xiii, 11-3 (21-7), 68-89. Cf. Daremberg and Saglio, iv, 319-21.
[5] Hor., *Sat.*, i, 4, 71 ; *Ars poet.*, 372-3.
[6] Cic., *Att.*, xiii, 12, 2.
[7] Mart., i, 117, 15. For details about the book-trade see Daremberg and Saglio, iii, 1232-4, or Stuart Jones, *op. cit.*, pp. 334-7.
[8] Pliny, xxix 1 (6), 12.

Even Italian midwives found their occupation gone, at least with wealthy clients, when Greek competitors appeared. Though Greeks of good position came to practise in Italy, most members of the profession were freedmen or slaves of Greek origin, and rich men often kept physicians of their own. The Romans had long considered agriculture, the profession of law, and the service of the State as alone worthy of a free citizen (though the men of business had within the last century compelled recognition by their wealth), and hence not only retail traders, but even architects, engineers, and physicians were regarded as inferiors. The medical attendant of Domitius Ahenobarbus, the bitter enemy of Caesar, was his slave ;[1] while a freedman, attached to his household, prescribed for the younger Cato.[2] The medical, like the scholastic, profession, was uncontrolled : no degree, no diploma was required ; any one who chose to call himself a physician or a surgeon might practise without question. The inevitable result was that quacks abounded. 'Medicine', said Pliny,[3] 'is the only vocation in which any one who sets up as an expert commands ready confidence, though in no other is imposture more dangerous. . . . Furthermore, there is no law to punish ignorance : medical men learn at the peril of their patients, and the physician alone may kill a man with impunity.' Still, among many charlatans there were competent practitioners who had a high standard of professional honour,[4] and some modern doctors would be astonished to learn how much their ancient predecessors knew. There were, as one might have expected, various schools of theorists,[5] while medicine and surgery were rarely practised by the same man. Specialists, moreover, existed even then. Oculists, who became numerous under the Empire, were perhaps already consulted :[6] dentistry, as we learn from a clause in the Twelve Tables,[7] had

[1] Suet., *Nero*, 2, 3.   [2] Plut., *Cato min.*, 70, 1.
[3] xxix, 1 (8), 17-8.   [4] See e. g. Cic., *Att.*, xii, 33, 2.
[5] Pliny, xxix, 1 (3-4), 5-6.
[6] Mart., viii, 74 ; *C. I. L.*, iii, 614 ; vi, pars ii, 3987, 8909-10, 9606-9 ; H. Dessau, *Inscr. Lat.*, 7807-9.   [7] x, 8 (Bruns, *Fontes*⁶, &c., 1893, p. 37).

existed in the early period of the Republic. Teeth bound together by gold have been found in many Italian tombs,[1] and one of Martial's epigrams[2] ridiculed a lady whose teeth had obviously been bought. Lithotomy was occasionally performed,[3] and the statement of Pliny[4] that the medical profession was the most lucrative of all is illustrated by a case which, although it occurred in the early Empire, may well have been paralleled in the later Republic. In the reign of Nero a famous surgeon was summoned from Massilia to perform an operation in Italy, and received a fee, including his travelling expenses, of two hundred thousand sesterces[5]—about two thousand pounds.

But if the Romans owed these benefits to the Greeks, the public health had in other respects been provided for from the earliest days of the Republic. Not only Rome, but most of the country towns had an ample supply of pure water.[6] Four aqueducts, of one of which the bridges and tunnels are still visible in the neighbourhood of Tivoli, supplied the capital from the river Anio and from the Sabine and Alban hills.[7] Sewers, which, in Rome, originated in the time of the monarchy and were doubtless due to Etruscan builders, drained the public buildings, while private houses and tenements usually had cesspools.[8] As, however, the sewers served to carry off refuse and rainwater as well as sewage, openings in the streets were necessarily frequent, and the air was laden with the odours which offend visitors in certain continental towns.[9]

Water-supply.

Drainage.

Not less important for the well-being of the population Baths.

[1] *Bull. dell' Inst.*, 1877, p. 64, n. 5 ; *Mittheil. d. Kaiserl. deutsch. archaeol. Inst.*, Roem. Abth., i, 1886, p. 26.
[2] v, 43. Cf. xii, 23, and Cic., *De leg.*, ii, 24, 60.
[3] Celsus, vii, 26, 1–3.
[4] xxix, 1 (1), 2.
[5] *Ib.*, 1 (8), 22. See S. Reinach's admirable article MEDICUS (Daremberg and Saglio, iii, 1671–97), and cf. Sir C. Allbutt, *Greek Medicine in Rome*, 1921, ch. iii.
[6] F. Haverfield, *Anc. Town-Planning*, p. 17.
[7] Pliny, xxxvi, 15 (24), 121 ; Frontin., *De aq.*, i, 5–8 ; T. Ashby in *The Builder*, 1908, pp. 37–9, 89–90, 111–2, 142–4, 174–5, 203–5, 234–7.
[8] Daremberg and Saglio, i, 1261–4 ; iii, 988, 990.
[9] R. Lanciani, *Anc. Rome*, p. 56.

were the public baths, in which the poorest citizen could bathe in chambers of graduated temperature, plunge, after perspiring in the hot room, into the swimming tank, and finally take gymnastic exercise—all at the cost of half a farthing. Many of these buildings were beautifully decorated; but people of refinement who disliked mixed company could be accommodated in private establishments, which were, of course, worked for the profit of the proprietors, while the rich had similar baths in their urban mansions and their country houses.[1]

Country life and agriculture.

Contrasting with the bustle of the capital and the provincial towns, the cultured leisure of the Alban villa, and the frivolities of Puteoli or Baiae, were the old-fashioned life of the country gentleman, who, managing his own estates, brought up his sons to be hardy, frugal, and industrious,[2] and the laborious existence of the ploughman, the vine-dresser, the wood-cutter, the herdsman, and the shepherd. Not only peasants in their cottages, but many burgesses in market towns still ate their meals before the hearth in a common living-room.[3]

49 B. C. Wealthy nobles still possessed vast demesnes, which they leased to tenant-farmers.[4] Domitius Ahenobarbus promised an allotment to every centurion and every legionary whom he commanded in Corfinium, if they would hold the fortress against Caesar—a distribution which would have amounted to not less than twenty thousand acres.[5] In consequence, however, of the successive agrarian laws and the foundation of colonies, numerous small holdings now existed side by side with estates, often not more than a hundred and fifty acres in extent,[6] a dozen or more of which were in some cases owned by a single wealthy landlord:[7] but the tenure of the veteran soldiers

---

[1] Cic., *Pro Cael.*, 26, 62; *Fam.*, xiv, 20; Hor., *Sat.*, i, 3, 137; Pliny, xxxvi, 15 (24), 121; Daremberg and Saglio, i, 651-62; *Paulys Real-Ency.*, ii. 2747-50.   [2] Nonius, p. 108, s.v. *ephippium*.

[3] Hor., *Sat.*, ii, 6, 65-7; Colum., xi, 1, 19.

[4] Caes., *B. C.*, i, 34, 2; 56, 3. Cf. Cic., *Fam.*, xiii, 11, 1; Att., xiii, 9, 2; *Pro Caec.*, 20, 57; Varro, *R. R.*, ii, 3, 7.

[5] Caes., *B. C.*, i, 17, 4.   [6] Varro., *R. R.*, i, 18, 1.

[7] Cic., *Pro Rosc. Amer.*, 2, 6; 7, 20. Varro (*R. R.*, i, 15; ii, pr. 6; iii, 3, 8; 13, 1) possessed several estates as well as sheep runs and ranches.

whom Sulla and Caesar and Pompey planted on lands which they confiscated or purchased out of national funds was often ephemeral ; and, as we have seen in the preceding chapter, many of the Gracchan allottees, tired of the monotonous toil of farming, were attracted by the artificial cheapness—and afterwards by the free distribution—of food, to share the amusements of Rome with manumitted slaves and needy artisans. Either for this reason or because malaria had increased in the Campagna,[1] towns, such as Gabii and Bovillae, which had once been populous, had so dwindled that they could hardly find representatives to attend the Latin festival.[2]

Within the last century Italian agriculture had greatly changed. Rome had never been a market for Italian corn, except what was grown in the adjoining parts of Latium, for, owing to the heavy cost of transport, it could not be sold at a reasonable price. The corn grown on each little farm was disposed of by the owner, after he had provided for his own family, in the nearest town.[3] When the population of Rome increased and its wants could no longer be supplied by Latium, it subsisted on grain imported from Sicily, Sardinia, and Africa, and occasionally, even as early as the Hannibalic War, from Egypt ;[4] and if cargoes were also distributed in country towns, the motive for raising corn in Italy was proportionately weakened. How then were land-owners to find

---

[1] Cic., *De rep.*, ii, 5, 11 ; H. Nissen, *Ital. Landeskunde*, i, 1883, p. 417 ; R. Lanciani, *Wanderings in the Roman Campagna*, 1909, p. 5 ; *Class. Rev.* xxiv, 1910, p. 166.

[2] Cic., *Pro Planc.*, 9, 23. H. F. Pelham (*Essays*, 1911, pp. 269–73) holds that ' the spread of malaria was the effect, and not the cause of the depopulation testified to by the writers of the first century ' B. C., because with the disappearance or decay, due to the incessant wars that accompanied the advance of Roman dominion, of the small communities that had studded the Campagna, cultivation had declined, while the silting up of soil on the coast produced stagnant pools and marshes. But was not malaria both effect and cause ?

[3] Cato, *De agri cult.*, 2 ; 22, 3 ; Varro, *R. R.*, i, 69, 1 ; G. Salvioli, *Le capitalisme dans le monde ant.*, 1906, pp. 173, 178–9, 183 ; H. Bolkstein, *De colonatu Rom.*, &c., 1906, p. 117.

[4] *Mém. de l'Inst.*. . . . *Acad. des Inscr.*, &c., xl, 1916, pp. 247–9 ; Polyb., x, 44, 1-2. Cf. Livy, xxvii, 4, 10.

a remunerative investment ? Nobles, men of business, and even retired centurions who had made money in the East invested what they did not spend on luxuries in buying land [1], and turned their attention to new methods of cultivation. In Apulia, Lucania, and elsewhere large tracts, unsuitable for tillage, afforded excellent pasturage : but only the rich could make them profitable ; for it was necessary to drive the beasts on to the uplands for the summer, and to bring them back to the lowlands for the winter,[2] and to work a ranch on such a scale required a large staff of herdsmen, who had sometimes to encounter brigands and, with the aid of their fierce dogs, to ward off the attacks of wolves.[3] On the more productive lands the industry that superseded the growing of corn was the cultivation of the vine and olive, which not only fetched much higher prices, but, owing to their smaller bulk, cost much less to transport ; and, since to raise them at a profit required both capital and scientific method, the plantations were in the hands of wealthy men, some of whom spent a large part of the year on their estates and personally supervised the workers.[4] On a property of about one hundred and fifty acres, such as that which the elder Cato [5] described, the few labourers—not more than fourteen—who tilled the land and attended to the live-stock were controlled by the bailiff, himself a slave, whose wife was the only woman in the establishment ; but those who were inclined to be refractory were sometimes forced to work in chains and confined at night in those subterranean barracks to which urban slaves were occasionally relegated by way of punishment.[6] When

Ranches.

Vineyards and olive-gardens.

---

[1] Varro, *R. R.*, i, 2, 1. 7 ; 5, 1 ; 37, 2.
[2] *Ib.*, ii, 5, 11.   [3] *Ib.*, 10, 1-3, 10-1 ; iii, 17, 9.
[4] G. Ferrero, *Grandezza e decadenza di Roma*, ii, 1902, pp. 206-8 (Eng. tr., ii, 1907, pp. 132-3). Cf. Prof. Stuart Jones's article in *Edin. Rev.*, ccxxiv, 1916, p. 64.
[5] *De agri cult.*, 10, 1. See also 1, 7, and 11, 1, and cf. Varro, *R. R.*, i, 18, 1. H. Gummerus in his admirable treatise *D. röm. Gutsbetrieb* (*Klio*, Beih. 5, 1906, p. 72) concludes that in Varro's time conditions did not differ materially from those described by Cato.
[6] Cato, 56-7 ; Plaut., *Captivi*, 110-8 ; Columella, i, 6, 3 ; Pliny, xviii, 6 (4), 36. Columella remarks with unconsciously (?) grim humour that *ergastula* should be as healthy as possible.

the fruits had to be gathered additional labour was required, and a contractor, who employed free labourers, was called in.[1] Varro,[2] indeed, recommended that in unhealthy regions such workers should be regularly hired instead of slaves.

The year in which Gaius Gracchus died was remembered long after the fall of the Republic for the abundance of the vintage;[3] and the Government had already been induced to protect the interests of the growers by forbidding the Ligurians of Transalpine Gaul to plant fresh vineyards or olive groves.[4] The produce of Italy was exported both to Gaul and Liguria;[5] and though Varro[6] remarked that in his time there were individuals who complained that the business did not pay, it may be that they were only a minority, who had failed through inexperience or ignorance.[7] By the time of Pompey's third consulship the cultivation of the olive had been so far developed that it was for the first time exported to the provinces.[8]

153 B.C.

Oil and wine indeed were almost the only products which Italians could offer to foreign buyers:[9] their imports, which greatly exceeded their exports in value, were paid for by the money which they had gained by conquest.[10] Woollen tunics, intended for hard wear, were imported from Gaul;[11] gold, silver, copper, tin, and lead from Spain;[12] tin from Britain;[13] timber and iron-ore

Exports and imports.

[1] Cato, 5, 4; 136.
[2] *R. R.*, i, 17, 2. Since I wrote the foregoing paragraphs Mr. W. E. Heitland's *Agricola* (1921) has appeared. He makes his readers (see pp. 151-99) transport themselves in fancy to the old *I*talian country-side.
[3] Pliny, xiv, 14 (16), 94.
[4] Cic., *De rep.*, iii, 9, 16. Cf. S. Reinach's article in *Rev. arch.*, 3e sér., xxxix, 1901, pp. 367-9.
[5] Cic., *Pro Font.*, 9; Strabo, iv, 6, 2; Athenaeus, p. 152 c.
[6] *R. R.*, i, 8, 1.
[7] Cf. G. Ferrero, *Grandezza e decadenza di Roma*, i, 122 (Eng. tr., i, 71).
[8] Pliny, xv, 1 (1), 3.
[9] Daremberg and Saglio, iii, 1772. Diodorus (v, 13, 1-2) says that *I*taly exported iron implements.
[10] The Government attempted, of course in vain, to prevent gold and silver from being exported (Cic., *Pro Flac.*, 28, 67; *In Vat.*, 5, 12).
[11] Livy, xxix, 3, 5; Strabo, iv, 4, 3.   [12] See p. 138.
[13] Rice Holmes, *Anc. Britain*, 1907, pp. 483-514.

from the Balkans and the Danubian region;[1] amber from the Baltic;[2] grain and oil as well as the wild beasts destined for the arena from Africa;[3] marble from Numidia and Greece;[4] wines from Greece and the Balearic Isles;[5] purple dyes from Tyre[6] and glass from Sidon;[7] paper and glass from Alexandria;[8] silk from Assyria and the island of Cos;[9] spices, perfumes, and precious stones from Arabia;[10] ivory from East Africa;[11] pearls from the Persian Gulf;[12] diamonds, emeralds, and other luxuries from Upper Egypt and from India.[3]

Merchant ships arrived in Italian waters between February and November, for navigation was normally suspended in the winter.[14] The principal ports were Brundisium[15] on the eastern, and Puteoli on the western coast. The latter was selected instead of Naples, which, as its inhabitants had refused the citizenship, was a Greek,

[1] Stuart Jones, *op. cit.*, p. 321.   [2] Pliny, xxxvii, 3 (11), 42–5.
[3] *Bell. Afr.*, 97, 3; Suet., *Div. Iul.*, 75, 3.
[4] Strabo, ix, 1, 23; x, 5, 7; Pliny, iv, 12 (22), 67; v, 3 (2), 22; xxxvi, 6 (5), 44.
[5] *Ib.*, xiv, 6, 71; 14 (17), 96.
[6] Strabo, xvi, 2, 23; Pliny, v, 19 (17), 76; ix, 39 (63), 137.
[7] *Ib.* and xxxvi, 26 (66), 193.
[8] *Ib.*, xiii, 11–3 (21–7), 68–89; Athenaeus, p. 784 c; Daremberg and Saglio, iv, 319–21.
[9] Propert., ii, 3, 15; Pliny, xi, 22 (25–6), 75–6; Daremberg and Saglio, i, 720; iv, 1252.
[10] Strabo, xvi, 4, 25; xvii, 1, 45; Pliny, xiii, 3 (5), 24; xxxvi, 8 (12), 62; xxxvii, 2 (9), 24; &c.
[11] Strabo, i, 2, 32; Pliny, vi, 29 (34), 173.
[12] Strabo, xv, 1, 67; xvi, 3, 7. Inferior pearls were imported from Britain (Pliny, ix, 35 (37), 116).
[13] *Ib.*, vi, 17 (19), 52; xxxvii, 4 (15), 55; Strabo, xv, 1, 69; xvii, 1, 45. Mr. R. Sewell (*Journ. Roy. Asiat. Soc.*, 1904, pp. 593–4) infers from the small number of recorded Roman coins (only 15) found in India up to 1904 that there was 'little trade between India and Rome in the years preceding the reign of Augustus'. Very likely; but Mr. G. F. Hill tells me that Roman imports from India may have been paid for by bullion.
We learn from Lucretius (iv, 1126) that the precious stones called *smaragdi*, which is generally translated by 'emeralds', were already imported in his time. It is believed, however, that they were not emeralds, but peridots which came from an island in the Red Sea. If emeralds were worn by Roman ladies, they must have come from the mines in Upper Egypt (Strabo, xvii, 1, 45).
[14] Pliny, xix, 47 (49), 122.
[15] *Ib.*, iii, 11 (16), 101; Strabo, vi, 3, 6.

not a Roman, port, where merchants would have been obliged to pay duties to the native as well as to the Roman government. The grain intended for the capital was there stored, and conveyed, as it was wanted, to Ostia, at the mouth of the Tiber, where, owing to the silting up of the harbour, it had to be unloaded and carried in barges, towed by oxen, to the commercial port at the foot of the Aventine. Goods imported from Spain and the Balearic islands were brought direct to Ostia, and forwarded in the same way.[1]

Italian financiers [2]—bankers, brokers, money-lenders— were established in various centres of the Mediterranean,— at Narbo in Gaul, at Utica in the province of Africa, in Alexandria, in the province of Asia, in short wherever there was business to be done and money to be made. They formed associations in provincial towns to protect their interests against natives or the interference of Roman governors, and did much to propagate Roman civilization throughout the Mediterranean world.[3] The magnitude of their operations is illustrated by a letter in which Cicero [4] recommends to a correspondent an acquaintance named Pinnius, to whom the city of Nicaea owed a sum equivalent to eighty thousand pounds. The dealings of a more famous operator, Rabirius Postumus, who went to Alexandria to adjust the affairs of Ptolemy Auletes, the father of Cleopatra, are known to us from the speech in which Cicero defended him against the charge of fraud.

Italian men of business abroad.

The internal trade of Italy gave employment to comparatively few Roman citizens. Workmen could rarely earn more than twelve asses (about seven pence halfpenny) a day,[5] and those who lived in Rome were tempted to supplement this pittance by selling their votes to candi-

Handicrafts and guilds.

---

[1] Strabo, v, 3, 5 ; Pliny, xix (1), 3–4 ; Marquardt, *Röm. Staatsverw.*, ii², 113 ; R. Lanciani, *Anc. Rome*, p. 236.   [2] *Negotiatores*
[3] Caes., *B. C.*, ii, 19, 3 ; iii, 9, 3 ; Sall., *Iug.*, 26, 3 ; A. Schulten, *De conventibus civium Rom.*, 1892 ; Stuart Jones, *op. cit.*, pp. 316–7.
[4] *Fam.*, xiii, 61.
[5] Cic., *Pro Rosc. com.*, 10, 28. Gummerus (*Paulys Real-Ency.*, ix, 1495–6) conjectures that labourers were provided with food as well.

dates for office. Indeed, though free labourers were in demand for harvesting, the only craft in which free artisans held a strong position was that of the fullers, whose services were indispensable for cleansing the woollen garments which every Italian wore.[1] From time immemorial citizens engaged in the several handicrafts had combined in guilds to protect their interests and to worship the deity by whose aid they hoped to prosper ;[2] but these associations had little in common with our trades unions. Their aim was not to obtain higher wages or shorter hours of work, for they were composed of master craftsmen or independent artisans ; and if they included men who worked for hire, it would have been hopeless to strike against an employer who belonged to the same guild when there were slaves ready to take their places. In the houses of the rich[3] as well as on large estates remote from towns slaves were employed as potters, weavers, and in other industries.[4] Indeed it was perhaps partly under such competition that, as we shall see in a later chapter, the guilds in the Ciceronian Age, like corporations whose objects were ostensibly religious and others which were merely electioneering clubs, turned their attention to securing the bribes which politicians were ready to give for their support.[5]

[1] Pliny, xxxv, 17 (57), 197–8 ; Daremberg and Šaglio, ii, 1352.
[2] Pliny, xxxiv, 1, 1 ; xxxv, 12 (46), 159 ; Plut., *Numa*, 17, 3–4.
[3] Corn. Nep., *Att.*, 13, 3 ; Cic., *Pro Planc.*, 25, 62 ; Plut., *Cato min.*, 21. Cf. E. Meyer, *Kleine Schr.*, 1910, p. 210, and *Paulys Real-Ency.*, ix, 1455–7. As Gummerus remarks (*ib.*, p. 1457), it cannot always be determined whether such slaves worked for the domestic requirements of their owner or for his profit in the workshop of an independent craftsman ; and it would appear from Asconius (ed. Clark, p. 43, ll. 13–4 [ed. Stangl, p. 38]) that the practice of making clothes in private houses was falling into disuse.
[4] Varro, *R. R.*, i, 16, 4–5. Cf. *Klio*, Beih. 5, 1906, pp. 69, 72, 94.
[5] Cic., *Q. fr.*, ii, 3, 5 ; *Pro Planc.*, 15, 37 ; 19, 47 ; Q. Cic., *De pet. cons.* 19. Cf. J. P. Waltzing, *Étude hist. sur les corporations prof. chez les Romains*, i, 1895, pp. 48–50, 78, 87–9 ; Daremberg and Saglio, i, 447, 1292 ; iv, 1372–3 ; *Klio*, Beih. 5, p. 94 ; *Paulys Real-Ency.*, ix, 1454. Journeymen in handicrafts were mostly slaves, the employment of free workmen being exceptional (*Dig.*, ix, 2, 5, 3 ; xiii, 6, 5, 7. Cf. *Paulys R.-E.*, ix, 1506–7) ; and the contempt with which handicrafts were regarded (Cic., *De off.*, i, 42, 150–1) resulted from the prevalence of slave labour (*Paulys R.-E.* ix, 1511). Many of the craftsmen, slaves or free, in Rome were Greeks or Orientals, though natives predominated in country districts (*ib.*, 1508–10).

IN THE CICERONIAN AGE

Various industries were specialized in divers parts of the peninsula. Comum and Sulmo were noted for iron works.[1] Wine-jars, bolts, locks, keys, and clogs were made in Rome; ropes at Capua; bronze goods at Capua and Nola; wagons at Suessa and in Lucania; iron implements at Cales, Minturnae, and Puteoli;[2] pottery at Arretium;[3] woollen goods in the valley of the Po[4]; while flax was grown and manufactured in the neighbourhood of Faventia,[5] and Genoa was a mart for timber, cattle, hides, and honey, produced by the natives of Liguria.[6] In ancient times, however, factories on a large scale did not exist; for the machinery which would have given them an advantage over lesser workshops had not been invented, and capital was never employed in developing an extensive business which would need time and organization to bring to a remunerative stage.[7] The shops which occupied the frontage of blocks of flats and even of the mansions of the nobility were sometimes owned by wealthy citizens and managed by their freedmen or by slaves, who paid them a fixed sum and kept the surplus profits for themselves.[8] Indeed connoisseurs who had a taste for artistic ornaments occasionally kept jewellers who designed and wrought exclusively for them. These craftsmen were of course Greeks, for Roman jewellers copied Greek models, just as English jewellers reproduce the creations of the Rue de la Paix.[9]

Specialized industries.

Besides the great trunk roads, which, though they had been designed for the movement of armies, facilitated trade, regional roads were made from time to time to meet the requirements of local traffic.[10] Like the aqueducts and other public works, they were constructed by slaves, working under contractors, whose tenders had been

Roads.

---

[1] Pliny, xxxiv, 14 (40), 144–5.   [2] Cato, De agri cult., 135, 1–3.
[3] Pliny, xxxv, 12 (46), 160.   [4] Strabo, v, 1, 7. 12.
[5] Pliny, xix, 1 (2), 9.   [6] Strabo, iv, 6, 2.
[7] G. Salvioli, op. cit., pp. 153, 205; Paulys Real-Ency., ix, 1454.
[8] Cic., Pro Cluent., 63, 178; Dig., xiv, 3, 3; 4, 1. 5; xv; xxxiii, 7, 19, 1; xl, 7, 14.
[9] Cic., Verr., iv, 24, 54; Klio, xv, 1918, pp. 259, 261.
[10] See the maps in Daremberg and Saglio, v, 790–1, 794,

approved by the censors and occasionally by officials called overseers of the roads.[1] Repairs were executed under the superintendence of the aediles, who, however, if we may judge from the complaints of Horace,[2] sometimes neglected their duties or could not obtain from the Treasury the necessary funds. Other administrative functions, upon which public security depends, were disregarded in a way which brought grave discredit upon the Government. The want of an organized postal system was, indeed, supplied by the messengers whom the tax-collectors in the provinces, as well as the governor, were obliged to employ, and who occasionally carried letters for private individuals who were not rich enough to keep couriers of their own;[3] but the aediles, who were not only responsible for supervising public baths, taverns, and brothels, and for such business as would now devolve upon a borough council, but were also, in a sense, police magistrates,[4] had not the means of preserving peace and order. The streets were dark at night, and pedestrians were liable to be waylaid. No adequate police existed; and, while political riots were now a matter of course, Rome as well as rural districts was infested by robbers.[5] Rich men who coveted their neighbours' lands sometimes employed armed slaves to drive them from their homes, and boundary disputes were frequently decided not by law but by violence.[6] The laws which protected Roman

Postal messengers.

Inadequate police.

[1] Livy, xxxix, 44, 5. 8; Polyb., vi, 17, 2-6. Whether these overseers were temporary or permanent is unknown. We learn from an inscription (*C. I. L.*, vi, 3824 = Dessau, *Inscr. Lat.*, 5799) that a section, 20 miles long, of the Caecilian way, the shortest route between Rome and the Adriatic, cost 150,000 sesterces (£1,500).

[2] *Sat.*, i, 5, 96. Cf. Ovid, *Ep. ex Ponto*, ii, 7, 41-5.

[3] Cic., *Att.*, i, 5, 3; 9, 1; v, 16, 1; vi, 2, 1; viii, 14, 1; *Fam.*, ii, 7, 3; xii, 30, 1; xvi, 9, 2. Cf. Miss A. M. Ramsay's interesting paper in *Journ. Rom. Studies*, x, 1920, especially pp. 81-5. W. Riepl (*D. Nachrichtenwesen d. Altertums*, 1913, p. 140) maintains that letter-carriers usually travelled on foot—even (p. 204) from the Channel across Gaul to Rome!

[4] Livy, viii, 18, 4; xxxix, 14, 10; *lex Iulia municipalis*, ll. 20-36 (Bruns, *Fontes*⁶, &c., 1893, pp. 105-6); Val. Max., vi, 1, 7; Tac., *Ann.*, ii, 85; *Paulys Real-Ency.*, i, 452-8.

[5] Varro, *R. R.*. i, 16, 1-2; Suet., *Aug.*, 32, 1: App., *B. C.*, v, 132, 546-7.

[6] Cic., *Pro Tull.*, 8; *Pro Caec.*, 1, 1; *Pro Cluent.*, 59, 161. Cf. Greenidge, *Legal Procedure*, &c., pp. 552-3.

citizens from capital punishment and even from stripes had been passed at a time when an alien and criminal population had not yet begun to encumber Rome: outlawry could generally be evaded by voluntary exile; and even Oppianicus, whose many murders are recorded by Cicero in that speech which depicts in dark colours the morals of Italy, was safe after his condemnation so long as he remained outside the city walls.[1] Jerry-built tenements occasionally collapsed, and frequently caught fire owing to the woodwork in their upper stories;[2] but, in default of a fire brigade, the only officials available to cope with the conflagrations were the so-called nocturnal commissioners and the public slaves whom they controlled.[3]

Conflagrations.

Even the national defences suffered from maladministration: for, as we shall see hereafter, the Senate was naturally jealous of the ambitious leaders into whose hands military power was tending to pass; and although throughout this period standing armies existed, they were not recognized as such. The Government could not or would not adopt measures for maintaining them under their control; and the efficiency which they attained was due to their commanders alone.[4] In such an outline of the military system as may enable readers to understand the subsequent narrative we may leave out of sight details which will be noticed in their proper place.

Military system.

Although Marius had found willing recruits among the poorest class, which had been excluded from service before his time, the law still held good that every citizen of military age was liable to be called out; and the compulsory levy, though it might be evaded by individuals

---

[1] Cic., *Pro Cluent.*, 62, 175. Cf. a striking passage in Prof. A. C. Clark's edition of *Pro Milone*, 1895, pp. xv–xvi. 'There is no trace', says Strachan-Davidson (*Problems of the Rom. Crim. Law*, ii, 1912, p. 24), 'in all the voluminous evidence supplied by Cicero's writings that a single Roman was ever put to death in his time by regular course of law.'

[2] Catull., 23, 9; Strabo, v, 3, 7.

[3] Livy, xxxix, 14, 10; 16, 12; 17, 5; Gell., xiii, 12, 6; Val. Max., viii, 1, *damn.* 5–6; Daremberg and Saglio, v, 412–3. The commissioners (*tresviri*) acted, or were supposed to act, as police at night; but the force at their disposal was inadequate.

[4] See G. L. Cheesman, *The Auxilia of the Rom. Imp. Army*, 1914, pp. 12–3.

who bribed the recruiting officers or obtained underhand influence,[1] was still frequently resorted to.[2] As a rule, however, the forces of the Ciceronian Age, especially those of Caesar, were largely composed of volunteers.[3] The men were probably attracted by the prospect of booty and obtaining bounties and grants of land after their discharge, for the pay was no more than one hundred and twenty *denarii* (less than five pounds) a year ; [4] and although Caesar, at least for his own men, virtually doubled this amount, it was even then no more than the wage of a day-labourer, and was subject to deduction of the cost of rations and of clothing.[5] Each legion consisted of ten cohorts ; and the cohort, formed of three maniples or six centuries, had replaced the maniple as the tactical unit of the legion.[6] From the earliest times the legion had been commanded by an officer called a military tribune. Six were assigned to each legion, and each one of the number held command in turn. But they now often owed their appointments to interest rather than to merit ; and no tribune in Caesar's army was ever placed at the head of a legion. Except when the office was a sinecure, bestowed by the general at the request of some influential friend, the tribunes still had administrative duties to

---

[1] *Bell. Alex.*, 56, 4 ; Sall. (?), *Ep. ad Caes.*, i, 8, 6.
[2] Cic., *In Cat.*, ii, 3, 5 ; *Pro Mil.*, 25, 67 ; *Att.*, vii, 21, 1 ; Caes., *B. G.*, vi, 1, 2 ; vii, 1, 1 ; Varro, *R. R.*, iii, 2, 4 ; Sall., *Cat.*, 30, 5 ; Dio, xxxix, 39, 1. 3 ; &c. Cf. *Paulys Real-Ency.*, v, 610–2.
[3] *Dig.*, xlix, 16, 4, 10.
[4] Polyb., vi, 39, 12 ; Pliny, xxxiii, 3 (13), 45.
[5] Suet., *Div. Iul.*, 26, 3 ; *Domit.*, 7, 3 ; Tac., *Ann.*, i, 17. Cf. Marquardt, *Röm. Staatsverw.*, ii², 92–6. The law by which C. Gracchus released soldiers from the obligation of paying for their clothes (p. 24, *supra*) was probably abrogated before the time of Caesar. See Tac., *Ann.*, i, 17.
[6] R. Cagnat (Daremberg and Saglio, iii, 1051) infers from Caesar, *B. G.*, i, 25, 2 (*milites . . . manipulos laxare iussit*), vi, 36, 6 (*si continere ad signa manipulos vellet*), and *B. C.*, i, 76, 1 (*Petreius manipulos circumit*), ii, 28, 1 (*legionesque eas transduxerat Curio . . . adeo ut paucis mutatis centurionibus idem ordines manipulique constarent*) that the maniple was still the tactical unit. But any one who reads these passages with the context will see that they are inconclusive ; and while *cohors* occupies more than nine columns of Meusel's *Lex. Caes.*, a few lines suffice for *manipulos*, which, moreover, is not to be found in *Bell. Alex.*, *Bell. Afr.*, or *Bell. Hisp. B. G.*, v, 15. 4, 34. 2, 35. 1 tell especially against Cagnat's view.

perform, and exercised subordinate commands.¹ But the principal officers were the *legati*, who might loosely be called brigadiers or generals of division. Their powers were not strictly defined, but varied according to circumstances and to the confidence which they deserved. A *legatus* might be entrusted with the command of a legion or of an army corps; he might even, in the absence of his chief, be entrusted with the command of the entire army. But he was not yet, as such, the permanent commander of a legion.² The officers upon whom the efficiency of the troops mainly depended were the centurions. They were chosen from the ranks—not always because they deserved promotion, for avaricious generals sold their patronage to the highest bidder;³ and their position has been roughly compared with that of our own non-commissioned officers. But their duties were in some respects at least as important as those of a captain; the centurions of the first cohort were regularly summoned to councils of war; and the chief centurion of the legion was actually in a position to offer respectful suggestions to the legate himself.⁴ Occasionally, indeed, though, it would seem, very rarely, a centurion might rise to be a military tribune.⁵ Every legion included a number of skilled artisans, called *fabri*, who have been likened to the engineers in a modern army; but they were not permanently enrolled in a separate corps.⁶ They fought in the ranks like other soldiers; but when their special services were required, they were directed by staff-officers called *praefecti fabrum*. It was their duty to execute repairs of every kind,⁷ to superintend the construction of permanent camps, and to plan fortifications and bridges; and it would seem that they also had charge of the

---

[1] Rice Holmes, *Caesar's Conquest of Gaul*², 1911, pp. 565–7.
[2] *Ib.*, pp. 563–5.
[3] Cic., *De imp. Cn. Pomp.*, 13, 37; *In Pis.*, 36, 88. Caesar probably alluded to this practice in *B. G.*, i, 40, 12.
[4] *B. G.*, iii, 5, 2; v, 28, 3; vi, 7, 8.
[5] *B. C.*, iii, 104, 2; Plut., *Pomp.*, 78, 1 Cf. *Paulys Real-Ency.*, vi, 292.
[6] Rice Holmes, *op. cit.*, p. 579.
[7] *B. G.*, v, 11, 3.

artillery,[1]—the *ballistae* and catapults which hurled heavy stones and shot feathered javelins against the defences and the defenders of a besieged town, and of which the lighter pieces were occasionally used like field guns. The descriptions of these weapons given by ancient writers have been elucidated by the allied labours of a German scholar and a German officer of artillery. It is impossible to state exactly what the difference between catapults and *ballistae* was; but both derived their power from the recoil of tightly twisted cordage, and

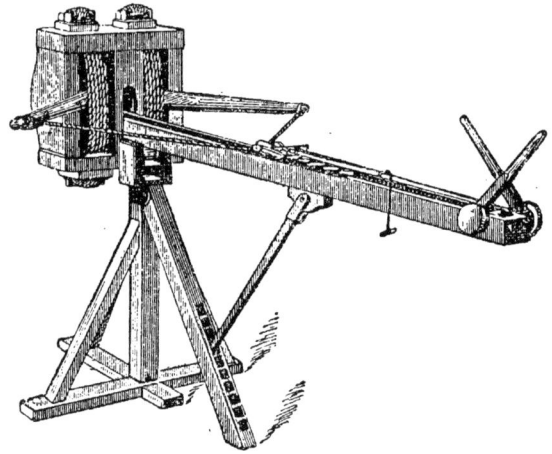

both could discharge either heavy stones or feathered javelins.[2] The two arms of the engine were passed through the skeins of cordage. A block, furnished with

[1] W. Rüstow, *Heerwesen u. Kriegführung C. J. Caesars*, 1855, p. 31; Fr. Fröhlich, *D. Kriegswesen Cäsars*, 1891, pp. 51-3. R. Schneider (*Paulys Real-Ency.*, vii, 1318) is right in saying that there was no special corps of artillerymen; but when he infers from Tacitus (*Ann.*, ii, 81; xiii, 39) and Vegetius (*De re mil.*, iii, 3) that *all* legionaries were competent to handle the engines he goes too far. Unskilled or clumsy men might injure the mechanism; and since Caesar 'selected skilled workmen from the legions' to repair damaged ships (*B. G.*, v, 11, 3), it seems probable that he did the same for the service of his artillery. Cf. Veg., *op. cit.*, ii, 11, and Daremberg and Saglio, iii, 956-7.

[2] R. Schneider (*Paulys Real-Ency.*, vii, 1297-1322); Col. E. Schramm (*Jahrb. d. Gesell. f. lothr. Gesch.*, &c., xvi, 1904, pp. 142-60; xviii, 1906, pp. 276-83). Cf. Stuart Jones, *op. cit.*, pp. 215-22, and *Class. Quart.*, xiv, 1920, pp. 82-6.

a hook which held the bowstring and which was itself held down by a trigger, could slide up and down in the groove. When the engine was loaded the block was forced back, despite the resisting cordage, by a windlass, and fixed by a catch which fitted into a row of teeth : when the missile was to be discharged the trigger was pressed, the bowstring was released, the recoil of the cordage caused the arms to fly back, and the missile sped on its way.

The legionary wore a sleeveless woollen shirt, a leathern cuirass protected across breast and back by bands of metal, strips of cloth wound round the thighs and legs, and, in cold or wet weather, a kind of blanket or military cloak, which, fastened on the right shoulder by a safety-pin, left his right arm free. His defensive armour, besides the cuirass, consisted of helmet, shield, and greaves : [1] his weapons were a short, two-edged, cut-and-thrust sword [2] and a javelin, the blade of which, behind the hardened point, was made of soft iron, so that, when it struck home, it might bend and not be available for return.[3] These, however, formed only a part of the load which he carried on the march. Over his left shoulder he bore a pole, to which were fastened in a bundle his ration of grain, his cooking vessel, cup, saw, basket, hatchet, sickle, pick, and spade.[4] For it was necessary that he should be a woodman and navvy as well as a soldier. No Roman army ever halted for the night without constructing a camp fortified with trench, rampart, and palisade.

The regular infantry, however, was the only arm that consisted of Roman citizens. Roman cavalry, which had formerly been brigaded with the several legions, ceased

---

[1] Fröhlich, *op. cit.*, pp. 66–8, 70–4 ; Daremberg and Saglio, iii, 1068; Rice Holmes, *op. cit.*, pp. 584–5.   [2] Fröhlich, *op. cit.*, pp. 61–2.

[3] *B. G.*, i, 25, 3–4. A. J. Reinach (Daremberg and Saglio, iv, 482) asserts without any evidence that this device was invented by Caesar. For a description of javelins (*pila*) found at Numantia, Alesia, and near Urso see A. Schulten's article in *Rhein. Mus.*, lxix, 1914, pp. 477, 485, 489, n. 5.

[4] Veg., *De re mil.*, ii, 25 ; Fröhlich, *op. cit.*, pp. 74–5 ; Rice Holmes, *op. cit.*, p. 585.

to exist after the time of Marius ; for, in consequence of the prolonged and inglorious wars in Spain, the wealthier Italians of whom it had been composed became more and more reluctant to serve.[1] Thenceforward the cavalry were furnished by various nations,—provincials, who were obliged to serve, subjects of dependent princes, Gallic, Thracian, Galatian, Numidian, or even German mercenaries, who served, for the most part, under their tribal chiefs, though individual squadrons were occasionally, and the whole division always, commanded by a Roman officer.[2] The light-armed auxiliary infantry—archers, slingers, and targeteers armed with broadswords, who figured in various campaigns—were raised from divers countries under Roman rule.[3] In the stress of the war between Caesar and Pompey not only cavalry,[4] but also infantry[5] were occasionally raised from slaves, whom even Catiline had forborne to arm ;[6] and legions were sometimes composed of provincials, who accordingly received the franchise.[7]

The column was of course accompanied by a host of non-combatants. Each legion required at least five or six hundred mules to carry its baggage ;[8] and the drivers and grass-cutters with other slaves, who waited on the officers, formed a numerous body.[9] Wealthy officers were often attended by their private surgeons, whom they probably allowed to minister to wounded men as well : at all events medical aid of some sort was provided for

[1] G. L. Cheesman, *The Auxilia of the Rom. Imp. Army*, 1914, pp. 9–10.
[2] Abundant evidence will be given in succeeding chapters. Cf. *Caesar's Conquest of Gaul*², pp. 579–81.
[3] Caes., *B. G.*, ii, 7, 1 ; *B. C.*, i, 39, 1 ; Tac., *Hist.*, i, 38 ; *Ann.*, xii, 35.
[4] Caes., *B. C.*, i, 24, 2 ; iii, 4, 4 ; *Bell. Afr.*, 19, 4.
[5] *Ib.*, 36, 1 ; *Bell. Hisp.*, 7, 4–5 ; *App.*, ii, 103, 427.
[6] Sall., *Cat.*, 44, 5–6.
[7] *B. C.*, ii, 20, 4 ; *Bell. Alex.*, 53, 4–5, &c. ; *Bell. Hisp.*, 10, 3 ; 12, 1 ; *Hermes*, xix, 1884, p. 13, n. 2 ; Marquardt, *Röm. Staatsverw.*, ii², 432–3.
[8] Caesar nowhere mentions that he used wagons or carts during the Gallic war ; but it seems certain that he must have used some, to carry artillery, material for sappers' huts, &c. See *Bell. Afr.*, 9, 1 ; 21, 2 ; Plut., *Pomp.*, 6, 4 ; Fröhlich, *op. cit.*, p. 89. The larger pieces of artillery were of course conveyed in parts, which were put together as occasion required.
[9] Fröhlich, *op. cit.*, pp. 56–7.

the rank and file.¹ Among the camp-followers were also dealers who supplied the wants of the army and were ready to buy booty of every kind.² How the Romans, in default of a national fleet, raised ships of war and the crews who manned them, will appear in the succeeding narrative.

The revenue required to defray administrative charges was derived from taxes or duties paid by Roman citizens, from property belonging to the State, from booty of war when the general was conscientious enough to transmit what was due into the treasury,³ from indemnities exacted from conquered peoples, and from tribute paid by the provincials. Since the subjugation of Macedonia the property tax formerly levied on Roman citizens had been remitted;⁴ customs duties, as we shall see hereafter, were abolished soon after the consulship of Cicero,⁵ though a few years later they were revived; and, except a tax on pillars imposed by Caesar during his third dictatorship,⁶ probably with the object of checking extravagance in building, the only direct impost, which, moreover, affected comparatively few, was a duty of five per cent. on the value of manumitted slaves.⁷ Rent was, however, paid by the tenants of the Campanian public land until they were evicted to make room for colonists, and by graziers for the privilege of feeding cattle upon public pastures; and funds were also raised from water rates, sewer rates, fishing rights, and tolls of various kinds.⁸

But the greater proportion of the revenue was derived from the provinces, which, as Cicero⁹ remarked, were regarded as the estates of the Roman People. The principles upon which the Senate organized the provincial governments were much the same as those which had

Revenue.

167 B.C.

Provincial administration.

¹ Cic., *Tusc.*, ii, 16, 38; Suet., *Aug.*, 11; *Nero*, 2, 3; Fröhlich, *op. cit.*, p. 131.
² *B. G.*, ii, 33, 7; vi, 37, 2.
³ Cic., *De lege agr.*, i, 4, 12; ii, 22, 59. See my edition of Caesar's *B. G.*, note on vii, 89, 5.
⁴ Cic., *De off.*, ii, 22, 76; Val. Max., iv, 3, 8; Pliny, xxxiii, 3 (17), 56; Plut., *Aem. Paul.*, 38, 1.
⁵ *Att.*, ii, 16, 1. ⁶ *Ib.*, xiii, 6, 1. ⁷ *Ib.*, ii, 16, 1.
⁸ Marquardt, *Röm. Staatsverw.*, ii², 151, 159. ⁹ *Verr.*, ii, 2, 3, 7.

guided them in dealing with the peoples whom they subdued in Italy, and in certain respects they find a parallel in the first century of Anglo-Indian rule. Roman statesmen were content to let well alone. They never interfered with religion, for intolerance of foreign deities was naturally unknown to polytheism, nor did they make any change in municipal or financial organization when they found it serviceable. But, acting on the time-honoured principle *Divide et impera*, they took care to prevent combination between communities which might give trouble ; and the roads which they constructed were planned, like the highways of Italy, with a single eye to military convenience.[1] The parallel with British India is particularly noticeable in the varieties of status which existed within the provinces. Not all were under the direct control of the proconsul or the propraetor. Client princes, like Ariobarzanes, the king of Cappadocia, were suffered to govern under the overlordship of Rome, doubtless in the expectation that their subjects would be gradually prepared to submit to Roman rule ; and if their government was oppressive, the paramount power, in this respect unlike the British, was too indifferent or too conscious of its own shortcomings to call them to account.[2] Roman colonies and municipalities which possessed Latin rights were obliged, unlike those of Italy, to pay taxes.[3] Certain towns which had rendered services to Rome in war were granted charters of freedom (which might, it is true, be revoked), and accordingly enjoyed immunity from ordinary taxation, internal autonomy, and exemption from the jurisdiction of the Governor as well as from the burden of housing and feeding troops.[4] Others, which had also shown themselves friendly to the paramount power, were

---

[1] Daremberg and Saglio, v, 783. Cf. Cic., *De prov. cons.*, 2, 4. Milestones were placed on provincial roads, as on those of Italy, before the time of C. Gracchus (Polyb., iii, 39, 8 ; O. Hirschfeld in *Sitzungsber. d. Königl. Preuss. Akad. d. Wiss.*, 1907, p. 167 and n. 4 ; *C. I. L.*, ii, p. 655 and No. 4956).

[2] See P. C. Sands, *The Client Princes of the Roman Empire*, 1908, pp. 157–62.

[3] Marquardt, *Röm. Staatsverw.*, i², 87–8.

[4] Cic., *De prov. cons.*, 4, 7 ; Tac., *Ann.*, xv, 45 ; *C. I. L.*, i, No. 204.

called federate towns because the same privileges were guaranteed to them by treaty : but in both cases these privileges were occasionally violated by unscrupulous rulers ;[1] and certain free and federate towns, though they were exempt from ordinary taxation, were obliged to contribute to the maintenance of the fleet required for the protection of the province.[2] The remaining communities were of course taxed; and the measure of internal independence which they were allowed depended upon the discretion of the Governor, who, if he was honest and capable, interfered with them no more than he found necessary.[3] Besides paying tribute, however, they, as well as certain free and allied towns, were liable to conscription,[4] and even dependent kings were required in emergencies to supply auxiliaries as well as money ;[5] for military service in foreign parts was unpopular in Italy,[6] and Rome, like England, which employs sepoys in conjunction with British troops, could not furnish enough legionaries for the little wars or the punitive expeditions which a provincial ruler might be obliged to undertake. The Governor was the supreme judge in all suits between inhabitants of communities other than the free and the allied towns; and against his decision there was no appeal.[7] Moreover, he was not merely the civil ruler, but also the commander-in-chief.[8]

In the matter of taxation the provinces were not all treated alike. Sicily and Asia paid tithes of the produce of the soil, the collection of which was farmed to the *publicani*,—syndicates of monied men, whose affairs were

[1] Cic., *Verr.*, ii, 2, 66, 160 ; 69, 166 ; iii, 6, 13 ; 40, 91–2 ; 73, 170 ; iv, 9, 20 ; *Pro Balbo*, 8, 22 ; 17, 39–40 ; *De off.*, iii, 22, 87 ; Plut., *Pomp.*, 10, 2.
[2] *Verr.*, i, 34, 86 ; 35, 89 ; iv, 9, 21 ; 34, 76 ; 67, 150 ; v, 19, 49. Cf. *Pro Flac.*, 12, 27 ; 13, 30.
[3] *Verr.*, iv, 65, 146 ; *Pro Flac.*, 19, 44 ; *Att.*, vi, 1, 15.
[4] Cic., *Att.*, vi, 5, 3 ; *Phil.*, x, 6, 13.
[5] Caes., *B. C.*, iii, 3, 2 ; Cic., *Fam.*, xv, 2, 4 ; Plut., *Cr.*, 17, 6 ; App., *Mithr.*, 64 ; *B. C.*, i, 102, 474–5 ; Dio, xli, 63, 1 ; xlii, 49, 1–2.
[6] Sall., *Iug.*, 85, 3.
[7] Cic., *Verr.*, ii, 2, 22, 53–5 ; 24–5 ; v, 11, 28 ; *Att.*, ii, 16, 4 ; v, 20, 1 ; 21, 9.
[8] This will appear in the course of the subsequent narrative.

managed by a director resident in Rome, and who, after paying a lump sum to the State for the privilege of collection, exacted from the provincials what they could, dealing with them through the several communities.[1] The remaining provinces—Sardinia (which also paid tithes [2]), Corsica, Spain, the greater part of Africa, Gaul, Macedonia, Illyricum, Achaia, Cilicia, and the four that were annexed within this period—Bithynia, Syria, Crete with Cyrenaica, and Gallia Comata—paid definite sums or definite quantities of goods, for the collection of which they were themselves responsible.[3] These provinces therefore were so far free from the intrusion of Roman tax-gatherers; and in the cases of Spain and Gaul at least one may suppose that the method was adopted because they had no cities and the Roman officials, in default of native assistance, would have found difficulty in raising what was due: but in all the provinces, as in Italy, the right of levying the customs, from which, however, in the provinces Italians were exempt,[4] and of collecting the rent for pasturing cattle on the public lands,[5] was farmed to *publicani*.[6] Moreover, when provincials were remiss in raising their tribute, *publicani* contracted for collecting the arrears,[7] and the revenues

[1] Cic., *Verr.*, iii, 7, 18; 27, 67; 32, 75; 37, 84; 38, 86; 42, 99.

[2] Livy, xxxvi, 2, 13; xxxvii, 2, 12; 50, 9; xlii, 31, 8. Though Sardinia paid tribute as well (Cic., *Pro Balbo*, 18, 41; Livy, xxiii, 32, 9; 41, 6), I can find no evidence that on the whole it was more heavily burdened than any other province.

[3] *Verr.*, iii, 6, 12; Pliny, xxi, 13 (45), 77; xxxiii, 3 (15), 51. The agrarian law of 111 B. C. (*C. I. L.*, i, No. 200 = Bruns, *Fontes*[6], &c., 1893, pp. 74–90), which related in part to Africa, illustrates the varieties of tenure from which the State derived revenue. Besides the public land, conquered by force of arms, which, except allotments granted to Roman colonists and others, yielded tithes and rent for pasture, both farmed by *publicani*, there were estates purchased by private individuals, who paid a nominal rent as an acknowledgement that the State retained a proprietary right. The bulk of the land (*ager stipendiarius*), which did not fall under these categories, had been restored after the annexation of the country to the natives (App., *Pun.*, 135), who paid a rent, but might be required at any time to give up possession. Cf. M. Rostovtceff, *Studien zur Gesch. d. röm. Kolonates*, 1910, pp. 315–8.

[4] Livy, xxxviii, 44, 4; *C. I. L.*, i, No. 204. Cf. Daremberg and Saglio, iii, 1772.

[5] *Verr.*, ii, 70, 169.   [6] *Q. fr.*, i, 1, 33.   [7] Cic., *Fam.*, iii, 8, 5.

of public lands were regularly farmed to them.[1] Finally, a poll-tax was levied in certain provinces,[2] perhaps to meet extraordinary expenditure ; and with the same object various other imposts were occasionally devised.[3] Such were the arrangements made for the administration of the provinces, and, except that the system of farming the taxes, while it yielded an inadequate revenue, had no merit except that of saving trouble, no great fault can be found with them ; but in practice they were vexatious to the last degree. It is true that the provincials derived benefits from the paramount power. Spain and Gaul and Africa, which were only half civilized when they were subdued, and were comparatively free from the extortion of the tax-collectors, after they settled down under their new masters took kindly to Roman rule : in course of time they became proud of their connexion with the world-famed empire, and their later history bears witness to the good which they derived from Roman discipline. Every province was practically freed from urban sedition and internecine war ;[4] and if they were not adequately protected from border raids,[5] and brigandage was not wholly checked,[6] these evils were greatly mitigated.[7] Even Roman taxation was not an unmixed evil : 'the Caunians,' wrote Cicero,[8] 'and all the islands made tributary to the Rhodians by Sulla recently ... petitioned the Senate to let them pay their taxes to us rather than to them.' Moreover, it must not be supposed that order and security were purchased by the loss of political life ; for such did not exist, and, especially under upright governors, municipal activity continued.[9] Nevertheless, when the apologist for Roman rule has urged every reasonable plea, it remains true that it inflicted

[1] Cic., *De lege agr.*, ii, 19, 50.
[2] *Fam.*, iii, 8, 15 ; *Att.*, v, 16, 2 ; Caes., *B. C.*, iii, 32, 2.
[3] *Ib.* ; *Fam.*, iii, 8, 15 ; xv, 4, 2.   [4] *Q. fr.*, i, 1, 25. 34.
[5] Cic., *De prov. cons.*, 2, 4 ; *In Pis.*, 40, 96 ; Dio, xxxix, 56, 1.
[6] *Fam.*, ii, 9, 1 ; x, 31, 1 ; *Att.*, vi, 4, 1 ; Varro, *R. R.*, i, 16, 2 ; *Bell. Alex.*, 42, 2 ; Strabo, iii, 4, 13.
[7] *Q. fr.*, i, 1, 25. 34 ; *B. G.*, v, 1, 5. 9.   [8] *Q. fr.*, i, 1, 33.
[9] See, for instance, *Q. fr.*, i, 1, 25 ; *Att.*, vi, 2, 4. Cf. F. Haverfield, *Some Roman Conceptions of Empire*, 1916, p. 17.

evils which demanded such radical reform as an imperial government, itself strengthened and regenerated, could alone supply.

If we probe the roots of the evil, we shall find that they were the love of money, which originated in the standard of luxury prevalent in Rome, which, in the case of the Governor, was stimulated by the consciousness that his period of office must soon end, and which, owing to the great distances that separated the provinces from Rome and the general lack of interest in provincial affairs, was not restrained by the Senate or by public opinion; the incompetence or inexperience of the average governor, which was not compensated by a permanent body of civil servants (for he took with him his staff, as untrained as he was himself); and the absence in the capital of an impartial judicial body. Provincial governors had no salary; and it has been said that this accounted for their often yielding to the temptation of using their power to enrich themselves.[1] Certainly no administration was ever more corrupt than that of the servants of the East India Company in the days when they were badly paid and before they were in some degree restrained by Clive. But proconsuls and propraetors were granted liberal allowances to cover their expenses, out of which they could without dishonesty save enough to live in comfort for the remainder of their lives; and when they were able to put pressure upon influential senators, the allowance might amount to an enormous sum. Caesar's father-in-law, Lucius Calpurnius Piso, received eighteen million [£180,000] sesterces, which he left to be invested by his agents in Rome;[2] and even Cicero, whose allowance was doubtless normal, and who actually returned a large proportion of it to the treasury,[3] was able, though his administration lasted barely a year, to lay by an amount equal to twenty-two thousand pounds.[4] But there was one influence which even those governors who were personally incorruptible found it difficult to withstand. 'The great difficulty',

[1] W. Cunningham, *An Essay on Western Civilization*, 1898, p. 166.
[2] Cic., *In Pis.*, 35, 86.   [3] *Att.*, vii, 1, 6.   [4] *Fam.*, v, 20, 9.

wrote Cicero to his brother Quintus, who was serving as propraetor in Asia, 'that besets your earnest endeavour to do right comes from the farmers of the taxes. If we oppose them, we shall alienate from ourselves and from the State a class which has served us both well, and which we have brought to associate itself with the common weal : if, on the other hand, we comply with all their demands, we shall be acquiescing in the ruin of those whose wellbeing, aye and whose interests we are bound to consult. This, if we look the facts fairly in the face, is the one difficulty in your whole government.'[1] So impressed was he by this difficulty that he advised his brother to urge the natives, for their own sake, not to insist overmuch upon their rights, but to keep on good terms with the tax-gatherers.[2] To a man like Cicero, who believed that unless the equestrian order were kept in good humour and made to feel that their interests were identical with those of the aristocracy, the State would fall under the dominion of an unscrupulous demagogue, this argument might seem sufficient ; but the average politician had more cogent reasons for dreading to offend this powerful class. The shareholders in the companies to which the taxes were farmed were very numerous.[3] During the ten years, indeed, that followed the dictatorship of Sulla the Senate had control of the courts at Rome ; and perhaps it was because Verres was confident that his brother senators would acquit him if he were prosecuted after his term of office, that, although he occasionally acted in collusion with the tax-collectors,[4] he had the hardihood to defraud them by exporting valuables of which he despoiled the Sicilians without paying duty.[5] But when, just after he was brought to trial, the knights regained the right of sitting on juries, the situation was entirely changed. The laws against extortion, the futility of which had been exemplified by the scandalous con-

---

[1] *Q. fr.*, i, 1, 32.
[2] *Ib.*, § 35. Cicero (*Fam.*, xiii, 9) begged a propraetor of Bithynia to allow a *publicanus* to fix his own price for letting pastures.
[3] Polyb., vi, 17, 3–4.
[4] *Verr.*, iii, 10, 25.   [5] *Ib.*, ii, 2, 74–5, §§ 182–5.

demnation of Rutilius,[1] became not merely useless, but positively injurious to the provincials. ' I fully believed ', said Cicero,[2] 'that foreign nations would send envoys to the Roman People to pray that the law against extortion might be abrogated.' Every provincial governor was aware that if he exerted his authority to prevent the tax-gatherers from exacting more than their due, they would probably suborn some rising politician to accuse him, and their colleagues on the jury would vote for his condemnation. No wonder that governors found it expedient to connive at extortion ; and if they chose to plunder on their own account, their risk, unless their guilt was as glaring as that of Verres or their prosecutor as eloquent as Cicero, was comparatively slight. So long as their office lasted they were beyond control, for they could not be brought to trial until they returned. 'There is such a press of business at Rome', said Cicero in one of his forensic speeches,[3] 'that people hardly give ear to what is happening in the provinces.' If a dishonest governor were prosecuted, the senatorial jurors would be on his side ; the knights, if he had conciliated them, would join in voting for his acquittal ; and if a majority of the jury were inclined to be obdurate, a part of his ill-gotten gains, expended in bribery, would doubtless mollify them. And even if a governor were strong enough to resist temptation, and the province throve under his rule, there was always the fear that his policy would be reversed by his successor. Want of continuity in administration caused the provincials to live in continual uncertainty.

Considering these things, one may wonder, not that many provincial governors were corrupt, but that some were incorruptible. 'In my opinion,' wrote Cicero,[4] thinking particularly of the Greek subjects of Rome, 'the whole aim of government should be the greatest happiness of the governed . . . we are under a special obligation to that people to practise in our dealings with those from whose maxims we have derived our culture what we have

---

[1] See p. 42.
[3] *Pro Planc.*, 26, 63.
[2] *Verr.*, i, 14, 41.
[4] *Q. fr.*, i, 1, 24. 28.

learned from them'; and in various letters [1] he testified that the Chief Pontiff Mucius Scaevola and Rutilius Rufus had left successors who realized his ideal. The law had indeed contrived a plan which was intended to ensure good government. Every governor was obliged before he entered upon office to publish an edict, stating the principles upon which he intended to govern. The document was generally based upon the regulations that had been originally framed for the administration of the province and upon such modifications or additions, made by his predecessors, as he might choose to adopt:[2] but an unscrupulous magistrate would often violate his own edict; and every one who has read the *Verrines* of Cicero is familiar with the various acts of oppression which the provincials suffered. If Verres was the most notorious criminal of his class, it does not follow that he was the worst; and Appius Claudius, who preceded Cicero as Governor of Cilicia, was apparently not much better.[3] The right, guaranteed to free and allied towns, of enjoying their own laws was often disregarded.[4] The unhappy provincials, except when an upright governor prohibited the practice, were constrained to incur the expense of sending deputations to Rome to eulogize the virtues of their oppressors.[5] The Syracusans endeavoured to propitiate Verres by holding a festival in his honour and erecting a statue with an inscription in which he was designated as the saviour of their city.[6] When Cicero took over the government of Cilicia, the natives, who had endured so much from Appius, could hardly believe in their good fortune.[7] A conscientious ruler needed uncommon vigilance and strength of character to restrain his subordinates and the young nobles who were attached to his household in order to learn the business of administration from

---

[1] *Ib.*, §§ 25, 38–40; ii, 9, 3; *Fam.*, i, 9, 26; *Att.*, vi, 1, 13. Cf. *Verr.*, ii, 2, 21, 50.

[2] *Verr.*, ii, 1, 45, 117; 46, 118; ii, 2, 27, 66; iii, 10, 25; v, 3, 7; *Fam.*, iii, 8, 4; *Att.*, v, 21, 11; vi, 1, 15.

[3] *Ib.*, v, 16, 2.　　　　　　　　　　[4] *Verr.*, ii, 2, 22–5.

[5] Cic., *Fam.*, iii, 8, 2–4.

[6] *Verr.*, ii, 2, 63, 154·　　　　　　[7] Cic., *Att.*, v, 18, 2.

committing depredations for their own profit;[1] and readers of Catullus[2] will remember the virulence with which he lampooned the praetor under whom he had failed to make a fortune. One practice, which appears to have been general, though free and federate communities were nominally exempt, and a merciful commander would do his best to mitigate the hardships which it inflicted, was that of quartering soldiers for the winter upon the inhabitants of towns.[3] The people of Cyprus paid two hundred talents to Appius Claudius to relieve them from this burden.[4] 'Do you suppose,' said Cicero to a popular assembly when he was praising Pompey for the restraint which he exercised upon his troops, 'that in recent years more hostile cities have been destroyed by the arms of your soldiers than allied communities by winter quarters?'[5] Another grievance, for which the Senate was responsible, although Cicero succeeded in passing a law for diminishing the suffering which it inflicted, was the institution called a 'free legation': senators who wished to travel or to transact business in the provinces were in the habit of obtaining from the Senate a permit which empowered them, as if they were officials engaged on public affairs, to demand board and lodging from householders through whose towns they passed.[6]

[£48,000.]

63 B. C.

The rapacity of the tax-gatherers, which made them universally detested,[7] is familiar to all who have the most rudimentary knowledge of Roman history or even of the Bible; but Zacchaeus was not the only honest man among them, and those who have studied Anglo-Indian history and can comprehend the paradox that to Orientals the very efficiency of Western government is obnoxious may be inclined to suspect that the hatred was due not so much to the amount of their exactions (which were

---

[1] Cic., *Att.*, vi, 1, 20; *Pro Cael.*, 30, 73; *Fam.*, viii, 4, 6; 9, 3-4; *Q. fr.*, i, 1, 26; *Verr.*, ii, 2, 10, 27-8.   [2] x, 9-13; xxviii, 6-10.
[3] Cic., *De imp. Cn. Pomp.*, 13, 38. Cf. Caes., *B. C.*, ii, 18, 5; iii, 31, 4; Plut., *Luc.*, 33, 4.   [4] Cic., *Att.*, v, 21, 7.   [5] *De imp. Cn. Pomp.*, 13, 38.
[6] Cic., *De lege agr.*, i, 3, 8; ii, 17, 45; *Pro Flac.*, 34, 86; *De leg.*, iii, 8, 18.
[7] Livy, xlv, 18, 4; Cic., *Q. fr.*, i, 1, 33. 35; *Pro Flac.*, 8, 18; Ps. Ascon. *in Verr.*, ii, 2, 3, 7, ed. Stangl, p. 258 (ed. Orelli, p. 205).

probably less than what had been demanded by native rulers) as to the inevitable regularity with which they were enforced.[1] In order to satisfy their demands the provincials were often obliged to borrow from Italian usurers on the spot; for a law passed soon after the first consulship of Caesar, perhaps with the object of conciliating these harpies,[2] forbade provincials to contract loans in Rome, where the highest interest allowable was twelve per cent.[3] Sometimes, indeed, it fell as low as four,[4] and the most cautious speculator could make a handsome profit by borrowing in Rome and lending at an enhanced rate abroad.[5] The people of Apollonia in Macedonia were reduced to such straits by debt that they were driven to bribe the Governor, Piso, with a hundred talents to excuse them from repayment.[6] It is true that provincial communities often enjoyed the patronage of influential Romans who attended to their interests;[7] but such protection was of little avail; and, though rising politicians were ready enough to prosecute offenders, their punishment, even if they were convicted, would bring little benefit to those whom they had oppressed. The only sure protection which a provincial could obtain was Roman citizenship, and individuals like those whom

58 B. C.

[£24,000.]

---

[1] Cf. Rice Holmes, *Hist. of the Indian Mutiny*⁵, 1913, p. 46.
[2] Cic., *Att.*, v, 21, 12. The law is commonly assigned to the year of Gabinius's tribunate—67 B. C.; but George Long (*Decline of the Roman Republic*, iv, 1872, p. 423, n. 6), remarking that in that year the tribune Cornelius proposed a similar measure, which the Senate rejected (Ascon., ed. Clark, p. 57, ll. 8–16 [ed. Stangl, p. 47]), thinks that the *lex Gabinia* was passed by Gabinius as consul. Cf. Th. Mommsen, *Röm. Strafr.*, 1899, p. 885. Long (*Cic. Orat.*, iii, 1856, p. 269) says that this law ' could have no other object than to prevent the precious metals from being carried out of Italy '. But would they not return with interest ? The explanation which I have given is surely probable.
[3] Tac., *Ann.*, vi, 16. Cf. P. Willems, *Droit publ. rom.*, 1884, pp. 58–9. Cicero in his edict announced that he would not recognize a higher rate than 12 per cent., and in 50 B. C. a law to the same effect was passed by the Senate (*Att.*, v, 21, ll. 13), which Cicero failed to enforce.
[4] Cic., *Att.*, iv, 15, 7.
[5] See P. Guiraud, *Études écon.*, &c., 1905, p. 209.
[6] Cic., *In Pis.*, 35, 86. Cf. *De prov. cons.*, 3, 5.
[7] Cic., *Verr.*, iv, 40, 86; 41, 89; *Fam.*, xiii, 64, 1; *De off.*, i, 11, 35; Sall., *Cat.*, 41, 4; App., ii, 4, 14.

Pompey enfranchised,[1] or cities, like Gades, which earned the distinction as a reward for loyal service,[2] were indeed fortunate ; but the prize fell to the lot of few. For historical facts Cicero is often an untrustworthy authority ; but when in an official dispatch addressed to the Senate he alludes to 'the harshness and injustice',[3] of Roman rule, his testimony is unimpeachable. Nor would it be safe, even though one remembers how Burke calumniated Hastings, to attribute overmuch to rhetorical exaggeration of the famous passages in which Cicero described the misery of the subject peoples and their hatred of Rome :—' Every province is in sorrow : every free community has its grievance : every realm protests against our cupidity and our misdeeds : this side of the Ocean there is now no spot so remote or so secluded that in this epoch the lust and the iniquity of our countrymen has not found it out. It is not the power, the arms, the resistance of the nations that the Roman People is unable to withstand, but their mourning, their tears, their lamentations.'[4] 'It is difficult, fellow-citizens, to express how bitterly we are detested by foreign nations for the unbridled passions and the iniquities of those whom in late years we have sent to govern them.'[5]

Enough has been said to fulfil the purpose of this chapter. But to those who have sojourned with inquiring minds in Rome and scanned the sepulchral monuments that line the Appian Way, who have ascended the slopes on which stood Cicero's Tusculan villa, who have roamed through the streets of Pompeii, from which, thanks to the eruption that wrought such ruin, we learn more of ancient life than from any other source, who have explored the battlefields of Caesar, breathed the air which the Romans breathed and ventured upon the seas which their vessels sailed, the tale which I am about to unfold will be invested with a reality which can hardly be felt by those to whom the Mediterranean region is unknown.

[1] Cic., *Pro Balbo*, 8, 19 ; 21, 48 ; 23, 52.
[2] Dio, xli, 24, 1.
[3] *Fam.*, xv, 1, 5.
[4] *Verr.*, iii, 89, 207.
[5] *De imp. Cn. Pomp.*, 22, 65.

CHAPTER III

POMPEY THE GREAT

WHEN a thoughtful man, reading Roman history for the first time, has come to that part which records the abdication and the death of Sulla, he asks himself whether the effort which the great reactionary had made to restore the authority of the Senate offered any prospect of permanent success. Evidently none unless the Senate should comprise men sufficiently able and public-spirited to utilize his gift; in other words, unless, despite the corruption which he had infused into public life, the soul of the nation could recover its pristine tone. Since venerable custom had not sufficed to uphold the authority of the Senate against the Gracchi, it was unlikely that laws would avail when the dreaded legislator was no more; and the violence with which he had achieved his aim would surely be renewed by leaders of the party which he had for the moment crushed. The Senate itself was not of one mind: moderate men like Gaius Aurelius Cotta were disposed to make concessions to popular demands. The knights, who requited Sulla's hatred, were eager to regain the influence of which he had despoiled them. The sons of the proscribed were ready to join any adventurer who could give them back what they had lost. The populace missed the doles of grain which Sulla had cut off. The people who dwelt between the Alps and the Po resented their exclusion from the suffrage which had been granted to the Italians: these newly enfranchised citizens had not forgotten the massacre of Praeneste, the punishment of Etruria, the devastation of Lucania and of Samnium; and since their citizenship was hardly more than nominal, they felt little interest in the political life which seemed to be not only centred in, but confined to, Rome. The veteran soldiers of Sulla,

78 B. C.
No prospect of permanence for the Sullan constitution.

78 B.C.

if they might be trusted to unsheathe their swords in defence of the party to which they owed their farms, were rather an element of unrest than a source of national strength ; for their past had not fitted them for the steady toil that was needed to strengthen the Italian yeomanry. Unless representatives of the ruling families should arise who would work, not for their own profit or the interests of their class, but for Italy and the empire, the disunion of their opponents could alone help the Senate to retain its power. And, even if the Senate were not found wanting, there remained that innovation which Marius had introduced in order to make head against Rome's enemies, and which Sulla had matured :— Roman armies, in proportion as they had become efficient, had ceased to be national. Sulla himself must have foreseen that his measures would provoke opposition. It began even before his death.

Attempted counter-revolution of Lepidus.

The first man who attempted a counter-revolution was Marcus Aemilius Lepidus, one of the consuls of 78 B.C., who had already served as Governor of Sicily and had only escaped impeachment for extortion by ingratiating himself with the popular party.[1] Immediately after entering upon office he began to quarrel with his colleague Catulus, harangued the populace in the Forum, denounced the violence of Sulla, and urged his listeners to follow him and to regain their liberties.[2] When the news of Sulla's death reached the capital Lepidus and his partisans attempted to prevent the public funeral ; but Pompey, who, young as he was, had already won a great reputation in the Civil War, succeeded, partly by influence, partly by threats, in preventing such an outrage.[3] Lepidus, however, could rely upon the aid of all who had suffered from the tyranny of the late dictator ; and he was doubtless encouraged by the victories which Sertorius, the famous Marian leader, had won in

---

[1] Cic., *Verr.*, ii, 2, 3, 8, and Ps. Ascon., ed. Stangl, p. 259 (ed. Orelli, p. 206) ; iii, 91, 212. Cf. Pliny, *Nat. Hist.*, xxxvi, 6 (8), 49.
[2] See p. 363.
[3] Plut., *Pomp.*, 15 ; *Sulla*, 38, 1 ; App., *B.C.*, i, 105, 493-4 ; 107, 501.

Spain over the Sullan officers who were sent to oppose 78 B.C. him. For the moment, indeed, he was too cautious to yield to the impetuous democrats who desired to restore the tribunician power; but the manifesto in which he outlined his programme was calculated to win the support of all who had nothing to lose by revolution. While he proposed a bill by which five pecks of corn were to be granted monthly to every citizen in Rome and distributed largesses from the money which he had wrung from the Sicilians, he announced his intention of rescinding the enactments of Sulla and repatriating all whom he had driven into exile, and promised in the event of victory to restore the estates of all whom he had dispossessed. The Senate was too timid to oppose the bill, although it contravened one of Sulla's laws.[1] No man, indeed, of any standing joined the demagogic consul. The youthful Gaius Caesar, who belonged to the party of Marius, hurried from Asia as soon as he heard of Sulla's death, to take part in the movement for reform; but when he arrived in Italy he perceived that Lepidus was not a leader to follow and, unmoved by his flattering overtures, left him alone.[2] In Etruria, however, the evicted landholders had already armed; the inhabitants of Faesulae attacked the Sullan veterans who had settled in their neighbourhood, killed many of them, and resumed possession of their estates. Marcius Philippus, who had opposed the younger Drusus, in vain urged the Senate to act: the expedient which commended itself to them was to send both consuls, the lawless as well as the loyal being entrusted with an army, to suppress the insurrection. Lepidus of course welcomed the insurgents, who flocked to join him, and even turned against his colleague; whereupon the Senate in desperation required the ill-assorted pair to bind themselves by a solemn oath to refrain from civil war. The reader who wonders why Lepidus obeyed may surmise that he found it best to

---

[1] See p. 62. The authorities for the attempted revolution of Lepidus are examined on pp. 363-9.
[2] Suet., *Div. Iul.*, 3.

keep the peace until his preparations should be complete. At length, believing, as we may suppose, that the Senate would quail before a mere display of force, he marched towards Rome. An envoy was dispatched to meet him. The Senate had mustered courage to demand that he should quit his army, enter the city, and preside in the ordinary course at the consular elections. Lepidus, who was not yet prepared to violate the constitution by entering with his army, and feared perhaps that if he came alone his liberty would be imperilled, refused to obey. Negotiations, however, continued, and Lepidus obtained for the following year the province of Transalpine Gaul. He would then have an army in Northern Italy; his position as the champion of the oppressed would attract more and more recruits to his standard in Etruria; and when Catulus was no longer consul he would be released from his oath and free to enforce his demands. All the discontented flocked to join him, and before the year ended he was master of a formidable host. Since the elections had not been held, when the new year came there were no consuls. As it was known that Lepidus intended to insist upon the restoration of the tribunician power and to demand for himself a second consulship, the Senate again ventured to order him to return; but they still hesitated to compel submission. Philippus was indignant. They did not realize, he told them, that by their pitiful slackness they were actually encouraging rebellion. They might easily have crushed Lepidus when he was a mere adventurer; but now he had the prestige and the power of a proconsul. There were troubles enough abroad besides rebellion at home: Spain was overrun by the armies of Sertorius; Mithradates was only waiting for an opportunity to renew the war. Were they going to wait until Lepidus again marched on Rome? His high-sounding professions were a sham: while he clamoured for the restoration of confiscated property to the proscribed, he took care to retain what he had himself acquired. The more anxious the senators showed themselves for peace, the more clearly would he see that they dreaded him. Philippus concluded by 77 B.C. moving formally that since Lepidus was leading the host which he had illegally raised against the capital, the interrex,[1] the ex-consul Catulus, and other notables should be authorized to take all necessary steps to secure the public safety. The motion passed, and Lepidus was declared a public enemy. Catulus, who, as a proconsul, had command of an army, and who could also count upon the aid of Sulla's veterans, was to remain and protect the city: Pompey, who, in default of other competent leaders, received an extraordinary command, was dispatched northward to deal with a force which Marcus Brutus, the lieutenant of Lepidus, had assembled in Cisalpine Gaul. Catulus detached a force to hold the Mulvian Bridge; and when Lepidus, confident that he could dictate terms, appeared on the outskirts of the city, he found the army of his former colleague drawn up on the Janiculan heights, barring his way. Catulus was no general, but he was more than a match for Lepidus, who was beaten off with heavy loss and forced to retreat into Etruria. Brutus was unable to support him. Blockaded in Mutina by Pompey, he soon surrendered and, though he was at first permitted to go free, was afterwards put to death; while the garrison of Alba Pompeia on the river Tanarus was starved into submission. Returning southward, Pompey overthrew the demoralized army of Lepidus near the port of Cosa in Etruria, but failed to follow up his victory; for the proconsul, contriving somehow to procure shipping and embark his troops, sailed for Sardinia. He hoped to make himself master of the island and to prevent the corn which it produced from reaching Rome; but the Governor, Valerius Triarius, had made preparations for

[1] See p. 58. Here and elsewhere in this chapter I have used speeches which Sallust in the extant fragments of his *History* ascribes to prominent actors. Everybody knows that these speeches were composed by Sallust; but those which he incorporated in his *Catiline* can be checked and will in essentials stand the test, and *I* believe that the speeches in the *History* were for the most part likewise founded upon fact. Cf. *Atene e Roma*, xiv, 1911, col. 149.

defence, and before the end of summer Lepidus, repulsed by the garrisons of the towns which he attempted to reduce, fell ill and died.

The Senate had been able—not without the dangerous aid of Pompey—to hold its own in Italy; but beyond sea the opposition had a formidable champion. Five years before, Quintus Sertorius, who, Marian though he was, vigorously protested against the inhumanity of Marius,[2] had been sent as propraetor to secure the province of Nearer Spain.[3] In his youth he had fought against the Cimbri and the Teutoni in the disastrous battle on the Rhône; he had served as a military tribune in Northern Spain; in the Social War he had lost an eye.[4] A Sullan governor was already in possession of Nearer Spain; but Sertorius was strong enough to oust him.[5] As, however, he could of course expect no support from Italy, he was forced to depend upon the resources of the province alone.

The inhabitants of the peninsula, notwithstanding the intestine quarrels which are universal in the tribal stage, had attained a considerable degree of material civilization even before their country was incorporated in the Roman empire. The western and north-western tribes, indeed, were comparatively backward; but those who dwelt near the Mediterranean had begun to assimilate the culture of their conquerors. Gold, silver, tin, copper, and iron were won from the mines in the south-east and in Galicia; and Polybius speaks of an Iberian king upon whose table were set wine-flagons of gold. The Celtiberians were rich enough to pay six hundred talents (equivalent to nearly a hundred and fifty thousand pounds sterling) to a Roman general. Corn, wine, oil, and esparto grass were exported to Italy. Fishing smacks ventured into the Atlantic Ocean. Even the remote Lusitanians traded with Sicily; merchantmen sailed up

---

[1] The chronology of the Sertorian War is discussed on pp. 369-75.
[2] Plut., *Sert.*, 5, 4.
[3] *Ib.*, 6, 1; App., i, 108, 505. See W. Stahl, *De bello Sert.*, 1907, p. 37.
[4] Sall., i, 88; Plut., *Sert.*, 3, 1-3; 4, 1-2.
[5] App., i, 86, 392; 108, 506.

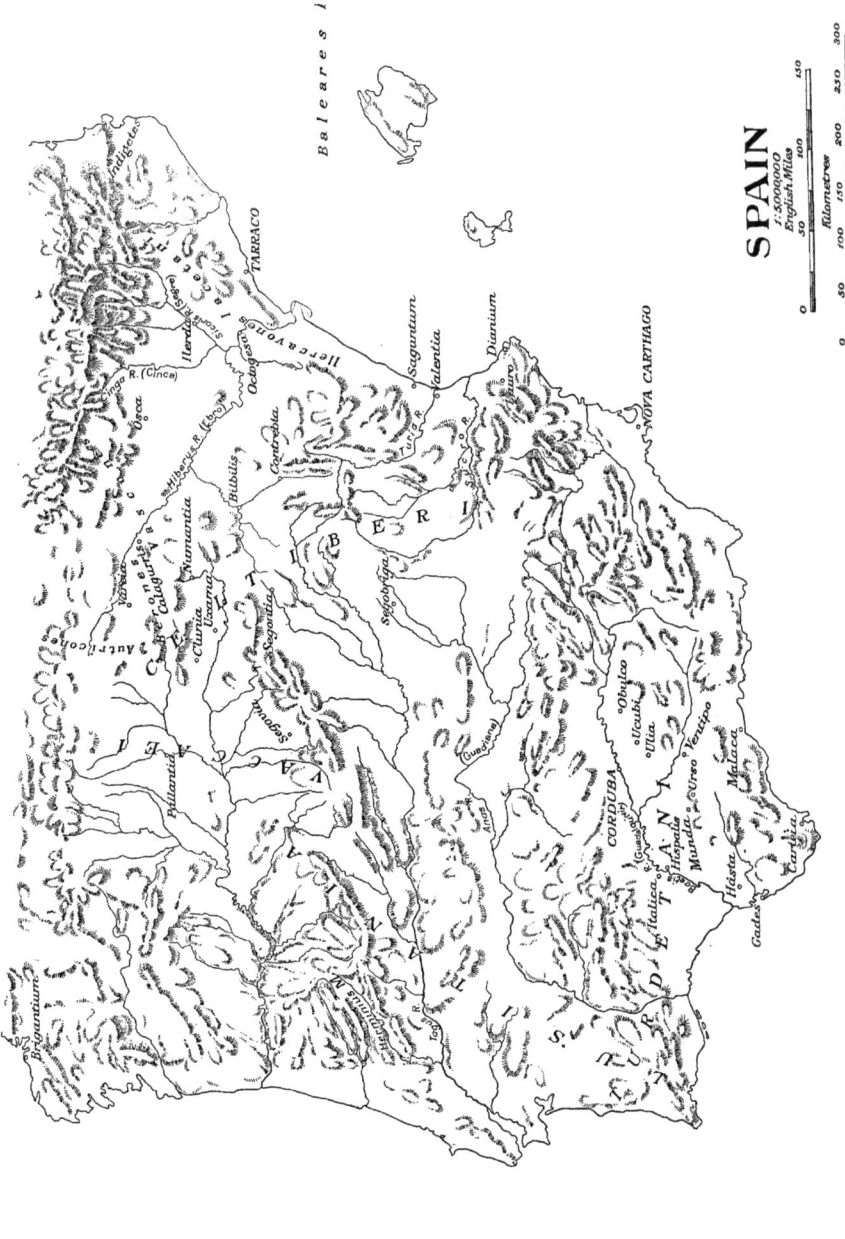

the Guadalquivir as far as Hispalis ; the ships of the [Seville.]
Turdetani, the most prosperous of the Spaniards, carried
their wares across the Western Mediterranean to Ostia
and through the Straits of Gibraltar. This tribe had not
only learned to speak Latin, but had a literature of
its own and a legal code expressed in metrical form.
Roman soldiers had settled after their discharge in
important towns : prominent natives had received the
gift of Roman citizenship ; in effect Southern Spain was
already Romanized.[1]

Finding that the natives had been alienated by the
tyranny and the rapacity of Roman proconsuls, Sertorius set himself to conciliate their goodwill. He 82-80 B.C.
achieved this by reducing taxation and by quartering
his troops in the outskirts of towns, where he could
better keep them under control, instead of billeting them
upon the townsmen. Meanwhile, as it was certain that
Sulla would eventually attempt to regain the province,
Sertorius armed the Roman residents who belonged to
his party and made other preparations for war.[2] About
the end of the year Sulla found time to attend to foreign
affairs, and a proconsul, Annius Luscus, was dispatched
with an army to Spain. He found the pass of the
Pyrenees blocked by a lieutenant of Sertorius : but this
officer was murdered by a traitor ; his troops, evidently
undisciplined levies, dispersed ; and Sertorius, whose
own force was still comparatively weak, was obliged to
flee the country and sailed with three thousand men
from New Carthage to Mauretania. After various [Cartaadventures by sea and land he joined a faction which had gena.]
dethroned a Moorish prince named Ascalis, besieged him
in Tingis (now Tangier), and repulsed an officer, Paccianus,
whom Sulla had sent to raise the siege. The troops of
Paccianus willingly enlisted under their conqueror,
whose fame had by this time spread throughout the

[1] Polyb., xxxiv, 8 ; 9, 3 ; Caes., *B. G.*, v, 1, 4 ; Diod. Sic., v, 34, 7 ;
35, 1–2 ; 38, 1 ; Strabo, iii, 1, 2. 6 ; 2, 3–6. 8–10 ; 4, 5. 13. 16 ; Archäol.
Anzeiger (*Jahrb. d. Kaiserl. deutschen archäol. Instituts*, xxvii, 1912), col.
431–2 ; *Comptes rendus . . . de l'Acad. des Inscr.*, &c., 1914, pp. 127–31.
Cf. M. Dubois, *Examen de la géogr. de Strabon*, 1891, p. 299, and *Paulys
Real-Ency.*, viii, 2039. [2] Plut., *Sert.*, 6, 2–4 ; Exup., 8.

West; and the Lusitanians, seeing an opportunity of throwing off the Roman yoke, invited him to be their leader. He promptly sailed, beat off a Sullan fleet which was cruising in the Straits to intercept him, and landed, probably near Cadiz. The force which he had brought with him numbered only two thousand six hundred including seven hundred Africans; but he speedily raised four thousand Lusitanian infantry and seven hundred horse, while recruits from the adjacent parts of Spain flocked to join him.[1] He had already won a battle on the Guadalquivir over Fufidius, the Governor of Further Spain, who had been sent from Rome to oppose him, when Quintus Caecilius Metellus, a son of the opponent of Jugurtha and the best general whom Sulla could select, took over the government of the province. During the next three years Sertorius and his lieutenants gained an unbroken series of victories.[2] Metellus, who established his head-quarters near the site of Cáceres, between the Tagus and the Guadiana,[3] captured a few forts and villages, but, failing to provoke Sertorius, who adopted guerrilla tactics, to fight a general action, he summoned Domitius Calvinus, the ruler of the Nearer Province, to assist him. The junction of the two armies was prevented by Hirtuleius, who overthrew Domitius on the Guadiana; Manlius, the Governor of Transalpine Gaul, who crossed the Pyrenees to aid his colleague, was driven back, after suffering a disastrous defeat, by the same officer; and when Metellus attempted to reduce Langobriga, a Lusitanian fortress the inhabitants of which supported the insurgents, he was compelled by Sertorius to retreat. While he remained inactive in the neighbourhood of Corduba, Sertorius advanced eastward, besieged Contrebia, only a few marches distant from the mouth of the Ebro, and, having captured it, went into winter-quarters not far east of the modern Cascante and

---

[1] Sall., *Hist.*, i, 107; Plut., *Sert.*, 7–10; 12, 2; Flor., ii, 10, 2.
[2] The evidence for the events of the Sertorian War is examined on pp. 379–84.
[3] A. Schulten (*Jahrb. d. Kaiserl. deutschen archäol. Inst.*, xxxiii, 1918, pp. 75–6, 79–81, 104).

near the lower course of the river. By this time he was 77 B.C. master of the greater part of the peninsula, and in the following year he would subdue the Celtiberian tribes that still adhered to the Senatorial Government. The first period of the war was over ; for it was evident that unless Metellus were strongly reinforced, Sertorius would soon be able, like another Hannibal, to advance from Spain to the conquest of Italy. But while the fragmentary records of his life tell us enough to whet our curiosity, tactical details, evidence for comprehending strategical movements, are rarely forthcoming. Only of the general methods which Sertorius adopted can we form a clear conception. While he permitted his native troops to pursue the guerrilla tactics to which they were accustomed, he developed their efficiency to the highest pitch by Roman discipline ; and the higher officers whom he appointed were all citizens of Rome.[1] Confronted by Metellus, his most formidable antagonist, whose forces were superior to his own, he steadily refused to fight a pitched battle, but persistently harassed his foragers and attacked his watering parties.[2] Utilizing a Spanish institution which Caesar afterwards described as prevalent among the Aquitanians, he attracted thousands of devoted followers with whom it was a point of honour and a sacred duty not to survive their lord.[3] He flattered the self-esteem of his soldiers by encouraging them to wear embroidered garments and to adorn their weapons with gold and silver.[4] He founded a school at Osca, [Huesca.] between the Ebro and the Pyrenees, where boys of noble birth might obtain, free of cost, the best education that Roman and Greek teachers could provide, and afterwards aspire to Roman citizenship ; and thus, without allowing his ulterior purpose to be discerned, he secured a sufficient number of hostages.[5] His manner was conciliatory and

---

[1] Plut., *Sert.*, 14, 1 ; 22, 4.   [2] *Ib.*, 12, 4 ; 13, 3.
[3] *Ib.*, 14, 4. Cf. Caes., *B. G.*, iii, 22.
[4] Plut., *Sert.*, 14, 1. 'The better you dress a soldier,' wrote Lord Wolseley (*The Soldier's Pocket-Book*[5], 1886, p. 4), 'the more highly he will be thought of by women, and consequently by himself.'
[5] Plut., *Sert.*, 14, 2-3.

winning; yet whenever he deemed it necessary to inspire fear he was absolutely ruthless. At a later time he executed a cohort of his Roman soldiers because they had made themselves odious by violating Spanish women; and he stabbed with his own hand a native who brought news of the defeat of one of his lieutenants lest he might spread the report and dishearten the army.[1] He knew, moreover, how to play upon the superstition of a half-barbarous people. A peasant gave him a white fawn, which grew so tame that it would follow him like a dog and come when he called. Sertorius declared that the fawn had been sent to him by Diana to reveal the movements of the enemy. Whenever he learned that any of his officers had been successful he exhibited his pet decked with chaplets, as if in celebration of a victory, and told his men to expect good news, which was presently announced.[2]

77 B.C.

Not long after the capture of Contrebia Sertorius received an unexpected reinforcement. Marcus Perperna, an ex-praetor of noble ancestry, collected the remnants of the army of Lepidus and, accompanied by many Marian refugees, sailed from Sardinia to Spain. Proud of his lineage and possessed by an overweening sense of his own importance, he intended to make war against Metellus on his own account; but he was ultimately compelled by the clamour of his men to place himself under the command of Sertorius. When the Senate learned that he had left Sardinia they became thoroughly alarmed. Metellus, who had failed to subdue Sertorius alone, would certainly be overcome by the combined forces of Sertorius and Perperna. The Ligurian and the Gallic tribes between Italy and the Pyrenees, excited by the victories of Sertorius and instigated by his emissaries, were ripe for insurrection.[3] The Vocontii took up arms

---

[1] Frontin., *Strat.*, ii, 7, 5; App., i, 109, 511.
[2] Val. Max., i, 2, 4; Pliny, viii, 32 (50), 117; Plut., *Sert.*, 11, 2–4; 20; Frontin., *Strat.*, i, 11, 13; Gell., xv, 22, 1–9; App., i, 110, 514; Polyaen., viii, 22.
[3] See Cic., *De imp. Cn. Pompei*, 11, 30; Sall., ii, 98, 4.

and the Volcae actually attacked the Roman colony of Narbo.[1] The consuls of the year had no military experience and prudently declined to take the field. Pompey, the one man in Italy who might be a match for Sertorius, had never held a public magistracy, and, moreover, had just shown that he was not disposed to submit to senatorial control. Returning to the outskirts of Rome from the field where he had defeated Lepidus, he was required to disband his army ; but, knowing that he was indispensable, he made excuses for evading compliance with an order[2] which the Government was powerless to enforce. The Sullan constitution was still in being ; and whereas a vote of the Roman People would formerly have been required for the appointment of a private citizen as general, the Senate was now supreme. But the Senate was itself forced to ignore the Sullan regulations for the assignment of provinces. On the motion of Philippus the House reluctantly consented to send Pompey with the rank of proconsul for an indefinite period to the province of Nearer Spain. A senator asked Philippus whether he thought it right to send so young a man, who held no public office, as proconsul. 'No,' replied Philippus, 'not as proconsul, but instead of the two consuls.'[3]

77 B.C.

The rise of Pompey.

Pompey proceeded forthwith to make his preparations, and in forty days he was ready to set out.[4] Before we follow him, let us see by what steps he had achieved a position so commanding and how he appeared to the great man who gave him his first start in life.

Pompey, says Plutarch, had a very winning and comely aspect, which spoke for him before he opened his lips, and his mistress, Flora, whose portrait adorned the temple of Castor and Pollux in the capital, was so

[1] Cic., *Pro Font.*, 6, 14 ; 9, 20 ; 20, 46. [2] See p. 378.
[3] *Non pro consule, sed pro consulibus.*—Cic., *De imp. Cn. Pomp.*, 21, 62 ; *Phil.*, xi, 8, 18 ; Plut., *Pomp.*, 17, 2 ; Oros., v, 23, 8. Perhaps Philippus reminded the Senate that the great Scipio had been appointed at the age of 24 in the Second Punic War to command in Spain before he held a magistracy. The extraordinary command which Pompey had himself held in Africa was another precedent. [4] Sall., ii, 98, 4.

enamoured of him that when he parted from her she suffered poignant grief. Even before his face lost the bloom of youth he had an air which compelled respect ;[1] and Cicero, who saw all the infirmities of his character, told Quintus that there was that in his countenance which awed a hostile crowd.[2] He had first gained distinction by seizing one of those opportunities which frequently occur in revolutionary times, but which only an able man can grasp. After he defeated the Marians, as a youth of twenty-two, with the troops which he had enlisted in Picenum, Sulla was so impressed by his energy, perhaps still more by his good fortune, that, when they first met, he dismounted and saluted him as Imperator.[3] Such an honour had never before fallen to the lot of one so young ; and the man who bestowed it was a judge of character. More compliant, however, than the youthful Caesar, Pompey consented to divorce his wife and marry a stepdaughter of Sulla.[4] Two years later, having expelled the Marians from Sicily, he was sent to deal with Sulla's enemies in Africa. He won a decisive battle, after which his troops hailed him by the title which Sulla had already conferred, and in forty days he reduced the whole province as well as the kingdom of Numidia to submission.[5] When he was about to embark for Sicily he received a dispatch from Sulla, ordering him to disband his army, except one legion, and to await the arrival of his successor. Sulla, it would seem, was anxious lest the popular hero, returning with his six legions, might prove a rival. Pompey's soldiers, who resented the order, became mutinous, and, whether it was withdrawn or not,[6] Pompey with his entire force

---

[1] Plut., *Pomp.*, 2, 1. 3–4.   [2] *Q. fr.*, ii, 3, 2.
[3] Plut., *Pomp.*, 8, 3 ; Val. Max., v, 2, 9   Cf. Sall., *Hist.*, v. 20.
[4] Plut., *Pomp.*, 9. 2.
[5] *Ib.*, 10–2 ; *Bell. Afr.*, 22, 2 ; Livy, *Epit.*, 89 ; Pliny, vii, 26 (27), 96; App., i, 95, 440 ; Eutrop., v, 9 ; Oros., v, 21, 11. 13–4.
[6] Plut., *Pomp.*, 13, 1-2. Cf. Sall., ii, 21 and Maurenbrecher's comment. Long (*Decline of the Roman Republic*, ii, 1866, p. 374), who thinks it ' strange that Sulla should have ordered the soldiers to be disbanded in Africa ', where ' they would be like so many hungry lions let loose on the people of the province ', suggests that ' Plutarch has misreported or misconceived

returned. When he was approaching Rome, Sulla, who 80 B.C. was too wise to flout popular sentiment, himself went out to meet him, and addressed him—perhaps with a touch of sarcasm—by the name by which he has ever since been known, Gnaeus Pompeius Magnus—Pompey the Great.[1] The young general, whose admirers assured him that he was destined to rival Alexander,[2] actually demanded the honour of a triumph. Sulla reminded him that such a distinction was never granted except to dictators, consuls, or praetors, who had defeated a foreign enemy, whereas he was a mere knight and, moreover, far too young to be qualified even for admission to the Senate. Even if he were himself disposed to make a concession, he could not afford to incur odium by defying precedent. Pompey, unabashed, retorted, 'More men worship the rising than the setting sun.' At first Sulla did not catch his words, but when a bystander repeated them, he said, 'Well, let him have his way.'[3] Evidently he saw that Pompey was a power; and against his judgement there is no appeal.

In the early autumn of 77 B.C. Pompey crossed the Alps by the pass of Mont Genèvre,[4] and, making his way through Southern Gaul, reduced one rebellious tribe after another to submission,[5] assigned the territory of the Ligurian Sallyes to their neighbours, the Massilians, as loyal friends of Rome,[6] and encamped for the winter beneath the northern slopes of the Pyrenees. The loyal Celtiberian tribes, which Sertorius was threatening, sent envoys to solicit his support; and when in the early 76 B.C. spring he emerged from the eastern pass and entered Spain, he received the submission of two maritime tribes, the Iacetani and the Indigetes. Sertorius, who

Sulla's orders'. *I* doubt whether Sulla troubled himself about the people of the province.
[1] According to Pliny (vii, 26 [27], 96, with which cf. Plut., *Pomp.*, 13, 3–4), Pompey was first called Magnus by his army in Africa.
[2] Sall., iii, 88.
[3] Plut., *Pomp.*, 14, 1–2. See pp. 375–6.   [4] See pp. 376–8.
[5] Cic., *De imp. Cn. Pomp.*, 11, 30 ; Sall., ii, 98, 5–6.
[6] Caes., *B. C.*, i, 35, 4.
2592.1

76 B.C.
Pompey and Metellus oppose Sertorius.

had spent the winter in preparing for the next campaign, manufacturing weapons and equipment and attending to every minute detail, was ready to encounter him. His chief object was to prevent Metellus from joining Pompey. When the weather became favourable he sent Perperna into the country of the Ilercavones, south of the lower Ebro, to join one of his lieutenants, Herennius, who was already there, and to protect the towns which were on his side, while Hirtuleius was to succour the friendly tribes of the Further Province against Metellus; but, as their forces were comparatively weak, he counselled them to avoid pitched battles and to content themselves with harassing their opponents and trying to cut off their supplies. Meanwhile he moved westward along the southern bank of the Ebro, against the tribes which had made overtures to Pompey, and, it would seem, captured one of their towns. Afterwards, but before the season was far advanced, he turned southward, marched past Saguntum and Valentia, and, crossing the river Sucro, or Jucar, laid siege to the fortress of Lauro, which may probably be identified with the modern Laury. Hard by on the Dianian promontory, where now stands the town called Denia, he had a dépôt, stored with the supplies which he received by sea from pirates.[1] Pompey, although his force, thirty thousand foot and a thousand cavalry, was weaker than that of his enemy,[2] was bound to make an effort to relieve the loyal garrison of Lauro. Perperna and Herennius, who had failed to prevent his passage of the Ebro, could not arrest his march; and on the river Palancia, which debouches near Saguntum, he concentrated his legions for the final advance. On his arrival he attempted to seize a hill which commanded the town, but Sertorius was too quick for him. Within the next few days Pompey sent a detachment to forage in a distant place, which Sertorius, in order to lure him into a sense of security, had forbidden his own foragers to approach. The only other

---

[1] Strabo, iii, 4, 6. Cf. Cic., *Verr.*, v, 56, 146.
[2] Oros, v, 23, 9.

spot where provender could be obtained was occupied 76 B.C.
by Spanish troops. Pompey's lieutenant, who neglected
scouting, fell into an ambuscade: the foragers were
routed; a legion which Pompey sent to the rescue was
caught between the infantry of the pursuers and their
cavalry, who had simulated flight; and when Pompey
himself was preparing to save it from annihilation, he
was deterred by the host of Sertorius, posted upon the
hill, and remained a passive spectator of the massacre.[1]
Even after he failed to seize the hill, he had told his
staff that Sertorius would find himself hemmed in between
the town and the relieving army: but Sertorius had six
thousand men on the plain besides the division that
occupied the hill; and Pompey saw that if he attempted
to attack them, he would himself be attacked in the
rear. 'I'll teach that pupil of Sulla', said Sertorius,
'that a general should look behind rather than before.'
Pompey had suffered, for the first time, a severe reverse.
He had been out-manœuvred and outwitted; he had
lost a large proportion of his army; and he could get
no fodder for his cattle. There was no course open to
him but to retreat. The garrison of Lauro surrendered
to Sertorius; and Pompey, who saw the flames leaping
from the town, returned to winter in the region of the
Pyrenees. Probably he could not count upon being able
to feed his troops except from the province of Gaul, for
the pirates of the Mediterranean were ready to intercept
corn-ships coming from Sardinia or Africa. Early in the
year he had detached a force to occupy New Carthage,
which might serve as a base of supply; but the town was
instantly blockaded, either by one of the lieutenants of
Sertorius or by a pirate fleet.

But the calculations of Sertorius were upset by the
disobedience of Hirtuleius, who, soon after the fall of
Lauro, attacked Metellus at Italica, near Seville, and
suffered a defeat. It was perhaps for this reason that
Sertorius, instead of remaining in the east, returned to
Lusitania; while Metellus moved northward to winter,

[1] Sall., ii, 29–30; Frontin., *Strat.*, ii, 5, 31. Cf. Stahl, *op. cit.*, p. 68.

76-75 B.C. like his colleague, near the Pyrenees. It would seem that even the resources of Roman Gaul were inadequate; for both complained that they could not procure sufficient food.¹

75 B.C. In the early spring Pompey recrossed the Ebro and advanced into the fertile plain which is known as the Garden of Valencia. There he would find supplies in great abundance, and perhaps he knew that he would be able to attack the hostile forces in detail; for Sertorius, who had sent on Perperna and Herennius from Lusitania, remained himself for some unexplained reason in their rear. Pompey encountered and defeated them on the southern bank of the Turia, or Guadalaviar, near Valentia; captured and destroyed the town; and moved on towards the Jucar, which enters the Mediterranean some five-and-twenty miles further south. Meanwhile Metellus had returned to his own province, for Hirtuleius was not yet crushed. Near Segovia he encountered his old enemy, who, untaught by experience, once more risked a battle. Metellus, observing that his best troops were posted in the centre, refused his own until, having overpowered the wings, he was able to close in. The victory was complete, and Hirtuleius himself was slain. This was the decisive battle of the war. Metellus was now free to join his colleague. The Pompeian garrison of New Carthage had successfully withstood the force which attempted to blockade it. Sertorius, who had not yet heard of the defeat of Hirtuleius, was moving swiftly to attack Pompey before Metellus could arrive, and Pompey was not less eager to win the sole credit of victory. The two generals met on the banks of the Jucar, and an indecisive battle followed, in which both armies suffered heavy loss. Next morning Sertorius was about to attack again when he learned that Metellus was approaching. 'If that old woman had not come up,' he said, 'I would have given the youngster a sound thrashing and sent him back to Rome.'²

¹ Sall., ii, 47, 6. Cicero (*Pro Font.*, 6, 14) speaks of the aid, in cavalry, money, and grain, which Pompey received from the Roman province of Gaul.
² Plut., *Sert.*, 19, 7. Anecdotes like this are intrinsically credible enough, but must obviously be taken for what they may be worth.

Weakened by the defeats of his officers and now heavily outnumbered, Sertorius was still formidable. Hoping to drive the joint commanders out of the rich country round Valentia, he contrived to cut off their convoys, and compelled them to take refuge near the stronghold of Saguntum. When they attempted to forage he again attacked them; but again the issue was uncertain. Sertorius now resolved to tire out his enemy by luring him far away from his base. Bidding his guerrillas disperse so that they might be safe from pursuit, he named as the rallying-point Clunia, a town on the upper Douro, two hundred miles and more to the north-west. Pompey and Metellus tramped doggedly after over the high table-land and endeavoured to blockade Clunia: but the Sertorians made frequent sallies, harassing the Roman foragers; pirates threatened their fleet and prevented them from getting adequate supplies; and as winter was approaching, Pompey was obliged to retire westward and encamp near the country of the Vaccaei, while Metellus retreated into Gaul. But Pompey still found it hard to get supplies, and, leaving one of his lieutenants to protect the friendly tribes of Celtiberia, he pushed on for the country of the Vascones, near the western Pyrenees. While he was encamped there some of his convoys were intercepted by brigands, and he was forced to borrow money in order to feed his men. Remarking that he was tired of sending dispatches which were disregarded, he wrote insistently to the Senate to complain that he had not been sufficiently provided either with money or with grain; that he had exhausted his own resources and his credit; and that unless the Government would assist him he would not be able to prevent his army from abandoning the struggle, or Sertorius from invading Italy.[1]

75 B.C.

[Now Leon.]

The Senate had troubles enough at home. The democrats were scheming for the overthrow of the Sullan constitution. In the previous year one of the tribunes, Lucius Sicinius, had delivered a series of inflammatory

Democratic agitation against the Sullan constitution.

[1] See p. 378.

harangues, in which he demanded the restoration of the tribunician power ;[1] and before Pompey's letter arrived the price of corn had risen so high in consequence of piracy that the populace, whose monthly doles had been withdrawn after the fall of Lepidus,[2] attacked the consuls, Lucius Octavius and Aurelius Cotta, in the Sacred Way and drove them to take refuge in Octavius's house.[3] Cotta, however, was not deterred from facing the people in the Forum. He made a conciliatory speech, emphasizing the difficulties with which the Government had to contend and appealing to his hearers to make allowances. Pompey and Metellus, he explained, were demanding reinforcements, money, and grain ; the attitude of Mithradates was so threatening that it was necessary to keep troops in Asia ; the revenues received from the provinces were diminished by war and insufficient to balance expenditure, and it was therefore impossible to maintain a fleet strong enough to protect the store-ships against the pirates. Really and truly the consuls were not to blame : they were doing their very utmost to fulfil the duties of a thankless office. He would entreat the people to support them and to endure hard times with patience.[4] But Cotta did not content himself with mere words. Another tribune, Quintus Opimius, was persistently fomenting popular discontent ; and Cotta, seeing that something must be done, succeeded, despite bitter opposition from the more reactionary senators, in carrying a law which permitted those who had served as tribunes to stand for higher magistracies. Thus the most important of Sulla's laws was partially abrogated.[5]

Early in the new year the dispatches from Spain were received, and Lucius Lucullus, one of the consuls, who was anxious to obtain the command against Mithradates

---

[1] Sall., iii, 48, 8 ; Cic., *Brut.*, 60, 217 ; Ps. Ascon. *in Div.*, § 8, ed. Stangl, p. 189 (ed. Orelli, p. 103).
[2] See p. 364. [3] Sall., ii, 45.
[4] *Ib.*, 47, 6–14.
[5] *Ib.*, 49 ; iii, 48, 8 ; Ascon., ed. Clark, p. 66, l. 20–p. 67, l. 4 (ed. Stangl, p. 53) p. 78, ll. 20–2 (ed. Stangl, p. 61) ; Ps. Ascon. *in Verr.*, ii, 1, 155, ed. Stangl, p. 255 (ed. Orelli, p. 200).

in the impending war, and feared that if Pompey carried 74 B. C.
out his threat he might be supplanted, exerted all his
influence to induce his fellow senators to comply with
Pompey's demands. His efforts were successful, and two
legions as well as funds were dispatched to Spain.[1]

Mithradates, who saw that his own prospects depended Treaty of
largely upon the prolongation of the Spanish war, had Sertorius
already sent ambassadors to negotiate a treaty with Mithradates.
Sertorius. He offered to supply him with money and 75 or
ships to cope with Pompey's fleet, and requested him to 74 B. C.
recognize in return his title, which Sulla had forced him
to renounce, to the province of Asia. Sertorius had
formed a council, which he called a senate, composed of
Marian refugees who had been members of the Senate of
Rome.[2] Loyal, so far as necessity would allow, to Rome
although he was in rebellion against the Roman Government, he refused the concession for which Mithradates
asked, but agreed to his annexing other lands which did
not belong to Rome. After some discussion a treaty
was arranged. Mithradates was authorized to take
possession of Bithynia, although the late king was said
to have bequeathed it to the Roman People, as well as
of Paphlagonia, Cappadocia, and Galatia, and Sertorius
was to send a general to assist him : in return, Mithradates was to supply Sertorius with forty ships and
three thousand talents (equivalent to about seven
hundred and thirty thousand pounds).[3] But it would
seem that the treaty was still-born ; and, perhaps in
consequence of the rumours which it occasioned, Metellus
offered a reward to any one who should put Sertorius
to death.[4]

The superior numbers of Pompey and Metellus were 74 B. C.
beginning to tell, and it was evident that the war could Failure
only end in one way. Osca and Ilerda, near the lower death of
Ebro, and Tarraco (now Tarragona) still held out ; but Sertorius.
the whole of Southern Spain, except the Dianian promontory, was lost to Sertorius. For some time he had not

[1] Plut., *Pomp.*, 20, 1 ; App., i, 111, 519.
[2] Plut., *Sert.*, 22, 4.   [3] See pp. 378-9.   [4] Plut., *Sert.*, 22, 1.

152 POMPEY THE GREAT CHAP.

74 B.C. been able to pay his troops.¹ Metellus captured several Celtiberian towns, the male inhabitants of which he ruthlessly deported, and although Sertorius forced Pompey to raise the siege of Pallantia and severely punished the combined armies when they attempted to blockade Calagurris on the Ebro, even compelling Pompey to retreat to Gaul, the Marian refugees were deserting him;² he incurred hostility by substituting a Celtiberian for a Roman bodyguard; his officers provoked revolts by heavy exactions which they made in his name; and he made himself odious by executing his hostages
74–73 B.C. to terrorize the malcontents. During the winter, indeed, Pompey was again straitened for supplies; but, though
73 B.C. in Galicia Perperna achieved some success, the initiative now belonged to him. One town after another in Celtiberia was taken, and Sertorius, who had become war-weary and addicted to wine and women, was invariably worsted. Perperna took advantage of his growing unpopularity to exacerbate the Roman refugees, and at last formed a plot against his life. In 72 the great commander, who for ten years had withstood all his enemies and had never been defeated in a general action, was treacherously murdered.

Why did Sertorius fail? The records of his life are so imperfect that to answer this question is not easy; and students of the art of war, who rightly demand that a military historian should make it clear why this movement failed and that succeeded, may perhaps complain that the labour which has been spent upon endeavouring to elucidate them is labour lost. Thanks to Plutarch, we see clearly that Sertorius was one of the few creative geniuses whom Ancient Italy produced; and our interest is not less keen because, like Hannibal and Vercingetorix, he was of the heroes who have failed. But the greatest general must yield in the long run when he is confronted

---

¹ Sall., ii, 47, 6.
² Maurenbrecher (*C. Sall. Crispi hist. rel.*, i, 1891, p. 34, n. 1) attributes the odium which Sertorius incurred with the Marian refugees and his Roman troops to his having made a treaty with Mithradates.

by armies better and more numerous than his own, if they are supported by adequate resources and led with tolerable skill. Sertorius was greater than Pompey; but his officers were incompetent or disaffected. Pompey had rare talents for war; he gained experience year by year; his colleague gave him a support which has not been sufficiently acknowledged; and both were backed, however tardily, by the available power of Rome.

Pompey's task was thenceforward easy. Perperna, who was soon overpowered, offered to produce letters written by prominent consulars to Sertorius if his life should be spared; but he was put to death, and Pompey, for reasons which statesmen will understand, ordered the documents to be burnt unread.[1] The few towns which still held out were speedily reduced, though Calagurris is said to have resisted until the garrison had killed and eaten their wives and children;[2] and the story may quicken our imagination of what Sertorians and Pompeians alike suffered in this bitter war. Gades, which had been a great commercial city since the days of the Phoenicians, had throughout remained steadfastly loyal, and Pompey bestowed Roman citizenship, which was subsequently recognized by the Senate, upon its leading citizens,[3] one of whom, Cornelius Balbus, became famous as a friend and confidential agent of Julius Caesar. Having settled the affairs of the peninsula, Pompey returned homewards, and on the highest point of the Col de Pertus, where he crossed the Pyrenees, erected a trophy bearing an inscription which recorded, with some elasticity of phrase, that from the Alps to Further Spain he had subdued eight hundred and seventy-six towns.[4] The name of Sertorius was judiciously omitted.

Pompey settles affairs in Spain.

71 B. C.

---

[1] Plut., *Sert.*, 27, 1–2; *Pomp.*, 20, 4; App., i, 115, 536–7.
[2] Sall., iii, 86–7; Val. Max., vii, 6, ext. 3; Flor., ii, 10, 9; Juv., xv, 93–6; Oros., v, 23, 14.
[3] Cic., *Pro Balbo*, 8, 19; 15, 34; 17, 40; Caes., *B. C.*, i, 61, 3; Pliny, v, 5, 36; Justin., xliii, 5, 11.
[4] Sall., iii, 89; Strabo, iii, 4, 1. 7. 9; iv, 1, 3; Pliny, iii, 3 (4), 18; vii, 26 (27), 96; Dio, xli, 24, 3. The precision of the figures sets one thinking, and *I* am rather inclined to believe that Pompey would have

71 B.C.
Continued agitation for the restoration of the tribunician power.
74 B.C.
73 B. C.

When Pompey arrived in Italy he found the Government distracted by fresh troubles. The concession which Cotta had extorted from the aristocracy had not satisfied the populace. Only a year later Lucius Quinctius, a tribune whom Cicero described as a voluble demagogue, renewed the agitation for the complete restoration of the tribunician power; but Lucullus, who vehemently denounced his conduct, prevailed upon him to desist.[1] In the following year renewed scarcity of grain, aggravated doubtless by piracy, gave an opportunity to another tribune, Licinius Macer, for reopening the question. The consuls, Marcus Terentius Varro Lucullus and Gaius Cassius, carried a law by which a sum equivalent to one hundred and twenty thousand pounds was voted for the purchase of corn in Sicily; and as the farmers were compelled to sell at the price which the Government fixed, a clause was added by which five pecks a month were to be distributed at a low charge to forty thousand needy citizens,[2] the consuls at the same time assuring them that something more should be done when Pompey returned from Spain. The grant only emboldened Macer to press his demands. In a speech of which the substance has probably been respected even by the rhetoric of Sallust he attacked the aristocracy as tyrants who ground down their fellow citizens and exploited the provinces for their own gain, while he reproached his hearers for their tame submission. As for Cotta, his concession had been prompted merely by fear. Had they not suffered the efforts of Sicinius to fail and remained passive as slaves when Lucullus was thundering against Quinctius? Were they going to rest satisfied with that wretched monthly dole, the allowance of malefactors in gaol? If the nobles wanted war for

contrived somehow by stretching the meaning of the word 'towns' to defend his statement. Perhaps some youthful German savant, in quest of the indispensable doctorate, will oblige the learned world by a dissertation on this and kindred inscriptions?

[1] Cic., *Pro Cluent.*, 28, 77; 29, 79; 39, 108; Sall., iii, 48, 11; Plut., *Luc.*, 5, 7; Ps. Ascon. *in Div.*, § 8, ed. Stangl, p. 189 (ed. Orelli, p. 103).

[2] Cic., *Verr.*, iii, 70, 163; v. 21, 52. See pp. 384-5.

their own selfish ends, let them fight themselves instead of making the poor fight for them—the poor who had all the toil, all the danger, and none of the reward. The one remedy was to restore that bulwark of popular liberty, the tribunician power ; but unless the people fought for liberty as resolutely as the nobles fought for tyranny, they would never succeed.¹ The harangues of Macer were supported by the eloquence of Caesar, perhaps not wholly without effect ; for although the tribunician power was not yet restored, a tribune named Plautius, backed by Caesar, carried a law which permitted the followers of Lepidus who had joined Sertorius to return to Italy ;² and in the following year the consul Lentulus Clodianus proposed a bill for recovering payment, which Sulla had remitted, from those who had bought the confiscated property of the proscribed.³ If, however, this bill became law, one may perhaps doubt whether influential purchasers were not able to find means for evading payment.⁴ But now that Pompey had returned, the agitation for the restoration of the tribunician power would be instantly renewed ; and while Lucullus had been fighting with Mithradates for three years, Italy was devastated by a war more terrible than any which had occurred since the time of Hannibal.

73 B.C.

72 B.C.

The half-savage herdsmen who tended sheep and cattle in Apulia, on the Apennines, and over the uplands of the southern peninsula were a constant source of danger. Where slavery exists the Government, if it is to rest secure, must be not only ruthless but also strong. But in Italy there was no standing army and no police. The servile insurrections of the previous century in Italy and in Sicily had been with difficulty suppressed, and since the death of Sulla the feebleness of the Government had invited revolt ; but hitherto the trained gladiators, who might be far more formidable, had given little trouble. Among them were descendants of the Cimbri

Spartacus.

---

¹ Sall., iii, 48, 6. 9. 11–12. 19. 21. 23. 26.
² Sall., iii, 47. See pp. 385–6.   ³ Cic., *Verr.*, iii, 35, 81 ; Sall., iv, 1.
⁴ See G. Long, *Decline of the Roman Republic*, iii, 1869, pp. 50–1.

and the Teutoni who had destroyed four Roman armies, and whom Marius alone had prevented from destroying Rome. In the early autumn of 73 there was living in a gladiatorial training school at Capua a Thracian, named Spartacus. He had served in Roman armies in Macedonia, but had deserted and become a brigand, and, having been arrested, had been sold into slavery. 'In intelligence and humanity', wrote Plutarch, 'he was above his lot and more like a Greek than a barbarian.' He persuaded his fellow gladiators, most of whom were Gauls or Thracians, to attempt escape. Seventy or more rose suddenly, beat off their warders, broke out of the building, seized knives from a cook's shop, captured a train of wagons, containing weapons, which they met outside the city-walls, and routed their pursuers. Spartacus, supported by two Gauls, Oenomaus and Crixus, led the little band to Mount Vesuvius, which was then believed to be an extinct volcano,[1] and encamped on the edge of the crater which formed its summit. Descending from time to time, they plundered the surrounding country; Spartacus was scrupulously fair in distributing the spoil; and slaves and desperadoes flocked to join him. The Government believed that they had only to deal with a gang of brigands; and the praetor Publius Varinius sent an officer named Claudius Glaber[2] with three thousand men, hastily levied in Campania, to block the only part of the mountain by which it seemed possible to descend. The insurgents appeared to be trapped. But wild vines were growing beneath the summit; and, fastening together their limber branches, the gladiators formed ladders by which they crept down unawares into a crater, and, emerging through a ravine,[3] fell upon the rear of the undisciplined levies, and put

---

[1] Strabo, v, 4, 8.
[2] See *Philol.*, lv, 1896, pp. 387-9.
[3] This is the inference which Groebe (W. Drumann's *Gesch. Roms*, iv², 1908, pp. 88-9, n. 1) draws from the words of Florus (ii. 8, 4),—(ibi cum obsiderentur . . .) *per fauces cavi montis* (vitineis delapsi vinculis ad imas eius descendere radices, &c.).

them to flight.[1] Encouraged by their success, the herds- 73 B.C. men of the Apennines began to reinforce them. Still the danger was underrated : raw recruits, dispatched under the lieutenants of Varinius against Spartacus, were routed near Vesuvius and near Herculaneum ; their arms and stores were looted ; and the rebels scoured the country as they pleased. The praetor's troops were panic-stricken ; many of the fugitives refused, despite a stringent proclamation, to rejoin their companies ; others were suffering from the unhealthy autumnal season ; and Varinius sent his quaestor, Thoranius, to Rome to represent the state of affairs. Not long afterwards Varinius, who had attempted to catch Spartacus at a disadvantage, was himself beaten ;[2] and his defeat was followed by that of Thoranius. The rebels overran Campania and Lucania. They could only subsist by plunder, and wherever they appeared the farmers and the peasants fled. Spartacus did his utmost to restrain the lust for vengeance, but in vain. Villages and homesteads were pillaged and burned ; travellers were robbed and murdered ; women were dragged out of their houses and ravished. Spartacus, who knew that, notwithstanding all his victories, he could not hope to withstand the reserved power of Rome, purposed to cross the Alps, whence his followers might disperse to their respective countries ; but Crixus insisted on remaining to plunder, and separated from him with the Gallo-German contingent. Spartacus passed the winter near Thurii in Lucania, preparing for the next campaign. Success brought him further reinforcements. Vagabonds and runaway slaves flocked to join the rebels, and they gained fresh recruits by breaking open the barracks in which chained slaves were confined by night and setting them

[1] Frontinus (*Strat.*, i, 5, 21), evidently following the statement of his authority as to the *original* number of the insurgents, says that Spartacus repulsed several cohorts with his seventy-four gladiators alone.

[2] Sall., iii, 96 B ; Frontin., *Strat.*, i, 5, 22. G. Rathke (*De Rom. bellis servilibus*, 1904, pp. 82-3) supposes that Varinius was defeated before he sent Thoranius to Rome ; but see Plut., *Cras.*, 9, 7, and Maurenbrecher (*op. cit.*, ii, 1893, p. 146).

free. They made shields of plaited osiers, which they covered with raw hides, and those who were skilled in metal-working forged the chains which they found in the barracks into swords and javelins. They collected the weapons of those whom they killed in battle, took possession of the riderless horses, and gradually formed a corps of cavalry.[1] In the new year the Senate, at length realizing the gravity of the danger, sent the consuls, Lucius Gellius and Lentulus Clodianus, with four legions into the field. Crixus was attacked by Gellius and the praetor Arrius near Mount Garganus in Apulia, and fell in the defeat which his headstrong folly had provoked. But Spartacus avenged his death. The horde, which no commander could have restrained from excesses in camp or on the march, obeyed him on the battle-field. Followed by Gellius, he was moving through the highlands of Picenum with the intention, which he had never abandoned, of crossing the Alps, when Lentulus appeared in front. Spartacus defeated him, then turned on his pursuers and defeated them. Although he strove to protect non-combatants from the rage and the lust of the liberated slaves, he had no compunction in teaching his enemies that fortune might reserve for them the fate for which they had destined him. In mockery of Roman usage he compelled three hundred of his prisoners to fight in pairs, to appease the ghost of Crixus. He now, we are told, intended to advance on Rome, but if he conceived such a design, he soon abandoned it, for, after inflicting another defeat upon the combined consular armies in Picenum, he pushed northward in pursuance of his original plan. Gaius Cassius, the Governor of Cisalpine Gaul, who tried to stop him, was beaten at Mutina. The Alps were now open; but, for some unrecorded reason—perhaps because his ignorant followers, intoxicated by success, would heed no warning—he

---

[1] Sall., iii, 91-8, 101-3; Livy, *Epit.*, 95; Vell., ii, 30, 5; Plut., *Cras.*, 8; 9, 1-8; Frontin., *Strat.*, i, 5, 21; 7, 6; Flor., ii, 8, 3-7; App., i, 116; Eutrop., vi, 7; Oros., v, 24, 1-3. The evidence for the later events of the war is examined on pp. 386-90.

marched southward towards Lucania. Probably he 72 B.C.
intended to invade Sicily, where supplies were abundant,
and where he would find recruits among the numerous
slaves, whose predecessors had twice offered a formidable
resistance to the armies of Rome.

It was time for the Government to exert all their
strength, for the public were nearly as alarmed as when
Hannibal had approached the walls of Rome.[1] In the
early autumn the consuls, who had failed so ignominiously,
were superseded; and the praetor, Marcus Licinius
Crassus, who had served under Sulla in the Civil War,[2]
was appointed to command in chief. Six new legions
were assigned to him; and his force, including the four
of which he took over the command, was as numerous as
that with which Caesar conquered Gaul. His aim was
to intercept Spartacus as he was marching southward.
One of his lieutenants rashly attacked the rebels, although
he had been ordered merely to watch their movements,
and was put to flight; but Crassus, having decimated
the cohort which had been the first to break its ranks,
pursued and destroyed a division of the insurgents,
and afterwards defeated Spartacus himself, who retreated
to the southern extremity of the peninsula. He found it
impossible to cross the Straits, for some pirates, who had
promised to transport his army, played him false; an
attempt which he desperately made to cross on rafts of
course miscarried; and Crassus proceeded to construct
an entrenchment from sea to sea to shut him in. While
the works were still incomplete Spartacus, whose supplies
were failing, cut his way out. The Roman populace were
becoming nervously impatient, and the Senate were
forced to acquiesce in a vote of the assembly, by which
Pompey was associated with Crassus in command.[3]
But Crassus was eager to prevent Pompey from getting

[1] App., i, 118, 549; Oros., v, 24, 5.
[2] Plut., *Cras.*, 6, 8.
[3] App., i, 119, 554. G. Ferrero (*Grandezza e decadenza di Roma*, i, 1902, p. 253, n. 2 [Eng. tr., i, 155, n. §]), distrusting, perhaps rightly, Appian's statement, says, 'It was probably the Senate, and not the people that recalled Pompey, but it was public opinion that forced the Senate', &c.

the credit for what he had himself achieved, and the folly of the Gauls in the rebel army gave him an opportunity. Spartacus intended to make his way to Brundisium, whence he might perhaps escape by sea; but hearing that a proconsular army had landed there from Macedonia, he was obliged to abandon his design. Dissensions broke out afresh between Spartacus and two of his Gallic officers, Castus and Cannicus, who moved northward into Lucania. Crassus overthrew them, but could not complete his victory, for Spartacus appeared in time to stop the rout. Soon afterwards, however, Crassus again encountered the two Gauls near the source of the river Siler in Lucania. Divining that Spartacus would try to rescue his rash colleagues, he concealed his powerful infantry beneath a hill, and sent a detachment of his cavalry to hold him, while the remaining squadrons were to retreat before the Gallo-German force towards the position which he himself had occupied. The unsuspecting rebels pursued the cavalry, and while Crassus suddenly attacked their front, twelve cohorts, posted behind the hill, fell upon their rear. The rebels were routed with enormous loss; five eagles, twenty-six manipular standards, and the consular insignia, which had been lost in former battles, were recovered.[1] The power of Spartacus was broken, and once more he retreated into the southernmost extremity of Italy. There he turned to bay and gained a last victory over a detachment which had pursued him. His followers were so elated that they insisted upon going back, and he reluctantly led them against the praetor's enormous army. Even Spartacus could not prevail against discipline and numbers. The desperate resistance of the insurgents was overborne; their ranks were shattered; and Spartacus, surrounded but fighting to the last after the rout began, was slain.

So perished the heroic gladiator, who had moulded herdsmen, brigands, and outcasts into a victorious army, supplied them with weapons and equipment, contrived during two years to feed them and to keep them together,

[1] Frontin., *Strat.*, ii, 5, 34.

done all that man could do to protect the innocent from their lust and vengeance, nine times defeated Roman armies, and compelled the Roman Government to put forth their whole available power and to commission their most illustrious general in order to subdue him. Five thousand of his scattered followers fell in with Pompey, and were annihilated; others, who escaped into the Bruttian hills, were destroyed piecemeal by Crassus; six thousand prisoners were crucified along the Appian Way, from Capua to Rome. The most terrible servile outbreak that history records was crushed; but Central and Southern Italy were devastated, and the warning was forgotten. Pompey boasted in his official dispatch that if Crassus had defeated the rebels, *he* had eradicated the rebellion.[1]

71 B.C.

Crucifixion of 6,000 prisoners.

It was April,[2] and in the next few months the consular elections would be held. Three courses were open to Pompey,—to follow the example of Sulla by seizing supreme power; to court the conservative aristocracy; or to ally himself with the populace and the knights. The first would entail a struggle with Crassus, who was master of ten legions, and was not only premature, but alien to Pompey's temperament: he could gain nothing by joining a party which had reluctantly used him to subdue its enemies; and, being minded to supplant Lucullus and obtain another extraordinary command, he had everything to gain by joining the popular party. All who had money to invest in the farming of the taxes were ready to support him, expecting that he would open the East to the financial enterprise of Rome.

Crassus was jealous of the fame of Pompey;[3] and Pompey, who could not bear an equal,[4] was perhaps uneasily conscious that he had reaped where Crassus had sown. But the two had need of one another. Crassus

Coalition of Crassus with Pompey.

---

[1] Plut., *Cras.*, 13, 12; *Pomp.*, 21, 2. Cf. Cic., *Verr.*, v, 2, 5; *De imp. Cn. Pomp.*, 10, 28; 11, 30; *Pro Sest.*, 31, 67.

[2] The war ended in the spring of 71, for, according to Appian (i, 121, 560), the command of Crassus lasted six months. On April 1 the people of Capua attended games in the amphitheatre (*C. I. L.*, x, pars ii, No. 8070, 3).

[3] Plut., *Cras.*, 7, 6.   [4] See vol. ii, p. 269, n. 2.

71 B.C.

had influence in the Senate; Pompey was the idol of the multitude.[1] Each expected a triumph and the consulship, though Pompey had never held any of the lower offices and was still six years below the legal age. His candidature was not welcome to the Senate;[2] for the democrats, to whom he looked for support, although they neither could nor cared to improve the condition of the poor, intended to use their votes in order to overthrow the Sullan constitution. But when the candidates appeared outside the gates of Rome at the head of their respective armies they were plainly irresistible; and many feared that Pompey would use his to make himself supreme.[3] The reforms of Marius had increased the efficiency of Roman legions; but that transformation of a national militia into a professional host, which prolonged service in foreign lands rendered inevitable, had dealt a blow, which Sulla had made fatal, at the stability of Roman government. The soldiers were devoted not to the State, which had lost credit, but to their generals: it was to them, not to the Government, that they swore allegiance when they were enlisted; and since the State gave them no pensions, it was to them that they looked for the bounties and the allotments which, when they had served their time, would enable them to subsist. Most of them belonged to rural districts; and as they could not afford to travel to Rome for the elections and were, moreover, ignorant, they may well have felt that they had no great stake in the welfare of the nation. It has been said that the best safeguard would have been a strong central executive, wielding the whole

How Roman armies endangered the Republic.

[1] Plut., *Pomp.*, 22, 2.

[2] There is no evidence for the assertions of Strachan-Davidson (*Cicero*, 1894, pp. 52–3) that the Senate at first refused to allow Pompey to triumph, and that when he demanded the privilege of standing for the consulship they 'foolishly haggled over the price'. However generous they might have been, they could not have induced Pompey to desist from restoring the tribunician power or reforming the jury-courts. We only know that they, no doubt reluctantly, passed resolutions authorizing the triumph and dispensing Pompey from observing the Sullan enactment about the minor magistracies (Cic., *De imp. Cn. Pomp.*, 21, 62; Livy, *Epit.*, 97; Plut., *Pomp.*, 22, 1–2; App., i, 121, 560–1). [3] Plut., *Pomp.*, 21, 3.

military force of the empire and strictly responsible to the Senate. But such a reform would have availed little if funds were not available to provide for discharged veterans; it would have been resisted by the leaders whose hopes of advancement rested upon the troops which they had already raised; and after fifty years of revolution, culminating in the demoralization for which Sulla was responsible, that public opinion which can make an adventurer feel that to clutch at tyranny would be hopeless did not exist.

71 B.C.

Pompey took care to avert suspicion by explaining that he was only awaiting the return of Metellus, who would triumph with him, and that he would then disband his troops: Crassus declared that for his part he was only waiting to follow Pompey's lead.[1] Pompey promised the tribunes that if he were elected consul, he would accomplish that reform on which their hearts were set,— the restoration of the tribunician power.[2] Crassus knew that Pompey, by reason of his great achievements, was far more popular than himself, and he solicited his support. Pompey for his part saw that the richest man in Italy could be useful, and did his utmost to recommend Crassus to the electorate. So strong was his position that the Senate passed a resolution suspending in his favour the law which fixed the age of candidates as well as that which required that whoever claimed a triumph should have held one of the higher magistracies; and the two generals were of course elected.[3] Pompey forthwith addressed a popular gathering outside the city, and, after renewing his promise to restore the power of the tribunes, declared that the provinces were misgoverned, that the juries, being composed exclusively of senators, used their privilege to screen the misdeeds of their own order, and that he was determined to remove this scandal. His speech was enthusiastically applauded,[4] and he knew

Pompey and Crassus consuls.

---

[1] Plut., *Pomp.*, 21, 4; App., i, 121, 561. [2] *Ib.*, § 560.
[3] Cic., *De imp. Cn. Pomp.*, 21, 62; Livy, *Epit.*, 97; Plut., *Cras.*, 12, 1-2; *Pomp.*, 22, 1-2.
[4] Cic., *Verr.*, i, 15, 45. Cf. Sall., iv, 43, and Ps. Ascon. in *Div.*, § 8, ed. Stangl, p. 189 (ed. Orelli, p. 103).

71-70 B.C.
Pompey backed by the populace and the knights.

that he could count on the support not only of the populace, but also of the knights; for while they resented the contempt with which Sulla had treated the equestrian order, they were bent upon obtaining control of the law-courts in order that they might get a hold over provincial governors who ventured to restrict their gains.

Towards the end of the year Crassus enjoyed the minor triumph, known as an ovation, which was all that the law allowed a general who had suppressed a servile insurrection; and on the last day of December Pompey and Metellus entered Rome in triumph for the pacification of Spain.[1]

70 B.C.

The memorable consulship of Pompey and Crassus began in due course on the 1st of January. Crassus held a festival, on which he expended a tenth of his huge fortune, in honour of Hercules; entertained the electors at a banquet for which ten thousand tables were laid; and gave every man who cared to accept it an allowance of grain sufficient to support him for three months.[2]

Restoration of the tribunician power.

Pompey introduced his bill for the restoration of the tribunician power; and Caesar, who was becoming known as a leader of the Marian party, exerted all his influence in support of it. The Senate reluctantly signified their assent; and the popular assembly passed the bill.[3]

Reform of the juries.

Caesar's maternal uncle, Lucius Aurelius Cotta, next proposed a measure for amending the qualification of jurors. Pompey's denunciation of the existing law was not exaggerated. Since Sulla had restricted the privilege of serving on juries to the Senate several jurors had been convicted of receiving bribes; and Cicero[4] related an instance in which a senator accepted money from the defendant to be shared with his fellow jurors and from the prosecutor to ensure conviction. If Verres, the Governor of Sicily, whom Cicero prosecuted, was condemned, notwithstanding the efforts which prominent

---

[1] Cic., *De imp. Cn. Pomp.*, 21, 62; *De div.*, ii, 9, 22; Val. Max., viii, 15, 8; Vell., ii, 30, 2; Plut., *Cras.*, 11, 13; *C. I. L.*, i², p. 178.
[2] Plut., *Cras.*, 12, 3.
[3] Cic., *Verr.*, i, 15, 44, and Ps. Ascon., ed. Stangl, p. 220 (ed. Orelli, p. 147); Cic., *De leg.*, iii, 9, 22; Vell., ii, 30, 4; Livy, *Epit.*, 97; Plut., *Pomp.*, 22, 2; Suet., *Div. Iul.*, 5.   [4] *Verr.*, i, 13, 39.

nobles made to save him, it was because his guilt was 70 B.C.
too flagrant to be denied. Cotta's bill was a compromise;
and it may reasonably be supposed that this was due to
the influence of Crassus as well as to the wishes of the
more liberal senators who supported Cotta, and that
Pompey acquiesced in their decision. Cotta proposed
that thenceforward juries should be eligible not only
from the Senate but also from the equestrian order and
from the *tribuni aerarii*, who had formerly acted as
paymasters of the army, but now, although they retained
their name, were only distinguished from the knights by
a lower pecuniary qualification.[1] He harangued the
people daily,[2] pointing out that the provincial governors,
who were all senators, plundered the provincials, and that
so long as jurors could be chosen only from the Senate
it would be useless to prosecute senatorial offenders.
Cicero in the pamphlet which he published after the
conviction of Verres dwelt upon the violation by provincial governors of the rights of Roman citizens; and
if the Roman populace cared little for the wrongs of
provincials, they were alive to those which might befall
themselves. The reactionaries in the Senate were again Sept.[3]
obliged to yield; and the bill was passed.[4] Catulus,
the staunchest of Conservatives, admitted that senatorial
jurors were corrupt, affirming that otherwise there would
have been no great demand for the restoration of the
tribunician power; and his opinion was confirmed by
that of Cicero.[5] As a concession to popular clamour and
with the object of further restraining judicial corruption,
the censorship, which had lain in abeyance for sixteen years,
was revived; and the censors expelled sixty-four members
from the Senate, among whom were the most notorious
of Sulla's partisans.[6]

[1] See pp. 391-5. [2] Cic., *Verr.*, iii, 96, 223.
[3] See W. Drumann's *Gesch. Roms*, v², 1912, p. 348, nn. 6-7.
[4] Cic., *Pro Cluent.*, 47, 130; *Att.*, i, 16, 3; Livy, *Epist.*, 97; Vell., ii, 32, 3; Plut., *Pomp.*, 22, 2; *Schol. Bob.*, ed. Stangl., p. 94 (ed. Orelli, p. 229); *Schol. Gronov.*, ed. Stangl, p. 328 (ed. Orelli, p. 386).
[5] *Div. in Caec.*, 3, 8; *Verr.*, i, 13, 38-9; 15, 44.·
[6] Cic., *Div. in Caec.*, 3, 8; Livy, *Epit.*, 98; Ascon., ed. Clark, p. 84,

166   POMPEY THE GREAT   CHAP.

<small>70 B.C.
The remnant of the Sullan constitution.</small> Thus the pillars of the Sullan constitution, which had tottered for nine years under repeated assaults, were overthrown. There survived only the one real reform which Sulla had made,—the law by which permanent courts had been established not only for the trial of provincial governors charged with extortion, but also for all the chief criminal offences. Nevertheless the influence of Sulla remained; and it was impossible to allay the dread that other revolutionaries would follow his example. The <small>Sulla's surviving victims still dangerous</small> sons of the proscribed, whom he had excluded from office, the men whose estates he had confiscated were ready to follow any leader who would help them to recover what they had lost. It remained to be seen whether the new jurors would be more conscientious than the old, and whether tribunes would use their restored powers to serve the purpose for which the tribunate had been established, or would sell them to the highest bidder.[1]

<small>Disputes between Pompey and Crassus patched up by a hollow reconciliation.</small> Crassus, whose sympathies were with the Senate, had obstructed Pompey's measures; but towards the end of the year, prompted by a well-meaning knight, he offered his hand to his colleague, who took it, but was not reconciled by the perfunctory overture.[2] Neither would accept a province; and we may safely presume that Pompey was looking for an opportunity of taking over the command, which Lucullus was then exercising, against Mithradates. The next two years, if we may judge from the silence of the chroniclers, were uneventful, and comparative peace apparently prevailed in Rome.

<small>67 B.C.</small> But in the following year the canvass of candidates for office was accompanied by so much violence that Cicero wrote to his friend Atticus, 'You can hardly believe what a great and sudden change for the worse from the state in which you left them you will find in public affairs'[3]; and a tribune, Gaius Cornelius, perhaps re-

<small>ll. 20-6 (ed. Stangl, pp. 65-6); Plut., *Pomp.*, 22, 4. The censors were the ex-consuls who had been superseded by the Senate two years before in consequence of their having ignominiously failed to quell the insurrection of Spartacus.
[1] Cf. Sall., *Cat.*, 38, 1, and Tac., *Ann.*, iii, 27.
[2] Plut., *Pomp.*, 22, 2; 23, 1. See pp. 390-1.   [3] *Att.*, i, 11, 3.</small>

POMPEY THE GREAT

membering the irregular exercise of power that permitted 67 B.C.
Pompey to stand for the consulship, succeeded in carrying
a law by which the senatorial practice of granting dispensations from existing laws was in some degree restricted. By this and other measures of reform he incurred Prosecution of Cornelius. the hatred of Conservatives, and two years later a charge
of treason was brought against him, of which he was
acquitted, thanks to the skilful advocacy of Cicero.[1]
Pompey, after his consulship, kept aloof from politics, Pompey in retirement. and on the rare occasions when he appeared in public he
was attended by a train of clients; for, says Plutarch,[2]
'he thought that it gave him an air of grandeur and of
majesty, and he was persuaded that his dignity should
be preserved uncontaminated by the familiarity and even
by the very touch of the multitude'. Probably he was
conscious that his temperament was unfitted for political
strife; but his military achievements were not forgotten,
and he was soon to have a chance of gaining fresh distinction.

Pirates had infested the Mediterranean from the earliest The Mediterranean pirates. historic times; and Thucydides remarks that piracy was
considered a respectable occupation. During the revolutionary period of Roman history the evil had increased;
for since the fall of Carthage the Romans, notwithstanding
their vast commercial interests, had no longer thought it
necessary to maintain a standing fleet. Five years before 75 B.C. the consulship of Pompey Servilius Isauricus had subdued the pirates who haunted the southern coast of Asia
Minor[3]: but his success was only temporary; and
Marcus Antonius, the father of Cleopatra's lover, who

[1] Dio, xxxvi, 39, 2–4; 40, 1; Ascon., ed. Clark, p. 58, ll. 3–25; 59, ll. 1–4 (ed. Stangl, pp. 47–8). Cf. P. Willems, *Le sénat*, &c., ii, 1883, pp. 118, 166. Dr. Hardy (*Journ. Rom. Studies*, vii, 1917, p. 155) believes that the laws of Cornelius were 'sanctioned, even if they were not actually supported by Crassus'. I doubt this. Crassus was never really a popular leader; and when he began to co-operate with Caesar, his motive was jealousy of Pompey.

[2] *Pomp.*, 23, 2.

[3] Cic., *Verr.*, ii, 1, 21, 56; Sall., ii, 87 B, ll. 11–3; Strabo, xii, 6, 2; xiv, 3, 3; Livy, *Epit.*, 93; Flor., i, 41, 4–5; Eutrop., vi, 3; Rufus Festus, 12, 3; Amm. Marc., xiv, 8, 4; Oros., v, 23, 21–2.

had been dispatched through the influence of Cethegus, an intriguing senator, to co-operate in the Mithradatic War by clearing the Eastern Mediterranean, robbed the provincials whom he was supposed to protect, and ignominiously failed to fulfil his mission.[1] The war with Sertorius, the war with Spartacus, the war with Mithradates, the reiterated menaces of the democratic leaders so distracted the Senate that the pirates, waxing more audacious from impunity, became the terror of the civilized world. Adventurers who had been proscribed or impoverished in the civil wars flocked to join them. Their chief strongholds were on the shores of Cilicia and in the harbours of Crete; but their depredations were carried as far as the Straits of Gibraltar. They virtually formed a great maritime power; and petty dynasts found it profitable to assist them. They had arsenals, dockyards, harbours, watch-towers; and their raids were executed not merely by single vessels, but also by organized fleets, each under its own admiral, and prepared, in case of need, to aid another. Cicero affirmed in one of his speeches that a flotilla commanded by a consul had been forced to surrender. When Verres was Governor of Sicily a piratical fleet defeated a Roman squadron and sailed unopposed into the harbour of Syracuse. Another entered the mouth of the Tiber, plundered Ostia, and burned the ships which were lying in the port. Crews occasionally marched inland, pillaged country houses, seized wealthy citizens, and held them for ransom. Timid travellers even avoided the Appian Way where it approached the sea. Two praetors in their purple robes of office were kidnapped with all their retinue. Roman troops, bound for the East, were delayed in Italy because they dared not cross the Adriatic until the winter, when navigation was generally suspended. Proconsuls, proceeding to the seat of government in

---

[1] Cic., *Verr.*, ii, 3, 8, and Ps. Ascon., ed. Stangl, p. 259 (ed. Orelli, p. 206); iii, 91, 213; Ps. Ascon. *in Div.*, § 55, ed. Stangl, p. 202 (ed. Orelli, p. 121); Sall., iii, 2–3; Livy, *Epit.*, 97; Vell., ii, 31, 3–4; Tac., *Ann.*, xii, 62; Flor., i, 42, 2–3; App., *Sic.*, 6.

POMPEY THE GREAT

Cilicia, were forced by dread of the marauders to land at Ephesus and undertake the long and wearisome journey overland.[1] Plutarch tells a story, presumably founded upon fact, to illustrate the humiliation which this monstrous power had brought upon Rome. A man who had been taken prisoner declared with naïve pomposity that he was a Roman citizen, whereupon his captors, pretending alarm, begged forgiveness and attired him in his toga, so that, as they said, they might never mistake him again. When they were tired of mocking him they lowered a step-ladder over the gunwale, wished him a pleasant journey, and pushed him into the sea. Only two years before, Delos, the great emporium of trade between Rome and the Levant, had been captured, and its prosperity irretrievably destroyed. The conduct of the war that was being waged against Mithradates was hampered by the assistance which he received from the corsairs. Commerce was crippled: the revenue from the port dues was greatly diminished; the remittances which the tax-collectors sent from the provinces were liable to be interrupted; and as the corn-ships from Sicily, Sardinia, and Africa were frequently attacked, the Roman populace was threatened with starvation.[2]

69 B.C.

There was only one man who could be relied upon to extirpate the evil; and the Senate, who did not realize that to conciliate him might secure their own position, were afraid to entrust him with a force which they fancied that he might use to make himself supreme.[3] But the restoration of the tribunician power had forged a weapon ready to the hand of any leader who could wield it. In January 67, Aulus Gabinius, one of the tribunes and an intimate friend of Pompey, proposed a bill providing that a man of consular rank should be appointed to wage war against the pirates; that his command should last three years and carry with it absolute dominion

Extraordinary powers for their suppression conferred upon Pompey.

---

[1] W. M. Ramsay, *Hist. Geogr. of Asia Minor*, 1890, p. 50.
[2] Cic., *Verr.*, iv, 46, 103; *De imp. Cn. Pomp.*, 12, 32–3; 18, 54–5; Livy, *Epit.*, 99; Plut., *Pomp.*, 24; 25, 1; *Luc.*, 13, 3; App., *Mithr.*, 91–3; Dio, xxxvi, 20–3; Phlegon, fr. 12; Eutrop., vi, 12; Oros., vi, 4, 1.
[3] Plut., *Pomp.*, 25, 3.

over the Mediterranean and authority equal to that of the proconsuls over the surrounding lands as far as fifty Roman miles from the coast; that he should receive a grant of six thousand talents,[1] and should be authorized to draw from the treasury and from the tax-farmers in the provinces as much more as he might require; and that he should be furnished with two hundred ships of war, as many men as he thought necessary, and fifteen lieutenant-generals, or vice-admirals, whom he might himself select from the Senate.[2] The proposal was received by the people with enthusiasm, for they knew what it meant: the 'man of consular rank' who would clear the sea for the corn-ships was Pompey the Great. But in the Senate the bill was of course opposed: Caesar was the only member who ventured to support it. Plutarch[3] observes that he backed Gabinius not because he cared for Pompey, but 'because it was his fixed purpose to worm his way into popular favour'. This was no doubt true enough. If Caesar already foresaw that Pompey was to be his rival, he had nothing to gain by thwarting a proposal which would inevitably be adopted; he might have much to gain by conciliating Pompey; and, like all great workers, he liked to see work done thoroughly.[4] Passions in the Senate were so inflamed that Gabinius, fearing or affecting to fear that his life was in danger, stole out of the House. The mob stormed the building; and the members fled. One of the consuls, Gaius Calpurnius Piso, was caught, and the rabble were about to murder him when he was saved by the intercession of Gabinius. The Senate attempted to gain the other tribunes; but only two—Roscius Otho and Lucius

---

[1] Nearly £1,500,000.
[2] Cic., *De imp. Cn. Pomp.*, 17, 52; Livy, *Epit.*, 99; Vell., ii, 31-2; Plut., *Pomp.*, 25, 2; App., *Mithr.*, 94; Dio, xxxvi, 23, 4-5; 37, 1.
[3] *Pomp.*, 25, 3.
[4] Groebe (*Klio*, x, 1910, p. 378) guesses that Caesar, who, he assures us, knew that Pompey would not try to seize autocratic power, was the real author of the law, his aim being to make an irreparable breach between Pompey and the Senate. Yet on the previous page he said that Gabinius was merely Pompey's tool.

Dio (xxxvi, 23, 4) sagely remarks that it is doubtful whether Gabinius was instigated by Pompey or desired to curry favour with him.

III POMPEY THE GREAT 171

Trebellius—dared to oppose the bill. Trebellius assured 67 B.C. the Senate that he would sooner die than allow it to become law.[1] On the day when it was to be submitted to the vote the Forum was densely thronged; and Pompey was acclaimed as the destined commander.[2] Gabinius presented him to the voters; and, if Cassius Dio is to be trusted, he told them that he was gratified by the honour which they desired to confer upon him, but that they could easily find others as capable as himself. Gabinius in a formal oration urged him to accept the offer, and, by way of suggesting that he should be presently entrusted with the conduct of the Mithradatic War, caused a picture to be displayed of the luxurious Tusculan villa of Lucullus—a hint that the general who was then in command was making a fortune dishonestly and spending it in self-indulgence.[3] When he had finished speaking, Trebellius attempted to reply; but as he was shouted down, he exercised his veto and forbade the bill to be submitted to the vote. Gabinius, following the unconstitutional precedent of Tiberius Gracchus, moved that Trebellius should be deposed. Seventeen out of the thirty-five tribes had already voted for the motion when Trebellius, seeing that he must otherwise be removed from office, withdrew his opposition. Roscius, unable to gain a hearing, held up two fingers to signify that another commander should be associated with Pompey, a gesture which provoked a roar of indignation. Gabinius, however, thought it expedient to ask Catulus, the most prominent of the conservative senators, to state his opinion. Catulus is remembered because he consistently strove to stem the irresistible forces that were undermining the Republic. His character commanded general respect, and he was listened to in silence. He paid Pompey graceful compliments, but insisted that the proposed appointment was both unconstitutional and dangerous to

[1] Ascon., ed. Clark, p. 72, ll. 10–2 (ed. Stangl, p. 57); Plut., *Pomp.*, 25, 4; Dio, xxxvi, 24, 1–3.
[2] Cic., *De imp. Cn. Pomp.*, 15, 44.
[3] Cic., *Pro Sest.*, 42, 93.

the State. It was not like the dictatorship, which could only be exercised in Italy, and the tenure of which was limited to six months. The wisest plan, he argued, would be to appoint divisional commanders who would be responsible, not to a commander-in-chief but to the Roman People, and who would therefore feel the strongest motive for performing their duties thoroughly.[1] After he sat down the meeting was adjourned; but when the voters reassembled, they passed the bill; and Pompey, taking advantage of the general enthusiasm, persuaded the assembly to increase his force by granting him power to raise five hundred ships of war, one hundred and twenty thousand legionaries, and five thousand cavalry.[2] The price of grain, which had been raised under the fear that the pirates would intercept supplies, instantly fell.[3]

Significance of the Gabinian law.

Let us consider the significance of this famous law. It is reasonable to suppose that Gabinius acted as Pompey's tool. Plutarch remarked that the law made Pompey 'not an admiral, but a monarch'[4]; and modern historians for the most part hold that it was a revolutionary measure, which tended towards the establishment of military autocracy. Perhaps, though the people were now clutching at the senatorial prerogative of appointing to extraordinary commands, it would be nearer the truth to say that it was a symptom of revolution. The immense power which it conferred upon Pompey did not itself lead to military rule; it was conferred because the evolution of Roman politics had long been heading towards that end. Unlimited power had been granted without protest to Antonius[5] because the senators had no fear that he would use it against themselves: they did fear Pompey because they failed to understand that what he desired was not despotism, but that all men should do reverence to Pompey the Great. One may doubt whether at any time during the past few years

---

[1] See pp. 396-7.
[2] Plut., *Pomp.*, 26, 2; App., *Mithr.*, 94.
[3] Cic., *De imp. Cn. Pomp.*, 15, 44; Plut., *Pomp.*, 26, 2.
[4] *Ib.*, 25, 2.   [5] Vell., ii, 31, 3.

piracy could have been extirpated unless discretionary 67 B.C. power had been conferred upon one commander; and if it was dangerous to the Republic to grant such power, the reason was that the Republic was already in danger. The Senate had become weakened and contained no one of great practical ability except Pompey himself, Crassus, and Caesar; its authority must have been shaken by the disgrace of Verres; it was not supported by the public opinion of Italy; and it no longer commanded the allegiance of the troops. The proposal of Gabinius was not merely a democratic measure—strictly speaking indeed there was no democratic party in Rome, only a coterie which used popular discontent as a weapon against the nobles: it was supported by politicians of all shades of opinion, except the extreme Conservatives whose spokesmen were Catulus and Hortensius. It was supported not only by Caesar, but also by Cicero,[1] who, although he lived and died for the Republic, justified the unconstitutional violence to which Gabinius had resorted, on the ground that in the public interest it was unavoidable. Pompey in the course of the Spanish War had suffered from senatorial incompetence; and it was not to be expected that he would assume responsibility aggravated by senatorial control, especially since many senators regarded him as a traitor to the Conservative cause. What really threatened the outworn Republic was the restored tribunician power, which had given him the position that he coveted, and might be used to exalt another whose aims were different from his.

During the winter the pirates were perforce idle; and Pompey had leisure to complete his preparations. He did his best to conciliate the Conservative party by selecting most of his lieutenants from their ranks; and it would seem that he found it unnecessary to collect as many ships or to raise as many men as he had been authorized to do. The ships and the rowers were for the most part furnished by the seaports and the islands of Greece and Asia, though the fighting men were Roman

[1] *De imp. Cn. Pomp.*, 17, 52-3; 20, 59-61.

soldiers. Pompey's plan was to assign a definite area of the Mediterranean to each of his admirals, so that if the pirates escaped one, they must run into the clutches of another: the Straits of Gibraltar, the Dardanelles, and the Bosporus were closed.[1] Ancient ships never kept at sea long; and when the pirate crews were forced to land for supplies or for repairs, the Romans would be able to prevent their return and to capture or destroy them. In the early spring,[2] while the admirals cruised within their respective limits, Pompey himself scoured the Tuscan Sea, coasted along Sicily and the African coast, and thence sailed to Sardinia, Corsica, Gaul, and Spain. Many pirates were captured: others sped before the westerly winds for the ports of Cilicia. At the end of forty days the western seas were completely cleared; corn-ships were sailing securely from Sardinia, Sicily, and Africa; and, after a short stay in Rome, where he was joyfully welcomed, Pompey travelled overland to Brundisium. Embarking with sixty of his best ships, which he had ordered to await him, he crossed the Adriatic, coasted round the Peloponnese, and steered for Cilicia. Many of the pirates surrendered, and although their strongholds were of course destroyed and their arms confiscated, they themselves were spared. The more desperate concentrated beneath the steep cliffs of Alaya and awaited Pompey's arrival; but they were defeated and driven to take refuge in the overhanging fortress of Coracesium, where they were compelled by hunger to submit. Just seven weeks after Pompey left Brundisium the war was at an end.[3]

Pompey's force was overwhelming; but he had conducted the war with skill, and he used his victory with

---

[1] See *Klio*, x, 1910, p. 388 and the accompanying map.
[2] Pompey sailed before March 10 (Cic., *De imp. Cn. Pomp.*, 12, 34, compared with Veg., *De re mil.*, iv, 39).
[3] Cic., *De imp. Cn. Pomp.*, 12, 33–5; Varro, *R. R.*, ii, prooem., 6; Strabo, x, 4, 9; Livy, *Epit.*, 99; Pliny, iii, 11 (16), 101; Vell., ii, 32, 4; Plut., *Pomp.*, 26, 3; 27; 28, 1–2; Flor., i, 41, 7–13, 15; App., *Mithr.* 94–6; Dio, xxxvi, 37, 3–4; Eutrop., vi, 12; Oros., vi, 4, 1. See p. 397.

moderation. To crucify the prisoners or to sell them to 67 B.C. the slave-dealers would have been in accord with precedent : Pompey distributed them in various parts of Asia Minor remote from the sea, in Achaia, and in Calabria, assigning them lands in the hope that they would settle down to an industrious life.[1] But he had still to deal with an aftermath of the war. Quintus Caecilius Metellus, a relation of the general who had served with him against Sertorius, had been dispatched two years before [2] to subdue Crete, which, as a hotbed of piracy, only less fertile than Cilicia, had with impunity defied Antonius. The wiser citizens had tried in vain to persuade their countrymen to accept the terms which the Senate dictated ; and Metellus had by this time overcome resistance. But Crete was included within the sphere of Pompey's command ; the Cretans, who had heard of the forbearance with which he treated the pirates, begged him to visit the island ; and he sent one of his lieutenants to supersede Metellus, at the same time writing to bid him desist from the war and warning the various communities not to recognize his authority. But Pompey was himself bound by that clause in the Gabinian law which gave him on land a power not absolute, but only equal to that of the proconsuls—a clause which could not but provoke disputes. Metellus disregarded the order, completed the conquest of Crete, and reduced it to the form of a Roman province ; for, although Pompey's dignity was wounded, he was not so foolish as to embroil himself in a civil war.[3] He was expecting an opportunity

---

[1] Livy, *Epit.*, 99 ; Strabo, viii, 7, 5 ; xiv, 3, 3 ; 5, 8 ; Vell., ii, 32, 5–6 ; Plut., *Pomp.*, 27, 4 ; 28, 3–4 ; Flor., i, 41, 14 ; App., *Mithr.*, 96 ; Dio, xxxvi, 37, 4–6 ; Servius *ad* Georg., iv, 127.

[2] Long (*Decline of the Roman Republic*, iii, 126) remarks that the campaign of Metellus ' lasted three years according to Velleius (ii, 34 [1]) ; or two years according to Orosius (vi, 4 [2]) '. The discrepancy is only apparent. Velleius, who is supported by Livy (*Epit.*, 98–100) probably meant that the war went on in each of three years—68, 67, and 66 B.C.—Orosius that its actual duration was two.

[3] Cic., *De imp. Cn. Pomp.*, 12, 35 ; 16, 46 ; Livy, *Epit.*, 99–100 ; Strabo, x, 4, 9 ; Diod. Sic., xl, 1 ; Vell., ii, 34, 1–2 ; Plut., *Pomp.*, 29 ; Flor., i, 42, 16 ; App., *Sic.*, 6 ; Eutrop., vi, 11.

67 B.C. of achieving distinction greater than any which he ha :
yet won ; for a faction in Rome had been intriguing t
deprive Lucullus of his command. Pompey therefore
leaving the bulk of his force in Cilicia, proceeded witl
a division to the province of Asia,¹ and there awaitec
events. Honours were conferred upon him by the grateful
inhabitants of commercial towns : a statue was erected
in the island of Delos ; in Syria the citizens of Pompeiopolis and Alexandria introduced a new era to date from
the year of their deliverance.²

It is now time to trace the course of the Third Mithradatic War. It will be remembered that the agreement
which Sulla had made with Mithradates was not expected
to last ; for Sulla, who was obliged to hasten back to
Italy, had been content to gain his immediate object.
The province of Asia was not secured against attack ;
the kings of Bithynia and Cappadocia were defenceless ;

Mithradates prepares to renew war with Rome.
83–81 B.C.

and Mithradates, whose resources were still great, was
left free to prepare for another war. In the three years
that followed the settlement the Governor of Asia had
made a series of wanton raids into his territory ; and
although Mithradates twice asked that the agreement
should be confirmed by a written treaty, the Senate
ignored his request, and on the second occasion did not
even observe the formality of granting his ambassadors
an audience³ ; he hated Rome as relentlessly as ever ;
and if he was not a great captain, he was a great organizer
of war. Everything favoured his enterprise. Sertorius
was detaining two large Roman armies in Spain. The
pirates of Cilicia were friendly.⁴ The mountaineers who
dwelt between the Aegean and the Danube were harassing
the province of Macedonia ⁵ ; and it seems probable that
they were hounded on by Mithradates. He had conquered
the kingdom of Bosporus ; and he persuaded his son-in-

---

¹ See pp. 426–7.
² W. Dittenberger, *Syll. inscr. Graec.*, i², 1898, No. 336 ; B. V. Head, *Hist. num.*², 1911, p. 716.
³ Cic., *De imp. Cn. Pomp.*, 3, 8 ; App., *Mithr.*, 64–7
⁴ Plut., *Pomp.*, 24, 1.
⁵ See p. 188.

law, Tigranes, the King of Armenia, to invade Cappa- 75 B.C.
docia. While his envoys were negotiating with Sertorius
he was completing his preparations. He collected three
million bushels of grain and stored it in dépôts on the
southern coast of the Black Sea. He raised more than
a hundred thousand men in his own country, in Armenia,
in Cappadocia, in the Crimea, and even in the valley of
the Danube, arming them with Roman swords and
shields and drilling them in the Roman fashion ; and he
could dispose of four hundred ships of war.[1] A pretext
had already presented itself. In 75 B.C. Nicomedes
Philopator, the King of Bithynia, died, and, as it was
said, bequeathed his kingdom to the Roman People.[2] Alleged
Mithradates, who affirmed that Nicomedes had left a son,[3] bequest
may well have surmised that the bequest was a forgery ; Bithynia
for the possession of Bithynia was essential to the Romans to the
if they intended to attack him. But certain individuals, People.
whose expenses we may suppose to have been paid by
the Roman Government, travelled from Bithynia to
Rome in order to testify that the young pretender was
a suppositious child [4] ; and their evidence was of course
accepted. Bithynia, which had already been occupied in
the interest of Rome by Ariobarzanes,[5] the King of
Cappadocia, was declared a Roman province ; and the
Roman tax-collectors made themselves so odious to the
natives that they were ready to welcome Mithradates.[6]
He could count upon the fidelity of the Greek colonies
on the Euxine, for they had thriven under his rule, and
they were not disposed to exchange it for Roman administration [7] : the burgesses of Heraclea indeed massacred

[1] Memnon, 37 ; Plut., *Luc.*, 7, 5 ; App., *Mithr.*, 67, 69. Kromayer
(*Philol.*, lvi, 1897, pp. 474-7) endeavours to prove that the ancient writers
exaggerated the size of the Pontic fleet ; but it seems to me probable that
various small craft and perhaps also ships employed in remoter parts of the
Black Sea, which may not have taken part in the recorded battles, were
included in the estimate.
[2] See p. 398. [3] Sall., iv, 69, 9. [4] *Ib.*, ii, 71
[5] *Schol. Gronov.*, ed. Stangl, p. 316 (ed. Orelli, p. 437).
[6] Plut., *Luc.*, 7, 5.
[7] See Th. Reinach, *Mithr. Eupator*, 1890, pp. 247-8, 348, and D. M.
Robinson, *Sinope*, 1906, p. 252.

the Roman tax-collectors as soon as they arrived.¹ In the spring of 74 ² Mithradates reviewed his fleet; offered sacrifice to Zeus Stratios, the god of battles, in the temple, the ruins of which are still standing, at Amasia ³; and, sending a detachment into Cappadocia to intercept the Romans if they invaded Pontus, marched through Cappadocia against Bithynia. The Roman residents—tax-gatherers, bankers, money-lenders, and officials—hearing that the King had crossed the frontier, hurried to take refuge in Calchedon, by the southern entrance of the Bosporus.⁴ The consuls, Lucius Licinius Lucullus and Marcus Aurelius Cotta, were instantly dispatched to the theatre of war ⁵. It was about the same time that Marcus Antonius was sent to support them by attacking the pirates of the Eastern Mediterranean; but, as the foregoing narrative has shown, he ignominiously failed.

Lucullus and Cotta dispatched to the theatre of war.

The manner in which Lucullus obtained the command, on which his heart had long been set, throws light upon the working of the senatorial government. The provinces originally assigned to the consuls were Cisalpine Gaul and Bithynia: the lot gave the latter to Cotta and the former to Lucullus. In the early spring of 74 the Governor of Cilicia died, and many consulars were anxious to succeed him; for Cilicia was conterminous with Cappadocia, and whoever held it would be in a position to act against the Pontic King. Everybody knew that the senator whose influence it was essential to obtain was the notorious Cethegus, the typical wire-puller of the later Republic, who had obtained for Antonius his command against the pirates; and Cethegus was himself under the influence of a beautiful courtesan, named Precia. Lucullus had often attacked Cethegus, whom he detested as an insolent demagogue; but, being a man of the world, he paid his court to Precia, giving her costly

How Lucullus obtained his command.

---

¹ Memnon, 38, 3.
² For the chronology of the war see pp. 398–403.
³ F. and E. Cumont, *Studia Pontica*, ii, 1906, p. 171, n. 4. See the photograph on p. 174.
⁴ Memnon, 37; App., *Mithr.*, 70–1; Eutrop., vi, 6.
⁵ See pp 398–403.

presents, whose value he enhanced by graceful compliments; and, flattered by the attentions of the polished aristocrat, she persuaded her lover to support him. The province of Cilicia, to which Asia was presently added, was assigned to Lucullus, and with it the command of the expeditionary force.[1] He had originally intended to march from Cilicia through Cappadocia against Pontus; but the news that Bithynia was invaded and that Asia was in peril compelled him to change his plan.[2]

Lucullus, who had served under Sulla in the Social War and against Mithradates, and had so won his confidence that he appointed him guardian of his son, was a cultivated noble of luxurious tastes, a distinguished speaker, and a devoted student of Greek literature. He had shown administrative ability in collecting ships of war from the Greek allies of Rome, and, commissioned by Sulla to collect the indemnity which he demanded from the province of Asia, he had endeared himself to the inhabitants by the considerate manner in which he discharged this duty.[3] He had not yet had an opportunity of showing that he could command an army; but he must have learned much from Sulla, and on his outward journey he spent his time in studying military history and questioning experienced officers who travelled with him.[4] His force was comparatively small, and the ancient historians, who apparently assumed that each of his legions was at its full strength, perhaps exaggerated when they reckoned his infantry at thirty thousand men.[5]

<small>His character and antecedents</small>

<small>His army.</small>

---

[1] Plut., *Luc.*, 6, 1–6. Cf. Cic., *Parad.*, v, 3, 40. G. Ferrero (*Grandezza e decadenza di Roma*, ii, 1902, p. 537 [Eng. tr., ii, 327]) insists that Lucullus had no authority in the province of Asia at the beginning of the war; but Velleius (ii, 33, 1) expressly says that he had, and none of the other authorities (Cic., *Pro Flac.*, 34, 85; Memnon, 37; Plut., *Luc.*, 7, 1; App., *Mithr.*, 72, 83) says anything which discredits his statement. Cf. L. Lange, *Röm. Alt.*, iii, 1871, p. 201, and Th. Mommsen, *Röm. Gesch.*, iii⁸, 1889, p. 56 (Eng. tr., iv, 1908, p. 324).

[2] See pp. 403–4.   [3] Plut., *Luc.*, 1, 6–8; 2, 1. 3; 3, 2–4; 4, 2.

[4] Cic., *Acad. prior.*, ii, 1, 2.

[5] Plutarch (*Luc.*, 8, 6) and Appian (*Mithr.*, 72), according to whom Lucullus had 30,000 infantry, presumably multiplied the number of his legions by 6,000—the full complement of one legion; but the four which he

74 B.C.

His strategical plans.

Disaster at Calchedon.

Mithradates resolves to besiege Cyzicus.

Four legions with sixteen hundred or, according to Plutarch, two thousand five hundred cavalry were already in Asia, and Lucullus was accompanied by one legion, which had only just been raised.[1] The four veteran legions, two of which had served under Servilius Isauricus and the others under the notorious Fimbria, had become demoralized by living idly at free quarters; and before Lucullus could take the field it was necessary to restore discipline, which he did with a vigorous hand.[2] His plan was that Cotta should hold in check the fleet of Mithradates, while he himself attacked by land. Cotta was therefore ordered to station his fleet at Calchedon, while Lucullus marched through Phrygia with the intention of invading Pontus. He had not advanced far when he was recalled by the news that Mithradates had made a rapid march westward, attacked Cotta, and forced him to take refuge behind the walls of Calchedon. Sixty-four Roman ships had been captured or burnt, and Cotta had lost three thousand men.[3] Mithradates, hearing that Lucullus was approaching, left Calchedon, which he had begun to besiege, and marched south-westward against the fortress of Cyzicus, situated on an island off the southern shore of the Sea of Marmara.[4] He apparently believed that if he could capture this stronghold, which Cicero called the gate of Asia, the whole province would lie at his mercy; and, moreover, he was eager to punish the Cyzicenes, who had assisted Cotta in the late battle.[5] Probably he counted upon receiving some assistance from the Greek communities on the western shore of the Black Sea; he hoped to incite the provincials against their Roman masters; and Marius, a Roman renegade whom Sertorius found in Asia must have fallen far below their ideal strength unless fresh drafts had been sent to reinforce them.

[1] Plut., *Luc.*, 7, 1; 8, 6; App., *Mithr.*, 72. Cf. *Klio*, x, 1910, p. 77.
[2] Sall., iii, 19; Plut., *Luc.*, 7, 1-3. Cf. W. Drumann's *Gesch. Roms*, iv², 1908, p. 149, n. 9.
[3] Memnon, 37; 39; Plut., *Luc.*, 8, 1-4; App., *Mithr.*, 71; Oros., vi, 2, 13. See pp. 403-4.
[4] Sall., iii, 26-7; Plut., *Luc.*, 9, 1; *C. I. L.*, i, p. 292 (= H. Dessau, *Inscr. Lat.*, 60).
[5] Cic., *Pro Mur.*, 15, 33.

had sent to join him, promised self-government and freedom from taxation to townships which would side with the invader. Some were inclined to accept the offer when Gaius Caesar, who had crossed from Rhodes on the outbreak of the war, raised a corps of volunteers, expelled the deputy of Mithradates, and induced the waverers to stand fast.[1] Followed by Lucullus, who hung upon his rear, engaging successfully in occasional skirmishes, Mithradates encamped opposite Cyzicus,[2] which was connected by a bridge with the mainland.[3]

74 B.C.

Caesar's coup in Asia.

Lucullus presently arrived. After reconnoitring the country he paraded his men and told them that they should see the huge host of Mithradates beaten, and not a drop of their blood should fall. Close to the King's encampment was an eminence which commanded the country in his rear. Taking advantage of his negligence, Lucullus seized this position, which he fortified, thus preventing the enemy from getting supplies except by sea. Mithradates, however, persevered. He stationed ships to guard the strait which separated Cyzicus from the mainland, occupied a suburb immediately south of the bridge, and then, crossing over, took possession of a hill which dominated the city on the north. After these preliminaries he proceeded, doubtless with the help of Roman renegades who had long been associated with him or of Greek engineers, to undertake a regular siege, encompassing the town and the harbours with earthworks, and assailing the walls with artillery and battering rams. As there was no sign of surrender he brought three thousand Cyzicene prisoners, who had been captured at Calchedon, in ships close up to the wall, hoping that pity for their threatened doom would move the garrison to yield. The prisoners with outstretched hands appealed

Lucullus outmanœuvres Mithradates.

---

[1] Plut., *Sert.*, 24, 2–3 ; Suet., *Div. Iul.*, 4, 2.
[2] Plut., *Luc.*, 9, 1–2 ; App., *Mithr.*, 72 ; Livy *Epit.*, 94. See pp. 403–4.
[3] Groebe (W. Drumann's *Gesch. Roms*, iv², 144, n. 14) points out that Frontinus (*Strat.*, iii, 13, 6), evidently following Sallust (iii, 30—*Unde pons in oppidum pertinens explicatur*), mentions only one bridge, though in the time of Strabo (xii, 8, 11) there were two. Cf. F. W. Hasluck, *Cyzicus*, 1910, p. 3.

to their fellow citizens for sympathy; but the commander bade his crier tell them that they must face death like men. Lucullus was powerless to attack the besieging force, but, foreseeing that it must ultimately succumb to famine, he entrusted a letter of encouragement to a private soldier, who crossed the sea on inflated skins and succeeded in entering the city; while he also contrived to send some legionaries in a vessel to join the garrison. When Mithradates endeavoured by means of a wooden tower, mounted on two galleys lashed together, to push a flying-bridge on to the wall, the defenders poured boiling pitch on to the ships. They broke the impact of the rams by hanging bales of wool from the wall, or seized the heads with nooses, or smashed them by dropping heavy stones. Winter had now set in. The King's ships could no longer keep his army supplied; many perished from hunger; and famine was aggravated by pestilence. He sent away some of his troops with the starving horses; but a Roman detachment overtook them while they were fording the Rhyndacus and captured all who escaped the sword. Even now Mithradates persisted; but the garrison, knowing the condition of his army, made frequent sallies, undermined the earthworks, and burned the engines; and early in the following year he was forced to abandon the siege.[1] Retreat towards Bithynia was barred. Part of the fugitives took the road for Lampsacus, some seventy miles westward, and those who were not slaughtered on the banks of the Aesepus or drowned in attempting to cross made good their escape.[2] The rest crowded tumultuously on board the ships, some of which capsized, and while the survivors sailed to Parium, hoping to rescue those who might have survived the rout, the Cyzicenes slaughtered the sick who had been left behind and pillaged the deserted

---

[1] Cic., *De imp. Cn. Pomp.*, 8, 20; *Pro Mur.*, 15, 33; *Pro Arch.*, 9, 21; Sall., iii, 19 D, 34, 38; Livy, *Epit.*, 95; Strabo, xii, 8, 11; Memnon, 40, 3; Plut., *Luc.*, 9–11; Frontin., *Strat.*, iii, 13, 6; iv, 5, 21; Flor., i, 40, 15–6; App., *Mithr.*, 72–6; Oros., vi, 2, 14–5. 19.

[2] According to Florus (i, 40, 17), Lucullus beat the fugitives on the Aesepus and again on the Granicus.

camp. From Parium Mithradates dispatched a squadron to Lampsacus, which succeeded in embarking the remnant of the fugitives; and, sending fifty ships under Marius into the Aegean, he crossed the Propontis in the hope of capturing Perinthus on the northern shore, where he would be within reach of his European allies, and whence he might threaten the flank of the Romans if they invaded Pontus; but his attempt was frustrated, and he was compelled to fall back upon Nicomedia, the capital of Bithynia.[1] *73 B.C.* *Mithradates, compelled to raise the siege, retreats to Nicomedia.*

When Mithradates attacked Cyzicus in the presence of the Roman general, he committed one of those errors which Fortune does not forgive; and Lucullus took instant steps to complete his overthrow. The Senate had offered him three thousand talents to build a fleet; but he assured them that he would drive the enemy from the sea with the ships of the allied communities alone.[2] Sending three of his lieutenants—Valerius Triarius, Barba, and Voconius—to secure Bithynia, he sailed himself with a fleet furnished by the province of Asia to destroy the Aegean squadron. Myrlea, Prusa, Cius, and Nicaea, the chief towns of Western Bithynia, were successively captured; Mithradates, hearing that Lucullus had routed his fleet, first off Tenedos and then near Lemnos, embarked at Nicomedia with the remnant of his army and, owing to the negligence of Voconius, who arrived too late to blockade the port, thus losing the opportunity of ending the war, sailed through the Bosporus under the eyes of Cotta and, though many of his ships were wrecked in a storm and he owed his own escape to a pirate named Seleucus, made his way along the shore of Bithynia to the independent seaport of Heraclea. Exhorting the Greek citizens to be true to him and reinforcing his exhortations by gifts of money, he left four thousand men to defend the town.[3] [£720,000.] *While Lucullus destroys his fleet he escapes to Heraclea*

[1] Memnon, 40, 3; Plut., *Luc.*, 11, 8; App., *Mithr.*, 76; Oros, vi, 2, 20.
[2] Plut., *Luc.*, 13, 4. The date is uncertain. Kromayer (*Philol.*, 1897, p. 474) fixes it after the time when Mithradates arrived at Heraclea. *I* infer from Plutarch's account that it was earlier. Cf. Th. Mommsen, *Röm. Gesch.*, iii², 1889, p. 57 (Eng. tr., iv, 1908, pp. 324–5).
[3] Cic., *De imp. Cn. Pomp.*, 8, 21; *Pro Mur.*, 15, 33; *Pro Arch.*, 9, 21; Sall., iii, 54; iv, 69, 14; Strabo, xii, 3, 6; Memnon, 41–2; Plut., *Luc.*,

73 B.C.
Lucullus
invades
Pontus.

Meanwhile Lucullus, who had joined Triarius and Cotta at Nicomedia, was preparing to invade Pontus. In order to secure his rear, he sent Cotta to besiege Heraclea, while Triarius, who was charged to prevent the ships which Mithradates still had in the Aegean from passing through the Hellespont, encountered them near Tenedos and gained a decisive victory.[1] The maritime power of Mithradates was wellnigh destroyed; but he resolved to make a stand at Cabira (the modern Niksar), where he had contrived to assemble forty thousand foot and four thousand horse.[2] If he could be expelled from this fortress, it would remain only to reduce the ports on the Black Sea, and he would be completely subdued. Lucullus, hoping to crush him before Tigranes could come to his relief, advanced through Bithynia into Galatia.[3] Thirty thousand Galatian porters, whom he had pressed into his service, carried his supplies. Invading Pontus by way of the Chiliokomon, between the Halys and the Lycus, he struck northward and began by laying siege to the commercial port of Amisus, hard by the site of the modern Samsoun. In order to elucidate the campaign which followed, it will be necessary to describe the country which lay between the Roman army and Cabira.

Amisus stood upon the seaward end, still covered with its ruins, of the headland north of the modern city, which gave shelter to the roadstead where ships from many ports found anchorage. Its situation, on the Euxine and between the two great Pontic rivers, had attracted numerous settlers and given rise to a prosperity which is attested not only by the words of Strabo, but also by numerous works of art and a marvellous variety of coins. Between Amastris, or Amasra, on the far west and Trapezus (Trebizond) on the far east it commanded the one opening in the mountain range which, steeply

12, 3-7; 13; Flor., i, 40, 18; App., *Mithr.*, 77-8. Appian and Orosius (vi, 2, 24) incorrectly say that after the storm Mithradates fled to Sinope and thence to Amisus.

[1] Memnon, 47. 1, 48. Cf. *Bull. de corr. hell.*, xi, 1887, pp. 265-7.
[2] App., *Mithr.*, 78.
[3] The evidence for the campaign of Cabira is examined on pp. 404-8.

overhanging the sea, severs the seaboard from the interior of Pontus; the one great road that runs from north to south connected it with Amasia, the inland capital, and was itself crossed by the great trunk road that led from Bosporus through Cabira to the Euphrates.[1] Amisus was the commercial capital of Pontus, as Sinope was its naval arsenal. Eastward of Amisus and watered by the Iris, stretched the fertile plain of Themiscyra, south of which and linked to it by the valley, but separated from it by a range of hills, lay another and higher plain, called Phanaroea. This higher terrace, forty miles long and four or five miles broad, through which the Lycus flows to join the Iris, is divided into an upper and a lower basin by hilly country which rises between Herek and Niksar. It has been called by a modern traveller [2] 'the heart of the whole kingdom'. About the middle of the lower and western basin, the Iris, rushing out of a rocky gorge, mingles its turbid waters with the Lycus.[3] On a knoll near the right bank of the Iris and just below the confluence stood a newly founded fortress, still incomplete, called Eupatoria, commanding the southern end of the pass of which the northern was guarded by Themiscyra, and dominating the bridge by which the great trunk road was carried across the stream. From Eupatoria the road extended over the level expanse of Phanaroea between the right bank of the Lycus and the Paryadres mountains and, crossing the hills which broke the continuity of the plain, and from which a branch road led across the river to Amasia, ran on again over level ground to Cabira.[4] Cabira itself stood upon a spur which projects from the Paryadres into the plain, on the northern bank of the Lycus.[5]

Throughout the winter the besiegers of Amisus could make no way, for Mithradates contrived to send supplies 73-72 B.C.

---

[1] *Journ. Hellen. Studies*, xxi, 1901, pp. 52-3; *Studia Pontica*, ii, 1906, pp. 112, 116-7; iii, 1910, p. 1.
[2] Mr. J. A. R. Munro.
[3] *Journ. Hellen. Studies*, 1901, pp. 53-4.   [4] *Ib.*, p. 57.
[5] W. J. Hamilton, *Researches in Asia Minor*, &c., i. 1842, pp. 346-7; *Royal Geogr. Soc. Suppl. Papers*, iii, 1893, p. 732; *Studia Pontica*, ii, 259-62.

72 B.C and reinforcements to the garrison. Lucullus saw that this support must be cut off, and also that before he could attack Cabira it would be necessary, in order to force

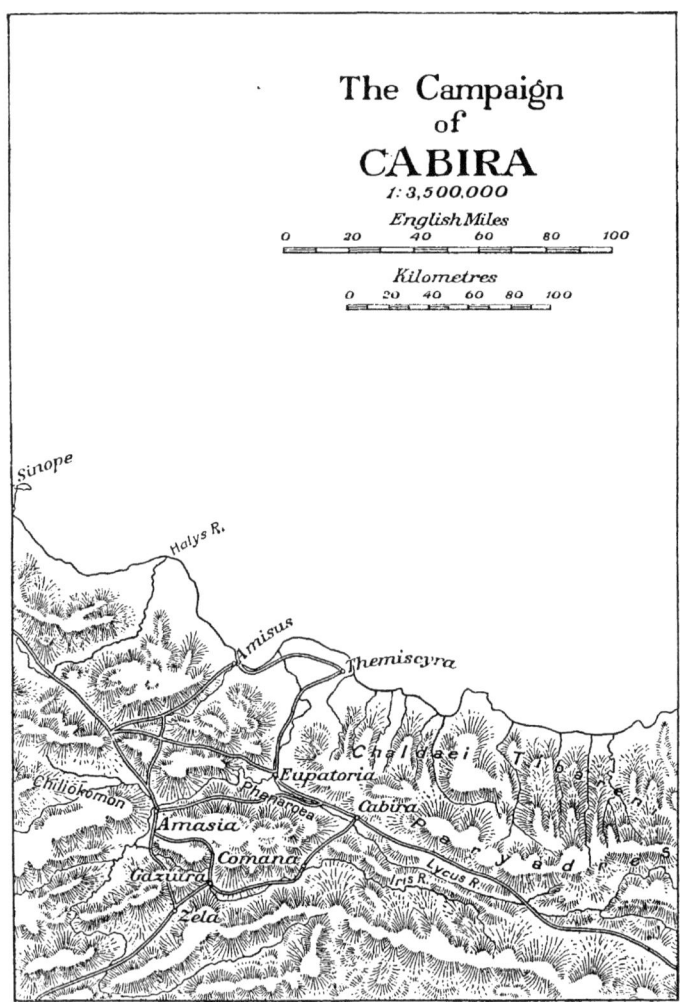

his way into the plain of Phanaroea, to capture Themiscyra and Eupatoria. Leaving one of his officers, Licinius Murena, to carry on the siege, he marched eastward with three legions in the early spring, got possession of Themiscyra and Eupatoria—the latter, by voluntary surrender—

and, gaining the great trunk road, turned eastward towards Cabira. Mithradates did not wait to be attacked. With his powerful cavalry he advanced over the hilly country, crossed the Lycus by the branch road, and menaced the flank of his opponents. The Roman cavalry forded the river, but in the ensuing combat they were worsted; and Lucullus, severed from his base and forced to quit the plain, took refuge in the hills. Guided by a native prisoner, he made his way over the crest of the ridge to a position, defended by a ravine, where he could block the road to Cabira and threaten the bridge by which Mithradates had crossed the Lycus. Mithradates, finding that his own communications were endangered, fell backward along the left bank and encamped opposite the Roman army. Lucullus could not advance, for his supplies were running out and the fertile plain was still closed to him by the Pontic horsemen. The friendly Cappadocians would supply him; but to fetch corn from them his foragers must cross the road commanded by the enemy. A convoy, guarded by ten cohorts under an officer named Sornatius, got through the pass which leads from Herek to Comana Pontica and beat off the force which Mithradates sent against it. When a second convoy started under Fabius Hadrianus, Mithradates sent the flower of his cavalry to await its return. The Pontic commander entered the pass, where his horsemen could not act, instead of charging the vanguard as it debouched, and was routed with heavy loss. Mithradates, on hearing of this reverse, determined to retreat and, fearing for the honour of his women, gave orders that his unmarried sisters, his wives and concubines should be put to death. His pursuers were on the point of seizing him when one of his mules, loaded with bullion, was caught, and while the Roman soldiers were plundering and quarrelling the King escaped and made his way to Comana, whence he fled to join Tigranes.[1] Lucullus, after subduing the Chaldaei and the Tibareni, two

72 B.C.

Mithradates forced to take refuge in Armenia.

[1] Cic., *De imp. Cn. Pomp.*, 9, 22; Plut., *Luc.*, 17, 5-7; 18, 2-3; 19, 1; App., *Mithr.*, 82.

188 POMPEY THE GREAT CHAP.

72 B.C.
Lucullus
captures
Cabira
and
Amisus
and
returns
to the
province
of Asia.

of the Pontic tribes, taking Cabira, and receiving the surrender of other forts, returned to Amisus, which he captured by assault, and the surviving inhabitants of which, although he could not at first restrain his troops from pillage and massacre, he treated with clemency, providing clothes for the Athenian settlers and sending them home with money for their journey. Then, leaving Cotta and Triarius to reduce the great coastal towns, he returned to the province of Asia, the affairs of which demanded his attention.[1]

His
brother
supports
him by a
successful
campaign
in Thrace.

By this time Marcus Lucullus, the proconsul whose return intimidated Spartacus,[2] operating in support of his brother but in a distant theatre, had succeeded in cutting off Mithradates from European aid. In order to understand how this result was achieved, we must revert to the period of Sulla's death. The province of Macedonia had long been exposed to raids from barbarous tribes which inhabited Illyricum on one side and on the other the region between the Lower Danube and the Aegean Sea. While Lepidus was disturbing Italy and Sertorius fighting in Spain, while Spartacus was routing consular armies and Mithradates was overrunning Bithynia, while pirates were plundering the vessels that carried corn for Rome, the distracted Senate were compelled to dispatch one force after another for the protection of the Macedonian frontier. Cosconius punished Illyricum.[3] Scribonius Curio[4] attacked the raiders whom Appius Claudius had already attempted to subdue[5]; but although he chastised the Dardani north of Macedonia and even penetrated as far as the Danube, his victories were not decisive. At last, however, Marcus Lucullus defeated the Thracians who dwelt in what is now Bulgaria, captured their fastnesses; subdued Moesia as he advanced across

[Prob.
78 B.C.]
[75-74
B.C.]

---

[1] Cic., *De imp. Cn. Pomp.*, 9, 22; Sall., iv, 12, 14–5; Strabo, xii, 3, 33; Memnon, 45; Plut., *Luc.*, 18, 1; 19, 2–9; 20, 1; App., *Mithr.*, 83.
[2] See p. 160.
[3] Eutrop., vi, 4; Oros., v, 23, 23. Cf. Maurenbrecher, *op. cit.*, i, 71.
[4] Sall., ii, 80; Livy, *Epit.*, 92; Oros, v, 23, 20. Cf. Maurenbrecher, i, 70; ii, 124.
[5] Livy, *Epit.*, 91; Flor., i, 39, 6–7; Eutrop., vi, 2; Oros., v, 23, 17–9.

the Balkans to the Danube, and, being resolved to stop 72 B.C. aggression by a terrible example, cut off the hands of his prisoners and then turned them loose. Moving eastward against the maritime tribes, he destroyed Apollonia and took five other Greek cities on the western shore of the Black Sea.[1] The effect of his campaign, the latter part of which one is tempted to attribute to the inspiration of his brother, was to prevent the Thracians and the European Greeks from reinforcing the Pontic King.

Lucullus was welcomed as a deliverer in Asia. The provincials, loaded with debt in consequence of the huge indemnity which Sulla had compelled them to pay, were suffering from the extortion of Roman tax-gatherers and Roman money-lenders, and many were obliged to sell their children as slaves in order to find the money. Lucullus, who had befriended them in Sulla's time, forbade the creditors to exact more than a third of the amount due, and, as usurers in the provinces demanded higher interest than the law allowed in Italy, fixed the rate at the Italian maximum of twelve per cent. The grateful provincials instituted a yearly festival in his honour[2]; the exasperated money-lenders bribed politicians at Rome to denounce him and exerted all their influence to wreck his reputation.

Lucullus by checking Roman extortion incurs enmity in Rome.

Meanwhile Lucullus had sent his brother-in-law, Appius Claudius,[3] to demand the surrender of Mithradates. Tigranes was then in Syria, engaged in subduing certain Phoenician towns. Appius, waiting for him at Antioch, spent the time in conciliating various chieftains, who chafed under Armenian rule, and encouraging them to resist. Before Tigranes began to reign Armenia had 95 B.C. suffered great losses from the Parthians; but since then he had not only recovered all that had been lost, but had also conquered Media, Northern Mesopotamia, and Syria, established his footing in Cappadocia and Cilicia,

---

[1] Sall., iv, 18; Livy, *Epit.*, 97; Strabo, fr. 79; Pliny, xxxiv, 7 (8), 39; Flor., i, 39, 6–7; App., *Ill.*, 30; Rufus Festus, 9, 2; Eutrop., vi, 7; Amm. Marc., xxix, 5, 22; Oros., vi, 3, 4. Cf. Maurenbrecher, ii, 124.
[2] Cic., *Acad. prior.*, ii, 1, 3; Plut., *Luc.*, 20; 23, 1; App., *Mithr.*, 83. See pp. 395–6.   [3] Not the one mentioned on p. 188.

and forced the Iberians and Albanians on the north to acknowledge his hegemony. His dominions now extended from the Caucasus to Palestine and from Mount Taurus to the farthest boundary of Media. Vassal kings waited on him at table and ran by his side when he rode: he had founded a great city, which he called Tigranocerta —'the city of Tigranes'—and he had assumed the title of King of Kings. Appius, who was not intimidated by the pomp of the court, delivered a written ultimatum from Lucullus :—Tigranes must surrender Mithradates; otherwise Lucullus would attack him. Tigranes, says Plutarch, was disconcerted by the first free speech which he had heard for five-and-twenty years; but he refused to betray his father-in-law and said that he was prepared for war.[1] He now sent for Mithradates, whom he had hitherto refused to see; and the two kings concerted their plans. It was agreed that Mithradates with ten thousand men, apparently subjects of Tigranes, should return to Pontus;[2] but Tigranes, whether from overconfidence or from sheer ineptitude, neglected to utilize the time that would elapse before Lucullus could arrive in preparing to repel invasion.

Tigranes refuses to surrender Mithradates.

Early in 69 Lucullus quitted Ephesus, where he had passed the winter, and rejoined the force which he had detached to besiege Sinope. The Heracleots, resisting desperately even after the fleet of Triarius prevented supplies from reaching them, even after famine was followed by pestilence, had been betrayed by treacherous officers after a two years' siege; and the fall of Heraclea was followed by that of Tieum and Amastris.[3] Sinope still held out, and when Lucullus arrived, he found that

Fall of Heraclea.

70 B.C.

---

[1] Sall., iv, 56; Pliny, vi, 28 (32), 142; Strabo, xvi, 2, 3; Memnon, 46, 2; Plut., *Luc.*, 21; 23, 1; Jos., *Bell. Iud.*, i, 6, 3; App., *Syr.*, 48, 69; *Mithr.*, 105. Groebe (Drumann's *Gesch. Roms*, ii², 1902, p. 173, n. 4) thinks it unlikely that both Appius Claudius and Publius Clodius accompanied Lucullus, and accordingly he identifies Appius with Clodius, although Plutarch differentiates them. *I* agree with Munzer (*Paulys Real-Ency.*, iii, 2849 (297)) and Fröhlich (*ib.*, iv, 82) that there is no reason to distrust Plutarch.

[2] Memnon, 55; Plut., *Luc.*, 22, 1-2.

[3] Memnon, 47-52; App., *Mithr.*, 82.

a fleet, laden with corn for the besieging army, had been 69 B.C.
captured by Seleucus, who had rescued Mithradates from
shipwreck two years before. Cleochares, the commander
of the garrison, determined to resist to the last, but was
opposed by Seleucus, who now, foreseeing the inevitable
end, hoped to make his fortune by betraying the town.
When Lucullus, reinforced by the troops of Cotta, who
had returned to Rome, was about to prosecute the siege,
Machares, the King of Bosporus, a son of Mithradates,
sent envoys with an offer of alliance. Lucullus accepted
the offer on the condition that Machares should refrain
from assisting Sinope ; and Machares not only agreed,
but sent supplies to the Roman camp. Cleochares and
Seleucus, seeing that resistance was hopeless, sailed away, Lucullus
and Sinope was soon taken by assault. Lucullus, though Sinope.
he could not wholly restrain the passions of his troops,
treated the inhabitants humanely, and, moved by the
sympathy which he always felt for the Greek settlers in
Asia Minor, granted freedom to the city, as he had done
already to Amisus. He saw that by generous treatment His
the Greek colonies might be converted into bulwarks of humane
the Roman power and serve as centres of culture to pre- of Greek
pare the Asiatics for Roman government. Through his colonies.
influence Cyzicus was rewarded by an extension of its
domain ; the Heracleots recovered their territory ; the
outlying possessions of Sinope and Amisus were enlarged.[1]

The conquest of Pontus was complete ; but Lucullus
did not feel that he had done enough. It was rumoured
that Mithradates and Tigranes were about to make an
incursion into Cilicia.[2] So long as the King of Kings was
undefeated Roman dominion in the East would be
insecure. Lucullus, therefore, notwithstanding the small-
ness of his force, resolved to invade Armenia and there
to bring the war to a decisive termination. His troops

[1] Livy, *Epit.*, 98 ; Strabo, xii, 3, 11 ; 8, 11 ; Memnon, 53–4 ; Plut., *Luc.*, 23, 2–3 ; 24, 1 ; Tac., *Ann.*, iv, 36 ; App., *Mithr.*, 83 ; Oros., vi, 3, 2–3. According to Appian, whose chronology is often confused, Lucullus captured Sinope and received the alliance of Machares before he returned to the province Asia !
[2] Plut., *Luc.*, 23, 7.

69 B.C.
His campaign against Tigranes.

were reluctant to follow him into the remote eastern land which no Roman army had yet penetrated, and perhaps he already knew that tribunes at Rome were endeavouring to excite public opinion against him; but he pursued his preparations unmoved. Leaving Sornatius with six thousand men to hold Pontus, he set out with eighteen thousand legionaries, three thousand cavalry, including some Thracian and Galatian mercenaries, and one thousand archers and slingers against Tigranes.[1]

Marching rapidly through Cappadocia, he received supplies from Ariobarzanes, who in the course of the winter had built a flotilla of small craft for the passage of the Euphrates,[2] and moving down the road which leads past Melitene, came to the river at Tomisa; but, as the current, swollen by the melting of the snow, was dangerously strong, the boats proved insufficient, and it was necessary to collect barges and to construct rafts. Lucullus now found himself in the Armenian province of Sophene, the inhabitants of which, conciliated by the forbearance of his disciplined troops, furnished him with grain, and, advancing south-eastward by way of Arghana and Amida (now Diarbekr), he crossed the western tributaries of the Tigris and pushed on towards Tigranocerta.[3] Hitherto Tigranes had been kept in ignorance of his approach. The first messenger who brought the news was beheaded. A courtier, named Mithrobarzanes, ventured notwithstanding to tell the King the truth, whereupon he was himself dispatched at the head of an army with orders to bring back Lucullus alive; but, attacking a detachment which Lucullus sent to watch his movements, he was defeated and killed. Tigranes now left Tigranocerta in charge of a Greek officer, and moved northward across the Masian range to collect fresh troops. Two of Lucullus's lieutenants, Sextilius and Murena, destroyed various bands as they were marching to join him; and Tigranes

[1] Plut., *Luc.*, 24, 1; Sall., iv, 58. See pp. 408–9.
[2] Sall., iv, 59.
[3] Strabo, xii, 2, 1; Memnon, 56, 1; Plut., *Luc.*, 24, 2–8; Tac., *Ann.*, xv, 26–7.

himself, as he was threading a defile, was deprived of all 69 B.C. his baggage. Lucullus, wishing to provoke him to fight and thus to avoid the labour of following him through the mountains, laid siege to his capital.[1]

Tigranocerta, situated in the plain, below the Pass of Siege of Mardin and some forty miles west of Nisibis, was pro- Tigranocerta. tected by walls seventy-five feet high, and partly surrounded by a river.[2] Sextilius, who directed the operations of the besiegers, constructed embankments of logs compacted with earth, carrying battering rams screened by sappers' huts as well as wooden towers which bore artillery destined to play upon the defenders, and also sunk galleries with the object of undermining the wall: but the working parties were harassed by frequent sallies; the garrison, setting fire to the woodwork, discharged naphtha to feed the flames; and, as the besiegers were too few to invest the fortress, a detachment sent by Tigranes managed to penetrate the lines and to carry off not only his concubines but also the greater part of his treasure.[3]

Meanwhile Tigranes was returning with his levies to relieve Tigranocerta. Mithradates had written, urgently warning him not to attack the Romans, but to utilize his cavalry in cutting off their supplies. But Tigranes, who fancied that his father-in-law was merely envious, allowed himself to be persuaded by his courtiers that he would gain an easy victory.[4] The estimates of his force which the ancient historians found in their authorities vary between three hundred thousand and eighty thousand; at all events it was far larger than the Roman army:[5] but it was a motley host, composed of divers nationalities

[1] Plut., *Luc.*, 25; 26, 1; App., *Mithr.*, 84. Cf. Drumann-Groebe, iv², 160, n. 6.
[2] I must warn the reader that the site of Tigranocerta is still disputed. On pp. 409-25 I give my reasons for the view which I tentatively adopt here.
[3] Sall., iv, 61, 63; Memnon, 56, 2; Plut., *Luc.*, 26, 2-4; App., *Mithr.*, 84-5; Xiphilinus (Melber's ed. of Dio, vol. i, p. 358). Eckhardt (*Klio*, 1910, p. 92) remarks that Lucullus certainly did not, as Memnon (56, 1) states, divide his army, which was already weak, by besieging other Armenian towns. Perhaps Memnon was thinking of the later siege of Nisibis.
[4] Plut., *Luc.*, 26, 5-7. [5] See p. 409.

—Armenians, Arabs, Medes, Albanians, and Iberians—who were not accustomed to act in unison. When the column appeared on the hills above Tigranocerta the garrison, crowding upon the walls, exultantly clapped their hands and pointed significantly in its direction. But Lucullus did not hesitate to encounter it with a fraction of his army. Leaving six thousand men to maintain the siege, he marched with the remainder—fifteen thousand including cavalry, archers, and slingers—and encamped on the western bank of the river. From his camp on the heights Tigranes surveyed the contemptible little army. 'If they are ambassadors,' he said, 'there are too many; if soldiers, too few.' The river made a bend towards the west, and Lucullus moved at daybreak in this direction, knowing that he would find a ford. 'You see', remarked Tigranes to one of his officers, 'those invincible Romans are in full retreat': but when he saw the foremost companies approaching the bank, he realized that he would have to fight and began to form his line. It was the 6th of October, the anniversary of the day on which a Roman army had been annihilated by the Cimbri; and one of Lucullus's lieutenants remarked that it was ominous. 'I', replied Lucullus, 'will make it a lucky day for Rome.'

At the foot of a hill, not far from the ford, the Armenian heavy cavalry were descried in front of the enemy's right wing, armed with spears and clad in coats of mail, even their horses being protected by coverings fringed with chain armour. Lucullus, noticing that his adversary had neglected to occupy the hill, saw instantly how the battle could be won. After crossing the river he ordered his Thracian and Galatian horse to attack the mailed squadrons on their flank, which Tigranes had left exposed, and to beat aside the spears—their only weapons—with their swords. Lucullus himself, while the bulk of his infantry were deploying in front of the enemy, led two cohorts unobserved behind to the summit of the hill. Seeing that the Armenian cavalry, as he had expected, were in disorder, he exclaimed, 'Men, the victory is ours', and told them not to use their javelins, but to close upon the rear of the cavalry and stab their thighs, which were unprotected, with their swords. The cohorts charged down the hill. Smitten from behind by these assailants, harassed on their flank by the Thracians and Galatians, confronted by the main body of the Roman infantry, the cavalry crowded on to their own infantry, and then followed utter rout. Jostling one another in the confined space from which they were struggling to extricate themselves, the Asiatics were slaughtered in thousands; and those who broke away were hunted until the sun went down.[1]

Tigranocerta was speedily captured, the Greek mercenaries who formed part of the garrison helping the besiegers to force an entrance. Lucullus permitted his soldiers to sack the town, and the bullion which had been left behind was so abundant that, after he had appropriated all that belonged to the King, he was able to give three thousand two hundred sesterces (equivalent to more than thirty pounds) to every man. The inhabitants, however, were considerately treated, the Greeks, like those of Sinope, being allowed to return home and supplied with money to defray the cost; and when the report spread that Lucullus had protected women, the Sopheni, the Gordyeni, and other peoples voluntarily submitted.[2] Gordyene contained so much treasure and its granaries were so full that Lucullus supplied his army and defrayed all charges without drawing upon the Roman treasury.[3] Nevertheless his enemies at Rome were as active as ever; and when, towards the end of the year, the news of the victory reached the capital, men asked why he had not instantly pursued Tigranes and made an end of the campaign. Sallust[4] relates that he bribed the demagogue Quinctius to resist any proposal for his supersession; but if the story is true, he underrated the forces that were

69 B.C.

Victory of Lucullus near Tigranocerta.

Tigranocerta captured.

Intrigues in Rome against Lucullus

[1] Sall., iv, 64-5, 67; Memnon, 57, 1-2; Plut., *Luc.*, 27-8; Frontin., *Strat.*, ii, 1, 14; 2, 4; App., *Mithr.*, 85; Oros., vi, 3, 6-7.
[2] Memnon, 57, 3; Plut., *Luc.*, 29, 3-8; App., *Mithr.*, 86; Dio, xxxvi, 2, 3.
[3] Plut., *Luc.*, 29, 10-1.
[4] iv, 71. Cf. Maurenbrecher, *op. cit.*, ii, 186.

69-68 B.C.

Mithradates constrains Tigranes to continue war.

arrayed against him. It was asserted that he was deliberately prolonging the war in order to retain his power, and at the instigation of the knights whose capital was invested with the tax-farming syndicates, the province of Asia was withdrawn from his control.[1]

Meantime Tigranes had been joined by Mithradates,[2] and, if he had ever been inclined to sue for peace, he was soon overborne by that indomitable man. Mithradates would not hear of surrender: he was determined to win back his own kingdom, and he urged his son-in-law to raise a new army, assuring him that all would yet be well. Tigranes acquiesced and left Mithradates a free hand. Mithradates directed the armourers to forge new weapons, ordered a general levy throughout Armenia, instructing his officers to train the recruits in Roman discipline; called upon the princes and the peoples of the East to join him in repelling the Western robbers; and advised Tigranes to purchase the support of Phraates, the Parthian King, by the cession of Mesopotamia. Phraates had already offered to join the Romans; but when Lucullus learned that he was negotiating with Mithradates and Tigranes,[3] he purposed to attack him, and, if we may believe Plutarch,[4] directed Sornatius to advance from Pontus and join the main army in Gordyene. The troops of Sornatius, Plutarch adds, refused to stir; those of Lucullus, who heard of their disobedience, were becoming restive; and accordingly Lucullus, abandoning his purpose, determined to march northward against Tigranes and Mithradates, who were now prepared to take the field.[5]

---

[1] Plut., *Luc.*, 24, 1; Dio, xxxvi, 2, 1-2.

[2] Memnon, 58, 1 (cf. 56, 2); Plut., *Luc.*, 29, 1-2. According to Frontinus (*Strat.*, ii, 1, 14; 2, 4), Appian (*Mithr.*, 85), and Orosius (vi, 3, 6), Mithradates was with Tigranes before and during the battle; but Memnon and Plutarch are evidently right.

[3] According to Memnon (58, 2), Tigranes offered to cede Mesopotamia to Phraates.

[4] *Luc.*, 30, 3-4. One finds it hard to believe that Lucullus would have denuded Pontus of the entire army of occupation, but he may have summoned a part of it

[5] Cic., *De imp. Cn. Pomp.*, 9, 24; Sall., iv, 69; Memnon, 58; Plut, *Luc.*, 30; 31, 1; App., *Mithr.*, 87; Dio, xxxvi, 3.

Another summer had begun before Lucullus was ready to set out. Crossing the mountains west of Lake Van by the Pass of Nardjiki,[1] he found the corn still green, but procured supplies by rifling the dépôts in which Tigranes had stored grain and capturing his convoys. As the kings avoided fighting, he advanced towards Artaxata on the Araxes, where Tigranes had placed his wives and children. The King marched to dispute his passage of the Arsanias, or Murad-Su; but Lucullus forded this river, routed the enemy's cavalry, and pushed on over the highlands which Xenophon and the Ten Thousand had crossed in their retreat. Though the autumnal equinox had not yet passed, the streams were so cold that the horses would not drink; snow fell almost continually; the men lay down at night upon damp ground; and their supplies were beginning to fail. When they remonstrated, Lucullus appealed to them to follow him and destroy Artaxata, the Armenian Carthage, which, he told them, had been built by Hannibal, the bitterest enemy of Rome. They flatly refused to advance. Lucullus therefore reluctantly retreated[2] by a different route,[3] round the eastern shore of Lake Van, to Nisibis, which, as it was still warm in that southern latitude,[4] he immediately besieged. Directed by a Greek engineer, the garrison resisted every attack until the approach of winter, when, believing that Lucullus would be forced to raise the siege, they became less vigilant, and the besiegers, taking advantage of a moonless and clouded night, assaulted the fortress in a thunder-storm and under drenching rain. A great quantity of treasure was found within the town, and there the army wintered.[5]

68 B. C.
Lucullus marches against Artaxata, [Ardas char.]

but is forced by mutiny to retreat.

He captures Nisibis,

---

[1] See *Zeitschr. f. d. Ethnologie*, 1899, p. 255; *Klio*, x, 1910, pp. 203–5; and Lehmann-Haupt, *Armenien einst u. jetzt*, 1910, pp. 327–32.
[2] Plut., *Luc.*, 31; 32, 1–5; Dio, xxxvi, 5; 6, 1; Eutrop., vi, 9.
[3] See *Klio*, 1910, pp. 226–31. Rufus Festus (15, 3) absurdly says that Lucullus returned via Melitene on the Euphrates.
[4] See p. 425.
[5] Sall., iv, 79–80; Plut., *Luc.*, 32, 6–8; Dio, xxxvi, 6, 2–3; 7; Eutrop., vi, 9; Oros., vi, 3, 7.

68-67 B.C. The career of Lucullus was drawing near its end. Marcius Rex, one of the consuls, had been appointed to supersede him as Governor of Cilicia. His troubles were aggravated by emissaries from his enemies in Rome and by his own brother-in-law, Publius Clodius, who reminded the mutinous troops that while they were worn with toil and hardship and got little booty, the general's wagons and camels were loaded with gold and precious stones.[1] Meantime the little force which he had left to hold Pontus had suffered a disaster.

but is superseded.
P. Clodius stirs up the soldiery against him.

Mithradates, after the battle of the Arsanias, returned with eight thousand men, of whom four thousand were lent to him by Tigranes, with the resolve of recovering his kingdom.[2] Fabius Hadrianus, who encountered him near the great trunk road, was driven to take refuge in Cabira; but Triarius, arriving opportunely from the province of Asia, forced Mithradates to raise the siege, pursued him along the road to Comana, and there defeated him. The two armies then went into winter-quarters, Mithradates retiring to the fortress of Zela, while Triarius encamped between him and Comana at Gazioura—now Turkhal[3]—where he commanded the road that led from Zela to Amasia and thence to Amisus. Early in the spring Lucullus would arrive from Nisibis; Triarius had only to hold fast and Mithradates must be finally overwhelmed. But Mithradates intended to deal with the lieutenant before the chief could arrive. The heavy baggage of the Roman army was stored in a fort called Dadasa, between Zela and Gazioura; and Mithradates, who was now reinforced, sent a detachment to attack it in the hope of seducing Triarius to fight. Triarius, who divined his object, refused to stir, until his troops, who

---

[1] Cic. (?), *De har. resp.*, 20, 42; Sall., v, 14; Plut., *Luc.*, 34, 1-3; Dio, xxxvi, 14, 4; 15, 1. If, as Appian (*Mithr.*, 90) says, Marcius Rex was appointed by the Senate, not by a popular decree, we may be sure that the Senate, which sympathized with Lucullus (Plut., *Luc.*, 35, 4), acted reluctantly under popular pressure.

[2] In regard to the events described in this and the next paragraph see pp. 425-6.

[3] See Strabo, xii, 3, 15; *Royal Geogr. Soc. Suppl. Papers*, iii, 1893, p. 736; *Studia Pontica*, i, 1903, pp. 69-70; ii, 1906, p. 249

were war-weary and thought only of saving their belongings, compelled him by mutinous threats to let them hurry to the rescue. On Mount Scotius, a few miles north of Zela, they were surrounded by the superior Pontic forces and utterly defeated. Twenty-four military tribunes, one hundred and fifty centurions, more than seven thousand men were said to have been slain. Lucullus, who was marching up the road from Melitene to Sebasteia, the modern Sivas, was unable to repair the disaster, for Mithradates took up a strong position on the heights above Talaura,[1] from which it was impossible to dislodge him and he could not be induced to stir.

67 B.C.

Mithradates recovers Pontus.

But sooner or later he must surrender if only Lucullus could hold his army firm. Why did not Lucullus invest Talaura? Perhaps he thought that the men, of whom he was no longer master, could only be kept to the semblance of obedience by being actively employed. At all events he resolved to make an effort to complete the subjugation of Tigranes. His troops, hearing that the consul Glabrio had been appointed to supersede him and instigated by that Fimbrian contingent whose loyalty had never been secure, declined to move. We are told that he humbled himself to go from tent to tent and to supplicate the Fimbrian mutineers, who spurned his prayers, although they allowed themselves to be persuaded by the other legions to remain with the standards for the time.[2] Throughout the summer he was compelled to remain inactive in his camp while Mithradates resumed control over his kingdom and while Tigranes overran Cappadocia.[3] Ariobarzanes, once more expelled from his dominions, entreated Lucullus to succour him. Lucullus could do nothing: Marcius Rex said that he could not help Lucullus because his army would not follow him; Glabrio remained idle in Bithynia. About this time commis-

Humiliation of Lucullus.

---

[1] The geographical position of Talaura is uncertain. See p. 426.
[2] Plut., *Luc.*, 35, 4–6. Cf. Cic., *De imp. Cn. Pomp.*, 11, 26; Sall., v, 13, and Dio, xxxvi, 14, 4.
[3] Cf. Th. Reinach (*Mithr. Eupator*, pp. 375–6), who remarks that, according to Appian (*Mithr.*, 91) and Dio (xxxvi, 19, 1), Mithradates also ravaged Cappadocia.

sioners arrived from Rome to settle the affairs of Pontus; for Lucullus had reported to the Senate that Mithradates was subdued. Among them were Marcus Lucullus, the conqueror of Macedonia, and Murena,[1] who had served under Lucius; but, well-disposed though they may have been to the unlucky General, they could only conclude that the province of Pontus did not exist.

Why and how far he failed.

So ended the first period of the last Mithradatic War. The confused compilations upon which the modern historian has to work, sometimes mutually contradictory, abounding in details which are neither instructive nor picturesque, deficient in essential information, do not enable us to understand completely the causes either of Lucullus's success or of his failure. We see from the story of Cyzicus and of Tigranocerta that he had the eye of a tactician and the courage to put everything to the hazard for a great end. With his little force he expelled Mithradates from Asia, from Bithynia, and from Pontus, destroyed his naval, shattered his military power, and humbled his arrogant ally. All this he accomplished without drawing upon the Roman treasury; yet he contrived to reward his soldiers and to enrich himself, while he gained the affectionate respect of the provincials and treated the peoples whom he conquered with rare generosity. It has been said that he did not attempt to gain the confidence of his soldiers, that he imposed on them onerous services, and that he was inexorable in punishing breaches of discipline.[2] The truth is that he was by temperament unfit to manage men who, when he took command of them, were thoroughly demoralized. The discipline which he enforced was strong until it was strained to the verge of breaking: what he failed to see was that that iron discipline which compels the obedience of war-weary troops, and which was congenial to his nature, could not, in his generation, be long maintained; for it cannot be applied to soldiers without patriotism who look up to their general alone, but only to those who

---

[1] Cic., *Att.*, xiii, 6, 4; Plut., *Luc.*, 36, 7-8.
[2] Plut., *Luc.*, 33, 2.

are the servants of a strong and stable government. Lucullus scorned to imitate Sulla, who, so long as his legions fought for *him*, allowed them every licence;[1] he had not that magnetism by which Caesar and Napoleon held the affections of their troops. Still, his army followed him to victory until he tempted fortune by an enterprise which was foredoomed to failure; and even then he was only prevented from achieving final conquest by the machinations of his enemies, which, however, were perhaps in part provoked by his own cupidity.

The supplanters of Lucullus were themselves about to be supplanted. Pompey, after he had subdued the pirates, remained in the province of Asia;[2] and, since he was free to return to Rome and letters were passing throughout the winter between Rome and Asia,[3] we must conclude that he was awaiting a fresh commission, and had instructed his agents to secure it. Early in the new year one of the tribunes, Gaius Manilius, proposed a bill for conferring upon him the command against Mithradates and Tigranes with the same powers which he already possessed under the Gabinian law. In other words, the authority over the Mediterranean and the Mediterranean coasts that had been granted to him for three years (of which two were still to run) was to be increased by unlimited authority to make war in the East.[4] Whether the bill was debated in the Senate we do not know; but several senators supported it before the popular assembly, and none ventured to oppose it except the two staunch Conservatives, Hortensius and Catulus, who had opposed the Gabinian law.[5] Their motives are not difficult to

67 B.C.

66 B.C. Unlimited authority in the East granted to Pompey by the Manilian law.

---

[1] Plutarch (33, 4) says that, according to Sallust, Lucullus incurred odium early in the war by keeping his troops during two successive winters in camp instead of quartering them in towns [where they would have been a nuisance to the inhabitants].   [2] See pp. 426-7.
[3] Cic., *De imp. Cn. Pomp.*, 2, 4.
[4] Livy, *Epit.*, 100; Vell., ii, 33, 1; Ascon., ed. Clark, p. 65, ll. 18-20 (ed. Stangl, p. 53); Plut., *Pomp.*, 30; *Luc.*, 35, 9; App., *Mithr.*, 97; Dio, xxxvi, 42-3. Authority was granted to Pompey over Phrygia, Lycaonia, Galatia, Colchis, Armenia, and the provinces of Asia, Bithynia, and Cilicia (Plut., *Pomp.*, 30, 1-2; Dio, xxxvi, 42, 4).
[5] Cic., *De imp. Cn. Pomp.*, 17, 51; 23, 68. Cf. Zonaras, x, 4.

fathom. Not only would the law give enormous power to one ambitious man, but if more territories were conquered, the problem of ruling them would put a breaking strain upon the constitution. Ten pro-magistrates were available each year to govern provinces; thirteen provinces existed; and it would become necessary either that one man should control more than one province, or that the same man should retain his office for successive years, or even, as had happened when Pompey was given his command in Spain, that some popular soldier should be appointed who had no lawful claim. There was a danger that the central government might lose its hold on the expanding empire and that civil authority might have to yield to military despotism.[1] The leading supporters of Manilius were Cicero, whose speech (in an elaborated form) has been preserved, and Julius Caesar.[2] Cicero, who was now praetor, intended to begin his canvass for the consulship in the following year,[3] and, since he was what the Romans called 'a new man', none of his family having ever held a great magistracy, and was therefore likely to be opposed by the nobility, his only resource was to ingratiate himself with the populace, whose idol was Pompey, and with the knights, whose financial interests Pompey was ready to promote. The tribute due from Asia during the last few years, as from Spain during the Sertorian War, must have seriously diminished; and the numerous shareholders whose savings were invested with the farmers of the taxes were doubtless eager to place in command the famous general who could be trusted to restore and augment their dividends. Cicero told the people that now that he was about to address them, as their praetor, for the first time, he could find no theme more congenial than the merits of Pompey. Roman dominion in the East was menaced by two mighty kings; the province of Asia,

---

[1] See N. Machiavelli, *Discorsi sopra . . . Tito Livio*, 1540, Bk. iii, ch. xxiv; P. Willems, *Le sénat*, &c., ii, 576-89; and *Ann. Rept. . . . Amer. Hist. Assn.*, i, 1915, p. 125.
[2] Dio, xxxvi, 43, 2.   [3] *Att.*, i, 1, 1.

a fruitful source of revenue, was in danger. The knights, 66 B.C. whose capital was invested in the province, were daily receiving letters which warned them of their peril; the kingdom of Cappadocia was in the power of the enemy. Lucullus had done great things, but he was now retiring: Glabrio was not prepared to continue his work. Mithradates had never been sufficiently punished for his crimes; he had even encouraged Sertorius; and the danger from Sertorius had been repelled by Pompey. The honour of Rome, her public credit, the safety of her subjects were all at stake. Pompey's career, from the time when, as a boy of seventeen, he had served in the Social War, had been one of unbroken success; and no words could do him justice. Italy, as Sulla testified, had been saved in the Civil War by his aid: he had pacified Sicily, recovered Africa, overthrown Sertorius: the mere expectation of his return had checked the Servile War, his arrival had put a stop to it: finally, he had extirpated piracy, which had threatened the very existence of the civilized world. He had proved that he possessed every quality of a great commander,—professional skill, indefatigable industry, courage of the highest kind, energy in action, wisdom in planning, swiftness in execution, integrity, good faith, urbanity, capacity for maintaining discipline, the prestige that inspired public confidence, and, above all, a double portion of that which had helped Rome's greatest generals to victory,—unparalleled, invariable, God-given good fortune. As for the objections of Hortensius and of Catulus, they had been refuted in advance by facts. Hortensius had opposed the Gabinian law on the ground that absolute power ought not to be entrusted to one man: was not the result of the war against the pirates a sufficient answer? Catulus urged that no innovation should be made in violation of precedent and of immemorial usage: had not extraordinary powers been conferred upon the younger Scipio Africanus and upon Marius? had not Pompey already received extraordinary commands with the approval of Catulus himself? Cicero concluded by protesting that he was

66 B.C.

not supporting the bill from interested motives, but, despite the enmities which he well knew that he had incurred, solely for his country's good.[1] Those who have read his speech and noticed how he magnified Pompey by ignoring Crassus and Metellus, how he appealed to the avarice of the knights and to the vanity of the populace, may conclude that the patriotism of the orator was calculated to further his advancement.

Pompey was still in the province of Asia when he received the news of his appointment.[2] It was not in his nature to show consideration for the man who, whatever his shortcomings may have been, had made his task easy. If Plutarch is to be trusted, he had an old grudge against Lucullus for having supplanted him in the favour of Sulla. 'He lost no opportunity', says the biographer, 'of showing the adherents of Lucullus that all his authority was gone.' Lucullus complained; and the common friends of the two generals, hoping to effect a reconciliation, persuaded them to meet.[3] The interview took place at Danala in Galatia,[4] whither Pompey's troops had marched from Cilicia.[5] They began by complimenting and congratulating one another; but courtesy was soon exhausted. Pompey accused Lucullus of lust of money: Lucullus accused Pompey of lust of power. As soon as they had parted each spoke of the other with contempt. Pompey sneered at the achievements of Lucullus, and said that the real fighting was only about to begin: Lucullus remarked, in words which contained truth enough to wound, that Pompey had usurped the credit that belonged of right to Catulus, to Metellus, and to Crassus, and that it was not surprising that the man who had contrived to obtain a triumph for having scattered runaway slaves, should now claim the glory of dealing a final blow at Mithradates and Tigranes.[6]

Stormy interview of Pompey with Lucullus.

---

[1] Cic., *De imp. Cn. Pomp.*, §§ 3–5, 7, 9–10, 17–9, 29–49, 52–3, 59–61, 71.
[2] See pp. 426–7.
[3] Plut., *Luc.*, 4, 6–7; 36, 2; *Pomp.*, 31, 1–2.
[4] Strabo, xii, 5, 2.   [5] See pp. 426–7.
[6] Vell., ii, 33, 2; Plut., *Pomp.*, 31, 4. 6–7; *Luc.*, 36, 2–4; Dio, xxxvi, 46, 1–2.

Pompey's force, whatever its numbers may have been, was far larger than the little army with which Lucullus had taken the field when the power of Mithradates was at its height; and the power of Mithradates was now brought low. Lucullus had no more than thirty thousand infantry and three thousand cavalry: Pompey retained the legions which had been raised for the war against the pirates, while he took over the greater part of his predecessor's troops;[1] and he could command the services of the three legions which belonged to the Governor of Cilicia.[2] The accounts of the prize-money which he distributed show that when the war was over he still had at least forty thousand men.[3] Before he put his troops in motion he had concluded a treaty with Phraates, confirming, it would seem, an agreement which Lucullus had made, by which the Euphrates was recognized as the Romano-Parthian frontier, and had, moreover, induced him to attack Tigranes.[4] Negotiations followed between Pompey and Mithradates, each perhaps desiring to gain time and to get information about the strength of his enemy. Mithradates, who, in order to ensure the fidelity of his subjects, had punished sundry deserters by burning them alive or gouging out their eyes, was looking to Phraates for assistance, but, learning that Pompey had secured his friendship, sent envoys to ask for terms. Pompey replied that he must surrender all deserters and lay down his arms. Mithradates was unable, if he desired, to comply; for his soldiers raised an outcry, and even threatened mutiny.[5]

66 B.C.
Pompey's army.

His treaty with Phraates.

Pompey began by distributing his squadrons along the coast from the Hellespont to Phoenicia, thus ensuring his communications against pirates, for not one Pontic galley remained in the open sea.[6] Marcius Rex with his

[1] *Ib.*, § 1; Plut., *Luc.*, 36, 4; *Pomp.*, 31, 1. 5.
[2] Sall., v, 14. [3] See pp. 427-8.
[4] Livy, *Epit.*, 100; Flor., i, 46, 4; Dio, xxxvi, 45, 3; Oros., vi, 13, 2.
[5] Dio, xxxvi, 45, 3-5; App., *Mithr.*, 97-8. According to Appian, Pompey also required that Mithradates should himself surrender.
[6] Plut., *Pomp.*, 32, 1. In regard to the events described in this paragraph, see pp. 428-33

66 B.C.

His successful campaign against Mithradates.

army was advancing from Cilicia to join him. The sequel proved that the peril encompassing the province of Asia with which Cicero had alarmed his audience was imaginary. Mithradates, who was apparently near Cabira, being now far too weak to resist, retreated, devastating the country as he went, down the great trunk road. Hoping to exhaust his pursuers by famine, he occupied a hill-fort, called Dasteira, in the Lesser Armenia, not far from Purkh, and harassed their foragers with his cavalry; but Pompey proceeded to form a contravallation round the hill, and, posting his light-armed troops with five hundred horsemen in a valley, sent the rest of his cavalry to lure the Pontic outposts by a feigned retreat into the ambush, where they were overwhelmed. When the Cilician force arrived, he sent a detachment into the district of Acilisene by the nearer bank of the Euphrates, to collect supplies and to bar any attempt which Mithradates might make to cross the river there. While the contravallation was still incomplete, the King, hearing that Pompey was now abundantly supplied and in possession of Acilisene, massacred his sick and wounded, left fires burning in his camp to avert suspicion, and, escaping through the gap, pushed eastward with the object of crossing the Euphrates and taking refuge with his son-in-law. Pompey followed him at dawn in the hope of forcing him to fight; but Mithradates, remaining obstinately in his new encampment throughout the day, moved on at nightfall and seized a strong position on a hill. Pompey was reluctant to attack by night in an unknown country, but, perceiving that Mithradates was determined not to fight by day, resolved to take the risk, and at noon, while the enemy were resting, marched on unperceived and occupied a line of heights commanding a valley through which they would be obliged to pass. They entered unsuspecting. Presently, when retreat was no longer possible, missiles rained down upon them in the darkness; soon the Roman soldiers were upon them with the sword; camels, horses, wagons became involved with the troops in inextricable confusion; and when the moon shone out, the trapped soldiers, striving desperately to resist, were dazzled by its rays. Many were killed and many taken prisoners; but Mithradates contrived to get away. Learning that Tigranes, who suspected that his son had been instigated by him to rebel, would not receive him, he made his way with the remnant of his force to Dioscurias on the north-eastern shore of the Black Sea. His active career was at an end; but he still dreamed of future conquest.

66 B. C.

Armenia was now open to the advance of Pompey, who pushed on for Artaxata; and Tigranes, whose rebellious son was leagued with Phraates, seeing that it was time to surrender, presented himself before the Roman camp. The lictors ordered him to dismount, and, giving up his sword, the King of Kings suffered himself to be led into the presence of the Roman General, who, when he prostrated himself in token of submission, compassionately raised him, replaced the diadem, which he had taken off, upon his head, and invited him to sit by his side.[1] Pompey had determined that Armenia should serve as a buffer between the newly acquired territories and Parthia. He therefore told Tigranes that he might retain his hereditary dominions, but must restore the lands which he had annexed to their former rulers, and pay six thousand talents as an indemnity and as the price of recognition of his title. Tigranes was so pleased with the concession that he presented every tribune in the Roman army with forty thousand sesterces, equivalent to four hundred pounds, every centurion with four thousand, and every private with two hundred.[2] His son, who had expected that Pompey would reward his rebellion by dethroning his father in his favour, was obliged to content himself with the province of Sophene; but as he claimed the treasure, belonging to Tigranes,

Tigranes surrenders: terms imposed upon him by Pompey

---

[1] Cic., *Pro Sest.*, 27, 58; Livy, *Epit.*, 100; Val. Max., v, 1, 9; Plut., *Pomp.*, 33, 1–3; Dio, xxxvi, 51, 1; 52; Eutrop., vi, 13. Appian (*Mithr.*, 104) distorts the order of events. Florus (i, 40, 27) wrongly says that Pompey captured Artaxata.

[2] Livy, *Epit.*, 101; Strabo, xi, 14, 10; Plut., *Pomp.*, 33, 3–4; App., *Mithr.*, 104–5; Dio, xxxvi, 53, 2.

which was there deposited, and the treasurer refused to surrender it without his sanction, Pompey made him a prisoner and detained him even when the money was given up. Phraates demanded his release in vain, and when he requested that the Euphrates should be formally recognized as the frontier between the Roman and the Parthian power, Pompey ambiguously answered that he would make such arrangements as were just.[1] No more important problem presented itself to Pompey; and his lack of judgement was fraught with consequences which were not realized until Crassus fell at Carrhae. After concluding these arrangements Pompey crossed the Araxes and marched northward to winter in the valley of the Kur. Mithradates was still at large, and there could be no security against the designs of that restless brain until he was hunted down: moreover, the Caucasian peoples had sent contingents to the host which encountered Lucullus at Tigranocerta [2], and Pompey could not afford to leave them unconquered in his rear. The Albanians, who inhabited what is now called Georgia, fearing that he intended to invade their country, attacked him, but were defeated and admitted to terms. In the following spring he subdued the Iberians, who possessed the upper part of the valley, south of the Caucasus and west of Albania. Thence he penetrated into Colchis with the intention of pursuing Mithradates, who had retired to the Crimea; but finding that such a march, through an unknown country inhabited by hostile tribes, would be impracticable, he sent orders to his admiral, whose fleet was lying off the mouth of the river Phasis, to prevent the King from escaping and to allow no supplies to be conveyed to him by sea. From Colchis he was recalled by a rising of the Albanians, which he easily repressed; and thence he returned into the Lesser Armenia, where ambassadors from Phraates and from the Parthian satrap of Elymais, who was bent upon throwing off the authority of Phraates, met him.[3] Gabinius, who was

---

[1] Plut., *Pomp.*, 33, 4; App., *Mithr.*, 105.   [2] Plut., *Luc.*, 26, 6.
[3] Livy, *Epit.*, 101; Vell., ii, 40, 1; Plut., *Pomp.*, 34-5; 36, 1; Flor.,

now one of Pompey's marshals, had been dispatched on a mission to Judaea; and since he took the route through Mesopotamia, we may infer that he had been instructed to watch the Parthians as well.[1] Phraates, impressed by the achievements of Pompey and learning that Gabinius had reached the Tigris, was anxious to conclude a treaty in pursuance of their agreement of the previous year. But Pompey, adhering to the traditional policy of Rome— to weaken native princes by whose aid she had humbled others, and thus to hold the balance between them— ignored the request of the ambassadors, merely writing to warn the King that he must surrender Gordyene, the possession of which he disputed with Tigranes; and before he could receive an answer he ordered his lieutenant Afranius to occupy that province. The envoys of the satrap, on the other hand, were welcomed [2]; and Phraates may well have felt that the Roman general was treating him not only with bad faith but with positive hostility. Pompey then returned to Pontus, and, taking up his quarters at Amisus, proceeded to make arrangements for the settlement of the conquered lands.[3]

{65 B.C.}
{He breaks faith with Phraates.}
{Early in 64[2] B.C.}

Although it was usual for a Roman conqueror to await the arrival of commissioners from the Senate and conjointly with them to fix the principles on which the newly acquired territory was to be governed, Pompey might reasonably assume that the absolute powers with which he had been invested under the Manilian law entitled him to act on his own authority; and in due course he would ask the Senate to confirm his measures. The work which he had to do demanded much deliberation, and the labour which it imposed upon his secretaries may be estimated from the fact that to collect and make an inventory of the treasures which were found in the

{His settlement of Pontus.}

---

i, 40, 28; Dio, xxxvi, 54; xxxvii, 1–5; 7, 5; Eutrop., vi, 14; Oros., vi, 4, 8–9. Appian (*Mithr.*, 103) distorts the order of events. See pp. 433–4.

[1] Jos., *Ant.*, xiv, 3, 2; Plut., *Pomp.*, 36, 1; Dio, xxxvii, 5, 2; Oros., vi, 6, 2.

[2] Plut., *Pomp.*, 36, 1; Dio, xxxvii, 5, 3–5.

[3] See *Hermes*, xiii, 1878, pp. 38–40, where Niese proves what appears to me self-evident, that Pompey returned to Amisus in 64 B.C. Cf. pp. 433–4.

fort of Talaura alone required thirty days.¹ Pompey had not only to form a new province out of those territories which it seemed expedient to annex, and to prescribe rules for the guidance of the local authorities,² but also to determine what communities, not yet ripe for incorporation in a province, should be empowered to manage their own affairs, to select the localities which would be suitable for the foundation of new, or the development of existing cities, to decide how the tribute to be exacted from the province, from dependent princes, and from self-governing communities should be raised, to make grants of territory to native rulers who deserved well of Rome or to reward them with honorific titles, and to advance loans to impoverished rulers who had not the means of supporting their dignity. Ariobarzanes was of course reinstated in Cappadocia, Sophene, of which the younger Tigranes was deprived, and Gordyene together with certain cities of Cilicia being annexed to his kingdom, which, however, he resigned in favour of his son ;³ and Pompey, who could appreciate a profitable investment, lent the new monarch a large sum of money from his own purse.⁴ The remainder of Cilicia together with Pamphylia and Isauria, which Servilius Isauricus had subdued, was formed into a new province ;⁵ and there, as in Bithynia, although the taxes were not, as in the province Asia, farmed, the natives, for want of the necessary organization, were obliged to invoke the aid of Roman publicans, who charged them heavily for helping them to collect the tribute.⁶ Deiotarus, a Galatian tetrarch, who had aided Lucullus in his first campaign,⁷ was recompensed with the title of king and with territory

¹ App., *Mithr.*, 115.
² Pompey's regulations for Bithynia were still observed in the time of Trajan (Plin., *Ep. ad Trai.*, 79, 1 ; 112, 1 ; 114, 1).
³ App., *Mithr.*, 105, 114.   ⁴ Cic., *Att.*, vi, 1, 3 ; 3, 5. See p. 486.
⁵ App., *Syr.*, 48, 50 ; *Mithr.*, 106, 118 ; Justin., xl, 2, 5. Servilius had enlarged the original province of Cilicia (Livy, *Epit.*, 93 ; Flor., i, 41, 5 ; Eutrop., vi, 3) ; the tract, taken from Tigranes, which Pompey added, was called *Cilicia campestris*.
⁶ Cic., *Att.*, v, 16, 2 ; *Fam.*, iii, 8, 5. Cf. pp. 124, 396.
⁷ See p. 124.

in that part of Pontus which adjoined the Lesser Armenia, including the country round Trapezus.[1] Other native potentates who had rendered services received lands round Comana, in Paphlagonia, and in Colchis.[2] The remaining parts of the Pontic kingdom were annexed to the province of Bithynia,[3] the various lands being assigned to eleven important townships.[4] Pompey, like Lucullus, saw that the higher culture of the cities would influence the Asiatics in the interest of Rome, and he pressed the people of the outlying villages to migrate to them.[5] In making his selection he showed that if he was neither a statesman nor a politician, he possessed not only the judgement that might have been expected from so experienced a soldier, but also the foresight of a great administrator. The cities all lay where facilities of communication would promote their trade or where they would dominate the conquered country. Nicopolis (perhaps not one of the eleven), Diospolis, which grew out of Cabira, Magnopolis the offshoot of Eupatoria, Neapolis, between the plain of Phanaroea and the river Halys,[6] Pompeiopolis, now represented by Tash Keupru on the Amnias—served to guard the great trunk road that traversed Pontus and Bithynia, and at the same time formed centres for the diffusion of Graeco-Roman civilization.[7] Nicopolis, which Pompey founded to commemorate the victory that terminated the career of Mithradates, and in which he settled a colony of war-worn soldiers, who were joined by natives from the surrounding country,[8] stood upon the site of the modern Purkh, some six miles from the Lycus, and not far from the fastness in which the King had made his final stand. None of the new foundations was more ideally situated. Standing upon

---

[1] Strabo, xii, 3, 13 ; App., *Mithr.*, 114. See p. 434. Eutropius (vi, 14) incorrectly says that Pompey gave Deiotarus the Lesser Armenia.
[2] App., *Mithr.*, 114 ; Eutrop., vi, 14.
[3] Strabo, xii, 3, 1.   [4] See pp. 434-5.
[5] Strabo, xi, 8, 4 ; xii, 3, 30. 38.
[6] *Studia Pontica*, i, 92.
  See the remarks of Mr. J. A. R. Munro in *Royal Geogr. Soc. Suppl. Papers*, iii, 1893, p. 739 and *Journ. Hellen. Studies*, 1901, pp. 60-1. Cf. *Studia Pontica*, i, 51, 86-7.   [8] Dio, xxxvi, 50, 3.

the lower slopes of a spur which projected from a wooded mountain mass, it was supplied with water by limpid streams ; below it lay a broad and fertile valley ; the great road connected it with the sea on one side, on the other with the Euphrates.[1] Thus endowed, it grew so rapidly that in the time of Augustus it was already a flourishing and populous city.[2]

64 B. C.

He annexes Syria.

In the following spring Pompey marched for Syria, preceded by Afranius, who prepared a way for him over the mountains of Eastern Cilicia by subduing the Arabs that held the passes.[3] Syria, paralysed by a long succession of feeble rulers, riven by anarchy and feud, could make no resistance. Antiochus, the last of the Seleucid dynasty, who, though he had recovered the kingdom on the withdrawal of Tigranes, had failed to maintain his authority against rivals and enemies, implored the conqueror to reinstate him on his ancestral throne, which Lucullus had permitted him to retain ; but Pompey, explaining that it was unreasonable that a descendant of a king who had been dethroned by Tigranes should possess the country rather than the Roman People, who had conquered Tigranes, declared Syria to be a Roman province.[4] His purpose was to shield the Greek cities, which would be useful to Rome, from attack and to establish orderly rule ;[5] but here again, as in Asia Minor, many cities, notably Antioch and Seleucia, although they were required to pay a tribute, raised in accordance with native methods of taxation, were allowed to retain their own jurisdiction and to manage their own affairs.[6] A petty dynast, Antiochus of Commagene, was likewise permitted to retain his possessions,

[1] *Studia Pontica*, ii, 305-6.
[2] Strabo, xii, 3, 28. Some of Pompey's territorial arrangements were afterwards modified (*ib.*, § 1). Cf. *Journ. Hell. Soc.*, 1901, p. 61, n. 1.
[3] Plut., *Pomp.*, 39, 2.
[4] *Ib.* ; Strabo, xvi, 2, 18 ; Vell., ii, 37, 5 ; App., *Syr.*, 49, 70 ; *Mithr.*, 106 ; Justin., xl, 2, 2. Cf. A. Kuhn, *Beitr. zur Gesch. d. Seleuk.*, 1891, p. 45.
[5] See E. R. Bevan, *The House of Seleucus*, ii, 1902, p. 267.
[6] Strabo, xvi, 2, 8.

including another Seleucia, which commanded the 64 B.C.
Euphrates ;¹ and through this dependent prince Pompey
controlled the two chief passages of the river, for the
other, at Melitene, had been granted by Lucullus to the
King of Cappadocia as a recompense for his services.²
Meanwhile ambassadors arrived from Phraates and from His treat-
Tigranes, who had quarrelled about the question of ment of Phraates.
Gordyene. Phraates was naturally indignant at the
treatment which he had received and, moreover, resentful
because Pompey declined to address him by his title,—
the King of Kings ; but Pompey, disregarding his complaints, sent his representatives to settle the dispute,
which related to the delimitation of the common frontier.³
The condition of Judaea, which demanded his attention,
made it easy for him to interfere. Under the vigorous rule
of the Maccabees the Jews had successfully resisted the
kings of Syria ; but since the death of Joannes Hyrcanus, 107 B.C.
a grandson of the great Mattathias, they had been
weakened by internal feuds ; and when Pompey entered
Syria, their king, Aristobulus, who was at enmity with
his brother, Hyrcanus, was besieged in Jerusalem by his
brother's ally, Aretas, king of the Nabataean Arabs.⁴
Hyrcanus, himself an indolent man, was backed by
Antipater, the father of Herod the Great, and by the
Pharisees,⁵ who intended through him to make themselves
supreme. Pompey's quaestor, Aemilius Scaurus, whom
he had dispatched in advance, and whose favour the two
brothers both tried to buy, accepted a bribe from Aristobulus, and ordered Aretas, on pain of being treated as
an enemy of Rome, to raise the siege.⁶ While Pompey
was still in winter-quarters at Antioch envoys from
Hyrcanus and Aristobulus presented themselves before
him. Postponing his decision, he directed that the disputants should meet him in the following spring at
Damascus, which two of his lieutenants had already

¹ *Ib.*, 3 ; App., *Mithr.*, 114. ² Strabo, xii, 2, 1.
³ Plut., *Pomp.*, 38, 1 ; Dio, xxxvii, 6 ; 7, 1–4.
⁴ Jos., *Ant.*, xiii, 11–xiv, 2, 1. ⁵ *Ib.*, xiii, 16, 2 ; xiv, 1, 4.
⁶ *Ib.*, 2, 3 ; *Bell. Iud.*, i, 6, 2–3. Josephus incorrectly refers the mission
of Scaurus to the time when Pompey was at war with Tigranes.

seized.¹ Early in the new year he quitted Antioch and, marching by way of Apamea, razed the forts in the mountains of Lebanon, from which brigands used to make raids on the people of the plains,² and thence advanced to Damascus, where he gave audience to the brothers. Aristobulus presented him with a golden vine,³ worth five hundred talents;⁴ Hyrcanus was supported by Antipater, who produced numerous reputable Jews to advocate the claims of his principal. Pompey learned that the nation favoured neither, but desired to be ruled by their priests alone. Fearing that Aristobulus, if he were to decide against him, might stimulate the populace to rise, he again reserved his decision and marched on, promising to settle the matter as soon as he had leisure. Aristobulus, who had returned to Judaea and doubtless saw that he had nothing to expect from further negotiations, abandoned without resistance various forts which Pompey ordered him to surrender, and retreated to Jerusalem. When Pompey was approaching the gates, Aristobulus came out to meet him, offering to give him money and to surrender the city. Pompey deputed Gabinius to receive the fulfilment of the offer ; but the soldiers of Aristobulus sent him away empty-handed, whereupon Pompey placed Aristobulus under arrest. The partisans of Aristobulus seized the temple and destroyed a bridge, spanning a ravine, which connected it with the city, while the supporters of Hyrcanus admitted the Roman army within the walls. The occupants of the temple refused to surrender. Pompey, who had not expected resistance and had therefore neglected to provide himself with siege material, was obliged to send to Tyre for the timber required for constructing engines and works of approach.⁵ The

---

¹ Jos., *Ant.*, xiv, 2, 3 ; 3, 2.
² Strabo, xvi, 2, 18 ; Jos., *Ant.*, xiv, 3, 2.
³ *Ib.*, 3, 1. Cf. Diod. Sic., xl, 2. Any one who reads the narrative of Josephus carefully will see that he mentions the golden vine in the wrong place and that his chronology is confused. Cf. *Hermes*, xi, 1876, p. 471 and E. Schürer, *Gesch. d. jüd. Volkes*, i⁴, 1901, p. 296, n. 15. ⁴ £120,000
⁵ Jos., *Ant.*, xiv, 3, 2-4 ; 4, 1-2 ; *Bell. Iud.*, i, 6, 5-6 ; 7, 1-2.

POMPEY THE GREAT

temple, situated on a steep hill, was defended by a strong wall and separated from the city on its west, from the Mount of Olives on its east, and from the stronghold Sion on the south, by deep ravines : as the bridge had been destroyed, it could not be attacked except from the north ; and even here a deep fosse had been cut out of the rock.[1] Pompey, having succeeded in partially filling up the fosse and the ravine, began to construct an embankment, on which he mounted his battering rams and the sappers' huts within which they were worked. He was able to complete these preparations without opposition by taking advantage of the scruple which forbade the Jews to attack on the Sabbath an enemy who was not actually attacking them. In the third month of the siege a breach was effected in one of the towers, and the temple was taken by assault. Many of the priests were slaughtered while they were offering sacrifices and burning incense : many of the garrison threw themselves down the precipices ; but most of those who perished were massacred by the partisans of Hyrcanus. Pompey presumed to enter the Holy Place ; but, knowing the temper of the Jews, he forbore to touch the treasures which it contained.[2]

Before the siege began Pompey had received news of an event which closed an era in Roman history.[3] Driven

63 B.C.

Autumn.

Last efforts of Mithradates.

[1] Strabo, xvi, 2, 40 ; Jos., *Ant.*, xiv, 4, 2 ; *Bell. Iud.*, i, 7, 1 Cf. Schürer, *op. cit.*, p. 298, and G. A. Smith, *Jerusalem*, ii, 1908, pp. 439, 443–5, 466.

[2] Cic., *Pro Flac.*, 28, 67–8 ; Jos., *Ant.*, xiv, 4, 2–4 ; *Bell. Iud.*, i, 7, 2–6 ; Dio, xxxvii, 16, 1–4 ; Oros., vi, 5, 2–3. The assault was delivered on a Sabbath (Strabo, xvi, 2, 40 ; Dio, § 4), and Josephus (*Ant.*, xiv, 4, 3), who copied Strabo, says that Jerusalem was taken on 'the fast-day' (τὴν τῆς νηστείας ἡμέραν) ; but, as Théodore Reinach points out (*Textes... relatifs au Judaïsme*, 1895, p. 104, n. 1), Strabo, like Suetonius (*Aug.*, 76, 2), fancied that the Jews fasted on the Sabbath. The passage which I have cited from Dio is decisive against the view of Max Radin (*The Jews among the Greeks and Romans*, 1915, pp. 399–400) that Strabo and Josephus meant the Day of Atonement. Nor was Pompey so stupid as to lose the advantage of attacking on a Sabbath.

[3] Jos., *Ant.*, xiv, 3, 4 ; *Bell. Iud.*, i, 6, 6. Plutarch (*Pomp.*, 41, 4–5) says that Pompey was not far from Petra when he heard the news of the death of Mithradates. He never went near Petra. See p. 435.

64-63 B.C. to take refuge at Panticapaeum, or Kertch, in the Crimea, compelled to remain passive while Pontus was being Romanized, Mithradates had sent envoys to Syria, offering to pay tribute on the condition that he should be secured in the possession of his ancestral kingdom. Pompey replied that he must come in person, as Tigranes had done, and sue for terms.[1] Indignantly rejecting the demand, Mithradates collected troops and manufactured weapons, while his agents wrung money from his long-suffering subjects. One Castor of Phanagoria, a town on the further side of the Kertch Strait, who had been affronted by one of the King's eunuchs, incited his fellow citizens to revolt ; and the inhabitants of other fortresses followed their example.[2] Mithradates remained undaunted. Encompassed by rebellion, he actually meditated an invasion of Italy, hoping that the Celts would join him before he crossed the Alps and that the Italians would welcome him as a deliverer. Although he found no encouragement for his wild schemes, not one of his officers ventured to remonstrate ; for the old man's anger was still terrible. But the worst enemies of Asiatic potentates are those of their own household. Pharnaces, the favourite son of Mithradates, formed a conspiracy against him ; and we may suppose that his motive was to ingratiate himself with Pompey as well as to usurp the throne. The plot was detected : his accomplices were tortured ; he himself was pardoned and left at liberty. He used it to resume his intrigues ; and Mithradates, finding himself beset by mutineers, fled for refuge into the fort of Panticapaeum, whence he sent messengers to his son to beg for mercy and permission to go into retirement. They did not return ; and the King, praying that the gods, if gods there were, might grant that his son's sons should conspire against *him*, took poison. Finding that it was not producing its effect (for he had fortified his constitution by antidotes), he induced one of his retainers, a Galatian Celt named Bituitus, to slay

His son Pharnaces plots against him : his death and character.

---

[1] App., *Mithr.*, 107.   [2] *Ib.*, 108.

him.[1] Twenty-five years had passed since he instigated 63 B.C. the universal massacre, which hardened the resolution of the Romans against him, of the Italians in Asia ; and from that day he had devoted his prodigious energy to his master passion,—hatred of Rome. In this alone he was the peer of Hannibal, whom he strove to emulate ; but he who can hate as Mithradates hated is no common man. When we contemplate the manly beauty of the portraits that adorn his coins ;[2] when we read in Appian[3] and Plutarch of his feats of strength and horsemanship, his innumerable amours, his love of letters and of music, his stupendous cruelties ; how he conquered an empire and, when he had been despoiled of it, bent all his force of mind and will to win it back ; how he mastered twenty-two languages in order to transact business without interpreters ;[4] how he raised armies and cemented alliances and hoped against fear to the last, we feel that he was one of the world's foremost men. 'Even in the midst of calamities', says Appian,[5] 'his spirit was always great, always indomitable'.

The conquest of the East was finished. The records are even more deplorable than those which chronicle the operations of Lucullus : like the astronomers who map in outline the plains and mountains of the moon, we can dimly trace the principal moves ; but to students of military history and to readers who ask only for details of human interest the story is equally barren. We can hardly appreciate Pompey's strategy or his tactics : we can only see that his work, which the urbane voluptuary who preceded him had made comparatively easy, was

[1] *Ib.*, 109-11 ; Pliny, xxv, 2 (3), 5 ; Livy, *Epit.*, 102 ; Val. Max., ix, 2, *ext.* 3 ; Vell., ii, 40, 1 ; Flor., i, 40, 26 ; Gell., xvii, 16, 5 ; Justin., xxxvii, 2, 6 ; Dio, xxxvii, 11-3 ; Galen, ed. C. G. Kühn, xiv, 1827, pp. 283-4 ; Ps. Victor., *De vir. ill.*, 76, 8 ; 77, 5 ; Rufus Festus, 16, 1 ; Eutrop., vi, 12 ; Oros., vi, 5, 2-6. Daremberg and Saglio (v, 713-5) give interesting information about ancient poisons. In regard to Mithradates's antidotes see Sir Clifford Allbutt's *Greek Medicine in Rome*, 1921, pp. 355-6.

[2] W. H. Waddington, E. Babelon, and Th. Reinach, *Rec. gén. des monn. grecques d'Asie Mineure*, i, 1904, pl. 2 and 3.

[3] *Mithr.*, 112. Cf. Sall., v, 5.

[4] Pliny, vii, 24, 88 ; xxv, 2 (3), 6. Cf. Gell., xvii, 17, 2.   [5] *Mithr.*, 112.

63 B.C.

Pompey's settlement of Syria.

rapidly and smoothly done. It only remained for him to complete his settlement of the conquered lands. Palestine was made a tributary dependency of Rome: Hyrcanus was reinstated in the high priesthood, being left free to administer internal affairs, though he was bound to defer to the Government of Syria; and Pompey commissioned Scaurus to rule the province and to reduce Aretas to submission.[1] The status of the new dependency was somewhat complex. All the cities in Coele-Syria— the region that extends eastward of Lebanon and of the Orontes—which had been conquered from Antiochus by the Maccabees, were withdrawn from Hyrcanus and made subject to the Government of Syria;[2] Many non-Jewish towns in the interior of Palestine, including the group called Decapolis, familiar to readers of the Bible, and certain maritime towns, of which Joppa was the most important, were declared autonomous, though, like the region subject to Hyrcanus, they were obliged to pay a tribute, which was levied by their own authorities;[3] while certain petty princes or emirs, Ptolemy the ruler of Chalcis in Coele-Syria, and Sampsiceramus, the ruler of Emesa, on the Orontes, were allowed, on payment of a lump sum or of yearly instalments, to retain their dominions, and were of course held responsible for the maintenance of order.[4]

He returns to Pontus and makes final arrangements.

From Palestine Pompey returned once more to Amisus,[5] where he made such arrangements as were required by the death of Mithradates. Pharnaces received the kingdom of Bosporus as the reward of parricide, and was honoured by the title of Friend and Ally of the Roman People; but Phanagoria, the inhabitants of which had begun the insurrection against Mithradates, was withdrawn from

---

[1] Vell., ii, 37, 5; Jos., *Ant.*, xiv, 4, 5; 5, 1; *Bell. Iud.*, i, 7, 7; Flor., i, 40, 29. 31; App., *Syr.*, 51; *Mithr.*, 118; *B. C.*, v, 10, 40; Dio, xxxvii, 16, 4; Oros., vi, 6, 4. Cf. *Acta soc. philol. Lips.*, v, 1875, p. 162. See pp. 453–6.
[2] Strabo, xvi, 2, 46; Jos., *Ant.*, xiv, 4, 4; App., *Syr.*, 50; *Mithr.*, 106, 114.
[3] Jos., *l. c.* and *Bell. Iud.*, i, 7, 7; B. V. Head, *Hist. num.*[2], 1911, pp. 786–7.
[4] Strabo, xvi, 2, 10. 18; Jos., *Ant.*, xiv, 3, 2; *Bell. Iud.*, i, 9. 2.
[5] Plut., *Pomp.*, 42, 1.

his control and received the status of a self-governing city, while Castor, who had incited them to revolt, was made a Friend of the Roman People.¹ Before his departure Pompey required the province of Asia to maintain a permanent fleet to safeguard commerce in case piracy should reappear ; and in the following year the Roman Senate at his suggestion decreed that squadrons should cruise for the same purpose in the Adriatic and off the western coast of Italy.² The constructive work of his life was finished : Caesar's was not begun.

62 B.C.

Looking back upon these fifteen eventful years, the reader, wearied perhaps by the tale of wars and of the conflicts between politicians at Rome, may well ask the writer why he has said so little about the people of Italy. Let him turn to the original authorities, such as they are, and he will find the answer. If Plutarch, Appian, Dio, and the rest found the records which they abridged so barren of information about those things which we are curious to learn, it was because, as I have remarked in the beginning of this chapter, the people of Italy felt so little interest in Roman politics, in foreign campaigns, or in the fate of the provincials whom they were supposed to rule. The citizenship which they had won in the Social War was not, indeed, a sham, for municipal residents could and did attain the highest honours in the State ; but of those who lacked the ability or the ambition to engage in a political career few probably cared, fewer still could afford, to journey to the capital and take their part in the elections. The force which they unwittingly exerted in shaping Roman history worked in silence. Unambitious nobles watched their fish-ponds ; men of the middle class, like the father of Marcus Cicero, lived on their estates in respectable obscurity ; local magnates busied themselves with details of municipal administration ; yeomen tilled their farms ; seamen conveyed Roman armies to their destinations or traded from port to port ; recruits left their cottages to join legions that fought for hire without patriotism ; Sulla's veterans

The people of Italy in this period.

¹ App., *Mithr.*, 113-4.   ² Cic., *Pro Flac.*, 12, 29 ; 13, 30-2.

squandered their gains and mismanaged their allotments ; idlers and broken men flocked into Rome and swelled the mob of venal electors ; brigands lay in wait for unwary travellers ; herdsmen slaves, appalled by those six thousand crucifixions that had lined the Appian Way, toiled for their wealthy owners in weariness to which hope was now denied. But what these classes thought, in so far as they thought at all, of the forces that were sapping the republican constitution, what proportion of the newly enfranchised citizens took the trouble to vote for the candidates whom they favoured, we cannot tell. We must wait for the guidance of Cicero's letters and of the other documents that illustrate the last days of the Republic before we can gain even an inkling of that wider knowledge which we crave.

Let us now watch the rise of Cicero and of Caesar and observe how politics had shaped themselves in Italy since the departure of Pompey, so that we may understand the situation with which he would have to deal when he returned to Rome.

CHAPTER IV

THE *ANNUS MIRABILIS* OF CICERO AND THE RISE OF CAESAR

DURING the period which we have just reviewed the two men rose to eminence who with Pompey and Marcus Cato were the foremost in the moribund Republic. Of the character of one we can discern little save the outlines : the other is more familiar than any other personage of antiquity, than almost any of all time.

Gaius Julius Caesar, a patrician of the bluest blood, was born on the 13th of July, 102 B.C.,[1] the year in which Marius destroyed the host of the Teutoni. His father's family claimed descent from Iulus, the son of Aeneas : his father's sister was the wife of Marius.[2] Like other Roman boys of gentle birth, he studied Greek as well as Latin literature [3] and wrote verses which Augustus judiciously suppressed.[4] At fifteen he was nominated by Marius and Cinna to fill the next vacancy as Flamen Dialis, or priest of Jupiter.[5] Four years later, after divorcing an heiress of lower station, to whom his parents had betrothed him while he was still a child,[6] he married Cornelia, a daughter of Cinna.[6] His relationship with Marius made him conspicuous, and Sulla required him to divorce his bride. He refused to obey, whereupon Sulla

Early life of Caesar.

[1] See pp. 436-42.
[2] Vell., ii, 41, 1 ; Plut., *Caes.*, 1, 1 ; Suet., *Div. Iul.*, 6, 1.
[3] Suet., *De gram.*, 7.   [4] Suet., *Div. Iul.*, 56, 7.
[5] See p. 442 and the interesting remarks of Dr. Warde Fowler (*The Religious Experience of the Roman People*, 1911, pp. 342-3).
[6] Suet., *Div. Iul.*, 1, 1. Prof. M. E. Deutsch (*Class. Philol.*, xii, 1917, pp. 93-6) points out that *dimissa* in Suetonius (*Aug.*, 62, 1 ; 63, 2 ; 69, 1 ; *Tib.*, 7, 2 ; 10, 1 ; 35, 1 : 49, 1 ; *Nero*, 35, 2 ; *Domit.*, 8, 3) and other writers means 'divorced' ; that it is never used in the sense of a broken engagement ; and that, unless Plutarch (*Caes.*, 5, 3) is wrong in saying that Pompeia was Caesar's third wife, the heiress, Cossutia, must have been the first.

confiscated Cornelia's dowry and deprived him of his priesthood.[1] Aware that he was marked by the Dictator's myrmidons, he fled from Rome and wandered over the Sabine hills, fearing for his life. At length he was arrested by a band which was scouring the country in search of Marian fugitives ; but their leader accepted a bribe, and influential friends interceded with Sulla, pleading that Caesar was too young to be feared. 'As you please,' said Sulla, yielding to their importunity ; 'but mark you, in that effeminately foppish boy there are many Mariuses.'[2] In Italy, however, there was no opening for any Marian. Leaving his girl-wife and her infant daughter, Caesar sailed for the province of Asia. Serving his first campaign under Minucius Thermus, he was entrusted with a mission to Nicomedes, the King of Bithynia, his relations with whom gave occasion throughout his life for scandal of that kind which is reprobated with indignation and listened to with zest.[3] In the assault of Mytilene he saved the life of a soldier, was rewarded with the much-prized decoration called the civic crown, and afterwards joined the staff of Servilius Isauricus in Cilicia.[4] After he returned to Italy and saw that he could gain nothing by supporting Lepidus, he strove to attain distinction in the usual way,—by prosecuting political opponents ; and although he failed to secure conviction, his listeners admired the eloquence which afterwards won for him a reputation second only to that of Cicero.[5] In the fashionable world he was becoming known. His pleasant

Vell., ii, 41, 2 ; Plut., 1, 1 ; Suet., 1, 1-2.
[2] Gell., vi, 12, 1-4 ; Dio, xliii, 43, 2. 4 ; Macrob., *Sat.*, ii, 3, 9. See pp. 442-3. Ferrero (*Grandezza e decadenza di Roma*, i, 1902, p. 169, note Eng. tr., i, 102, note]) asserts that the story is apocryphal.
[3] Plut. (whose chronology is wrong), 1, 2 ; Suet., 2 ; Ps. Victor, *De vir. ill.*, 78, 1. Although the persistent attacks of Caesar's enemies on the score of unnatural vice deserve to be recorded as a sign of the times, their charges must be regarded as Not Proven. See vol. ii, p. 152, n. 3.
[4] Suet., 2, 3.
[5] Val. Max., viii, 9, 3 ; Ascon., ed. Clark, p. 26, ll. 13-8, p. 84, l. 16 (ed. Stangl, pp. 27, 65) ; Plut., 4, 1 ; Suet., 4, 1 ; 55, 1. See p. 443, and, in regard to Caesar's eloquence, Cic., *Brut.*, 72, 252 ; Plut., 3, 2 ; Quint., *Inst.*, x, 1, 114.

manner won many friends ; he entertained lavishly ; his amours were already notorious.[1] But his purpose never wavered ; and to perfect his oratorical powers he again left Italy in the winter of 75, intending to study rhetoric at Rhodes under the famous professor, Apollonius.[2] Near Pharmacussa, now called Farmaco, an islet off the coast of Caria, the ship was captured by pirates ; and in connexion with this adventure Plutarch found in some authority one of those anecdotes which, however much we may suspect them, we cannot always reject without the risk of missing what is both characteristic and true. The pirates demanded fifty talents as Caesar's ransom.[3] Some of his companions were allowed to go to Asia to obtain the money ; and during their absence Caesar spent nearly forty days with his captors, reading and writing diligently, but joining in their sports and telling them genially that some day he would crucify them all. When the ransom had been paid he sailed to Miletus, manned some ships which were lying in the harbour, returned to Pharmacussa, captured many of the pirates, and imprisoned them at Pergamum. The Governor of the province, whom he asked to deal with them, replied that he would consider the matter at his leisure, whereupon Caesar went back to Pergamum and fulfilled his threat.[4] At the outset of the Mithradatic War he crossed, as we have seen,[5] from Rhodes to Asia, and induced certain communities, which were inclined to revolt, to remain loyal. Meanwhile through the influence of his friends at

---

[1] Plut., 4, 2 ; Suet, 50 ; &c. [2] Plut., 3, 1 ; Suet, 4, 1.

[3] Plutarch (2, 1, with which cf. Polyaenus, viii, 23, 1) says that the pirates demanded 20 talents, but that Caesar, telling them that they did not know who their captive was, offered 50 ! Valerius Maximus (vi, 6, 15) and Suetonius (4, 2) say that he paid 50. Caesar was not vain ; and if there was any foundation for the story which imposed upon the innocent biographer, I would suggest that Caesar offered 20, but that the pirates knowing that he was somebody, would not take less than 50.

Plutarch (1, 2) wrongly says that Caesar was captured in the life-time of Sulla and before he returned to Rome from his first campaign. The incident is also narrated by Velleius Paterculus (ii, 42, 2–3) and Ps. Victor (*De vir. ill.*, 78, 3).

[4] Plut., 2. Suetonius (74, 1), giving instances of Caesar's clemency, assures us that before the pirates were crucified their throats were cut.

[5] See p. 181.

Rome he had been elected a member of the pontifical college. Pirates swarmed in the Adriatic, and, knowing what he might expect if he were caught, he determined not to be taken alive; but he engaged a fast quadrireme and reached Brundisium in safety.[1] Of the next few years of his life—the period in which Pompey was campaigning against Sertorius and Crassus against Spartacus, in which the Sullan constitution was overthrown and Pompey, after his first consulship, was living in retirement—we know little, except that he joined in the movement for the restoration of the tribunician power and that, with the purpose of buying popular support, he borrowed and spent on a prodigious scale.[2] In the year that preceded the enactment of the Gabinian law he was appointed quaestor under the Governor of Further Spain. Just before he started, his aunt, the widow of Marius, and his wife, whom he had refused to divorce at Sulla's bidding, died. When the funeral procession entered the Forum there was observed among the images of the ancestors of the deceased a bust of Marius, a reminder that liberty had been restored. Some of the spectators raised an outcry, but they were silenced by the plaudits of the populace. Mounting the platform to deliver the customary eulogy, Caesar told his listeners, upon whose credulity he knew how to play, that Julia was descended on her father's side from Venus, on her mother's from King Ancus Martius; and we may be sure that he dwelt upon the victories of Marius and lauded Cinna as a champion of the poor.[3] In Spain, where he gathered experience of judicial and financial business, he must have met provincials who had known Sertorius; and perhaps it was admiration of the lieutenant of Marius that made him eager, as he afterwards said,[4] to serve his quaestorship in that country and to do what he could for its inhabitants. There is no reason to ridicule the story told by Suetonius [5] that when he saw a portrait of Alexan-

---

[1] Vell., ii, 43, 1-2. [2] Plut., 5, 4; Suet., 5.
[3] Plut., 5, 3; Suet., 6, 1. [4] *Bell. Hisp.*, 42, 1.
[5] *Div. Iul.*, 7, 1. The story is told by Plutarch (11, 3) with reference to Caesar's government of Further Spain. Plutarch forgot that in 62 B. C.,

der the Great in the temple of Hercules at Gades, he lamented that at the age when Alexander had conquered the East he had himself done nothing memorable. Returning to Italy, he passed through Cisalpine Gaul, which had been formed, perhaps by Sulla, into a province.[1] While the people who lived south of the Po had received Roman citizenship, those on the north still possessed only Latin rights. This distinction was of course resented by the Transpadanes, more especially as the Italians had won the suffrage; and they were now agitating for its removal. Caesar went from town to town, fomenting the agitation; but though he never forgot the Transpadanes, the time had not come when he could attempt to satisfy their aspirations.[2] We have seen how he supported both the Gabinian and the Manilian law; but when we learn that, immediately after the expiration of his quaestorship, he married a lady named Pompeia,[3] we may reject the inference which at first seems obvious, for Pompeia was only a distant relative of Pompey. As a commissioner for the maintenance of the Appian Way, he defrayed the cost of repairs in part out of his own purse.[4] In 65 B. C. he was elected one of the curule aediles, who were responsible for preserving order in the capital and for superintending the public games. These officers generally expended large sums in making the entertainments more attractive with the view of conciliating the electors when they should stand for higher posts. Caesar determined to outdo his

He supports the agitation of the Transpadanes for Roman citizenship.

His aedileship.

when Caesar was propraetor, he was several years older than Alexander had been when he died.

[1] Dr. Hardy (*Journ. Rom. Studies*, vi, 1916, pp. 65-7) rejects the prevalent opinion, and argues that Cisalpine Gaul was made a province early in the Social War—90-89 B.C.

[2] Suetonius (8) says that Caesar 'would have incited [the Transpadanes] to make some audacious attempt if the consuls had not detained for a time the legions raised for service in Cilicia in order to prevent him'. *I* agree with Long (*Decline of the Roman Republic*, iii, 1869, pp. 217-8) and Dr. Hardy (*Journ. of Philol.*, xxxiii, 1914, p. 107) in rejecting this statement, which implies that Caesar was devoid of common sense. Hardy remarks that it 'may be classed with the story current about him and Crassus in connexion with the [Catilinarian] conspiracy . . . and was no doubt the invention of his political opponents at a later time'.

[3] Plut., 5. 3; Suet., 6, 2.   [4] Plut., 5, 4.

predecessors. At his own expense he decorated the Forum and the surrounding buildings, exhibited three hundred and twenty pairs of gladiators for the delectation of the populace, and armed the criminals who were condemned to encounter the wild beasts in the arena with weapons adorned with silver.[1] Early one morning people entering the Forum were amazed to see statues of Marius and figures symbolical of his victories, all glittering with gold. Crowds came thronging to the spectacle, and every one guessed who had done the deed. Conservatives muttered that Caesar was making a bid for power; but the surviving partisans of Marius, among whom there must have been veterans who had fought under him, exulted, and some even wept for joy:[2] Sulla had removed the trophies of his enemy's prowess, but the man who in boyhood had defied Sulla had now replaced them. Feeling that he could count upon popular support, Caesar soon afterwards attempted, through the agency of tribunes who were on his side, to obtain a command in Egypt.[3] It would seem that he was acting in collusion with Crassus,[4] who, taking advantage of a prevalent belief that the late King had bequeathed his kingdom to the Romans,[5] purposed to make Egypt a tributary dependency. This project was perhaps not unwelcome to the populace and the knights, who always favoured a policy of annexation, though they may have suspected that it was directed against Pompey. But when, after reading the one short sentence in which Caesar's biographer records his scheme, we examine the theory which modern historians have built upon it,[6] we may at first feel sceptical. Caesar could not hope to play in Egypt the part which Sertorius

---

[1] Plut., 5, 4 ; Suet., 10.   [2] Vell., ii, 43, 4 ; Plut., 6 ; Suet., 11.

[3] Suetonius (11) wrongly says that Caesar took advantage of the fact that the Alexandrians had expelled their King [Ptolemy Auletes], a 'Friend and Ally' of the Roman People. Ptolemy came to Rome after his expulsion in 58 B. C.   [4] Plut., *Cras.*, 13, 2.

[5] Cic., *De lege agr.*, i, 1, 1 ; ii, 16–7, §§ 41–4. P. C. Sands (*The Client Princes of the Roman Empire*, 1908, p. 147) suspects that the rumour about the bequest was originated by Sulla. Cf. App., *B. C.*, i, 102, 476.

[6] Th. Mommsen (*Röm. Gesch.*, iii³, 1889, pp. 177–8 [Eng. tr., iv, 1908, p. 467]) and his disciples.

had played in Spain or to counterbalance the power of Pompey, unless he too were entrusted with a great fleet and a great army; and one can hardly believe that he, who looked without prejudice at fact, could have dreamed at that stage of his career that such power would be conferred upon an untried man. He may, however, have expected that if the contemplated annexation were carried out, it would become necessary to maintain an army in the province, of which, sooner or later, he would be able to make use. But he and his associate were both rebuffed. Crassus was denounced by Catulus;[1] Cicero argued in the interest of Pompey that Egypt had not been bequeathed to Rome;[2] and Caesar was not yet strong enough to overbear the opposition of the aristocracy.

He fails to obtain a command in Egypt.

So far we have been obliged to study the career of Caesar though the medium of compilers whose statements are not always trustworthy and often vague. The outlines, however, apart from anecdotes which, though they must be taken with reserve, read true to character, are clear enough. Caesar had become the leader of the party to which he belonged by birth, and to which, since he was not minded to rally to a lost cause, if he desired to regenerate the Roman commonwealth, he was bound for the time being, no matter what his sympathies may have been, to adhere. But he was oppressed with debt; in general estimation he ranked immeasurably below Pompey, who stood apart from and above all parties; his military genius was unknown; and even if Pompey, who seemed to have it in his power to determine the fate of the Republic, should leave an opening, some years must pass before he could obtain an office which might enable him to fulfil his destiny.

His political standing in 65 B.C.

Let us now attempt to trace the rise of Cicero, who was at this time beginning to canvass for the consulship.

Marcus Tullius Cicero was born on the 3rd of January, 106 B.C.[3]—the year of Pompey's birth—in his father's

Marcus Cicero.

---

[1] Plut., *Cras.*, 13, 2.
[2] *Schol. Bob.*, ed. Stangl, p. 92 (ed. Orelli, p. 350).
[3] Cic., *Brut.*, 43, 161; Plut., *Cic.*, 2, 1; Gell., xv, 28, 3

country house by the river Fibrenus, about three miles from Arpinum.[1] This town, the birth-place of Marius, was situated in the Volscian highlands, on the borders of Latium and Campania ; the tourist who enters it will see above its gate an inscription which the burgesses have set up in honour of the famous soldier and the famous orator. Cicero's mother belonged to a noble family ; his father, a studious valetudinarian, was a simple knight.[2] He was a Roman citizen, however, even when his elder son was born ; for Arpinum had received the franchise just a century before the Social War.[3] Marcus attended a school in Rome, where his ability was soon recognized ; and Plutarch relates that the parents of his schoolfellows came to see the prodigy of whom they had heard so much and to watch him at his work.[4] Afterwards, when he was speaking as counsel for the Greek poet Archias, he told the jury that it was his client who had first encouraged him to devote himself to oratory.[5] He had been listening for some time to the great speakers of the day when the Social War broke out, and as a boy of seventeen he served under Pompey's father and also under Sulla.[6] After the first campaign he studied philosophy under teachers of various schools and rhetoric under Apollonius, who was then in Rome, took daily lessons in elocution, and at the same time gained some knowledge of law from the Chief Pontiff, Scaevola.[7] When the Civil War was over he began at the age of twenty-five to practise at the bar.[8] In the following year his opportunity came. Sextus Roscius, a rich citizen of Ameria, had recently been murdered, and the murderers induced Chrysogonus, one of Sulla's favourites, to have his name inserted in the list of the proscribed. His estate, worth six million sesterces, was confiscated and sold at a mock auction for

---

[1] Cic., *De leg.*, ii, 1, 1. [2] *Ib.*, § 3 ; Plut., *Cic.*, 1, 1 ; 11
[3] Livy, xxxviii, 36, 7-9. [4] Plut., 2, 1.
[5] *Pro Arch.*, 1, 1.
[6] Cic., *De div.*, i, 33, 72 ; *Phil.*, xii, 11, 27 ; Plut., 3, 1.
[7] Cic., *Fam.*, xiii, 1, 2 ; *Brut.*, 89, 306-7 ; 90, 309 ; *De nat. deor.*, i, 3, 6 ; *De amic.*, 1, 1.
[8] *Pro Quintio*, the first of Cicero's extant speeches, was delivered in 81 B. C.

eight thousand to Chrysogonus,[1] who divided it with his friends. Fearing that the murdered man's son might sooner or later call them to account, they accused him of the crime. It was not likely that any one would venture to defend him against the Dictator's favourite and before a jury composed entirely of senators, themselves creatures of the Dictator. But Cicero did. He began his speech by explaining that he might presume to undertake a case which his illustrious seniors had declined, just because he was young and obscure, and while he exposed the villainy of Chrysogonus he contrived to exonerate Sulla. The defendant was acquitted, and Cicero left the court a famous man. 'From that moment,' he afterwards wrote, 'no case was deemed too important to be committed to my charge.'[2] But, notwithstanding the reputation which he had gained, he was aware that he had much to learn. He did not yet know how to modulate his voice; he was in poor health; and, if Plutarch is to be believed, he dreaded the resentment of Sulla.[3] Accordingly he left Rome and spent two years in the East, attending lectures on philosophy, practising under famous orators in Athens and the province of Asia, and finally studying at Rhodes under his old teacher, Apollonius.[4] No man ever longed more ardently or toiled more indefatigably for fame. About the time when the rebellion of Lepidus was suppressed he returned to Rome, and became at once one of the leaders of the bar.[5] In the following year he was elected a quaestor, and served at Lilybaeum in Western Sicily. At a later time, when he was addressing a jury, he told a story, which retired Anglo-Indians would appreciate, to illustrate Roman indifference to provincial affairs. 'To tell the truth,' he said, 'I thought that people in Rome were talking of nothing but my quaestorship. The Sicilians had paid me unheard-of compliments, and

He studies in the East.

77 B.C.

76 B.C.

He tells a story against himself.

---

[1] *Pro Rosc. Amer.*, 2, 6; Plut., 3, 2.   [2] *Brut.*, 90, 312.
[3] Plut., 3, 3. Prof. Reid (*M. T. Cic. Acad.*, 1885, p. 3) disbelieves Plutarch, because 'Cicero himself . . . never assigns any other cause for his departure than his health'.
[4] Cic., *De nat. deor.*, i, 3, 6; 21, 59; *De fin.*, i, 5, 16; *Brut.*, 91, 316; Plut., 4, 1.   [5] *Ib.*, 5, 2.

230   ANNUS MIRABILIS OF CICERO   CHAP.

I left the island in the expectation that the Roman People would come and lay the world at my feet. It happened that in the course of my journey I arrived at Puteoli, in the height of the season, when it was thronged with fashionable visitors. Gentlemen, I almost fainted when one of them came up and asked when I had left Rome and what was the latest news. " I'm returning ", I answered, "from my province." " Oh yes, of course," said he : " from Africa, isn't it ? " " No," said I, intensely irritated, " from Sicily." Some one, by way of showing that he was posted up in everybody's doings, interjected : ".What, don't you know that our friend has been quaestor at Syracuse ? " To cut a long story short, I swallowed my vexation and mingled with the crowd who had come to take the waters.' Cicero profited by his lesson. ' I saw ', he said, ' that though the ears of the Roman People were dull, their eyes were sharp : so I ceased thinking of what men might hear about me and took care that in future they should see me every day.' [1]

70 B. C.
His prosecution of Verres.

Another opportunity presented itself. In the first consulship of Pompey the Sicilian communities requested Cicero to undertake the prosecution of their late Governor, the notorious Verres, whose name symbolizes the worst iniquities of Roman provincial administration. Cicero obtained permission to visit Sicily for the purpose of collecting evidence, on the condition that he should not spend more than one hundred and ten days in the island.[2] In fifty he returned to Rome with documents and witnesses.[3] Verres and the senators who were interested in preventing the exposure of his crimes made desperate efforts to secure the appointment of an incompetent prosecutor, and afterwards to postpone the trial. Verres himself expended much of the money of which he had despoiled the Sicilians in trying to prevent Cicero from obtaining the office, for which he was a candidate, of curule aedile. But Cicero had won the election when he appeared in court. The trial began on the 5th of August.[4]

---

[1] *Pro Planc.*, 26–7, §§ 64–6.   [2] *Verr.*, ii, 1, 11, 30.
[3] *Ib.*, i, 2, 6.   [4] *Ib.*, 10, 31.

Verres still hoped that, owing to numerous festivals, on which the court could not sit, it might be possible to spin out the proceedings until the following year, when one of his friends would preside; or if not, that through influence and bribes he would be able to secure acquittal. Among the witnesses were many who had heard him boast that he would make a fortune in the first year of his governorship, hand over the plunder of the second to the advocate who would defend him and to his other supporters, and distribute that of the third among the jury.[1] Within nine days the trial ended. The evidence was so overwhelming that before the prosecution closed Verres left Rome for Massilia,[2] the favourite asylum of wealthy Roman exiles.

Cicero was now recognized as the foremost advocate in Rome;[3] but he did not begin to take an active part in politics until the time when, as praetor, he delivered his famous speech in support of the Manilian law.[4] Two years earlier he had written the first of his extant letters, which enable us henceforth to observe all the workings of his mind, while, along with the letters of his correspondents, his orations, and the memoirs of Caesar, they form, what hitherto we have rarely found, original sources of Roman history. Many of them were addressed to his old schoolfellow Pomponius Atticus,[5] a wealthy man of business, with whom he had first become intimate at Athens, who rejoiced in his prosperity, upon whom he leaned in adversity, who relieved him of innumerable burdens—truest, most generous, most unselfish, most devoted of friends.[6]

Now that Cicero is about to reveal himself, let us try to picture him in his environment. The bust, which stands in the Royal Gallery of Madrid,[7] portraying the kindly,

66 B. C.

Beginning of his correspondence with Atticus.

Cicero in his environment.

---

[1] *Ib.*, 14, 40.
[2] *Ib.*, ii, 1, 60, 156; Ps. Ascon., ed. Stangl, pp. 205, 223, 225 (ed. Orelli, pp. 126, 153, 156).
[3] *Brut.*, 93, 320.   [4] See p. 202.   [5] Corn. Nep., *Att.*, 1, 4.
[6] See my article in the *British Review*, xii, 1915, pp. 211-25.
[7] See J. J. Bernoulli, *Röm. Ikonogr.*, i, 1882, pp. 135-7. Compare the Apsley House bust, figured in A. Hekler's *Greek and Roman Portraits*, 1912, No. 159.

meditative, eager countenance of one who cannot but see every aspect of a question, and whose intellect is out of all proportion with his will, might depict some scholarly dean or academic dignitary of our own day. He was now in easy circumstances, though, being always careless about money, he was frequently in debt. From his father he had inherited a small estate.[1] His wife, Terentia, that unsympathetic woman of whom he said that she was more ready to meddle in politics than to let him have a voice in domestic affairs,[2] had brought him a dowry equivalent to four thousand pounds;[3] and although, under a law which was virtually obsolete, advocates were forbidden to accept fees,[4] grateful clients gave handsome presents and left substantial legacies.[5] Cicero had already bought a villa at Formiae,[6] near the Appian Way, and another, which had belonged to Sulla,[7] near Tusculum, on the slopes above the modern Frascati and commanding a view of the Campagna and of Rome. This was his favourite residence. Hard by was the villa of Lucullus, in whose society he delighted, and whose famous library was always open to him.[8] 'Here only,' he told Atticus, ' I find perfect rest from all worries and all toils.'[9]

66 B. C.
Catiline.

While Cicero was still a praetor and just before Caesar entered upon his aedileship, the notorious conspirator whose fortunes were destined to be linked with theirs, and whose biography illuminates the social and the political conditions of the time, began to play a prominent part in the public life of Rome.

Lucius Sergius Catilina, a patrician belonging to a noble family, which had once been famous but for two centuries had remained obscure, was endowed with a personality that wrought upon the imagination of his contemporaries and of posterity, and still exercises the judgement of the

[1] Plut., 8, 2.   [2] *Ib.*, 20, 2.   [3] *Ib.*, 8, 2.
[4] Livy, xxxiv, 4, 9; Tac., *Ann.*, xi, 5. Cf. P. Willems, *Le sénat*, &c., i, 1878, p. 205.
[5] R. Y. Tyrrell, *The Correspondence of Cicero*, i², 1885, pp. 34-6.
[6] *Att.*, i, 4, 3.   [7] Pliny, *Nat. Hist.*, xxii, 6 (6), 12.
[8] Cic., *Acad. Prior.*, i, 2, 4; Plut., *Luc.*, 41, 4; 42, 1. 5.
[9] *Att.*, i, 5, 7. See p. 444.

learned world. Virgil [1] ratified the condemnation which 66 B.C. Cicero and Sallust [2] had pronounced. But neither the portrait drawn by the historian nor the invective of the orator enables us to understand him. A list of qualities, an inventory of vices, a catalogue of crimes do not re-create a character : even Plutarch could not make more of Catiline than a conventional villain of melodrama. The one document that gives a real insight into his mind is a letter written when he was quitting his house on the Palatine, which shows that his last thought, when he was going to his doom, was for the welfare of the woman for whose sake he was reputed to have committed a monstrous crime.[3] Whether he was really guilty of the abominations with which Cicero charged him to his face without, as we are told, eliciting denial [4]—whether he committed fratricide and perpetrated massacre when he attached himself to Sulla, attempted to debauch Cicero's sister-in-law, the Vestal virgin Fabia, and murdered his own son because his mistress, Orestilla, would not marry him till she was relieved of the encumbrance—these problems we need not attempt to solve, for the life of Catiline concerns us only so far as it belongs to the history of Rome. But a novel phenomenon of our time may impel those who have been accustomed from childhood to regard him as a political monster to reflect : the objects which he purposed, if it were possible, to achieve by constitutional means had much in common with those which conspirators in more than one European country, who aim at destroying constitutional government, openly avow, without the least risk of prosecution, without any fear that their rulers will pass an ' ultimate decree ' to save the State from *them*.

When Pompey was beginning his career in Asia Catiline was governing the province Africa, and in the course of the year a deputation appeared before the Senate to complain of his administration. Soon afterwards Catiline himself returned to Rome to canvass for the consulship ; but as he had received notice of prosecution from the

[1] *Acn.*, viii, 668-9.   [2] *Cat.*, 14-6.   [3] *Ib.*, 35.   [4] See p. 240.

youthful Publius Clodius for malversation in his province, the consul Volcacius Tullus, after consultation with leading senators, who perhaps suspected that Crassus and Caesar were prepared to back him, decided that with this charge impending he must not be allowed to stand. After the election the successful candidates, Publius Autronius Paetus and Publius Cornelius Sulla, were disqualified for bribery; and the candidates who had lately been defeated, Lucius Aurelius Cotta and Lucius Manlius Torquatus, were elected in their stead.[1] But the Government had neither soldiers nor police, and there were many discontented men in Italy who could be relied upon to abet a revolution. A plot was formed—the so-called first conspiracy of Catiline—the details of which, even when Sallust endeavoured to unravel them, were not completely known.[2] With Gnaeus Calpurnius Piso (an impoverished noble), Autronius, and perhaps also Sulla, Catiline conspired to murder the new consuls on the 1st of January, when they were to enter upon office. Autronius and Sulla were to seize the consular insignia, and Piso was to take possession of the provinces of Spain. The plot was abortive, for the day before it was to take effect Catiline rashly displayed the armed men whom he had engaged, and the Senate provided the consuls with a bodyguard. Though certain senators desired to take action, a tribune exercised his veto, perhaps because it was suspected that influential persons, whom it might be imprudent to provoke, were implicated: moreover, incredible as it may at first sight appear, Piso by a senatorial decree was actually sent to Spain, because Crassus and other senators, who pressed for his appointment, hoped that he would serve as a drag upon the dreaded power of Pompey. Enemies of Caesar, whose testimony is eagerly accepted by his chief admirer[3] and contemptuously rejected by his sternest critic,[4] asserted that he and Crassus were not only privy to, but the prime movers in the plot; and since

---

[1] See pp. 445-6.   [2] See pp. 446-9, where the evidence is discussed.
[3] Mommsen. See p. 449.
[4] Strachan-Davidson, *Cicero*, 1894, p. 91.

it was through the influence of Crassus that the ulterior design of the conspirators was carried out, we may reasonably infer that he and probably also Caesar, if they were wise enough to keep clear of murder, gave their countenance to the intended *coup d'état*.[1] Anyhow, we may gather from Caesar's later conduct that he was prepared, if the plot succeeded, to turn it to account.

65 B. C.

Catiline did not stand for the consulship this year, for at the time of the election his trial had not begun; but Cicero, who had refused to accept a province because, in view of his own candidature, he desired to keep himself before the public, began in July to canvass for the election which was to be held in the following year. 'Catiline', he told Atticus, 'will be sure to stand, if the jury finds that it is not broad day at noon.'[2] A few days later he wrote again, 'At present I am thinking of defending my competitor, Catiline. We have the very jurors we require, and the prosecutor is most obliging. I hope, if he is acquitted, he will join me more closely in canvassing; but if it happens otherwise, I will bear it with resignation.[3] It is essential for me that you should come, and that speedily, for there is a very strong opinion prevalent that friends of yours in high position will be opposed to my election, and I see that to conciliate their support your help will be invaluable.'[4] Cynics may ask whether Cicero, when he wrote this letter, was aware of the murders, the attempted massacre of consuls, the incest, and the other crimes which he afterwards denounced. He decided, after all, to take no part in the defence;[5] but, owing to the collusion between Clodius and Catiline, at which he hinted, the bribes that were administered to needy jurors, and perhaps also the support of distin-

Cicero's canvass for the consulship.

· G. Ferrero (*Grandezza e decadenza di Roma*, ii, 1902, p. 545 [Eng. tr., ii, 333]), thinks that one motive of Crassus was to have the consuls on his side and by their aid to accomplish his design of annexing Egypt. But we do not know whether that design had yet been formed.

The plot was wholly abortive. Piso failed to conciliate the provincials and was assassinated.

[2] *Att.*, i, 1, 1.   [3] *Ib.*, 2, 1. See p. 449, n. 7.
[4] *Att.*, i, 2, 2.   [5] See pp. 449-50.

236 ANNUS MIRABILIS OF CICERO CHAP.

65 B.C. Catiline acquitted of malversation. guished men, who testified to the excellence of the defendant's character, Catiline was acquitted. Incredible as it may appear, his counsel was the same Torquatus whom he had planned to murder.[1] We are assured by the learned commentator, Asconius, who cleared up obscurities in Cicero's orations, that the senatorial jurors voted against Catiline, the knights and the 'pay-masters' in his favour;[2] and if we hesitate to accept the conjecture[3] that the senators voted to save their credit for integrity, but bribed their colleagues to save a member of the Senate, we cannot deny that such a proceeding would have been characteristic of the times.

Candidates for the consulship. The elections of 64 were near. Catiline, despite his acquittal, did not fulfil Cicero's hope by joining in his canvass. Besides these two there were five candidates; but only one of them, Gaius Antonius (an uncle of Mark Antony) was considered formidable.[4] Catiline joined with Antonius to defeat Cicero: both were supported by Crassus and Caesar,[5] who were doubtless confident that they would be able to make use of them, whereas Cicero was known to be devoted to Pompey, whom Crassus detested and whose power was a bar to the rise of Caesar. Caesar and Crassus had long been scheming to procure the election of their candidates not only for the consulship **65 B.C.** but also for the tribunate. In the preceding year, when Caesar was an aedile, Crassus and Catulus were censors.[6] Crassus desired, in pursuance of the policy which Caesar

---

[1] Cic., *Pro Sulla*, 29, 81; *In Pis.*, 10, 23.
[2] Ed. Clark, p. 89, ll. 16-9 (ed. Stangl, p. 69). H. Wirz (*Catilina's u. Cicero's Bewerbung*, &c., 1864, p. 11. Cf. E. Meyer, *Caesars Monarchie*[2], 1919, p. 23), remarking that the law (*lex Fufia*) by which senators, knights, and *tribuni aerarii* voted separately was not passed till 59 B.C. (see p. 319), maintains that Asconius was wrong. It is probable, however, that, notwithstanding the ballot, the manner of voting leaked out. See *Q. fr.*, iii, 4, 1, where Cicero, speaking of the trial of Gabinius for bribery, says, 'Domitius Calvinus voted so openly for acquittal that every one could see'. Cf. Vell., ii, 47, 5.
[3] G. Long, *Decline of the Roman Republic*, iii, 1869, p. 202.
[4] Cic., *Att.*, i, 1, 1; Ascon., ed. Clark, p. 82, ll. 4-17 (ed. Stangl, p 64); Q. Cic., *De pet. cons.*, §§ 7-8.
[5] Ascon., ed. Clark, p. 83, ll. 2-4 (ed. Stangl, p. 64).
[6] Plut., *Cras.*, 13, 1.

had adumbrated on his return from Spain, to obtain the enfranchisement of the Transpadanes: Catulus was strongly opposed to such a measure; and the dispute between the two became so acrimonious that both resigned.[1] But why? They would not have resigned on a mere difference of opinion. The ingenuity of an English scholar [2] has suggested a satisfactory explanation of what had puzzled generations of commentators. The censors could not give effect to their respective views unless a bill for the contemplated enfranchisement were passed, when the time would come for enrolling the new citizens in the electoral register. Caesar evidently hoped that one of the tribunes who supported him [3] would succeed in passing such a bill; and the censors were doubtless aware of his intention. We may conjecture that Crassus threatened to block every official act of Catulus unless the bill were carried, or that Catulus declared that if it were carried, he would refuse to sanction the enrolment of the new electors. The bill, if indeed it was drafted, was not passed; but Caesar did not abandon his intention. The censors of the following year belonged to the popular party, and Caesar hoped that if a reform bill could be passed, they would see to it that the Transpadanes were enrolled before the time of the elections. But the Conservatives again frustrated the design. Certain tribunes belonging to their party vetoed the first act of the new censors—the revision of the list of senators—and a tribune named Gaius Papius carried a law by which all aliens then resident in Rome, except those who were permanently domiciled in Italy as distinct from Cisalpine Gaul, were compelled to leave. Thus even if the Transpadanes were enfranchised, they would be excluded from the poll. The censors, like their immediate predecessors, of course resigned.[4]

65 B. C.
Caesar and Crassus fail to procure the enfranchisement of the Transpadanes.

64 B. C

[1] Suet., *Div. Iul.*, 8 ; Dio, xxxvii, 9, 3. Cf. Plut., *Cras.*, 13, 2.
[2] Dr. E. G. Hardy (*Journ. Rom. Studies*, vi, 1916, pp. 63–82).
[3] Suet., 11.
[4] Dio, xxxvii, 9, 5. The other important passages in which the Papian law is mentioned are (Cicero) *Pro Arch.*, 5, 10 ; *Pro Balbo*, 23, 52 ; *De off.*, iii, 11, 47. Prof. R. W. Husband (*Class. Philol.*, xi, 1916, pp. 326–7) says

238   ANNUS MIRABILIS OF CICERO   CHAP.

64 B.C.
Q. Cicero advises Marcus about the conduct of his canvass.

A few months before the consular election Cicero's younger brother Quintus, who had himself had experience of electioneering, sent him a letter, which he called *The Candidates' Handbook*,[1] to help him in his canvass. Cicero found it very useful.[2] While it contains many passages which would be applicable to our own times, it shows that the labour which a candidate had to face and the demands that were made upon his purse were far greater then than now. Cicero was a 'new man'.[3] None of his paternal ancestors had held any of the offices of state; the great families, for the most part, were opposed to him;[4] and he could not afford to neglect any means of conciliating the electors. On the other hand, the equestrian order, to which he himself belonged, supported him; his eloquent advocacy had laid various public men under obligation, while many of the rising generation were his warm admirers; and his only formidable rivals were suspected men.[5] They would assuredly resort to bribery; but his conscience and his reputation forbade him to follow their example. Notwithstanding the fatigue, the slowness, and the expense of travelling, he must go far afield to solicit the votes of those who could afford to

that 'nobody can believe that Dio's opinion'—that the object of the law was 'the expulsion of those who did not have legal residence in *I*taly'—' is correct. It would be absurd to think that for . . . fifteen years [i. e. until the enfranchisement of the Transpadanes in 49 B.C.] inhabitants of the provinces, as well as those who lived outside the Roman Empire, were forbidden to take up their residence in Rome '. The passages cited from Cicero, he continues, ' are quite out of harmony with the idea that the law was intended to secure the departure of aliens from Rome '. Are they ? Read the passage in *De officiis* :—*Male etiam qui peregrinos urbibus uti prohibent eosque exterminant, ut Pennus apud patres nostros, Papius nuper: Nam esse pro cive qui civis non sit rectum est non licere . . . usu vero urbis prohibere peregrinos sane inhumanum est.* As Hardy says (*op. cit.*, p. 81), ' the only " peregrini " domiciled in *I*taly at this time were foreigners . . . and all of these . . . were unaffected by the Papian law. On the other hand, any " peregrini " domiciled outside *I*taly, and therefore any Transpadani from the Latin colonies in the Cisalpine, who happened to be in Rome, would have to leave '.

[1] See pp. 450-1. [2] *Q. fr.*, i, 1, 43.
[3] Q. Cic., *De pet. cons.*, § 1 ; Cic., *De lege agr.*, ii, 1, 3.
[4] Sall., *Cat.*, 23, 6.
[5] *De pet. cons.*, §§ 3, 8–10 ; Ascon., ed. Clark, p. 82, l. 17 ; p. 83, ll. 1–2 (ed. Stangl, p. 64).

come to Rome.¹ He must convince Conservatives that he shared their views and that, if he was despised by the nobility, he was no demagogue.² He must not merely appeal to the gratitude of clients whom his professional skill had saved, but must let others know that they could count upon his assistance if they gave him their support.³ He must take the trouble to become acquainted with electors of every rank and to gain the assistance of the political clubs.⁴ ' One has great need ', Quintus reminded him, ' of a flattering manner, which, wrong and discreditable though it may be in other walks of life, is indispensable in seeking office.' ⁵ Every elector was entitled to the satisfaction of being personally solicited for his vote.⁶ Marcus must not be over-scrupulous. He must not refuse his services to those who asked for them merely because he knew that he would be unable to keep his promises, for, as Quintus observed, human nature being what it is, ' all men prefer a false promise to a flat refusal.' ⁷ Moreover, ' at the worst, the man to whom you have told a falsehood may be angry. That risk, if you make a promise, is uncertain and deferred, and it only affects a few ; but if you refuse, you are sure to offend many, and that at once.'⁸ ' You must take care ', Quintus added, ' to let every one know that Pompey is strongly in your favour, and that your success would entirely suit his plans. . . .'⁹ Contrive, if possible, to get some new scandal started against your rivals for crime or immorality or corruption, according to their characters.' ¹⁰

This last injunction Cicero diligently observed. It was notorious that Catiline and Antonius were bribing the electors on a prodigious scale,¹¹ and those who remembered

---
¹ Cic., *Att.*, i, 1, 2.   ² *De pet. cons.*, § 5.
³ *Ib.*, §§ 20, 22.   ⁴ *Ib.*, §§ 16–9.   ⁵ *Ib.*, § 42.
⁶ *Ib.*, § 43.   ⁷ *Ib.*, § 46.   ⁸ *Ib.*, §§ 47–8.
⁹ E. Meyer (*Caesars Monarchie*², 1919, p. 11, n. 1) remarks that no such relations existed then between Cicero and Pompey as those to which Quintus alludes. How does he know ? We may infer from Cicero's speech *De lege agr.*, ii, 18, 49 (*quam* [dignitatem] *ego, etsi libente illo, tamen absente illo . . . consecutus sum*) that Pompey approved his candidature.
¹⁰ *De pet. cons.*, §§ 51–2.
¹¹ Ascon., ed. Clark, p. 83, ll. 6–7 (ed. Stangl. p. 64)

what Catiline had attempted in the previous year might expect that his supporters would try more drastic methods. A decree was therefore passed for the dissolution of all electioneering clubs, besides religious and other associations whose members might resort to violence or exercise undue influence;[1] and various senators urged that the existing law against bribery should be strengthened by fresh penalties. A tribune, Mucius Orestinus, vetoed the proposed bill, a step which provoked general indignation. Thereupon Cicero, taking advantage of the temper of the House, delivered an invective against the tribune and the candidates whom he was endeavouring to screen; nor did he shrink from covertly attacking the powerful financier who was supporting Catiline. He plainly hinted that Crassus had been the author of the plot to murder the consuls of the previous year. He assailed Catiline with the stock charges which have made him the arch-villain of Roman history—murder, tyranny, bribery, adultery, marriage with the daughter whom an adulterous mistress bore him, attempted incest, intended massacre. Catiline and Antonius retorted with abuse, and as they could not confute the orator, derided him as an outsider who had come to lodge in Rome.[2] Alarming rumours were afloat about the designs of Catiline, probably also about those of Caesar; and if Cicero had in the past opposed the Senate, he could be trusted to support it now. In politics indeed he had always been eclectic: though he had acted with the popular party on behalf of Pompey, though he had defended Cornelius in his struggle with the Optimates, he had never been a demagogue.[3] Perhaps

---

[1] Cic., *In Pis.*, 4, 8; Ascon., ed. Clark, p. 7, ll. 9–14; p. 75, ll. 13–9 (ed. Stangl, pp. 15, 59). It is now generally admitted that the *senatus consultum* referred to by Asconius in the former passage, which has occasioned needless controversy, was passed in 64, not 65 B. C.; for, as the second passage shows, the clubs in question still existed in 65. See J. P. Waltzing, *Étude hist. sur les corporations prof. chez les Romains*, i, 1895, pp. 98–9, and *Paulys Real-Ency.*, iv, 406.

[2] *Oratio in toga candida* and Asconius's comments, ed. Clark, p. 83, ll. 10–26, p. 84, ll. 1–11, p. 85, ll. 1–6, p. 86, ll. 23–7, p. 91, ll. 14–26, p. 92, ll. 11–4, p. 93, ll. 24–5, p. 94, l. 1 (ed. Stangl, pp. 64–7, 70–2).

[3] Cf. G. Boissier, *Cicéron et ses amis*, 1892, pp. 50–3; *La conjuration de*

he may have been asked to give some definite pledge; 64 B.C.
at all events Conservatives who had before frowned upon
his candidature now used their influence on his behalf.
In the election which followed he received the suffrages Cicero
of all the tribes; Antonius obtained a small majority elected.
over Catiline.[1]

But Catiline was determined to try again; and, if we
may trust Cicero,[2] he made repeated attempts to compass
his assassination before he entered upon office. A fresh
prosecution, which Cicero had warned him in the Senate
that he would not be able to escape,[3] overtook him before
the end of the year; but fortune again befriended him.
He was accused before Caesar, who had been appointed
president of the permanent commission which heard
charges of murder, of having committed that crime in
the proscription of Sulla; and since Caesar had already
treated as murderers those who had received money from
the treasury for the heads of proscribed persons, although
they had been expressly indemnified by Sulla,[4] modern Catiline
historians have not unreasonably assumed that he screened acquitted
Catiline from conviction because he intended to employ court of
him as a tool.[5] murder.

Caesar himself, though he had failed to secure the
consulship for Catiline, was not at the end of his resources.
Towards the end of the year the Chief Pontiff, Quintus
Caecilius Metellus, died, and Caesar, although he was still
comparatively young, resolved to become a candidate for
the vacancy. The office was tenable for life, and the
holder had great authority in deciding questions of
religious law, with which politics were closely intertwined.

Catilina, 1905, pp. 87–9; and R. Heinze (*Abhandl. d. philol.-hist. Kl. d.
Königl. Sächs. Gesellsch. d. Wiss.*, xxvii, 1909, p. 948).
  [1] Ascon., ed. Clark, p. 94, ll. 3–6; Plut., *Cic.*, 10, 1; 11; App., ii, 2, 5.
  [2] *In Cat.*, i, 5, 11; 6, 15. Cf. Sall., *Cat.*, 26, 1.
  [3] Ascon., ed. Clark, p. 87, ll. 5–8 (ed. Stangl, p. 67).
  [4] Suet., 11. 'Caesar', says Strachan-Davidson (*Problems of the Rom. Crim.
Law*, ii, 1912, p. 34), 'appears to have held that the' law of Sulla directed
against murder (*lex de sicariis*) 'abrogated the immunity which Sulla's
previous law had given to his agents'.
  [5] Dio, xxxvii, 10, 2–3; Ascon., ed. Clark, p. 91, ll. 11–3 (ed. Stangl,
p. 70).

242 ANNUS MIRABILIS OF CICERO CHAP.

64 B.C.
The right of electing the Chief Pontiff restored through Caesar's influence to the people.

Caesar had two formidable rivals, Catulus and Servilius Isauricus, and under the existing regulation, by which the appointment belonged to the college of pontiffs, he would have no chance of success. He therefore persuaded one of the tribunes, Titus Labienus, who had served with him against the pirates of Cilicia,[1] to propose a bill for restoring the election to the people, from whom it had been withdrawn by Sulla.[2]

Rullus proposes an agrarian law in the interest of Caesar and Crassus.

Another tribune, Servilius Rullus, was employed to introduce a measure which, if it were carried, would place in the hands of Caesar and Crassus a power not inferior to that of Pompey. All that we know about this bill, which was promulgated in December, is derived from the hostile criticisms of Cicero; but although he mentioned neither Caesar nor Crassus, it is evident to all who have read his speeches that they were the powerful demagogues of whom, as he broadly hinted, Rullus was the tool.[3]

Ostensibly the bill was an agrarian law on a colossal scale. Estates were to be purchased from private owners who might be willing to sell; the Campanian land and the adjoining Campus Stellatis—the only public lands that remained in Italy—were to be taken over by the State for distribution; and on all of them indigent citizens, and in the future veteran soldiers, were to be settled. The avowed purpose of granting allotments to the poor was to relieve the capital of its superfluous proletariate. The purchase-money was to be raised by selling certain tracts in nine provinces [4] of the empire and in all lands outside Italy which since the first consulship of Sulla had become domain of the Roman People, as well as buildings and other property, the sale of which had been authorized by the Senate eighteen years before; by an extraordinary tax which was to be levied in every province; by requiring all general officers in future or

---

[1] Cf. Suet., 3, with Cic., *Pro Rab.*, 7, 21. [2] See p. 62.

[3] Cf. *De lege agr.*, i, 7, 22, with ii, 9, 23; 18, 49–50; and iii, 4, 16. The best commentary on these speeches of Cicero is that of Dr. Hardy (*Journ. of Philol.*, xxxii, 1913, pp. 223–60).

[4] Sicily, Spain, Africa, Cyrene, Achaia, Macedonia, Asia, Bithynia, Cilicia.

during the next five years to surrender all the booty of 64 B.C. war which they had acquired; and by appropriating the produce of all the taxes which might result from further annexations. The administration of the law was to be entrusted to ten commissioners, who were to be elected by seventeen only of the thirty-five tribes,[1] and were to be invested with military power; and Pompey was virtually excluded by a clause which provided that all candidates must personally give in their names. Although the funds which it was proposed to raise were avowedly to be expended only in the purchase of lands for distribution, they would be so large that a surplus would be available for any object which the most influential of the commissioners might desire to attain. Moreover, the vaguely worded clause which entitled the commissioners to dispose of lands outside Italy would empower Caesar and Crassus, in the sure event of their election, to establish their authority in Egypt; and they would be able to raise an army for service there on the pretext of carrying out the annexation. While this force and the money which they would have at their disposal would serve to check any ambition which Pompey might entertain when he returned to Italy, the farms to be reserved for assignment to old soldiers would enable them to make terms with him when he found himself obliged to provide for his disbanded veterans.[2] Two of the provisions were undeniably statesmanlike. The systematic peculation that had been practised by generals like Lucullus was to be stopped, and the legal status of the lands which Sulla had confiscated was to be finally determined. All the agrarian measures of Sulla rested upon the Valerian law, which sanctioned in advance whatever he might himself enact, but which, having been proposed without due notice and by an official who had no authority to legislate, was itself illegal. It might therefore have been

---

[1] A. W. Zumpt (*M. T. Cic. orat. tres de lege agr.*, 1861, p. ix) thought that the object of this provision (*De lege agr.*, ii, 7-8, §§ 16-21) was to prevent favouritism and bribery. Cf. Hardy, *op. cit.*, p. 244.

[2] See Hardy, *op. cit.*, pp. 257-9.

argued that the lands which Sulla had granted to his veterans and those which, after he had confiscated them, remained unsold or unassigned and had probably been appropriated by his favourites, were public property; and a rash legislator, in the position in which Caesar now found himself, would have been tempted to mark them for distribution under his agrarian law. But Caesar, who saw that to cancel Sulla's acts would be a quixotic policy which could only lead to inextricable confusion, decided to confirm the titles of all who had profited by his legislation.[1]

But the power which the law would place in Caesar's hands was so enormous that no one can read the orations of Cicero without wondering whether Caesar could have had any confident expectation of success. At all events whatever chance he had he forfeited by his selection of an instrument and by the unskilfulness with which he or the agent whom he employed drafted the bill. Some of the clauses were so loosely worded that they invited misrepresentation, and Rullus inspired no confidence.

Cicero saw his opportunity. His colleague, Antonius, was in favour of the bill;[2] but Cicero contrived a plan for disarming his opposition and, what was more important, for detaching him from his connexion with Catiline. The provinces which had been assigned by the Senate to the consuls were Cisalpine Gaul and Macedonia. Cicero determined not to accept either, and resigned his claim to Macedonia in favour of Antonius,[3] at the same time taking steps to ensure that he should fulfil his bargain. The quaestor attached to Antonius was a young man named Publius Sestius. Cicero charged him to watch the

[1] Hardy, *op. cit.*, p. 247.
[2] Plut., *Cic.*, 12, 2.
[3] See p. 457. It is well known that two years later a sum of money was paid by Antonius to Cicero through an agent whom Cicero calls 'Teucris' (*Att.*, i, 12, 1-2; 13, 6; 14, 7). Whether, as Long (*Decline of the Roman Republic*, iii, 238) and E. Meyer (*Caesars Monarchie*², 1919, p. 29, n. 1) think, Cicero had stipulated for a share of the profits which Antonius would make in Macedonia, or, as Tyrrell supposes (in his note on *Att.*, i, 12, 1), Antonius had promised to pay Cicero 'for resisting attacks made on him in the senate for misgovernment', matters little.

movements of his chief and to report to him any which might appear suspicious.¹

Before the end of the year the bill of Rullus was posted, according to custom, in the Forum.² On the 1st of January—the first day of his consulship—Cicero brought its provisions before the notice of the Senate.³ He described, with the aim of ensuring its rejection, what its authors really purposed to attain. The ambitious men who two years before had tried in vain to get control of Egypt were now attempting to gain their object by clandestine means. 'Are you going to give them Alexandria', he asked, 'when they are trying to get it surreptitiously, you who resisted them when they openly fought for it?'⁴ After sketching the political features of the measure, he concluded by announcing that he did not intend to accept a province, but to remain and keep watch over the State, for, though it was not threatened by foreign enemies, there were evil-minded citizens who were scheming to effect its ruin.⁵ But to convince the Senate was an easy task: the test of Cicero's oratory would come when he had to persuade the people to reject a law which was on the face of it intended for their benefit.

Cicero sincerely believed that the bill of Rullus was dangerous to the State;⁶ and those who blame him for having misled his audience forget that a Roman mob was not to be convinced by sober and impartial reasoning. Congratulating himself and thanking the electors for having preferred him, a 'new man', to his noble rivals, he warned them that they were living in anxious times, when financial credit was shaken by the machinations of unscrupulous men, and assured them that he intended to be a people's consul in the best sense of the term.⁷ Against an agrarian law, as such, he had nothing to say: had not those illustrious patriots, the brothers Gracchi, settled the poor on public lands?⁸ When he heard that

64 B. C.

63 B. C.
Cicero's speeches against the bill.

---

¹ *Pro Sest.*, 3, 8; *In Pis.*, 2, 5.   ² *De lege agr.*, ii, 5, 13.
³ *Ib.*, i, 8, 26.   ⁴ *Ib.*, 1, 1.   ⁵ *Ib.*, 8–9, §§ 24–6.
⁶ *Fam.*, xiii, 4, 2.   ⁷ *De lege agr.*, ii, 1–4, §§ 3–9.   ⁸ *Ib.*, 5, 10.

the law of Rullus was contemplated, he had hoped that it would prove a useful measure, which he might honestly support. But when he had invited the confidence of those who were framing it, his overtures had been scornfully rejected.[1] What was it that this Rullus—this tribune who affected the long hair, the flowing beard, and the shabby clothing of a typical demagogue—wished the people of Rome to pass? Nothing but a cunningly disguised scheme for creating ten kings to dispose of the treasury, the public revenues, the provinces, the entire commonwealth—in short, for setting up ten irresponsible masters over the Roman world. And this bill, which gave the Roman People nothing and certain individuals everything, which offered allotments and took away freedom, was the work of tribunes,—those magistrates who had been established as the guardians of popular liberty![2] To begin with, the unheard-of method by which the commissioners were to be elected was a gross infringement of electoral rights: evidently Rullus intended so to manipulate the lot, by which the seventeen tribes were to be selected, as to get a majority which would elect those candidates, including Rullus himself, whom Rullus wished to be appointed. Why was Pompey excluded from the list? Simply because those crafty individuals who were behind Rullus knew that if the people were allowed to use their right of choice, Pompey was the man of all others whom they would choose.[3] Nominally, the commissioners were to hold office for five years; but that really meant for ever; for with their military authority and their vast resources, it would be impossible to get rid of them.[4]—Having thus cleared the way, Cicero proceeded to attack the various provisions by which the commissioners were to be empowered to raise the funds which they required. He assumed of course that they would be corrupt self-seeking scoundrels. What was there to prevent them from tampering with the public records and forging senatorial decrees, so as to add to the list of

[1] *De lege agr.*, ii, 5, 11–12.   [2] 5–6, §§ 13–6.
[3] 7–9, §§ 16–24.   [4] 13, 32–4.

those properties which they would be entitled to sell ?[1] 63 B.C. Without straining the truth Cicero could tell the people, as he had told the Senate, that those who two years before had endeavoured openly to get themselves invested with the control of Egypt were now seeking to attain the same end secretly ; but though he knew, and even unguardedly admitted, that the Senate had already decided that the will by which Egypt was said to have been bequeathed to the Roman People was genuine, he insisted that the commissioners would take it upon themselves to settle the question as they pleased.[2] The clauses that provided for the sale of lands and the imposition of new taxes were easy to misrepresent to an audience few of whom had taken the trouble to read the bill. The commissioners, Cicero explained, were to be empowered to sell the whole province of Asia, the whole of Bithynia, and many other tracts which he was careful to enumerate ;[3] and if the bulk of his hearers were not affected by the prospect which he conjured up, it may well have alarmed those who had invested their savings with the tax-collecting syndicates. Then, he continued, there was the clause, from which Pompey was conspicuously excepted—to do him honour or to bring him into odium ? —that provided for the surrender of all booty of war : was it not intolerable that the commissioners should assume the functions of the collectors of tolls and rummage the valises of Roman generals to see whether they had hidden anything ?[4] As for the purchase of estates— from those forsooth who were willing to sell—what an opening for jobbery ! What a chance for those friends of the commissioners who wanted to dispose of worthless property or property their title to which was doubtful ! Rullus's own father-in-law, for instance, had lands which he had got from Sulla, and would be glad to exchange the odium which they entailed upon him for a substantial sum.[5] The allotments that were offered to the poor were a snare and a delusion. Rullus had affirmed in the Senate

[1] 14, 37. [2] 16, 41–3. [3] 15, 38–40.
[4] 22–3, §§ 59–61. [5] 25–6, §§ 66–9

that the superfluous proletariate of Rome ought to be drained away : the fellow had the impudence to compare his respectable fellow-citizens to the bilge-water of a ship. If they would take his advice, they would remain in Rome, where they could use their votes and enjoy the public holidays, the public amusements, and the other advantages of the city, unless indeed they preferred to exchange those benefits for the arid fields or the malarious swamps which Rullus proposed to allot to them.[1] His plan for settling old soldiers on the land was simply a scheme for filling Italy with garrisons, which would be a standing menace to popular liberty. What was there to prevent him from planting a colony on the Janiculan hill and thence overawing the city ? The Campanian land, which even Sulla had not dared to touch, but which Rullus proposed to occupy with settlers who would be ready for any violence, was a most valuable source of revenue, which the State could not afford to lose. Moreover, it was already occupied by industrious and worthy tenants, and it would be monstrous injustice to dispossess them in favour of the turbulent satellites of the commissioners.[2]—If there were men below the platform who could discriminate between the specious and the true, they probably concluded that this plea for the Campanian land was one of the few sound arguments of a sophistical speech.

But Cicero understood his audience. He was obliged, indeed, to make a further effort, for Rullus addressed the people in his absence [3] and challenged him to say frankly whether he wished to question the titles of Sulla's allottees. Cicero admitted that he did not, but he contrived to distort the purport of the clause by which Rullus intended to confirm them, and he concluded by warning the people that the real object of the bill was to raise an army against Pompey and against their liberty.[4] Lucius Caecilius, a Conservative tribune, announced that he would block the bill ; [5] and if it was not rejected by

[1] *De lege agr.*, ii, 26–7, 70–1.　　[2] 27–31, §§ 73–86.　　[3] iii, 1, 1.
[4] 2–3, §§ 6–12 ; 4, 16.　　[5] Cic., *Pro Sulla*, 23, 65.

the assembly,[1] it was dropped. Cicero had gained a victory over Caesar; and Caesar doubtless profited by the lesson.[2]

63 B.C. Cicero wins an oratorical triumph.

Fresh from this success, Cicero achieved another oratorical triumph in defence of a principle which he constantly endeavoured to maintain, and which he regarded as the buttress of the constitution,—harmony between the Senate and the equestrian order. A few years before, a tribune, Roscius Otho, had revived an old statute by which certain seats in the theatre were to be reserved for the knights. Not long after the failure of the bill of Rullus Otho himself, appearing in the theatre, was hissed by the populace, who resented the favour which he had shown to their superiors. The knights countered the hisses by loud applause, and the disturbance was likely to end in riot. Hearing the uproar, says Plutarch, the consul entered the theatre and called upon the people to follow him into the temple of Bellona, where he explained the purpose of the statute with such persuasive force that when they returned to their places they vied with the knights in applauding Otho.[3]

67 B.C.

Meanwhile, however, Caesar had devised a scheme which, if it succeeded, might atone for the defeat of the agrarian bill and strengthen the position of his party. It will be remembered that in the rebellion of Lepidus the consul Catulus and other notables had been invested by the 'ultimate senatorial decree' with full power to secure the public safety. Since Opimius had been acquitted on the charge of having put to death Roman citizens when he was empowered to act against Gaius Gracchus, the decree, although it was regarded by the popular party with suspicion, had become recognized as constitutional.[4] Caesar himself, if not then, in the

The prosecution of Rabirius.

---

[1] Plut., Cic., 12, 3. Pliny (vii, 30 [31], 117), apostrophizing Cicero, says, *te dicente legem agrariam, hoc est alimenta sua, abdicarunt tribus.*

[2] The three speeches, and especially the second, should be studied by all politicians who aspire to become proficient in the art of misrepresentation.

[3] Cic., *Att.*, ii, 1, 3; *Pro Mur.*, 19, 40; *Phil.*, ii, 18, 44; Livy, *Epit.*, 99; Pliny, vii, 30 (31), 117; Vell., ii, 32, 3; Plut., *Cic.*, 13, 2; Dio, xxxvi, 42, 1.

[4] Strachan-Davidson (*Problems*, &c., i, 241-2) remarks that the *populares*, when they had the upper hand in the Senate, occasionally, e.g. in 83 B.C. against Sulla (Exup., 7), used the *senatus consultum ultimum*.

250   ANNUS MIRABILIS OF CICERO   CHAP.

63 B. C. maturity of his career, held that although it ought not to be used except in extreme peril, it was in such circumstances legitimate.¹ But the Senate might be tempted to use it not only to restrain public enemies, but also to coerce political opponents; and Caesar may have expected that it would be used without scruple in the unrest with which Catiline was menacing the State. At all events, whether he was then opposed on principle to the ultimate decree or only to that view of it which would invest the executive with absolute power of life and death, the stroke which he now contemplated was designed to give the Senate pause. His plan was to prosecute an aged man on the charge of having committed a murder
100 B. C. under the shelter of the ultimate decree thirty-seven years before. When Marius called upon all citizens to arm against Saturninus, among those who obeyed was a knight named Gaius Rabirius.² Whether Saturninus perished after he had surrendered under a guarantee of safety, and whether Rabirius had killed him, is irrelevant: that was the current version of the story and the one which it suited Caesar to adopt. Its truth being assumed, it seemed evident that Rabirius had abused the protection afforded by the ultimate decree.

It was open to Caesar to instruct Labienus, who again acted as his agent, to conduct the prosecution in the ordinary way, in which case the defendant, if he were condemned, could appeal to the people assembled in their centuries; but he preferred to revive the legendary procedure of King Tullus Hostilius in the trial of Horatius. The King, as we learn from Livy, had appointed two commissioners, who were to condemn and sentence the accused for a crime which was not denied. He might appeal to the people; but if the appeal failed, he was to be scourged and then hanged upon a cross erected in the Field of Mars. Evidently Caesar chose to adopt this formality, for which in the history of the Republic there

¹ *B. C.*, 1, 5, 3; 7, 5. See pp. 452-3.
² All questions relating to the prosecution of Rabirius are discussed on pp. 452-5.

was no precedent, in order to impress the imagination of 63 B.C.
the people; but nobody supposes that he intended that
the sentence should be carried out.

The first step was to appoint the two commissioners.
Since the King had named his own deputies, and the
sovereignty of the King had devolved upon the people,
Labienus promulgated a bill, providing that the urban
praetor should select a certain number of individuals from
whom the commissioners were to be chosen by lot. During
the interval between the promulgation of the bill and the
day on which it was to be submitted to the assembly it
provoked turbulent discussions in the Forum; but in due
course it became law, and the lots fell upon Caesar and
his kinsman Lucius, an ex-consul. Caesar himself would
probably have preferred, as he had done in the case of
Rullus, to remain in the background; but he and his
colleague of course pronounced the sentence. Whether
the cross was actually erected, is uncertain: at all events
the obsolete procedure was repugnant to the spirit of the
age, and Cicero induced the Senate to exert their prerogative and decree 'that the Roman People were not
bound by the law' of Labienus. Thus the sentence was
quashed; and if Rabirius had appealed, his appeal became
unnecessary and lapsed.

But Caesar, though he perhaps realized his tactical
error, was not checkmated. Labienus, doubtless intending
to prejudice Rabirius in view of the impending trial, had
summoned him to appear before his court on various
minor charges, the penalty fixed for conviction being
a heavy fine. Now that Cicero had baffled him, he determined, on the advice of Caesar, to convert this prosecution into a capital impeachment—in other words, to
proceed as he might have originally done. Rabirius was
condemned and appealed to the assembly of the centuries,
in whose presence on the Field of Mars Cicero delivered
in his behalf the celebrated oration which is still extant.
Incredible though it may appear to a modern lawyer,
Labienus was both prosecutor and president. Cicero
assumed that Labienus (for he did not mention Caesar)

was bent upon depriving the Senate of the right to pass the ultimate decree;[1] he dwelt, as he had done in the case of Rullus, upon the plots that were being formed against the State;[2] and he declared that, if it were necessary, he would not hesitate to follow the example of Marius and arm loyal citizens against public enemies.[3] He took for granted that Saturninus had been killed in open war;[4] but, he argued, even if he had received a pledge of safety, Rabirius was not bound by an act of which he was ignorant, and Marius had no right to act without authority from the Senate. But these arguments, which may have impressed an unreflecting audience, were superfluous; for before the people could give judgement the trial was abruptly and dramatically closed. In the days when Rome was exposed to attack from neighbouring tribes the Janiculum was guarded by armed men; and when an assembly on the Field of Mars was about to be dissolved a red flag was lowered on the hill. The Romans, like ourselves, clung to old forms which had long lost their meaning, and the flag was still kept hoisted when the centuries were gathered on the field below. Suddenly the praetor Metellus Celer, doubtless in collusion either with Cicero or with Caesar, ordered it to be taken down: the centuries dispersed; and Rabirius was free. Whether Cicero feared that his speech might not succeed, or Caesar wished to avoid the rebuff which an acquittal would involve, we cannot tell: at all events Caesar, although he had advertised a principle, had again failed to achieve his aim.

Meanwhile Caesar was taking advantage of the law which Labienus had enacted in his favour. Popular though he was with the electors, and already burdened with debt, he contracted fresh loans for bribery. Catulus offered him a large sum to withdraw from candidature; but he replied that he would prefer to borrow more. The day fixed for the election was the 15th of March.[5]

---
[1] *Pro Rab.*, 1, 2; 2, 4.
[2] *Ib.*, 12, 33.   [3] *Ib.*, § 34.   [4] *Ib.*, 6, 19.
[5] Tyrrell (*The Correspondence of Cicero*, i², 1885, p. 19) refers the election

Every one knows the story that when Aurelia, anxious and tearful, embraced her son as he was leaving home, he told her that unless he were elected, he would not come back :—'To-day, mother, you will see your son either Chief Pontiff or an exile.' He was returned by a huge majority.¹

63 B.C.

Caesar elected Chief Pontiff.

The time had not yet come for the work that was to make the consulship of Cicero illustrious ; but he found enough to keep him busy both in the Senate and in the Forum. He successfully defended Gaius Calpurnius Piso, who had been prosecuted at the instance of Caesar for extortion in the province of Transalpine Gaul and for having illegally punished a Transpadane.² When a tribune proposed that the sons of those who had been proscribed by Sulla should be restored to their civil rights, Cicero refused his sanction ; for, though he admitted that to exclude innocent men from public life was hard, he doubtless knew that among them were adherents of Catiline, and he argued that in the public interest the enactment of Sulla must be upheld.³ Even Caesar waited fourteen years before he gave effect to the proposal of the tribune.⁴ One measure Cicero carried the value of which was beyond dispute. The privilege allowing senators who had occasion to go abroad to apply for a ' free embassy ', which enabled them to travel at the expense of the provincials, had been so abused as to become a scandal ; and Cicero, who would have abolished it altogether if he had not been balked by the interference of a tribune, succeeded in limiting its tenure to a year.⁵

Cicero defends Gaius Calpurnius Piso,

opposes the rehabilitation of the sons of men proscribed by Sulla,

and limits the duration of ' free embassies '.

During these earlier months of Cicero's consulship Catiline was maturing his preparations,⁶ and it is time

Catiline's designs and his supporters.

to ' the *I*des of March ' (March 15), but gives no authority. Some years ago I lighted upon the Latin text which verifies his statement, but omitted to make a note of it. *I* have failed to find it since. In Ovid, *Fasti*, iii, 415-20, not Caesar, but Augustus is meant (*C. I. L.*, i², p. 311).

¹ Vell. Pat., ii, 43, 3 ; Plut., *Caes.*, 7, 1 ; Suet., 13. Dio (xxxvii, 37, 2) dates the election incorrectly.
² Cic., *Pro Flac.*, 39, 98 ; Sall., *Cat.*, 49, 2. As to Piso see p. 170.
³ *Att.*, ii, 1, 3 ; *In Pis.*, 2, 4 ; Pliny, vii, 30 (31), 117 ; Plut., *Cic.*, 12, 1 ; Dio, xxxvii, 25, 3 ; Quint., *Inst.*, xi, 1, 85.
⁴ Plut., *Caes.*, 37, 1. ⁵ *De leg.*, iii, 8, 18. ⁶ See pp. 455-7.

63 B.C. to form a judgement on the nature of his enterprise. For this purpose the gap of two years in Cicero's correspondence, the loss of the narratives which he published of his administration and even of the work, perhaps more outspoken, which he reserved for posthumous publication,[1] are of little moment : if there was anything noteworthy to be told besides what he related in his speeches, one may presume that it belonged to the personal, not to the historical aspect of the crisis. We might be glad to know more of what he thought of the character of Catiline and of the attitude of Caesar ; but the extant materials reveal both the origin of the conspiracy and the aims of the conspirators, and the vexed question, whether Sallust was a conscientious historian or a biased apologist of Caesar, need not disturb our view.

Catiline was heavily in debt, and debt or poverty would impel adventurers of every class to join him.[2] If he won the consulship, he could accomplish his designs under the forms of law and restore his fortunes by the plunder of a province : if he lost it, he could resort to violence. The elements of revolution were ready to his hand. Rome abounded with nobles who had wasted their inheritance in luxury, who were reluctant to pay their debts by selling their estates, and of whom many coveted offices which they had no chance of obtaining without his aid.[3] The veterans whom Sulla had settled throughout Italy and especially in Etruria, had spent recklessly what they had lightly gained ; they had failed to make a competence from their farms ; and, harassed by usurers, they were looking for fresh opportunities of enrichment from rapine.[4] Yeomen who had been evicted to make room for them were eager to share the spoil. Rome was full of idlers attracted by cheap food and free amusement, bad characters of every kind, and hooligans who were

---

[1] Ascon., ed. Clark, p. 83, ll. 21-2 (ed. Stangl, p. 65) ; Dio, xxxix, 10, 2-3. Cf. *Hermes*, xxxii, 1897, pp. 558-9.
[2] Q. Cic., *De pet. cons.*, 3, 10 ; Cic., *In Cat.*, i, 6, 14 ; *De off.*, ii, 24, 84.
[3] *In Cat.*, ii, 8, 18 ; 9, 19 ; Sall., *Cat.*, 14, 2 ; Plut., *Cic.*, 10, 3.
[4] *In Cat.*, ii, 3, 5 ; 9, 20 ; Sall., 16, 4 ; 28, 4 ; Plut., 14, 1.

always ripe for mischief ; in all parts of Italy there were 63 B. C. criminals, brigands, debtors, paupers, desperadoes, who had nothing to lose and everything to gain from the success of Catiline.[1] The sons of the proscribed, rebuffed by the Government, could look for restoration to him alone.[2] Others, who remembered how Sulla had raised private soldiers to the Senate and had made them rich, hoped that Catiline would do as much for them.[3] He was the hero of impressionable youths whom he had attracted by pandering to their vices, by inspiring them with ambitious dreams, and by that power of becoming all things to all men which, as his contemporaries observed, gave him an ascendancy over every one whom he cared to win.[4] In the inner circle of his associates were senators, such as Publius Lentulus Sura, an ex-consul, who had been expelled from the House for flagrant immorality, but as praetor had regained admission, Autronius and Vargunteius, who had been involved in the first conspiracy, Gaius Cethegus, Lucius Cassius Longinus, Marcus Porcius Laeca ; sundry knights, of whom Lucius Statilius, Gabinius Capito, and Cornelius were the most conspicuous ; and prominent men belonging to country towns.[5] The programme which Catiline unfolded to these trusted followers was to obtain for them the honours, the great offices of state, and the reversion of rich provinces, which had hitherto been monopolized by a few noble families, to cancel all debts, to carry out, after the example of Sulla, a proscription of the rich, and to confiscate their property.[6]

Was Catiline, as a modern writer [7] has affirmed, 'the successor in direct order of the Gracchi, of Saturninus,

[1] Cic., *Pro Tull.*, 2, 8; *In Cat.*, ii, 4, 7–8; Sall., 14, 3; 16, 4; 28, 4; 33, 2 ; 37, 7 ; 48, 1.
[2] *Ib.*, 37, 9.
[3] *Ib.*, § 6 ; 51, 34. Cf. Dion. Hal., v, 77.
[4] Sall., 14, 4–6 ; 17, 6 ; Cic., *In Cat.*, ii, 10, 22–3 ; Plut., 10, 3 ; App., ii, 2, 4.
[5] Sall., 17, 3–5 ; Vell., ii, 34, 4 ; Plut., 17, 1 ; Dio, xxxvii, 30, 4. The cognomen of Gabinius, according to Cicero (*In Cat.*, iii, 3, 6), was Cimber.
[6] Sall., 20, 7–8. 11–5 ; 21, 2–4.
[7] E. S. Beesly, *Catiline*, &c., 1878, pp. 18–9.

of Drusus, of Sulpicius, and of Cinna'? For this assertion, long since discredited, there is no evidence. Catiline was not the leader, but a tool, to be used if occasion offered, of the real leader, Julius Caesar. He was, indeed, a revolutionary leader, but of those only, whether high or low, whose aim was to repudiate their debts and to prey upon all who were more fortunate than themselves. Though he posed as the champion of the wretched,[1] he had not, so far as we can tell, any political principle. Nor had he any qualification except courage, bodily strength, and the power of working upon plastic minds. He could not discern what was attainable. He failed to see that even bribery and the baits which he dangled before the poor would not influence more than a small proportion even of the Roman populace to vote for him. Even if he became consul and Caesar could not keep him within bounds, any revolutionary measures which he might pass would be annulled on the return of Pompey. If his candidature failed, he might perhaps at first succeed by violence, for Italy was without an army and without police, and Pompey would not return for a year or more. But his success would be short-lived. Cicero could rely not only upon the influence of the great families, but also upon the knights, the shop-keepers in Rome and in the country towns, in fine, upon all respectable men whose safety or whose property would be menaced by the collapse of established rule : [2] the Government, which had raised troops to subdue Spartacus, was not defenceless against Catiline ; and since the only forces upon which he could rely, besides a miscellaneous rabble, were the discontented veterans of Sulla, the resources of the State would be enough to crush him before Pompey with his legions reappeared.

But the danger, for a time, was real. While Cicero was engaged in the Senate, in the Forum, and on the Field of Mars, Catiline was canvassing for the consular election, preparing to overawe his opponents, and scheming, in

---

[1] Cic., *Pro Mur.*, 25, 51 ; Sall., 35, 3.
[2] *In Cat.*, iii, 2, 5 ; iv, 8, 17.

case of failure, to achieve his aims by force. Besides 63 B.C. fresh adherents of every class he had attracted ladies of fashion, by whose influence he hoped to enlist the services of their slaves, while Manlius, who had served as a centurion under Sulla,[1] was recruiting in Etruria. Prominent among the women was Sempronia, the mother of Decimus Brutus, who was famed not only as a beauty and a graceful dancer, but also for her wit, her taste in literature, and a conversational charm which made the reputation of her salon.[2] Three other candidates were standing against Catiline,—Servius Sulpicius, a famous jurist, Junius Silanus, who had nothing but his family to recommend him, and Lucius Murena, who had won distinction as a lieutenant of Lucullus.[3] Cicero, doubtless in the hope of checkmating Catiline, carried a law which made it penal to receive as well as to offer bribes and, in addition to the existing penalties, provided that those convicted of corruption should be banished for ten years.[4] Murena was backed by the soldiers who had come to witness the triumph of Lucullus;[5] Sulpicius was so busy in procuring evidence of bribery against his rivals that he neglected to pay court to the electors;[6] Catiline paraded the streets at the head of Sullan veterans and of men who had been dispossessed by Sulla's violence, whom Manlius had brought from Etruria to support him.[7] It was reported that in a private gathering of his followers he had proclaimed himself the champion of the poor and the oppressed, and that he intended to assassinate Cicero in the confusion of the polls.[8] Even now he did not shrink from appearing in the Senate, and when Cato

[1] Plut., 14, 1 ; Dio, xxxvii, 30, 5.   [2] Sall., 24, 3–4 ; 25.
[3] See p. 192.
[4] Cic., Pro Mur., 2, 3 ; 3, 5 ; 22, 45 ; 23, 46–7 ; 32, 67 ; 41, 89 ; Pro Sest., 64, 133 ; In Vat., 15, 37 ; Pro Planc., 34, 83 ; Dio, xxxvii, 29. Cf. A. H. J. Greenidge, Legal Procedure, &c., 1901, pp. 425, 512, n. 4, and Paulys Real-Ency., vi, 1684. In Pro Mur., § 89, Cicero loosely calls banishment (relegatio), which did not involve loss of citizenship, exilium, which did, but which was not itself a punishment, but a means of avoiding outlawry. See p. 331, n. 2.
[5] Pro Mur., 18, 37.   [6] Ib., 24, 48–9.
[7] Ib., § 49 ; Plut., Cic., 14, 1.   [8] See p. 258, n. 4.

2592.1

threatened him with prosecution, he replied in stilted metaphor that 'if a conflagration were kindled against his fortunes, he would quench it not by water but by ruin'.[1] Cicero had for some time been kept informed of his intentions by a lady named Fulvia, the mistress of Quintus Curius, one of the conspirators,[2] and when he heard what he had said in the private meeting and that he designed to murder him, he summoned the Senate and reported the state of affairs. The consular election had been fixed for the next day, but on his motion it was postponed in order that the Senate might have an opportunity of discussing his report.[4] Next day therefore the Senate reassembled. Catiline was present, and Cicero challenged him to explain his conduct. Catiline, who knew that certain senators were on his side, replied that there were two bodies in the State, one feeble with a weak head, the other strong, but with no head : so long as he lived that strong body, if it deserved one, should not want a head. Members who understood that by the 'weak head' Catiline meant Cicero murmured in indignation ; but some of them, so Cicero thought, did not yet realize the danger, while others were too timid to repel it : at all events the Senate did not act, and Catiline stalked out of the House in triumph.[5] Cicero, seeing that

---

[1] *Pro Mur.*, 25, 50–1 ; Val. Max., ix, 11, 3.
[2] Sall., 23, 1–4 ; 26, 3. The word 'conspirators' will not, *I* think, be misunderstood. See pp. 457, 460, n. 5.   [3] See pp. 458–61.
[4] Dr. Hardy (*Journ. Rom. Studies*, vii, 1917, p. 180) suggests that Cicero's real object was to protect himself against assassination. Presently, however (p. 183), arguing that 'the evidence for this . . . murder scheme is hardly worth considering', for Cicero 'omitted to mention it in the Senate', he insists that 'Even the breastplate which he put on, he admits was not to protect his life [*non quae me tegeret*, which, as the context shows, really means ' not to cover my *body*], but to create the impression that his life was in danger '; but in quoting the passage on which this assertion rests he omits the words that follow *tegeret—etenim sciebam Catilinam non latus aut ventrem, sed caput et collum solere petere* ('for *I* was aware that Catiline's practice was to aim not at the chest or stomach, but at the head and throat'). Finally, he adds that 'Cicero's information may have been well founded ' ! What does Dr. Hardy really mean ? Where did he learn that Cicero omitted to mention the 'murder scheme' in the Senate ? Dio (xxxvii, 39, 3) expressly says that he did there mention it.
[5] *Pro Mur.*, 25, 50–1 ; Plut., *Cic.*, 14; 2 ; Dio, xxxvii, 29, 3.

he must rely upon himself, enlisted a bodyguard of loyal men, who habitually escorted him when he appeared in public, and donned a cuirass to advertise his peril. On the day of the election he entered the Field of Mars with his defenders. Catiline and his gang were overawed : the electors who supported him were comparatively few, and Silanus and Murena were returned.² In the city the seditious element was evidently weak.

63 B. C.

Early in Oct. ?¹

His candidature fails.

Catiline now determined to use the weapons which he had kept in reserve. He sent back Manlius to Faesulae, while two of his lieutenants proceeded to raise fresh levies in Picenum and Etruria.³ On the 27th of October Manlius was to raise the standard of rebellion ; a massacre of the leading Conservatives, including Cicero, was planned for the 28th ; and on the 1st of November Praeneste, a centre of the Marian party and one of the strongest towns in Latium,⁴ was to be seized.⁵ Cicero's house was at that time on the Oppian hill,⁶ not far east of the Forum. On the night of the 20th of October he was roused from his sleep, and Crassus, accompanied by two other nobles, Marcus Marcellus and Caecilius Metellus Scipio, handed to him several letters, which had been delivered to his hall porter by an unknown individual. Crassus had opened only one of the letters, which was anonymous and gave warning of the intended massacre.⁷ Whether it confirmed information which Cicero had already received from Fulvia and perhaps also from Caesar, who at some time gave him particulars of the conspiracy,⁸ is uncertain : at all events, on the following morning Cicero convened the Senate, and the letters were read. A resolution was immediately made that a state of war existed in Italy. Next day the Senate reassembled.

He purposes to resort to violence

Crassus furnishes Cicero with evidence against him.

---

¹ See pp. 458–61.
² *In Cat.*, i, 5, 11 ; *Pro Mur.*, 26, 52 ; *Pro Sulla*, 18, 51 ; Sall., *Cat.*, 26, 4–5 ; Plut., *Cic.*, 14, 3 ; Dio, xxxvii, 29, 3–4 ; 30, 1.
³ Sall., *Cat.*, 26, 5 ; 27, 1.
⁴ Strabo, v, 3, 11.   ⁵ *In Cat.*, i, 3, 7–8.
⁶ Cf. Cic., *Q. fr.*, ii, 3, 7, with *Fam.*, v, 6, 2, and Plut., *Cic.*, 8, 3.
⁷ Plut., *Cras.*, 13, 4 ; *Cic.*, 15, 1–2 ; Dio, xxxvii, 31, 1.
⁸ Suet., *Div. Iul.*, 17, 2.

A member, named Quintus Arrius, who was in Caesar's confidence,[1] announced that troops were being levied in Etruria;[2] Cicero, if we may believe the written version of his most famous speech,[3] foretold that Manlius would appear in arms on the 27th and affirmed that the massacre had been planned for the 28th.[4] These revelations produced the effect which he desired. The Senate, which had been so supine when he challenged Catiline, were now aroused, and after prolonged discussion passed the ultimate decree, empowering the consuls, from one of whom no more than acquiescence could be expected, to provide for the safety of the State.[5] Cicero immediately arranged that a guard of volunteers should be in readiness on the 28th to protect the threatened notables,[6] and dispatched another to occupy Praeneste.[7] For the moment Catiline was checked. About the end of the month a senator named Lucius Saenius communicated to the House a letter, which he had just received from Faesulae, stating that Manlius had actually taken the field on the 27th; and at the same time news arrived that slaves were in revolt at Capua and in Apulia.[8] The Senate accordingly decreed that Marcius Rex, the ex-Governor of Cilicia, and Metellus, the conqueror of Crete, who were waiting outside the city in the expectation of their triumphs, should proceed respectively to Faesulae and to Apulia, and the praetors, Pompeius Rufus and Metellus Celer, to Capua and Picenum; but as no troops were ready, they were obliged first to raise recruits. At the same time rewards were offered to any who should give information about the conspiracy—freedom and one hundred thousand sesterces[9] to slaves, a free pardon and

---

[1] Cic., *Att.*, i, 17, 11.   [2] Plut., *Cic.*, 15, 3.
[3] Cicero did not publish his first Catilinarian oration and his other speeches of 63 B.C. till 60 (*Att.*, ii, 1, 3).
[4] *In Cat.*, i, 3, 7.
[5] Cic., *in Cat.*, i, 1, 3; 2, 4; Plut., 15, 3; Dio, xxxvii, 31, 2. See *Journ. Rom. Studies*, vii, 1917, pp. 189–90, and p. 458, n. 5, *infra*.
[6] Dr. Hardy (*Journ. Rom. Studies*, vii, 192, n. 1) shows that Sallust (30, 7) post-dates this precaution.
[7] *In Cat.*, i, 3, 7–8; Dio, xxxvii, 31, 3.   [8] Sall., 30, 1–2.
[9] £1,000.

two hundred thousand to citizens—while arrangements 63 B. C. were made for keeping the gladiators at Capua out of mischief by billeting them in small parties on the neighbouring towns.[1] Perhaps it was at this time that, as Cicero relates,[2] the slaves of suspected persons were tortured in order to wring from them evidence against their masters. The sight of the piquets which Cicero posted in the city caused great anxiety.[3] Credit was destroyed, and valuable property became unsaleable. In these circumstances a money-lender named Quintus Considius, who had sums equivalent to one hundred and fifty thousand pounds on loan, forbore to press any of his debtors for repayment; and the Senate passed a resolution thanking him for his generosity, which had allayed the prevalent alarm.[4] Before the consulars and the praetors were ready to set out for their respective districts, Lucius Aemilius Paullus, a son of the notorious Lepidus, gave notice of his intention to prosecute Catiline for violent crime.[5] Catiline offered successively to place himself in custody, with Manius Lepidus, an ex-consul, with Cicero himself, and finally with Metellus Celer. All declined to receive him; but the threatened prosecution came to nothing, for it did not suit Cicero's purpose to allow Catiline to be tried.[6] Catiline had already determined to leave Rome and direct the operations of the insurgent force. On the night of the 6th of November he assembled the leading conspirators at the house of Laeca. Explaining that he was about to join Manlius, he requested those whom he had selected for divisional commands to proceed to Etruria, Picenum, and Cisalpine Gaul while others, including Lentulus and Cethegus, remained in Rome to arrange for the burning of specified regions of the city and the massacre of certain individuals. Finally he impressed upon the gathering that before he started Cicero must be put to death. Cornelius and

Financial crisis.

Catiline instructs his accomplices in the house of Laeca.

[1] Sall., 30, 3–7; Plut., 16, 1.   [2] *De part. orat.*, 34, 118.
[3] Sall., 31, 1–2. Cf. Cic., *In Cat.*, i, 1, 1.
[4] Val. Max., iv, 8, 3. The exact date of Considius's action is uncertain. It seems reasonable to refer it to this time.
[5] Sall., 31, 4; Dio, xxxvii, 31, 3.   [6] *In Cat.*, i, 8, 19; Dio, xxxvii, 32, 1.

262 ANNUS MIRABILIS OF CICERO CHAP.

63 B. C.

Abortive plot to assassinate Cicero.

Vargunteius volunteered to visit the consul in the morning on the pretext of paying their respects, and to assassinate him there and then. The traitor Curius instantly informed his mistress, who lost no time in warning Cicero. When the assassins reached the house they found it strongly guarded, and were obliged to abandon their attempt.[1] Cicero probably expected that Catiline, in accordance with his plan, would leave Rome that night and thus reveal his guilt ;[2] but Catiline changed his mind.

Nov. 8.[3]

Cicero's first oration against Catiline.

Next day[3] Cicero assembled the Senate in the temple of Jupiter Stator at the foot of the Palatine, having taken the precaution of surrounding the building with armed knights.[4] Catiline took his place ; but when he sat down the benches near him were at once deserted.[5] Cicero then delivered the invective[6] which was to become the most famous of all his orations. Though (if the published version represents in substance what he said) he not only recounted what had passed at the house of Laeca, but also charged Catiline with having made more than one attempt to murder him ;[7] though he affirmed that a rebel army was then assembled in Etruria ;[8] though he insisted that the ultimate decree empowered him to put Catiline to death,[9] he confessed that there were senators present who could not or would not believe him guilty.[10] He could not yet produce irrefragable evidence of Catiline's connexion with the rebels ; he knew that to send him to execution would bring upon himself a storm of obloquy, while the other conspirators would still be formidable ; and he felt that the best course would be to let him leave the city, where he was dangerous, to wait until his guilt became evident to all before striking

---

[1] Cic., *In Cat.*, i, 1, 1 ; 4, 8-10 ; ii, 3, 6 ; *Pro Sulla*, 6, 18 ; 18, 52 ; Sall., 27, 3-4 ; 28, 1-3 ; Plut., 16, 1 (inaccurate) ; Dio, xxxvii, 32, 3-4 ; 33, 1 ; 34, 1. See pp. 461-4. Every student of Roman history knows that Sallust misdated the meeting in the house of Laeca. Appian (ii, 3, 8-12) confounds the orders which Catiline gave there with those which he gave before leaving Rome (p. 263). [2] See p. 464. [3] See pp. 461, 464-5.
[4] *In Cat.*, i, 8, 21 ; Plut., 16, 2. [5] *In Cat.*, i, 7, 16 ; ii, 6, 12.
[6] Sall., 31, 5-6 ; Plut., 16, 2. [7] *In Cat.*, i, 1, 2 ; 4, 9 ; 5, 11 ; 6, 15.
[8] *Ib.*, 2, 5. [9] *Ib.*, §§ 4, 5. [10] *Ib.*, 12, 30. Cf. ii, 2, 3-4.

IV AND THE RISE OF CAESAR 263

a decisive blow, and meanwhile to employ the resources of the State in holding him and his followers in check.¹

Catiline went back immediately to his house, urged Lentulus and Cethegus to procure the assassination of Cicero and to carry out the instructions which he had given at Laeca's house, and, promising to return at the head of an army, left Rome at midnight with a few followers to join Manlius.² On the way he wrote to leading men in Rome, telling them that as he was a victim of false charges and could not contend against a hostile faction, he was going in voluntary exile to Massilia.³ A like report was spread by his accomplices who remained behind,⁴ and doubtless the object was to throw discredit upon Cicero. Catulus read in the Senate a letter which Catiline had written to him just before he started, and of which Sallust ⁵ has preserved a copy. The writer recalled acts of kindness which he had received from Catulus at a certain crisis in his life, and explained that, as he had been stung by wrong and insult, and had been unable to win the position in the State to which his birth and merit had entitled him, he had come forward as the champion of the wretched. 'I commend to you Orestilla,' he concluded, 'and commit her to your protection. In the name of your own children I ask you to defend her from all injury.'

Meanwhile Manlius had sent a message to Marcius Rex, which, if the substance has been faithfully reported, illustrates the motives of the Sullan veterans and of the evicted yeomen who had joined them. He called Heaven to witness that he and his followers had not taken up

63 B. C.

Catiline joins his adherents in Etruria.

Manlius appeals to Marcius Rex.

---

¹ *Ib.*, i, 2, 5–6 ; 12, 29–30. Cf. iii, 7, 16. Sallust (31, 7–9) says that Catiline replied to Cicero ; but the words which he ascribes to him were spoken, according to Cicero (*Pro Mur.*, 25, 51), some weeks earlier in answer to Cato (see p. 258). Cicero himself (*De or. part.*, 34, 129) says that Catiline did not answer him ; and, if we may believe Diodorus (xl, 5), he merely said that he would go into voluntary exile. Dio (xxxvii, 33, 1. Cf. Diodorus) incorrectly states that the Senate ordered Catiline to quit Rome.

² *In Cat.*, ii, 1, 1 ; 4, 6 ; Sall., 32, 1–2 ; Plut., *Cato min.*, 22, 1 ; *Cic.*, 16, 2–3 ; App., ii, 3, 10–1 ; Dio, xxxvii, 33, 2.

³ See pp. 465–6.

⁴ *In Cat.*, ii, 6, 14 ; 7, 16 ; Sall., 34, 2.   ⁵ *Ib.*, § 3 ; 35.

264   ANNUS MIRABILIS OF CICERO   CHAP.

63 B. C. arms against their country, but to save themselves from the rapacity of their creditors, against whom he begged Marcius and the Government to protect them. Marcius advised them to lay down their arms, repair to Rome, and invoke the compassion of the Senate, to whom none had ever appealed in vain.[1]

Cicero informs the people of the state of affairs. Nov. 9.
Respectable people in the city were naturally anxious for information, and since no official gazette as yet existed, it was for the consul to enlighten them. On the day after Catiline's departure he addressed an informal assemblage in the Forum. He told the story of the nocturnal meeting, the attempted murder, the dramatic scene in the Senate. The arch-villain had departed, and the city was well rid of him. He ought long ago to have been put to death; but there were many who would not believe the evidence of his guilt, and who, if he had been punished as he deserved, would have denounced the consul and prevented him from dealing firmly with the conspirators who remained. Now the quarrel would be fought out in the open field, and the wretched levies of Catiline with his body-guard of catamites would in vain contend against the forces of the State. The report that he was going to Massilia was false: he was about to join Manlius. But there was no cause for alarm. The safety of the city was provided for: the yeomen and the country towns had been duly warned and would protect themselves; the gladiators were in safe keeping; Metellus Celer had been dispatched to safeguard Picenum and Cisalpine Gaul. As for the conspirators who remained in Rome, they had best beware.[2]

A few days later news arrived that Catiline, preceded, like a consul, by twelve lictors, with whom he doubtless hoped to impress the populace, had reached the camp of

Catiline proclaimed a public enemy.
Manlius.[3] Forthwith the Senate proclaimed Catiline and his lieutenant public enemies, at the same time offering an amnesty to their followers if, before a fixed day, they

[1] Sall., 32, 2; 33; 34, 1.
[2] *In Cat.*, ii, 1, 1; 2, 3–4; 3, 5; 4, 6–8; 7, 16; 12, 26–7.
[3] *Ib.*, 6, 13; *Pro Sulla*, 5, 17; Sall., 36, 1; Plut., *Cic.*, 16, 3; Dio, xxxvii, 33, 2.

laid down their arms, and ordered Antonius, who apparently superseded Marcius Rex,[1] to raise recruits and to advance as soon as possible against the rebels.[2] The promised amnesty and the rewards that had been offered to informers were alike futile : not a man deserted Catiline ; not one came forward to give evidence.[3] Meanwhile Lentulus and his colleagues were maturing their plans. Lentulus was heard to boast that the Sibylline Books contained a prophecy that three Cornelii, of whom he, after Cinna and Sulla, was the third, were to be masters of the Roman world. Cethegus, blind to the self-evident truth that it would be vain for the conspirators in Rome to strike unless Catiline and Manlius came to their support, was eager for instant action ; but Lentulus, who was not wholly without sense, overruled him. He arranged that on the 16th of December a tribune, Lucius Bestia, should convene the people and charge Cicero with having provoked hostilities by accusing innocent men. On the night of the 17th,[4] amid the licence of the Saturnalia, the conspirators were to carry out their several instructions :—Statilius and Gabinius with their underlings were to fire the city in twelve places, in order that in the consequent confusion it might be easier to get at Cicero and the other notables who were marked down as victims ; then Cethegus was to attack Cicero in his house ; and finally the conspirators were to leave the burning city in the tumult and meet Catiline, who, it was expected, would then with his army be close at hand.[5] Even Lentulus, however, failed to

63 B. C.

His accomplices plan an outbreak in Rome.

---

[1] *Journ. Rom. Studies*, vii, 199.
[2] Sall., 36, 2–3 ; Plut., 16, 3 ; Dio, xxxvii, 33, 3.   [3] Sall., 36, 5.
[4] The date of the Saturnalia was *a. d. xiv. Kal. Ian.* =Dec. 17 (Macrob., i, 10, 2).
[5] *In Cat.*, ii, 1, 1 ; 3, 6 ; iii, 4, 10 ; 7, 17 ; *Pro Sulla*, 11, 33 ; 19, 53 ; Sall., 39, 6 ; 43, 1–2 ; Plut., *Caes.*, 7, 2 ; *Cato min.*, 22, 1 ; *Cic.*, 17, 1. 4 ; 18, 1 ; Flor., ii, 12, 8 ; App., ii, 3, 11–2 ; Dio, xxxvii, 34, 1. See p. 466. Though, as Dr. Hardy says (*Journ. Rom. Studies*, vii, 196), Cicero (*Pro Sulla*, 6, 19) grossly exaggerated when he said that the conspirators intended to burn the whole city, one may infer from what Dr. Hardy calls the 'sane and clear account' of Sallust that more was planned than the destruction of the houses of 'leading men'. Plutarch (*Cato min.*, 22, 1) makes a groundless charge against Catiline.

realize that if the forces of the State were handled with ordinary skill, Catiline would not be able to elude them. In Picenum, Apulia, and the Bruttian peninsula, even in the Gallic provinces, weapons were being stored; but the agents responsible for these measures were unwary, and many were arrested.[1] Towards the end of November,[2] while Cicero was trying to procure evidence which would warrant him in arresting the conspirators, his attention was distracted by the ill-timed zeal of two senators who ought to have supported him. The consul-elect Murena was charged with having violated the new law concerning bribery, and Cicero was called upon to defend him.

An event had lately occurred which Cicero turned to good account. Metellus Nepos, a brother of Metellus Celer, who had served under Pompey against the pirates [3] and in the East,[4] had been sent home to promote his interests and, as later developments will show, to bring about some understanding with Caesar.[5] Marcus Porcius Cato, learning that he was a candidate for a tribuneship, and feeling sure that he and Pompey had some sinister design, resolved, with the support of the Conservatives, to stand against him.[6] Metellus and Cato were both elected.

Sulpicius, one of the unsuccessful candidates for the consulship, was the prosecutor of Murena, and he was zealously assisted by Cato. When the illustrious jurist, whose character was above suspicion, and the uncompromising Stoic, whose proverbial integrity was honoured by those who deplored his impracticable scrupulosity, united in bringing a charge the evidence for which they had diligently collected,[7] the jurors might not unreasonably assume the guilt of the accused. But Cicero was too clever for his opponents. As usual, he spoke last of the counsel for the defence,[8] for he had no rival in

---

[1] Sall., *Cat.*, 42 ; Cic., *Pro Sulla*, 19, 53.
[2] Cf. *Pro. Mur.*, 37. 79, 39. 84; *In Cat.*, ii, 3, 6 ; and *De domo*, 52, 134.
[3] Flor., i, 41, 10 ; App., *Mithr.*, 75.
[4] Jos., *Ant.*, xiv, 2, 3 ; *Bell. Iud.*, i, 6, 2.
[5] See pp. 285-6. [6] Plut., *Cato min.*, 20, 1-2.
[7] See p. 257, and Plut., *Cato min.*, 21, 3-4. [8] *Pro Mur.*, 23, 48.

awakening the sympathies of a jury.¹ He reminded 63 B.C. Cato that another tribune designate (he meant Metellus Nepos) had only the day before harangued the populace in words which menaced the authority of the Government.² But he could also discourse in a more playful vein. While he dwelt seriously upon the urgent need, in view of the pressing peril of the time, of having two consuls ready to take office on the first day of the coming year,³ he ridiculed Sulpicius and kept the jury in good humour by bantering Cato. Complimenting him as the mainstay of the prosecution and confessing that he dreaded the authority of his name more than his charge, he asked them to consider what would be the effect of applying Stoical maxims to Roman politics.⁴ Turning to the jury, who were in fits of laughter, Cato dryly remarked, 'What a witty fellow our consul is!'⁵ Whatever they may have thought about the merits of the case, they voted unanimously for acquittal.⁶

The trial was hardly over when the evidence which Cicero had sought was put into his hands. Two envoys from the Allobroges, the most disaffected tribe of Transalpine Gaul, had lately come to Rome to complain of the tyranny of the Governor and the extortions of the Italian usurers.⁷ Lentulus commissioned one Umbrenus, who had had commercial dealings in Gaul, to approach the envoys. Why should they not persuade their Government to foment a rebellion and send a contingent of the famous Gallic cavalry to Catiline? Umbrenus assured them that if they would join the conspirators, all their grievances should be redressed. They listened eagerly, and, to satisfy them that his offer was duly authorized, Umbrenus sent for Gabinius, in whose presence he communicated to them the names of the chief

He obtains evidence against the conspirators,

---
¹ Cic., *Orator*, 37, 130.   ² *Pro Mur.*, 38, 81.
³ *Ib.*, 37, 79; 38, 82; &c.
⁴ *Ib.*, 28, 58; 36, 76-7. Cf. *De fin.*, iv, 27, 74, and Quint., *Inst.*, xi, 1, 69.
⁵ Plut., *Cato min.*, 21, 4.
⁶ See Cic, *Pro Flac.*, 39, 98.
⁷ Sall., 40, 1. 3; Plut., *Cic.*, 18, 3; App. ii, 4, 13.

conspirators and details of the conspiracy.¹ Presently, however, they began to hesitate. The resources of the Roman Government were great, and they would certainly be well rewarded if they joined the stronger side. They therefore revealed what they had learned to Fabius Sanga, the recognized patron of their tribe,² who promptly informed Cicero. Now at last there was a chance that sceptical senators would be convinced. Cicero told Sanga to go back to the envoys and instruct them to feign enthusiasm for the conspiracy, communicate with the ringleaders whom they had not yet seen, and promise the help that was required of them.³ Gabinius introduced them to the ringleaders, and a parley followed. The envoys insisted that Lentulus, Cethegus, Statilius, and Cassius should give them sworn promises in writing, sealed with their several seals, to deliver to their principals: without this guarantee they would not be able to induce them to embark on so serious an enterprise. Lentulus, Cethegus, and Statilius unsuspectingly complied: Cassius, more wary than his colleagues, explained that he was going to Gaul himself, and immediately left Rome.⁴ On the night of the 2nd of December the envoys were to start on their homeward journey. Lentulus enjoined them to meet Catiline on the way and conclude with him a formal treaty of alliance: at the same time he directed one Volturcius to accompany them and entrusted him with a letter, in which he urged Catiline to enlist every available man, not excluding the lowest of the low. The letter was not signed, but Lentulus prefaced it by explaining that Volturcius would disclose the identity of the writer, and charged him to tell Catiline that, since he had already been declared a public enemy, he was over-scrupulous in refusing to arm slaves, that all his instructions had been duly carried out, and that he ought to return without delay.⁵

[1] *In Cat.*, iii, 2, 4 ; 4, 9 ; Sall., 40.   [2] See p. 131.
[3] Sall., 41 ; App., ii, 4, 14.   [4] Sall., 44, 1–2.
[5] *In Cat.*, iii, 2, 4 ; 5, 12 ; Sall., 44, 3–6 ; Plut., 18 ,3 ; App., ii, 4, 14.
No one who compares Sallust's version of the message with that of Cicero

The envoys had of course apprised Cicero of the time 63 B.C. fixed for their departure. He immediately sent for two of the praetors, Lucius Valerius Flaccus and Gaius Pomptinus, took them into his confidence, and requested them to proceed with an armed force to the Mulvian bridge, which crossed the Tiber on the Flaminian Way, two miles north of the city, to wait in concealment for the envoys, and to arrest them. Towards evening the praetors reached the spot and posted their men in two houses, one on each side of the bridge. About three Dec. 3. o'clock in the morning the envoys with their retinue reached the bridge : the Romans rushed out of the houses, and on both sides swords were drawn ; but the envoys, grasping the situation, surrendered to the praetors, who called off their men ; and Volturcius, who had attempted to resist, finding himself deserted, followed their example.[1]

The praetors instantly dispatched orderlies to inform Cicero, and just before sunrise brought the envoys and Volturcius to his house. The letters, of which they had of course taken possession, were handed to him with the seals unbroken. He immediately sent officers to summon who are the chief conspirators to his presence. Gabinius, who arrested suspected nothing, came first : Statilius followed, and brought before the then Cethegus ; Lentulus, fatigued after his nocturnal Senate. interview with the envoys, was somewhat late. Prominent politicians, who had heard of the arrest of the envoys, called at the house and urged Cicero to open the letters at once, arguing that if they contained nothing that would incriminate the conspirators, he would be blamed for having raised a false alarm ; but, being well aware of their purport, he replied that it was his duty to deliver them unopened to the House. Before going to meet the Senate, which was to assemble in the temple of Concord, at the foot of the Capitol, he sent one of the praetors on

will hesitate which to prefer. Cicero was not quoting the actual words of Lentulus, but explaining to his audience the instructions to which Lentulus of course merely alluded.

[1] Sall., 45 ; Plut., 18, 4 ; App., ii, 4, 15. Mr. A. M. Cook in a note on *Cat.* 45, 3, corrects G. Long's attempt (*Decline of the Rom. Rep.*, iii, 309) to impugn the veracity of Cicero (*In Cat.*, iii, 2, 6) and the text of Sallust.

the advice of the envoys to search the house of Cethegus, where a large quantity of weapons was discovered.¹ Then, taking Lentulus by the hand, out of respect for his official rank, he led him into the temple, while the other conspirators and Volturcius followed in custody. The envoys were also conducted into the building, but remained for the present in the background. The temple, which Cicero had surrounded with guards, was densely thronged. Four senators, skilled in the art of writing with abbreviations—the Roman equivalent of shorthand ² —were commissioned by the consul to record the evidence. He brought forward Volturcius first and proceeded to examine him. In evident alarm Volturcius tried to dissemble, but when Cicero, with the sanction of the House, promised him a free pardon, he revealed the designs of the conspirators, protesting, however, that he had only been admitted into their confidence a few days before and knew no more than the Gallic envoys. He recounted the plans that had been formed for incendiarism and massacre, related how Lentulus had entrusted him with a letter for Catiline, and described the oral message with which he had been charged to supplement it. The envoys were then introduced. Naming the chief conspirators, they spoke of the letters, confirmed by oath, that had been given to them for delivery to their principals and the request which the conspirators had made for the loan of Gallic cavalry. The letters were then produced. Cicero showed Cethegus his seal. Cethegus admitted that it was his. Cicero cut the string and read the letter aloud. Cethegus had stated, when Cicero asked him to account for the weapons which had been discovered in his house, that he had been in the habit of collecting choice specimens of such things ; but when

---

¹ *In Cat.*, iii, 3 ; Sall., 46, 3–5 ; Plut., 19, 1.
² Cic., *Pro Sulla*, 14, 41–2. In regard to Roman shorthand see Cic., *Att.*, xiii, 25, 3 ; 32, 3 ; Daremberg and Saglio, *Dict. des ant. grecques et rom.*, iv, 105 ; *Archiv f. Stenogr.*, N.F., i, 1905, pp. 5–6 ; Jahresb. d. philol. Vereins (*Zeitschr. f. d. Gymnasialwesen*, xii, 1908), p. 32 ; Chr. Johnen, *Gesch. d. Stenogr.*, i, 1911, pp. 165–9, 173–4 ; *Hermes*, li, 1916, pp. 189–210 ; and *Neue Jahrb. f. d. klass. Altertum*, xxxvii, 1916, pp. 493–4.

he heard the letter read he lost all presence of mind 63 B.C. and had nothing to say.[1] Statilius, who was next brought forward, likewise acknowledged his seal and, when his letter also was read, confessed his guilt. It was now the turn of Lentulus. Cicero showed him the letter which bore his seal and asked him whether he recognized it. Lentulus nodded assent. The letter was then read, and Cicero invited him to explain. At first he denied that he had written it, but when all the evidence had been recited, he asked the envoys what dealings he had had with them and why they had come to his house. They replied briefly and firmly that Umbrenus had introduced them to him and that they had visited him repeatedly; and they in their turn asked him whether he had not spoken to them about the Sibylline oracle. Practised debater though he was, he lost all self-control and, to the amazement of the House, admitted that he had. Suddenly Volturcius asked that the letter which, he said, had been given to him by Lentulus for Catiline should be produced. Lentulus, utterly confounded, acknowledged his seal and handwriting. Gabinius was then called. He answered brazenly at first, but, on being pressed, did not deny the truth of what the envoys said.[2]

The evidence being now closed, Cicero invited the House to consider the situation. A resolution was passed, thanking him for having by his energy, judgement, and foresight, saved the State from extreme peril; the services of the praetors, Flaccus and Pomptinus, were duly recognized; and, with an irony which can hardly have been unconscious, the consul Antonius was commended for having avoided all connexion with the conspirators. The Senate then resolved that Lentulus, and are who was constrained to resign his office, Cethegus, committed Statilius, Gabinius, Cassius, and other conspirators of to the custody of senators.

[1] Whoever reads Cicero's words, *Tum Cethegus . . . studiosum fuisse* (*In Cat.*, iii, 5, 10), carefully will see that the 'discrepancy' which Long (*op. cit.*, iii, 313) points out is imaginary.

[2] *In Cat.*, iii, 4-5; *Pro Sulla*, 13, 36; Sall., 46, 6; 47, 1-3; Plut., 19, 1; App., ii, 4, 15.

272   ANNUS MIRABILIS OF CICERO   CHAP.

63 B.C.

An extraordinary honour conferred upon Cicero.

lesser note should be committed to the charge of prominent senators, Caesar being made responsible for Statilius and Crassus for Gabinius. Finally, a thanksgiving service was decreed in the name of Cicero—the first such honour that was ever conferred for civil services.[1]

The day was far advanced, but Cicero had more work to do. He directed that copies of the evidence should be circulated throughout Italy,[2] and immediately after the session he went down to the Forum, where the people were anxiously awaiting him. Now that conclusive proofs had been obtained of the conspiracy, there was a revulsion of feeling among the dregs of the populace, and he was loudly cheered; for even the rapscallions who had hoped that the success of Catiline would give them a chance of plunder did not relish the prospect

He addresses the people.

of being burned in their beds.[3] Cicero related how he had learned of the intrigues of the conspirators with the Gauls, how he had got possession of the incriminating letters, and how he had compelled the criminals to confess their guilt. All danger, he assured his hearers, was now at an end. He did not forget to dwell upon the honour which the Senate had conferred upon him, remarking that while Pompey had extended the Roman dominion to the uttermost parts of the earth, he had saved the heart of the empire from destruction; he gave a significant hint of the doom that might be in store for Lentulus; and in his peroration he bade his fellow-citizens to offer up their prayers to Jupiter, the protector of the city.[4]

Dec. 4.

L. Tarquinius calumniates Crassus.

Next day the Senate met again. An obscure individual, named Lucius Tarquinius, was introduced and offered to give information about the plot if his own safety were guaranteed. Cicero told him to speak out. After repeating what Volturcius had said about the preparations for massacre and incendiarism, he affirmed that Crassus had ordered him to convey a message to Catiline, exhorting

[1] App., ii, 5, 16; *In Cat.*, iii, 6; iv, 5, 10; 10, 20; *In Pis.*, 3, 6; Sall., 47, 4; Plut., 19, 1.
[2] *Pro Sulla*, 15, 42.   [3] Sall., 48, 1–2; Dio, xxxvii, 34, 3.
[4] *In Cat.*, iii, 6, 14–6; 11, 26; 12, 28.

him to hasten to Rome and liberate his friends. Senators 63 B.C. who owed money to Crassus exclaimed that the fellow was a liar and demanded that the accusation which he had brought should be instantly dealt with by the House. Cicero accordingly put the question. The Senate decided that the evidence of Tarquinius was false and that he should be detained in custody until he confessed who had prompted him to tell so monstrous a lie. Crassus himself afterwards assured Sallust that Tarquinius had been instigated by Cicero, but omitted, for obvious reasons, to substantiate the charge. If Sallust [1] had evidence for saying that Catulus and Piso urged Cicero to have Caesar incriminated by some informer, Cicero avoided the folly of acceding to their request. Before the session closed the evidence of the Gallic envoys and of Volturcius was formally accepted; rewards were voted to them; and the conspirators in custody were declared public enemies.[2] Meanwhile efforts were being made to set free the ringleaders. The dependants of Lentulus incited artisans and mob-leaders to rescue him; Cethegus sent messengers to urge his slaves and freedmen to make a combined attack upon the house where he was confined and enable him to escape. To frustrate these attempts Cicero posted piquets, and convened the Senate for the following day to decide the fate of the conspirators.[3]

The conspirators declared public enemies: attempts to release them.

Early in the morning Cicero directed that all patriotic citizens should take the military oath in the presence of the praetor, in case additional forces might be required.[4] The Forum, the adjoining temples, the approaches to the temple of Concord, in which the session was to take place, were guarded by armed volunteers.[5] A band of knights, who held the slope of the Capitol, was headed by Atticus.[6] Among the senators were observed the

Dec. 5. Debate in the Senate on their punishment.

---
[1] 49, 1.
[2] *In Cat.*, iv, 3, 5; Sall., 48, 3–9; 50, 1. 3; Dio, xxxvii, 35, 1-2.
[3] *In Cat.*, iv., 8, 17; Sall., 50, 1–3; App. (whose over-condensed narrative is confused), ii, 5, 17; Dio, xxxvii, 35, 3.
[4] *Ib.*, § 4. Cf. Cic., *Phil.*, ii, 7, 16.
[5] *In Cat.*, iv, 7, 14–5; Sall., 50, 3; Dio, xxxvii, 35, 3.
[6] Cic., *Att.*, ii, 1, 7.

consuls designate, fourteen ex-consuls, Tiberius Nero, the grandfather of the emperor Tiberius, Caesar, now a praetor elect, and Cato, the most conspicuous of the newly chosen tribunes; but Crassus was not in his place.[1] When all were assembled, and the customary religious rites had been performed,[2] Cicero invited the senators to state their pleasure as to what punishment should be awarded to the prisoners. The Senate had in strict law no right to decide the question;[3] but Cicero, who relied upon the authority conferred by the ultimate decree, doubtless desired the moral support of the august assembly. The consul-designate Silanus was asked first for his opinion.[4] He replied that the five who were in custody and likewise Cassius, Umbrenus, and two others, Publius Furius and Quintus Annius, in case they were apprehended, should be put to death. One after another, the consul-designate Murena and all the prominent consulars said the same. Caesar, when he was called upon, made a carefully premeditated speech, the substance of which has been preserved. He doubtless felt that his own position was delicate, for he must have known that he was suspected of being concerned in the conspiracy. He began by insisting upon the duty of considering the question in a spirit free from passion, and he recalled instances in which the Roman Government had treated their enemies, despite gross provocation, without vindictiveness, thinking only of what was worthy of themselves. No punishment could be sufficiently severe for the crimes of the conspirators; but that which Silanus had proposed was foreign to the constitution. It was unnecessary, for their illustrious consul had provided a strong defensive force; indeed it was no punishment, for death was the end of human ills, and beyond there was neither happiness nor woe.

---

[1] *In Cat.*, iv, 5, 10. [2] Gell, xiv, 7, 9.

[3] Prof. G. W. Botsford (*Class. Weekly*, March 1, 1913, p. 131), citing Polybius (vi, 13, 4), holds that, on the assumption that the prisoners, who had been declared public enemies, had ceased to be citizens, the Senate had jurisdiction over them.

[4] The evidence for the debate is examined on pp. 467-9.

It would be dangerous to establish a precedent on the strength of which some future consul might take advantage of the ultimate decree to execute men who were unjustly charged. The advice which he would tender to the consul was that the property of the prisoners should be confiscated, that they should be incarcerated in the strongest Italian towns, which should be held strictly responsible for their detention, and that no one should thereafter make any motion in the Senate or address the people on their behalf, on pain of being proclaimed a public enemy.[1] May one not suppose that when Caesar proposed this punishment he believed that under another consul it would be easy to procure the release of the prisoners and the restoration of their property?

Caesar's arguments produced a great effect. Many senators professed their agreement with him,[2] and Cicero thought it time to intervene. He reviewed the speeches of Silanus and of Caesar and called attention to weak points in the latter: it would be unfair to order the municipal towns to receive the prisoners, while merely to ask them would involve a difficulty—in other words, as Cicero evidently meant, they would decline so invidious a responsibility. Again, by making it penal to propose a mitigation of their punishment Caesar was depriving the prisoners of all hope—the one consolation of the miserable. Surely he was aware that the Sempronian law, which forbade the infliction of capital punishment, had been passed in the interest of Roman citizens, and that public enemies,

---

[1] *In Cat.*, iv, 4, 8; Sall., 51 (especially §§ 1–7, 15–20, 26–7, 35–6, 43). See p. 469. Strachan-Davidson (*Cicero*, pp. 141–2) holds that imprisonment was not recognized as a punishment, 'but only as a harsh method of safe-keeping', and therefore that ' Caesar's motion may be held to "Keep on the windy side of the law"'. But what about confiscation? Inconsistently with his earlier view Strachan-Davidson maintained (*Problems*, &c., i, 244) that the Sempronian law did not 'expressly prescribe the necessity of a trial for treason', otherwise Cicero could not 'with any plausibility' have argued (*In Cat.*, iv, 5, 10) that Caesar pronounced on the conspirators despite the Sempronian law because he knew that by their crimes they had forfeited their citizenship.

[2] Dio's statement (xxxvii, 6, 2), with which Plutarch's (*Caes.*, 8, 1) virtually agrees, that every one assented to Caesar's proposal is surely exaggerated.

as such, forfeited their citizenship. If the Senate adopted the proposal of Caesar, who was a popular favourite, he himself would have nothing to fear from a popular ebullition : but the proposal of Silanus was really the more merciful of the two ; and if the Senate shrank from adopting it because they feared the reproach of undue severity, they ought rather to fear that by relaxing the punishment due to relentless enemies they might be deemed guilty of cruelty to their own country.[1]

When Cicero sat down his hearers must have felt that if his speech was in form judicial, he himself was in favour of the punishment of death. His friends, if Plutarch was well informed, supported Caesar's plan, because they thought that it would save Cicero from obloquy.[2] Tiberius Nero, however, suggested that the prisoners should be kept in custody, the guards in the city being reinforced, until Catiline was defeated and further evidence obtained.[3] Silanus, seeing that he was likely to be in the minority, protested that he had been misunderstood : he had not really meant that the prisoners ought to be put to death, but only that their punishment should be imprisonment, the severest sentence known to Roman law, and he intended to vote for the amendment of Tiberius. Finally Cato rose. Pouring contempt upon the tergiversation of Silanus [4], warmly praising Cicero,[5] and hinting broadly that Caesar was himself involved in the conspiracy,[6] he insisted that the municipalities would not be strong enough to prevent the rescue of the prisoners. Upon the decision of the Senate depended the issue of the struggle ; if they showed the least sign of weakness, Catiline and his followers would be emboldened. Catiline was threatening

---

[1] *In Cat.*, iv, especially 4, 7-8 ; 5 ; 6, 11. 13.

[2] *Cic.*, 21, 1. Dr. Hardy (*Journ. Rom. Studies*, 1917, p. 215, n. 3) thinks that Plutarch was mistaken ; for, he remarks, ' Cicero's opening sentences show that his friends had already manifested their anxiety on his account.' Even if they do, that is hardly a sufficient reason.

[3] At what stage in the debate Tiberius Nero spoke is disputed. See pp. 468-9.

[4] Plut., *Cato min.*, 23, 1. Plutarch says that Cato's speech was taken down as he delivered it.

[5] Cic., *Att.*, xii, 21, 1.   [6] Plut., *Cic.*, 21, 2.

the city while enemies were within the walls ; and unless the Senate made an end of the conspirators, the conspirators would make an end of them. Cato concluded by formally proposing the punishment of death and sat down amid rounds of applause.[1] Not only the consulars but many of the other senators agreed with him, and members who had been influenced by Caesar changed their minds.[2] But Caesar was not to be silenced. It was unjust, he contended, to adopt the severer part of his own proposal—the confiscation of the property of the prisoners—while rejecting the more merciful ; and as many of his fellow senators opposed him, he appealed, but in vain, to the tribunes.[3] While he was arguing with Cato a letter was delivered to him. Cato insinuated that it contained something treasonable, and Caesar was called upon to read it. He immediately handed it to Cato, who, seeing that it was a love-letter, written by his half-sister Servilia, the mother of Marcus Brutus and the wife of Silanus, flung it back, exclaiming, 'Take it, you sot!'[4] After this interruption Cicero, withdrawing the proposal for confiscation, put Cato's motion to the vote. The House divided, and the motion was carried by a large majority.[5] When Caesar was leaving the temple many of the guards who had been placed outside closed upon him with swords drawn, looking for orders to Cicero, who raised his hand and checked them.[6]

Night was falling, and Cicero determined to act at once, lest a second attempt might be made to liberate the prisoners. The three officials who carried out executions were ordered to get ready ; piquets were posted to keep disturbers of the peace in check ; and while the praetors fetched the other prisoners, the consul, escorted by a bodyguard, conducted Lentulus through the silent and

---

[1] Sall., 52 (especially §§ 15, 18, 26–7, 35–6) ; 53, 1 ; Cic., *Pro Sest.*, 28, 61.
[2] Plut., *Cato min.*, 23, 2 ; Suet., 14, 2 ; Dio, xxxvii, 36, 3.
[3] Plut., *Cic.*, 21, 2.   [4] Plut., *Cato min.*, 24, 1.
[5] Cic., *Att.*, xii, 21, 1 ; Sall., 53, 1 ; Plut., *Cato min.*, 23, 2 ; *Cic.*, 21, 2.
[6] Sall., 49, 4 ; Plut., *Caes.*, 8, 2. Suetonius (14, 2) incorrectly says that Caesar was attacked while the debate was still going on.

63 B.C.

Controversy on the conduct of Cicero reviewed.

awestruck crowd along the Sacred Way and across the Forum to the prison, which is now approached beneath the steps of the church of San Pietro in Carcere, opposite the arch of Severus. Lentulus was lowered through a hole in the floor into the subterranean dungeon called the Tullianum, where he was strangled;[1] Cethegus, Statilius, Gabinius, and one Caeparius perished in the same way.[2] Leaving the prison, Cicero turned to the multitude and said, 'They have lived their life.' The people followed him homeward through the Forum, saluting him with shouts of applause as the saviour and second founder of the State ; women clustered on the house-tops to do him honour ; and lamps and torches were displayed at every door.[3]

'No State trial,' said the late Master of Balliol,[4] 'except that perhaps of Charles the First, has ever been the subject of so much controversy as that which consigned Lentulus and his companions to the executioner.' The controversy has centred upon the conduct of Cicero ; and opinions will always differ, for agreement will never be reached on the kernel of the question,—whether the danger was so great as to require the punishment of death. None would now assent to the verdict of the German historian, that Cicero committed 'an act of the most brutal tyranny'[5] : Mommsen was young when he wrote those words, and in the zenith of his powers he held that Cicero was legally justified by the ultimate decree.[6] The Porcian law[7] allowed any Roman citizen who had been condemned to death to appeal to the Roman people; the Sempronian law[8] enacted that, except by the people, no Roman citizen might be so condemned. The legal question, as Cicero virtually admitted,[9] was whether Lentulus and his

[1] See p. 470.
[2] Sall., 55 ; Plut., *Cic.*, 22, 1–2. Cf. App., ii, 6, 22, and G. Long, *Decline of the Roman Republic*, iii, 352.
[3] Plut., 22, 2–3 ; App., ii, 6, 22.
[4] J. L. Strachan-Davidson, *Cicero*, 1894, p. 151.
[5] Th. Mommsen, *Röm. Gesch.*, iii⁸, 1889, p. 191 (Eng. tr., iv, 1908, p. 484).
[6] *Röm. Staatsr.*, iii, 1887, p. 1246 ; *Röm. Strafr.*, 1899, pp. 256–7.
[7] Cic, *De rep.*, ii, 31, 54 ; Greenidge, *Legal Procedure*, &c., pp. 320–2.
[8] See p. 23.   [9] *In Cat.*, iv, 5, 10. Cf. i, 11, 28.

companions were citizens or not. The acquittal of 63 B.C. Opimius had established the principle that any one bearing arms against the State was an enemy, and might be lawfully killed under the decree.[1] The popular party, it would seem, insisted that this precedent did not justify the execution of any except overt enemies: the Senate, maintaining that those who had co-operated with armed criminals were themselves public enemies, had branded Lentulus and his associates as such.[2] The defenders of Cicero hold that Lentulus, Cethegus, and the rest were as dangerous as Catiline and Manlius, and therefore that the Senate was justified: those who condemn Cicero reply that Lentulus and his fellows had not accomplished any of their designs; that on the sole legally established precedent—that of Opimius—only armed and active enemies could be legally put to death; and that Cicero had no precedent for inflicting that punishment upon men whose guilt did not extend so far.[3] All these propositions the advocates of Cicero admit. What then is the difference between the disputants? If, says an able critic of Cicero,[4] he could have shown that the State could only be saved by the execution of the prisoners, there might have been some justification for his conduct; but it would have established a dangerous precedent, and Caesar pointed out to him a practicable alternative. This is the vital question, and this is where the parties disagree.

Was Caesar's proposal likely to safeguard the State against the danger which Cicero had revealed? Granted

[1] See p. 31.
[2] Those 'whom the Senate declared public enemies' (*quos senatus hostes iudicavit*) were deemed to have forfeited their citizenship (*Dig.*, iv, 5, 5, 1).
[3] *Journ. Rom. Studies*, iii, 1913, p. 55; *Journ. of Philol.*, xxxiv, 23. When Dr. Hardy says (*Journ. Rom. Studies*, 1917, p. 212) that 'Opimius did not violate the *lex Sempronia* when he killed Gracchus ... because the latter was, or was said to be, an open enemy under arms', he is putting the cart before the horse. Opimius did violate the *lex Sempronia*, but was acquitted; and his acquittal created a precedent. Greenidge (*Legal Procedure*, p. 405) says, 'it was the very possibility of such a declaration'— that the prisoners were public enemies—'that the Gracchan law denied'. But this argument would tell equally against Opimius, whose action had been legally sanctioned.
[4] *Journ. Rom. Studies*, 1913, p. 55.

that it was within the competence of Cicero to intern the prisoners in Italian towns, what security was there that their internment would be valid ? Later events proved that Caesar's proposal for preventing any magistrate from procuring their release was absolutely worthless.[1] But, even supposing that their internment could be ensured, what would be the effect upon the criminals who remained at large in Rome and upon the adherents of Catiline in Italy ? We know the effect of the penalty of death. When the fate of the prisoners became known, the criminals dispersed [2] and Catiline's force was reduced from twelve thousand to three thousand men.[3] It has been said that Cicero never regarded the rising in Etruria as dangerous, for he was anxious that Catiline should join it.[4] But why did Cicero desire that ? Because when he urged Catiline to depart, he was unable to produce evidence against him which none would be able to gainsay, and therefore felt that his best course would be to push the quarrel to extremities and leave him free to go where he must either surrender or encounter the armies of the State. No doubt he expected that those armies would defeat him ; but, for the most part, they were composed of raw recruits,[5] and since Catiline with his diminished force was able to make a desperate resistance, the execution of the prisoners, which caused the bulk of his followers to disperse, was the best way of providing for the safety of the State. The death of Lentulus and his companions saved the lives of many honest men. Cicero could not afford to take the risk, made evident the day before, that interned prisoners might be rescued by their retainers or

---

[1] See *Journ. Rom. Studies*, 1913, p. 58. Dr. Hardy gives his case away when, observing (*op. cit.*, p. 215) that Caesar's proposal ' was a very usual precaution ', he admits that it was ' generally a futile one ', and he does not save his face by adding that ' till the end of the crisis ' it ' might have been enforced, but no longer '.

[2] So Sallust says, but Dr. Hardy knows better : ' it is obvious ', he says (*op. cit.*, p. 221) ' that not terror of punishment, but conviction of failure caused the dispersal ', &c.

[3] Sall., 57, 1. Cf. Plut., *Cic.*, 22, 4 ; Dio, xxxvii, 39, 2 ; 40, 1.

[4] *Journ. Rom. Studies*, 1913, p. 55.

[5] Sall., 56, 2-3 ; 59, 5. Cf. App., ii, 7, 23.

released by demagogues;[1] nor could he ignore the certainty that if he accepted the advice of Caesar, the conspirators and their adherents both in Rome and in the country would attribute his choice to fear. The danger that threatened Rome was apparent from the precautions which he had taken to guard the Senate against violence.[2]

But there is another aspect of the case, which has not received due attention. To argue that Catiline, because he commanded an army, which had not yet struck a blow, was a public enemy, but that Cethegus, who had stored his house with weapons, to be used either by that army or against his countrymen in Rome,[3] was entitled to the privileges of a citizen, is a subtlety, not distinguishable from hair-splitting, which will impose upon no sensible man. And, even supposing that the immediate danger had been removed, was no danger to be apprehended in the future? Roman statutes made no provision for the adequate punishment of such criminals: martial law, provided for by the ultimate decree, was the only safeguard. To execute them not merely in retribution for their crimes, but to deter others from following their example, was a duty, from which Cicero, to his honour, did not shrink. Though jurists may still question the justice of his conduct, men of action who have been confronted by rebellion will

[1] Dr. Hardy admits (*op. cit.*, p. 209) that 'so long as' the conspirators 'were confined in the city' the attempt that had been made on Dec. 4 to release them 'might be repeated'. Would he deny that it might have been repeated with far greater prospect of success if they had been confined in municipal towns? [*I* am glad to find that my question was anticipated by Cato (Sall., 52, 15).]

[2] When Dr. Hardy asserts (*op. cit.*, p. 207) that 'it was clear after the Senate's decrees [on Dec. 3] and Cicero's public statement [*In Cat.*, iii, 7, 16] that the safety of the republic was no longer involved in the decision', does he not forget that Cicero's business was to reassure the people, and that the Senate, in decreeing a vote of thanks to Cicero for having saved the State, by no means implied that if the conspirators were treated with undue leniency, danger might not recur?

[3] Dr. Hardy says (*op. cit.*, pp. 205-6), 'even the weapons found with Cethegus might have been for dispatch to the army outside'. What does that matter? When Dr. Hardy admits that it was 'proved beyond a doubt that there was a conspiracy in Rome connected with Catiline, an open and declared enemy of the State', does he not virtually throw up his case?

282   ANNUS MIRABILIS OF CICERO   CHAP.

63 B.C.

Sequel of the execution.

endorse his words, 'The highest law must be the safety of the State.'[1]

Cicero had not long to wait before the attack which he anticipated in his speech[2] began. In the Senate, indeed, he was treated with all honour. Cato and Catulus called him the father of his country; Lucius Gellius, an ex-censor, said that he deserved the 'civic chaplet', that coveted decoration which Caesar had gained for saving a comrade's life.[3] But Metellus Nepos, who had just entered upon office, declared in a public meeting that one who had punished others without trial ought not himself to be allowed to speak;[4] and it would seem that the lower classes were impressed by the remark.[5] If Plutarch[6] can be trusted, Caesar attempted in the Senate to clear himself from suspicion of complicity with Catiline, but was interrupted by shouts of disapproval; as the session was unusually prolonged, a crowd beset the House, demanding that Caesar should be allowed to leave; and Cato, fearing that the poor, who worshipped Caesar, would raise disturbances, persuaded the Senate to appease them by renewing monthly doles of grain at the lowered price fixed by the obsolete law of Gracchus.[7] At all events Sestius, whom Cicero, after the arrest of the conspirators, had summoned from Capua to Rome, was able with his troops to restrain the unfriendly tribunes from attempting violence.[8]

Cicero attacked by Metellus Nepos.

But Metellus was not deterred from using the tribunician power to humiliate the consul. Cicero, who was aware of his intention, asked Mucia, the wife of Pompey,

---

[1] *Salus rei publicae suprema lex esto* (*De leg.*, iii, 3, 8).
[2] *In Cat.*, iv, 5, 9. Cf. 6, 11.
[3] Cic., *In Pis.*, 3, 6; Pliny, vii, 30 (31), 117; Plut, 23, 2; Gell., v, 6, 15; App., ii, 7, 24.
[4] Cic., *Fam.*, v, 2, 7. Cf. Plut., 23, 1.   [5] Cf. Dio, xxxvii, 38, 1.
[6] *Caes.*, 8, 3–4; *Cato min.*, 26, 1. Suetonius (14, 2) incorrectly, in my opinion (see p. 277, n. 6), says that Caesar did not venture to appear again in the House before the end of the year.
[7] See p. 385. *I* agree with Groebe (W. Drumann's *Gesch. Roms*, v², 1912, pp. 174 n. 3, 175 n. 13) that Cato's proposal was made in December, 63. Lange (*Röm. Alt.*, iii, 1871, p. 258) refers it to 62, but gives no reasons.
[8] Cic., *Pro Sest.*, 4–5, § 11.

and Clodia, the sister-in-law of Metellus, to appeal to his 63 B.C.
good feeling;[1] but if they tried to influence him, their
efforts were ignored. On the last day of December, when
Cicero, in conformity with precedent, was about to
address the people on laying down his office, Metellus
forbade him to say anything beyond taking the customary
oath that he had faithfully discharged his duty. Ascending the platform, Cicero swore in a loud voice that he,
and he alone, had saved the State : the people with one
universal shout declared that he had told the truth ; and
when he left the Forum, he was escorted to his house by
the loyal citizens of Rome.[2] Three days later Metellus, 62 B.C.
evidently intending an impeachment, attacked him Jan. 3
furiously in the House ; but the assembled senators
passed a decree indemnifying all who had acted against
the conspirators and declaring that any one who ventured
to prosecute should be treated as a public enemy.[3]

[1] *Fam.*, v, 2, 6.
[2] *Ib.*, § 7 ; *Pro Sulla*, 11, 34 ; *In Pis.*, 3, 6–7 ; *De rep.*, i, 4, 7 ; Plut., *Cic.*, 23, 1 ; Dio, xxxvii, 38. The remark of Dio, that Cicero was all the more hated for his oath, is obviously one of his many malignant inventions.
[3] Cic., *Fam.*, v, 2, 9 ; Dio, xxxvii, 42, 3.

CHAPTER V

THE DISILLUSIONMENT OF POMPEY AND THE CONSEQUENT TRIUMVIRATE

62 B. C.

Cicero's self-laudatory letter to Pompey.

Jan. 3.

Caesar, as praetor, courts Pompey's favour.

WHEN the new year began Catiline and Manlius were still at large, though the forces of the Republic were closing in upon them; and Pompey, upon whose absence Catiline had based his hopes, was counting on the prospect of being summoned to deal the death-blow to the rebellion.[1] Metellus Nepos was preparing to introduce a measure in his favour.[1] Cicero, who, when the death of Mithradates was announced, had proposed that a thanksgiving service should be held in Pompey's honour,[2] and who imagined that he would be glad to hear that the conspiracy of Catiline was crushed, wrote him a letter of portentous length, in which with much self-glorification he narrated the achievements of his consulship.[3] Persuading himself that he had established in the face of the common danger that harmony between the Senate and the knights on which, as he believed,[4] the stability of the Republic rested, he was confident that Pompey, who was so deeply indebted to his eloquence, would co-operate with him in preserving such harmony for ever. At the same time he denounced Metellus in the Senate,[5] forgetting perhaps that to wrangle with Pompey's agent would not recommend him to the esteem of Pompey. Caesar was more circumspect. Catiline, whom he had planned to mould in the event of his becoming consul, was now doomed. In his own person he had consistently supported Pompey; and if he had been foiled in veiled attempts to gain an authority which might counterbalance his, that was itself a reason for conciliating his good-will. Some

---

[1] See p. 467. [2] *De prov. cons.*, 11, 27. Cf. *Pro Mur.*, 16, 34.
[3] *Pro Sulla*, 24, 67; *Pro Planc.*, 34, 85; *Schol. Bob.*, ed. T. Stangl, p. 167 (ed. Orelli, p. 271). Cf. *Fam.*, v, 7, 3.
[4] *In Cat.*, iv, 7, 15.   [5] *Fam.*, v, 2, 8.

DISILLUSIONMENT OF POMPEY

weeks before, on his suggestion, Labienus and another tribune, Titus Ampius, had carried a bill, which Cato of course opposed, for conferring a special honour upon Pompey;[1] and on the 1st of January, when Caesar entered on his praetorship, he took another opportunity of posing as his friend. Catulus, to whom Caesar owed a grudge, had been appointed to complete the work, which Sulla had left unfinished, of rebuilding the temple of Jupiter on the Capitol; Caesar had given notice of a proposal for transferring the honour from Catulus, whom he intended to press for an account of his expenditure, to Pompey and of erasing the name of Catulus, for which that of Pompey was to be substituted, from the wall. The attempt, indeed, failed, for while Caesar was haranguing the populace the supporters of Catulus came down in force, and opposed him so energetically that he was obliged to drop his bill;[2] but the demonstration doubtless served its purpose, and it was promptly followed up. Metellus, who was working in unison with Caesar, proposed in the Senate that Pompey and his army should be recalled in order to save Rome from Catiline.[3] Since two armies were already hemming in the rebels and their speedy overthrow was certain, the object of the proposal was self-evident, and Cato, reasoning with Metellus, attempted to induce him to withdraw it. Metellus answered that he would achieve his aim despite the Senate: Cato retorted that while he lived Pompey should not enter Rome with troops. Caesar had certainly no wish that a bill which would give Pompey supreme power should pass; but he may have seen that its defeat would widen the breach between Pompey and the Senate, and so prepare the way for an alliance between Pompey

62 B.C.

Metellus Nepos, in collusion with Caesar, proposes the recall of Pompey to save the State. Cato opposes Metellus: uproar in the Forum.

---
[1] Vell., ii, 40, 4; Dio, xxxvii, 21, 4.
[2] Suet., *Div. Iul.*, 15; Dio, xxxvii, 44, 1-2.
[3] See p. 467. Strachan-Davidson (*Cicero*, 1894, p. 163) thinks that the proposal of Metellus in Jan., 62 to recall Pompey to restore order (Dio, xxxvii, 43, 1) was distinct from the proposal, which (p. 160) he refers to December, 63, to recall him to crush Catiline. Plutarch evidently regards them as one and the same. Perhaps the proposal was originally made in 63; but the bill was submitted to the people in the following year, when Catiline was still in the field.

and himself. When the bill was about to be submitted to the people, Metellus and Caesar took their places in the temple of Castor while armed men occupied the steps. Cato, accompanied by his friends and by a brother tribune, Minucius Thermus, entered the Forum and walked towards the temple. The guards respectfully made way for the two tribunes, and Cato sat down between Caesar and Metellus. The clerk produced the bill; but Cato, in virtue of his tribunician power, forbade him to proceed. Metellus took the bill and himself began to read it; Cato snatched it from his grasp, and when Metellus tried to recite the words from memory Thermus put his hand upon his mouth, whereupon Metellus signalled to his guard, who scattered the followers of the tribunes. Pelted with sticks and stones, Cato refused to budge; but the consul Murena, whom he had tried to exclude from office, wrapped his own toga round him and managed to get him inside the temple. Metellus, supposing that his adversaries were cowed, dismissed his guards and was about to read the bill when Cato's partisans rushed back into the Forum; the remaining adherents of Metellus fled; and Cato was left in possession of the field. On the same day the Senate, assuming the garb of mourning as for a national calamity, again passed the ultimate decree, and carried a resolution suspending Caesar and Metellus from office. Metellus forthwith summoned the assembly, declaimed against the action of the Senate, and left the city, in violation of the law, to rejoin his chief. Caesar, ignoring the decree, continued to adminster justice in his court, but soon afterwards, learning that he would be forcibly ejected, quietly went home. Next day a mob collected outside his house and volunteered to back him in asserting his authority; but he declined the offer and persuaded them to disperse. The Senate, which had assembled in expectation of a riot, sent a deputation to thank him for his self-restraint, invited him to attend the House, and reinstated him.[1]

[1] Plut., *Cato min.*, 27–8; 29, 1–2; Suet., 16; Dio, xxxvii, 43. Cf. Cic., *Fam.*, v, 2, 9; *Pro Sest.*, 29, 62; and P. Groebe (W. Drumann's *Gesch. Roms*, iii², 1906, p. 169, n. 2).

By this time Catiline had found his fate. Before the 62 B.C. arrest of Lentulus and Cethegus he had raised two legions,—about twelve thousand men ; but only three thousand were properly equipped, and when, after the execution of the conspirators, the bulk of his followers deserted, he was heavily outnumbered. Abandoning the offensive, he hoped to get across the Apennines, intending, it would seem, to make his way in the early spring into Transalpine Gaul. He had reached Pistoria, close to the southern slope, when he found his progress stopped by Metellus Celer, who, on learning his intention from deserters, had moved with three legions from Picenum and blocked the northern outlets of the passes. Despair may have prompted him to turn and attempt a raid on Rome : but the army of Antonius, who had been compelled by the remonstrances of his second-in-command, Petreius, and of the quaestor, Sestius, to bestir himself, barred the way ; and his supplies were almost consumed. Compelled to risk a battle, he formed his line on level ground, confined between the mountains and rugged rocks, where the enemy would be unable to outflank him. Antonius, who was ill or simulated illness, deputed Petreius to command. The Sullan veterans fought Defeat desperately, and it was not until Petreius brought up and death of his body-guard and pierced their centre that they were Catiline. overthrown, when Catiline, seeing that all was lost, rushed into the hostile ranks to die.[1]

The remaining insurgents in divers parts of Italy were Adherents soon subdued ;[2] and various conspirators, amongst others of Catiline condemned. Autronius, Porcius Laeca, at whose house the plot for

---

[1] Cic., *Pro Sest.*, 5, 12 ; Sall., *Cat.*, 56–61 ; Vell, ii, 35, 5; Flor., ii, 12, 12 ; App., *B. C.*, ii, 7, 23 ; Dio, xxxvii, 39, 1–3. Sallust (57, 1-3) appears to mean that when Metellus Celer, who, he says, was in Picenum, heard that Catiline was marching [from Faesulae] to Pistoria, he moved thither and intercepted him. That, as the map will show, was impossible. Metellus, if he was ever in Picenum, presumably moved thence when he first heard of, or divined, Catiline's intention. Dio, who says that Antonius and Metellus blockaded Faesulae and prevented Catiline from advancing [towards Rome ?], and that he moved against Antonius, whose camp was separated from that of Metellus, does not say where the battle took place.

[2] Dio, xxxvii, 41, 1 ; Oros., vi, 6, 7.

murdering Cicero had been formed, and the two assassins, Vargunteius and Cornelius, were brought to trial and condemned.[1] A common informer, Lucius Vettius, who had himself been engaged in the conspiracy, ventured to lay an information against Caesar, who, as praetor, was immune from prosecution,[2] before one of the quaestors, Novius Niger ; while Curius, to whom a reward had been promised for the disclosures which he had made through Fulvia, denounced him in the Senate. Curius named Catiline as his authority, and Vettius promised to produce a letter in Caesar's handwriting addressed to Catiline. Caesar appealed to Cicero to testify that he had spontaneously informed him about the plot ; and Cicero confessed his obligation.[3] Curius of course forfeited his reward : Vettius, who failed to make good his promise, was committed by Caesar to prison, perhaps in order to save him from the mob, who threatened to lynch him ; and the quaestor, who had violated the law by allowing the praetor to be indicted, was punished in the same way.[4]

About this time a final dispatch arrived from Pompey, and Cicero received an answer to the letter in which he had recounted the achievements of his consulship. He read it with a disappointment which he did not attempt to conceal. 'From your official dispatch,' he replied, ' I have derived, like every one else, the most intense satisfaction.... But I am bound to tell you that your old enemies— now posing as your friends [5]—have received a staggering blow from the dispatch : their far-reaching hopes are shattered, and they are simply prostrate. Though your letter to me contained but a meagre expression of your goodwill, I can assure you that it gave me pleasure, for there is nothing which I delight in more than the consciousness of having served my friends ;

---

[1] Cic., *Pro Sulla*, 2, 6 ; *Pro Cael.*, 29, 70 ; Dio, xxxvii, 41, 2–3.

[2] Dr. Hardy (*Journ. Rom. Studies*, vii, 1917, p. 222) conjectures that 'the disclosures of Vettius' were 'almost certainly prompted by men like Catulus and Piso'. See p. 273, *supra*.

[3] This is implied, though not expressly stated, by Suetonius.

[4] Suet., 17 ; Dio, xxxvii, 41, 2.

[5] Evidently Cicero is alluding to Caesar, and probably also to Crassus.

THE CONSEQUENT TRIUMVIRATE 289

and if in any case I do not get a fair return, I am quite 62 B.C.
content to have the balance in my favour. Of one thing
I am sure—even if my great efforts on your behalf have
done little to unite you to me, the public interest will
bring us together and cement our union. To let you know
what I missed in your letter, I will write frankly, as my
disposition and our friendship demand. What I have
achieved led me to expect some congratulation ... let me
tell you that what I did to save the country is approved
by the verdict and the testimony of all the world. You
are a much greater man than Africanus, but I am not
much inferior to Laelius ; and when you return you will
find that I acted with a judgement and a force of character
which will make you ready enough to be associated with
me in public affairs as well as in private friendship.'[1]
Pompey when he read this effusion must have smiled at
the simplicity of Cicero, who did not see that the 'achievements' for praise of which he thirsted had stultified the
mission of Metellus Nepos and frustrated the ambition
of Pompey the Great.

Pompey was now about to return. Despite his dis- Pompey's
appointment he evidently felt that he was exalted above journey.
the law, for in the course of the summer messengers
arrived in Rome to request that the consular elections
should be postponed in order that he might support the
canvass of his lieutenant Pupius Piso. The Senate was
disposed to yield ; but Cato, who suspected Pompey,
persuaded them to refuse.[2] It was generally believed
that Pompey, when he appeared with his irresistible

---

[1] *Fam.*, v, 7.
[2] There is a conflict of evidence between Plutarch (*Cato min.*, 30, 1), whom
I have followed, and Dio (xxxvii, 44, 3), who says that Pompey sent Piso
to stand for the consulship, that the elections were deferred until his
arrival, and that Piso was unanimously elected. Dio ascribes the postponement to the prevailing fear that Pompey would not disband his army.
His ascription of motives is almost always to be distrusted, and if the elections had been held a few days later than usual, he would not have hesitated
to write what he did. The refusal of the Senate, as described by Plutarch,
is quite in harmony with their usual attitude towards Pompey. Dr. Hardy
(*op. cit.*, p. 227), who accepts Dio's statement, finds it 'impossible not to
detect in this episode the influence of Crassus and Caesar'.

2592.1 U

army, would follow the example of Sulla and seize supremacy.[1] His journey resembled the progress of an absolute king. Halting at Mytilene, he bestowed upon it autonomy, in honour of his secretary, Theophanes, who was a native of the city, and listened to the recital of prize poems written to celebrate his deeds. While his legions were marching towards Ephesus, where they were to embark, he sailed to Rhodes and visited the philosopher Posidonius. The illustrious Stoic was in bed, suffering from gout; but when Pompey, after paying him many gracious compliments, remarked how sorry he was that he could not hear him lecture, he replied, 'You shall! I will not allow bodily pain to make a great man visit me for nothing'; and when the pangs became severe, he exclaimed in the midst of his discourse, 'It won't do, Pain: plague me as much as you please, but I will never admit that you are an evil.' The minor philosophers, who apparently were not invited to hold forth, received a talent apiece from the conqueror,[2] whose sense of humour, if he had one, must surely have been tickled then. At Ephesus, before the troops embarked, he distributed the prize-money, sixteen thousand talents in all. The generals and the quaestors were awarded one hundred million sesterces—the equivalent of a million sterling; and every private drew six thousand, or about sixty pounds.[3]

Towards the end of the year the transports reached Brundisium: the troops, after they disembarked, were assembled on parade; and Pompey, bidding them farewell, forthwith dismissed them to their homes.[4]

What were the motives of Pompey for reducing himself to impotence we do not know, nor even whether the thought of seizing supreme power had ever dawned upon his mind. To rail at him for having 'timidly clung to formal right'[5] is as gratuitous as to commend him for

[1] Vell., ii, 40, 2; Plut., Pomp., 43,1; App., Mithr., 116; Dio, xxxvii, 44, 3.
[2] Cic., Tusc., ii, 25, 61; Strabo, xiii, 2, 3; Plut., Pomp., 42, 3–5.
[3] See p. 427.
[4] Vell., ii, 40, 3; Plut., Pomp., 43, 2; App., Mithr., 116.
[5] Th. Mommsen, Röm. Gesch., iii⁸, 1889, p. 204 (Eng. tr., iv, 1908, p. 499). Caesar, who was careful to put himself legally in the right in 50–49 B.C.,

self-restraint.¹ When we reflect that fortune had never 62 B.C. failed him and that his career had been unprecedently splendid; that he was beyond all question the foremost man in the Roman, indeed in the inhabited world; that consulars or tribunes had been ever ready to promote his aims; that his flatterers had likened him to Alexander the Great, and that the greatest of Roman orators had encouraged him to believe that he was the greatest Roman who had ever lived; we may suppose that he felt confident that without his army he could bend Lucullus and the Senate to his will, that Caesar, whom he rated far below himself, and who, moreover, had lately courted him, would remain subservient, and that Crassus, his old enemy, might safely be ignored.² On the other hand, the necessity of remaining to complete his work in Asia had prevented him from retaining his army, when he returned to Italy, on the pretext of restoring order; and perhaps he felt that the task of rebuilding the Roman constitution and governing the Roman empire, which, if he made himself dictator, he could not shirk, was above his strength.

Just before Pompey reached the capital two incidents, trivial in themselves, but destined to produce momentous consequences, were being talked about in all classes of society; and one of them, which, as Cicero wrote to Atticus,³ occasioned extraordinary scandal, was already begetting political unrest. Pompey had divorced his wife,⁴ and Caesar, whose name was sure to be coupled with that of any attractive woman suspected of adultery,⁵ was said to be her lover. He himself had reason for complaint. In the first week of December⁶ the festival of

would have been too prudent to seize the opportunity which the historian whom Bismarck derided as 'a greenhorn in politics' sneered at Pompey for having missed. ¹ Strachan-Davidson, *Cicero*, p. 171.

² Dr. Hardy (*op. cit.*, p. 227) suspects 'that Pompey's resignation of his military command ... was ... in conformity with previous understandings arrived at with Caesar and Crassus'. But see p. 467.

³ *Att.*, i, 12, 3.

⁴ Ascon., ed. Clark, p. 20, l. 2 (ed. Stangl, p. 23); Plut., *Pomp.*, 42, 6.

⁵ See Suet., 50–1, 52, 1; &c.

⁶ Plut., *Cic.*, 19, 2; Dio, xxxvii, 35, 4; Warde Fowler, *Roman Festivals*, 1899, pp. 255–6.

292 DISILLUSIONMENT OF POMPEY AND CHAP.

62 B. C.
Clodius enters Caesar's house in female dress during a religious festival.

the Good Goddess, which it was sacrilege for men to behold, was celebrated in his official residence [1] in the Sacred Way. His mother Aurelia and his wife Pompeia presided. While the ceremony was being performed, Clodius, who was enamoured of Pompeia, came to the door, dressed as a woman, and was admitted by one of Pompeia's maids, who, being privy to his intrigue, ran to tell her mistress. Another maid met and questioned him, recognized his sex by his voice, and, rushing into the throng of worshippers, exclaimed that she had discovered a man. Aurelia instantly stopped the service and searched the house; but Clodius, helped by the maid who had admitted him, contrived to escape. The Vestal Virgins performed the rites anew; but the story of course spread, and a senator, Cornificius, called attention to it in the House.[2] The question was referred to the college of pontiffs, who pronounced that a sin had been committed against the religion of the State. The matter could not be allowed to rest; but this particular form of sacrilege was unprecedented,[3] and there was no standing court of justice which could deal with it. The consuls therefore,

Bill for the appointment of a commission to try him for sacrilege.

acting on a senatorial decree, promulgated a bill for the appointment of an extraordinary commission; and Caesar immediately divorced his wife. The bill provided that the praetor who was to preside at the trial should himself select the jurors from the existing list.[4] On the

61 B. C.

27th of January, after Pompey had arrived, Cicero wrote to Atticus that while one of the consuls, Valerius Messalla, was in earnest, the other, Pupius Piso, Pompey's nominee, was doing his best to get the bill, for which he was himself responsible, rejected by the popular assembly; that respectable citizens, yielding to the importunity of Clodius, were inclined to hold aloof; and that Clodius was hiring rowdies to intimidate opponents who might

---

[1] Though Caesar occupied the house as Chief Pontiff, it was because he was also urban praetor that the festival was celebrated there.
[2] Cic., *Att.*, i, 12, 3; 13, 3; *De har. resp.*, 21, 44; Plut., *Caes.*, 10, 1-3; Cic., 28; Dio, xxxvii, 45, 1; App., ii, 14, 52. Cf. W. Drumann, *Gesch. Roms*, ii², 1902, p. 177, n. 8.
[3] Cic. (?), *De har. resp.*, 18, 38.   [4] Cic., *Att.*, i, 13, 3; 14, 1.

THE CONSEQUENT TRIUMVIRATE 293

attempt to vote. 'I myself,' Cicero added, 'though I was a veritable Lycurgus at first, now feel my indignation every day subsiding. Cato is insisting on stern measures. To put the matter in a nutshell, I fear that between the indifference of decent folks and the backing given to it by rascals, this scandal may be a source of great evils to the State.' Then followed a first impression of Pompey.—'Outwardly he is now quite fond of me, makes much of me, loves me like a brother, praises me to my face, while secretly (but still transparently) he is jealous of me. There is no courtesy in the man, no candour, no sense of honour in politics, nothing high-minded or vigorous or frank.'[1]

_{61 B. C.}

_{Cicero's unfavourable opinion of Pompey.}

Meanwhile Piso was inciting one of the tribunes, Fufius Calenus, to wreck the bill. People were waiting to hear what Pompey would have to say. As he could not lawfully enter the city before his triumph,[2] it was necessary that all meetings at which his presence was desired should be held outside the walls. The letter in which Cicero chronicled his first utterance is lost; but on the 13th of February he had much to relate to Atticus. 'I have already', he wrote, 'described to you Pompey's first public speech. It did not please the poor, nor satisfy radicals, nor appeal to the well-to-do; nor was it sound enough for the friends of order: therefore it fell flat. Afterwards, instigated by the consul Piso, that worthless tribune, Fufius, introduced Pompey to the assembly. The meeting was in the Flaminian Circus. . . . Fufius asked him to say whether he approved of jurors' being selected by the praetor, who was himself to take them as his panel. . . . The tone of Pompey's speech was thoroughly aristocratic: his answer, given at great length, was that in his judgement the authority of the Senate in all matters was and always had been paramount.' A meeting of the Senate followed, in which the consul Messalla invited Pompey to state his opinion on the bill. Evading the question, he pronounced a comprehensive panegyric on

_{Pompey invited to speak on the bill.}

---
[1] *Att.*, i, 13, 3–4. Cf. *Phil.*, ii, 5, 12.
[2] Cic., *Fam.*, i, 9, 25; Th. Mommsen, *Röm. Staatsr.*, i³, 1887, p. 641, n. 3.

the Senate. His speech was received with cheers. As he sat down he turned towards Cicero and said, ' I think my answer was explicit enough about your administration.' [1] Cicero understood that Pompey was awkwardly attempting to express that approval of his consulship which he had omitted in his recent letter. Crassus, noticing how the House had ratified Pompey's implied commendation, and perhaps anxious to dispel suspicions of his own complicity with Catiline, promptly rose : ' he spoke of my consulship', wrote Cicero naïvely, ' in the most enthusiastic terms, going so far as to say that he owed it to me that he was still a senator, a citizen, a free man—aye, that he was still alive; that he never beheld wife, home, or country without recognizing my beneficent hand . . . I was sitting next to Pompey. I noticed that the man was annoyed, either that Crassus should come in for the gratitude which he had himself neglected, or that my achievements were important enough for the Senate to be so glad to hear them praised. . . . This day has made me a close ally of Crassus ; yet I was glad to receive any compliment, open or veiled, that the other paid me.' [2] Cicero himself, eager, as he told his friend, to impress Pompey, exerted all his eloquence to celebrate the extinction of the conspiracy, the restoration of credit, the reestablishment of peace—above all, the harmony of the Senate with the knights and the unanimity of Italy. It was this harmony and this unanimity that might, he feared, be disturbed by the contests about the approaching trial. When the day came for submitting the bill to the assembly, the young men of fashion who were friends of Clodius—' all the Catiline herd,' as Cicero called them, ' with that girl, young Curio, at their head '—came down to the Forum, and urged the people to have none of it. Piso, its joint author, was not ashamed to speak against it. The bravoes whom Clodius had hired were grouped in front of the polling places, and, if we may trust Cicero, those who had the courage to confront them found that

---

[1] *Att.*, i, 14, 1-2. Cf. *De off.*, i, 22, 78.
[2] *Att.*, i, 14, 3-4.

the only voting tickets to be had were 'Noes'.[1] 'Cato', he wrote, 'rushed on to the platform and delivered a magnificent invective against Piso—if you can call it an "invective" when it was really an oration, weighty, authoritative, and full of the most salutary counsel.' Hortensius and others followed Cato's lead. In consequence of their resistance the meeting was dissolved, and the Senate was hastily convened. A motion was made that the consuls should exhort the people to pass the bill. Piso opposed the motion; Clodius implored members, one after another, to vote against it; and the elder Curio proposed as an amendment that the Senate should abstain from taking action : but four hundred or more voted for the decree, while only fifteen supported Curio. In the face of this majority Fufius, who had blocked the decree, gave way, reserving, however, the right to interpose his veto when the bill should be again submitted to the people. Another meeting of the assembly followed. Clodius, introduced by Fufius, inveighed against Messalla and Hortensius, and, repeating a gibe which had become the vogue, sneered at Cicero for having repeatedly boasted that he had 'discovered' the designs of Catiline. The Senate resolved to transact no business until the bill was brought before the people,[2] and Cicero, stung by the raillery of Clodius, attacked the policy of Piso and defended the authority of the House. 'How often', he told Atticus, 'I wished that you were there, not only to help me with your advice, but to see what a glorious fight I made!'[3] But his exultation was premature. Hortensius, fearing that the authority of the Senate would be weakened if Fufius vetoed a bill which was to be proposed to the assembly by its decree, persuaded them to accept a compromise : let Fufius, he suggested, himself introduce a bill, identical with the existing one except that the jurors should be chosen by lot in the ordinary way; the guilt of Clodius was so notorious that any jury must convict him—' a leaden sword would do to cut *his* throat '. Cicero gave up the case. Hortensius, he wrote, 'failed

61 B. C.

The bill shelved : Clodius to be tried by a jury.

[1] *Ib.*, §§ 3, 5.   [2] *Ib.*, § 5.   [3] *Ib.*, 16, 1.

296 DISILLUSIONMENT OF POMPEY AND CHAP.

61 B.C.

to see that it was better to leave Clodius in disgrace and humiliation than to trust the issue to a rotten jury.'[1]

The trial.

The tribune's bill was of course passed; and the trial began. The penalty named in the bill was 'interdiction from fire and water', which could only be escaped by voluntary exile.[2] The prosecutor, Cornelius Lentulus Crus,[3] exercising his right of challenge, rejected the most disreputable of the jurors, and the defendant the most respectable. Fifty-six remained. Among them were senators who, if they had not been formally disgraced by the censors, were under a cloud, and knights who had been reduced to poverty. 'There never was a viler crew', wrote Cicero, who saw them, 'round a table in a gambling hell.' 'However,' he admitted, 'there were a few honest men among them,' who 'were intensely disgusted at having to rub elbows with such rascals'. Still, the case for the prosecution was so strong that in the preliminary proceedings the jury again and again decided the questions that were referred to them against the defendant. Lucullus was not ashamed to produce female slaves to testify that Clodius had committed incest with Clodia, his younger sister, before her husband, Lucullus, had divorced her.[4] Hortensius was jubilant. The prosecutor demanded that certain slaves of Clodius should be examined, as was usual, under torture; but all whose evidence was likely to tell against him had been sent into the country.[5] The defence was an attempt to prove an *alibi* : one Gaius Causinius swore that on the night of the festival in Caesar's house Clodius had been staying with him at Interamna, ninety miles from Rome. Among the witnesses were Caesar and Cicero. Caesar deposed that he knew nothing about the case. 'Why then', asked the prosecutor, 'did you divorce your wife?' The reply, by which Caesar intended to remind the court

---

[1] *Att.*, i, 16, 2. Cf. Greenidge, *Legal Procedure*, &c., p. 388.
[2] Cic., *Parad.*, iv, 32. Cf. Strachan-Davidson, *Problems*, &c., ii, 41.
[3] *Schol. Bob.*, ed. Stangl, p. 167 (ed. Orelli, p. 330).
[4] Cic., *Pro Mil.*, 27, 73 ; Plut., *Cic.*, 29, 2 ; *Luc.*, 38, 1.
[5] *Schol. Bob.*, ed. Stangl, p. 91 (ed. Orelli, pp. 338-9).

that his wife was the wife of the Chief Pontiff, has become 61 B.C.
proverbial—'Because my wife must be above suspicion'.
When Cicero appeared, the supporters of Clodius raised
an uproar ; but the jurors gathered round him and showed
that they intended to defend the man who had saved the
State. His evidence was brief : Clodius had called to see
him three hours before the time when he was charged with
having been in Caesar's house.[1] Clodius and his counsel,
the elder Curio, were dumbfounded. The jurors, with
one dissentient, announced before they left the court that
they would not return unless they were protected by
a guard ; and every one concluded that they intended to
convict. Their request was referred to the Senate, who
complimented them and granted it. But Crassus, if not
also Caesar, resolved that Clodius must be saved ; and
a later chapter of this history may warrant a suspicion
that both had reason to believe that he would prove
a serviceable instrument. Crassus invited the jurors to Crassus
an interview, made them an offer, and paid a deposit to bribes
those who would accept it: 'even the favours', wrote jurors to
Cicero, 'of certain ladies and introductions to youths of acquit Clodius.
noble family helped with some of the jurors to balance
the account.' When they were dismissed to consider of
their verdict the Forum was occupied by slaves, and no
respectable citizens ventured to appear. Yet Clodius Acquittal
narrowly escaped. The majority in his favour was only by a small majority.
six ; and his friends admitted with cool cynicism that
his guilt was patent and that the jurors had been bought.
'Why,' asked Catulus, when he met one of them, 'did you
apply to us for a guard ? For fear you might be robbed
of your money ? ' To Cicero the matter was too ominous
for sarcasm. 'That settlement of the State', he wrote,
'which seemed fixed and established by the unanimity
of all honest men and by the precedent of my consulship—

[1] E. Meyer (*Caesars Monarchie*², 1919, p. 48) sees no reason for rejecting the story of Plutarch (*Cic.*, 29, 1) that Cicero had been a friend of Clodius, but was egged on to give evidence against him by Terentia, who suspected that Clodia wished Cicero to marry her. Terentia may have been jealous of Clodia ; but *I* distrust Plutarch's attribution of motives, and Cicero's account of the trial shows that he gave his evidence *con amore*

that, I assure you, unless Providence takes pity on us, has by this one verdict, if verdict it is to be called ... slipped from our grasp.'[1]

Cicero denounces the corrupt jurors and inveighs against Clodius.

He strove, however, to counteract its ill effects. Knowing that those who had sympathized with Catiline were exulting, he inveighed so vigorously against the corrupt jurors and their backers that Piso was deprived of Syria, the rich province which the Senate had allotted for his proconsulship. Reminding the House that Lentulus Sura and Catiline had both been twice acquitted, and that the jurors had now let loose another criminal, he turned upon him and exclaimed, 'You are mistaken, Clodius : it is not for public life, but for the dungeon that the jurors have reprieved you ; they did not mean to keep you in the State, but to deprive you of the privilege of exile.' Up sprang Clodius ; and then followed a verbal duel. Cicero returned taunt for taunt. 'The jurors', Clodius shouted, ' didn't trust you on your oath ! ' 'Yes,' Cicero retorted, 'twenty-five did trust me; thirty-one did not trust you, for they pocketed their money in advance.' The thrust was loudly cheered, and Clodius sat down silenced.[2]

Caesar was now able to leave Rome and take over the government of Further Spain, the province in which he had served his quaestorship and which the lot had committed to his charge. But his creditors were becoming impatient and, hoping perhaps that the fear of seeing his prospects ruined would compel him to find some means of discharging his obligations, insisted upon immediate payment. He had always kept on good terms with Crassus, who, despite the hollow reconciliation that closed his consulship, was still an enemy of Pompey, and could well afford to advance a sum which would assure

---

[1] *Att.*, i, 16, 3–6, 11 ; Val. Max. (who is unnecessarily explicit), ix, 1, 7; Ascon., ed. Clark, p. 49, ll. 11–7 (ed. Stangl, p. 42) ; Plut., *Caes.*, 10, 3–4 ; *Cic.*, 29 ; Dio (who incorrectly says that Clodius was tried on other charges besides that of adultery, with which he was not charged at all), xxxvii, 46, 1–3. Cf. Greenidge, *op. cit.*, pp. 386–8.

[2] *Att.*, i, 16, 7–10 ; *Schol. Bob. in Clod. et Cur.*, fr. xxvi, ed. Stangl, p. 90 (ed. Orelli, p. 338).

THE CONSEQUENT TRIUMVIRATE

political support and which might, sooner or later, be repaid. Caesar is said to have remarked that he wanted just one hundred million sesterces—about a million sterling—to be worth exactly nothing.[1] Crassus placed eight hundred and thirty talents—nearly two hundred thousand pounds—at his disposal, enough to satisfy the more importunate of his creditors ; and before midsummer he was free to start.[2]

Meanwhile Pompey, whose reception had not been flattering, must have been in some anxiety. Since he had chosen to disband his army, he had to rely upon the Senate, in which he had many enemies, for the confirmation of his settlement of Asia, and, above all, for the grant of the allotments which he had promised to his soldiers. Cato, who had baffled both him and his lieutenants, was manifestly a rising man ; and Pompey made overtures for a marriage with one of his relations. Suspecting Pompey's motives and not foreseeing that a statesman who allowed no scruples to weaken policy might seize the opportunity which he neglected, Cato refused the offer, which the women of his family were eager to accept.[3] The eloquence of Cicero, however, might be useful ; and Pompey, willing to heal the wound inflicted by his frigid letter, condescended to make himself agreeable. 'The wretched starveling mob', wrote Cicero to Atticus, 'fancies that I am the special favourite of "the Great", and indeed we really have had much pleasant intercourse —so much that the boon-companions of the conspiracy, our young friends with the little chin-tufts, talk of him as Gnaeus Cicero.' 'We are all', he continued, 'looking forward to the elections : much to every one's disgust, our friend "the Great" is backing Aulus junior,[4] not with the weapons of prestige or influence, but by the means with which Philip used to say that every fortress could be taken—if only an ass could get up to it with a load of

61 B.C.

Crassus enables Caesar to satisfy his creditors and assume the government of Further Spain. Pompey anxious for confirmation of his arrangements in the East.

---
[1] App., ii, 8, 26.
[2] Plut., *Cras.*, 7, 7 ; *Caes.*, 11, 1. Cf. Suet., 18, 1.
[3] Plut., *Pomp.*, 44, 2–3 ; *Cato min.*, 30, 2–4.
[4] i.e. Lucius Afranius.

300 DISILLUSIONMENT OF POMPEY AND CHAP.

61 B. C.

gold '. The Senate was doing its best to baffle Pompey. Two decrees had just been passed, at the instance of Cato and of his brother-in-law Domitius,—one providing that the houses of magistrates might be searched for evidence that money was deposited therein for bribery, the other that any one who harboured bribery agents in his house should be deemed a public enemy. 'Mark you,' Cicero concluded, 'if this fellow is elected, even my consulship, which Curio used to call the apotheosis of the office, will become a byword.'[1]

The decrees were as futile as every law directed against bribery had been. Afranius was elected; and his patron, who expected him to prove his gratitude for the expenditure which had purchased his success,[2] was preparing to impress upon the popular imagination the magnitude of his own achievements. After his final dispatch was read Cicero had carried a motion for holding a second thanksgiving in his honour;[3] and on the last two days of September, of which the second was the anniversary of his birthday, he celebrated his final triumph, the most gorgeous that had ever been seen in Rome. The time did not suffice to display all the treasures which he had brought from the East. Conspicuous among the trophies was one bearing an inscription which, as if in memory of the triumphs that had commemorated his exploits in Africa and Spain, declared him the conqueror of the world. Banners, borne in the procession of the opening day, informed the spectators that Pompey the Great, after restoring to the Roman People the dominion of the seas, had subdued Asia, Pontus, Armenia, Paphlagonia, Cappadocia, Cilicia, Syria, Albania, Iberia, Crete (which had been subdued by Metellus), and other lands (which Pompey had never seen); that he had vanquished Mithradates and Tigranes, taken a thousand forts, nearly nine hundred towns, and eight hundred ships, founded thirty-nine

He celebrates his third triumph.

---

[1] *Att.*, i, 16, 11–3 ; Plut., *Pomp.*, 44, 3.
[2] The fact is self-evident, but is attested by Dio (xxxvii, 49, 1).
[3] *De prov. cons.*, 11, 27, my interpretation of which is confirmed by W. Sternkopf (*Rhein. Mus.*, xlvii, 1892, pp. 468–72).

V THE CONSEQUENT TRIUMVIRATE 301

cities, brought twenty thousand talents into the treasury, 61 B.C. and raised the national revenue from two hundred million to three hundred and forty million sesterces. A long train of wagons carried the gold, the silver, and the captured weapons; a gilded bust of Mithradates, eight cubits high, contrasted with a bust of Pompey, made throughout of pearls. Tigranes, the son of the Armenian king, and Zosime, his wife, five sons and two daughters of Mithradates, the king of the Colchians, Aristobulus, the humbled rival of Hyrcanus with his son Antigonus, princes, satraps, military commanders, pirate chiefs, and hostages —three hundred and twenty-four in all—walked in orderly array. Pictures represented the blockade of Mithradates, his nocturnal flight, and his tragic death. Pompey followed in his triumphal car, which glittered with precious stones; and last of all, some mounted, some on foot, came the generals, the admirals, and the subordinate officers who had served under his command. But it was not only for its splendour that this triumph was remembered. When Pompey ascended the Capitol he disregarded precedent, and would not allow his captives to be led to execution : except the royal personages, who were detained as a precaution, they were sent back at the public cost to their respective homes.[1]

By this time Caesar was exercising his first command. His province comprised Lusitania as well as the remoter parts of Spain, and his commission empowered him to make war upon recalcitrant tribes.[2] Two legions, the regular army of the Governor, had awaited him, and on his arrival he had raised a third.[3] The Lusitanians were doubtless as reluctant as ever to submit to alien rule, for, notwithstanding the insinuations of Cassius Dio, it is

Caesar's operations in Further Spain.

---

[1] Cic., *Verr.*, v, 30, 77; Livy, *Epit.*, 103; Diod. Sic., xl, 4; Pliny, vii, 26 (27), 98; xxxvii, 1 (5), 11; 2 (6), 13–6; Vell., ii, 40, 3–5; Plut., *Pomp.*, 45; App., *Mithr.*, 116–7; Dio, xxxvii, 21, 1–3; Eutrop., vi, 16; *C. I. L.*, i, p. 460, xxvii. Appian incorrectly says that Aristobulus and Tigranes were afterwards put to death. G. Beseler (*Hermes*, xliv, 1909, p. 352, n. 1) conjectures that the execution of the captive general was in its inception a form of human sacrifice.
[2] App., *Hisp.*, 102. [3] Plut., *Caes.*, 12, 1.

incredible that Caesar wasted time and money in attacking tribes who desired to live in peace. He compelled the mountaineers of the Herminian range, between the Tagus and the Mondego, to quit their fastnesses, pursued them when they afterwards rebelled to the Atlantic, and, sailing northwards with ships furnished by the friendly citizens of Gades to the Bay of Betanzo, received the submission of Brigantium.[1] We need not regret that the narrative of Dio, the only ancient writer who attempted to describe the operations, is unintelligible, for, although Caesar's soldiers saluted him as Imperator, he did not care to record his exploits in his *Commentaries*; and though Suetonius, who eagerly ransacked the memoirs written by Caesar's enemies, relates that he plundered towns which voluntarily surrendered,[2] the most cynical reader may be inclined to doubt whether such booty in Lusitania was worth the trouble of removal.[3] That Caesar accepted presents from the ' allies ',[4] if by that term the biographer meant the Gaditanians, is not improbable. However this may be, he did his best to ameliorate the condition of the natives, persuading mutually hostile tribes to settle their disputes,[5] inducing the Senate to remit the taxes which Metellus had imposed in the Sertorian War,[6] and enacting that debtors who, in consequence of those taxes, were harassed by the demands of Italian money-lenders should be free to retain one-third of their annual incomes, while they handed over the remainder to their creditors until their debts were paid.[7] He was assisted by the local knowledge and the influence of Cornelius Balbus, one of the Gaditanians upon whom Pompey had bestowed Roman citizenship as a reward for service in the Sertorian War. After his enfranchisement Balbus had removed to Rome, cultivated the friendship of his patron, and attached himself to Caesar, who, discerning his trustworthiness, his worldly wisdom, and

---

[1] Plut., *Caes.*, 12, 1; Dio, xxxvii, 52-3. [2] *Div. Iul.*, 54, 1.
[3] See the sensible remarks of Long, *Decline of the Roman Republic*, iii, 1869, p. 394. [4] Suet., *l. c.*.
[5] Plut., 12, 2. [6] *Bell. Hisp.*, 42, 2-3. [7] Plut., 12, 2.

his tact, took him on his staff to Spain. With Balbus at his side Caesar did much for Gades. The city was enlarged and modernized ; the inhabitants, who enjoyed self-government secured by treaty, were induced to accept reforms and to abolish an old barbarous usage, which we may perhaps suppose to have been human sacrifice.[1]

But Caesar had more important work in view. The Senate had granted him the right to triumph for his victorious campaign.[2] Less than a year after he left Rome he started on his homeward journey, intending to present himself as a candidate for the consulship.[3] In order to understand the situation with which he had to deal, it is necessary to review the events that had followed Pompey's triumph.

On the 5th of December, 61 B. C., Cicero wrote to Atticus, deploring an outburst of ill feeling between the Senate and the knights.[4] A good understanding between the orders seemed to him essential for the stability of the Republic, and to promote it was his constant aim. A few days before, when he was absent from the House, a senator had moved that all who had taken bribes as jurymen should be prosecuted. The knights, knowing that the mover was thinking of the trial of Clodius, were indignant, for they had always claimed immunity from such a charge,[5] and Cicero urged the Senate for the sake of concord to rescind the resolution. 'Considering', he told Atticus, 'that my case was not a good one, I spoke with weight and eloquence. But', he added, 'here is another piece of almost intolerable impudence on the part of the knights.'[6] The syndicate which had contracted for the collection of the taxes in the province of Asia complained that they had offered an excessive sum, and, encouraged

---
[1] Cic., *Pro Balbo*, 19, 43 ; 28, 63 ; Strabo, iii, 5, 3. Cf. G. Long, *Cic. orat.*, iv, 1858, p. 141. Prof. J. S. Reid in his edition of the speech *Pro Balbo* (1904, p. 83) gives what seems to me a less probable explanation of *inveteratam quondam barbariam* : 'The Punic element in the population no doubt oppressed the non-Punic, and Caesar's reforms gave all classes equal rights before the law.'   [2] App., ii, 8, 28.
[3] Suet., 18, 1 ; Dio, xxxvii, 54, 1.   [4] *Att.*, i, 17, 8.
[5] Cic., *Pro Rab. Post.*, 7, 16. Cf. Strachan-Davidson, *Cicero*, pp. 34–5, 185.   [6] *Att.*, i, 17, 9.

by Crassus, requested the Senate to annul the bargain. The request was considered on the 1st and the 2nd of December, and Cicero earnestly supported it. 'It was an odious affair', he admitted, 'and the demand was disgraceful'; but, he pleaded, 'there was a great risk that, if they got no concession, they would be alienated from the Senate.' The business was not settled, though members generally were inclined to side with Cicero: Metellus Celer, one of the consuls-designate, was the only senator who answered him, for Cato, whose turn was to come later, was prevented from speaking by the adjournment of the House.[1] But Cato, although even he occasionally thought it right to sacrifice his principles to manifest expediency, was not disposed to bribe the knights to support the Senate. 'One man', wrote Cicero on the 20th of January, 'has it in him to do good—I mean Cato; but, as it seems to me, he has more firmness and integrity than judgement or ability. He has been worrying the unhappy knights, who were once devoted to him, for the last three months.'[2]

Cicero, seeing that the 'harmony of the orders' was in danger of disruption, had been trying to find some other way of serving his country and securing his own position. 'I am making', he confided to Atticus, 'what I may call a road, which will, I hope, be safe, to maintain our power. . . . I cultivate the closest intimacy with Pompey.'[3] Pompey had expected that Afranius, for whom his influence and his gold had won the consulship, would secure confirmation of the arrangements which he had made in Asia and obtain allotments for his impatient soldiers. But Afranius lacked the energy and the ability to overcome the resistance of the Senate; his colleague was offended because Mucia, one of his relations, had been divorced by Pompey; Crassus was unforgiving; Lucullus and Metellus, the conqueror of Crete, had not forgotten Pompey's insolence, and when Lucullus demanded that his own settlement of Asia, which Pompey

[1] *Att.*, i, 17, 9. [2] *Ib.*, 18, 7. [3] *Ib.*, 17, 10.

THE CONSEQUENT TRIUMVIRATE 305

had annulled, should be considered, Cato took his side.[1] 61-60 B.C.
If Pompey's troops were left destitute, he would forfeit
their devotion and that of all who might thereafter have
to serve under his flag. A tribune, Lucius Flavius,
proposed an agrarian law, which was intended to secure
for him the same advantages that Caesar had designed
to offer, for a price, under the law of Rullus. Pompey,
in accordance with whose dictates the bill was evidently
drafted, intended to procure grants not only for his
veterans, but also for needy citizens, in the hope that
they would vote for it and eventually for his Asiatic
settlement. The bill provided that all the lands, besides
the Campanian, which had been declared public in the
tribunate of Tiberius Gracchus, certain others which
Sulla had confiscated but had not allotted, and the
estates which Sulla had granted to his adherents should
be made available for distribution, and that additional
lands should be purchased with the revenue which during
the next five years would accrue from the conquests in
the East. Cicero could not afford either to offend Pompey
or to disappoint the poor: on the other hand, he desired
to protect the landed gentry, who were the mainstay of
his party, and whose interests were endangered by the
bill. In a public meeting he argued with such force as
to persuade his hearers that all the clauses ought to be
rejected, except that which provided for the purchase
of allotments. Metellus Celer, backed by the Senate,
opposed the measure as a whole, and although the tribune
actually incarcerated him, and when Pompey had the
good sense to press for his release, threatened to forbid
him from proceeding to his province. Metellus was
undaunted, and the bill was dropped.[2] For the present Pompey
Pompey could do nothing; and since no letters of his fails to
or Caesar's, belonging to this period, are extant, one can allotments
only wonder whether it had occurred to him that he veterans.
might soon find a coadjutor upon whom he could rely.

[1] *Ib.*, 12, 3; Plut., *Pomp.*, 46, 3; *Cato min.*, 31, 1; Dio, xxxvii, 49; App., ii, 9, 31.
[2] *Att.*, i, 18, 6; 19, 4; ii, 1, 8; Dio, xxxvii, 50, 1-5. Cf. p. 242.

306 DISILLUSIONMENT OF POMPEY AND CHAP.

61-60 B. C.

Ariovistus and the Helvetii in Gaul.

Meanwhile disquieting rumours were coming from beyond the Alps. In the previous year a rebellion of the Allobroges had been repressed with a ruthlessness which left them embittered against Rome;[1] and outside the frontier of the Roman Province a struggle was in progress which the Roman Government could not afford to disregard. The Aedui, who nearly a century before had entered into friendly relations with the Roman People, had for many years been enemies of the Arverni, whose name survives in the modern Auvergne. The Arverni in conjunction with the Sequani, who inhabited the country between the Saône, the Jura, and the Rhine, hired a German chieftain, Ariovistus, to assist them. The Aedui were beaten, and in 61 B. C. one of their leading men, the famous Druid Diviciacus, went to Rome to solicit help. He made the acquaintance of Cicero,[2] with whom he discussed religion and philosophy, but although he was received by the State as an honoured guest,[3] his mission failed: all that the Senate would do was to decree that the Governor of the Transalpine Province and his successors should take care, so far as the interest of the Republic would permit, to safeguard the Aedui and the other allies of the Roman People.[4] Ariovistus was not a mere mercenary leader: he had come to conquer Gaul, and he compelled his Sequanian paymasters to cede to him the fertile plain of Alsace. Combining with the Aedui too late, the Sequani struggled to get rid of the invader, but suffered a defeat.[5] The news reached Rome before Caesar returned from Spain; and about the same time it was reported that invaders from Helvetia—that part of Switzerland which is bounded by the Rhine, the upper Rhône, the Lake of Geneva, and the Jura—were raiding the Roman Province. The Senate resolved that the consuls should be sent to take charge respectively of the Cisalpine and the Transalpine province; that troops should be raised forthwith; and that commissioners

---

[1] Livy, *Epit.*, 103; Dio, xxxvii, 47-8.
[2] Cic., *De div.*, i, 41, 90.   [3] *Paneg. Vet.* (ed. Baehrens), v, 3, 2.
[4] Caes., *B. G.*, i, 35, 4.   [5] *Ib.*, 31, 10. 12; 40, 8; Cic., *Att.*, i, 19, 2.

should be dispatched to dissuade the various Gallic 60 B.C. tribes from joining the Helvetii. The commissioners were selected by lot from senators of consular rank ; and among the names were those of Cicero and Pompey. Neither was permitted to go. Cicero thought that he and his illustrious friend were considered too valuable to be sent on a mission which might prove dangerous ;[1] but we may perhaps conjecture that the Senate was unwilling to give Pompey an opportunity of obtaining another military command. It is doubtful, however, whether the commissioners were ever called upon to act ; for Cicero soon afterwards informed Atticus that the danger had passed away. ' Metellus ', he remarked, ' is an excellent consul : the only fault I have to find with him is that he is not much pleased with the news that Gaul is calm.'[2]

Such was the state of affairs that confronted Caesar when, early in June,[3] he appeared outside the gates of Rome. Whether he had accepted bribes in Spain or not, he had no money to expend in bribing the electors. Several months before, however, he had arranged with Lucius Lucceius, a wealthy senator, that they should stand conjointly for the consulship, Lucceius paying for them both and Caesar using his influence on Lucceius's behalf.[4] Cicero was aware of his design, and the prospect filled him with anxiety.[5] Atticus had gently remonstrated with him for being too intimate with Pompey ; but he replied that in the public interest it was the only course which he could follow. He had, indeed, confided to his friend what he really thought of Pompey : ' he has nothing great, nothing elevated in his nature, nothing that is not low and temporizing.'[6] But, he explained, ' the state of affairs is such that if we chanced to disagree, there would inevitably be violent party quarrels.' Cicero believed that he could exercise a wholesome influence on Pompey :—' You must know that he speaks

Caesar's candidature for the consulship alarms the Senate : attitude of Cicero.

[1] Ib., §§ 2–3.   [2] Ib., 20, 5   [3] Ib., ii, 1, 9.
[4] Ib., i, 17, 11 ; Suet., 19, 1.
[5] Att., i, 17, 11.   [6] Ib., 20, 2.

308 DISILLUSIONMENT OF POMPEY AND CHAP.

60 B. C.

in far higher terms of my achievements, which many people urged him to attack, than of his own. . . . What if I convert Caesar also, who is now sailing triumphantly before the wind?' Few of the nobles, as Cicero used to say, cared anything for politics so long as the mullets in their fish-ponds would come to feed out of their hands. 'Do you not see', he asked, 'that I am doing some considerable service if I can take the will for mischief from those who have the power? You do not love Cato more than I do; but still, with the best intentions and the most sterling honesty, he sometimes does positive injury to the country. He talks as if he were in the Republic of Plato, not in the sink of Romulus.'[1] What, then, could Cicero do but make common cause with Pompey and hope for the best from Caesar? The Conservatives were opposed to both alike. Fearing that Caesar, if he were elected consul, would introduce revolutionary measures, they subscribed large sums to assist Bibulus, who had been Caesar's colleague in the aedileship, in opposing him. Even Cato, though he knew that the money was to be spent in corrupting the electors, decided that on this occasion the end justified the means. At the same time the Senate provided for the chance of failure by enacting that the successful candidates should be entrusted with the government of provinces in which

Coalition of Caesar, Crassus, and Pompey.

ambition would find no scope.[2] Caesar knew that Pompey would gladly coalesce with him in return for the confirmation of his Asiatic measures and for a law which would reward his veterans; and if Crassus could be induced to join the coalition, the three would be irresistible.[3] Self-interest and Caesar's tact might induce Pompey and Crassus to patch up their quarrel. The mere wealth of Crassus was a power. No one, he used to say, was really rich who could not afford to maintain a legion out of income.[4] With the gains which he had acquired from Sulla's confiscations he had bought at

---

[1] *Att.*, ii, 1, 6-8. Cf. i, 19, 7.   [2] Suet., 19. See p. 474.
[3] See pp. 474-6.
[4] Cic., *De off.*, i, 8, 25   Pliny, xxxiii, 10 (47), 134.

a low rate numerous houses which had collapsed from faulty construction or had been destroyed by fire, had rebuilt them, and had thus become the landlord of a large part of the capital. By these and other means he had increased the patrimony with which he began life to seven thousand one hundred talents—over one million seven hundred thousand pounds. But he was not only endowed with the genius or the cunning that makes a great financier. He made it his constant business to conciliate new acquaintances among high and low, rich and poor. He was a practised speaker, if not an orator, and readily undertook to plead causes which Cicero declined; he was always willing to lend money without interest to friends who could be useful; and his influence in the Senate was considerable.[1] Though he and Pompey were not yet even outwardly reconciled, they both supported the candidature of Caesar. The day for the election had been fixed. Caesar, who wished to enjoy his promised triumph, and would be obliged in the ordinary course to remain outside the city until the last day for notifying his candidature should have passed, requested the Senate to permit him to dispense with this formality and to stand for the consulship in absence. There were several precedents;[2] but Cato, though he was prepared to recognize them in favour of a friend, determined not to allow the benefit to Caesar. He was a master of the art of parliamentary obstruction, and obstruction under the rules of senatorial debate was easy; for a senator might speak at any length and on any topic, however irrelevant. On the last day on which candidates might give in their names he deliberately talked on to prevent the Senate from coming to a decision. Caesar of course abandoned the triumph, for which he had made every preparation, entered the city, and handed in his name. Lucceius spent his money, but lost his election: Caesar and Bibulus were returned.[3]

60 B.C.

Caesar and Bibulus elected consuls.

[1] Plut., *Cras.*; 2, 2–8; 3, 1–5.
[2] Drumann (*Gesch. Roms*, iii², 1906, p. 176) gives a list.
[3] Plut., *Caes.*, 13; *Cato min.*, 31, 2; Suet., 19, 2; App., ii, 8, 28–30; 9, 33; Dio, xxxvii, 54.

†

310 DISILLUSIONMENT OF POMPEY AND CHAP.

60 B.C. Historians have blamed the Senate for having failed to see that by thwarting Pompey they were depriving themselves of an ally who might defeat the intrigues of Caesar ;[1] and doubtless they lacked that foresight which is the rarest of statesmanlike qualities. But since the same historians insist that the Republic was doomed to perish unless it could invent a fresh machinery of government,[2] which Pompey, at all events, could not do, the question arises whether the Senate, in resisting him, was guilty of a fatal blunder. Those who maintain its guilt must prove that he could be trusted to rest content with that privileged position which, by their own admission, he demanded,[3] that military government was not then inevitable, and that, if either Pompey or Caesar was to be the master, Pompey was likely to prove the better of the two. To demonstrate these theses might strain the ingenuity of the sternest critic of Caesarism.

Caesar was engaged during the months that followed his election in drafting a bill by which he intended to obtain grants for Pompey's soldiers and for needy citizens and in preparing other measures which he had in view. He intended to do his utmost to conciliate his opponents in the Senate ;[4] and Cicero now had to consider what course he should himself adopt. He had reason to believe that the land bill would offend his principles ; but he was tempted to join the coalition. In December he wrote to Atticus : ' I must either firmly resist the agrarian law, which would cost a struggle, but a glorious one, or remain passive . . . or actually support it, which, I am told, Caesar confidently expects me to do. For I have had a visit from Cornelius (I mean Balbus, Caesar's intimate friend), who said positively that Caesar would avail himself of my advice and Pompey's in everything, and that he intended to do his best to reconcile Crassus with Pompey. The last course offers these advantages,—

[1] H. F. Pelham, *Outlines of Rom. Hist.*², 1895, p. 229 ; Strachan-Davidson, *Cicero*, pp. 169, 183-4, 251.
[2] *Ib.*, p. 168. [3] *Ib.*, p. 169.
[4] Dio, xxxviii, 1, 1.

a close alliance with Pompey and, if I choose, with Caesar too, reconciliation with my enemies, peace with the multitude, tranquillity for my old age. But I am greatly moved by the finale of the last canto of my poem. . . . I cannot doubt that I shall always hold that

"The best of omens is our country's cause." '.[1]

60 B. C.

Cicero disinclined to accept Caesar's overtures.

---

[1] *Att.*, ii, 3, 3. The line which Cicero quoted—
Εἷς οἰωνὸς ἄριστος ἀμύνεσθαι περὶ πάτρης—
is in the *Iliad* (xii. 243).

[NOTE.—As readers may have inferred, one can only conjecture whether Flavius (see p. 305) proposed to compensate the occupants of the lands scheduled in his bill for distribution.]

CHAPTER VI

THE FIRST CONSULSHIP OF CAESAR AND THE EXILE OF CICERO

59 B. C.

THAT part of the first consulship of Caesar which followed his agrarian legislation presents little difficulty to historical research; the earlier is not wholly clear.[1] We can form a general notion of his measures and of the circumstances in which they took effect; but the narratives of the Greek compilers upon which we have chiefly to depend are, as usual, so loose that, even with the aid of Cicero's letters, which are fewer, less explicit, and more wanting in detail than one might wish, it needs great care to fix the sequence of events, and even the essential facts are not fully known.

Caesar's agrarian laws.

Caesar's first object, and the one in which he might expect most opposition, was to provide for Pompey's veterans and, it would seem, to gain favour with the populace by granting allotments of land to the deserving poor. He was of course anxious to avoid disturbing vested interests and to dispel the fears of the aristocracy. When he was about to introduce his bill he began by assuring the assembled senators that he was reluctant to give offence to any one. His intention, he explained, was to purchase land from those who were willing to sell, and to pay for it partly out of the proceeds of existing taxes, partly out of the revenue with which Pompey had enriched the State. Promising to amend any clause that might seem objectionable, he proceeded to read the bill aloud. No one, we are told, openly opposed it; even Cato raised no objection, except that the bill was needless; but, apart from the group which regularly supported Caesar, all disliked it, because they believed that its real object was simply to strengthen the hold which Caesar had established on

[1] See pp. 476-9.

THE FIRST CONSULSHIP OF CAESAR 313

the populace. Every effort was made to obstruct the passage of the bill,[1] Lucullus, Bibulus, and Cato being conspicuously active.[2] In one of the debates Cato, pursuing his usual tactics, continued speaking at such length that Caesar, losing patience, ordered him to be removed to prison. Senators, accompanied by respectable citizens, followed him in silent indignation, Petreius, however, shouting that he would rather be in gaol with Cato than in the House with Caesar; and since Cato forbore to appeal to the friendly tribunes, Caesar, feeling that he had made a false step, suborned one of his own tribunes to release him.[3] At length, finding that he was unable to conciliate the Senate, Caesar determined to submit his measure to the popular assembly.[4] On one occasion, after haranguing the people in the Forum and trying in vain to mollify his colleague, he turned to Pompey and Crassus, and asked them to declare their opinion. Both of course expressed their warm approval, and Pompey, some of whose discharged veterans had assembled,[5] added that, if it were necessary, he would support the bill by armed force.[6] Three of the tribunes were on the side of Bibulus,[7] but against the popular opposition they could give him no effective aid; and, finding that all other methods were unavailing, he gave notice that so often as the assembly met he would discern unfavourable portents in the sky, on account of which, as Roman law prescribed, the assembly must be dissolved. Caesar, taking no notice of this threat, which indeed was itself irregular, fixed the day on which the voting was to

59 B. C.

[1] Plut., *Caes.*, 14, 1; *Cato min.*, 31, 3; App., *B. C.*, ii, 10, 34–5; Dio, xxxviii, 1–2; 3, 1.

[2] Plutarch (*Cato min.*, 31, 3) adds the name of Cicero; but there is no other evidence that he was present while the bill was being discussed.

[3] Plut., *Caes.*, 14, 5; Gell., iv, 10, 8; Dio, xxxviii, 3, 2–3. Valerius Maximus (ii, 10, 7) and Plutarch (*Cato min.*, 33, 1–2) misdate this incident.

[4] Plut., *Caes.*, 14, 2; App., ii, 10, 36; Dio. xxxviii, 3, 3. Appian and Dio (4, 1) incorrectly say that Caesar never again consulted the Senate in his consulship.

[5] Plut., *Pomp.*, 48, 1. Cf. *Caes.*, 14, 5.

[6] *Ib.*, § 2; App., ii, 10, 36; Dio, xxxviii, 4, 4–6; 5, 1–3.

[7] *Ib.*, 6, 1; Cic., *Pro Sest.*, 58, 113, and *Schol. Bob.*, ed. Stangl, p. 135 (ed. Orelli, p. 304).

314 THE FIRST CONSULSHIP OF CAESAR CHAP.

59 B.C. take place. In the night the populace occupied the Forum. While Caesar was haranguing the assembly from the temple of Castor, Bibulus, followed by his lictors and accompanied by Lucullus, Cato, and the three tribunes, entered the Forum and advanced towards the temple. Respecting his rank, the crowd made room for him to pass; but when he mounted the steps and was beginning to denounce the bill, a basket of dung was emptied on his head, some of the Pompeian veterans broke the *fasces* of the lictors, Bibulus was thrown down the steps, and two of the tribunes were wounded.[1] Bibulus got up, uncovered his neck, and shouted to his assailants to dispatch him, but was persuaded by his friends to withdraw into an adjoining temple : Cato shouldered his way through the crowd and was beginning to speak when he was forcibly removed by Caesar's men, but presently returned by another way only to be removed again.[2] After this scene the people proceeded to vote, and the bill was passed.[3] Next day Bibulus made a formal complaint in the Senate about the treatment which he had suffered, and urged the House to annul the law; but no one ventured to make any motion.[4] In accordance with the precedent of Saturninus every senator and every citizen was required under a heavy penalty to swear that he would observe the law. A few refused at first to take the oath; but even Cato at last yielded to the arguments of his friends, among them Cicero, and his ape Favonius followed his example.[5] The Senate indeed was powerless to withstand the people and their confederate leaders; for there was no police, and the only soldiers in the city were at the beck of Pompey. Moreover, the Senate was

---

[1] Plut., *Pomp.*, 48, 1; *Cato min.*, 32, 1; *Luc.*, 42, 6; App., ii, 11, 38; Dio, xxxviii, 6, 2–3.

[2] App., ii, 11, 39–41. Cf. Plut., *Cato min.*, 32, 1; Suet., *Div. Iul.*, 20, 1.

[3] Plut., *Pomp.*, 48, 2; *Cato min.*, 32, 2; Dio, xxxviii, 6. 4. Appian (ii, 10, 36) seems to mean that the voting took place before Bibulus was attacked; but the apparent error was probably due to his loose style of writing.

[4] Suet., 20, 1; Dio, xxxviii, 6, 4.

[5] Cic., *Pro Sest.*, 28, 61; Plut., *Cato min.*, 32, 2–3; App., ii, 12, 42; Dio, xxxviii, 7, 1. Plutarch says that Favonius remained obdurate.

VI THE FIRST CONSULSHIP OF CAESAR 315

not a united body: besides avowed adherents of the 59 B.C.
triumvirs there were doubtless men who hoped to obtain
from them lucrative or influential posts. Bibulus in
despair ceased to attend the meetings. Shutting himself
up in his house, he announced in accordance with his
threat that he had observed the sky, and issued proclamations in which, inveighing impartially against
Caesar and against Pompey, he declared that Caesar
had been involved in the first conspiracy of Catiline, and
that, as he had once been the 'queen' and consort of
Nicomedes, so he was now aspiring to be a king.[1]

Caesar now introduced another bill for distributing the
Campanian public land, which was already occupied,
among twenty thousand citizens who had three children
each or more, with the proviso that for twenty years the
allotments should be inalienable.[2] Resistance was manifestly hopeless. It was enacted that all candidates for
office should swear that they would never move that the
land should be held on terms other than those which the
law defined; and one Juventius Laterensis, a candidate
for a tribuneship, rather than take the oath retired from
the contest.[3]

Such, as far as I can gather, was Caesar's agrarian
legislation. It is not certain whether or how far his
earlier law was carried out;[4] but since he allotted the
public land, which he had originally forborne to touch,
it is probable that he could not obtain land enough by
purchase. What must strike every one who studies the
original authorities is that only one[5] of them even alluded
to the Pompeian veterans, to provide for whom was
Caesar's chief concern. But as it is certain that ten years
later many of them were settled in Campania,[6] we must
infer that they were included among 'the poor' for whose
benefit, according to the historians, the Campanian law

---

[1] Cic., *Att.*, vi, 8, 5; Vell., ii, 44, 5; Plut., *Pomp.*, 48, 4; Suet., 9, 2; 20, 1; 49, 2; App. ii, 12, 45; Dio, xxxviii, 6, 5.
[2] App., iii, 2, 5. See pp. 476-8.   [3] Cic., *Att.*, ii, 18, 2.
[4] See *Journ. of Philol.*, xxxii. 1913, p. 260.
[5] Plut., *Cic.*, 26, 3.   [6] See p. 478.

was passed. One noteworthy consequence of the law was that Capua, which, as a punishment for its defection in the war with Hannibal, had been deprived of its municipal constitution, became a Roman colony.[1] Not one of the authorities said a word about the Campanian farmers, the tenants of the State, who were evicted to make room for the new occupants ; but we may suppose that for the most part they flocked to Rome, to subsist on the cheap grain that was there distributed. Apart from the question of humanity, a measure which dispossessed industrious cultivators in favour of new-comers, of whom many, according to all experience, were likely to be restless and unfit for husbandry, was an economic crime, only to be excused by the pressing necessity of providing, in default of pensions, for discharged soldiers who would otherwise be a perennial source of trouble : on the other hand, to include needy Roman citizens among the new settlers— in other words, to relieve Rome of a part of its proletariat only to encumber it with ejected yeomen who would be forced to exchange industry for idleness, and who would, moreover, be embittered by the destitution which they had not deserved—would have been not only a crime but a blunder, of which it is hardly possible to believe Caesar guilty. One would rather suppose that the allotments reserved for the proletariat were purchased lands. Were the evicted tenants compensated ?[2] There

[1] Caes., *B. C.*, i, 14, 4 ; Vell. ii, 44, 4 ; C. Lachmann, *D. Schr. d. röm. Feldmesser*, i. 1848, p. 231.
[2] The comments of Long (*Decline of the Roman Republic*, iii, 424), however sweeping they may be, are still worth reading. After remarking that ' all the circumstances . . . which we know, are against this supposition '—that the Campanian cultivators received compensation—he continues, ' there remains the single fact that a fruitful territory was cleared of an industrious population, who had been born on the land which they cultivated, whose ancestors were buried on it, and whose burying places would be desecrated by the new settlers. Men, women, and children with their household goods, their furniture and their cattle were driven out of their homes, and would be compelled to part with their movables for any price they could get. This monstrous, this abominable crime was committed to serve a party purpose ; and the criminal was a Roman consul . . . too intelligent not to know what he was doing, and unscrupulous enough to do anything that might serve his own ends '. E. Meyer (*Caesars Monarchie*², &c., 1919,

VI THE FIRST CONSULSHIP OF CAESAR 317

is no evidence except that Caesar offered a fair price for those lands which he proposed to buy, and that, if civilians were settled upon the Campanian land, it was against his interest to provoke the hatred of one set of cultivators by displacing them without compensation for another. While the laws were being debated Cicero, whose eloquence had frustrated the agrarian bill of Rullus and who disapproved equally the bills of Caesar, forgot the line of Homer which he had taken as his motto.[1]

59 B.C.

Meanwhile Caesar, who had much still to do, was taking steps to strengthen his position. Cicero, before leaving Rome, undertook to defend his former colleague, Gaius Antonius, who, on returning from Macedonia, was prosecuted by a young plebeian, Marcus Caelius Rufus, probably on a charge of having extorted money from the people of that province.[2] In the course of his speech Cicero unguardedly made remarks derogatory to Caesar.[3] On the same day Caesar arranged with the assistance of Pompey, who, as an augur, officiated in the necessary religious ceremony, that Clodius, who, though he was a patrician, desired to stand for a tribuneship, should be adopted by a plebeian and thus become qualified for election.[4] Caesar's action may or may not have been prompted, as Cicero thought,[5] by a misleading report which he heard of Cicero's remarks; at all events his object in securing the adoption of Clodius was unmistakable. Clodius, though he had attempted to debauch

Clodius qualified by the aid of Caesar to become a tribune.

---

p. 65) conjectures that the evicted tenants remained as labourers in the service of the allottees. Perhaps some did.

[1] Meyer (*op. cit.*, p. 74, n. 3), remarking that Cicero was still in Rome two days after Metellus swore to observe the first agrarian law (*Pro Cael.*, 24, 59), regrets that the absence of his letters in the earlier part of the year (did he write any?) prevents us from knowing what part he took in the debates. *I* reply that as neither Cicero himself nor any other authority, except Plutarch in one passage, says that he resisted Caesar, we may reasonably infer that his resistance, if he made any, was feeble.

[2] According to Dio (xxxviii, 10, 3), Antonius was charged with having been concerned in the conspiracy of Catiline; but see Cic., *Pro Cael.*, 7. 15, 32. 78, and Long, *op. cit.*, p. 411.

[3] *Pro Cael.*, 19, 47; Suet., 20, 4; Dio, xxxviii, 10, 4.

[4] Cic., *Att.*, ii, 12, 1–2; *De domo*, 16, 41; *De prov. cons.*, 19, 45–6.

[5] *De domo*, 16, 41.

his wife, might as a tribune be very useful, and the sequel may suggest that Caesar contemplated that he might restrain Cicero if Cicero should attempt to undo the acts of Caesar's consulship. Cicero was indignant when he heard of the adoption. 'This', he told Atticus, 'is really tyranny and intolerable.'[1] A young friend of his, Scribonius Curio, assured him that Clodius himself threatened to annul Caesar's acts and that Caesar denied that he had taken part in the adoption;[2] but Pompey, who happened to meet Cicero,[3] admitted that he had himself taken the auspices at the ceremony. If Clodius did not intend to deceive Cicero when he declared himself hostile to Caesar, Caesar knew how to bring him to his senses: he had only to disavow his own part in the affair. Cicero did not yet suspect what Clodius had in store for him: he assured Atticus that he was ready and eager for a fight;[4] if Clodius wanted to attack him, 'let him attack'.[5] When he heard from Atticus that 'the talk' against Caesar had 'died out at Rome', he replied, 'I can tell you it has not died out in the country: no, the country cannot stand the despotism you are suffering . . . how our friend Magnus is detested! His surname is becoming as obsolete as that of Crassus, "Dives"'.[6] But a little later, after the bills had become law, he heard from Atticus a disquieting report. 'Sampsiceramus',[7] he replied, 'is plainly preparing a tyranny. For what is the meaning of this sudden marriage union that you mention ? . . . That little strain of vanity and love of admiration in my nature—it is good to know one's faults—is tickled by a certain pleasure. It used to

[1] *Att.*, ii, 12. 1.   [2] *Ib.*, § 2.
[3] According to the MSS. (*Att.*, ii, 12, 1), at Antium. But Mr. C. L. Smith (*Class. Quart.*, i, 1907, pp. 273–4) shows that Pompey almost certainly made the statement here attributed to him before Cicero went to Antium. He explains that *Anti* got into the text because Cicero really wrote *Balbi Ati*, the Balbus mentioned in the letter being M. Atius Balbus.
[4] *Att.*, ii, 7, 2.   [5] *Ib.*, 9, 1.
[6] *Ib.*, 13, 2. The Crassus whom Cicero mentions here was the praetor P. Licinius Crassus. Cf. Val. Max., vi, 9, 12.
[7] Cicero nicknamed Pompey 'Sampsiceramus' after the Syrian emir mentioned on p. 218.

sting me that six centuries hence the services of Sampsiceramus to his country might seem greater than my own ; from that anxiety at least my vanity is now quite free.'[1] The meaning of the marriage union was transparent. While Caesar married his fourth wife, Calpurnia, the daughter of Lucius Calpurnius Piso, whose support he had secured and for whom he intended to secure the ensuing consulship, he gave his daughter Julia, though she was betrothed already, in marriage to Pompey.[2] Cato insisted that these matrimonial alliances corrupted public life ;[3] but Caesar had bound Pompey to himself for years to come.

Meanwhile Caesar was preparing measures which were not demanded by his confederates, but were designed to benefit the State. He had already introduced an innovation by which he gained a hold over the Senate while all classes were kept informed of current events :—the proceedings of the Senate and the popular assembly were briefly recorded, and the record was posted in the Forum for the information of the public.[4] The praetor Fufius Calenus, doubtless under Caesar's influence, amended the Aurelian law passed in the consulship of Pompey[5] by providing that in criminal trials the three classes of jurors—senators, knights, and *tribuni aerarii*—should vote separately, in order that it might be known whether each class—not the individual jurors, who were protected by the ballot—had voted for conviction or acquittal.[6] The object perhaps was to ascertain how far the lowest class of jurors could be trusted. More important was the ' Julian law concerning extortion ', by which Caesar attempted to remove the notorious abuses of provincial administration, and which Cicero more than once described as ' a most excellent law '.[7] Repeating former enact-

59 B. C.

Pompey marries Caesar's daughter.

The 'Daily Gazette'.

Amendment of the law relating to juries.

Caesar's attempt to purify provincial administration.

---

[1] *Att.* ii, 17, 1-2.
[2] Vell., ii, 44, 3 ; Plut., *Caes.*, 14, 4 ; *Cato min.*, 31, 3 ; Flor., ii, 13, 13 ; Suet., 21 ; App., ii, 14, 50-1 ; Dio, xxxviii, 9, 1. Dio dates these marriages several months too late, and invents a false motive for them.
[3] App., ii, 14, 51. Cf. Plut., *Caes.*, 14, 4.
[4] Suet., 20, 1. Cf. Cic., *Att.*, iii, 15, 6 ; vi, 2, 6.   [5] See p. 165.
[6] Dio, xxxviii, 8, 1.   [7] *Pro Sest.*, 64, 135 ; *In Pis.*, 16, 37.

ments and introducing many that were new, it was above all designed to prevent extortion and corruption. Provincial magistrates were forbidden under heavy penalties to accept presents, to sell or arbitrarily to withdraw justice or privileges, to demand from provincials anything except what was allowed by existing law or custom, the various exceptions being precisely defined ; governors were forbidden to transgress the limits of their provinces with or without their armies, or to interfere in matters which did not belong to their administration.[1]

Throughout the spring and the summer Cicero continued to comment on public affairs, in which he took no part. Occasionally he alluded in his letters to the threats of Clodius, which he still despised, or affected to despise.[2] Caesar, who, though he was determined to restrain him if he attempted opposition, desired to protect him from his enemy, invited him to become one of his lieutenants in his coming proconsulship or to accept an 'unofficial embassy' ;[3] but Cicero hesitated to undertake the duty, and, though he accepted the sinecure, made no use of it.[4] 'I don't like running away,' he told Atticus ; 'I am longing to fight' ;[5] and when Caesar asked him to be one of the commissioners who were to superintend the distribution of allotments, he refused.[6] He caught at every sign, or what he interpreted as such, that the three great men were making themselves unpopular. 'Bibulus', he wrote, 'is praised to the skies. . . . Pompey, once my hero, has, to my infinite sorrow,

[1] Cic., In Vat., 12, 29 ; In Pis., 21, 50 ; 37, 90 ; Pro Rab. Post., 4, 8 ; Att., v, 10, 2 ; 16, 3 ; Fam., viii, 8, 3 ; Dig., xlviii, 11, 1. 3. 6. Cf. B. Kübler; C. I. Caes. comm., &c., iii, 1897, pp. 172-5. Dio (xxxviii, 7, 6) says that Caesar passed many other laws without opposition (cf. App., ii, 13, 46), but that it is needless for his purpose to mention them !

It is uncertain whether Caesar's law about 'unofficial embassies' (de liberis legationibus [see pp. 130, 253, supra], which Cicero mentions (Att., xv, 11, 4), was part of his law concerning extortion or a separate enactment passed in 46 B. C. ; but as Cicero omits to mention it in De leg., iii, 8, 18 (written in 52 and 46), I am inclined to infer that it belonged to the later year.

[2] Att., ii, 19, 1. 4. 5 ; 20, 2 ; 21, 6 ; &c.
[3] See p. 253.   [4] Att., ii, 18, 3 ; 19, 5.   [5] Ib., 18, 3.
[6] Ib., 19, 4 ; De prov. cons., 17, 41.

VI THE FIRST CONSULSHIP OF CAESAR 321

extinguished himself.'[1] Popular feeling was most plainly shown in the theatre and at the games. 'At the festival of Apollo', wrote Cicero,[3] 'the actor Diphilus made a saucy attack upon our friend Pompey:

59 B.C. July 13 ?.[2]

"'Tis through our misery that thou art Great."

He was encored again and again; and amidst the plaudits of the whole theatre he declaimed,

"A time will come when thou shalt rue that power".

... The lines indeed are such that one would think they had been composed for the occasion by an enemy of Pompey.' Caesar, when he entered, was received in silence; the youthful Curio, who followed him, and who, alone among public men, had dared to inveigh in the Forum against the three confederates, was welcomed with shouts of applause. The confederates, if Cicero was not misinformed, were so exasperated with the people for applauding Curio, that they threatened to repeal the law by which special seats were reserved in the theatre for the knights and the law by which the proletariat received cheap corn.[4] In June they had been 'popular with the multitude', but in July, so Cicero believed, they were 'universally detested';[5] and Pompey, who was 'not used to unpopularity', saw that to persevere in his alliance with Caesar would be dangerous, but shrank from drawing back, lest he should be taunted with vacillation. He was greatly worried by the scurrilous edicts of Bibulus, which attracted such attention that, as Cicero reported, 'one couldn't get past the place where they are posted up for the crowd of readers'. On the 25th of July Cicero saw Pompey addressing the assembly about the edicts, and the spectacle moved him to tears:—
'he who had been accustomed to show himself so proudly on the Rostra, in full possession of the affection of the people and the goodwill of all, how humble, how down-

---

[1] *Att.*, ii, 19, 2.
[2] Warde Fowler, *Roman Festivals*, 1899, pp. 179-80.
[3] *Att.*, ii, 19, 3; Val. Max., vi, 2, 9.
[4] *Att.*, ii, 19, 3. Presumably Cicero meant the recent law of Cato. See pp. 282 and 385. [5] *Att.*, ii, 21, 1.

322 THE FIRST CONSULSHIP OF CAESAR CHAP.

cast was he then; he seemed as much dissatisfied with himself as his hearers were with him. It was a sight which could give pleasure to Crassus alone.'[1] Varro, though he accepted a post in the land commission,[2] denounced the triumvirs in a pamphlet, *The Three-headed Monster*.[3] Bibulus had given notice that the consular elections were to be postponed till the 18th of October, and Cicero gathered that Caesar, who knew that such postponements were generally unpopular, thought that the populace might be incited to attack his colleague's house; but, he added, 'though he spoke at great length and with extreme violence, he failed to extract one word from any one'.[4] The cautious reader of Cicero's correspondence may wonder whether these reports were based upon personal knowledge or partly upon hearsay, which he was too ready to believe. Caesar for his part cared nothing for the abuse of Bibulus; and just as Bibulus himself complained that he had been eclipsed by Caesar in their joint aedileship,[5] so it was commonly remarked that there was but one consul. Facetious citizens, appending their signatures to legal documents, added, 'In the consulship of Julius and of Caesar'.[6] If Cicero was not identifying the few whose murmurs he heard or heard of with 'the multitude', Caesar knew how to regain at least the favour of the knights. Since the Senate had not vouchsafed an answer to that request of the tax-collectors which Cicero, though he denounced it as shameful, supported, because to grant it was necessary in order to prevent a breach between the senatorial and the equestrian order, Caesar summarily settled the matter because it was necessary for his purpose to conciliate the latter. The arrangement which he made, with the consent of the popular assembly alone,

Caesar conciliates the farmers of the taxes.

---

[1] *Att.*, ii, 21, 3–4.
[2] *R. R.*, i, 2, 10; Pliny, *Nat. Hist.*, vii, 52 (53), 176.
[3] App., ii, 9, 33. Appian appears to assign this brochure to 60 B.C.; but his chronology is notoriously loose, and the triumvirate was then only inchoate. I agree with Meyer (*op. cit.*, p. 80) in referring the work to 59.
[4] *Att.*, ii, 20, 6; 21, 5.   [5] Suet., 10, 1.
[6] *Ib.*, 20, 2   Dio, xxxviii, 8, 2.

VI THE FIRST CONSULSHIP OF CAESAR 323

was to remit one-third of the sum which the syndicates 59 B.C.
had contracted to pay ; at the same time he recommended
them to refrain in future from bidding beyond their
means.[1] Pompey's settlement of the East was of course Pompey's
confirmed, also by the popular assembly ;[2] but Pompey, settlement of
if Cicero understood his mood, was not quite happy the East
under the obligation : 'Sampsiceramus', he wrote, 'is confirmed.
utterly sick of his position, and longing to be restored to
the place from which he is fallen . . . he confides his
trouble to me and is openly seeking for a remedy.'[3]
The only remedy which Cicero could suggest was to break
with Caesar![4]

The consular elections were approaching ; and with The mysterious
them was perhaps connected a mysterious incident, the affair of
reports of which have baffled every commentator.[5] The L. Vettius.
candidates were Caesar's father-in-law Calpurnius Piso,
Aulus Gabinius, the steady supporter and former lieutenant
of Pompey, and Lucius Cornelius Lentulus. On the
13th of May Bibulus had warned Pompey to be on his
guard against assassins, and Pompey duly thanked him.
Some time afterwards Cicero wrote to Atticus that, as August?
far as he could make out, the informer, Lucius Vettius,

---

[1] Cic., *Pro Planc.*, 14, 35 ; App., ii, 13, 47–8 ; Suet., 20, 3 ; Dio, xxxviii, 7, 4. From a somewhat obscure passage in Cicero's oration against Vatinius (12, 29)—*volo uti mihi respondeas . . . eripuerisne partes illo tempore carissimas partim a Caesare, partim a publicanis*—the general sense of which is that Vatinius cheated both Caesar and the tax-collectors, Prof. Reid (*Hermathena*, xiii, 1905, p. 373) infers that 'part of the money lost to the treasury . . . by the remission granted to the publicani went into the pockets of Caesar', &c. How would Caesar's career have been affected if he had accepted a bribe from one of the most powerful bodies in the State ? Vatinius could afford to stoop to such a job ; could his master ? From the same passage Ferrero (*Grandezza e decadenza di Roma*, i, 1902, p. 443, n. 1 [Eng. tr., i, 286]) infers that 'the directors' of the *publicani* allotted Caesar 'a large number of shares in the company'.

[2] *Bell. Alex.*, 68, 1 ; Vell., ii, 44, 2 ; Plut., *Pomp.*, 48, 3 ; App., ii, 13, 46 ; Dio, xxxviii, 7, 5. Prof. E. T. Sage (*Amer. Journ. of Philol.*, xxxix, 1918, p. 372) thinks that the relief of the *publicani* and the ratification of Pompey's acts may have come 'early in the year'. Certainly not while the agrarian laws were being discussed. *I* do not believe that the knights would have made a hostile demonstration against Caesar in July (see p. 321) if he had already placed them under an obligation.

[3] *Att.*, ii, 23, 2.   [4] *Phil.*, ii, 10, 23.   [5] See pp. 479–82.

who three years before had denounced Caesar as an accomplice of Catiline, had promised Caesar that he would bring the younger Curio under suspicion of violent crime. If Cicero's information was correct, Vettius told Curio that he had resolved to assassinate Pompey; Curio told his father, who informed the Senate; Vettius was brought before the Senate and inculpated various public men, including Bibulus, Lucullus, and Lentulus, as his instigators and accomplices: but, as he contradicted himself under cross-examination and the charge which he brought against Bibulus was manifestly absurd, he was committed to prison to await his trial. Three years later Cicero, in the famous oration which he delivered against Vatinius, charged him, without naming Caesar, with having murdered Vettius 'lest any proof of fabricated evidence should come to light'. Whether the charge was true or false, the murder was ordered by some one whose official position gave him access to the prison; and though there is no evidence that Caesar made away with the informer, he has not been exonerated from suspicion. It may be, as more than one writer has suggested, that a plot was really formed against Pompey by some hot-blooded young aristocrats; but, if Cicero knew and told the truth, the affair was a scheme for discrediting Lentulus and thus securing the election of Gabinius. At all events Gabinius and Piso, the tools of the three confederates, were elected consuls for the ensuing year.[1]

Meanwhile Caesar, who took care to amuse the populace with spectacular displays,[2] arranged that the provinces which he desired, not that which the Senate had impotently named, should be assigned to him. While he was busy with legislation his attention was also fixed upon the political situation in Gaul. In the course of the year, if not before,[3] envoys from Ariovistus arrived in Rome to solicit for their master the friendship of the Roman

---

[1] Plut., *Pomp.*, 48, 3; App., ii, 14, 50–1.   [2] *Ib.*, 13, 49.
[3] Cf. C. Jullian, *Hist. de la Gaule*, iii, 1909, pp. 163, 165, n. 4, and Rice Holmes, *Caesar's Conquest of Gaul*², 1911, p. 40.

VI THE FIRST CONSULSHIP OF CAESAR 325

People. Caesar, who intended that his provinces should 59 B.C.
be Cisalpine and Transalpine Gaul, was aware that the
Helvetii would give trouble, and that it would be as
much as he could do to deal with them without making
Ariovistus his enemy. He therefore induced the Senate Caesar
to confer upon Ariovistus the titles of King and Friend honours
of the Roman People.[1] Satisfied with these honours, vistus.
the barbarian chief would keep quiet until Caesar should
be free to expel him and his Germans from Gaul. Caesar's
faithful henchman, the tribune Vatinius, invited the
assembly to confer upon him the provinces of Cisalpine
Gaul and Illyricum with three legions for five years,
and to give him the right, which Pompey had received
under the Gabinian law, of appointing his lieutenants.
Bibulus of course declared that he had observed the sky
and that no business must be done ; but Vatinius was
backed not only by Pompey but by the consuls designate,
and the assembly accepted his proposal. Caesar let it He ob-
be known that he desired the Transalpine Province also, tains the
and accordingly his supporters in the Senate moved that of Gaul.
Gallia Comata—' the land of the long-haired Gauls '—in
other words, the whole of Transalpine Gaul, including the
Roman Province, with the legion quartered in the latter,
should be assigned to him likewise for the same period ;
and the Conservatives knew that if they opposed the
motion, the people would fulfil Caesar's wish themselves.[2]

[1] Caes., B. G., i, 35, 2 ; 43, 4 ; Plut., Caes., 19, 1 ; Dio, xxxviii, 34, 3.
P. C. Sands (The Client Princes of the Roman Empire, 1908, p. 138) has no
doubt that Ariovistus paid Caesar for his title.
[2] Cic., De prov. cons., 17, 42 ; In Vat., 15, 35–6 ; Vell. ii, 44, 5 ; Plut.,
Pomp., 48, 3 ; Caes., 14, 5 ; Cato min., 33, 3 (inaccurate) ; Suet, 22, 1 ;
App., ii, 13, 49 ; Dio, xxxviii, 8, 5 ; Eutrop., vi, 17 (inaccurate). Cf. Cic.,
Att., viii, 3, 3. Orosius (vi, 7, 1) incorrectly says that, under the Vatinian
law, Illyricum, Cisalpine Gaul, and the Transalpine Province were granted
to Caesar with seven legions. In regard to the time of year when the law
was passed see Amer. Journ. of Philol., 1918, pp. 378–80. If Prof. Reid
(Hermathena, xiii, 1905, pp. 378–9) is right in thinking that Cicero, when
he complained to Atticus in April (Att., ii, 9, 1) that ' immense sums ' had
been given to ' a small coterie ', was referring to money voted to Caesar for
his expenses in Gaul, the Vatinian law had been already passed. Cf. Cic., In
Vat., 15, 36.
A. Klotz (Neue Jahrb. f. d. klass. Alt., xxxv, 1915, p. 622) insists that

326 THE FIRST CONSULSHIP OF CAESAR CHAP.

59 B. C.

Thus, if the term 'Gallia Comata' was used in its proper sense,[1] Caesar's commission practically empowered him to act in what was then independent Gaul. Under the law of Vatinius or another by which he supplemented it, Caesar was authorized to settle new colonists, who were to receive the franchise, at Comum, thenceforward to be called Novum Comum, a Latin colony which the father of Pompey had established by the Lake of Como.[2] Thus reinforced, the colony would form an outpost against the turbulent Alpine tribes, and Caesar would be able to offer to the Transpadanes a first instalment of the Roman citizenship which, seven years before, he had encouraged them to hope for.[3]

His bargain with Ptolemy Auletes.

One act of Caesar's consulship remains to be recorded, of which it is impossible to fix the date. By a decree of the Senate Ptolemy Auletes was recognized as King of Egypt and as a Friend and Ally of the Roman People.[4] The recognition was of course purchased at a heavy

there is no evidence that the action of the Senate was prompted by Caesar's friends, and asserts that he could easily, if he had wished, have induced the people to give him the province of Transalpine Gaul. Klotz therefore concludes that Caesar originally intended to remain near Rome, as Pompey did in 55 B.C. when he received the province of Spain. Does Klotz forget that the evidence which he desiderates is supplied implicitly by Suetonius (22) and explicitly by Dio (xxxviii, 8, 4–5), and that Cicero (*Att.*, viii, 3, 3) says that Pompey, who presumably acted in accordance with Caesar's expressed wish, supported the grant of Transalpine Gaul? Undoubtedly Caesar intended to remain for a time near Rome, for the reason which I have stated in the text (p. 327); and even without that reason he would not have crossed the Alps until the weather made it possible to move his army: but that he intended to remain permanently in *I*taly is incredible, for he knew that, sooner or later, he would have to deal with the Helvetii.

Ferrero (*op. cit.*, p. 449, n. 4 [Eng. tr., i, 290, n. †]), remarking that C. C. L. Lange (*Röm. Alt.*, iii, 1871, p. 283) has shown [or rather asserted] that Caesar was appointed to the command of Cisalpine Gaul in consequence of the death of Metellus Celer, concludes that 'this provides the only possible explanation why Caesar's *imperium* dated from March 1, 59, and Narbonese Gaul was added later by the Senate'.

[1] Cf. *Caesar's Conquest of Gaul*[2], p. 41, n. 2, and Cic., *Fam.*, x, 1.

[2] See vol. ii, pp. 317–20. Meyer (*op. cit.*, p. 92, n. 4) thinks it improbable that Novum Comum was expressly mentioned: in other words, he supposes that Caesar was generally authorized to found Roman colonies. In that case we should have heard of others. [3] See p. 225.

[4] Caes., *B. C.*, iii, 107, 2; Cic., *Pro Rab. Post.*, 3, 6; Dio, xxxix, 12, 1.

VI THE FIRST CONSULSHIP OF CAESAR 327

price; but the details of the transaction are somewhat doubtful. Plutarch[1] relates that eleven years later seventy million sesterces (seven hundred thousand pounds), which Ptolemy had owed to Caesar, remained unpaid; that Caesar exacted forty millions for the maintenance of his army, and waived the remainder of his claim. Suetonius,[2] remarking that Caesar sold alliances and thrones, asserts that he took nearly six thousand talents[3] from Ptolemy for himself and Pompey. The discrepancy matters little; but was the money which Caesar claimed demanded wholly in his consulship or partly four years later, when Ptolemy, who had been expelled by his own subjects, was restored by Gabinius to his throne?[4] We only know that Ptolemy was obliged to pay both for his recognition and for his restoration.[5]

59 B. C.

For a short time after his consulship Caesar remained in Rome. If he was aware that the Helvetii were already preparing to invade Transalpine Gaul, he knew that they could not move before the end of winter; and he was determined to ensure that Cicero should not be able in his absence to attack the Campanian law. Two of the praetors, Gaius Memmius and Lucius Domitius, attempted to impugn the validity of his acts, and he himself, relying upon the influence which he could command and upon the tribunes whose veto was at his disposal, requested the Senate to pronounce judgement; but they declined, and he left the city to await in the suburbs

58 B. C. He resolves to prevent Cicero from invalidating his laws.

Futile attacks on Caesar after his consulship.

---

[1] *Caes.*, 48, 5.
[2] 54, 3. Cf. Cic., *Fam.*, i, 9, 7; *Att.*, ii, 9, 1; 16, 2; *Q. fr.*, ii, 10, 2; *Pro Sest.*, 30, 66; *In Vat.*, 12, 29. Cicero charges Vatinius with having negotiated these sales; but he evidently meant that the consul was behind the tribune.
[3] £1,444,000.   [4] See vol. ii, p. 149.
[5] Cic., *In Pis.*, 21, 49; *Pro Rab. Post*, 11, 30; Dio, xxxix, 12, 1; 56, 3. Suetonius (*l. c.*) says that Caesar in his first consulship stole 3,000 pounds' weight of gold from the Capitol and replaced it by gilded copper; but, as Long remarks (*Decline of the Roman Republic*, iii, 440), he ' was too prudent to commit a disgraceful theft, which would be immediately detected'. Long (v, 241) regards the other statement of Suetonius as equally improbable, and conjectures that Ptolemy undertook to pay the 6,000 talents into the treasury; but, if Cicero (*Pro Sest.*, 30, 66; *In Vat.*, 12, 29) can be trusted, Caesar sold honours to other foreigners.

328 THE FIRST CONSULSHIP OF CAESAR CHAP.

58 B. C.

developments which he foresaw.[1] Immediately afterwards his quaestor was threatened with prosecution, 'as an example', says Suetonius,[2] 'of what was to happen to himself'; but the threat apparently came to nothing. The confederates had not been able to prevent the election of some hostile magistrates, and a tribune, Lucius Antistius, gave notice of his intention to bring Caesar himself to trial; but this ebullition was foredoomed: the college of tribunes was successfully appealed to, on the ground that Caesar was absent from the city 'on the public service' and therefore immune from prosecution.[3] These attacks may have strengthened Caesar's determination to use every means while he was in Gaul to secure the election of magistrates devoted to his interests; but for the present he was perfectly safe. Clodius, who had been elected tribune by his agency, was wayward, but amenable to control; and, animated by desire for revenge, though he was not incapable of generosity,[4] he was scheming to ruin the man whose eloquence might prove dangerous to Caesar.

Cicero fears the hostility of Clodius,

Cicero, after prolonged hesitation, had declined Caesar's offer of a military command, believing that it was not necessary to secure his safety.[5] In the latter half of Caesar's consulship, however, he had become more anxious about the hostility of Clodius. Pompey repeatedly endeavoured to reassure him;[6] but he was inclined to suspect that Pompey was being deceived by Clodius, and, explaining that he felt it risky to trust his guarantee, begged Atticus to return to Rome and to find out through Clodia whether Pompey was sincere. 'You can scarcely believe', he added, 'how much I confide in your counsel, your wisdom, and above all in your affection and fidelity.'[7] Clodius himself made no secret of his

---

[1] Cic., *In Vat.*, 6, 15, and *Schol. Bob.*, ed. Stangl, p. 148 (ed. Orelli, p. 317); *Pro Sest.*, 18, 40, and *Schol. Bob.*, ed. Stangl, p. 130 (ed. Orelli, p. 297); Suet., 23, 1.
[2] *Ib.*   [3] *Ib.*
[4] See Val. Max., iv, 2, 5.
[5] *De prov cons.*, 17, 41. Plutarch (*Cic.*, 30, 2-4) is inaccurate.
[6] Cic., *Att.*, ii, 20, 2; 22, 2.   [7] *Ib.*, 23, 3.

threats; 'while disclaiming them to Sampsiceramus', wrote Cicero, 'he openly avows and parades them to others'. Cicero consoled himself by reflecting that the three confederates were still unpopular and that his own services were gratefully remembered : ' I am supported', he told his friend, ' by the strongest goodwill of all.'[1] But towards the end of October there was a scene in the Forum which should have warned him that he had failed to gauge public opinion aright. One Gaius Porcius Cato, whom he described as 'a young man of no sense', had determined to prosecute Gabinius for bribery; and, as the praetors refused to hear him, he ascended the Rostra, addressed the people, and denounced Pompey as 'an unofficial dictator'. The crowd attempted to lynch him; and Cicero reported that he was within an ace of being killed.[2] Still Cicero remained hopeful :—' if Clodius impeaches me, all Italy will rush to my support . . . if he attempts violence, I hope, by the zeal not only of friends but also of opponents, to repel force with force. Every one promises to place not only himself, but also his friends, dependants, freedmen, slaves, and— to crown all—his money at my disposal. . . . Pompey makes every promise, and so does Caesar;[3] but I don't trust them enough to relax any of my preparations.'[4]

but is reassured by Pompey.

Clodius was maturing his. On the last day of the year, when Bibulus presented himself, according to custom, before the assembly, and, after taking the oath that he had done his duty in his consulship, was about to speak on the political situation, Clodius silenced him as, four years before, Metellus Nepos had silenced Cicero.[5] Immediately afterwards Clodius introduced four bills, which were designed to prepare the way for the attack which he had planned.

Legislation of Clodius.

The first, calculated to gain the favour of the rabble,

---

[1] *Ib.*, 25, 2.   [2] *Q. fr.*, i, 2, 15.
[3] Was Cicero alluding to promises which Caesar had made to him in person, or merely repeating what Pompey had told him ?
[4] *Q. fr.*, i, 2, 16.   [5] Dio, xxxviii, 12, 3.

provided that grain should thenceforward be distributed to all citizens who cared to ask for it, free of charge.[1] Next, evidently intending to prevent official opposition to his contemplated attack, Clodius proposed that no magistrate should be allowed to 'observe the sky', and thus to stop proceedings, when the assembly was convened for public business.[2] He then proceeded to legalize the formation of political clubs of the kind which six years before had been suppressed [3]—in other words, to encourage citizens of the lowest class and even slaves to band together in associations and hire out gangs of roughs to any politician who wished to intimidate a political opponent, to prevent the election of a rival candidate, or to carry a revolutionary bill.[4] Finally, Clodius enacted that the censors in constituting the Senate should not omit the name of any existing senator, nor place their official ban upon any citizen unless he had been tried and convicted by them both.[5] By this law he not only secured his own protection and the support of every senator and knight whose status might have been threatened by the censors, but also weakened the power of the Senate.[6]

Before Clodius proceeded further he gained over both the consuls by promising, in defiance of the law, under which the consular provinces had already been assigned, to obtain by decree of the people for Gabinius the province of Syria, and for Piso that of Macedonia with the addition of territories which Caesar's provincial law had recognized as free.[7] Perhaps he relied also upon the

[1] Cic., *Pro Sest.*, 25, 55; Ascon. *In Pis.*, ed. Clark, p. 8, ll. 12-6 (ed. Stangl, pp. 15-6); Dio, xxxviii, 13, 1.
[2] *Ib.*, §§ 3-6; Cic., *Cum senatui*, &c., 5, 11; *Pro Sest.*, 15, 33; *In Pis.*, 4, 9; Ascon., ed. Clark, p. 8, ll. 17-8 (ed. Stangl, p. 16).
[3] See p. 240.
[4] Cic., *Att.*, iii, 15, 4; *Pro Sest.*, 25, 55; *In Pis.*, 4, 8-9; Ascon., ed. Clark, p. 7, ll. 14-5, p. 8, ll. 22-3 (ed. Stangl, pp. 15-6); Dio, xxxviii, 13, 2.
[5] *Ib.*; Cic., *Pro Sest.*, 25, 55; *De prov. cons.*, 19, 46; *In Pis.*, 4, 9; *De har. resp.*, 27, 58; Ascon., ed. Clark, p. 8, ll. 24-6. See Long's correction (*Decline of the Roman Republic*, iii, 448-9) of Cicero and Dio.
[6] The law was repealed six years later. See vol. ii, p. 236.
[7] *Pro Sest.*, 10, 24; *De prov. cons.*, 2, 3; 4, 7; *In Pis.*, 16, 37; 24, 57; *De domo*, 9, 23; *Att.*, iii, 1; Plut., *Cic.*, 30, 1.

VI THE EXILE OF CICERO 331

enmity which Cicero had provoked from the victims of his sarcastic tongue.¹ He now proposed a bill by which any one who had put to death a Roman citizen uncondemned or any one who thereafter did so should be 'interdicted from fire and water', in other words, declared an outlaw.² Every one of course understood that although the bill named nobody, it was directed against Cicero alone; but it may be that Clodius was not merely actuated by personal animosity and the motive of preventing Cicero from assailing Caesar's laws, but also intended to attack the 'ultimate decree', under which Cicero had been empowered to act against Catiline.³ Cicero's judgement and his nerve were paralysed by the shock. 'If', he wrote later, 'when the bill was published, I had chosen to commend it or to ignore it . . . it could have done me absolutely no harm.'⁴ Discarding his senatorial dress in token of affliction, he went from place to place, begging all who had any influence to befriend him.⁵ Clodius, haranguing the populace in the Forum, told them that Pompey approved what he had done, that Caesar and Crassus were both hostile to Cicero, and that the three confederates were ready to use force.⁶ Cicero did not believe this talk; but as the confederates did not contradict it, he became alarmed: evidently, he thought, Caesar was unwilling to offend the tribune who was the idol of the multitude, for fear the acts of his consulship might be rescinded. Besides, Caesar was waiting outside Rome, and Cicero well knew why he was there.⁷ When he ventured out of doors the myrmidons of Clodius insulted him and pelted him with mud and stones.⁸ Nevertheless most of the knights put on mourning to show their sympathy with the orator who had espoused their cause; Publius Crassus, the son of Marcus, who

58 B.C.

His bill directed against Cicero.

General sympathy with Cicero.

---

¹ Dio, xxxviii, 12. Cf. Plut., *Cic.*, 24, 1; 25-8.
² See p. 483 and Strachan-Davidson, *Problems of the Rom. Crim. Law*, ii, 1912, pp. 24-7, 40, 51-74.
³ See Dio, xxxviii, 14, 5, and *Klio*, xiii, 1913, p. 381.
⁴ *Att.*, iii, 15, 5.   ⁵ Plut., 30, 4; Dio, xxxviii, 14, 6-7.
⁶ *Pro Sest.*, 17, 39.   ⁷ *Ib.*, 18, 41.
⁸ Plut., *Cic.*, 30, 4. Cf. App., ii, 15, 55-7.

revered him, did the same and induced many of the younger men to follow his example; a crowd of these enthusiasts accompanied Cicero through the streets, mingling their entreaties with his; and he received messages of encouragement from all parts of Italy.[1] The knights sent a deputation, which was joined by two senators—the famous advocate Hortensius and Scribonius Curio, the father of Cicero's young friend—to plead with the Senate on his behalf. Gabinius refused to receive the deputation, and when the two senators attempted to address the people a gang of ruffians, whom Clodius had engaged, fell upon and beat them. Lucius Ninnius, a tribune who had steadily supported Cicero, was forbidden by Clodius to speak,[2] and a senator who had accompanied Hortensius was so roughly handled that he died.[3] Cicero implored Piso to assist him. Piso replied that it was useless to appeal to himself or to his colleague; the latter was in debt and must have a province, which he could not get unless he adhered to Clodius.[4] A day or two later Clodius presented the consuls to the assembly and asked them what they thought of Cicero's consulship and of the bill. Piso answered, alluding to the execution of the Catilinarian conspirators, 'No savage or cruel deed commends itself to me';[5] Gabinius merely blamed the knights and the senators for interference.[6] The Senate, as a body, in pursuance of a resolution which they had passed, put on mourning to manifest their sorrow[7]: the consuls forbade them to wear it—an exercise of power which was not only tyrannical but infringed the law.[8]

Clodius, who had not yet obtained the opinion of Caesar, summoned the people to assemble outside the gates and questioned him. Caesar replied that, as every-

---

[1] *Att.*, iii, 15, 7; *Pro Sest.*, 11, 26; 14, 32; Plut., *Cras.*, 13, 5; *Cic.*, 31, 1.
[2] Cic., *Pro Sest.*, 12, 27; 13, 30; Dio, xxxviii, 16, 2-4.
[3] Cic., *Pro Mil.*, 14, 37. [4] *In Pis.*, 6, 12.
[5] Dio, xxxviii, 16, 5-6. Cf. *In Pis.*, 6, 14. [6] Dio, *l.c.*
[7] They took off their purple-striped togas (see Pliny, ix, 36 [60], 127) and assumed the narrow-striped garb of knights (Dio, xxxviii, 14, 7).
[8] Cic., *Pro Sest.*, 14, 32; *In Pis.*, 8, 18; Plut., *Cic.*, 31, 1; Dio, xxxviii, 16, 3.

THE EXILE OF CICERO

body knew, he disapproved the execution of the Catilinarian conspirators, but that he equally disapproved a bill which enacted a heavy penalty for a deed that was past and done.[1] Crassus, if we may believe Dio,[2] sided with 'the crowd'. Pompey behaved in a way which Cicero could not forget. Again and again he had assured the orator, who had helped to make him what he was, that Clodius would not be suffered to do him any harm. He had retired to his villa on the Alban hills, and had thus avoided the ordeal of being asked for his opinion on the bill. Cicero's friends, among them Marcus Lucullus and the praetor Lentulus Crus, travelled from Rome to see him and entreated him not to abandon Cicero or neglect the interest of the State. He replied that without authority from the Senate he could not resist an armed tribune; let them appeal to the consuls: if the consuls under the sanction of a senatorial decree would defend the State, he would take up arms.[3] He knew as well as they that the consuls had to earn their reward. Cicero himself knelt at the feet of Pompey and implored his favour: Pompey would not raise the prostrate suppliant, but said that he could not oppose the will of Caesar. Cicero, who himself described this incident,[4] has left it uncertain whether it happened in Pompey's villa or at Rome; but, if we may trust Plutarch,[5] he went to call on Pompey, who, ashamed to look him in the face, stole out of the house by another door.

Time pressed, and Cicero had to come to a decision. Lucullus and others advised him to remain in Rome and face his enemy; Cato, Hortensius, and Cicero's own family counselled him to depart.[6] He accepted their

58 B. C.

Pompey fails him.

He goes into voluntary exile.

---

[1] *Ib.*, 17, 1-2; Plut., *Cic.*, 30, 4.   [2] xxxviii, 17, 3.
[3] Cic., *Q. fr.*, i, 4, 4; *Att.*, viii, 3, 3; ix, 5, 2; 9, 1; 13, 3; *In Pis.*, 31, 77; Plut., *Cic.*, 31, 1; Dio, xxxviii, 17, 3.
[4] *Att.*, x, 4, 3.   [5] *Cic.*, 31, 2.
[6] *Ib.*, § 3; Cic., *Q. fr.*, i, 3, 8; 4, 4; *Pro Sest.*, 17, 39; Plut., *Cic.*, 31, 3; Dio, xxxviii, 17, 4. Cicero in a letter to Atticus (iii, 15, 2) seems at first sight to imply that Cato did not, as Plutarch and Dio affirm, advise Cicero to leave *I*taly; but, Strachan-Davidson (*Cicero*, p. 234, n. †) notwithstanding, *I* do not think that his testimony is necessarily at variance with theirs.

334 THE EXILE OF CICERO CHAP.

58 B. C.

March 16 (Julian).

advice and, taking from his home a small statue of Minerva, placed it in the temple of Jupiter on the Capitol, adding the inscription MINERVAE VRBIS CVSTODI—'To Minerva, the guardian of Rome'.[1] About the 20th of March he left his house, intending to go in the first instance to Southern Italy.[2] On the same day[3] Clodius, in violation of a statute that forbade laws to be enacted against individuals,[4] presented a bill to the assembly, in which he proposed that Cicero should be 'interdicted from fire and water' within the limits of the empire, that his property should be confiscated, and that his house should be destroyed.[5]

Journeying slowly down the Appian Way, Cicero halted somewhere in Southern Latium,[6] where he received a copy of the bill. He saw that he must leave Italy and wrote to the friend who never failed him : 'I beg you to make it your business to follow and overtake me instantly'. Perhaps it might be advisable to cross from Brundisium to Epirus, where Atticus had influence and could befriend him. Travelling through Campania, he learned that his friends were trying to get the law amended in his favour and, hoping that after all he might be suffered to remain in Italy or near it, he resolved to go, not to Brundisium

[1] Dio, xxxviii, 17, 4–5; Plut., *Cic.*, 31, 4.
[2] Plut., *l. c.* For the date see *Harvard Studies in Class. Philol.*, vii, 1896, pp. 77–8.
[3] Cic., *Cum senatui*, &c., 7, 17 ; *Pro Sest.*, 10, 25 (*promulgantur uno eodemque tempore rogationes ab eodem tribuno de mea pernicie et de provinciis nominatim*) ; 24, 53. Groebe (W. Drumann's *Gesch. Roms*, ii², 1902, p. 219, n. 5), following Sternkopf (*Philol.*, lix, 1900, p. 276), holds that the law which, as Cicero says, was *proposed* (not, as Sternkopf and Groebe say, carried) in order to ruin him (*de mea pernicie*) was not the one that named him, but the earlier one (see p. 331). This law had been proposed—there is no evidence that it was ever carried—before Cicero left Rome (*Att.*, iii, 15, 5). Otherwise he would not have gone !
[4] Clodius's bill was a *privilegium* because Cicero was not summoned to stand his trial. The bill which Fufius had directed against Clodius in 61 B.C. (see pp. 295–6), though Cicero (*Paradoxa*, iv, 32) called it a *privilegium*, did not violate law, because the sentence which it imposed was conditional on the verdict of a jury. Cf. Cic., *Att.*, iii, 15, 5, *De domo*, 17, 43, and Strachan-Davidson, *Problems*, &c., ii, 41–2. [5] See p. 483.
[6] *Harvard Studies*, &c., 1896, pp. 80–1. For the order of the events described in this paragraph see pp. 482–5.

but to Vibo, in the south of the Bruttian peninsula. 58 B.C. Begging Atticus to follow him, he could not refrain from Apr. 6. adding, 'I hope to see the day when I may thank you for having forced me to remain alive : so far I regret it keenly'; but on the 10th of April he wrote from Thurii, 'if you are at Rome, you cannot now catch me up'. Arriving at Vibo, he was welcomed by a friend named Sica, who had a villa near the town, and who counted the danger of sheltering him as nothing. He intended to cross the Straits, but Gaius Vergilius, the Governor of Sicily, with whom he had long been intimate, wrote forbidding him to come,[1] and, unwilling to expose Sica to further risk, he bade him farewell and started for Brundisium. On the road he learned that the efforts of his friends had been successful : the bill had been amended, and he was free to take up his abode wherever he pleased, provided that the place was not less than five hundred miles from Italy.[2] Arriving at Brundisium on the 17th,[3] Apr. 13. he was welcomed by another friend. Just before he started for Dyrrachium he wrote a letter to his family :—' when I write to you or read your letters, I am so worn by weeping that I cannot bear it. . . . I have been thirteen days at Brundisium with Marcus Laenius Flaccus, a most excellent man, who, thinking of my safety, counted as naught the risk to his own fortunes and to his civil status, and has not been led by the penalty fixed by a most iniquitous law to refuse me the rights and the kind offices of hospitality and friendship. May I be able some day to prove the gratitude which I shall always feel. . . . My Terentia, most faithful and best of wives, my darling little daughter, my little Cicero, last hope of our family, good-bye.'[4] From Dyrrachium he resolved to go to Macedonia and join his friend Plancius, the quaestor of that province. Plancius, as soon as he heard that Cicero had landed, put on mourning, travelled post up the Egnatian Way to meet him, and took him back to his official residence, which they reached on the 23rd of

[1] Plut., *Cic.*, 32, 1.   [2] See pp. 483-5.   [3] *Att.*, iii, 7, 1.
[4] *Fam.*, xiv, 4, 1. 2. 6.

336 THE EXILE OF CICERO CHAP. VI

58 B. C.
May 18.

May.[1] Sica, Flaccus, Plancius—Cicero remembered them as well as Pompey and lived to prove his gratitude : still, after two thousand years, a few students of the past feel the influence of their charity and learn from it that even in the decadence of the Republic there were upright men in Rome.

Already in the far West a drama was beginning to unfold itself which was to affect for all time the trend of European history. Unconsciously Cicero had left Rome just in time to suit the plans of Caesar, who knew that the acts of his consulship, so long as Cicero remained in exile, were secure from attack. Simultaneously a sensational announcement reached him. The Helvetii, reinforced by allies from beyond the Rhine, were about

March 24. to enter Gaul, and on the 28th of March they were to assemble opposite Geneva, ready to cross the Rhône.

Caesar then goes to encounter the Helvetii.

Instantly the proconsul started.[2] The ex-tribune Labienus, who had served him five years before in the prosecution of Rabirius, and whom, discerning perhaps his military genius, he had selected as his chief lieutenant, had probably preceded him. Did Caesar reflect, as he sat in his travelling carriage, that Clodius had let loose forces that would make for anarchy ?

[1] Cic., *Pro Planc.*, 41, 98-9. Rabirius Postumus, the famous financier, also befriended Cicero (*Pro Rab. Post.*, 17, 47).
[2] *B. G.*, i, 6, 4 ; 7, 1.

PART II

THE AUTHORITIES OF OUR AUTHORITIES

MANY years ago, conversing with a curate, who is now Bishop of Burnley, I dilated upon the researches by which Bessel, Henderson, and Struve had endeavoured to calculate the parallaxes of the nearer stars. Remembering that he had an elementary knowledge of astronomy, I hoped that he would share my interest in what Sir John Herschel called 'the greatest and most glorious triumph which practical astronomy has ever witnessed'. To my surprise and disappointment he dismissed the subject with impatient contempt: the *Nautical Almanac* was useful, but whether 61 Cygni was sixty billions (60,000,000,000,000) of miles away, as Struve calculated, or, as Bessel insisted, only forty billions, mattered not a brass farthing. The Bishop is a sound classical scholar, and I have often wondered what he would have thought of the treatises which learned Germans, who almost monopolize this field of inquiry, have produced in what they call Q*uellenforschung*, or Q*uellenkritik*—the investigation of the sources from which the ancient writers whose works form the staple of our knowledge of Roman history derived theirs. Maurenbrecher, one of the most indefatigable of *Quellenforscher*, at the close of an exhaustive review of Sallustian literature, in which he argued that this and that author had derived his information from Sallust's *Histories*, made this significant admission: 'That for the criticism of Sallust it would be not unimportant to be able to ascertain from what sources *he* drew, and what reliance is to be placed upon *his* narrative, is assuredly clear; but on this point as little as for his *Catilina* and *Iugurtha*... certain results have hitherto been obtained.'[1] That they never will be is a safe prophecy. To the historian as such Q*uellenforschung* is of no value, except in so far as it may enable him to appraise the credibility of his materials.

How far can it serve that end? When the historian has satisfied himself that Valerius Maximus, Velleius Paterculus, Frontinus, Florus, Obsequens, Pseudo-Aurelius Victor, Eutropius, Orosius, Cassiodorus, and Granius Licinianus, all used Livy or an epitome of Livy, that Licinianus, Exuperantius, and Orosius used Sallust, and that some epitomizers copied others, is he any the wiser? Does he gain much from Suetonius's mention of authorities whose works no longer exist, or from the admitted fact that Suetonius also used Caesar and Cicero, whose works he can study for himself? He may be thankful when he is able to detect errors in these writers by comparison with authentic sources; but those statements of theirs which by this

[1] Bursian's *Jahresbericht*, cxiii, 1902 (1903), p. 258.

means he can neither verify nor refute can only be appraised at their apparent worth. I am not, however, arguing that the investigation of sources can *never* be useful to the historian. If, for instance, V. Ussani [1] had succeeded in proving that Appian, Dio, and Orosius copied Lucan instead of going direct to Livy, Lucan's source, their credit would sink lower than it is. Again, something is perhaps gained when, after an exhaustive criticism of the authorities for the conspiracy of Catiline, H. Willrich [2] concludes that the most trustworthy are Cicero, Sallust, Plutarch, Suetonius, Dio, and Asconius : at all events the historian who may be tempted to appeal to Plutarch [3] as confirming two famous paragraphs of Sallust [4] will pause when he is convinced that Sallust himself was the authority whom Plutarch, directly or indirectly, followed. But he might perhaps arrive at this conviction without the assistance of a *Quellenforscher.*

The writers about whose sources there has been the most controversy are Plutarch, Appian, and Dio ; and, as H. Peter truly says, [5] in the case of Dio—he might have added the other two—it has led to no certain result. The historian who has followed it, even if he is sure of his own conclusions, will find that they do not help him, for here again the sources are such as he cannot control. What will he have gained when he has decided whether Plutarch and Appian used the lost work of Asinius Pollio directly or only through a Greek médium ? It is satisfactory to know that they both derived much of their information, directly or indirectly, from a writer who was contemporary with the events which he described, and whose intimacy with Caesar may have enabled him to learn the truth : still, we have no guarantee of his own accuracy except that he censured the alleged inaccuracies of Caesar.[6] And even if it could be proved that Plutarch,[7] when he said that Sulpicius sold the citizenship, followed the *Memoirs* of Sulla, Sulpicius's enemy, it would be rash to conclude that the statement was untrue.

I doubt whether a historian who ignored *Quellenkritik*, if he were able to weigh evidence, would make more mistakes than the most industrious of *Quellenforscher.*[8] If I have any acumen in testing the

---

[1] *Sul valore storico del poema Lucaneo*, 1903, pp. 9 ff.
[2] *De coniurationis Cat. fontibus*, 1893.
[3] *Cic.*, 10.   [4] *Cat.*, 17, 21.
[5] *D. gesch. Litt. über d. röm. Kaiserzeit*, &c., 1897, ii, 269.
[6] Suet., *Div. Iul.*, 56, 4.   [7] *Sulla*, 8, 2.
[8] *I* have just lighted upon the third volume of E. A. Freeman's *History of Sicily*, and am glad to find that in the matter of *Quellenkritik* we are of one mind. 'At last', he says (p. 591), 'one almost comes instinctively to shrink from all discourses about *Quellen.* One begins to suspect forgetfulness of the truth that the final cause of a source is not simply to show our ingenuity in finding the way to it, but to draw something from it when it is found.' Again (p. 607), 'Where did Diodôros and Plutarch get their materials ? We cannot say, except when they tell us themselves. . . . For the rest we may, within certain bounds of possibility, guess anything that we please, and nobody can prove to absolute demonstration that we are wrong'. Finally (p. 615), he says substantially what *I* have said, ' In all this *Quellenfrage* . . . *I* have found nothing whatever in any way to affect my notions of any point of Sicilian history of the slightest moment '. Warde Fowler (*Eng. Hist. Rev.*, xx, 1905,

credibility of my authorities, I attribute it partly to having gained experience, before I approached the serious study of Roman history, by investigating the history of the Indian Mutiny and that of Sir Charles Napier's conquest and administration of Sind; for in checking the original records, printed and manuscript, by the testimony of survivors who had seen or had taken part in the events which I narrated, I learned how mistakes in detail arise and what kinds of statements are open to suspicion.

THE UNREFORMED AND THE JULIAN CALENDAR

As students of Roman chronology are aware, all dates between February 24, 700 (54 B.C.)—if not also between 691 (63 B.C.), the year of Cicero's consulship—and the last day of 708 (46 B.C.) can be referred with absolute certainty to the corresponding day of the Julian calendar, with a possible error of one day. The possibility of this minute error lies in the fact that it is not quite certain whether the Kalends of January, 709—the first year of the Julian calendar— corresponded with January 1, 45 B.C. or with January 2. In *Ancient Britain* (pages 714–26) I gave reasons for believing that *Kal. Ian.*, 709, fell upon January 1, 45 B.C. One book, however—the third volume of the revised edition of Drumann's *Geschichte Roms*, which appeared in 1906, just before the manuscript of *Ancient Britain* went to the printer—was then unknown to me. I will now examine the reasons which the editor, Paul Groebe,[1] has given for accepting the view that the first day of 709 was January 2, 45.

Groebe starts from the date—*a. d. V. Kal. Apr.* (March 28, 696)— which, according to Caesar,[2] the Helvetii fixed for their general muster on the banks of the Rhône. It is agreed by all chronologists and is certain that this day corresponded either with March 24 or with March 25, 58 B.C. If with the latter, *Kal. Ian.*, 709 equals January 2, 45.

Groebe truly, if needlessly, observes that Caesar translated the Helvetian date into one which would be intelligible to his readers: he argues that the Helvetii intended to assemble at new moon, which was considered lucky;[3] and he insists that by new moon we are to understand the day on which the crescent first became visible. There was a new moon on March 24, 58 B.C., at 4.40 p.m.;[4] and Groebe remarks that, according to observations made with the naked eye

---

p. 210) credits *Quellenforscher* with the discovery that Plutarch, Appian, and other late writers derived information either from ' memoir-writers ' of the Gracchan age or from ' works in which those memoirs [or rather statements based thereon] were to be found at second hand '. Self-evidently they derived it, if not from the former, from the latter source.

[1] W. Drumann, *Gesch. Roms*, iii², 1906, pp. 774–9.
[2] *B. G.*, i, 6, 4.
[3] Cf. *B. G.*, i, 50, 5, with Tac., *Germ.*, 11.
[4] Cf. *'Class. Quart.*, 1912, p. 79 and n. 5, with Drumann-Groebe, iii, 776.

by F. J. Schmidt at Athens, the crescent can be seen between 29 and 63 hours after new moon.[1] Evidently, then, if those observations are to be accepted as a basis of calculation, it would have been invisible before March 26 : Groebe, who asserts that it was visible on the 25th, seems to forget that by 9.40 p.m. on that day, 29 hours after new moon, the orb had set! Since March 26, as Groebe himself remarks, is out of the question, it follows that the hour at which the crescent would become visible did not coincide with the fixed date ; and, since it was obviously impossible to foretell at what time it would become visible, or even, in cloudy weather, that it would be visible at all, the Helvetii probably fixed their assembling, as nearly as they could tell, for new moon itself. It must be remembered that they had not arranged to *start* on a. d. V. Kal. *Apr.*, but to arrive at their place of muster. Even if they had not had to reckon with Caesar, they could not have started before the following day at the very earliest ; and we need not suppose that they intended to move before March 26, when, if the sky were clear, the crescent would be discerned.

The difficulty which Groebe's theory involves is further illustrated by what he says about the first day of the Julian calendar. He finds support in the statement of Macrobius [2] that Caesar took account of the phases of the moon (*annum civilem Caesar habitis ad lunam dimensionibus constitutum edicto palam posito publicavit*). There was a new moon on January 2, 45 B. C., at 1.26 a.m. : therefore, says Groebe, the crescent was visible on January 2. Was he dreaming ? Visible, though it set before 6 p.m., when it was less than 17 hours old ! Perhaps, as Dr. Fotheringham has suggested,[3] Caesar ' may have calculated ' the new moon ' for the 1st ' of January ; but, supposing that the calculation was approximately correct, the hour may well have been counted as included in January 1, for in popular usage the Roman day was reckoned, not from midnight to midnight but from dawn to dawn.[4]

[Dr. Fotheringham,[5] commenting on the foregoing note in the form in which it appeared in the *Classical Quarterly*, remarks that, as ' the moon stood 14 degrees vertically above the setting sun at Geneva ' on March 25, 58 B.C., she ' ought therefore in normal [or abnormally fine ?] weather to have been visible that evening, and Groebe is fairly entitled to say that the first appearance of the new moon was on the evening of the day which he equates with a. d. V. Kal. Apr.' But the question remains whether the Helvetii would have counted upon seeing a moon less than 29 hours old ; for, as Dr. Fotheringham has said,[6] ' Hitherto it has been the practise to assume that [in the

---

[1] Groebe adds that the astronomical tables of the Babylonians of the third century B. C. fix the time between 19 and 50 hours ; but account must be taken of the relative clearness of the atmosphere.
[2] i, 14, 13.
[3] *Journ. of Philol.*, xxix, 1903, pp. 98–9.
[4] See *B. G.*, vi, 18, 2, and Drumann-Groebe, iii, 777, n. 3.
[5] *Class. Quart.*, xiv, 1920, pp. 97–9.
[6] *Monthly Notices Roy. Astron. Soc.*, 1910, p. 531.

early spring or the winter and in favourable weather ?] the moon becomes visible on the first evening when she is more than 30 hours old at sunset.'

Dr. Fotheringham, of course, freely admitted that the second date on which I joined issue with Groebe must be decided in my favour, and went on to give a new and interesting reason for believing that 'the inaugural day of the Julian calendar' was January 1, 45 B.C.]

Thus every date which we find mentioned in our authorities between February 24, 700 (54 B. C.), and January 1, 709 (45), can be expressed in terms of the Julian calendar; and the correspondence can also be established for the period between February 24, 696 (58), and February 23, 698 (56); for it is now admitted by all chronologists that in that period there was no intercalary month.[1] It is certain that in the intervening time—February 24, 698, to February 24, 700 —there was one and only one intercalation.[2] Which of the three years, 56, 55, 54, was distinguished by an intercalary month? Before we attempt to solve this problem I may remind the reader that the time for intercalating was between the 23rd and the 24th of February.

Ludwig Holzapfel[3] holds that the disputed year was 700 (54 B. C.). Considering first 698, he observes that when Cicero wrote to his brother on February 15[4] it was still winter, whereas, if an intercalary month was inserted, the beginning of spring—February 24, according to the Julian calendar—must have immediately preceded the day on which the letter was written. Again, in a letter of April 4,[5] Cicero remarks that navigation, which commonly opened on March 10 of the Julian calendar,[6] had not yet begun; and on April 8, when he again wrote to his brother, the weather was apparently still unsettled.[7] The inference, says Holzapfel, is that the calendar was then nearly a month in advance of solar time. Still greater was the difference in 699. In this year Crassus left Rome for Syria about November 15:[8] therefore he must have embarked at Brundisium about the 25th. When he reached Brundisium the weather was stormy.[9] That he delayed his departure after the day which corresponded with November 11 of the Julian calendar, when rough weather was to be expected, can hardly be supposed. Most probably, as his voyage would last 15–20 days, he reached Brundisium before October 20 of the perpetual Julian calendar.

Holzapfel apparently forgets that *hiems* does not necessarily mean 'winter': commonly it means 'wintry (or stormy) weather'. Cicero[10] says that in 58 B. C., on a day later than April 10,[11] which

---

[1] See *Jahrb. f. class. Philol.*, cxxix, 1884, p. 582.
[2] *Class. Quart.*, vi, 1912, p. 74.
[3] *Röm. Chron.*, 1885, pp. 320–3.   [4] *Q. fr.*, ii, 3, 7.
[5] *Ib.*, 4, 7. The date results from comparison of 5, 1 with 4, 2.
[6] Veg., *De re mil.*, iv, 39.
[7] *Q. fr.*, ii, 5, 3 (*tu . . . primam navigationem, dummodo idonea tempestas sit, ne omiseris*). A similar proviso might have been made in July!
[8] Cic., *Att.*, iv, 13, 2.   [9] Plut., *Cras.*, 17, 1.
[10] *Pro Planc.*, 40, 96.
[11] Cf. *Pro Planc.*, 40, 96, with p. 335 of this volume.

corresponded with April 6 of the Julian calendar, *hiemis magnitudo* prevented him from going by sea from Vibo to Brundisium. If navigation had not begun on April 4, 698, we can only conclude that the weather was bad. In practice navigation did not begin or end on a fixed day : the time varied according to the atmospheric conditions, the hardihood of the shipmasters, or the necessities of the case, and seamen were occasionally forced to venture out even in midwinter. Still, though Holzapfel reasoned badly, his conclusion, as far as it related to 56 B. C., was right. G. F. Unger,[1] indeed, argues that the year in question was 56. Cicero, in his speech on the consular provinces,[2] speaking of the successor of Piso, says, ' In January and February he will have no province : on the 1st of March his province will come into being ' (*Ianuario, Februario provinciam non habebit : Kalendis ei denique Martiis nascetur . . . provincia*) ; that there would be no intercalary month in 699 could be presumed, says Unger, if one had been inserted in the year of the speech (698), but not otherwise. Unger failed to see that Cicero was not speaking of 699, but of 700. But Unger has other arguments in reserve. In 56 the consul Lentulus Marcellinus had the *fasces* in January [3] and again in April [4] ; therefore there must have been an intercalary month. Here Unger makes a mistake. The second letter in which Cicero implied that Marcellinus then had the *fasces* was written not in April, but in March,[5] and therefore tends to show that in 56 there was no intercalary month.

[1] *I.* von Müller, *Handbuch d. klass. Altertumswiss.*, i², 1892, p. 812.
[2] *De prov. cons.*, 15, 37.
[3] Cic., *Fam.*, i, 1, 2. [4] *Q. fr.*, ii, 4, 4.
[5] Mommsen held that §§ 3–7 of *Q. fr.*, ii, 6, were really a continuation of *Q. fr.*, ii, 4, 2 ; and since in § 6 Cicero mentions the acquittal of Sextus Clodius, which occurred ' a few days ' (*his paucis diebus*) before the trial of Caelius (*Pro Cael.*, 32, 78), that is shortly before April 4, Mommsen inferred that the whole letter was written at the end of March or the beginning of April. Rauschen, however (*Eph. Tull.*, 1886, pp. 39–40), argues that Mommsen, whose arrangement has been followed by almost all editors, was wrong ; that §§ 1–2 were written soon after the acquittal of Sestius, which, as we learn from § 1, took place on March 11 ; and that §§ 3–7 form a second letter, the beginning of which he believes to have been lost. Cicero, he suggests, alluded to the lost section when on April 8 he reminded Quintus (*Q. fr.*, ii, 5, 1) that he had already written to tell him that Tullia was betrothed on April 4. Rauschen's reasons are these : first, if Mommsen is right, Cicero, who told his brother ' as the latest news ' that Sestius had been acquitted, must have withheld that news until after the acquittal of Clodius, that is, as Rauschen infers from the words *his paucis diebus*, for at least a fortnight ; secondly, Mommsen's arrangement implies that Cicero muddled the order of events, for, after mentioning in § 2 that builders were hard at work on Quintus's house and his own, and then speaking about other things, he returns in § 3 to the matter of building with the remark, ' *I* am building on three different sites and doing repairs as well '. The third reason is not worth mentioning, for it depends upon the assumption, which Rauschen has already made, that a fortnight or more elapsed between the acquittal of Sestius and the acquittal of Clodius. In my opinion he has failed to upset Mommsen's arrangement. In Cicero's mouth *his paucis diebus* means, within reason, anything you please : *paucis ante diebus* in *In Cat.*, iii, 1, 3, means 24 days, and even if Clodius was acquitted towards the end of March, Cicero may have begun the letter several days earlier and afterwards finished it, for since he remarks in § 7 that ' the sea is still closed ' (*adhuc clausum mare fuisse scio*)—in other words, that navigation

THE JULIAN CALENDAR 343

Early in 698 (56) Cicero wrote to Quintus, ' The builders are hard at work both on your house and mine. . . . I hope we shall be together before winter ' (*Spero nos ante hiemem contubernales fore* [1]). Unger,[2] believing that the letter was written on April 3, which, if there had been no intercalation in that year, would have corresponded to March 9, 56 B. C., maintained that in that case Cicero would have written ' before next winter ' (*ante proximam hiemem*). No, replied Gerard Rauschen,[3] the words in question were written about the middle of March, that is, if there was no intercalation, at the end of February, 56, when the Italian winter was over. The houses, I may add, were not yet ready, and Quintus, who was in Sardinia, would not be back in Italy for some weeks.[4] Cicero was evidently thinking of the next winter, though he did not say *proximam*. Why should he? Moreover, there is proof positive that there was no intercalation in this year; for in a letter [5] written on February 12 Cicero appends the postscript ' February 15 ' (*XV. Kal. Mart.*), and if there was an intercalary month, such a date was impossible: it would have been *a. d. X. Kal. interc.* Unger [6] could only extricate himself from this difficulty by guessing that the words *XV. Kal. Mart.* form the beginning of some other letter; and Rauschen confuted him. The year 56, then, may be ruled out; and there is a sufficient reason for excluding 54. Writing to Quintus on February 15, Cicero said, ' Appius holds that on the comitial days following the Quirinalia [February 17] he is not prevented by the Pupian law from holding a meeting of the Senate, and that by the Gabinian law he is actually bound to grant an audience of the Senate to the ambassadors every day from the 1st of February to the 1st of March: thus it is supposed that the elections are postponed till March ' (*Comitialibus diebus qui Quirinalia sequuntur Appius interpretatur non impediri se lege Pupia quo minus habeat senatum, et, quod Gabinia sanctum sit, etiam cogi ex Kal. Febr. usque ad Kal. Mart. legatis senatum cotidie dare: ita putantur detrudi comitia in mensem Martium* [7]). If there was to be an intercalary month between the 1st of February and the 1st of March this sentence would be unintelligible: the Gabinian law provided

---

is hazardous—he may well have had to wait some time before a messenger could start. The double mention of building operations will not, *I* think, present the slightest difficulty to any sensible reader, especially if he consults Tyrrell's notes; but if it does, the suggestion that Cicero began to write immediately after the acquittal of Sestius and finished later will remove it. Rauschen failed to observe that if § 4 was written in April, Lentulus must have had the *fasces* then, whereas if, as Rauschen rightly holds, there was no intercalation in 56, he would in the ordinary course have had them in March. [I find that Tyrrell and Purser in their second edition (*The Correspondence of Cicero*, ii, 1906, p. 48) argue in much the same strain as *I* have done. Sternkopf (*Hermes*, xxxix, 1904, pp. 383–418; xl, 1905, pp. 1–49), who rightly vindicates Mommsen's arrangement in substance, unnecessarily supposes (p. 407) that §§ 3–7 were a second letter, written towards the end of March; for he forgets to allow for the risks of navigation and the consequent delay in the transmission of letters.]

[1] *Q. fr.*, ii, 4, 2. [2] *Jahrb. f. class. Philol.*, 1884, p. 585.
[3] *Eph. Tull.*, p. 20. [4] Cf. *Q. fr.*, ii, 5. [5] *Ib.*, 3, 7.
[6] *Op. cit.*, pp. 584–5. [7] *Q. fr.*, ii, 11, 3.

that foreign embassies should have audience of the Senate on every day of February, but not of an intercalary month. I am forced therefore to conclude with Rauschen that the year in question was 699 (55).[1] It may be objected that the intercalation was generally made in a year of which the number was even : but, as Tyrrell and Purser remark in a note on Q. fr. ii, 11, 3, ' In the year 699 (55) everything had been done irregularly, through the high-handed action of the consuls Pompeius and Crassus ; ' and as they were not elected before January or February, they may well have arranged for an intercalary month in order to gain time.

THE EQUIVALENTS IN OUR MONEY OF THE SESTERCE, THE DENARIUS, AND THE TALENT

When we read that Crassus was worth 7,100 talents,[2] or that while Caesar was hard pressed by the lieutenants of Pompey in Spain the price of grain rose to 50 *denarii* a *modius* [3]—about fifty times its normal price—we want to know the modern equivalents of these sums. A *denarius* (4 sesterces) contained about the same amount of silver as a shilling or a mark ; but as silver was in Roman times worth one-twelfth of gold—a considerably higher ratio than the modern— a German metrologist has fixed the value of the sesterce at 17·5 pfennigs (about twopence), and therefore of the denarius at 70 pfennigs (about eightpence).[4] In this country, on the other hand, 100 sesterces are sometimes reckoned as equivalent to £1—' a rough compromise,' as Strachan-Davidson explained,[5] ' between the weight of gold and the weight of silver in the sums named.' So far this estimate appears the more accurate of the two ; indeed it is substantially that which German and French historians commonly adopt. H. Schultz, however, who regards all such calculations as unsatisfactory, has set himself to determine the ratio between the purchasing power of Roman and German money ; and from various statements in Cicero's letters and other documents he arrives at the conclusion that if a *denarius* in one sense was worth no more than 70 pfennigs, its real value was about three times as much, say 2 marks.[6] Thus, he observes, when we read [7] that Caesar spent 60 millions of sesterces, or 10,500,000 marks (£525,000) on the improvements which he contemplated in the Roman Forum, we should multiply this amount by 3.

If Schultz means that the German historian should state that 60,000,000 sesterces were equivalent to 31,500,000 marks, I cannot

[1] Groebe (*op. cit.*, p. 777), who thinks that 700 is the most probable, refers to Holzapfel, who ignores *Q. fr.*, ii, 11, 3.
[2] Plut., *Cras.*, 2, 2.   [3] *B. C.*, i, 52, 2.
[4] Fr. Hultsch, *Griech. u. röm. Metrologie*², 1882, pp. 173, 297-9.
[5] *Cic.*, 1894, p. 30, note.
[6] *Sokrates*, ii, 1914, pp. 75-84.   [7] Cic., *Att.*, iv, 16, 8.

follow him. The result of such calculations would be mere confusion. In every successive edition the historian would be obliged to revise his figures. In the three years that have elapsed since Schultz published his article (I am writing on the 5th of December, 1917) [1] the purchasing power of money in this country has diminished, so far as food and drink are concerned, by about one half. When we learn that William Beckford, the famous author of *Vathek*, on becoming of age in 1780, came into possession of ' a million of money and £100,000 a year ',[2] we accept those numbers : we do not think it necessary to multiply them because the purchasing power of money has diminished since Beckford's time. It seems to me therefore that the only rational course for the historian is to base his calculations upon the assumption that 100 sesterces (25 *denarii*) were approximately equivalent to £1, to supply the reader with data sufficient to show what the purchasing power of 100 sesterces then was, and to leave him to compare it with whatever it may be in his own country[3] at the time when he reads. But he should bear in mind that while in the Ciceronian age necessaries were, measured by our standards, cheap, certain luxuries were at least as dear as they are now.[4]

LAWS OF THE PERIOD 133–81 B. C.

The alleged law of C. Gracchus for reforming the Senate.—

According to the Epitome of Livy,[5] Gracchus passed a law that 600 knights should be added to the Senate, which then comprised only 300 members (*ut sescenti ex equite in curiam sublegerentur et, quia illis temporibus CCC tantum senatores erant, DC equites CCC senatoribus admiscerentur, id est, ut equester ordo bis tantum virium in senatu haberet*). Diodorus,[6] Velleius,[7] and Appian[8] state that Gracchus transferred the right of serving as jurors from the Senate to the knights ; Plutarch,[9] that he associated 300 knights with the existing 300 senators as jurors. Plutarch apparently means that these knights were incorporated in the Senate.[10]

Mommsen[11] accepted the essential part of the epitomizer's statement, but, having regard to the testimony of Plutarch, supposed that Gracchus intended to add 300, not 600, knights to the Senate. What

---

[1] Now (14. 4. 22), when one pound sterling is worth about 1,300 marks, Schultz's calculations need revision.
[2] *Dict. Nat. Biogr.*, iv, 1885, p. 82.
[3] *I* say ' in his own country ' advisedly. The difference between English and German standards may be gauged from one fact which Schultz emphasizes : the lowest income subject to income-tax in Germany immediately before the war was 900 marks (£45) ; in England £160.
[4] Many examples have been given in ch. ii. According to Suetonius (*Div. Iul.*, 50, 2), Caesar paid 6,000,000 sesterces (£60,000) for one pearl for Servilia!
[5] 60.   [6] xxxv, 25, 1.   [7] ii, 6, 3 ; 13, 2 ; 32, 3
[8] *B. C.*, i, 22, 92. Cf. Pliny, xxxiii, 2 (8), 34, and Tac., *Ann.*, xii, 60.
[9] *C. Gr.*, 5, 1 ; *Agidis et Cleomenis cum Gracchis comp.*, 2, 1.
[10] ὁ δὲ τριακοσίους τῶν ἱππέων προσκατέλεξεν αὐτοῖς οὖσι τριακοσίοις, &c.
[11] *Röm. Staatsr.*, iii, 1887, p. 530, n. 1.

is certain is that in consequence of the Gracchan legislation the knights remained for many years in sole possession of the courts.

Dr. Warde Fowler [1] says, ' It is perfectly plain that the Epitomator was struck by the story as he read it in Livy . . . and that for once in a way he took the trouble to make it perfectly clear that Livy . . . had described a scheme of reform which involved an increase of the Senate . . . I know of no other such sentence in these Epitomes, in which the writer says a thing three times over, so that there shall be no mistake about his meaning.' Then, remarking that Plutarch's ' somewhat similar account . . . must be taken on the whole as bearing out the statement of the Epitomator,' Dr. Warde Fowler accounts for the absence in the other authorities of any mention of the law which the epitomator describes by ' the very obvious reason that neither Romans nor Greeks troubled themselves much about what a statesman wished to do, but only about what was actually done '. Unhappily he weakens this explanation by suggesting that Gracchus did actually pass the law, though he adds the conjecture that in consequence of the defection of his supporter, the consul Fannius, he perceived that it would prove unworkable, and substituted the plan, described by Appian and others, of putting the knights in control of the courts.[2] But on this theory Livy and Plutarch ignored the plan!

Very different is the view of Strachan-Davidson.[3] Ridiculing ' the hopeless entanglement ' into which Mommsen was led by attempting to combine the statements of the epitomizer and of Plutarch, he rejects their ' stories ' as mutually contradictory, and prefers the statements of Appian and Velleius. He explains, however, that he is not throwing Livy overboard, ' but only some careless scribe . . . the same scribe . . . who says [*Epit.*, 97] of the lex Aurelia that it transferred the jury courts to the *equites* '—a statement which, I may

---

[1] *Eng. Hist. Rev.*, xx, 1905, pp. 426-31.

[2] Strachan-Davidson (*Problems of the Roman Crim. Law*, ii, 1912, pp. 82-4) reminds us that the author of the famous *lex Acilia* (C. G. Bruns, *Fontes iuris Rom.*[6,] 1893, pp. 55-73) found no list of jurors in existence, and entrusted the duty of forming one not to Gracchus, who, according to Plutarch (*C. Gr.*, 6, 1), named the jurors under his own law, but, annually, to the praetors. As, moreover, there is no hint in the *lex Acilia* that senators had already been excluded from the courts, he concludes that it was the first law that substituted knights for senators as jurors ; that Acilius was a colleague of Gracchus ; and that he proposed the law on his account, just as Aurelius Cotta proposed the *lex Aurelia* of 70 B.C. (see p. 164, *supra*) on account of Pompey. Dr. Warde Fowler (*op. cit.*, pp. 429-30) is substantially of the same opinion. The *lex Acilia* (22) mentions the *lex Rubria*, which authorized the foundation of the colony of Carthage, and was therefore later ; and if Strachan-Davidson is right in supposing that the Gracchan law directed against judicial corruption— *ne quis iudicio circumveniretur* (Cic., *Pro Cluent.*, 55, 151 ; 56, 154)—followed the lines of the *lex Acilia*, it was of course later still. Strachan-Davidson believes that this latter law and the *lex Acilia* constituted that transfer of the courts from senators to knights which Appian thought had been effected by a single law. Did they ? The *lex Acilia* was not a judiciary law, but concerned extortion ; and the judiciary law of Gracchus was passed in his first tribunate. As to the law *ne quis*, &c., see p. 23, n. 2.

[3] *Problems*, &c., ii, 76-8.

LAWS OF THE PERIOD 133-81 B. C.   347

remark, though it is not the whole truth, is perfectly true [1]—but he makes no attempt to refute Warde Fowler's defence of the epitomizer.[2] Dr. Hardy [3] concludes that 'while the epitomator and Plutarch are equally wrong in their description of the measure actually passed, the former . . . is giving a correct version of the original scheme, while the latter merely assumes that Gaius was carrying out the design of Tiberius.'

Von Stern,[4] remarking that there is no evidence that Gracchus passed more than one judiciary law, argues that the [partial] accuracy of the *Epitome* is confirmed by the Acilian law,[5] under which 450 knights were to be selected as jurors for the trial of charges of extortion, senators being expressly excluded. It follows, he insists, that for other trials senators were eligible. (This, I may parenthetically remark, is inconsistent with a well-known statement of Cicero.[6]) Further, von Stern continues, the Acilian law shows how far the epitomizer needs correction : the equestrian jurors did not become senators.[7] Doubtless Livy misunderstood his authority, which probably said that the 600 equestrian jurors were to have the same rights as the senators with whom they were associated. The privilege, entrusted to Gracchus,[8] of selecting jurors from the knights, would, if they had been made senators, have been an unheard-of innovation.

I need add nothing to what I have said in my narrative,[9] except that since the alleged bill, as described by the epitomizer and Plutarch, certainly did not take effect, it is hardly explicable that, if it was passed or even proposed, none of our authorities has recorded more than one. The one which is indisputable transferred judicial power from the senators to the knights.

The date of the Gracchan colonial law.—According to Plutarch,[10] Gracchus carried his law for establishing colonies after his re-election ; according to Livy [11] and Appian,[12] in his second tribunate, that is, after December 10, 123 B. C. Eutropius [13] and Orosius [14] wrongly ascribe the foundation of Carthage, Velleius [15] of all the colonies to 123.

Eduard Meyer [16] holds that Plutarch mentioned the re-election of

[1] See p. 165.
[2] Cf. W. Judeich's defence (*Hist. Zeitschr.*, cxi, 1913, p. 493). Citing Gellius (ix, 14, 16. Cf. Festus, p. 236), who refers to the speech which Gracchus made 'about bills which he had promulgated' (*de legibus a se promulgatis*), he concludes, rashly in my opinion, that Gracchus in the beginning of his first tribunate introduced simultaneously in one composite bill (*per saturam*) the corn law, the law (mentioned by Plutarch and Appian) relating to the *I*talians, the agrarian law, the judiciary law, and the law in favour of soldiers.
[3] *Journ. of Philol.*, xxxii, 1913, pp. 98-9.
[4] *Hermes*, lvi, 1921, pp. 281-3.   [5] §§ 12, 16, 21.
[6] *Apud* Ascon., ed. Clark, p. 79, ll. 3-6 (ed. Stangl, p. 61). Cf. *Verr.*, i, 13, 38.
[7] Cf. Judeich, *op. cit.*, p. 493, n. 1.   [8] According to Plutarch (6, 1).
[9] p. 25.   [10] *C. Gr.*, 8, 3.   [11] *Epit.*, 60.
[12] i, 23, 98.   [13] iv, 21.   [14] v, 12, 1.
[15] i, 15, 4.
[16] *Untersuch. zur Gesch. d. Gracchen*, 1894, p. 19, n. 4. Meyer, whose view has been generally accepted, observes in this note that Appian, when he assigned all the laws of Gracchus, except the corn law, to his second tribunate,

Gracchus where he ought to have mentioned his entry upon office. Kornemann [1] maintains that Plutarch's words, ' when he saw that the Senate was openly hostile and that Fannius was cooling in his friendship, he tried to conciliate the people by other laws ' (ἐπεὶ δὲ ἑώρα τὴν μὲν σύγκλητον ἐχθρὰν ἄντικρυς, ἀμβλὺν δὲ τῇ πρὸς αὐτὸν εὐνοίᾳ τὸν Φάννιον, αὖθις ἑτέροις νόμοις ἀπήρτησε τὸ πλῆθος [2]) are best explained on the assumption that when Fannius became estranged and Gracchus passed his colonial law, Fannius had already entered office. Accordingly he refers the law to the beginning of 122, and rejects the statements of Velleius, Eutropius, and Orosius. Meyer, on the other hand, so far accepts their testimony that he ascribes the law, though not its fulfilment, to 123.

The attempts of C. Gracchus to extend the franchise.—The measures by which Gaius Gracchus endeavoured to raise the status of the Latins and the Italian allies of Rome have occasioned much controversy. According to Velleius,[3] who ignores the Latins, he gave, or attempted to give, Roman citizenship to all Italians. Plutarch [4] says that in his first tribunate he carried a law for granting the same right of voting at elections to Italians as to Romans, and that after his re-election he granted full citizenship to the Latins ; [5] but in a later chapter [6] he remarks inconsistently that the Senate had been exasperated by his having bestowed equal rights of voting upon the Latins.[7] Plutarch states, further, that after Gracchus returned [in his second tribunate] from Carthage the consul Fannius expelled all persons who were not citizens from Rome.[8] Appian [9] relates that Gracchus in his second tribunate encouraged the Latins to claim Roman citizenship, and attempted to grant the suffrage to the Italian allies in the hope that they would help him to carry future laws,[10] which, except as regards the date, agrees with the first statement of Plutarch. He goes on to say that the Senate in alarm decreed that the consuls should exclude non-citizens from Rome while the recent bills were being voted upon ; but, unlike Plutarch, he assigns their exclusion to a time earlier than the departure of Gracchus for Africa.

Warde Fowler,[11] remarking that 'Drusus at the beginning of 122... carried a bill intended to please the Latins and make them dissatisfied confused his entry upon office with his re-election, which had occurred in midsummer (cf. App., i, 14, 58).

[1] *Klio*, Beih. i, 1903, p. 47.
[2] *C. Gr.*, 8, 3.   [3] ii, 6, 2.   [4] *C. Gr.*, 5, 1.
[5] *Ib.*, 8, 2. Plutarch is speaking loosely, for the bill was not passed.
[6] *Ib.*, 9, 2.
[7] It is of course conceivable that Plutarch by a slip of the pen wrote Λατίνοις for 'Ιταλιώταις.
[8] *Ib.*, 12, 1.   [9] *B. C.*, i, 23, 99.
[10] According to Strachan-Davidson (*Appian: Book I*, 1902, p. 26), Appian meant that only the restricted Latin right of voting in a single tribe was to be given to the Italians. Perhaps ; but his words—τῶν τε ἑτέρων συμμάχων, οἷς οὐκ ἐξῆν ψῆφον ἐν ταῖς 'Ρωμαίων χειροτονίαις φέρειν, ἐδίδου φέρειν ἀπὸ τοῦδε ἐπὶ τῷ ἔχειν καὶ τούσδε ἐν ταῖς χειροτονίαις τῶν νόμων αὐτῷ συντελοῦντας—seem to me consistent with the supposition that he meant the same as Plutarch.
[11] *Eng. Hist. Rev.*, 1905, pp. 423-5.

LAWS OF THE PERIOD 133-81 B. C. 349

with Gaius ',[1] infers that 'what he [Gracchus] had done so far concerned the Latins only '—in other words, that Plutarch is wrong in saying that he had already given the same right of voting to Italians as to Roman citizens. Appian, he continues, ' joins the proposals affecting Latins and Italians in a single sentence, in a way which strongly suggests two several enactments, about the details of which the writer was in a state of mental confusion.' Finally, he reminds us that the Latins ' could not record their votes except in a single tribe ', which, as there were thirty-five tribes, rendered their voting power insignificant : ' Remembering these facts ', he feels justified in correcting the original authorities. Plutarch, he believes, ' simply made the natural mistake of confusing Latins with Italians, and his account becomes quite intelligible if we can only substitute Latins for Italians in ch. 5 and Italians for Latins in ch. 8.' Accordingly he holds that Gracchus in his first tribunate was content ' to extend the Latin vote over the whole thirty-five tribes ', that is, to place the Latins as voters on an equality with Roman citizens ; that after he returned from Africa he ' brought forward a more sweeping measure ', proposing to give full Roman citizenship to all Italians, including Latins ; and that it was in prospect of the voting on this bill that Fannius was persuaded by the Senate to expel aliens from the city. He assures us [2] that Gracchus was ' a man of weight and good sense ', who would not have ' attempted what had signally failed two years before '—to enfranchise all Italians [3]—' before he had secured his ground and felt his way ' ; yet he insists that, after his comparatively mild proposal in favour of the Latins had been nullified by Drusus, he proposed a far ' more sweeping measure ' at a time when ' his influence was on the wane '. Warde Fowler himself refers [4] to the well-known fragment of a speech delivered by Fannius, in which he dissuaded the Romans from granting citizenship to the Latins.[5] Does it not confirm the evidence of Plutarch and Appian ?

Judeich,[6] though he accepts the testimony of Plutarch, holds with Kornemann and Warde Fowler that among the bills which Gracchus introduced after he returned from Carthage was one offering citizenship to all the Italian allies. He says that the date of this law is proved by the fact that Fannius, who was consul in 122, made a speech against Gracchus *de sociis et de nomine Latino*, and by the fact that the aliens were expelled from Rome. Doubtless the aliens were expelled after Gracchus returned from Carthage ; but there is no evidence that Fannius made his speech then, and I shall show that he made it before.

The only direct evidence that Gracchus proposed a bill for enfranchising the Italians is that of Velleius, and Greenidge [7] may perhaps be right in supposing that when he wrote that Gracchus *dabat civitatem omnibus Italicis*, he meant by *civitatem* simply Latin rights. More probably, I should say, he meant what he said. Let us consider

[1] See p. 27.   [2] *Op. cit.*, p. 423.   [3] See p. 21.
[4] *Op. cit.*, p. 213.   [5] See p. 27.   [6] *Hist. Zeitschr.*, cxi, 1913, p. 488.
[7] *Hist. of Rome*, i, 1904, p. 233, n. 3.

whether there is any reason to believe him. It is generally admitted that Appian was wrong in stating that the aliens were expelled before Gracchus went to Africa ;[1] but we need not distrust his statement that Drusus vetoed the bill for granting citizenship to the Latins. The speech of Fannius was directed against that bill, and we may infer from his extant words that when he spoke there was no question of extending the same boon to the Italians. Therefore, even if Gracchus did subsequently attempt to legislate on their behalf, it is clear that the speech was not delivered then, but in connexion with the measures of Drusus ; and it follows that Appian was wrong in linking the expulsion of aliens with the law which Drusus vetoed. But an important question remains :—can the expulsion of aliens be accounted for except on the assumption that a bill for granting citizenship to the Italians had just been introduced ? Certainly it can if Plutarch was right in saying that the suffrage had already been conferred upon them ; and anyhow the consul may have feared that aliens might succeed in passing themselves off as citizens or might create disturbances. Still, I do not deny that the expulsion may tend to confirm the assertion of Velleius, or that Kornemann, Warde Fowler, and Judeich may not unfairly appeal to it in support of their opinion.

[Von Stern[2] imagines that Gracchus, warned by the failure of Flaccus,[3] delayed dealing with the franchise until after he had carried his other measures, but that in his second tribunate, although his influence was waning, he felt obliged to introduce the bill which he had outlined in his programme. The purpose of that bill, von Stern maintains, was to confer citizenship not upon the Italians, but only upon the Latins ; but his explanation acquits Gracchus of the headstrong folly which Warde Fowler's view seemed to me to imply.]

The law of Drusus exempting Latins from the punishment of flogging.—We learn from Sallust[4] that one Turpilius was scourged and beheaded in the war with Jugurtha by order of Metellus, *nam is civis ex Latio erat*, which one would at first sight translate, ' for he was a [Roman] citizen from Latium ' ; and this rendering is supported by Appian,[5] who expressly says that Turpilius was a Roman citizen. Strachan-Davidson,[6] who cannot believe that Sallust would have said ' that a man was scourged . . . because he was a Roman ', thinks that *civis ex Latio* must mean ' simply a citizen of a Latin town and not of Rome '. Professor Stuart Jones,[7] condemning this translation as both forced and inconsistent with the statement of Appian, observes that *nam* ' does not . . . here possess the explanatory force which belongs to it in ordinary classical usage, but is employed in the elliptical construction (" I say this, for . . . ") so familiar in Latin comedy '. Mr. Caspari, who discussed the passage [8] before

[1] E. Meyer, *Untersuch. zur Gesch. d. Gracchen*, p. 19, n. 4.
[2] *Hermes*, 1921, pp. 287-9.
[3] See p. 21. [4] *Iug.*, 69, 4. [5] *Num.*, 3.
[6] *Problems of the Rom. Crim. Law*, i, 1912, pp. 115-9.
[7] *Eng. Hist. Rev.*, xxviii, 1913, pp. 141-3.
[8] *Class. Quart.*, v, 1911, pp. 115-6.

LAWS OF THE PERIOD 133-81 B. C. 351

the professor offered this explanation, takes *nam* in its ordinary sense, and accordingly concludes that under the law of Drusus Latins were exempt, while Roman citizens remained liable to scourging. That such an anomaly should have been suffered to continue, as Mr. Caspari thinks, for seventy years or more, is surely incredible. Appian, I believe, drew a false inference from the statement of Sallust. If Sallust had meant that Turpilius was a Roman citizen, the remark that he came from Latium would have been pointless unless he had acquired citizenship by holding a local magistracy. I therefore have little doubt that Strachan-Davidson was right,[1] and that the law of Drusus was no longer observed. If so, Sallust must have believed that in the time of Metellus, Roman citizens, even on military service, were exempt from scourging; but, legally or illegally, they were occasionally scourged to death in the last century of the Republic.[2]

The lex Thoria.—Mommsen [3] argued that the agrarian law passed by the tribune Spurius Thorius [4] belonged to 119 or 118 B. C., because Appian [5] says that the results of another agrarian law enacted not long afterwards became evident fifteen years after the legislation of [Tiberius] Gracchus (ὅθεν ἐσπάνιζον ἔτι μᾶλλον ὁμοῦ πολιτῶν τε καὶ στρατιωτῶν καὶ γῆς προσόδου καὶ διανομῶν καὶ νομῶν, πεντεκαίδεκα μάλιστα ἔτεσιν ἀπὸ τῆς Γράκχου νομοθεσίας, ἐπὶ δίκαις ἐν ἀργίᾳ

---

[1] The word *civis* is often used, for instance, by Caesar (*B. G.*, vii, 77, 3; *B. C.*, ii, 6, 1) in a sense other than that of a Roman citizen.

[2] R. Cagnat (Daremberg and Saglio, *Dict. des ant. grecques et rom.*, ii, 1896) says that about 108 B. C., in consequence of a *lex Porcia*, generals were deprived of the right of executing Roman citizens; but the existence of the said law is merely inferred from the relevant passage in Sallust and from a coin of P. Porcius Laeca, the interpretation of which is notoriously disputable. A. H. J. Greenidge (*Class. Rev.*, x, 1896, pp. 226-33; xi, 1897, pp. 437-40. Cf. his *Legal Procedure*, 1901, pp. 414-5) argued, rightly in my opinion, that Mommsen (*Röm. Staatsr.*, ii³, 1887, p. 117, n. 2) was wrong in holding that Cicero, when he said 'On military service there must be no appeal against the general' (*Militiae ab eo qui imperabit provocatio ne esto* [*De leg.*, iii, 3, 6]), was referring only to earlier times. Strachan-Davidson, however (*op. cit.*, pp. 118-9), remarks that 'a strong distinction was drawn between a regular scourging . . . (*virgis caedi*) and a caning', and points out that, according to Livy (*Epit.*, 57), Roman soldiers received the latter 'for an offence for which the ally is *virgis caesus*'. He admits (p. 121) that 'actual instances' of scourging are recorded (Cic., *Phil.*, iii, 6, 14; *Bell. Hisp.*, 27, 6), but he thinks that 'perhaps Crassus and Caesar', who executed men under their command (Plut., *Cras.*, 10, 3; Dio, xli, 35, 5), 'would have justified their action on the ground that soldiers abdicated their citizenship' by cowardice or mutiny. Cf. Julius Paulus, *Sent.*, v, 26, 2, and Greenidge, *Legal Procedure, l. c.* Strachan-Davidson remarks, further, that the Acilian law (78) 'in recounting the privileges granted, as a substitute for the Roman citizenship, to the ally who does not care to accept that citizenship . . . names *provocatio* [the right of appeal] without limit of place amongst them', and he infers that the citizenship 'guaranteed the same privilege'. But it may have been understood that service in the field was an exception, and the Acilian law was passed several years before the alleged *lex Porcia*.

[3] *Ber. . . . d. Königl. sächs. Gesellsch. d. Wiss.*, philol.-hist. Cl., ii, 1850, pp. 90-4.

[4] App., i, 27, 122. It is universally admitted that instead of (Σπούριος) Βόριος or Βούριος in the MSS. we should read Θόριος; for Appian was evidently referring to Spurius Thorius, whom Cicero mentions. [5] *Ib.*, § 124.

352   LAWS OF THE PERIOD 133–81 B. C.

γεγονότες). If the reader cannot extract any meaning from the last five words, he may console himself with the assurance that the editors are not less helpless, though the latest, P. Viereck, conjectures that ἐπὶ δίκαις means 'in consequence of litigation'; but Mommsen assumed that Appian was referring to the paralysis of the land commission appointed by Tiberius.[1] Kornemann,[2] however, objects that the commission did not become inactive until 129, when its judicial powers were abolished,[3] and holds, rightly in my opinion, that the obscure words are closely related to the passage where Appian[4] says that the commissioners found their occupation gone (ἐπὶ ἀργίας ἦσαν). Thus the date of the law in question would be 114 B. C. The words ἀπὸ τῆς Γράγχου νομοθεσίας, which may present a difficulty, must be understood in a loose or general sense—'from the time of the Gracchan legislation' [and of its proximate results]—for Kornemann's alternative suggestion, that they were interpolated, is not acceptable.[5]

But a passage in Cicero has suggested the question whether the *lex Thoria* was not really the last of the three laws which Appian successively describes. According to Appian, it enacted that no more public land should be allotted, but that the existing holders should be left in undisturbed possession on condition of their paying rent. Cicero[6] says that Spurius Thorius *agrum publicum vitiosa et inutili lege vectigali levavit*. Unbiased readers might translate, 'relieved the public land from rent by an invalid and useless law'; [7] but this translation applies to the third law, under which, as Appian[8] says, the rent imposed by the law of Thorius was abolished. Mommsen[9], however, insists that what Cicero meant was, 'by imposing a rent relieved the public land of an invalid and useless law.'

Dr. Hardy,[10] who accepts Mommsen's rendering, says that the third law, which was certainly identical with the well-known *lex agraria* of 111 B. C.,[11] 'did not relieve any public land from' rent. It is true, he admits, that the existing holders no longer paid a rent, but that was because their holdings had become private property. Besides, he continues, the alternative translations of Cicero's words

[1] See p. 19. [2] *Klio*, Beih. i, 1903, pp. 52–3.
[3] See p. 19. [4] i, 19, 80.
[5] Mr. Caspari (*Klio*, xiii, 1913, pp. 185-6, 191) goes further than Kornemann and argues that the *lex Thoria* was enacted in 112. His point is that as Gaius Gracchus revived his brother's agrarian law, 'it follows . . . that the land commission was revived . . . and continued its work during the two years of Gaius's supremacy in Rome', and therefore that, although it remained inactive for fifteen years [or rather, for two distinct periods amounting to fifteen years] from 129 B. C., its final extinction was deferred till 112. *I* am not impressed by this reasoning or by the conjectures with which Mr. Caspari reinforces it.
[6] *Brut.*, 36, 136.
[7] Strachan-Davidson's translation—'relieved the public land from an invalid and useless law which had subjected it to a rent-charge'—agrees with the one in the text as regards the substance of the law, though it transfers Cicero's criticism to the one that had preceded it.
[8] i, 27, 123. [9] *C. I. L.*, i, p. 77.
[10] *Journ. of Philol.*, xxxi, 1910, p. 281. Cf. xxxii, 1913, pp. 105–6.
[11] *C. I. L.*, i, No. 200 (=C. G. Bruns, *Fontes iur. Rom.*[6], 1893, pp. 74–90).

LAWS OF THE PERIOD 133-81 B.C.

imply that he regarded either Appian's second law or the law of 111 as mischievous. 'Not quite accurately,' he explains, Cicero represented that Thorius by requiring the payment of a rent practically repealed the useless law of Tiberius Gracchus : what he ought to have said was that he 'relieved the public land of a useless law by abolishing the land commission'.

Mr. Caspari cannot conceive what was the law which, according to Mommsen's translation, Thorius abolished. 'The only conceivable reference', he says (so far agreeing with Dr. Hardy), 'is to the land law of Tiberius Gracchus . . . but on what grounds could it be called *vitiosa* ?' (Surely on the ground that it was passed by unconstitutionally deposing a tribune.) Besides, 'Appian's mistakes . . . are so numerous that one blunder more or less does not weigh in the scale'.[1] Mr. Caspari proceeds to argue[2] that another passage,[3] in which Cicero mentions the *lex Thoria*—*cum ageretur de agris publicis et de lege Thoria et premeretur Lucilius ab iis qui a pecore eius d e p a s c i agros publicos dicerent*, &c.—proves that it was the law of 111, for we learn from the said passage that Lucilius [Hirrus] was charged with allowing his cattle to devour '*all* the public pasturage'. 'Now', says Mr. Caspari, 'there are . . . clauses [24–6] in the statute of 111 B.C. which distinctly assert the right of all . . . to graze cattle up to a certain number . . . and consequently forbid the monopolizing of public pastures[4] . . . the second law, so far as Appian describes it, contains nothing . . . concerning the use . . . of public domains ; and it is unlikely that it comprised, besides the provisions mentioned by Appian . . . other clauses on miscellaneous agrarian topics, for if such had been the case there would have been no subsequent need for a comprehensive regulating act like that of 111 B.C.' Dr. Hardy,[5] says Mr. Caspari, 'uses the passage in Cicero as evidence against the identification of the Lex Thoria [with the law of 111] on the ground that according to Cicero the Lex Thoria forbade the use of common pasture, whereas the act of 111 . . . permitted it. But all that is implied in Cicero's text is that the Lex Thoria prohibited the monopolization of common land (*depasci*).' Finally, Mr. Caspari has to meet Dr. Hardy's objection[6] that Cicero would not have been guilty of 'a reckless and ignorant disparagement' of so sound a law as that of 111, and he does so in the following way : 'if the Lex Rubria [which authorized the foundation of a colony at Carthage[7]] was *nefas*, so was the law of 111 . . . in so far as it confirmed the Lex Rubria'. This does not meet the objection that Cicero would not have called the law 'useless' ; but, accepting Strachan-Davidson's translation—'relieved the public land from an invalid and useless law which had subjected it to a rent-charge'—I think it may fairly

---

[1] *Klio*, 1913, pp. 188-90. [2] *Ib.*, 190-1. [3] *De orat.*, ii, 70, 184.
[4] E. Meyer (*Caesars Monarchie*², 1919, p. 67, n. 3), remarking that it is now generally admitted that the *lex Thoria* was identical with the *lex agraria* of 111, points out that Cicero's statement agrees with §§ 14-5 and 26 of the latter.
[5] *Journ. of Philol.*, 1913, p. 106.
[6] *Ib.*, p. 105. [7] See p. 28.

be argued that Cicero might have called Appian's second law useless, and that, as a rhetorician, he would not have hesitated to couple with *inutili* the epithet *vitiosa*. Since the law of 111 not only relieved the holders of land which had once been public from the obligation of paying rent, but also allowed every one to feed a certain number of cattle on the public pastures rent-free, and since what Cicero says of the law of Thorius agrees so far with the law of 111, I am convinced that the two were identical and that Appian here made one of his many chronological mistakes.

The judiciary law of Q. Servilius Caepio.—What was this law, and was it ever enacted? The only statements about its scope come from Tacitus, who says that it restored the control of the law courts to the Senate,[1] and from Obsequens[2] and Cassiodorus,[3] who agree that Servilius gave the right of serving conjointly on juries to the senators and the knights. Strachan-Davidson[4] rejects the evidence of Obsequens and Cassiodorus on the grounds that 'Cicero[5] tells us that the first time when senators and knights sat together on the bench was in 89 B. C.', and that it is incredible that if 300 knights had been added to the Senate, 'some trace of the increase would not have been found in ancient writers'; but if the bill was not actually passed, these arguments collapse. Strachan-Davidson, however, accepting the statement of Tacitus, infers that the law was passed, but was soon repealed. Greenidge,[6] on the other hand, thinks that Obsequens and Cassiodorus can be reconciled with Tacitus if we suppose that Caepio, like Gaius Gracchus,[7] intended to enlarge the Senate by admitting knights, and to give the control of the courts to the reconstituted body; but, like Strachan-Davidson, he believes that the law was carried. But Cicero's remark, quoted by Strachan-Davidson, that senators and knights sat together as jurors *for the first time* under the *lex Plautia* (89 B. C.), is precise; and since his authority is better than that of Obsequens, who, indeed, may only mean that Caepio introduced a bill, I conclude that that bill never became law.[8]

The laws of Saturninus.—1. A. H. J. Greenidge[9] assumes that the corn law was passed in the second tribunate of Saturninus. F. W. Robinson[10] rightly assigns it to the first, because the colleague of Caepio, who, as one of the urban quaestors, protested against the

---

[1] Cum Semproniis rogationibus equester ordo in possessione iudiciorum locaretur, aut rursum Serviliae leges senatui iudicia redderent (*Ann.*, xii, 60).
[2] 41 [101].
[3] *Chron.* (*Mon. Germ. hist.*, t. xi, vol. ii, 1894, p. 132).
[4] *Problems*, &c., ii, 80–1.   [5] Ascon. ed. Clark, p. 79, ll. 3–4.
[6] *Hist. of Rome*, 1904, pp. 477-82. Cf. A. H. J. Greenidge, *Legal Procedure*, &c., 1901, p. 435.
[7] If the *Epitome* of Livy (60) can be trusted. See pp. 345-7.
[8] This is also the opinion of Dr. Hardy (*Journ. of Philol.*, xxxii, 1913, pp. 102–4), who, while he agrees with Greenidge as to the purport of the bill, holds, unlike him, that in 106 B.C. 'there was a boom of popular and anti-senatorial feeling'.
[9] *Sources for Rom. Hist.*, 1903, p. 84.
[10] *Marius, Saturninus u. Glaucia*, 1912, pp. 63–4.

expense which the measure would entail,[1] was L. Calpurnius Piso,[2] whereas in 100 B. C. C. Saufeius was one of the two quaestors,[3] and also because in 104, the year before the first tribunate, there was a scarcity of corn.[4]

2. Cicero [5] says that Saturninus authorized Marius to create three Roman citizens in each colony. 'Obviously', says Strachan-Davidson,[6] 'no such petty matter would justify Appian's statement that "the allies had the chief advantage in the law"'. We must suppose, then, that other clauses opened avenues to enfranchisement wider than that of nomination by Marius.' May we suppose that the nomination was designed to make the colonies Roman, but that Italians were permitted to settle therein, who might ultimately become citizens?[7] As Professor J. S. Reid remarks,[8] when the Roman colonies of Parma and Mutina were founded [9] (183 B. C.), 'the franchise was conferred, under ... a law similar to that of Saturninus, on a few Latins'.[10]

R. Maschke,[11] followed by Robinson,[12] identified the *lex Bantina*, which Mommsen [13] regarded as a law, otherwise unknown, enacted between 133 and 118 B. C., with the agrarian law of Saturninus. I agree with Warde Fowler [14] that 'even if we accept the hypothesis ... the gain for the history of ... 100 is not very great'.

The judiciary law of the younger Drusus.—We read in the *Epitome* of Livy [15] that Drusus, in order to meet the desire of the Senate to regain control over the courts, carried a law by which judicial power was to be shared equally between the Senate and the equestrian order. Appian [16] says much the same, adding that as Drusus could not simply restore the power to the Senate, he proposed a bill for incorporating with the senators, who numbered barely 300, an equal number of knights. Velleius [17] states that the aim of Drusus was to restore the dignity of the Senate and to transfer the judicial power to it from the knights. Strachan-Davidson [18] prefers the authority of Velleius, and, citing the passage of Cicero,[19] which I have used in my narrative,[20] argues that the attack made by the consul Philippus on the Senate 'as it now is' (*illo senatu se rem publicam gerere non posse*) and its defence by Drusus and Lucius Crassus 'would have been absurd, if the very point of Drusus's

---

[1] Ps. Cic., *Ad Herenn.*, i, 12, 21.
[2] *Paulys Real-Ency.*, iii, 1387, No. 89.
[3] App., *B. C.*, i, 32, 143. Cf. Cic., *Pro Rab.*, 7, 20.
[4] Cic., *Pro Sest.*, 17, 39 ; *De har. resp.*, 20, 43.
[5] *Pro Balbo*, 21, 48. [6] *Appian : Book I*, 1902, p. 34.
[7] Cf. F. W. Robinson, *Marius*, &c., pp. 68-9.
[8] In his edition of *Pro Balbo*, p. 87. [9] Livy, xxxix, 55, 7.
[10] Cf. Cic., *Brut.*, 20, 79.
[11] *Zur Theorie u. Gesch. d. röm. Ackergesetze*, 1906, pp. 75-8, 92-108.
[12] *Op. cit.*, pp. 80-2. [13] *C. I. L.*, i, 45-7.
[14] *Eng. Hist. Rev.*, xxviii, 1913, p. 144.
[15] 71. [16] *B. C.*, i, 35, 157-8. [17] ii, 13, 1-2.
[18] *Problems*, &c., ii, 78-9.
[19] *De or.*, iii, *I*, 2. W. Strehl (*M. Livius Drusus*, 1887, pp. 2-6) argues on insufficient grounds that Cicero's account is not historical. [20] p. 44.

proposal had been to revolutionize the Senate by doubling its numbers'. Accordingly he rejects Appian's account 'as a mere antedating of what Sulla afterwards accomplished'. Dr. Hardy,[1] on the other hand, can see no inconsistency between Cicero and Appian. It was impossible, he argues, for Drusus to do more for the Senate, though he was its champion, than what Appian says that he did. For since there were only 300 senators, while under the *lex Acilia*[2] 450 jurors were required for the single court which tried charges of extortion, there was no way of restoring judicial power to the Senate except increasing its numbers. This argument is unanswerable, and if Strachan-Davidson had thought twice, he would have seen that what Velleius said is perfectly consistent with the statements of the *Epitome* and Appian; for if, as Appian says and the epitomizer evidently means, the judicial power was to be shared equally between the 300 existing senators and the 300 knights who were to be added to the Senate, that power was transferred, as Velleius says, from the equestrian order to the Senate.[3]

The Julian law (90 B. C.).—According to Appian,[4] the new citizens enrolled under the Julian law were distributed, not among the thirty-five existing tribes, lest their superior numbers should give them an advantage at the polls, but in ten new ones, in which they were to vote after the others. Velleius,[5] on the other hand, who gives the same reason for the arrangement which he describes, says that they were enrolled in eight tribes. A fragment of Sisenna[6] tells us that L. Calpurnius Piso added two new tribes; and if Velleius meant that the eight of which he speaks were new, Sisenna confirms his statement. Two years later, as we learn from Appian,[7] the Lucanians and Samnites received the citizenship, and were enrolled in the same tribes as the other Italians with the same object.

It seems to me that the authorities can be reconciled on the assumption that Velleius omitted to state that his eight tribes were new, and that Appian carelessly conveyed the impression that ten new tribes were created simultaneously, whereas in reality eight were created first and two added later. Mommsen[9] prefers Appian to Velleius, for he supposes the latter to mean that the new citizens were enrolled in eight old tribes, and in that case, as he remarks, the old citizens in those tribes would have been outvoted. But why accuse Velleius without evidence of a blunder aggravated by a self-evident contradiction?

[1] *Class. Rev.*, xxvii, 1913, pp. 262-3.
[2] C. G. Bruns, *Fontes*[6], &c., 1893, p. 60 (12), &c.
[3] Replying to Strachan-Davidson's argument about the Senate 'as it now is', Dr. Hardy says that the words of Philippus, as reported by Cicero, seem to him to imply that ' the idea of a new Senate was in the air. Philippus', he adds, ' may well have argued ... "The only part of the tribune's scheme for which anything can be said is the reconstitution of the Senate, for with the present Senate government is impossible ". On the other hand, Drusus would naturally defend the present Senate because his scheme of reconstruction implied not qualitative but quantitative incapacity'.
[4] *B. C.*, i, 49, 214.   [5] ii, 20, 2.   [6] H. Peter, *Hist. Rom. fr.*, p. 179. 17.
[7] i, 53, 231.   [8] *Röm. Staatsr.*, iii, 1887, p. 179, n. 1.

LAWS OF THE PERIOD 133-81 B. C.   357

Did Sulla absolutely deprive the tribunes of legislative power?—
The prevalent view is that Sulla, while he greatly weakened the
power of the tribunes, permitted them to propose bills which had
been approved by the Senate ; but a Swedish scholar, J. M. Sundén,
has argued that he did not leave them even this semblance of initiative. The direct evidence is for the most part vague. ' I heartily
approve Sulla ', wrote Cicero, ' for having by his legislation deprived
the tribunes of the power of doing mischief, while he left them free
to succour ' [persons who might appeal to them for protection]
(*vehementer Sullam probo, qui tribunis plebis sua lege iniuriae faciendae
potestatem ademerit, auxilii ferendi reliquerit* [1]). Caesar remarks that
' Sulla, although he reduced the power of the tribunes to a nullity,
nevertheless left their right of veto unimpaired ' (*Sullam nudata
omnibus rebus tribunicia potestate, tamen intercessionem liberam
reliquisse* [2]). The epitomizer of Livy [3] emphatically says that Sulla
not only weakened the power of the tribunes, but absolutely deprived
them of the right of legislation (*tribunorum potestatem minuit et omne
ius legum ferendarum ademit*) ; but the extreme conciseness of the
Epitome and the looseness with which the word *omnis* is sometimes
used must be taken into account. Velleius [4] observes that Sulla
left the tribunes the shadow without the substance of power (*imagi-
nem sine re reliquerat*) ; Suetonius [5] that he lessened the force of the
tribunician power (*tribuniciae potestatis, cuius vim Sulla diminuerat*).
Appian [6] states that the dictator reduced the power of the tribunes
to the extremity of weakness, indeed virtually abolished it (τὴν δὲ
τῶν δημάρχων ἀρχὴν ἴσα καὶ ἀνεῖλεν, ἀσθενεστάτην ἀποφήνας) ; but
in an earlier passage [7] he tells us that Sulla as consul (in 88 B. C.,
six years before his dictatorship) enacted that no bill should be
brought before the people which had not been first submitted to the
Senate. Mommsen [8] relies partly upon this passage, but still more
upon a well-known law, the *lex Antonia de Termessibus*,[9] ' which was
proposed by the tribunes with the approval of the Senate ' (. . .
tr[ibuni] pl[ebei] de s[enatus] s[ententia] plebem *ioure rogaverunt*),
certainly during the last Mithradatic War after 72 B. C. and, as he
argues, in 71, that is before the tribunician power was restored by
Pompey. If the date is correct, Mommsen's view must be accepted.
But Sundén tried to prove that it was wrong.

Mommsen's date rests upon the fact that only those persons who
had been citizens of Termessus before the 1st of April, 682 (72 B. C.)
were to be admitted to the privileges of the law ; and he contends
that as this clause was evidently intended to prevent aliens from
entering the town in the hope of enjoying those privileges, the law
was passed not long afterwards. The argument is obviously inconclusive ; and Sundén,[10] gives a strong reason for rejecting it. We

[1] *De leg.*, iii, 9, 22.   [2] *B. C.*, i, 7, 3. See vol. ii, p. 330.   [3] 89.
[4] ii, 30, 4.   [5] *Div. Iul.*, 5.   [6] *B. C.*, i, 100, 467.   [7] *Ib.*, 59, 266.
[8] *C. I. L.*, i, p. 115. Cf. *Zeitschr. f. d. Alterthumswiss.*, iv, 1846, col. 107.
[9] *C. I. L.*, i, p. 114 (=H. Dessau, *Inscr. Lat.*, 38).
[10] *De tribunicia potestate a L. Sulla imminuta* (printed in *Skrifter utgifna af
K. Humanist. Vetenskapsamfundet i Upsala*, v, 1897, pp. 14-5).

358   LAWS OF THE PERIOD 133-81 B. C.

learn from an inscription [1] that an individual, whose name is uncertain, repaired a road in conjunction with nine colleagues, whose names are given. Three of the names are identical with those of three tribunes who are mentioned as having proposed the *lex Antonia de Termessibus*; and accordingly Mommsen concluded that the other seven were also tribunes, and therefore that the inscription belongs to the same year as the law. But, says Sundén, that being the case, the law cannot have been passed in 71 B. C.; for the name of Palicanus, who was unquestionably a tribune in that year, is absent. This argument compels assent; but Sundén failed to prove that the law was not passed in 70 B. C. Antonius is therein called *C. Antonius M. f.* (= *Marci filius*) : accordingly scholars agree that he was the Gaius Antonius who was praetor in 66 B. C. and Cicero's colleague in the consulship in 63. Now Mommsen,[2] pointing out that in 16 of 22 instances recorded for the fifty years from 217 to 167 there was an interval of four years between the tenure by the same individual of the tribuneship and the praetorship, infers that that interval was usual; and Ludwig Holzapfel concludes that the *lex de Termessibus* was passed not later than 70 B. C.[3] The conclusion is not more than probable ; but Sundén, who himself suggests [4] that the law belonged to that year, apparently forgot that in that case it may have preceded the measure by which Pompey restored the tribunician power.

But what about the law authorizing the return of the partisans of Lepidus (*lex Plotia de reditu Lepidanorum*), which is commonly assigned to 73 B. C. ? I have discussed its date elsewhere.[5] Sundén,[6] remarking that it is not expressly stated to have been proposed by a tribune, and finding it hardly credible that the partisans of Lepidus should have been repatriated before Pompey returned to Rome from the Sertorian War, concludes that the law was most probably passed in the consulship of Pompey, after the tribunician power had been restored, and that the only certain inference to be drawn from the passage in which Suetonius [7] mentions it is that it was passed before Caesar's quaestorship, that is before 68 or 69 B. C. To me it seems not at all incredible that the law should have been passed as a concession to popular sentiment in 73, when the tribune Licinius Macer was clamouring for reform and when the Senate cheapened the price of corn to appease popular discontent ; [8] but even if Sundén could prove that no tribune proposed a law in the ten years that followed Sulla's dictatorship, it would not necessarily follow that Sulla absolutely forbade tribunes to legislate : for it might have happened that no tribune could obtain the consent of the Senate to any law which he wished to propose.[9] One asks oneself whether Sulla, whose

---

[1] *C. I. L.*, i, pp. 171-2 (= Dessau, 5800).
[2] *Röm. Staatsr.*, i³, 1887, p. 552 and n. 3.
[3] *Berl. philol. Woch.*, 1898, col. 751.   [4] *Op. cit.*, p. 14.
[5] See pp. 385-6.   [6] *Op. cit.*, p. 20. Cf. p. 21.
[7] *Div. Iul.*, 5.   [8] See p. 154
[9] Sundén (*op. cit.*, p. 9), anticipating this argument, replies that even the

rigour was not headstrong but calculated and moderate, would have abolished the legislative power of the tribunes when he could gain his object better by leaving them the semblance of power without the reality ; and when Cicero heartily approves Sulla's policy and at the same time says that he does not like to blame Pompey for having reversed it, but cannot praise him (*Pompeiumque nostrum ceteris rebus omnibus semper amplissimis summisque ecfero laudibus, de tribunicia potestate taceo ; nec enim reprehendere libet nec laudare possum* [1]), I am inclined to infer that so cautious a man would hardly have ventured to imply that Sulla had been right in *annihilating* the tribunician power. But it is to Appian that Sundén and those whom he criticizes alike turn. Appian, as we have seen, states that Sulla in his first consulship enacted that no bill should be brought before *the people* (ἐς τὸν δῆμον, not ἐς τὸ πλῆθος, the plebs) until it had first been approved by the Senate ; and he remarks that this was an old constitutional usage, which had for some time been violated (νενομισμένον οὕτω καὶ πάλαι, παραλελυμένον δ' ἐκ πολλοῦ)[2]. Sulla, he continues, enacted further that the elections should thenceforth be held not by tribes but by centuries, in accordance with the classification of King Servius Tullius (καὶ τὰς χειροτονίας μὴ κατὰ φυλὰς ἀλλὰ κατὰ λόχους, ὡς Τύλλιος βασιλεὺς ἔταξε, γίγνεσθαι) : but he proceeds to explain that Sulla believed that if by these two laws the assent of the Senate were required before a law could be proposed to the *plebs* (ἐς τὸ πλῆθος) and if the elections were in the hands not of the poor and turbulent but of the well-to-do and well-disposed, civil strife would be avoided. He adds that Sulla strengthened the Senate by the addition of 300 members selected from the aristocracy.

Now Appian,[3] in describing the measures which Sulla passed seven years later as dictator, says that he increased the Senate by the addition of 300 members chosen from the knights ; and since in describing Sulla's consular measures he says that ' in many other ways he curtailed the power of the tribunes ' (πολλά τε ἄλλα τῆς τῶν δημάρχων ἀρχῆς . . . περιελόντες), it has been inferred that he wrongly ascribed to the earlier year the events of the later.[4] If this view is right (Dr. Hardy[5] has, I think, confuted it), Sundén is wrong : Sulla did not absolutely deprive the tribunes of the right of legislation. Sundén, however, holds [6] that the law which required the

consuls could not legislate without the previous sanction of the Senate. Manifestly this, even if it were true, would be no answer.
[1] *De leg.*, iii, 9, 22.
[2] The true explanation of these words has, *I* think, been given by Mr. Strachan-Davidson (*Eng. Hist. Rev.*, i, 1886, p. 213). He believes that Appian had in mind the ' customary and constitutional right ' which the Senate had established during the period of the great wars, ' to be consulted before any magistrate proposed a measure for the acceptance either of the *populus* or the *plebs* ', a usage on which Tiberius Gracchus had trampled (παραλελυμένον δ' ἐκ πολλοῦ), and correctly denoted by the word νενομισμένον, which does not connote any *legal* disability. [3] i, 100, 468.
[4] See J. L. Strachan-Davidson's *Appian, Book I*, 1902, p. 62.
[5] *Journ. Rom. Studies*, vi, 1916, pp. 59-62. [6] *Op. cit.*, p. 35.

previous assent of the Senate was passed in 88, and the other, regulating the elections, which, he maintains, Sulla would not have been strong enough to carry in 88, in 81. Its object, he urges,[1] was almost certainly to deprive the assemblies of the *plebs*, over which the tribunes presided, of the power of making laws. But, he complains, this explanation would not suit those who hold that Sulla left the tribunes some power of legislating ; and accordingly they maintain that the law which required that no bill should be submitted to the people unless it had received the assent of the Senate concerned the tribunes only and not the higher magistrates ; but this will not do, for since the second law can only refer to the assemblies of the *plebs*, the first cannot refer *only* to the tribunes of the *plebs*.[2]

Has Sundén succeeded in grasping Appian's meaning ? I think not. To begin with, it is clear that, rightly or wrongly, Appian regarded the two laws as parts of one scheme ; for he represents Sulla as contemplating the effect which they were jointly to produce. Secondly, although the words ἐσηγοῦντό τε μηδὲν ἔτι ἀπροβούλευτον ἐς τὸν δῆμον ἐσφέρεσθαι, taken by themselves, undoubtedly mean, as Sundén says, that no magistrate, high or low, might propose any measure without the approval of the Senate either to the people as a whole (*populus*) or to the *plebs*, there is, as Mr. Strachan-Davidson[3] remarks, ' no trace in the years following Sulla's restoration of any such legal limitations on the consuls or praetors ' ; and (though he has not noticed the point) Appian in the very next sentence substitutes ἐς τὸ πλῆθος for ἐς τὸν δῆμον. This law, then, whether it was passed in 88 or in 81, applied to the tribunes alone and restricted, but did not absolutely destroy their legislative power.[4]

THE POPULATION OF ROME

Various attempts have been made by writers who agreed in discarding earlier calculations to estimate the population of Rome ;[5] but as the arguments relate mainly to various periods of the Empire, we may ignore them except in so far as they bear, directly or indirectly, upon the time of Caesar. The starting-point of the inquiry is the statement of Suetonius[6] that the recipients of free corn in

---

[1] *Op. cit.*, p. 24.   [2] *Ib.*, p. 28.   [3] *Appian: Book I*, p. 62.
[4] When Appian says that ' the votes should be given not by tribes but by centuries ', he seems to mean that all magistrates were to be elected in the Comitia Centuriata, not in the Comitia Tributa ; but this is untrue (Cic., *Fam.*, vii, 30, 1). Mommsen, however (*Röm. Staatsr.*, iii, 1887, p. 270, n. 1), infers from the words ' in accordance with the classification of King Tullius ' that what Appian meant was simply that Sulla abolished the division of the Comitia Centuriata according to tribes, which existed in 211 B.C. (Livy, xxvi, 22, 12-3), and restored the old arrangement. *I* am disposed to agree with Strachan-Davidson, who thinks that ' Appian has only a very confused idea of the measure which he attempts to describe ', and doubts whether Mommsen's explanation can be safely accepted.
[5] See J. Marquardt, *Röm. Staatsverw.*, ii², 1884, pp. 120-5.
[6] *Div. Iul.*, 41, 3.

46 B.C. numbered 320,000. It is certain that this number comprised only males. Beloch,[1] however, maintains that it included not only citizens resident in Rome, but also those who lived within a radius of 20 or 30 miles and who would have found it worth while to fetch their monthly ration; and as Suetonius [2] says that Augustus distributed largesses to boys under ten, although only those above that age had hitherto received them, he infers that it was the inferior limit for those entitled to receive free corn before Caesar reduced the number of participants. Women, he continues, were far less numerous than men, because they had not the motive—the desire to obtain food for nothing—which attracted needy immigrants to the city; and it may be added that Dio [3] expressly affirms their numerical inferiority. The number of children, then, Beloch argues, must have been comparatively small. Even in modern Rome, when he was writing, there were on an average only 796 females to 1,000 males, and of 1,000 males only 137 were boys under ten. On the basis of these figures, the free Roman population in 46 B.C. would have been 320,000 males over ten, 50,900 boys under ten, and 295,200 females—in all 666,100. This proportion of females, however, Beloch, for the reason already given, thinks too large: accordingly he conjectures that in 5 B.C., when 320,000 males received the bounty of Augustus,[4] the entire free Roman population was not more than half a million. He does not attempt to fix the number for 46 B.C.; but, as he holds that the only boys included in the 320,000 of that year were over ten, he would of course have offered a somewhat higher estimate. He next proceeded to number the resident aliens and the slaves, and though his calculations were only made for the year 5 B.C., he would not perhaps have altered them materially for the earlier date. In default of direct evidence he examined sepulchral inscriptions, and, finding that those in Latin occurred in thousands while those of Greeks were only hundreds, he provisionally computed the foreign element as 60,000 or 70,000. Again, remarking that Rome was not a manufacturing town, he argues that the proportion of industrial slaves was much smaller than in Pergamum, where in the second century of our era slaves of all sorts formed one-third of the inhabitants, but that the proportion of domestic slaves must have been greater. Accordingly he conjectures that in 5 B.C. there were about 280,000 slaves, and therefore that the whole population amounted to 850,000.

But his calculations are vitiated by two serious mistakes. The fanciful conjecture that suburban residents shared in the doles of corn is refuted not only by the statement of Appian [5] that only the poor in the city received rations, but also by Augustus, who said that his gifts were bestowed upon the urban populace.[6] Moreover,

---

[1] *D. Bevölkerung d. griech.-röm. Welt*, 1886, p. 400.
[2] *Aug.*, 41, 2.
[3] liv, 16.
[4] *Res gestae divi Augusti* ², 1883, ed. Th. Mommsen, 3, 15.
[5] *B. C.*, ii, 120, 506.
[6] *Res gestae*, &c., 3, 15-6. Cf. L. Friedlaender, *Darstell. aus d. Sittengesch. Roms*, i⁸, p. 71.

only males who possessed the franchise, not boys under age, were entitled to free corn.¹ The question, however, remains whether persons who were not citizens had contrived before 46 B.C. to get their names entered on the list of recipients; and that this was the case is clearly implied by Dio.² What, then, becomes of Beloch's estimate of the foreign population?

Calculations which depend largely upon guesswork are not satisfactory; but Beloch arrives at the same result by another method. By measuring on Kiepert's map he finds that the area of Rome within the wall called after Aurelian was 1,230 hectares, or 3,040 acres, and he says that in the most densely peopled quarters there were in 1881 as many as 969 inhabitants to a hectare. In the time of Augustus, he observes, the proportion must have been greater, but not so great as in Naples, the most populous quarter of which in 1881 had 1,470 inhabitants to a hectare. Why not so great? Because Beloch's results would then refuse to coincide? Striking the average which suits his purpose between the fashionable quarters and the slums, he reaches the precise result to which his former method led.³ Ludwig Friedlaender, on the other hand, insists that, considering the narrowness of the streets and the height of the tenements occupied by the poor, the density of the population must have been greater than in modern Naples as a whole, and accordingly, rejecting Beloch's average—650 to the hectare—as too low, he concludes that the inhabitants of Rome in 5 B.C. numbered about 1,000,000—how much more or less he judiciously declines to say.⁴

One more clue remains. Pseudo-Victor⁵ relates that under Augustus Egypt sent yearly 20,000,000 *modii* of corn to Rome; and Friedlaender⁶ gives good reasons for accepting this statement. Marquardt,⁷ remarking that in the time of Josephus⁸ Egypt supplied Rome for four months in the year, and assuming that the same proportion holds good for the Augustan period, concluded that Rome then received 60,000,000 *modii* a year. Friedlaender⁹ reminds us that in the time of the elder Cato¹⁰ slaves received from 4 to 4½ *modii* a month, and, as women and children would eat less, he supposes that the average monthly consumption was 4 *modii*, which implies a population of 1,250,000. But, granting that the total import was 60,000,000, the question arises whether a considerable proportion was not destined for country towns.¹¹ Moreover, an early commentator on Lucan, whose information may

---

¹ O. Hirschfeld (*Philol.*, xxix, 1870, p. 6). Cf. Cic., *Tusc.*, iii, 20, 48.
² xliii, 21, 4.
³ *Op. cit.*, pp. 404–11. In a later paper (*Jahrb. f. Nationalökon. u. Statistik*, 3. Folge, xiii, 1897, p. 329) Beloch computed that the population under Augustus was about 1,000,000—perhaps 100,000 or 200,000 less.
⁴ *Op. cit.*, pp. 64, 67.   ⁵ *Epit. de Caes.*, 1, 6.
⁶ *Op. cit.*, pp. 65–6.   ⁷ *Op. cit.*, p. 126, n. 6.
⁸ *Bell. Iud.*, ii, 16, 4.   ⁹ *Op. cit.*, pp. 66–7.
¹⁰ *De agri cult.*, 56. In 78 B.C. the monthly allowance in Rome was 5 *modii* (Sall., *Hist.* ed. B. Maurenbrecher, i, 55, 11; Licinianus, ed. M. Flemisch, p. 34, ll. 3–5).
¹¹ See p. 107.

or may not be trustworthy, affirmed that the daily consumption of the capital was no more than 80,000, which, on Friedlaender's reckoning, would imply a population of 608,000.
But this estimate is certainly too low. Considering that in Caesar's time there were at least 320,000 *adult* males in Rome, besides those who were too prosperous or too proud to accept charity, and also women, children of both sexes, a considerable number of aliens, and a host of slaves, it seems not unreasonable to conclude that the population amounted at least to the lowest estimate—not much less than a million.[1]

THE ATTEMPTED REVOLUTION OF LEPIDUS

Sallust's report of the speech of Lepidus.—The extant speech attributed to Lepidus,[2] however closely it may represent the substance of what he said, was obviously composed by Sallust.[3] One would gather from it that Lepidus made the speech when he was actually consul,[4] and that Sulla, against whom he inveighed, was still dictator.[5] But Lepidus was consul in 78 B.C., and it appears from the testimony of Plutarch,[6] Appian,[7] and Orosius[8] that Sulla abdicated in 79. Unless Sallust, when he put into the mouth of Lepidus the concluding words, ' Come, Quirites, and ... follow your consul Marcus Aemilius to recover freedom ', meant that Lepidus was only consul designate, we must assume either that he made a gross blunder, or that in representing Sulla as still dictator he sacrificed truth to rhetorical effect. The latter alternative is the more probable ; and it would appear from the first extant fragment of Sallust's history[9] that he began by describing the consulship of Lepidus and Catulus.[10]

The corn laws of 78 and 73 B. C.—The corn law passed by Lepidus

---

[1] The latest estimate, so far as I can ascertain, is that of G. Cardinali (E. de Ruggiero, *Dizionario epigr. d. antichi*, iii, 1904, pp. 310-1),—at least 1,000,000.
[2] Sall., i, 55 (ed. B. Maurenbrecher).
[3] Cf. H. S. von Carolsfeld, *Ueber die Reden u. Briefe bei Sallust*, 1888, p. 59.
[4] § 27,—adeste, Quirites, et . . . M. Aemilium consulem . . . sequimini, &c.
[5] § 7,—Agundum . . . est, Quirites . . . nisi forte speratis taedium iam aut pudorem tyrannidis Sullae esse, &c.
[6] *Sulla*, 34, 6-7.   [7] *B. C.*, i, 103, 478.   [8] v, 22, 1.
[9] Res populi Romani M. Lepido Q. Catulo consulibus ac deinde militiae et domi gestas composui. Cf. i, 54.
[10] J. Francke (*Jahrb. f. class. Philol.*, cxlvii, 1893, pp. 49-50) doubts whether Lepidus would have dared to make this speech while Sulla was alive, and remarks that Licinianus does not say that he attempted reform before Sulla died. It would be rash, however, to deny that he spoke on the subject earlier ; and Florus (ii, 11, 1), Plutarch (*Pomp.*, 16, 1), and Appian (*B. C.*, i, 107, 501), to whom Francke appeals, are alike inconclusive. Appian indeed (105, 491) says that Sulla had hardly resigned when discord broke out afresh, and that Lepidus began to quarrel with his colleague immediately after he took office, from which, he adds, it was evident that trouble was impending ; and Sulla was at that time alive.

has occasioned controversy. Licinianus[1] says that he 'carried a corn law with no opposition, to the effect that five *modii* [about 4¾ pecks] should be given to the people' [monthly] (⟨*le*⟩*gem frumentari*⟨*am*⟩ *nullo resistente* ⟨*tuta*⟩*tus est, ut annon*⟨*ae*⟩ *quinque modii popu*⟨*lo*⟩ ⟨*da*⟩*rentur*). Mommsen[2] infers that the corn law passed in 73 B. C. by the consuls Marcus Terentius Lucullus and Gaius Cassius Varus,[3] to which Sallust[4] refers, 'did not first re-establish the [grant of] five *modii*, but only secured the distribution of grain by regulating the purchases of Sicilian corn' : in other words, he holds that the law of Lepidus was still in force in 73. He maintains that the corn law of Gaius Gracchus must have been modified, in the sense that corn was distributed to a minority only of the Roman populace, because we learn from Cicero[5] that in 70 the monthly allowance amounted to only 198,000 *modii*, that is, that the recipients numbered not much more than 40,000 ; and this alteration, he insists, must have been adopted in the law of Lepidus.

J. Francke,[6] commenting on Mommsen's argument, points out that, according to Licinianus, five *modii* of corn were to be distributed [monthly] to 'the people'—that is to every citizen—not to a fraction of the people. It would have been extremely foolish of Lepidus to make an invidious distinction ; for it was his interest to engage the whole people on his side instead of offending the majority. In the passage of Sallust—an extract from the speech which he attributes to the tribune Macer—there is no mention of Lepidus as the author of the law : on the contrary, Macer violently inveighed against the nobles who by an ill-considered law had fancied that they could satisfy the populace—*Nisi forte repentina ista frumentaria lege munia vestra pensantur ; qua tamen quinis modiis libertatem omnium aestimavere, qui profecto non amplius possunt alimentis carceris.* The expression *repentina lex*—a law suddenly proposed— does not fit the law which Lepidus had passed in 78 B. C. Besides, Philippus in the contemporary speech ascribed to him by Sallust[7] referred to the corn law passed by Lepidus with the words, 'I saw that the state was being ruined by lavish distributions' (*largitionibus rem publicam lacerari videbam*) : this criticism could hardly have been made if Lepidus had dangled his bait not before the whole people but only a minority.[8] Finally, says Francke, it is not credible that the Senate, after the rebellion of Lepidus had been crushed, would have been so afraid of the populace as to let his law remain in force when it was dangerous to them. Francke therefore conjectures with good reason that the law did not long survive its author.

[1] The text which I follow is that of M. Flemisch.
[2] *Röm. Gesch.*, iii⁸, 1889, p. 25, n. **. (Eng. tr., iv, 1908, p. 289, n. 1).
[3] See pp. 154, 384–5.   [4] iii, 48, 19.
[5] *Verr.*, iii, 30, 72.
[6] *Jahrb. f. class. Philol.*, cxlvii, 1893, p. 53.   [7] i, 77, 6.
[8] Prof. J. S. Reid (*Journ. Rom. Studies*, v, 1915, p. 223) supposes that Lepidus reinstated 'the scheme of Gracchus', under which corn was to be sold at an 'artificially reduced price'.

ATTEMPTED REVOLUTION OF LEPIDUS

The rebellion of Lepidus.—The original records of the period between the death of Sulla and the end of the last Mithradatic War leave much to be desired, but those of the rebellion of Lepidus are perhaps the worst : ' it is absolutely impossible ', wrote George Long,[1] ' to construct any clear narrative from the miserable fragments that remain '. Long was too easily discouraged ; but I have found the task so difficult that it is not enough to support my narrative by mere references : I must place the evidence before the reader and ask him to join with me in working out the problem. In the following conspectus the *Epitome* of Livy (90), which gives no independent information, is ignored.

SALLUST[2]	EXUPERANTIUS[3]	LICINIANUS[4]
i, 55 (*Oratio Lepidi*), 18. Lepidus complains that he is taunted with having acquired property which had belonged to men proscribed by Sulla. He was intimidated into purchasing the property ; but he intends to restore it to the former owners (see Maurenbrecher's note in fasc. ii, p. 25).	c. 6. *Exuperantius begins by stating that Lepidus was defeated in a battle by Catulus, and then gives a summary of what led to this result and what followed it*.—Assembling those who had been dispossessed by Sulla, Lepidus raised an army, promising, in the event of victory, to restore their estates ; he also ingratiated himself with the populace by private largesses and by grants bestowed in the name of the Government. In Etruria he achieved some success ; but Pompey, returning from Gaul, so utterly overthrew his troops, who were retreating in disorder [evidently after the defeat which they had suffered from Catulus], that he fled to Sardinia, intending to cut off the supplies [of corn] which the Romans received thence and to recruit and refit his army. The Governor,[5]	Ed. M. Flemisch, p. 33, l. 14–p. 35, l. 10. When the tribunes met the consuls in order to restore the tribunician power, Lepidus demurred ; and when he declared in the assembly that the restoration was impolitic the majority assented. Lepidus supported a corn law, to the effect that five *modii* should be granted monthly to the people [i. e. to each citizen], and made many other promises, undertaking to repatriate exiles, to rescind the enactments of Sulla, and to restore to their former owners the lands which Sulla had assigned to his veterans. The Faesulans attacked the strongholds of the veterans and, after killing many of them, restored the lands. The consuls [Lepidus and Catulus] with an army which had been assigned to them marched in obedience
i, 65. A great number of men had assembled, who had been evicted from their estates [by Sulla] or outlawed.		
i, 66. Lepidus and Catulus with the armies assigned to them were to set out for Etruria as soon as possible.		
i, 67. The Etruscans and their sympathizers, thinking that they had secured a leader [Lepidus], originated the war with enthusiasm.		
i, 69. Etruria with Lepidus was suspected of having planned a rebellion.		
i, 77 (*Oratio Philippi*), 3. The Senate does not realize that by its inaction its own		

---

[1] *Decline of the Roman Republic*, ii, 1866, p. 438.
[2] The references are given according to the edition of B. Maurenbrecher (1891-3).
[3] An epitomizer of Sallust, whose fragments his narrative supplements.
[4] Fragments only remain of the chronicle which Licinianus based upon the *Histories* of Sallust and perhaps also the narratives of Livy and others (see O. Dieckmann, *De Gr. Liciniani fontibus*, 1896, pp. 12 ff., especially 58-71, 86-8).
[5] Cf. Ascon. ed. Clark, p. 18, l. 20 ; p. 19, ll. 1-2 (ed. Stangl, p. 22).

ATTEMPTED REVOLUTION OF LEPIDUS

SALLUST

dignity is impaired and Lepidus emboldened.

§ 6. Philippus, seeing that Etruria was plotting and that the proscribed were being recalled and the state ruined by lavish distributions [of corn], was from the outset in favour of a vigorous policy: Lepidus had raised troops on his own initiative to crush liberty.

§ 7. At first Lepidus was a mere brigand, backed by a few cutthroats: now he is a proconsul, and all the scum are flocking to join him.

§ 10. Are the Senate going to wait till Lepidus again marches upon Rome?

§ 14. Lepidus insists that confiscated property should be restored; yet he retains what he himself acquired. Moreover, he says that the tribunician power is to be restored.

§ 15. Lepidus is aiming at a second consulship.

§ 17. How long is the Senate going to hesitate? The more anxious they show themselves for peace, the more Lepidus will see that they are afraid of him.

§ 21. Since Lepidus is leading the army which he has raised without sanction against Rome, Philippus moves that the interrex Appius Claudius, Catulus, and others should provide for the public safety.

[The speech of Philippus was delivered, as we may infer from §§ 7, 21, early in 77 B. C.]

EXUPERANTIUS

however, encountered him in a series of combats; he was repulsed by the garrisons which he attacked, and at last fell ill and died.[1] [The decisive battle, in which Pompey defeated Lepidus, was fought, as we may gather from Sallust,[2] near Cosa, a Tuscan port, from which Lepidus sailed for Sardinia. How he contrived to embark a beaten army, the remnant of which, after his death, is said to have amounted to 53 cohorts[3] (more than 5 legions), and how he procured ships, is one of the puzzles of Roman history.]

LICINIANUS

to orders into Etruria Lepidus withdrew his army into the mountains. As the preservation of peace was doubtful, the Senate bound [Lepidus and Catulus] by solemn oaths not to fight. When Lepidus was approaching Rome the Senate dispatched an envoy [to negotiate].

---

[1] Despite the agreement of Exuperantius, Florus, Plutarch, and Appian, Prof. M. E. Deutsch (*Univ. Calif. Publications Class. Philol.*, v, 1918, pp. 59-68) argues, on unsubstantial grounds, that Lepidus met a violent end. What does it matter?

[2] i, 82.

[3] Plut., *Sert.*, 15, 2.

ATTEMPTED REVOLUTION OF LEPIDUS

FLORUS, ii.11.	PLUTARCH, Pomp., 16.	APPIAN, B. C., i, 107.	OROSIUS, v, 22.
§ 2. Lepidus attempted to rescind the enactments of Sulla; (§ 3) recalled the survivors of the proscribed; and restored to them their confiscated property. § 5. After delivering seditious harangues he started for Etruria, raised troops there, and marched on Rome; but (§ 6) Catulus and Pompey had occupied the Janiculum and the Mulvian bridge; (§ 7) he was driven back, and, having been declared by the Senate a public enemy, retreated with heavy loss to Etruria, and thence to Sardinia, where he perished from disease and chagrin.	§ 1. Immediately after the death of Sulla Lepidus took up arms, collecting and reanimating the survivors of the Marian party. Catulus was considered more fit for civil than for military duty, and the crisis demanded the aid of Pompey. Pompey unhesitatingly joined the *optimates* and was appointed to command against Lepidus, who had already stirred up many parts of *I*taly and held Cisalpine Gaul with the army of Brutus. § 2. Pompey, after easily subduing 'the rest', blockaded Brutus in Mutina. Meanwhile Lepidus marched on Rome, encamped outside the city, demanded a second consulship, and terrorized the inhabitants. § 3. They were relieved, however, by a dispatch in which Pompey announced that he had finished the campaign without a battle: Brutus had in fact surrendered, and had been put to death by Pompey. § 4. Lepidus forthwith fled to Sardinia, where he fell ill and died.	The consuls quarrelled immediately after Sulla's funeral, the favour of the populace being divided between them. Lepidus, to conciliate the *I*talians, promised to restore the lands of which Sulla had deprived them. The Senate made both consuls swear not to take up arms against one another. Lepidus, having obtained by lot Transalpine Gaul for his province, did not return for the elections, intending to make war upon the Sullan party in the following year, when he would be released from his oath. Being recalled by the Senate, who were aware of his designs, and knowing why he was recalled, he came with his whole force,[1] intending to seize Rome, and as he was prevented summoned his men to arms. Catulus did the same, and a battle followed in front of and not far from the Field of Mars. Lepidus was beaten and, being unable to hold out much longer, went to Sardinia, where he fell ill and died.	§ 16. Lepidus, rising in the Marian interest after Sulla's death against the Sullan leader Catulus, rekindled the embers of the civil war, and two pitched battles were fought. § 17. Alba was blockaded and starved into surrender; Brutus, fleeing into Cisalpine Gaul, was pursued by Pompey, and put to death at Regium.

Let me state the questions that arise. (1) Can we reconcile the alleged statement of Philippus, recorded in a fragment of Sallust's *Histories*,[2] that Lepidus demanded the restoration of the tribunician power, with the statement of Licinianus, who abridged the *Histories*, that Lepidus declared in the Assembly against the restoration? I have no doubt that both statements are true: Lepidus opposed the restoration soon after the death of Sulla and before he

---

[1] Mommsen (*Röm. Gesch.*, iii⁸, 1889, p. 27 [Eng. tr., iv, 1908, p. 290]) says, 'When at length, in the beginning of the following year (677 [77 B.C.]), Lepidus was expressly enjoined by the Senate to return without delay, the proconsul haughtily refused obedience', &c. This contradicts Appian.

[2] i, 73.—*Plebei tribuniciam potestatem.* Cf. B. Maurenbrecher, *C. Sall. Crispi hist. rel.*, fasc. ii, p. 22.

left Rome; he probably pressed for it when he first marched on Rome and formulated his demands, and certainly demanded it when he returned. (2) When did Lepidus make the first advance against Rome which is implied in the question of Philippus (§ 10), 'Are you going to wait till he *again* puts his army in motion, and attacks the city with fire and sword?' (*An expectatis dum exercitu rursus admoto ferro atque flamma urbem invadat?*)? I believe that he took this step in 78 B.C., after the Senate had made him and Catulus swear to keep the peace.[1] (3) When was Pompey appointed to command against Lepidus? The answer, I think, must be, early in 77, immediately after Philippus had moved the 'ultimate decree' (§ 21) and before Lepidus advanced for the second time on Rome.[2] (4) Is the statement of Florus that Catulus and Pompey occupied the Janiculum and the Mulvian Bridge, and drove off Lepidus consistent with the statement of Plutarch that Pompey was in Cisalpine Gaul when Lepidus marched on Rome, and with the statement of Appian that Catulus alone defeated Lepidus near the Field of Mars? We may infer from the speech of Philippus as well as from our other authorities that only one battle was fought there; [3] Livy,[4] Valerius Maximus,[5] Exuperantius, and Appian ascribe the victory to Catulus alone; and it follows that in mentioning Pompey Florus went astray and that the battle to which he refers was identical with that which Appian chronicles and which, as the Mulvian Bridge and the Janiculum were occupied by Catulus, must have taken place on the right bank of the river.[6] Evidently the two battles to which Orosius alludes were the one in which Catulus defeated Lepidus and that which Pompey won near Cosa. (5) Where was the Alba which Orosius mentions? Long [7] says that it was the town of that name 'on the river Tanarus in Cisalpine Gallia'; Hülsen [8] identifies it with Alba Fucentia in Central Italy: neither gives any reason. Groebe,[9] who apparently adopts Hülsen's view, argues that if Pompey had blockaded the Alba in Cisalpine Gaul, he must, as its geographical position proves, have done so after the fall of Mutina; for, according to Orosius, Brutus fled from Mutina to Regium, that is in the direction of the Tanarus, but the narrative of Orosius shows that the capture of Alba preceded the blockade of Mutina. This objection is

[1] Cf. Maurenbrecher, fasc. i, p. 14.
[2] Drumann (*Gesch. Roms*, iv², 1910, p. 353), referring to Cicero's speech *Pro Cael.*, 29, 70 (*quam legem Q. Catulus armata dissensione civium rei publicae paene extremis temporibus tulit*), affirms that in 78 B.C. Catulus extended the provisions of the *lex Plautia de vi* (cf. p. 386, *infra*), and concludes that the appointment of Pompey followed immediately. But Pompey presumably marched for Cisalpine Gaul soon after he took command; and if he had already done so, Philippus would not have upbraided the Senate so bitterly for their inaction.
[3] If Lepidus was twice defeated outside Rome, he fought the first battle in his consulship; but Appian implies that he intended to keep the peace until his consulship expired.
[4] *Epit.*, 90. [5] ii, 8, 7.
[6] The Campus Martius extended to the left bank of the Tiber.
[7] *Op. cit.*, ii, 439.
[8] *Paulys Real-Ency.*, i, 1300.   [9] Drumann, *op. cit.*, p. 356, n. 5.

ATTEMPTED REVOLUTION OF LEPIDUS 369

easily answered: there is no evidence that Pompey blockaded Alba, and the operation may well have been entrusted to one of his lieutenants. Orosius must have referred to the town on the Tanarus, which was known as Alba Pompeia; for Alba Fucentia was remote from the theatre of the war. Whether Alba fell before or, as W. Stahl[1] holds, after the death of Brutus, cannot in my opinion be determined.

THE CHRONOLOGY OF THE SERTORIAN WAR

1. When did Sertorius go to Spain?—Compare the 86th chapter of Appian's first book on the Civil Wars, in which he relates the departure of Sertorius, with the opening words of the 87th—' The consuls for the following year [82 B. C.] were Papirius Carbo ... and Marius, the nephew[2] of the famous Marius ' (Τοῦ δ' ἐπίοντος ἔτους ὕπατοι μὲν ἐγενέσθην Παπίριός τε Κάρβων αὖθις καὶ Μάριος ὁ ἀδελφιδοῦς[2] Μαρίου τοῦ περιφανοῦς)—and you will see that Appian meant to fix the event in 83. Plutarch,[3] on the contrary, immediately after saying that Marius became consul adds that Sertorius went to Spain; and Exuperantius[4] also apparently refers his departure to 82.

P. von Bieńkowski,[5] however, argues that the words of Exuperantius do not bear out this interpretation. According to Exuperantius, ' Marius and Carbo became (or " were elected ") consuls, the former for the seventh time.[6] Then Sertorius ... came to Rome. ... Then the consuls dispatched him to Nearer Spain ' (*facti sunt Marius septies et Carbo consules. Tunc Sertorius ... Romam venit ... Tum consules misere in citeriorem Hispaniam*). ' If ', says von Bieńkowski, ' we ponder what Sallust says about the second consulship of Marius —" After the war in Numidia was over ... Marius *was elected consul in his absence,* Gaul was assigned to him as his province, and *on the 1st of January* as consul he celebrated his triumph (*sed postquam bellum in Numidia confectum ... Marius consul absens factus est et ei decreta provincia Gallia isque calendis Ianuariis ... consul triumphavit*) "[7]—we see that *consul factus est* means " was elected consul ", and the words of Exuperantius must be understood in the same sense. Thus Exuperantius agrees with Appian, and the departure of Sertorius must be referred to 83.'

Is not von Bieńkowski inconsistent? Does not Exuperantius, after saying that Marius and Carbo *facti sunt consules,* add that the consuls—not the consuls-designate—dispatched Sertorius to Spain? His statement agrees with that of Plutarch; and it therefore seems to me that the date 82 is more probable than 83.[8]

2. The final return of Sertorius to Spain.—It is somewhat

---

[1] *De bello Sert.*, 1907, p. 55.
[2] Son, according to all the other authorities.   [3] *Sert.*, 6, 1.
[4] 7–8.   [5] *Wiener Studien*, xiii, 1891, p. 134.
[6] An obvious blunder. Exuperantius confounded the younger Marius with his father.
[7] *Iug.*, 114, 3.   [8] Cf. W. Stahl, *De bello Sert.*, pp. 35–6.

2592.1   B b

difficult to decide whether Sertorius returned to the peninsula in 81 or in 80 B. C.; but from Plutarch's narrative [1] I infer the latter date. If, as I believe, Sertorius did not arrive in Spain from Italy till 82, his wanderings could hardly have been finished within the following year.[2]

3. The departure of Metellus for Spain.—Sulla and Metellus were consuls in 80 B. C. Appian [3] says that Sulla, having dispatched Metellus to Spain, himself administered affairs in Rome, which seems to imply that Metellus started in the year of his consulship; and Pseudo-Victor [4] expressly says that he did: but Stahl [5] insists that this is a mistake because it is evident from Cicero's speech *Pro Plancio* [6] that Metellus in the year of his consulship was in Rome at the time of the praetorian elections, which then took place in August. It does not follow that he did not start for Spain later in the year; but Stahl also urges that by the *lex Cornelia de provinciis ordinandis*, passed in 81 B. C., it had been enacted that consuls should not leave Rome during their term of office. It is doubtful, however, whether the law contained such a clause; [7] and it seems to me therefore that the question cannot be settled, though Metellus certainly did not take the field before 79.

4. The junction of Perperna with Sertorius.—Appian [8] and Plutarch [9] differ as to the time when Perperna joined Sertorius. Plutarch says that when he entered Spain he intended to act against Metellus independently, but that his troops were indignant at this selfishness and, hearing that Pompey was actually crossing the Pyrenees on his way to reinforce Metellus, compelled him to join Sertorius. According to Appian, the Senate did not commission Pompey until they heard that Sertorius, reinforced by Perperna, was likely to invade Italy. It seems to me probable that Plutarch told the truth, and that the Senate, ignorant of the jealousy of Perperna and supposing that he had actually joined Sertorius, decided to let Pompey go.

5. The date of Pompey's arrival in Spain.—Mommsen [10] affirms that Pompey reached Spain in 77 B. C. That he started then is certain; for, as will presently appear, it would be impossible to account for the time which he must otherwise have spent in Italy after he defeated Lepidus. I am inclined, however, to believe that he arrived in 76; for Appian [11] remarks that after he failed to relieve

---

[1] *Sert.*, 6-11. [2] Cf. Stahl, *op. cit.*, p. 43. [3] i, 97, 450.
[4] *De vir. ill.*, 63, 2. [5] *Op. cit.*, p. 46. [6] 29, 69.
[7] Th. Mommsen (*D. Rechtsfrage*, &c., 1874, pp. 29-34) thinks that it did; P. Willems (*Le Sénat*, &c., ii, 1883, p. 578) that it did not.
[8] i, 108, 508.
[9] *Sert.*, 15, 1-2. Plutarch says (§ 2) that Perperna, when he joined Sertorius, had 53 cohorts—more than 5 legions. We are not told that he had raised any troops besides 'the greater part' of the scattered forces of Lepidus, which he had brought from Sardinia (App., i, 107, 504); and unless he had done so—where?—the statement of Plutarch seems hardly credible, for with such a force Perperna could surely have overpowered the Governor of Sardinia.
[10] *Röm. Gesch.*, iii³, 1889, p. 29 (Eng. tr., iv, 1908, p. 293).
[11] i, 110. 512.

CHRONOLOGY OF THE SERTORIAN WAR

Lauro—the first operation which he undertook—the armies went into winter-quarters, and if he had crossed the Pyrenees in 77 he would have been obliged to winter in Spain before he took the field; but we are not told that he did, and we may perhaps infer from the letter [1] which he wrote to the Senate in 75 that he had passed only one winter there.

Von Bieńkowski,[2] however, insists that Mommsen's chronology is verified by the following passage in Pompey's letter,—' during three years you have hardly met my expenses for a single year ' (*a vobis per triennium vix annuus sumptus datus est* [3]). The rebellion of Lepidus, he continues, ended in the spring of 77; and immediately afterwards Pompey returned with his army to Rome in order to extort for himself the command in Spain. The negotiations which followed did not last long, and Pompey after his 40 days' preparations could have started in the summer and arrived in the late autumn. But the passage on which von Bieńkowski relies, if it proves that Pompey set out for Spain in 77, is not enough to prove that he arrived in the same year. B. Maurenbrecher [4] argues that since Lepidus, after Pompey had defeated him at Cosa, crossed to Sardinia and continued to fight there in conjunction with Perperna, and since Perperna after the death of Lepidus crossed to Liguria [?] before he departed for Spain, Pompey, if he had reached Spain in 77, would have forestalled Perperna, whereas in fact Perperna had been fighting in Spain for some time before Pompey arrived. Evidently therefore Pompey spent the winter of 77–76 in Gaul and did not enter Celtiberia before the spring of the latter year. Again, when Pompey wrote, ' I spent the winter in camp in the midst of ruthless enemies ' (*hiememque castris inter saevissimos hostes . . . egi* [5]), he plainly alluded to the winter (76–75) which followed his defeat at Lauro. Maurenbrecher goes on to remark, as I have done, that Pompey mentioned only one winter, and concludes that his words are unintelligible unless he meant the first winter which he passed in Spain.[6]

Stahl,[7] however, is not convinced. It is true that Maurenbrecher has the authority of Orosius [8] for saying that Perperna fought in Liguria: but Exuperantius [9] distinctly says that he crossed over from Sardinia to Spain; one cannot conceive that he had any motive for going to Liguria after the rebellion of Lepidus had been suppressed; and Orosius does not say that he went to Liguria from Sardinia. Furthermore, Stahl reminds us that Pompey did not allude to the winter of 77–76 at all, whether he spent it in Spain or in Gaul; and he cannot see why the passage which Maurenbrecher

---

[1] Sall., ii, 98, 5.
[2] *Op. cit.*, p. 210. Cf. G. Dronke (*Zeitschr. f. d. Alterthumswiss.*, xi, 1853, col. 505).   [3] Sall., ii, 98, 2.
[4] *C. Sall. Crispi hist. rel.*, fasc. i, pp. 23–4; fasc. ii, p. 227.
[5] Sall., ii, 98, 5.
[6] Maurenbrecher (*op. cit.*, pp. 227–8) adduces another argument, based upon Cic., *Pro Font.*, 7, 16, which Stahl (*op. cit.*, pp. 61–2) confutes.
[7] *Op. cit.*, pp. 53, 64–6.   [8] v, 24, 16.   [9] 7.

quotes should be deemed unintelligible unless it is understood as referring to the first winter which Pompey passed in Spain. The question is difficult; but I believe that Maurenbrecher is probably right. Maurenbrecher,[1] with whom Stahl [2] himself agrees, maintains, rightly in my opinion, that the final defeat of Lepidus in Italy could not have occurred before the middle of the summer: Perperna certainly did not leave Sardinia until the fighting which followed the arrival of Lepidus was at an end; and Pompey was not appointed to his command until the news of Perperna's arrival had reached Rome. His preparations lasted 40 days, and his long march, delayed by fighting and by negotiation, must have lasted many weeks.

6. **On Livy,** *fr.* 91.—The question whether the siege of Contrebia and the subsequent events recorded in the extant fragment of Livy's 91st book occurred in 77–76 or in 76–75 B. C. is closely connected with that which I have discussed in the preceding section: Mommsen,[3] von Bieńkowski,[4] and Stahl [5] connect the fragment with the earlier, Maurenbrecher [6] with the later winter.

That Livy's fragment relates to the winter of 77–76 results, says von Bieńkowski, from the fact that, as we read there, Sertorius intended to exclude Pompey from the territories of the Ilercaones and the Contestani. For this implies that Pompey was still on the northern bank of the Ebro, and so he was in the winter of 77–76, but only then: after the disastrous campaign of 76 he could not have dreamed of invading the territory from which Sertorius intended to exclude him, nor would Livy have ascribed to Sertorius the words, ' Perperna had been placed in command on the seaboard [i. e. in the country of the Ilercaones] in order to *protect the districts that were still unravaged by the enemy*' (*Perpernam in maritimam regionem superpositum, ut ea quae integra adhuc ab hoste sint tueri posset*). Secondly, we are told that during the siege of Contrebia the Berones and the Autricones solicited the aid of Pompey. This could only have happened in the winter of 77–76, for Sertorius spent the following winter in Lusitania,[7] which is inconsistent with Livy's narrative. Finally, Sertorius, according to Livy's account of the instructions which he gave to his lieutenants, never alluded to his victory at Lauro, but expressed the hope that Pompey would not risk a pitched battle: this would be almost inconceivable if Pompey had already suffered a severe defeat.

Now it must of course be admitted that if, as Appian says, Sertorius spent the winter of 76–75 in Lusitania, Livy's fragment cannot relate to that year; for according to Livy Sertorius wintered in the valley of the Ebro. If Maurenbrecher is right, Appian must have made one of the careless mistakes of which he was often guilty.[8] But von Bieńkowski's first argument at all events is

[1] *Op. cit.*, fasc. i, p. 15.
[2] *Op. cit.*, p. 55.
[3] *Op. cit.*, p. 29 (Eng. tr., iv, 1908, p. 293).
[4] *Op. cit.*, pp. 211–2.
[5] *Op. cit.*, pp. 64–6.
[6] *Op. cit.*, fasc. i, p. 25.
[7] App., i, 110, 512.
[8] Orosius (v, 23, 7) says that Sertorius after he captured Lauro transferred

inconclusive. For after the disaster at Lauro Pompey retreated northward to winter in the Pyrenees, and moved southward again in the following spring,[1] just as he had done in the spring of 76, when he attempted to rescue Lauro : obviously the narrative of Livy might be correlated with this movement, and von Bieńkowski's objection therefore fails. The conclusion which he draws from the mention of Perperna shall be examined later. Meanwhile let me ask this question :—why should Sertorius have boasted—why should Livy have recorded such a boast—about the victory of Lauro, and why is it inconceivable that after having beaten Pompey there he should have expressed the hope that Pompey would not fight ? Is it not notorious that Pompey afterwards incurred that risk several times ? Maurenbrecher pointed out [2] before von Bieńkowski's article was published that Perperna and Herennius, who, according to Livy, were ordered by Sertorius to attack Pompey, did actually encounter him in 75, whereas there is no evidence of their having done so in the previous year ; and he urged that Sertorius would have had no reason for hoping that Pompey would avoid a battle unless he had already beaten him at Lauro. Stahl, however, replies that what led Sertorius to believe that Pompey would avoid a battle was not that he had been defeated at Lauro, but that, as Livy says, he expected without fighting to reduce Sertorius by famine. Still, if Maurenbrecher is right in believing that Pompey did not arrive in Celtiberia until the spring of 76, one may ask whether the Berones and the Autricones would have applied to him for help in the preceding winter ; for at that time he was still *ex hypothesi* on the northern side of the Pyrenees. Groebe,[3] indeed, argues that the words of Livy, ' envoys had been sent [by the Berones and the Autricones] to indicate the roads to the Roman army ' (*missosque qui itinera exercitui Romano monstrarent*), are meaningless unless Pompey was then beyond the mountains. But why ? If Pompey was in Spain, he perhaps did not yet know the roads that led into the country of the Berones and the Autricones ; and he would not have needed their envoys to point out the well-known pass of the Eastern Pyrenees.

The question is the most difficult of all the chronological problems that beset the study of this war ; but I am forced to conclude that the fragment refers to the earlier winter. Apart from the testimony of Appian, which, in the absence of strong reasons for rejecting it, it would be rash to attempt to explain away, it seems to me evident from the *Epitome* (91 and 92) that in the former book Livy described the events of 77-76 and in the latter those of 75 ; for 91 recorded the dispatch of Pompey from Italy and the capture by Sertorius of several towns [including Contrebia and Lauro], and the epitome ends with the words, ' Q. Metellus . . . defeated L. Hirtuleius,' &c.

(*traduxit*) the prisoners to Lusitania ; and it is conceivable that the record of this fact might have led Appian astray.
[1] App., i, 110, 512.   [2] *Op. cit.*, fasc. i, p. 25.
[3] W. Drumann's *Gesch. Roms*, iv², 373-4, n. 1.

(Q. *Metellus* ... *L. Hirtuleium* ... *cecidit*), an event which happened in 76 : 92 begins by recording the battles of 75. I have assumed that the epitomizer referred to the battle of Italica ; but if any one objects that he was thinking of the battle of Segovia, which occurred in 75, there remains that argument of von Bieńkowski which I reserved, and which seems to me decisive. If Livy had been describing the events of the winter that followed the capture of Lauro, how could he have said that the maritime districts south of the Ebro 'were still unravaged by the enemy'? Pompey had already traversed them when he was marching to Lauro from the Pyrenees.

7. The battle of Segovia.—Von Bieńkowski [1] endeavours to prove that the battle of Segovia was fought four years before that of Italica, —in 80 B. C.[2] The authority is Florus, who says, 'The earlier combats were directed by the subordinate leaders, for Domitius and Thorius on the one side, the Hirtulei on the other, indulged in preliminary skirmishes ; soon, after the latter had been overthrown at Segovia, and the former on the Guadiana, the commanders-in-chief in person hazarded battle in turn at Lauro and at Sucro, and balanced their respective losses' (*prima per legatos habita certamina, cum hinc Domitius et Thorius, inde Hirtulei proluderent ; mox his apud Segoviam, illis apud Anam flumen oppressis, ipsi duces comminus invicem experti apud Lauronem atque Sucronem aequavere clades* [3]). Remarking that earlier writers have taken *oppressis* in the sense of *interfectis* and have accordingly identified the battle of Segovia with that in which Hirtuleius fell,[4] von Bieńkowski points out that Florus, for instance in ii. 13, 19, also uses *opprimere* in the sense of 'to overthrow'. Florus, he continues, unquestionably places the battle of Segovia in the first period of the war, as is proved by the words *prima certamina per legatos habita* and by the word *proluderent*, which gives us to understand that the battle at Segovia was only a preliminary affair. But, as Maurenbrecher argues,[5] no victory could have been gained over the Sertorians in 80 B. C., for in that year Further Spain joined Sertorius :[6] moreover, Florus neglects chronological order, and, as the word *oppressis*—whether it means 'killed' or 'overthrown' matters nothing—and the antithesis between Hirtuleius and Domitius show, he was evidently referring to the decisive defeat of 75. Furthermore, as Stahl [7] points out, all our other authorities agree that in the earlier years of the war Sertorius and his lieutenants were invariably victorious ; if Hirtuleius had then suffered a disastrous defeat they would not have ignored it ; and the theory of Bieńkowski would lead to the conclusion that Florus ignored the decisive battle in which Hirtuleius was slain.

8. The battle of Valentia.—It would be superfluous to demon-

[1] *Op. cit.*, pp. 146–7.
[2] Maurenbrecher (fasc. i, pp. 26, 36), von Bieńkowski (p. 216), and Stahl (p. 69) agree in assigning the battle of *I*talica to 76 B. C. The date is certain.
[3] ii, 10, 6–7.   [4] Oros., v, 23, 12.
[5] Bursian's *Jahresbericht*, cxiii, 1902 (1903), p. 243.
[6] Metellus, who won the battle of Segovia, did not take the field until 79 B.C. See p. 370.   [7] *Op. cit.*, pp. 45–6.

strate that the battle of Valentia was fought in 75 B. C. if Bieńkowski [1] had not argued that the date was 76. It is evident from Plutarch's narrative [2] that this battle immediately preceded that of the Sucro; and it is incredible that Pompey immediately after he had been disastrously beaten at Lauro should have pushed on to Valentia and fought there. Moreover, Bieńkowski is implicitly contradicted by Appian.[3]

10. The treaty between Sertorius and Mithradates.—H. Bernhardt,[4] says Stahl,[5] infers from a remark which Plutarch [6] made in describing the negotiations—'Sertorius demurred, but said that he had no objection to Mithradates' taking Bithynia and Cappadocia, countries which had long been under kingly rule and in no sense belonged to the Romans' (. . . οὐκ ἠνέσχετο ὁ Σερτώριος, ἀλλὰ Βιθυνίαν μὲν ἔφη καὶ Καππαδοκίαν λαμβάνοντι Μιθριδάτῃ μὴ φθονεῖν ἔθνη βασιλευόμενα καὶ μηδὲν προσήκοντα 'Ρωμαίοις)—that Nicomedes, the last king of Bithynia, was still alive; and Maurenbrecher has made it probable that he died in the summer of 75.[7] I may add that a comparison of the 77th fragment of Sallust's Second Book—*Illi tertio mense pervenere in Pontum multo celerius spe Mithridatis* ('The envoys [who had been sent to Sertorius] reached Pontus in the third month, much earlier than Mithridates had expected ')—with the 93rd, which describes events belonging to the autumn of 75, suggests that the treaty was signed in that year.

THE DATE OF POMPEY'S FIRST TRIUMPH

Pompey was born on the 29th of September, 106 B. C.[8] According to the *Epitome* [9] of Livy, he celebrated his first triumph at the age of 24 (that is, between September 29, 82 and September 29, 81); according to Licinianus,[10] when he was 25, on March 12, that is in 80 B. C.; according to Eutropius,[11] in his 24th year; according to Pseudo-Victor,[12] at the age of 26. Plutarch [13] says that he subdued Africa in his 24th year. The epitomizer, Eutropius, and Plutarch are manifestly wrong, for the African campaign, which preceded the triumph, occurred in 81.

Mommsen [14] agrees with Pseudo-Victor. O. Dieckmann [15] believes

[1] *Op. cit.*, p. 217. Mommsen originally made the battle of Valentia precede the siege of Lauro (!) (see Eng. tr., iv, 1875, p. 28), but afterwards expunged the passage (*Röm. Gesch.*, iii⁸, 1889, p. 30).
[2] *Pomp.*, 19, 1.
[3] i, 109, 511. Bieńkowski (pp. 217, 220) argues that the battle of Valentia mentioned by Plutarch (*Pomp.*, 18, 3) was distinct from the one recorded by Pompey (Sall., ii, 98, 3). Stahl (pp. 73-4) takes the trouble to refute this phantasy.
[4] *Chronol. d. Mithr. Kriege*, &c., 1896, p. 18, n. 1. Appian (*Mithr.*, 68-70) apparently thought that the treaty was made before the death of Nicomedes.
[5] *Op. cit.*, p. 72.   [6] *Sert.*, 23, 3.   [7] See pp. 400-1.
[8] Pliny, xxxvii, 2, 13.   [9] 89.   [10] Ed. Flemisch, p. 31, ll. 2-3.
[11] v, 9.   [12] *De vir. ill.*, 77, 2.   [13] *Pomp.*, 12, 5.
[14] *C. I. L.*, i², p. 178.
[15] *De Granii Liciniani fontibus*, &c., 1896, p. 42.

THE DATE OF POMPEY'S FIRST TRIUMPH

that Licinianus was right, because Plutarch [1] tells us that Servilius Vatia strongly opposed Pompey's claim, and, as consul-designate for the year 79, he may be supposed to have been asked his opinion first. But Dieckmann seems to forget that, according to Appian,[2] Vatia was nominated consul at the beginning of 79. Nevertheless, accepting the date—March 12—given by Licinianus, I am inclined to believe that the year in question was 80: for Sulla, who was still dictator and consul when Pompey demanded a triumph, abdicated early in 79; [3] and I can at present see no reason for supposing that the triumph was deferred until the year after that in which the claim was made.

THE PASS BY WHICH POMPEY CROSSED THE ALPS

According to Sallust,[4] Pompey wrote to the Senate, 'I opened up a new route across the Alps, different from that of Hannibal and for us more convenient' (*per eas iter aliud atque Hannibal, nobis opportunius, patefeci*).[5] It is now generally believed that this was the pass that leads over Mont Genèvre. The conclusion is based partly upon the fact that this route, which Caesar afterwards used,[6] answered in point of convenience to Pompey's description, partly upon statements of Varro and Appian. Varro, whose evidence is important because he accompanied Pompey to Spain,[7] says that the Alps could be crossed by five routes,—along the coast; the pass by which Hannibal crossed; the pass by which Pompey marched to Spain; that by which Hasdrubal invaded Italy; and that which is known as the Graian Alps (*Alpes . . . quinque viis transiri posse, una quae est iuxta mare per Ligures, altera qua Hannibal transiit, tertia qua Pompeius ad Hispaniense bellum profectus est, quarta qua Hasdrubal de Gallia in Italiam venit, quinta quae quondam a Graecis possessa est, quae exinde Alpes Graiae appellantur*).[8] Appian,[9] who agrees with Varro that Pompey's route was different from that of Hannibal, adds that he marched ' by the sources of the Rhône and the Po, which rise in the Alps not far from one another '

---

[1] *Pomp.*, 14, 4.   [2] *B. C.*, i, 103, 480.   [3] *Ib.*; Oros., v, 22, *I.*
[4] ii, 98, 5. Cf. Cic., *De imp. Cn. Pomp.*, 11, 30.
[5] Mommsen (*C. I. L.*, v, pars ii, p. 809) interprets the statement which Sallust ascribes to Pompey as meaning that he constructed a new road over the pass. It seems to me more than doubtful whether he had time for a work of such magnitude, though he may have done something to improve the existing road; but at all events the conclusion is not warranted by the word *patefeci*. In *B. G.*, iii, 1, 2, Caesar says, *iter per Alpes, quo magno cum periculo magnisque cum portoriis mercatores ire consuerant, patefieri volebat*, which plainly means, 'he was anxious to *open up* the route over the Alps, by which traders usually travelled at great risk and with the obligation of paying heavy tolls': that is to say, the road which Caesar desired to open up already existed.
[6] *Caesar's Conquest of Gaul*[2], 1911, pp. 430-2.
[7] Sall., ii, 69. Cf. Stahl, *op. cit.*, p. 13.
[8] Serv. *ad Aen.*, x, 13.   [9] *B. C.*, i, 109, 509.

PASS BY WHICH POMPEY CROSSED THE ALPS

(ἀμφὶ ταῖς πηγαῖς τοῦ τε 'Ροδανοῦ καὶ 'Ηριδανοῦ, οἳ ἀνίσχουσι μὲν ἐκ τῶν Ἀλπείων ὀρῶν οὐ μακρὰν ἀπ' ἀλλήλων). Now the source of the Po is more than 150 miles in a straight line from the source of the Rhône ; and it therefore seems certain that Appian or his authority confounded tributaries of the two rivers with the rivers themselves. Mommsen indicated a way of solving the difficulty. Strabo [1] observes that in the country of the Medulli there are two springs not far apart, from one of which the Durance flows into the Rhône, while [from the other] the Duria flows through the country of the Salassi and joins the Po (πηγαὶ δύο οὐ πολὺ ἄποθεν ἀλλήλων, ὧν ἐκ μὲν τῆς ἑτέρας εἰσὶν ὁ Δρουεντίας ποταμὸς . . . ὃς ἐπὶ τὸν 'Ροδανὸν καταράττει, καὶ ὁ Δουρίας εἰς τἀναντία· τῷ γὰρ Πάδῳ συμμίσγει, κατενεχθεὶς διὰ Σαλασσῶν). Strabo blundered about the Duria, for the river of that name—the Dora Baltea—which flowed through the country of the Salassi rose near Mont Blanc ; but the other Duria—the Dora Riparia—with which he confounded it, does rise close to the source of the Durance. Mommsen accordingly conjectured that Appian mistook the Dora Riparia and the Durance for the Po and the Rhône, into which they respectively flow.[2] If the conjecture was right—and in no other way can Appian's statement, which of course rested upon some authority, be explained—Pompey marched by way of Mont Genèvre.

By what route Hannibal crossed the Alps is a question which fortunately does not concern the present inquiry : all that matters to us is by what route did Varro believe that he had come. Perhaps, as Strachan-Davidson suggests,[3] he shared the opinion which Livy [4] said was general, namely, that Hannibal came by the Great St. Bernard. If so, however, he did not enumerate the five passes in geographical order.

Camille Jullian [5] rejects the prevailing view. Maintaining that Hannibal actually crossed by Mont Cenis, he is inclined to believe that Pompey went by the Little St. Bernard : for he holds, first, that that was the most convenient route for the Romans, 'as is proved by the later construction of the great road from Milan to Vienne and Lyons ' ; secondly, that this route was new, whereas Mont Genèvre had long been used by traders ; thirdly, that Appian would not have thought of the source of the Rhône if Pompey had crossed further south than Mont Cenis ; and, lastly, that on the route by the Little St. Bernard the warlike tribes which he encountered [6] were to be found. Now, considering that Caesar unquestionably used Mont Genèvre, I cannot attach any weight to the first reason ; the evidence [7] which Jullian [8] quotes to prove that Mont Genèvre had long been in use proves nothing except that it was regularly used many years after Pompey died, and, however long it

---

[1] iv, 6, 5.   [2] *C. I. L.*, v, pars 2, p. 809.
[3] *Appian, Book I*, 1902, p. 128.
[4] xxi, 38, 6.   [5] *Hist. de la Gaule*, iii, 1909, p. 108, n. 8.
[6] Sall., ii, 98, 4.
[7] Strabo, iv, 1, 3 ; Pliny, ii, 108 (112), 244 ; Amm. Marc., xv, 10, 8.
[8] *Op. cit.*, i, 46, n. 2.

may have been in use, Pompey might claim that he had ' opened ' it, just as Caesar intended to open up the route over the Great St. Bernard, although it had long been used by traders; the words of Appian, in their literal sense, are meaningless whatever route Pompey may have chosen; and Jullian knows that Caesar when he went by Mont Genèvre encountered three warlike tribes before he reached the Rhône.[1] If Pompey went by the Little St. Bernard, we must reject the testimony of Varro, who expressly distinguishes the Graian Alps, that is the Little St. Bernard, from the route which Pompey chose; but that Varro could not identify the pass which he and his chief had trodden is plainly incredible. I follow Mommsen because Appian's statement is the only direct evidence which we possess and Mommsen's conjecture is the only one which can explain it.

POMPEY'S LETTER TO THE SENATE

Pompey complains, if we may believe the letter which Sallust[2] ascribed to him, that during three years the Senate have hardly defrayed his expenses for a single year (*a vobis per triennium vix annuus sumptus datus est*). But, says Long,[3] 'Even if Pompeius left Italy at the end of B. C. 77 [which he certainly did[4]], he had not been more than two years in Spain, for this letter was written in B. C. 75,' &c. No doubt; but, as we learn from Plutarch,[5] Pompey, before he left Italy, made excuses for retaining the army with which he had acted against Lepidus, although Catulus had ordered him to disband it. Long[6] 'can hardly believe' Plutarch; for it seems to him inconceivable that the Senate would have paid an army which was kept under arms without its consent. But during a considerable part of the year that army was fighting against Lepidus; and if during the short time that elapsed before Pompey was appointed to command in Spain the Senate withheld payment, Pompey or his supporters may have found the money. Besides, since Pompey left Italy in the autumn of 77, he might, counting what remained of that year as the first of the three years, 77, 76, 75, have written *triennium* conformably with the looseness of Roman chronological phraseology.

THE TREATY BETWEEN SERTORIUS AND MITHRADATES

According to Plutarch,[7] Mithradates offered to aid Sertorius with ships and money if Sertorius would recognize his claim to the province of Asia, which in his treaty with Sulla he had ceded to Rome. Sertorius refused, but said that he had no objection to the

[1] *B. G.*, i, 10, 4.   [2] ii, 98, 2.
[3] *Decline of the Roman Republic*, ii, 1866, p. 471.   [4] See p. 370.
[5] *Pomp.*, 17, 2.   [6] *Op. cit.*, p. 458.   [7] *Sert.*, 23, 2-3; 24, 1.

king's taking possession of Bithynia and Cappadocia. Accordingly a treaty was made on those terms. Appian[1] says that Sertorius consented to cede the province of Asia as well as Bithynia, Paphlagonia, Cappadocia, and Galatia. We may suppose that Plutarch carelessly omitted Galatia and Paphlagonia; but though Sertorius was rebelling against the Roman Government, he was loyal to Rome, and it is hard to believe that he would have yielded Asia as well. Stahl[2] suggests that Appian probably confused the terms proposed by Mithradates with those to which Sertorius agreed. The only alternative that I can think of is that Sertorius originally rejected the king's demand and afterwards yielded in order to obtain his aid. But this is hardly probable.

THE WAR OF SERTORIUS

The materials for the history of the Sertorian War are as deplorable as those from which we derive our knowledge of the Servile Insurrection or of the campaigns of Lucullus and Pompey in the East. Appian gives a consecutive narrative in chronological order, but omits many important events: the epitome of Orosius, which supplements it, is of course extremely bald; Plutarch, intent on portraying the character of Sertorius, can hardly be said to narrate at all; the fragments of Sallust's history are what their name implies; Florus sets chronology at defiance; and some of the incidents recorded by Frontinus can neither be dated nor referred to any known place.[3] Feeling therefore that I should not be justified in merely offering such an imperfect narrative as I could piece together, I resolved to collect the various scraps of evidence and thus enable readers to control what I have written. I omit the few trustworthy tactical details, for example those of the operations at Lauro, which I have narrated in the text. My object is simply to get at the record of the principal moves: my method is to reproduce the statements of Appian in the form of a table of contents, and to complete it from those of other writers, which I enclose in brackets { }.

(Appian, *B. C.*, i, 108) Sertorius, incorporating Celtiberians with his Italian troops, makes a splendid fight against Metellus. {*The following details are given by other writers:*—Sertorius before the arrival of Metellus defeats Cotta in a naval battle in the Straits near Mellaria [thus gaining access to Lusitania], and in the same year defeats Fufidius, the Governor of Further Spain, on the Baetis[4] (Guadalquivir). Metellus [taking the field in the following year] 79 B. C.

79–78 B. C.

80 B. C.

[1] *Mithr.*, 68.
[2] *De bello Sert.*, p. 72. Additional notices of the treaty are to be found in Cicero, *De imp. Cn. Pomp.*, 4, 9, *Pro Mur.*, 15, 32, and Orosius, vi, 2, 12.
[3] See Frontin., i, 5, 1. 8; ii, 12, 2; iv, 5, 19. Stahl (*De bello Sert.*, 1907, p. 67) is perhaps right in referring i, 4, 8 to Pompey's passage of the Ebro in 76 B. C., and (p. 75) ii, 1, 3 to some event which occurred soon after the battle of the Sucro. [4] Plut., *Sert.*, 12, 3.

sends for the proconsul M. Domitius from Nearer Spain.¹ Domitius is defeated and slain by Hirtuleius, a lieutenant of Sertorius, on the Anas ² (Guadiana). L. Manlius, Governor of the Province of Gaul, comes to assist Metellus, but is defeated by Hirtuleius, flees to Ilerda,⁴ and, returning to his province, is attacked by Aquitanians and put to flight.⁵ Plutarch ⁶ adds that Metellus laid siege to the stronghold of the Langobritae,⁷ the inhabitants of which had helped the rebels, but was compelled by Sertorius to retreat. *From Sallust* ⁸ *we learn that* Metellus captured Dipo in Lusitania and passed the winter of 77–76 in Corduba.} Reinforced by Perperna, Sertorius is believed to be about to invade Italy, when the Senate, fearing such a contingency, sends Pompey to Spain with a new army.⁹ As *Pompey did not supersede Metellus,*¹⁰ *it may be inferred that his province was Nearer Spain.*¹¹ {*The following details are supplied only by Fragment 91 of Livy:*—Sertorius besieges and captures Contrebia [while Pompey is advancing through Gaul (?)]. Leaving L. Insteius, one of his lieutenants, to hold it, he moves to Castra Aelia ¹² on the Ebro, goes into winter-quarters there, and prepares for the next campaign. Early in the spring he sends Perperna with a detachment into the country of the Ilercaones, ordering him to guard the seaboard there (near the mouth of the Ebro) and instructing him how he is to defend friendly towns which Pompey may attack and to harass Pompey's column on the march. At the same time he sends instructions to Herennuleius,¹³ who is also in the country of

¹ Sall., i, 111 (ed. B. Maurenbrecher). The epitomizer of Livy (90) and Florus (ii, 10, 6) wrongly call Domitius a lieutenant (*legatus*) of Metellus. Cf. Eutropius, vi, 1, and see Maurenbrecher, fasc. i, p. 22.
² Flor., ii, 10, 6–7. Cf. Livy, *Epit.*, 90; Eutrop., vi, 1; Oros., v, 23, 3; and Maurenbrecher, *op. cit.*, i, 22, n. 3. In what year Hirtuleius besieged Consabra (Frontin., iv, 5, 19) is unknown.
³ For the date see Stahl, *op. cit.*, p. 48, n. 3.
⁴ Oros., v, 23, 4. Cf. Sall., i, 122; Livy, *Epit.*, 90; and Plut., *Sert.*, 12, 3.
⁵ Caes., *B. G.*, iii, 20, 1. Long (*Decline of the Roman Republic*, ii, 1866, p. 455) remarks that the statement of Orosius 'does not agree with Caesar'. There is no inconsistency. Caesar, whose subject was the Gallic War, omitted the earlier misfortunes of Manlius; Orosius, who was summarizing the events of the Spanish War, the later. If Plutarch (*Sert.*, 12, 3) is to be believed, Manlius came to assist Metellus because the latter had already suffered many defeats from Sertorius.
⁶ *Sert.*, 12, 3.
⁷ The geographical position of this town is unknown; but, as Stahl (*op. cit.*, pp. 50–1) observes, it was doubtless [like Dipo] in Lusitania; for the province of Metellus was Further Spain.
⁸ i, 113; ii, 28. Cf. Stahl, *op. cit.*, p. 51.
⁹ Cf. App., *Hisp.*, 101. Camille Jullian (*Hist. de la Gaule*, iii, 1909, p. 107, n. 9) infers from Livy (*Epit.*, 90), Plutarch (*Sert.*, 12), and Orosius (v, 23, 4) that what led to the dispatch of Pompey was the defeat of Manlius. Doubtless, like other defeats, it influenced the resolve of the Senate.
¹⁰ Val. Max., viii, 15, 8.
¹¹ See Stahl, *op. cit.*, p. 51.
¹² It results from the narrative of Livy that Castra Aelia was on the lower Ebro, somewhere SE. of Cascantium (Cascante), for in 76 B. C. Sertorius marched from Castra Aelia north-westward through the territory of the Cascantini.
¹³ Called Herennius by Sallust (ii, 98, 6).

the Ilercaones, and to Hirtuleius, who is in the Further Province. Hirtuleius is to protect friendly tribes, but on no account to fight a battle with Metellus, whom he is not strong enough to encounter. Sertorius, who intends to avoid meeting Pompey in a pitched battle, proceeds to march westward up the valley of the Ebro against the Berones and the Autricones, who harassed his troops during the siege of Contrebia, and who have, moreover, solicited aid from Pompey. Halting at Calagurris Nasica (Calahorra), he sends one of his lieutenants into the country of the Arevaci, to enlist recruits and collect grain, and dispatches Insteius to Segovia, to raise horsemen and thence to return to Contrebia.¹ Marching on into the country of the Berones, he comes to Vareia . . . *Here the fragment abruptly ends.* We learn from Sallust² that Pompey was joined by the Indigetes and the Iacetani, who dwelt between the Pyrenees and the Ebro.} (109) Sertorius captures and destroys Lauro ³ in the presence of Pompey.⁴ (110) The armies go into winter-quarters. 75 B. C. In the early spring Metellus and Pompey move from their quarters in the Pyrenees, Sertorius and Perperna from Lusitania. {Soon 76 B. C. after the fall of Lauro Hirtuleius is defeated by Metellus at Italica (Santeponce, near Seville) and flees with a few survivors into Lusitania.⁵ Pompey [moving northward from Lauro ?] captures Belgida in Celtiberia.⁶ Pompey [having moved southward from his winter- 75 B. C. quarters] defeats Herennius and Perperna on the Turia (Guadalaviar) at Valentia : he captures and destroys Valentia.⁷ Meanwhile

¹ *Contrebia, (quae) Leucada appellatur* (Livy, *fr.* 91). Groebe (Drumann's *Gesch. Roms*, iv², 1910, p. 378, n. 7) concludes, perhaps hastily, that Livy distinguished this Contrebia from the town of the same name which Sertorius had captured.
² ii, 98, 5.
³ Lauro was evidently south of the Palancia (see the next foot-note), and Forbiger (*Handb. d. alt. Geogr.*, iii, 1848, p. 68, n. 60) was probably right in identifying it with the modern Laury. Cf. Stahl, *op. cit.*, pp. 67–8.
⁴ Cf. Sall., ii, 29–30 ; Plut., *Sert.*, 18, 3–7 ; *Pomp.*, 18, 3 ; Frontin., ii, 5, 31 ; Oros., v, 23, 6–7. Orosius says that Pompey assembled his troops at Palantia before he advanced to relieve Lauro. This is an obvious blunder. Palantia (Palencia) is north of the Douro ; and it is inconceivable that Pompey should have gone so far out of his way. Orosius confounded Palantia with Pallantias, the river now called Palancia, which debouched near Saguntum (Ptol., *Geogr.*, ii, 6, 15).
Cicero (*Pro Balbo*, 2, 5) mentions incidentally that New Carthage was blockaded [evidently by Sertorius or one of his lieutenants]. Maurenbrecher holds that this event, to which Sallust (ii, 56) refers, occurred in 75 B. C., remarking that the Pompeians could not have advanced so far southward as New Carthage after the disaster at Lauro in 76. Stahl (*op cit.*, pp. 66–7) attributes it, rightly *I* believe, to 76, pointing out that Pompey's quaestor, Memmius, who was in the town during the blockade, was present at the battles of the Sucro and the Turia (Cic., *op. cit.*), which occurred in 75. He also conjectures that New Carthage was attacked by pirates, who, as Plutarch says (*Sert.*, 21, 5), supported Sertorius ; for the situation of the town was such that it could most easily have been reduced by a fleet.
⁵ Livy, *Epit.*, 91 ; Oros., v, 23, 10. Cf. Frontin., ii, 1, 2.
⁶ The capture of Belgida is mentioned by Orosius (v, 23, 11) only, and its geographical position is unknown.
⁷ Sall., ii, 54, 98. 6 ; Plut., *Pomp.*, 18, 3.

Metellus, having returned from his winter-quarters to Further
Spain, defeats Hirtuleius at Segovia,[1] and thence marches eastward
to join Pompey.} (110 continued) In a battle near Sucro (on the
river Sucro,[2] or Jucar, south of Valentia) Metellus defeats Perperna,
while Sertorius defeats Pompey. [*Appian here blunders : for* Metellus
read Afranius.[3] *Metellus had not arrived from Segovia when the
battle of the Sucro was fought.*] Not long afterwards a battle is fought
at Segontia (Siquenza) with a similar result, Sertorius again defeating
Pompey and Metellus defeating Perperna : next day Sertorius
reinforced by many natives, unexpectedly attacks the camp of
Metellus, and is about to invest it when Pompey comes to the
rescue. The armies go into winter-quarters. {*The battle which
Appian wrongly locates at Segontia is evidently identical with that
which Plutarch*[4] *describes as having been fought in the plains of
Saguntum* (ἐν τοῖς τῶν Σαγουντίνων πεδίοις) *north of the Turia; and,
as the reader who consults the original authorities will see, this was the
same battle which Plutarch in a previous chapter*[5] *cursorily mentioned
as having been fought ' near the Tuttia* [*or rather Turia*] (περὶ Τουττίαν).
Plutarch gives the following details :—Sertorius reduces the enemy
to sore straits, and when they come to forage in the plains a battle
ensues. Sertorius defeats the army of Pompey ; Metellus overcomes
the Spaniards [under Perperna [6]] opposed to him. Thus the Romans
are on the whole successful. *Plutarch is silent about the attack,*

[1] Flor., ii, 10, 7. Cf. Frontin., ii, 3. 5, 7. 5 ; Oros., v, 23, 12.
[2] Pliny, *Nat. Hist.*, iii, 3 (4), 20.
[3] Cf. Cic., *Pro Balbo*, 2, 5; Sall., ii, 98, 6 ; Plut., *Sert.*, 19 ; Flor., ii, 10, 7.
Plutarch's account of the battle of the Sucro is fuller than Appian's. At first,
he says, Sertorius on the right wing encountered Afranius, who commanded
the Pompeian left. Hearing that his own left was being beaten by Pompey,
he went to the rescue and routed Pompey's troops. Returning to his own
right wing, he found that the Afranians had won, but attacking them while
they were plundering his camp, he defeated them. On the next day he offered
battle again, but, learning that Metellus was approaching, returned to his
camp. In his life of Pompey (19, 3) Plutarch says that on the approach of
Metellus the army of Sertorius deliberately dispersed [doubtless to get food]
with the intention of concentrating again (cf. Frontin., ii, 13, 3). This evidently
happened after the battle ' in the plains of Saguntum ', which Plutarch here
ignores (otherwise known as the battle of the Turia [cf. Cic., *Pro Balbo*, 2, 5],
but not to be confounded with the earlier battle of Valentia on the Turia).
Afterwards, he says (§ 4), Sertorius succeeded in preventing the armies of
Metellus and Pompey from communicating with one another, cut off their
supplies by devastating the country, and, getting command of the sea, prevented them from being supplied by ships, so that they were forced to quit
Spain and to go ' into other provinces ' [presumably Gaul].
    Long (*op. cit.*, p. 469) says that Appian ' appears to have confounded ' the
battle of the Sucro ' with a subsequent engagement at Saguntum ' ; but
Appian mentioned a subsequent engagement—at Segontia.
    The epitomizer of Livy (92) mentions (1) a battle in which Pompey fought
indecisively with Sertorius and (2) a battle in which Metellus defeated Sertorius
and Perperna, while Pompey, who wished to share the victory, was unsuccessful. Apparently the former was the battle of the Sucro and the latter
the battle in the plains of Saguntum.
[4] *Sert.*, 21, 1-4.
[5] *Ib.*, 19, 1.
[6] Livy, *Epit.*, 92 ; Oros., v, 23, 12.

THE WAR OF SERTORIUS

mentioned by Appian, which Sertorius made on the following day on the camp of Metellus, but relates that in order to secure his retreat and to gain time for reinforcements to arrive, Sertorius retired into a mountain stronghold, the defences of which he strengthened. This fortress, *as we may gather from a comparison of Plutarch with the Epitome of Livy*,[1] was Clunia (Penalva del Castro).—Blockaded in Clunia, Sertorius makes frequent sorties and inflicts heavy loss upon the besiegers, harasses their foragers, and by means of his 'piratical vessels' prevents them from getting supplies by sea:[2] thus they are compelled to abandon the siege and to separate, Metellus retiring into Gaul and Pompey going into winter-quarters in or near the country of the Vaccaei,[3] whence he writes to the Senate, threatening to withdraw his army unless he is supplied with funds.[4] *Sallust*[5] *adds the following important facts :*—Pompey is forced, in order to get supplies, to move on [from the neighbourhood of the Vaccaei] into the country of the Vascones; but orders his lieutenant Titurius to winter with 15 cohorts in Celtiberia and protect friendly tribes. While Pompey is encamped among the Vascones many of his convoys are cut off and he is compelled to borrow money. *Maurenbrecher*,[6] *comparing this last statement with the words which Sallust*[7] *attributes to Pompey,* ' I have exhausted not only my private resources, but also my credit ' ('Ego non rem familiarem modo, verum etiam fidem consumpsi'), *concludes that the letter which Pompey dispatched to the Senate was written in the country of the Vascones.*—In this year probably Sertorius concluded a treaty with Mithradates.[8]}—(111) The Romans send two new legions to Spain.[9]   74 B. C.
Thus reinforced, Metellus and Pompey move down from the Pyrenees. Sertorius and Perperna advance against them from Lusitania. Many Sertorians desert to Metellus. (112) Exasperated by this, Sertorius treats many of his followers with barbarous cruelty [10] and consequently incurs odium with his troops, who, however, are not altogether alienated. Metellus captures many of the towns held by Sertorius.[11] Pompey besieges Pallantia (Palencia), but is forced by Sertorius to raise the siege, and, after destroying the walls, rejoins Metellus. Sertorius repairs the walls, attacks the combined armies while they are blockading Calagurris, and destroys 3,000 men {, compelling Metellus to retreat into Further Spain and Pompey into Gaul.[12] In the course of the autumn, or perhaps in the following

---

[1] 92.   [2] *Ib.*; Sall., ii, 88–90.   [3] Plut., *Sert.*, 21, 5.
[4] Sall., ii, 98. Cf. 47, 6.   [5] *Ib.*, 93–4, 96–7.
[6] *Op. cit.*, fasc. ii, p. 97.   [7] ii, 98, 9.
[8] Cic., *De imp. Cn. Pomp.*, 4, 9; Livy, *Epit.*, 93; Plut., *Sert.*, 23; Oros., vi, 2, 12.   [9] Cf. Plut., *Pomp.*, 20, 1; *Luc.*, 5, 5.
[10] Cf. Livy, *Epit.*, 92; Plut., *Sert.*, 25, 3–4.
[11] Strabo (iii, 4, 13) says that Metellus and Sertorius fought in the neighbourhood of Segobriga and Bilbilis in Celtiberia, from which Stahl (*op. cit.*, p. 52) first somewhat rashly concludes that in 77 B. C. Sertorius made himself master of those towns, and afterwards (p. 78) affirms that they were captured by Metellus in 74. His second thoughts derive some support from App., i, 112 compared with Sall., ii, 70, and Livy, *Epit.*, 93.
[12] Sall., iii, 45; Livy, *Epit.*, 93. Cf. Cic., *Pro Font.*, 7, 16, and Stahl, *op. cit.*, p. 79.

384 THE WAR OF SERTORIUS

73 B.C.
72 B.C.

year,[1] Perperna captures Cales in North-Western Spain.[2] During the winter Pompey is hard pressed for supplies.[3]} (113) In the following spring Metellus and Pompey successfully attack the towns still held by Sertorius;[4] but no pitched battle occurs. Next year they continue the offensive with growing contempt, for Sertorius becomes lazy and addicted to wine and women; accordingly he is invariably beaten. He also becomes suspicious and cruel, in consequence of which Perperna plots against and murders him.[5] (115) Metellus, believing that Pompey can easily dispose of Perperna, departs for a remote part of Spain. After several days' skirmishing a battle is fought in which Pompey overthrows Perperna.[6]—{Pompey destroys Uxama (Osma) and Afranius Calagurris, while the remaining towns surrender.[7]}

THE CORN LAW OF TERENTIUS AND CASSIUS AND THE DISTRIBUTION OF CORN IN 62-58 B.C.

Professor Rostovtseff[8] infers from the words which Sallust ascribes to the demagogue Macer—that the services of the proletariat could not be recompensed by, nor their liberty bartered for, a monthly dole of five pecks of corn[9]—that under the law of Terentius and Cassius this amount was to be distributed gratis. Asconius,[10] speaking of the law by which Clodius afterwards (58 B.C.) distributed corn gratuitously, says that it had before (*antea*) been sold at [the artificially reduced price of] $6\frac{1}{3}$ asses per peck—the price which, according to Livy,[11] was fixed by the corn law of Gaius Gracchus. Greenidge[12] thought that by *antea* Asconius meant 'under the

---

[1] Cf. Stahl, *op. cit.*, p. 80. Bieńkowski (*op. cit.*, p. 228) assigns the capture of Cales to 72 B.C., but gives no reasons.
[2] Sall., iii, 43.
[3] *Ib.*, 46. Cf. Stahl, *op. cit.*, p. 79.
[4] Cf. Livy, *Epit.*, 94. Strabo (iii, 4, 10) says that Sertorius, after he was expelled from Celtiberia, carried on the last part of the war in Ilerda, Osca, Calagurris, the country round Tarraco, and Hemeroscopium (on the Dianian promontory).
[5] Cf. Sall., iii, 83; Plut., *Sert.*, 25-6. Strabo (iii, 4, 10) and Velleius (ii, 30, 1) inform us that Sertorius was murdered at Osca (Huesca). The murder occurred in the tenth year of the war according to Orosius (v, 23, 13), in the eighth of his command according to the *Epitome* of Livy (96) and Eutropius (vi, 1); but the epitomizer adds that Perperna was defeated and killed about ten years after the war began. The latter date is apparently reckoned from 81 B.C., when Luscus was sent to oppose Sertorius; the former from 79, when Metellus took the field. Cf. Stahl, *op. cit.*, p. 84.
[6] Cf. Plut., *Pomp.*, 20, 3, and Stahl, *op. cit.*, p. 82.
[7] Oros., v. 23, 14. Cf. Sall., iii, 86-7, Flor., ii, 10, 9, and Exup., 8.
[8] *Paulys Real-Ency.*, vii, 174.
[9] *Hist.*, iii, 48, 19.—'Nisi forte repentina ista frumentaria lege munia vestra pensantur, qua tamen quinis modiis libertatem omnium aestumavere', &c.
[10] Ed. Clark, p. 8, ll. 15-7 (ed. Stangl, pp. 15-6).
[11] *Epit.*, 60.
[12] *Sources*, &c., 1903, p. 206.

lex Terentia Cassia'; but I believe that he had particularly in mind the four years that preceded the law of Clodius, for, according to Plutarch,[1] Cato at the end of 63 B. C. persuaded the Senate to distribute corn monthly to the people. Plutarch does not say that this distribution was to be gratuitous : if it was, it must, as the comment of Asconius proves, have been soon annulled ; and since Plutarch says that the annual cost of Cato's measure was 7,500,000 *denarii* or 1,250 talents (£300,000), while the law of Clodius cost nearly one fifth of the annual revenue,[2] that is nearly £680,000,[3] it seems clear that Cato proposed to revive the obsolete system of Gracchus[4] by selling the corn at the reduced price of $6\frac{1}{3}$ asses,[5] which agrees with the statement of Asconius.

Although there is no evidence, except the remark which Sallust ascribes to Macer, that the *lex Terentia Cassia* authorized free distribution, Rostovtseff argues that the small number of the recipients—40,000[6]—can be best explained by supposing that it did. I believe on the contrary that in 73 B. C. the Government, burdened by the expense of the Sertorian and Mithradatic wars, could not, with diminished revenues,[7] afford to feed even this number for nothing ; and I would ask Rostovtseff whether he does not build too much upon the rhetoric of Sallust.

THE *LEX PLOTIA* (OR *PLAUTIA*) *DE REDITU LEPIDANORUM*

The late Dr. Greenidge[8] affirmed that 'the date of this law is unknown', although he 'followed Lange[9]... in assigning it to 73.' I have independently inferred the same date from the only direct evidence,—that of Suetonius,[10] who says, 'In his [Caesar's] military tribuneship, the first office which fell to his lot on returning to Rome [from Asia], he zealously supported those who were agitating for the restoration of the tribunician power. Moreover, by the Plotian law he secured the return of L. Cinna ... and the other followers of Lepidus who, after that consul's death, had fled with him to Sertorius, and he himself harangued the assembly on the bill' (*Tribunatu militum, qui primus Romam reverso ... honor optigit, actores restituendae tribuniciae potestatis ... enixissime iuvit. L. etiam Cinnae ... et qui cum eo ... Lepidum secuti post necem consulis ad*

---

[1] *Caes.*, 8, 4 ; *Cato min.*, 26, 1. [2] Cic., *Pro Sest.*, 25, 55.
[3] Plut , *Pomp.*, 45, 3.
[4] The date of the corn law of M. Octavius (Cic., *Brut.*, 62, 222), which repealed or modified the law of Gracchus, is unknown ; but it was certainly much earlier than 63.
[5] Prof. Reid, who holds, as *I* do, that Cato ' restored the Gracchan system ' (*Journ. Rom. Studies*, v, 1915, p. 223), conjectures that he did so ' either by increasing the amount of the dole or by lowering the price or by both devices '. This is irreconcilable with the statement of Asconius. I suppose that the corn law which, according to Cicero (*Att.*, ii, 19, 3), the triumvirs threatened to repeal in 59 B.C. was Cato's law. [6] See p. 154, *supra*
[7] Cf. Sall., *Hist.*, ii, 47, 6-7. [8] *Sources*, &c., 1903, pp. 228-9.
[9] *Röm. Alt.*, ii³, 1879, p. 703. [10] *Div. Iul.*, 5. Cf. Gell., xiii, 3, 5

386 THE LEX PLOTIA (OR PLAUTIA)

Sertorium confugerant, reditum in civitatem rogatione Plotia confecit, habuitque et ipse super ea re contionem). The last Mithradatic War began in 74;[1] and Caesar returned to Rome in the same year. In 73 Licinius Macer was agitating for the restoration of the tribunician power, and there is no evidence that the agitation was renewed until 71, when Pompey was standing for the consulship. It would seem, then, that the *lex Plotia* was passed in 73 [2] or perhaps in 72.[3] Mommsen,[4] however, holds that this *lex Plotia* was merely a part of the *lex Plautia de vi*. Remarking that Catiline was prosecuted under this law in 63,[5] and that the law under which Caelius was prosecuted in 56 was designated by Cicero [6] as a law 'concerning crimes of violence, which Quintus [Lutatius] Catulus carried ... when the State was almost in extremity of peril' (*de vi, quam legem Q. Catulus ... rei publicae paene extremis temporibus tulit*), he concludes that this law was promulgated after Catulus suppressed the insurrection of Lepidus (78–77 B. C.), and was probably the same law which, after the death of Lepidus, extended an amnesty to his followers,—in other words, the *lex Plautia de reditu Lepidanorum*. The amnesty, he argues, may well have been coupled with a threat of criminal prosecution in the event of further breach of the peace. But how could a law carried by Lutatius Catulus be called *lex Plautia*? Mommsen gets over this difficulty by supposing that Catulus, who, as proconsul (77 B. C.), was precluded from introducing a bill himself, employed a tribune named Plautius to do it for him: at the same time he admits that on this hypothesis it is surprising that Cicero should have used the word *tulit*. It is; and if any one less eminent than Mommsen had contended that a bill which Caesar supported in 73 had been passed in 77, his argument would have been ignored.

SPARTACUS

The original accounts of the last two years of the Servile War differ in important details. In order to help the reader to control my narrative, I reproduce in outline the statements of the two chief authorities, omitting all merely picturesque details. Statements in either narrative which are omitted in the other are enclosed in brackets { }—

	PLUTARCH	APPIAN
72 B. C.	*Cras.*, 9, 9. The Senate send the consuls [Gellius and Lentulus] into the	*B. C.*, i, 117. The consuls are sent into the field {with four

[1] See pp. 398–403.
[2] See p. 358.
[3] P. Groebe (W. Drumann's *Gesch. Roms*, iii², 1906, p. 134, n. 3) remarks that, according to Niccolini (*Fast. trib.*, App., p. 42), Plautius was tribune in 72 B.C. I cannot check Groebe's statement, for I have not been able to see the work to which he refers; but in 'Fasti tribunorum plebis' (*Studi storici*, iv, 1895, pp. 370–1) Niccolini, citing Lange and Maurenbrecher, expresses the opinion that Plautius was a tribune in 73, not 72. Unless he has since discovered direct evidence that the date was 72, what did Groebe gain by quoting his borrowed opinion?
[4] *Röm. Strafr.*, 1899, p. 654, n. 2.
[5] Sall., *Cat.*, 31, 4.
[6] *Pro Cael.*, 29, 70.

SPARTACUS

PLUTARCH

field. § 10. Gellius destroys the German contingent, separated from their comrades; {Spartacus defeats the lieutenants of Lentulus.} § 11. Spartacus moves towards the Alps {The Governor of Cisalpine Gaul tries to stop him, but is defeated.[1]} 10, 1. The Senate supersedes the consuls and appoints Crassus Commander-in-Chief. § 2. {Crassus occupies a position near the country of the Picentini [on the north-west frontier of Lucania] to intercept Spartacus, ordering Mummius to follow Spartacus, but not to fight:} Mummius disobeys and is defeated. § 3. Crassus decimates the cohort (500 men) which set the example of flight.[2] § 4. He then marches against Spartacus, who retreats through Lucania to the sea, intending to invade Sicily, but (§§ 4-5) being unable to transport his army across the Straits,[3] retires {to the peninsula of Rhegium.} §§ 6-7. Crassus proceeds to blockade him by constructing an entrenchment from sea to sea. § 8. Spartacus fills up a part of the trench {and thereby extricates one-third of his army. 11, 1-2. Crassus, fearing that Spartacus intends to march on Rome, attacks a number of his followers, who, having quarrelled with their chief, are encamped separately by a lake in Lucania,[4] and dislodges them, but cannot pursue because Spartacus [, having extricated the remaining two-thirds of his force,] stops the rout.} §§ 3-4. Crassus, anxious to forestall Pompey in case of his being appointed to a command,[5] {sends 6,000 men to attack Canicius and Castus, separated from Spartacus.[6] The movement of the

APPIAN

legions}. Crixus with 30,000 men is defeated by one of them {near Mount Garganus [in Apulia]}. Spartacus, marching through the Apennines towards the Alps with the intention of entering Gaul, successively defeats both consuls, {one of whom was trying to stop him, while the other was hanging on his rear. After sacrificing 300 captives in honour of Crixus he intends to march on Rome.[7] The consuls attack him near Picenum [?], but are again defeated. Finding that his army is not fit to attack Rome and that no town will help him, he abandons his intention,} captures and obtains supplies from Thurii[8] [in Lucania], {and again defeats the Romans.} 118. Crassus marches against Spartacus {with the two consular legions [previously commanded by Gellius and Lentulus] and six new ones.} He decimates the two consular legions in punishment for the defeats which they had suffered[9] [under Gellius and Lentulus.] {Afterwards he attacks 10,000 of the rebels, separated from Spartacus,} who retreats towards the sea, intending to cross over to Sicily. Crassus begins to blockade him. 119. Spartacus attempts to break the blockade {in the hope of reaching Samnium, but is repulsed;} afterwards he makes sorties at various points and by throwing fascines into the trench and igniting them

---

[1] Cf. Flor., ii, 8, 10, and Oros., v, 24, 4.
[2] Cf. Sall. (ed. Maurenbrecher), iv, 22.
[3] Florus (ii, 8, 13) says that Spartacus made an abortive attempt to cross on rafts. Cf. Cic., *Verr.*, v, 2, 5.   [4] Cf. Sall., iv, 37-8.   [5] Cf. *ib.*, 39.
[6] The epitomizer of Livy (97) is speaking of the same battle when he says that Crassus defeated 35,000 Gauls and Germans under Castus and Gannicus. Cf. Frontin., *Strat.*, ii, 4, 7; 5, 34; Oros., v, 24, 6. According to Frontinus, the defeat of Castus and Cannicus (this is the true form [A. Holder, *Alt-celt. Sprachschatz*, i, 735-6]) took place at Camalatrum (near the source of the Silarus in Lucania): according to Orosius, who alone mentions the Silarus, Spartacus himself was beaten there. The two accounts are not necessarily irreconcilable, for ancient writers sometimes loosely ascribed the actions of subordinate officers to the commander-in-chief.
In my narrative (p. 160) *I* have followed the description given by Frontinus.
[7] Cf. Flor., ii, 8, 9. 11.
[8] The capture of Thurii is perhaps implied in Plutarch's statement that Spartacus retreated through Lucania.
[9] Appian reports further from hearsay the still more incredible story that Crassus decimated the entire army, putting to death 4,000 men.

C C 2

PLUTARCH	APPIAN
6,000 men is detected, but they are rescued by Crassus, who in the ensuing battle slays 32,000 of the enemy.} § 6. Spartacus {, hearing of this disaster,} retreats {to the Petilian hills: L. Quinctius and Tremellius Scrofa pursue him, but are beaten. § 7. The rebels, elated by this success, force Spartacus to lead them back into Lucania.} § 8. The approach of Pompey is announced. § 9 Crassus, eager to forestall him, encamps opposite Spartacus: the rebels attack Crassus's troops while they are entrenching their camp. §§ 10-11. In the ensuing battle Spartacus is slain. § 12. Pompey cuts up the fugitives whom he encounters.	impedes the efforts of Crassus. 120. Crassus is anxious to forestall Pompey. {Spartacus proposes to negotiate: Crassus rejects the offer.} Spartacus breaks the blockade [1] and retreats, pursued by Crassus, towards Brundisium. But {, hearing that [M.] Lucullus has returned to Brundisium from Asia,} he becomes desperate and fights a battle, in which he is slain. {Crassus pursues many of the fugitives into the hills and destroys all except 6,000, who are crucified along the road from Capua to Rome.}

According to Plutarch and Appian, the German contingent—that is, the army commanded by Crixus—was beaten by one of the consuls; [2] according to the *Epitome* of Livy,[3] by the praetor Arrius. The explanation may be that the consul Gellius and the praetor acted together or that the praetor acted in obedience to the consul. This point, however, is unimportant; but the statement of Appian, who omits all mention of Mutina, that Spartacus intended, before he defeated the consuls near Picenum, to march on Rome, is at variance with that of Florus,[4] according to whom Spartacus formed this design later, after he had defeated Cassius at Mutina. We may, I think, reject the statement of Florus, for it is improbable that Spartacus, who had marched into Cisalpine Gaul with the object of quitting Italy, and had doubtless only abandoned his purpose because his followers were eager to remain and plunder, would then have committed himself to so rash an undertaking as a march against Rome. I doubt whether he ever entertained such a project at all, which may only have been attributed to him by rumour.

If Appian is right, Spartacus, after he retreated from Mutina to Thurii in Lucania, advanced northward again into the country of the Picentini. This seems unlikely, and although it is perhaps confirmed by Sallust,[5] I am tempted to suspect that Appian confounded the order of events. Again, who were the Romans whom Spartacus, according to Appian (117), defeated in Lucania? The consuls, if they had not already been superseded, were far to the north. Perhaps Appian was thinking of the victory (which he does not expressly mention) that Spartacus afterwards gained over the lieutenants of Crassus. When we read in Plutarch that Crassus occupied a position πρὸ τῆς Πικηνίδος in order to intercept Spartacus, and in Appian that the consuls attacked Spartacus περὶ τὴν Πικηνίτιδα γῆν and were defeated by him, a twofold problem arises. First, are two distinct events here described, or did one of the two writers blunder? Secondly, does Πικηνίς or Πικήνιτις

---

[1] Cf. Frontin., i, 5, 20.
[2] Orosius (v, 24, 4) says the same.
[3] 96. [4] ii, 8, 10. [5] Cf. iv, 20 with 22.

SPARTACUS

mean Picenum, or does it signify the territory of the Picentini, on the northern frontier of Lucania ? Or does Πικηνίς mean the former and Πικήνιτις the latter ? Strabo calls Picenum ἡ Πικεντίνη [1] and the chief town of the Picentini Πικεντία; [2] Ptolemy calls the people of Picenum Πικηνοί [3] and the Picentini Πικέντινοι.[4] We must, I think, conclude that two events are recorded, for Plutarch is describing what happened after, Appian what happened before the appointment of Crassus. Plutarch evidently believed that Spartacus, after he defeated the Governor of Cisalpine Gaul, moved southward, and either Picenum or the territory of the Picentini would accord with his narrative ; but when I read that immediately after the defeat of Mummius Spartacus retreated through Lucania I am disposed to conjecture that the scene of Mummius's defeat was the country immediately north of Lucania, that is, the country of the Picentini.[5] On the other hand, since, according to Appian, Spartacus was moving northward through the Apennines when he purposed to march on Rome, and since he then defeated the consuls περὶ τὴν Πικηνίτιδα γῆν, it would seem that Appian located that victory near Picenum ; for the country of the Picentini is too far south to fit his statement.

Appian, as Rathke [6] has pointed out, was wrong in saying that Crassus took the field in the third year of the war (71 B.C.) ; for we learn from Cicero [7] that the consuls, whom he superseded, were at Rome in November, 72. Rathke also remarks [8] that Appian most probably made another mistake when he said that Crassus took over only two legions from the consuls ; for it was customary, when two consuls simultaneously took the field, for each to command two legions. Probably, as Viereck, the latest editor, suggested, Appian found in his authority the words *cum binis legionibus* (' with two legions each ') and mistook *binis* for *duabus*.

The statement of Appian (118) that Crassus, after he inflicted the punishment of decimation, but before Spartacus retreated to the Straits, first defeated 10,000 of the rebels, separated from Spartacus, and afterwards defeated Spartacus himself, is hardly credible. No other writer mentions these defeats. I believe that when Appian spoke of the first he was thinking of the victory which, according to Plutarch (11, 1-2), Crassus gained near a lake in Lucania, and that he confounded the second with the victory which Crassus

[1] v, 4, 2.
[2] *Ib.*, § 13.
[3] *Geogr.*, iii, 1, 45.
[4] *Ib.*, § 60.
[5] This, I find, is also the view of Groebe (W. Drumann's *Gesch. Roms*, iv², 1908, p. 91, n. 10), who says, ' Plutarch speaks of Picenum, a mistake pardonable in a Greek '.
[6] *De Rom. bellis servilibus*, 1904, pp. 85–6. Appian, after remarking that ' it was now the third year of the war ', says that no candidate would come forward at the praetorian elections until Crassus undertook the office. Evidently he was referring to the elections of the previous year (72), for in 71 Crassus was elected to the consulship, which he held in 70.
[7] *Verr.*, ii, 2, 38–9, 95.
[8] *Op. cit.*, pp. 83–4.

390 SPARTACUS

gained over Castus and Cannicus near the source of the Silanus, for he mentions neither of these battles in its proper place.[1] The movement of Spartacus, described by Plutarch, towards the Petelian hills was probably identical with the movement, described by Appian, towards Brundisium; and Plutarch's account of the operations that followed the blockade of Spartacus, though it is much fuller than that of Appian, does not contradict it. Appian, as all who are familiar with Roman history will have observed, mistook M. Lucullus, who had returned to Italy from Thrace—not Asia—for his famous brother, the conqueror of Mithradates. No critical reader will give the slightest heed to the statements as to the numbers of the slain;[2] and all will see that the extant narratives of the Servile War, like those of the war waged by Sertorius, have no military value.[3]

THE FIRST CONSULSHIP OF POMPEY AND CRASSUS

Did Pompey and Crassus retain their armies during their first consulship?—Mommsen asserts that Pompey and Crassus throughout their consulship kept their troops under arms, and that 'for a moment it seemed as if the armies ... would come to blows before the gates of the capital'.[4] These statements are apparently based upon the narrative of Appian,[5] who relates that the two consuls after their election did not dismiss their armies, Pompey explaining that in view of his impending triumph he was awaiting the return of Metellus, while Crassus insisted that Pompey ought to disband first.[6] Appian then, ignoring the events of this momentous consulship, relates that 'the people', seeing that matters were tending towards revolution, and fearing the armies, entreated the consuls to be reconciled, whereupon, after some hesitation on the part of both,

---

[1] I find that G. Gundermann, the editor of Frontinus, shares my opinion. Cf. Frontin., ii, 4. 7, 5. 34 with pp. 148–9 of his edition.

[2] The Germans after their annihilation (Plut., *Cras.*, 9, 10) revive, but only to be destroyed again (*ib.*, 11, 5)! Plutarch (*Pomp.*, 21, 1) says that 12,300 men fell in the final battle; Livy (*Epit.*, 97) and Orosius (v, 24, 7) raise the number to 60,000!

[3] After writing these words I have lighted upon the following remark of Col. G. Veith (*Klio*, viii, 1908, p. 131)—'Military events for our knowledge of which we have to rely solely upon writers like Herodotus, Livy, Plutarch, Cassius Dio, Appian, &c., must, for the strictly scientific and professional study of war, be treated as irrevocably lost'.

[4] *Röm. Gesch.*, iii⁸, 1889, pp. 105–6 (Eng. tr., iv, 1908, p. 383).

[5] *B. C.*, i, 121, 561. Cf. Plut., *Pomp.*, 21, 4. If Mommsen relied upon Caesar's *B. C.*, i, 7, 2, he was leaning upon a broken reed. Cf. Meusel's edition, p. 305.

[6] Mommsen wrongly says that 'the pretext under which Pompey refused to dismiss the army was that he distrusted Crassus and therefore could not take the initiative'. Moreover, the pretext in question was put forward not, as Mommsen implies, during, but before the consulship.

FIRST CONSULSHIP OF POMPEY & CRASSUS 391

Crassus offered his hand to Pompey, who took it, and both disbanded their troops. The reconciliation, as we learn from Plutarch,[1] took place towards the end of the consulship. Thus Appian leaps in one sentence over a period of nearly a year and a half; and since Plutarch distinctly says that Pompey resigned his command during his consulship,[2] I suspect that Appian made one of his many blunders. If, however, both consuls retained their armies throughout, the question arises how the money was found for feeding and paying the men. We all know that Crassus boasted by implication that he was rich enough to maintain a legion;[3] but we may doubt whether even his resources would have been strained by supporting ten legions for an entire year, and Pompey certainly could not afford such an outlay. Nor is it easy to believe that the Senate was bullied into finding the money against its own interest from a depleted treasury.

The 'equites' and the 'tribuni aerarii' mentioned in the Aurelian law.—Formerly it was believed that the 'Knights' (*equites*) and the *tribuni aerarii* from whom under the law of Aurelius Cotta two-thirds of the jurors were to be chosen, were to be distinguished by a pecuniary qualification alone, the property of the former being not less than 400,000,[4] of the latter not less than 300,000 sesterces; and in accordance with this belief a gap in the text of the *lex Acilia*, where the qualifications of jurors were defined, was conjecturally filled up in the first five editions of Bruns's *Fontes Iuris Romani* as follows: quei in hac civit[ate HS CCCC n(ummum) plurisve census siet]: but, as we shall presently see, in the sixth edition the emendation was changed. The census of the *tribuni aerarii* is not directly attested: that it ranged between 300,000 and 400,000 sesterces is merely a conjecture, based upon comparison of a note written by the scholiasta Bobiensis [5] with a statement in Suetonius's Life of Augustus.[6] The *tribuni aerarii* were originally officials who collected the poll-tax (*tributum*) from Roman citizens and paid the troops;[7] but, as is well known, after 167 B. C. the tax was no longer required. So also the *equites*, for the most part, were in 70 B. C., when the Aurelian law was passed, and later 'Knights' only in name: in fact they were

[1] *Cras.*, 12, 4–5; *Pomp.*, 23, 1.   [2] *Ib.*, 22, 3. Cf. 21, 4.
[3] Pliny, *Nat. Hist.*, xxxiii, 10 (47), 134.
[4] Suet., *Div. Iul.*, 33; Hor., *Ep.* i, 1, 57; Pliny, *Ep.*, i, 19.
[5] *Schol. Bob. in Clod. et Cur.*, fr. xxx, ed. Stangl, 1912, p. 91 (Orelli, p. 339)— *ut posthac lege Aurelia iudex esse non possit*. Commenting on this, the scholiast says, *negat iudices illos Tullius pecuniam* [bribes] *quam acceperint reddituros, ne postea in numero iudicum lege Aurelia esse non possint: sive quod se pecuniam reddendo faterentur esse corruptos, sive quod amissis tricenis vel quadringenis millibus quae a reo acceperant in egestatem revolverentur ac propterea in iudicum.* . . .
[6] 32, 3.—*Ad tris iudicum decurias quartam addidit ex inferiore censu, quae ducenariorum vocaretur, iudicaretque de levioribus summis*, &c. J. B. Mispoulet (*Les inst. pol. des Romains*, ii, 1883, p. 209) suggests that the *tribuni aerarii* may have been identical with the *ducenarii*. But surely the 'three decuries of jurors' to which Augustus added a fourth were senators, *equites*, and *tribuni aerarii*. The *tribuni*, indeed, were removed from the panel by Caesar; but presumably they were afterwards restored.
[7] Varro, *De ling. lat.*, v, 181; Gell., vi, 10, 3.

the men of business who formed the middle class. Although after the Jugurthine War the cavalry of the Roman army was raised from foreign nations, the Eighteen Centuries, which in earlier days had formed the mounted corps, still survived, and the 1,800 ' Knights ' who composed those centuries served on horses provided by the State in the ' praetorian cohort ' or as field officers : the name of *equites* was borrowed by all, senators excepted, whose property— 400,000 sesterces or more—qualified them for enrolment in the centuries, even though they were contractors, money-lenders, or farmers of the taxes. The champions of the old theory,[1] which Mommsen was the first to challenge, urged that there was no evidence that the *tribuni aerarii* in the later period of the republic had any official position, and pointed to the passage in which Cicero,[2] emphasized the pecuniary qualification defined by the Aurelian law both for *equites* and *tribuni aerarii* ; but, as Strachan-Davidson [3] observed, ' it does not follow that the possession of the 400,000 or 300,000 was the only qualification.' He points out that Asconius,[4] after mentioning the senators, *equites*, and *tribuni aerarii*, who under the Aurelian law composed the juries, goes on to say that Pompey in his second consulship (55 B. C.) ordained that ' cases should be tried by jurors selected on a novel principle *from the wealthiest members of the centuries*, but, as before, from those three orders ' (*ut a m p l i s s i m o e x c e n s u e x c e n t u r i i s aliter atque antea lecti iudices, aeque tamen ex illis tribus ordinibus res iudicarent*). ' Now,' says Strachan-Davidson,[5] ' if Pompey could raise the property qualification without disturbing the balance of the orders, it seems clear that there must have been some criterion other than wealth to distinguish between the one order [*equites*] and the other ' [*tribuni aerarii*]. Not necessarily ; suppose that Pompey raised the qualification to 500,000 sesterces for the *equites* and to 350,000 for the *tribuni aerarii* : what becomes of the alleged ' criterion ' ? But let Strachan-Davidson proceed. ' If,' he adds,[6] ' with Mommsen (*Staatsrecht*, iii, p. 192, n. 4) we take " amplissimo ex censu " to mean the equestrian census of 400,000 sesterces, the [monetary] distinction would disappear altogether.' In other words, Strachan-Davidson held that ' the monetary qualification was . . . superimposed on the members of each *ordo*, [it was] not the qualification which constituted a man *ipso facto* a member of that *ordo*. There are other indications,' he continues, ' that the *tribuni aerarii* were often, so far as wealth was concerned, of the equestrian census, and therefore belonged to the *equester ordo* in its wider . . . sense.' The scholiasta Bobiensis calls the *tribuni aerarii* ' men of the same order ' (*eiusdem ordinis viri*) as the *equites* : Cicero, addressing ' the non-official members of the jury ' in his speech for Rabirius Postumus,[7] calls them all *equites*, including under that term

---

[1] J. N. Madvig, *Opusc. acad. altera*, 1842, pp. 251–3. Cf. A. W. Zumpt, *Das Criminalrecht d. röm. Republik*, ii, part 2, 1869, pp. 192–3.
[2] *Phil.*, i, 8, 20.
[3] *Problems of the Rom. Crim. Law.*, ii, 1912, p. 91.
[4] Ed. Clark, p. 17, ll. 7–10 (ed. Stangl, p. 21).
[5] *Op. cit.*, pp. 91–2.   [6] *Ib.*, p. 91, n. 4.   [7] 6, 14.

FIRST CONSULSHIP OF POMPEY & CRASSUS

the *tribuni aerarii*, whom he manifestly did not mean to ignore.

Mommsen[1] believed that the *tribuni aerarii*, who, he holds, possessed as a rule 400,000 sesterces or more,[2] continued after they ceased to be paymasters, to act as the *curatores tribuum* (administrative chiefs of their respective tribes), of whom there were 350. This is a mere hypothesis, and the *tribuni aerarii* were certainly more numerous ;[3] was Mommsen right in affirming[4] that under the Aurelian law the only distinction between the *tribuni aerarii* and the *equites* was that the latter had, the former had not horses provided by the State—in other words, that the *equites* were 'unquestionably *equites equo publico*', that is, selected from the 18 centuries of 'Knights'? Strachan-Davidson[5] points out that in the famous letter *De petitione consulatus* (8, 33), which is commonly ascribed to Quintus Cicero, the *equitum centuriae* 'are expressly distinguished from the *equester ordo*', and that since they are described as ' mainly composed of young men ', they could not have been jurors, who under the lex Acilia[6] were over 30 years of age. Mommsen[7] could only extricate himself from this difficulty by denying the authenticity of the treatise ; and, as I shall presently show, there is a further reason for rejecting his view.[8]

Strachan-Davidson[9] holds that 'we can only differentiate the *equites* and the *tribuni aerarii* [he means those members of both orders who served on juries] by dwelling on the original significance of the phrases '. Remarking that 'there was nothing in law to prevent a revival of the *tributum* ' which the *tribuni aerarii* had originally collected and disbursed as paymasters, he conjectures that they ' may well have continued to be elected to what was . . . meantime an insignificant office ; which, however (like the Stewardship of the Chiltern Hundreds . . .), might afterwards come in useful for another purpose '. His conclusion[10] rests not only upon this supposition, but also upon the restoration of the missing words in the Acilian law which Mommsen substituted in the sixth edition of Bruns's *Fontes* for his original conjecture—quei in hac civit[*ate equum publicum habebit, habuerit*] (whoever in this state shall have or shall have ever had a public horse). ' According to the theory which I advocate,' he says, ' all persons who had ever served, all past and present members of the equestrian centuries, so far as they were not disqualified by age, by office, or by loss of property, might be called upon to act as jurors. . . . In a similar way the *ordo* of *tribuni aerarii* is to be taken to include all who have ever held that annual [?] office.' I doubt whether this theory will win general

---

[1] *D. röm. Tribus*, 1844, pp. 45, 51–2.   [2] Cf. *Paulys Real-Ency.*, vi, 291.
[3] Cic., *Pro Planc.*, 8, 21.
[4] *Röm. Staatsr.*, iii, 530, n. 2 ; *Röm. Strafr.*, 1899, p. 210.
[5] *Op. cit.*, pp. 87–8.
[6] C. G. Bruns, *Fontes iuris Rom.*⁶, 1893, p. 61, l. 6.
[7] *Röm. Staatsr.*, iii, 484, n. 3.
[8] I find that I am supported by Bursian's *Jahresbericht*, clxxvi, 1918, p. 224.
[9] *Op. cit.*, p. 93.   [10] *Ib.*, pp. 94–5.

acceptance ; rather it will provoke amazement at the rashness which could build so elaborate a structure upon a doubtful conjectural emendation. I see no reason to discard the old view that the *equites* who received from Gaius Gracchus the right of serving on juries valued that privilege because it gave them a hold over provincial governors who belonged to the aristocracy, and would have been by no means satisfied if, instead of belonging to the equestrian order in its widest sense, it had been confined to those who served or had once served with ' a public horse ' ; and I find confirmation of this opinion in a passage from a letter [1] which Cicero wrote to Atticus in 61 B. C.—' I suppose you have heard that our friends the Knights are all but estranged from the Senate. Their first grievance was the promulgation of a bill ... for the trial of those who had taken bribes for giving their verdict ' [as jurors] (*Credo enim te audisse nostros equites paene a senatu esse disiunctos, qui primum illud valde graviter tulerunt, promulgatum ... fuisse ut de eis qui ob iudicandum accepissent quaereretur*). To any one who reads the next section of the letter it will be obvious that *equites* is to be understood in the widest sense ; and the great body of men of business would not have been so indignant with the Senate unless their own interests—not merely those of the *equites equo publico*—had been threatened by the bill. As to the *tribuni aerarii*, even supposing that some of them were still elected to an office which had no duties, I find it hard to believe that the ex-officials whose existence Strachan-Davidson postulates were sufficiently numerous to furnish a large body of jurors, nor, considering Cicero's statement that the most important [if not the sole] qualification was property, can I understand why they should have been selected to the exclusion of other members of the order who were equally affluent.

Before I became acquainted with Strachan-Davidson's theory I concluded that the *equites* mentioned in the Aurelian law were *equites* in the widest sense, and that the *tribuni aerarii* must have been either holders of an office which was merely nominal, or officials who discharged duties of which we know nothing, or members of an order composed of all citizens whose property was between 300,000 and 400,000 sesterces, and whose qualification, like that of our Special Jurors, related to pecuniary status alone. But that all the numerous *tribuni aerarii* were even nominally officials is incredible ; and if only those who were *ex hypothesi* acting officials were eligible as jurors, they were too few. The last hypothesis then seems to be by far the most probable ; for I can see no reason to doubt, despite the lack of direct evidence, that the pecuniary qualification, the existence of which is certain, was between that of the *equites* and that of the fourth order, created by Augustus, whose minimum census was 200,000.

The statement of the scholiast that the *tribuni aerarii* were ' men of the same order ' as the *equites* requires explanation. That there was some distinction between them is self-evident. Even if Strachan-

[1] *Att.*, i, 17, 8. Cf. 18, 3.

Davidson is right in supposing that *tribuni aerarii* occasionally possessed the property required for admission to the order of *equites*—the sole evidence for the supposition is the statement of the scholiast—the majority certainly did not. Madvig[1] held that they were classed with the *equites* because both were registered in the list of jurors with reference to property; but, Mommsen[2] objects, granted that the *tribuni aerarii* had a definite monetary qualification, the alleged discrepancy between it and that of the *equites* was hardly a sufficient reason for identifying the two classes. Zumpt[3] accounted for the scholiast's remark by the fact that the distinction between *equites* and *tribuni aerarii* was unimportant, whereas the *equites* were markedly distinguished from the senators; and he holds that the title of *equites* was conceded to them by courtesy. This seems to me the most probable explanation.

Did Sulla abolish the farming of taxes in Asia, and was it restored by Pompey?—Both these questions were answered in the affirmative by Mommsen;[4] and Professor Tenney Frank[5] has attempted to demonstrate what Mommsen affirmed. It is evident, he argues, from one of Cicero's letters,[6] that Sulla took away the taxation of the province of Asia from the *publicani*; and Cicero's *Third Verrine*[7] proves that by 70 B.C.—the year of Pompey's first consulship—it had been restored. Marquardt,[8] indeed, thinks that it was restored soon after Sulla's death; but, Frank urges, the Senate from 80 to 70 B.C. 'kept the Knights in subjection'; and from 74 to 70 Lucullus, an enemy of the Knights, managed the finances of Asia according to his own views. Therefore the change must have been made in 70, after Pompey had been elected consul 'by the plutocratic—democratic bloc'. The Knights desired the restoration of the censorship, which Pompey carried out, because it would restore their old privilege of collecting the taxes in Asia.

Professor Frank does not adequately represent Marquardt's views. Marquardt thought that the evidence that Sulla withdrew the collection of the taxes from the *publicani* was insufficient; and the passage from which he inferred that the withdrawal, if it ever occurred, was only transitory, is the very sentence in Cicero's letter which Professor Frank quotes in support of his own thesis. Marquardt also cites a passage from Appian[9] in which Sulla is said to have told the taxpayers of Asia that they were 'to pay immediately five years' tribute': Sulla, he says, may only have meant a lump sum fixed

---

[1] *Op. cit.*, pp. 256–8. [2] *D. röm. Tribus*, p. 55. [3] *Op. cit.*, p. 196.
[4] *Röm. Gesch.*, ii⁸, 1889, p. 346; iii⁸, 1889, p. 102 (Eng. tr., iv, 1908, pp. 110–11, 480). Mommsen's footnote (ii, 346) is not intended to prove his assertion; for one of the facts which he there emphasizes is that 'the Sullan apportionment was assumed as a basis in the case of subsequent imposts (Cic., *pro Flacc.*, 14, 32)', and Flaccus was Governor of Asia in 62 B.C.—eight years after the time when, according to Mommsen, the system of farming the taxes was restored.
[5] *Class. Philol.*, ix, 1914, p. 191. Cf. T. Frank's *Roman Imperialism*, 1914, pp. 316, 326, n. 5.
[6] *Q. fr.*, i, 1, 33. [7] 6, 12. [8] *Röm. Staatsverw.*, i², 1881, p. 338.
[9] *Mithr.*, 62, μόνους ὑμῖν ἐπιγράφω πέντε ἐτῶν φόρους ἐσενεγκεῖν αὐτίκα.

according to the previous yield of the taxes as farmed. V. Chapot [1] thinks it probable that Sulla merely imposed a special contribution on the province by way of punishment for the massacre of the Italians in Asia and of indemnity for the cost of the war, and that this exaction left the existing arrangements for the collection of the ordinary taxes unaltered. More than probable, I should say; for since Sulla only levied five years' tribute and levied it not yearly but as a whole, self-evidently Appian did not mean that he made any change in the existing system of taxation. In the *Third Verrine* there is nothing about the restoration of the taxes of Asia to the *publicani* : Cicero only says that by the Sempronian law it was granted to them. The passage in Cicero's letter runs as follows : *Nomen autem publicani aspernari non possunt, qui pendere ipsi vectigal sine publicano non potuerint, quod iis Sulla aequaliter discripserat* (' They [the Asiatics] cannot spurn the designation *publicanus*, for without his aid they were unable to pay the impost which Sulla had equitably assessed '). These words obviously mean not, as Frank imagines, that Sulla had deprived the *publicani* of the privilege of collecting the taxes, but that the people of Asia had not the organization necessary for raising the indemnity exacted by Sulla (which had nothing to do with ordinary taxation) without the assistance of professional tax-collectors.

My conclusion is that there is no evidence that Sulla abolished the system of farming the taxes in Asia, and therefore none that Pompey restored it.

Were the 'Knights' opposed to the Gabinian law?—Mommsen says that ' the mercantile aristocracy, which felt its exclusive rights endangered by such a radical revolution ', was violently opposed to the Gabinian law.[2] Is this statement based upon the opposition of the tribune Roscius, who in 67 B. C. carried the law restoring to the Knights the privilege of having seats reserved for them in the theatre ?[3]

The debate on the Gabinian law.—Dio Cassius [4] differs from Plutarch [5] about the order in which the speeches on the Gabinian law were delivered, and both omit to mention that Hortensius spoke against it.[6] According to Plutarch, who ignores the speeches of Pompey, Gabinius, and Trebellius, Catulus was followed by Roscius : according to Dio, Pompey spoke first, and was followed successively by Gabinius, Trebellius, Roscius, and Catulus. Both relate the grotesque incident of the falling crow (which I have not noticed in my narrative) immediately after describing the abortive demonstration of Roscius. Drumann [7] holds that Dio perverted the order of events.

[1] *La prov. rom. d'Asie*, 1904, p. 328.
[2] *Röm. Gesch.*, iii⁸, 1889, p. 114 (Eng. tr., iv, 1908, p. 393).
[3] See p. 249. Mommsen (*op. cit.*, p. 107) asserts that by this law the Senate tried to gain over the Knights, who 'had made common cause with' the populace in 70 B.C.
[4] xxxvi, 25–30.   [5] *Pomp.*, 25, 4–5.
[6] Cic., *De imp. Cn. Pomp.*, 17, 52.
[7] *Gesch. Roms*, iv², 1910, p. 418, n. 3.

FIRST CONSULSHIP OF POMPEY & CRASSUS 397

Perhaps he did; but with all his faults he was better acquainted with Roman affairs than any other Greek who wrote under the Empire, and Drumann does not explain what was his motive for perversion.

Hortensius may have followed Catulus, for there is a gap in Dio's history after his version of the latter's speech. Asconius [1] says that 'Trebellius withdrew his veto, and accordingly Gabinius carried his bill'. George Long [2] is hardly justified in inferring from this that Trebellius was the last speaker, for the bill was not carried till a later day.

POMPEY AND THE MEDITERRANEAN PIRATES

That Pompey actually enrolled 120,000 legionaries [3] for the war against the pirates is most improbable; for of the twenty-four or twenty-five admirals whom he was empowered to nominate [4] only thirteen appear to have served.

Plutarch [5] says that Pompey appointed one commander to each of thirteen regions. Evidently he drew a hasty inference from the number of the admirals; and I prefer the precise statement of Appian, [6] who specifies nine regions and names the thirteen officers to whom they were assigned. The narrative of Florus [7] is inaccurate.

The statement of the epitomizer of Livy [8] that Pompey cleared 'the whole sea' (*toto mari*) in 40 days, obviously refers only to the Western Mediterranean and to the first period of the war. The second lasted 49 days.[9]

It would be waste of time to comment on the glaringly discordant, though minutely precise statements of Strabo,[10] Pliny,[11] Appian,[12] and others,[13] concerning the number of the ships which Pompey captured or destroyed. When Pliny informs us that Pompey himself claimed to have accounted for 846, we may suppose, not that he was romancing, but that every little boat was made to swell the total: [14] so when he recorded on his Pyrenean trophy that he had taken 876 towns,[15] every hamlet was doubtless reckoned.

---

[1] Ed. Clark, p. 72, ll. 12–21 (ed. Stangl, p. 57).
[2] *Decline of the Roman Republic*, iii, 1869, p. 118.   [3] See p. 172.
[4] Plut., *Pomp.*, 26, 2; App.. *Mithr.*, 94. Dio (xxxvi, 37, 1), perhaps thinking of the original bill, says fifteen. P. Willems (*Le sénat*, &c., ii, 1883, pp. 614–15), remarking that the Gabinian law infringed for the first time the traditional right of the Senate to appoint *legati*, argues that Pompey must have submitted his list of nominees to the Senate for approbation; for, according to Cicero (*In Vat.*, 15, 36), Vatinius was the first to flout the authority of the Senate by nominating himself under his *plebiscitum* in 59 B.C. a *legatus* of Caesar. Cf. Th. Mommsen, *Röm. Staatsr.*, ii³, 1887, p. 680, n. *I*.   [5] *Pomp.*, 26, 3.
[6] *Mithr.*, 95. Cf. Varro, *R. R.*, ii, prooem., 6.   [7] i, 41, 9–10.
[8] 99.   [9] Cic., *De imp. Cn. Pomp.*, 12, 35. Cf. Plut., *Pomp.*, 28, 1.
[10] xiv, 3, 3.   [11] *Nat. Hist.*, vii, 25 (26), 93.
[12] *Mithr.*, 96. Cf. 117.   [13] Plut., *Pomp.*, 45, 2; Zonaras, x, 5.
[14] Cf. *Philol.*, lvi, 1897, p. 431.   [15] Pliny, vii, 26 (27), 96.

WAS BITHYNIA BEQUEATHED TO ROME?

That Nicomedes Philopator bequeathed Bithynia to the Romans is stated by the epitomizer of Livy,[1] Velleius,[2] Arrian,[3] Appian,[4] Ampelius,[5] and Eutropius.[6] Velleius, Ampelius, and Eutropius, however, copied Livy. On the other hand, we read in a scholium[7] that Nicomedes died intestate; and Maurenbrecher[8] remarks that the scholiast apparently derived this, like most of his statements, from Sallust. In Bursian's *Jahresbericht*[9] Maurenbrecher affirms that the story of the bequest was a false Livian tradition, originally derived from some writer who desired to whitewash the Roman Government; and, he argues, since Sallust[10] leaves it an open question whether the pretender who claimed to be the son and successor of Nicomedes was legitimate or not, he could not have related in his history the conventional fable of the will. In view of the statement of the scholiast and of the fact, recorded by Sallust, that 'many persons eagerly hurried from Bithynia [to Rome] to testify that the son was a supposititious child' (*Quos adversum multi ex Bithynia volentes accurrere falsum filium arguituri*[11]), it must be admitted that the Roman annexation of Bithynia was at least suspicious.

LUCULLUS IN THE THIRD MITHRADATIC WAR

The chronology of the war.—When the records of a war leave room for doubt even as to the year in which this or that campaign occurred, one cannot expect satisfactory information about strategy or tactics. Such are the materials for the history of the campaigns of Lucullus. First of all, we have to inquire in what year Nicomedes, King of Bithynia, died, and when the war began.

Appian, after describing the Spanish campaign of 75 B.C., says at the beginning of the next chapter[12] that 'In the following year, the 176th Olympiad, the Romans acquired two provinces by bequest, Bithynia, left by Nicomedes, and Cyrene,' &c. (Τοῦ δ' ἐπιόντος ἔτους, ἕκτης ἑβδομηκοστῆς καὶ ἑκατοστῆς ὀλυμπιάδος οὔσης· δύο μὲν ἐκ διαθηκῶν ἔθνη 'Ρωμαίοις προσεγίγνετο· Βιθυνία τε, Νικομήδους ἀπολιπόντος καὶ Κυρήνη). Appian does not necessarily mean that Nicomedes died in 74, for Cyrene was bequeathed in 96: he may only mean that Bithynia was occupied by Rome in 74. According to Eutropius,[13] however, Nicomedes died in the consulship of Lucullus and Cotta, that is in 74 B.C.

Cicero observes that Lucullus and Cotta were dispatched to the

---
[1] 93. [2] ii, 4, 1; 39, 2. [3] *Fragm. hist. Graec.*, ed. C. Müller, iii, 591.
[4] Mithr., 7, 71; *B. C.*, i, 111, 517. [5] 33, 3. [6] vi, 6.
[7] *Schol. Gronov.*, ed. Stangl, p. 316 (ed. Orelli, p. 437).
[8] *C. Sall. Crispi hist. rel.*, fasc. i, p. 59.
[9] cxiii, 1902 (1903), p. 246. [10] ii, 71; iv, 69, 9.
[11] ii, 71. [12] *B. C.*, i, 111, 517. [13] vi, 6.

seat of war during their consulship ; [1] the epitomizer of Livy [2] and Eutropius [3] add that they began military operations in that year, and, as H. Bernhardt [4] points out, the epitomizer, chronicling the events of the same year, calls Lucullus a proconsul. Cicero in another passage [5] says, '[Lucullus] administered his consulship ... in such a manner that all praised his industry and recognized his ability ; afterwards, having been dispatched to the Mithradatic War, &c. (*consulatum ... ita gessit ut diligentiam admirarentur omnes, ingenium agnoscerent ; post ad Mithridaticum bellum missus*, &c.). On the other hand, Velleius [6] says that seven years before the enactment of the Manilian law, that is, it would seem, in 73 B. C., Lucullus obtained the province of Asia after (?) his consulship and encountered Mithradates (*Cum ... L. Lucullus, qui ante septem annos ex consulatu sortitus Asiam Mithridati oppositus erat ... idem bellum adhuc administraret, Manilius ... legem tulit*).

Plutarch,[7] after describing the intrigue by which Lucullus obtained the province of Cilicia, states that ' Cotta, his colleague [in the consulship]... was sent with a fleet to guard the Propontis ' (Κόττας ὁ συνάρχων αὐτοῦ ... ἀπεστάλη μετὰ νεῶν τὴν Προποντίδα φυλάξων).

Appian [8] informs us that Mithradates invaded Bithynia ' just after the death of Nicomedes ' (Νικομήδους ἄρτι τεθνεῶτος), and that ' Lucullus, appointed consul and commander-in-chief in this war, left Rome with a legion ' (Λούκουλλος, ὑπατεύειν καὶ στρατηγεῖν αἱρεθεὶς τοῦδε τοῦ πολέμου, τέλος μέν τι στρατιωτῶν ἦγεν ἐκ Ῥώμης).[9]

According to Phlegon,[10] Lucullus, who was besieging Amisus in the first year of the 177th Olympiad (72 B. C.), left Murena to prosecute the siege and marched himself against Cabira, where he passed the winter. ' Further,' Phlegon continues, 'he ordered [his lieutenant] Hadrian to attack Mithradates, and defeated him ' (Λεύκολλος δὲ Ἀμισὸν ἐπολιόρκει, καὶ Μούρηναν ἐπὶ τῆς πολιορκίας καταλιπὼν ... αὐτὸς ... προῆγεν ἐπὶ Καβείρων, ὅπου διεχείμαζε. Καὶ Ἀδριανὸν ἐπέταξε πολεμῆσαι Μιθριδάτῃ καὶ πολεμήσας ἐνίκησε).

According to Théodore Reinach,[11] the war began in 73 B. C. ; Amisus was besieged in the winter of 72–71 ; Lucullus defeated Mithradates near Cabira in 71. Mommsen,[12] who is supported by Maurenbrecher [13] and others, held that the war began in 74, and dated the subsequent events accordingly.

Reinach affirms that in the British Museum are coins of Nicomedes Philopator, which bear the Bithynian date 224. That year, he

[1] *Pro Mur.*, 15, 33, 'Ad quod bellum duobus consulibus ita missis ut alter Mithridatem persequeretur, alter Bithyniam tueretur,' &c.
[2] 93–4. [3] vi, 6. [4] *Chronol. d. Mithr. Kriege*, &c., 1896, p. 19.
[5] *Acad. prior.*, ii, 1, 1. I have quoted from Prof. J. S. Reid's translation.
[6] ii, 33, 1. Bernhardt (*l.c.*), asserting that *ex consulatu* is to be taken in a causal, not a temporal sense, explains that as the Manilian law was passed in the beginning of 66, *ante septem annos* means 'in the year 74 '. Arithmetically the explanation is no doubt defensible, *septem annos* meaning seven years and so many months. [7] *Luc.*, 6, 7. [8] *Mithr.*, 70. [9] *Ib.*, 72.
[10] Fr. 12. [11] *Mithr. Eupator*, 1890, pp. 318, n. 2 ; 321, n. 1.
[12] *Röm. Gesch.*, iii³, 1889, p. 57 (Eng. tr., iv, 1908, p. 325).
[13] *C. Sall. Crispi hist. rel.*, fasc. i, 1891, p. 47 ; fasc. ii, 1893, pp. 228–31.

explains, began in October, 74 B. C.; and, as we learn from Appian [?] and Eutropius that Nicomedes died in 74, it follows that the date was between October and December, and that the war did not begin until the following year. Reinach, of course, takes account of the relevant passages in Cicero, Livy, and Eutropius; but he insists that all three writers expressed themselves loosely, and in support of this view quotes passages from Livy[1] and Cicero[2] in which proconsuls were incorrectly called consuls. Plutarch's narrative, he continues, shows that the province of Cilicia was substituted for that which Lucullus would have held in the ordinary course on the expiration of his consulship, and that Lucullus did not leave Italy until he had ceased to be consul: Cicero in his *Academica* says the same. Reinach[3] admits that the testimony of Phlegon is not consistent with the date (71) which he assigns to the campaign of Cabira; but he disposes of this difficulty by altering the text.[4]

Maurenbrecher finds no difficulty in refuting the alleged evidence of the Bithynian coins. He suggests that they were struck, not by Nicomedes Philopator, but by his son, who was proclaimed King by the Bithynians after his father died; they bear the image of Nicomedes the Second, not of Philopator, and there is no difference between the coins which were minted under the former and those which were issued by the latter. Sallust, who in his Second Book[5] alludes to the death of Philopator and the treaty concluded between Mithradates and Sertorius before inserting the letter which Pompey wrote to the Senate in 75 B. C.,[6] plainly shows that Philopator died in that year and not in 74. As to the argument that Cicero, Livy, and Eutropius loosely described proconsuls as consuls, one might not unreasonably suppose that one of the three was capable of making such a mistake, but who will believe that in this case all were equally careless? Furthermore, Eutropius,[7] in the chapter in which he narrates the events of 73 mentions consuls again, which shows that in the preceding chapter he, like his authority Livy, was narrating what happened in the consulship of Lucullus and Cotta.[8] Ridiculing Reinach's correction of Phlegon's text, Maurenbrecher notes that Arthur Tilley[9] strove to turn the obstacle which Phlegon presents to Reinach's theory by asserting that Lucullus 'advanced against Cabira in the same winter' (72–71), which is stultified by Plutarch's words, 'after the winter' (μετὰ τὸν χειμῶνα)[10] and Appian's, 'when fine weather set in' (ἱσταμένου δ' ἦρος),[11] that is in the spring of 72. Maurenbrecher then undertakes to show that Phlegon made no mistake, and that there is no real discrepancy

---

[1] xxvi, 33, 4. 7.   [2] *Verr.*, ii, 16, 39.   [3] *Op. cit.*, p. 336, n. 2
[4] 'Au reste', he says, 'il faut peut-être corriger le texte ainsi: προῆγεν ἐπὶ Καβείρων, ὅπου διεχείμαζε [Μιθριδάτης].
[5] Fr. 71, 79.   [6] *Ib.*, 98.   [7] vi, 7.
[8] Maurenbrecher might have made his point more forcibly if he had said that Eutropius ascribes the outbreak of the rebellion of Spartacus, which began in 73, to the year following the dispatch of Lucullus to the East
[9] *Eng. Hist. Rev.*, vii, 1892, p. 338.
[10] *Luc.*, 15, 1.   [11] *Mithr.*, 79

THIRD MITHRADATIC WAR

between his statement and the statements of our other authorities. When Phlegon, speaking of the 177th Olympiad (July, 72–July, 71) says, 'Lucullus, who was besieging Amisus, left Murena to prosecute the siege with two legions and marched himself with the remaining three against Cabira', he is describing the lapse of an entire *Roman* year from one winter to the next : at the beginning of 72 Lucullus was blockading Amisus ; in the spring he marched for Cabira, near which he passed the winter of 72–71 ; in the spring of 71 he, or rather his lieutenant Hadrian, defeated Mithradates. Finally, Maurenbrecher denies [1] that there is any inconsistency between the statements which Cicero made in his *Pro Murena* and in his *Academica* : Lucullus might justly be said to have gone to Asia after his consulship even though he went in 74, for he remained in Rome as consul until after the death of Octavian, whom he succeeded in the proconsulship of Cilicia.

Now Reinach's numismatic argument is certainly inconclusive ; but when Maurenbrecher urges that because Sallust alluded to the death of Nicomedes before he inserted his version of Pompey's letter, we must reject the testimony of Eutropius and refer the event to 75, I cannot follow him. Is it not conceivable that Sallust in lost fragments of his Second Book, which may have preceded the one that refers to the death of Nicomedes, described events in Asia that occurred in or before 75, and then proceeded to describe events connected therewith that occurred in 74 ? In that case he might without any violation of historical perspective have afterwards resumed his narrative of the Spanish campaign of 75.[2] Maurenbrecher's argument, however, is not essential to his chronology of the war : if Nicomedes died early in 74, that chronology is so far undisturbed. Again, when Reinach discerns in Plutarch's narrative proof that Cilicia was substituted for the province which Lucullus would normally have held *on the expiration of his consulship*, his mind is possessed by the notion that consuls might not leave Italy during their consulship.[3] But the authority to whom Maurenbrecher in the last resort appeals is Phlegon. Maurenbrecher reminds us [4] that, according to Plutarch,[5] the sieges of Cyzicus and Amisus occurred in two successive winters : he interprets Phlegon as meaning that the second of these winters was that of 73–72 ; therefore, he argues, the first must have begun in 74. Granted ; but that does not prove that Hadrian defeated Mithradates in the spring of 71. According to Maurenbrecher, the campaign which took place on the line between Eupatoria and Cabira—a distance of 27 miles—lasted an entire year or more ! That is alike ridiculous and incredible. There is not the faintest indication in Plutarch, Appian, or Memnon that the campaign, which began in spring, lasted through the winter into the following spring, and it is transparently clear that it ended with the defeat and flight of Mithradates in the course of the year in which

---

[1] Bursian's *Jahresbericht*, cxiii, 1902 (1903), p. 246.
[2] The chronology of Sallust's *Catiline* is more than once perverted.
[3] See p. 370 and n. 7.   [4] *Op. cit.*, i, p. 47.   [5] *Luc.*, 33, 4.

it began. How, then, Maurenbrecher may ask, do you explain the passage in Phlegon ? I believe that Phlegon meant what he said—that Amisus was being besieged in the first year of the 177th Olympiad (which he doubtless identified with the Roman year 682 [72]); that Lucullus, leaving Murena to prosecute the siege [which had begun in the previous autumn], marched to Cabira and there spent the winter of 72–71 ; and that his lieutenant, Hadrian, defeated Mithradates. If he meant that Hadrian gained his victory after Lucullus reached Cabira, he blundered grossly : anyhow his account is misleading.[1]

Nevertheless I agree with Maurenbrecher that the war began in 74. All the authorities, except perhaps Velleius, say that Lucullus took the field while he was still consul ; Bernhardt may be right in holding that when Velleius wrote *ex consulatu* he did not mean *post consulatum*; and it is much more likely that Cicero in his *Academica* meant that Lucullus left Rome after he had discharged his administrative duties, but in his consulship, than that in his speech *Pro Murena* he meant *proconsul* though he said *consul*. That, referring to a fact which all his readers knew, he contradicted in the *Academica* what he had said in *Pro Murena* is simply incredible. Orosius [2] says that in the year in which Mithradates fled to Sinope and Amisus,[3] that is in the second year of the war, Catiline was prosecuted for ' incest ' ; and since we learn from Cicero [4] that 63 B. C. was the tenth year ' after the acquittal of the [Vestal] virgins ', with one of whom Catiline was charged with having committed adultery, it is probable that the prosecution occurred in 73. It is clear, says Bernhardt,[5] from Phlegon's statement that Lucullus passed the winter of 72–71 in Cabira ; reckoning back, we come to 74 as the date of the outbreak of the war. Bernhardt, differing from Maurenbrecher, and anticipating my conclusion, takes Phlegon's words as meaning that Lucullus wintered in Cabira after he had captured it and therefore after he had defeated Mithradates and forced him to flee for refuge

---

[1] Maurenbrecher holds that, as Mithradates, after he fled from Cabira, spent twenty months in Armenia before Tigranes would see him (Memnon, 55), and as Lucullus began his march against Tigranes in the spring of 69, the defeat of Mithradates near Cabira must have occurred in the summer of 71. If this were true, the siege of Amisus would have begun in the winter of 72–71 ; the siege of Cyzicus in the winter of 73–72 ; and the war in 73, not, as Maurenbrecher maintains, in 74. But there is no sufficient evidence that the twenty months terminated in 69. Memnon leaves the date uncertain. Appian (*Mithr.*, 85), whose chronology is frequently confused, says that Tigranes declined to see Mithradates until [in the autumn of 69] he marched against Lucullus, who was besieging Tigranocerta ! Plutarch (*Luc.*, 22, 1) clearly implies that he saw him just after Appius Claudius, having accomplished his mission to Tigranes (see p. 190), started to return to Lucullus, a movement which cannot be dated later than 70. Maurenbrecher must admit that Lucullus could not enter Cabira until Hadrian had defeated Mithradates (Plut., *Luc.*, 18, 1) and apparently did not until he himself, after subduing the Chaldaei and the Tibareni, was returning to prosecute the siege of Amisus (cf. Memnon, 45, 1–2 with Plut., *Luc.*, 19, 2).

[2] vi, 2, 24 ; 3, 1.
[3] A geographical blunder.
[4] *In Cat.*, iii, 4, 9.
[5] *Op. cit.*, p. 20.

into Armenia. Phlegon, I may add, though he alludes to the campaign in which Lucullus defeated Mithradates after relating that Lucullus wintered in Cabira, does not expressly say that it followed that winter; and I suspect that the allusion was an afterthought. Bernhardt [1] argues, further, that the operations which Mithradates undertook in the Propontis [2] after he failed at Cyzicus, that is in the second year of the war, would have had small prospect of success in 72; for Marcus Lucullus was then fighting in Thrace, whereas in 73 Mithradates could count on the support of the still unconquered Thracians. The argument is ingenious, if not conclusive: at all events the balance of probability is greatly in favour of the date for which Bernhardt contends.

The alleged invasion of the province Asia by Mithradates.—Ferrero,[3] relying on a statement of Plutarch in his life of Sertorius,[4] argues that Mithradates ' accompanied the division of the army which entered Asia and not that which invaded Bithynia ', but afterwards invaded Bithynia in person in order to attack Cotta. But there is no evidence that any division entered Asia, except a force commanded by Marius, the emissary of Sertorius,[5] until Mithradates was about to besiege Cyzicus.[6] Plutarch in his life of Lucullus [7] says that Mithradates invaded Bithynia (which he would of course have traversed if he intended to invade Asia), and Appian [8] says the same, neither mentioning an invasion of Asia; for Plutarch, when he says in the chapter of his *Sertorius* to which Ferrero appeals that Mithradates took some towns in Asia, evidently means that some towns were induced to side with him by Marius, the emissary of Sertorius. It would have been folly for Mithradates to invade Asia until he had subdued Bithynia, and it was with that aim that he besieged Cyzicus, the capture of which, he expected, would open the way to Asia.[9]

The earlier operations of Lucullus.—The original accounts of the earlier operations of Lucullus are on certain points obscure. To begin with, modern commentators are not agreed as to the place from which Lucullus began his march! Maurenbrecher,[10] apparently arguing from the fact that his province was Cilicia, affirms that he moved from Cilicia into Phrygia. But he also had charge of the province of Asia,[11] to which Memnon [12] says that he was in the first instance sent; Mithradates expected him to invade Cappadocia; and if he started from Cilicia, it is impossible to explain why he was in Phrygia when he heard that Cotta was in peril. Evidently he had set out from Asia to invade Cappadocia and Pontus. Plutarch [13] says that Cotta, hearing that Lucullus was approaching, forced on a battle because he was eager to gain a victory before Lucullus, who was in

---

[1] *Ib.*, p. 28, n. 1. Bernhardt spoils a good case by some bad arguments.
[2] See p. 183.
[3] *Grandezza e decadenza di Roma*, ii, 1902, pp. 540–2 (Eng. tr., ii, 329–30).
[4] 24, 2.   [5] Plut., *Luc.*, 8, 7.   [6] See the next section.
[7] 7, 5.   [8] *Mithr.*, 71.   [9] Cic., *Pro Mur.*, 15, 33.
[10] *C. Sall. Crispi hist. rel.*, fasc. ii, p. 116.   [11] See p. 179, n. 1.
[12] 37.   [13] *Luc.*, 8, 2.

Phrygia, could forestall him. But this implies that Lucullus was marching to join Cotta, whereas, as Memnon [1] expressly says—and Plutarch [2] unwittingly confirms his statement when he tells us that Lucullus's soldiers were anxious to invade Pontus—he was recalled by the news that Cotta had been beaten.

The part which Deiotarus played is so uncertain that I have refrained in my narrative from referring it to any definite time. The epitomizer of Livy,[3] immediately after stating that Lucullus (evidently before the siege of Cyzicus) engaged in successful cavalry skirmishes with Mithradates, adds that Deiotarus defeated the king's officers in Phrygia, that is in the province of Asia. Mommsen,[4] remarking (apparently on the evidence of Plutarch [5]) that 'A considerable number of cities in Asia Minor opened their gates to the Sertorian pro-praetor who was placed at the head of the Roman province' and (apparently on the evidence of Appian [6]) that 'they massacred... the Roman families settled among them: the Pisidians, Isaurians, and Cilicians took up arms against Rome', adds that if Deiotarus had not come to the rescue, 'Lucullus would have had to begin with recapturing the interior of the Roman province' and that 'even as it was, he lost in pacifying the province and driving back the enemy precious time, for which the slight successes achieved by his cavalry were far from affording compensation'. Mommsen believed all this to have happened before Lucullus advanced towards Calchedon. But there is no evidence that he lost any time in pacifying the province or in driving back the enemy, and the only evidence as to the time when Deiotarus intervened is that of Appian,[7] who says, rightly or wrongly, that it synchronized with the siege of Cyzicus, and according to whom the Pisidians, Isaurians, and Cilicians, so far from taking up arms 'against Rome', were defeated by a lieutenant of Mithradates ! Those who share Matthew Arnold's view that history is a 'Mississippi of falsehood' would chuckle if they compared Mommsen's narrative with that of Théodore Reinach [8] and with our precious original authorities.

The operations between Amisus and Cabira.—Plutarch and Appian relate in considerable detail the operations that ended with the flight of Mithradates in 72 B. C.; and Mr. J. A. R. Munro,[9] who is thoroughly familiar with the ground, has attempted to explain what they left obscure. In order that readers may be able to form their own opinions of the explanation, which shall be presently transcribed, I reproduce the statements of the authorities, omitting everything which is not essential. The narrative of Memnon (43-5) as a whole is not helpful, though it contains one statement of which we shall have to take account.

[1] 39. [2] *Luc.*, 8, 4. [3] 94.
[4] *Röm. Gesch.*, iii⁸, 1889, p. 57 (Eng. tr., iv, 1908, pp. 325–6).
[5] *Sert.*, 24, 2–3.
[6] *Mithr.*, 75.
[7] *Ib.* The services of Deiotarus are noticed by Cicero, *Phil.*, xi, 13, 33.
[8] *Mithr. Eupator*, pp. 321–4.
[9] *Journ. Hell. Studies*, xxi, 1901, pp. 56–8.

PLUTARCH	APPIAN
Luc., 14, 1. Lucullus marches through Bithynia and Galatia into the kingdom of Mithradates. § 2. As he at first suffers from lack of provisions, Galatian porters carry corn for his army; but advancing and subduing the inhabitants, he finds abundant supplies. §§ 2-7. Having plundered the country as far as Themiscyra (15, 1), he lays siege to Amisus (apparently to humour his troops, who are eager for loot), but does so sluggishly on purpose: at the end of winter he leaves Murena to prosecute the siege, and marches against Mithradates, who is encamped at Cabira, having there collected 40,000 foot and 4,000 horse. § 2. Mithradates with these troops crosses the Lycus, and defeats the Romans in a cavalry combat. § 3. Lucullus avoids the plain on account of the enemy's superiority in cavalry, yet fears to take the difficult wooded route through the hills: a Greek prisoner, however, offers to guide him to a suitable position, where there is a fort, dominating Cabira. § 4. Lucullus trusts him, gets through the pass in the night, occupies the position, and becomes visible to the enemy. §§ 5-8. Accident is said to have brought on a partial engagement, in which the Romans were at first worsted; but Lucullus restored the battle, and the enemy were beaten. 17, 1. Sornatius, sent with 10 cohorts to get corn, is pursued by a lieutenant of Mithradates, whom he defeats. § 2. Hadrian, dispatched on a like errand, is said to have virtually annihilated a strong force which had been sent against him. §§ 3-8. Mithradates escapes alone. 18, 1. The capture of Cabira is mentioned.	*Mithr.*, 78. Lucullus advances [from Bithynia] into the interior, and there finds abundant supplies. He besieges Amisus, Eupatoria, 'which Mithradates founded close to Amisus', and Themiscyra. The Roman mining parties at Themiscyra are baffled by the ingenuity of the garrison. Mithradates, who is collecting a new army (40,000 foot and 4,000 horse) at Cabira, sends supplies to Amisus. 79. In the early spring Lucullus marches over the hills against Mithradates. Emerging from the hills, he descends on Cabira, but is beaten in a cavalry combat and returns to the hills. On several successive days Mithradates offers battle, but as Lucullus will not descend into the plain, he endeavours to find a way of approaching him. 80 Lucullus, fearing to descend into the plain on account of the enemy's superiority in cavalry, and being unable to find a circuitous route, captures a hunter and, guided by him, moves round by unbeaten tracks above Mithradates, descends, and encamps in rear of a torrent. Lack of supplies forces him to send into Cappadocia for corn,[1] which leads to skirmishes with the enemy. In one of these combats the enemy flee, but are rallied by Mithradates, who came to the rescue from his camp, and drive the Romans into the hills.[2] Mithradates orders the flower of his cavalry to lie in wait for the foragers returning from Cappadocia. 81. The Pontic cavalry encounter the vanguard of the foragers in the pass, impatiently attack them there, where their own horses are useless, instead of waiting till they emerge into the plain, and are beaten. Mithradates, hearing of this disaster and expecting to be attacked in force by Lucullus, flees with a few followers and (82) escapes to Comana, and thence to Tigranes.

The reader will have noticed that Plutarch omits to mention the sieges of Eupatoria and Themiscyra; that Appian assigns to Eupatoria a position different from that of the known town of the same name; that the two narratives differ as to the site of the first cavalry

---

[1] Cf. Sall. (ed. B. Maurenbrecher), iv, 8.

[2] Maurenbrecher (*op. cit.*, fasc. i, p. 62) remarks that 'in the second battle' Appian, whose authority, he thinks, was Strabo, makes the Pontic troops victorious, Plutarch, who followed Sallust, the Romans. He may be right, but it is not certain that the two combats were the same.

combat; that Appian says nothing about the fort which Plutarch mentions; that he apparently ignores the combat which Plutarch describes in 15, 5–8, and does not chronicle the victory of Sornatius; and that Plutarch apparently ignores the skirmish, mentioned by Appian, in which the Romans were beaten.[1]

'Mithridates', says Mr. Munro, 'took up his position at Cabira (Niksar) . . . and organised a fresh army. Lucullus, much hampered by lack of transport and provisions, advanced slowly through Galatia, and probably entered Pontus by way of Chorum and the Chiliokomon. . . . He left Amasia and the Phanaroea, which were occupied by Mithridates's troops, on his right, and marched straight down the great north road to Amisus, to which he laid siege. . . . Mithridates contrived to aid the besieged with supplies and reinforcements. . . . It was doubtless partly to check this assistance, partly to open the way for his attack on Cabira, that Lucullus, leaving . . . Murena to blockade Amisus, marched . . . against Themiscyra and Eupatoria, which guarded the lower and upper ends of the pass. The fortress of Eupatoria . . . stood just at the mouth of the gorge on a rocky knoll by the right bank of the Iris a little below its junction with the Lycus, and commanded not only the pass down the river, but also the bridge which carried the great trunk road across it. The capture, by storm or by treachery, of these two strongholds admitted Lucullus to the Phanaroea.[2] He turned eastwards along the trunk road to attack Mithridates.

[1] Memnon (43, 3) mentions both.
[2] Mr. Munro remarks (p. 57, n. 1) that 'the route followed by Lucullus is defined only as having lain " through the mountains ", and no relation is recognized between it and his attacks on Themiscyra and Eupatoria. We are left in the dark as to the fate of Themiscyra, which must have been taken before Lucullus could proceed. The capture of Eupatoria is falsely involved with the siege of Amisus. *If* there really was a second Eupatoria, a suburb of Amisus . . . it might explain this misapprehension and the contradiction between Memnon, who tells how Eupatoria was carried by . . . assault, and Appian, who implies that it surrendered to the Romans (*Mithr.*, 115). But I am inclined to believe that the root of the confusion may have been that the story of the siege of Amisus was reserved to the date of the capture of the city, and with it the attack on Eupatoria (cf. Memnon's order), so that the latter was divorced from the march of Lucullus, and falsely connected with Amisus. . . . Memnon's account of the storming of Eupatoria looks like a reduplication of the capture of Amisus', &c.

The question which Mr. Munro raises can be easily answered. There was only one Eupatoria. Long (*Decline of the Roman Republic*, iii, 23) insists that 'As Cabira was so near to Eupatoria at the junction of the Lycus and *Iris*, it was not the place of that name which Lucullus was besieging; and besides Strabo [xii, 3, 30] informs us that this Eupatoria was only a half-finished place when Pompeius some years later was in these parts'. The first reason depends upon the assumption that Appian was right in calling the Eupatoria which Lucullus besieged a suburb of Amisus: the second is no better. Long must have forgotten the passage (*Mithr.*, 115) in which Appian says that Mithradates [when he regained possession of Pontus in 68–67 B.C.] destroyed Eupatoria, to punish its inhabitants for having surrendered to Lucullus. Appian also says that Eupatoria was the town which Pompey afterwards called Magnopolis; and this town, as we learn from Strabo, was at the confluence of the *Iris* and the Lycus. Therefore, considering the gross carelessness of Appian, I have no doubt that

'From Eupatoria to Cabira the road runs through level ground between the right bank of the Lycus and the foot of the Paryadres range. But about 15 miles from Eupatoria and 12 from Cabira it has to cross the broken ridge of hilly country which divides the Phanaroea into two basins. The Lycus has cut a channel through the ridge, but neither the Eupatoria road on the right bank nor the Amasia road on the left, can follow the river at all closely. The latter road crosses the Lycus a little above the gorge on a bridge, which ... seems to be Roman in parts, and probably represents a still older original. Mithridates advanced over the bridge along the Amasia road, and threatened the flank of Lucullus's column on its march from Eupatoria. In response to this challenge the Roman cavalry seems to have crossed the river, which is easily forded in summer, and an engagement ensued, in which the Pontic horsemen were victorious and gained control of the whole plain on both sides of the Lycus right up to the Paryadres. Lucullus was driven up the slope, leaving the road in possession of the enemy, who cut him off from Eupatoria. But ... by a night march along the hillside he circumvented the king, and entrenched himself in a strong position above the plain, out of reach of the cavalry and defended by a ravine. This position must, I think, be sought on the ridge between the two basins,[1] perhaps near the village of Manas, where there is a deep watercourse spanned by a ... bridge resting on possibly ancient foundations. In this situation Lucullus blocked the direct road to Cabira and threatened the bridge on the Amasia road. Mithridates fell back to protect his communications. He encamped on the left bank of the Lycus opposite to Lucullus, but probably rather farther east and nearer to the bridge. From this station he dominated both plains with his cavalry and held his antagonist pinned against the wall of the Paryadres. The Romans soon began to suffer from famine. To draw supplies from the west along the length of the Phanaroea was impossible. Lucullus was reduced to the desperate expedient of revictualling his army from Cappadocia, across the ... road commanded by the enemy. He probably used the pass from Herek to Comana. The first convoy, escorted by ... ten cohorts, fought its way through. Mithridates sent his cavalry to waylay the second, but his officers made the mistake of attacking in the pass instead of in the open, and their force was almost

when he called Eupatoria a suburb of Amisus he either misinterpreted his authority or else used the word παρῳκοδύμησε in an elastic sense. I have heard an eminent educational reformer call Southend a suburb of London.

[1] 'It is true', says Mr. Munro (p. 57, n. 2), 'that Plutarch (*Luc.* 15) speaks of Lucullus having got through a " pass " and occupied a position " overhanging Cabira ", but these expressions seem to me not unnatural exaggerations. The passage between the river and the hills, or even the whole valley at this point, may reasonably be called a pass. Lucullus had got over the crest of the ridge and overlooked the plain of Niksar. It must be remembered that he cannot be thrust too far eastwards, for he has to communicate with Cappadocia, and the road from Cabira to Comana must have been in Mithridates's hands (Appian, *Mithr.*, 82). The ridge was the ... most obvious point for Lucullus to seize, and in every way fits the rest of the narrative.'

annihilated. Having lost the best part of his cavalry, Mithridates was in danger of being cut off from Cabira ; for the plain was now open to the Roman infantry, and Lucullus held the shorter road. Retreat was necessary, but it became a rout. The king escaped with difficulty to Comana. . . . He probably intended to gain Cabira by the bridge higher up the Lycus on the Comana road, but was headed off. . . . Our authorities . . . are miserably vague as to localities. I have given the interpretation . . . suggested to me by the topography.' The interpretation seems to me as satisfactory as such miserable vagueness will allow. One question, however, not in Mr. Munro's interpretation but in the authorities, presses for an answer, which I cannot give. If Lucullus succeeded in ' the desperate expedient of revictualling his army from Cappadocia, across the . . . road commanded by the enemy ', why was it impossible ' to draw supplies from the west along the length of the Phanaroea ' ?

Memnon,[1] differing from Appian and Plutarch, who imply that Mithradates was present in camp during the final battle, says that when his lieutenants were defeated he was at Cabira ; this version, remarks M. Théodore Reinach,[2] ' just because it is less dramatic, may well be nearer the truth'. Anyhow it seems probable that Memnon, who wrote from an Asiatic standpoint, was better informed than the other historians about the personal movements of the king.

The numerical strength of the armies of Lucullus and Tigranes.— Lucullus, says Plutarch,[3] set out on his campaign against Tigranes with ' 12,000 foot and less than 3,000 horse ' ; Appian[4] assigns him two legions and 500 horse. Plutarch in a later chapter[5] says that Lucullus, leaving 6,000 men to continue the siege of Tigranocerta, attacked Tigranes ' with 24 cohorts, numbering not more than 10,000 men, besides the whole of his cavalry and about 1,000 archers and slingers '. It would appear, then, that when Lucullus started he had 16,000 foot and 1,000 archers and slingers, besides the 3,000 cavalry. Eckhardt[6] points out that Plutarch must have forgotten to reckon in his first statement the 6,000 men whom Lucullus left to continue the siege of Tigranocerta : thus the number of legionaries whom Plutarch accounts for is 18,000, and this estimate is confirmed by Eutropius[7] and Rufius Festus,[8] who, although they say that Lucullus defeated Tigranes with 18,000 legionaries, evidently meant that that was the force with which he began the campaign. Frontinus,[9] who states that Lucullus had 15,000 ' armed men ' in the battle, must have included the cavalry and light-armed auxiliaries. The only real discrepancy between Frontinus and Plutarch (who, like the Roman writers, derived his information from Sallust and ultimately from Lucullus himself[10]) is that according to the latter 14,000 men took part in the battle, according to the former 15,000.

[1] 43, 5 ; 44. [2] *Mithr. Eupator*, p. 340, n. 1. [3] *Luc.*, 24, 1.
[4] *Mithr.*, 84. [5] *Luc.*, 27, 2. [6] *Klio*, x, 1910, p. 78.
[7] vi, 9. [8] *Brev.*, 15, 3. [9] *Strat.*, ii, 1, 4.
[10] H. Peter, *D. Quellen Plutarchs*, &c., 1865, pp. 106-9 ; B. Maurenbrecher, *C. Sall. Crispi hist. rel.*, fasc. i, p. 53.

As to the Armenian force the authorities differ widely. According to Plutarch,[1] Tigranes had 150,000 infantry, 55,000 cavalry, of whom 17,000 were heavy-armed, and 20,000 slingers and archers; according to Appian,[2] 250,000 infantry and 50,000 cavalry. Nobody will accept these figures; but one is not obliged to suppose that Lucullus lied.[3] It is often impossible to get accurate information about an enemy's force. Colonel G. F. R. Henderson[4] says that in the American Civil War 'Patterson reported to his Government that he had been opposed by 3,500 men, exactly ten times Jackson's actual number'. Memnon[5] and Phlegon[6] are certainly nearer the truth when they respectively estimate the whole Armenian force at 80,000 and 70,000 men.

Tigranocerta.—That the problem which we have to attack is difficult may be inferred from the controversies which it has provoked. The geographer Kiepert successively identified Tigranocerta with four sites—two on the left, two on the right bank of the Tigris. The son who continued his last work adopted the original choice which his father had discarded half a century before.

Strabo[7] mentions Tigranocerta in conjunction with Nisibis (now Nisibin) among the towns possessed by the Mygdones in Mesopotamia; and he says that both were situated at the foot of the Masian range.[8]

According to Pliny,[9] Tigranocerta was on high ground (*in excelso*); and when he says[10] that the Tigris receives the Nicephorio (on which, as we learn from Tacitus,[11] Tigranocerta was situated) 'from Armenia', he evidently means that that tributary entered it through its left, or northern, bank.

Plutarch informs us that Lucullus, when, after crossing the Euphrates, he was marching through Sophene against Tigranes, pointed to the distant range of the Taurus and told his soldiers that there was the stronghold which they had to destroy.[12] Lucullus, he continues, making forced marches, crossed the Tigris and entered Armenia;[13] Tigranes abandoned Tigranocerta, moved towards the Taurus, and assembled his forces from all parts;[14] on his way back to Tigranocerta he crossed the Taurus and descried the Roman army which was blockading the town, while his own army was observed by the garrison, who triumphantly pointed it out to the Romans.[15] Plutarch gives the following topographical details. On the day before the battle Lucullus, leaving a part of his army to prosecute the siege of Tigranocerta, marched against Tigranes and encamped close to 'the river' in 'a great plain'. Tigranes was on the eastern side of the river, which there made a westward bend and was easily

---
[1] *Luc.*, 26, 8. [2] *Mithr.*, 85.
[3] T. Frank (*Roman Imperialism*, 1914, p. 311) suggests that he counted non-combatants.
[4] *Stonewall Jackson*, i, 1898, p. 158. [5] 57, 1.
[6] 12. Phlegon's estimate is of the combined forces of Tigranes and Mithradates, but the latter was not present in the battle
[7] xvi, 1, 23. [8] xi, 12, 4. [9] *Nat. Hist.*, vi, 9 (10), 26.
[10] *Ib.*, 27, 129. [11] *Ann*, xv, 4. [12] *Luc.*, 24, 8.
[13] *Ib.* Cf. Oros., vi, 3, 6. [14] *Luc.*, 25, 7. [15] *Ib.*, 27, 1.

fordable.[1] Before the battle his heavy cavalry were arrayed in front of his right wing at the foot of a knoll (λόφῳ τινί), crowned by a level space, the ascent to which, four stades in length, was neither difficult nor steep.[2] Lucullus, after his victory, entered Gordyene [in the valley of the Tigris, north of the Masian range], and, marching northward against Tigranes, crossed the Taurus.[3]

Tacitus states that Tigranocerta was 'strong from the number of its defenders and the great size of its walls' (*urbem copia defensorum et magnitudine moenium validam*); that the Nicephorius, a river 'of no mean width' (*haud spernenda latitudine*), flowed round a part of the walls; and that the city was 37 miles from Nisibis.[4]

From Appian[5] we learn that the rout of the Armenian army was visible to Mancaeus, who commanded the garrison of Tigranocerta. Tigranocerta, according to Eutropius,[6] was in Arzanene; and this statement is confirmed by the Armenian historian, Faustus[7] of Buzanta,[8] who wrote about the end of the fourth century.

Ptolemy[9] computed the latitude of Tigranocerta as 39° 40'.

It would appear from the statements of Strabo and Tacitus that Tigranocerta was south of the Tigris; Pliny, Ptolemy, Eutropius, and Faustus evidently located it (or a town of the same name) on the northern bank; and Plutarch, when he said that Lucullus crossed the Tigris, apparently implied the same. E. Sachau infers from the words of Tacitus—*urbem copia . . . validam*—that the site was not naturally strong.[10]

1. Amida, now represented by Diarbekr, about 80 Roman miles north-west of Nisibin, would probably never have been mentioned in connexion with this problem if it had not been supposed that Faustus identified it with Tigranocerta.[11] The reason of this supposition is that, according to Faustus, Shapur, commonly called Sapor the Second, captured Tigranocerta, while Ammianus Marcellinus[12] relates that Sapor besieged and captured Amida. May Amida have been one of the other strongholds which, according to Faustus, Sapor captured?[13] Faustus, as we have seen, says that Tigranocerta was in Arzanene, whereas Amida was in Sophene. W. Ainsworth,[14] however, who visited Diarbekr, identified it with Tigranocerta on the

---

[1] *Luc.*, 27, 5. Cf. App., *Mithr.*, 85.   [2] *Luc.* 28, 2.   [3] *Ib.*, 29, 10.
[4] *Ann.*, xv, 4–5.   [5] *Mithr.*, 86.   [6] vi 9.   [7] iv, 24.
[8] *Klio*, viii, 1908, p. 514.
[9] *Geogr.*, v, 13, 22.
[10] *Abhandl. d. Königl. Akad. d. Wiss. zu Berlin*, 1880, p. 44. In the following discussion I shall ignore absurd and obsolete guesses. Th. Reinach (*Mithr. Eupator*, 1890, p. 345, n. 5), remarking that Tell Ermen, the site proposed by Sachau, hardly agrees with the statement of Tacitus, says 'Je préférerais donc un emplacement tel que Midiyâd, au N.N.E. de Nisibis'; but he does not develop this view, which, so far as I know, has never since been noticed. On p. 361 he says that just before the battle of Tigranocerta 'Les deux armées étaient séparées par le Tigre (!), qui . . . faisait un coude vers l'occident'; in his map (at the end of the volume) he locates Tigranocerta on the site of Tell Ermen !
[11] iv, 24. Cf. my article in *Class. Quart.*, vii, 1917, p. 122, n. 2.
[12] xix, 1–8.
[13] Cf. Amm. Marc., xx, 6; 7, 1–16.
[14] *Travels . . . in Asia Minor*, ii, 1842, p. 362.

THIRD MITHRADATIC WAR 411

ground that the topography corresponds with the description of Plutarch ; but it is now universally admitted that he was wrong. ' One consideration alone ', says W. Belck,[1] ' will suffice to show that this identification is an absolute impossibility. . . . Diarbekr is one of the oldest towns in the world and figures in the earliest Assyrian inscriptions under the name Amid. . . . Moreover, Diarbekr was well known to the Romans under the name Amida ', &c.

2. Sir Henry Rawlinson, followed by Kiepert [2] and originally by Mommsen,[3] decided for Tell Abad, which is about 43 miles north of Nisibin, and in the northern part of the Masian range, not, as Strabo says of Tigranocerta, below it and on its southern side. Rawlinson, reporting in the *Athenaeum* (February 14, 1863, page 228) the recent travels of Consul John Taylor in Armenia, emphasized ' his most remarkable discovery of the ruins of *Kefr Joze*, which he describes as an immense city . . . and the great treasure house, from which the larger portion of the Greek and Parthian coins and gems current in northern Mesopotamia are procured, thus leading to the conclusion that we have at last found the site of Tigranocerta '. Two years later Taylor himself published an account of his travels in the *Journal of the Royal Geographical Society*; and I turned eagerly to his article for details of the ' remarkable discovery '. What was my disappointment to find that he apparently attached little or no importance to what he had seen. ' Tell Biat ' [otherwise Tell Abad], he says, ' is of some extent and formed of the débris and remains of former buildings, which, I was told at Keffr Joze, yielded numerous medals and intaglios.' That is all ; [4] and in truth there is nothing to be said in favour of Tell Abad.[5] Its geographical position answers to the data neither of Strabo, nor of Pliny, nor of Tacitus, nor of Plutarch,[6] nor of Eutropius ; and the necessary river is not to be found. Sachau, indeed, who visited the spot, says that a tiny brook flows near the south of Tell Abad : but, he adds, in many places it can easily be jumped : except after heavy snow-storms it is generally dry ; and it is never more than one foot deep.[7]

3. We now come to the one site on the right bank of the Tigris which deserves serious consideration. The hill of Tell Ermen, selected by Sachau in the course of a journey which he made through Armenia,[8] and adopted by Kiepert after he had successively

---

[1] *Zeitschr. f. Ethnologie*, xxxi, 1899, p. 267.
[2] *Hermes*, ix. 1875, pp. 143, 148
[3] See the map facing p. 134 of *Hermes*, 1875, where Mommsen calls Tell Abad ' Tell Bejâd '.
[4] ' I offered a high price ', says Sachau (*Abhandlungen*, &c., p. 71), ' and not one single coin could they show me '. For the last clause of Taylor's notice he says (p. 75) that he would substitute, ' which, *I* was told at Kefr-Joze, never yield medals nor intaglios '.
[5] See E. Sachau, *Reise in Syrien*, &c., 1883, p. 416.
[6] The plain in which, according to Plutarch, Lucullus encamped before the battle is nowhere to be found (Sachau, *Abhandlungen*, &c., pp. 19–20).
[7] *Ib.*, pp. 71–2.
[8] *Ib.*, pp. 1–92. George Rawlinson (*The Sixth Great Oriental Monarchy*, 1873, p. 141, n. 3) had already pointed to the neighbourhood of Tell Ermen.

adopted and discarded Meiafarkin, Arzen, and Tell Abad, by the late Professor Pelham,[1] by Mr. Bernard Henderson, tentatively by Mr. J. G. C. Anderson,[2] and even by Mommsen himself,[3] is situated near the southern slopes of the Masian range at the junction of several roads, about 40 Roman miles west of Nisibin, and on a river called the Gyrs. It thus corresponds with the statements of Strabo, and perhaps closely enough with the position indicated by Tacitus. The so-called hill, which is from top to bottom a conglomerate of the remains of buildings,[4] rises about 150 feet above the plain : the channel of the river, which winds round the northern slope, is 30 metres broad and from two to three deep, sometimes, as Sachau says,[5] dry, sometimes filled by a strong stream. Close to Tell Ermen it receives a small tributary, the Zrgan, and below the confluence the river is called by that name.[6] A few miles to the north-east lies the Pass of Mardin, through which, if Sachau's choice was right, Tigranes must have marched when, after he had assembled his army, he recrossed the Taurus on his way to relieve Tigranocerta. Sachau[7] admits that he could find no traces of ancient walls or columns or blocks of stone : but brick and potsherds were visible everywhere both on the hill and in the surrounding plain ; the natives assured Sachau that whenever they dug on the hill or in the neighbourhood they unearthed antiquities ; and in almost every peasant's house ancient coins, for instance of Caracalla and Constantine the Great, were to be seen. Mr. Henderson has vigorously advocated the claims of Tell Ermen.[8] He observes that it is ' conspicuous far over the plain ', implying that it would have been easily discerned by the soldiers of Lucullus when he pointed towards the stronghold which they must attack ; and while he admits that ' as regards " finds " or " ruins " the evidence is practically *nil* ', he affirms that the site ' is just 37 miles from Nisibis ', and that the fact of its being ' by no means impregnable or precipitous . . . suits the Tacitus description of the city '. Moreover, ' the site suits Plutarch . . . better than any other '. Lucullus ' would march from the Tigris about Diarbekr viâ the Rubbut pass on Tell Ermen. Tigranes would retire Northwards viâ the Mardin pass. . . . Returning with reinforcements by this same route he would be visible some miles away. . . . Just above Tell Ermen the river takes a turn to the west. Lucullus marching to cross here seems to Tigranes to be retreating.' Again, says Mr. Henderson, the strategical advantages of the site would

[1] See *Journ. of Philol.*, xxix, 1903, p. 115.
[2] *Asia Minor* (Murray's Handy Classical Maps), 1903.
[3] *Hist. of Rome*, iv, 1875, p. 47. note. In the eighth German edition this note disappears, and Mommsen (iii, 68, note) says that Sachau has proved 'that Tigranocerta was ' in the neighbourhood of Mardin ', though his identification of it with Tell Ermen ' is not free from doubt '.
[4] Sachau, *Reise*, &c., pp. 402, 425.
[5] *Abhandlungen*, &c., pp. 81–2.
[6] *Reise*, &c., p. 425. Sachau says (*Abhandlungen*, &c., p. 81) that traces exist of a trench which was filled with water from the river ; but it is impossible to tell whether this was the moat which Tacitus describes.
[7] *Abhandlungen*, &c., p. 79. [8] *Journ. of Philol.*, 1903, pp. 114–6.

have recommended it to Tigranes when he was about to found Tigranocerta; for, 'guarding as it does the two passes over Taurus, the Rubbut Pass and the Mardin Pass, it blocks all hostile inroad from the South into the Upper Tigris valley, and thus into the heart of Armenia. And Tigranes' chief foes when he founded the city were the Parthians. The soil is fertile and water abundant.' Finally Mr. Henderson argues that Tell Ermen answers perfectly to the Tacitean description of the Armenian campaign in the reign of Nero; for 'Vologeses . . . at Nisibis is clearly in close touch with his forces besieging Tigranocerta in A. D. 61 (*Ann.* xv. 4. 5) . . . and Tel Ermen would satisfy this requirement excellently. . . . Tacitus states that Vologeses' cavalry during this Nisibis-Tigranocerta campaign were sorely in straits for food owing to the plague of a locust swarm. And the prevalence of such locust swarms precisely in this Mardin-Nisibis district is specially noticed by Taylor.'[1]

Those who have read Plutarch's *Lucullus* may be amused by Mr. Henderson's insistence upon the fact that the Roman soldiers on their march could have seen Tell Ermen from afar if it and Tigranocerta were one.[2] It is not true that Tell Ermen 'is just 37 miles from Nisibis': it is more than 40, and Mr. Henderson may only claim that it is the one site which even approximately answers to the statement of Tacitus.[3] The discrepancy, however, is unimportant; for Corbulo, from whom Tacitus presumably derived his information, may have roughly computed the distance between the outskirts of the two towns. Mr. Henderson wisely admits that little stress can be laid upon the story of the locusts; and unless it can be proved that in the time of Nero the country between Nisibis and Mardin was the only part of Armenia which they infested, I fear that they are quite irrelevant. Moreover, he was apparently unaware that a series of objections had been brought against Tell Ermen by scholars who had explored the theatre of the war, and who, moreover, adduced arguments in favour of another site, which he ignored.

Belck[4] gives the following reasons for rejecting Sachau's choice. First, the site of Tell Ermen was strategically bad, because it was exposed to attack from the Parthians. Secondly, Plutarch[5] says that just before the battle of Tigranocerta Lucullus encamped 'by

[1] *Journ. Roy. Geogr. Soc.*, 1868, pp. 356, 359.
[2] Plutarch, says Mr. Henderson (*op. cit.*, p. 107), supports the theory that Tigranocerta was south of the Masian range, for 'a city north of the Tigris would not be within eyesight of an army on the northern slopes'. But Plutarch says nothing about 'eyesight'; and Mr. Henderson's argument is as naïve as that of the scholars who by way of proving that Hannibal crossed the Alps by the Col du Clapier quote the passage in which Polybius (iii, 54, 2–3) says that from the summit of the pass he pointed out the plain of Lombardy to his troops. Read Plutarch's words (*Luc.*, 24, 8) : ' " There," said Lucullus, pointing to the distant Taurus, " is the stronghold which we have to destroy " ' ('Εκεῖνο, ἔφη, μᾶλλον τὸ φρούριον ἡμῖν ἐκκοπτέον ἐστί, δείξας τὸν Ταῦρον ἄπωθεν ὄντα).
[3] I have three times measured with a map-measurer the distance from Nisibin to Tell Ermen *via* Amudis—that is by the shortest road—each time with the same result, 60 kilometres or 40½ Roman miles. See R. Kiepert's *Karte von Kleinasien* ($\frac{1}{400000}$), sheets C. VI and D. VI.
[4] *Zeitschr. f. Ethnologie*, 1899, pp. 264–6. 601.   [5] *Luc.* 27, 3.

the river, in a great plain'. But since *ex hypothesi* he was already in Mesopotamia, this statement would have been superfluous. Rightly understood, it implies that the terrain which Lucullus left before he pitched his camp was not a plain at all, and that the 'great plain' contrasted both with the hill on which Tigranocerta stood and with the country which surrounded it. Thirdly, since Lucullus was obliged to look for a ford before he could cross the river, the water was evidently deep: this condition is not satisfied by the Gyrs. Fourthly, in Tell Ermen no remains of a large fortified city are recognizable. This cannot be explained by assuming that Tigranocerta was built of brick; for every one who knows the methods of building in vogue with the Armenians, who spared no expense in procuring the best stone, will acknowledge that the mere absence of ruins is enough to prove that Tigranocerta is not represented by Tell Ermen. Fifthly, according to Sachau, Lucullus, after he had captured Tigranocerta, marched into Gordyene [1] by way of Nisibis: why did he not besiege Nisibis then instead of deferring the siege until after he returned from his campaign against Artaxata? Sixthly, Tell Ermen does not even approximately correspond to Ptolemy's statement about the latitude of Tigranocerta. Lastly, the dimensions of Tell Ermen are too small.

Not one of these objections—not even all of them combined—appear to me conclusive. Every fortress is exposed to attack, or it would not have been built; surely the best site for a fortress intended to protect Armenia from a Parthian invasion was near the Armenian frontier on a road by which the Parthians might advance; and a fortress at Tell Ermen would have been a formidable obstacle, for unless the Parthians captured it, they could not enter the Pass of Mardin. Belck's second objection is plausible; but it implies that Plutarch had mastered the geography of Armenia and Mesopotamia, whereas he probably knew no more than he could collect from Sallust, who himself knew little. Even Lucullus in his dispatch might pardonably have alluded to the 'great plain', for, however pointless the words might have been, they were true. Does not Polybius [2] observe, with equal truth and equal ineptitude, that Hannibal, marching from Spain towards the Rhône, had 'the Sardinian Sea' on his right? The third objection is even more feeble. The Gyrs at Tell Ermen is many times wider than the Farkin-Su at Meiafarkin, which Belck identifies with Tigranocerta; and Taylor has emphasized the shallowness of that stream: [3] when Sachau saw the Gyrs it was unfordable; [4] and although it is sometimes very low, Belck cannot prove that to search for a ford would have been unnecessary when Lucullus was about to fight. Taylor has pointed out that at Sert and at Meiafarkin the remains of ancient buildings are probably buried underground: [5] why not also at Tell Ermen? And why does Belck omit to add that, except one solitary block of stone, the

---

[1] See Plut., *Luc.* 29, 10.   [2] iii, 41, 7.
[3] See p. 420, *infra*.   [4] *Abhandlungen*, &c., p. 45.
[5] *Journ. Roy. Geogr. Soc.*, 1865, pp. 24, 30.

ruins of Nisibis, whose site is certain, are nowhere visible?[1] That
Lucullus, if he had marched from Tell Ermen into Gordyene, would
have besieged Nisibis on the way may seem at first sight evident;
but think again. The siege would inevitably be prolonged; Lucullus,
who was about to march against the remote city of Artaxata, had no
time to spare; and he may well have determined to postpone the
siege until after his return. It is true that if we identify Tigranocerta
with Tell Ermen, we must reject the evidence of Ptolemy; but
Mommsen[2] and Kiepert,[3] who differed on many points, agreed that
Ptolemy's calculations are utterly untrustworthy.[4] Finally, although
the tumulus of Tell Ermen is itself not much more than a mile in
circuit,[5] the city which it represents extended far, as Sachau has
explained, in all directions round it.

More serious are the objections which Kurt Eckhardt brings
against Tell Ermen. We have seen that Lucullus crossed the Tigris.
Look at the map and you will find that if Tigranocerta was on the
right bank, he would not have crossed the Tigris, properly so called,
at all. He would have advanced by way of Kharput, Arghana, and
Diarbekr to Mardin; in doing so he would have crossed affluents of
the Tigris thrice; and after he had crossed the third he would still
have been in Sophene, which Plutarch implicitly distinguishes from
Armenia.[6] 'I do not believe,' says Eckhardt,[7] 'that Plutarch would
have laid stress upon the triple passage. . . . No; the passage
[of the Tigris] resulted in an invasion of Armenia, and therefore
implies that Lucullus remained on the left bank; and, moreover,
it must have taken place at a point where it could be regarded as an
event worth mentioning.'

This argument is reasonable, but hardly, as Eckhardt thinks, conclusive. He expects from Plutarch, whose strong point was not
meticulous accuracy, a degree of precision such as one might find in
a dispatch addressed by von Hindenburg to the All Highest.
Plutarch's narrative is certainly the best extant; but from what was
it derived? From Sallust's history, which was itself presumably
based, directly or indirectly, upon dispatches written by Lucullus.[8]
Lucullus may have mistaken an affluent for the main stream of the
Tigris; and even if he did not, such a mistake may easily have
insinuated itself into the second-hand narrative of Sallust or the
third-hand narrative of Plutarch.[9] And when Eckhardt objects

[1] Sachau, *Reise*, &c., pp. 392, 403   Lehmann-Haupt (*Zeitschr. f. Ethnologie*,
1899. p. 606) implicitly contradicts his colleague Belck. Remarking that
Tell Ermen, like Meiafarkin, forms an Armenian enclave in a region where
a different language is spoken, he concludes that an Armenian town was
founded there, and that its founder was Tigranes.
[2] *Hermes*, 1875, p. 133
[3] *Monatsb. d. Königl. Preuss. Akad. d. Wiss.*, 1873, pp 202–210, with which
cf. *Hermes*, 1875, p. 145.
[4] Cf. *Studia Pontica*, i, 1903, pp. 14, 91, n. 3.
[5] See the plan (Taf. 1) in *Abhandlungen*, &c.
[6] *Klio*, x, 1910, pp. 85–6, 88.   [7] *Ib.*, p. 86
[8] Plut., *Luc*., 26, 9. Cf. H. Peter, *D. Quellen Plutarchs*, 1865, pp. 106–9.
[9] Lehmann-Haupt himself says when it suits his purpose, 'Very often . . .

that Lucullus, after his final crossing, would still have found himself in the province of Sophene, his argument is less destructive than he thinks. For when Plutarch said that Lucullus, after crossing the Tigris, invaded Armenia, he made a statement which was in any case misleading : Lucullus invaded Armenia when he crossed the Euphrates. And although, strictly speaking, he was in Mesopotamia if, after crossing a tributary of the Tigris, he traversed the Masian range, Eckhardt might have remembered that his master, Lehmann-Haupt, insisted that ' Armenia ' and ' Mesopotamia ' were not merely geographical but also administrative terms, and that the northern part of Mesopotamia, being subject to the Armenian king, might be truly called Armenia.[1]

But Eckhardt keeps his strongest argument until the last. Sachau, he observes, found it impossible to reconcile the topography of the country near Tell Ermen with Plutarch's description of the battle. He supposed that Tigranes, after emerging from the Pass of Mardin, encamped above the Romans on the spurs of the hills, his right flank resting on the pass, while his centre and left extended to Horrîn. The Roman army, blockading Tigranocerta, was on both banks of the river. Leaving Murena with 6,000 men to continue the blockade, Lucullus crossed the river and encamped between Mishmish and the western bend. Why, asks Eckhardt, should he have done this when the bulk of his army was already posted on the same side of the river as his enemy ? To this question there can be but one answer. Sachau was obliged to force his theory into agreement with Plutarch's narrative. Accordingly he made Lucullus move westward, that is in the wrong direction, from before Tigranocerta, needlessly cross the river, and then recross it lower down ! Again, the plateau below which Sachau placed the heavy cavalry of Tigranes is on the left by Gos and Horrîn, not, as Plutarch requires, on the right. Sachau himself was aware of the contradiction, but he could only extricate himself by saying, ' The bulk of the Armenian heavy cavalry stood, it is true [according to Plutarch], on the right wing, therefore near the Pass of Mardin ; nevertheless I am inclined to place the scene of the decisive struggle not between the pass and Goli, but in the neighbourhood of Horrîn.' [2] ' That ', says Eckhardt, ' is quite simple, but it does not agree with Plutarch, and there is not the slightest ground for supposing that the heavy cavalry were suddenly transferred to the left wing.' [3]

The movement of Lucullus, as it must have been directed if Tigranocerta is represented by Tell Ermen, does not to my mind present an insuperable difficulty. In the case supposed a division of the Roman army was on the western bank of the Gyrs, blockading that side of the city, before Lucullus decided to advance against Tigranes. When that division moved south-westward Tigranes may

affluents are incorrectly regarded as . . . branches of larger rivers ' (*oft genug* . . . *Zuflüsse ungenauer Weise als* . . . *Arme von grössern Flüssen betrachtet werden* [*Zeitschr. f. Ethnologie*, 1899, p. 605]).

[1] See pp. 420-1.
[2] *Abhandlungen*, &c., pp. 31-3   [3] *Klio*, 1910, p. 110.]

well have fancied, as Plutarch says,[1] that Lucullus intended to retreat; and if Plutarch implies that the whole army, except the 6,000 men who were left to prosecute the siege, forded the river, it is quite conceivable that he misunderstood or misrepresented his authority. The difference between Plutarch's description and Sachau's reconstruction of the battle is more serious, and, if Plutarch made no mistake, if Sachau observed the terrain with a practised eye, I do not see how Eckhardt's criticism can be met. Sachau indeed affirms that Plutarch's description applies to the whole ground;[2] but without an authoritative map on a large scale, which does not exist, and in default of photographs, with which Sachau

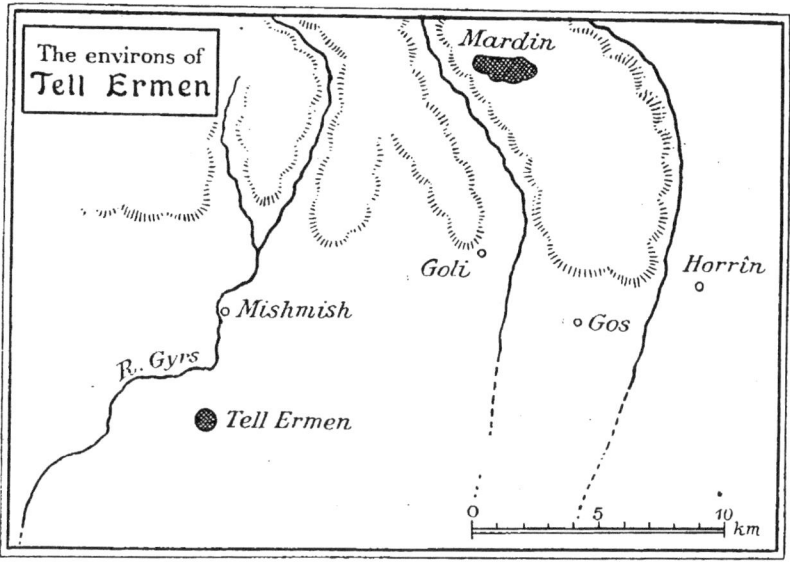

omitted to support his argument, one cannot decide whether his statement is correct.

One more objection must be noted, which was anticipated by Sachau himself. Since Tell Ermen is not really a hill at all, but a tumulus composed of ruins, it was not *in excelso*;[3] but this description is given by Pliny alone, and, as the reader knows, we have to choose between the irreconcilable statements of Pliny on the one hand and of Tacitus and Strabo on the other. Were they describing different towns of the same name?

Let us now explore the northern bank of the Tigris.

4. D'Anville, the famous French geographer of the eighteenth century, identified Tigranocerta with Sert, on the grounds that

---

[1] *Luc.*, 27, 5. [2] *Abhandlungen*, &c., p. 32.
[3] Sachau (*Abhandlungen*, &c., p. 49) remarks that in relation to Tell Ermen *in excelso* can only mean that the citadel dominated the surrounding plain. That was not what Pliny meant.

the distance of Sert from Nisibin corresponds with the distance, stated by Tacitus, between Nisibis and Tigranocerta, and that the Armenian term 'Kert' denotes a city of great importance.[1] Now we have seen that, according to Tacitus, Tigranocerta was 37 Roman miles from Nisibis; Sert is fully 80 miles NNE. of Nisibin. D'Anville's other reason is no better. Ainsworth,[2] indeed, was wrong when he reported that there were 'no remains of antiquity at or near . . . Sert'; for, as Taylor remarked, 'he probably was unaware that the whole of the town has been constructed from the remains of old buildings that have been exhumed from a depth of many feet below the soil.' But Taylor himself gives a conclusive reason for rejecting Sert : its topographical features do not correspond in the least with Plutarch's description, and 'the banks of the river are so rugged and steep that at present there is only one road leading to it, which a small number of men could easily defend against hostile thousands seeking to reach the plain'.[3]

5. Kiepert, after he had successively adopted and rejected Meiafarkin and Tell Abad, declared for Arzen, on the left bank of a river of the same name.[4] It stands, as Taylor says, 'on what appears a natural platform of some little elevation,' and close to the ruins of Arzen the river is fordable.[5] This ruined town, said Kiepert, 'by its position on a river corresponding to the description of Tacitus and by the regularity with which its fortifications were designed appeared to satisfy all the requirements for identifying Tigranocerta.'[6] But, replies Belck, except that the river is fordable in autumn, the topography corresponds in no respect to Plutarch's description; and ancient ruins are entirely wanting.[7] The ruins might perhaps be found by excavation; but Kiepert once more changed his mind and finally rejected Arzen in favour of Tell Ermen.

6. Meiafarkin, or, as the Armenians call it, Farkin, about 30 miles WNW. of Arzen, is situated on the Farkin-Su, an affluent of the

[1] *L'Euphrate et le Tigre*, 1779, p. 84.
[2] *Travels . . . in Asia Minor*, ii, 361–3.
[3] *Journ. Roy. Geogr. Soc.*, 1865, pp. 30–1.
[4] *Monatsb. d. Königl. Preuss. Akad. d. Wiss.*, 1873, pp. 186–90.
[5] *Journ. Roy. Geogr. Soc.*, 1865, pp. 26–7. 'So many medals in gold and silver', says Taylor, 'are found here [at Arzen] that the fellahs who till the ground are paid nothing by the owner for their labour, and they give him in addition half of everything they may find.'
[6] *Hermes*, 1875, p. 142.
[7] *Zeitschr. f. Ethnologie*, 1899, p. 267. Lehmann-Haupt (*Armenien einst und jetzt*, 1910, p. 385) raises two objections against Arzen. The Arzen-Su, he says, flowing past the western side of the town, would have been no protection against an enemy from the east; but Tigranes evidently came from that side. What then? If the reader can perceive the force of this argument, which implies that Tigranes was an enemy of his own capital, and, moreover, ignores the moat, he is more acute than *I*. Again, says Lehmann-Haupt, the plain in which Lucullus encamped before the battle is not to be found. Not close to Arzen; but the plain in which Lucullus, according to Lehmann-Haupt, encamped was twelve miles south of Farkin, and a great plain stretches southward from a point some eight miles S. by W. of Arzen (R. Kiepert, *Karte von Kleinasien*, C. VI). Indeed a plain four or five miles wide extends opposite the western bend which the river makes just below the town.

Batman-Su, which flows into the Tigris from the north. More than
70 years ago von Moltke identified it, without, however, giving any
reasons, with Tigranocerta ;[1] Belck and Lehmann-Haupt, who have
explored the length and breadth of Armenia, claim to have established
its identity beyond dispute. In the reign of Theodosius the Second
the town, whatever it may have been called before, received the
name of Martyropolis ;[2] and Faustus of Buzanta[3] tells us that
St. Epiphanius, coming from Sophene, founded a church in Tigranocerta in honour of the martyrs. That Farkin is far older than the
early Christian period has been attested by Consul Taylor, who had
no theory to support ;[4] but the foundation does not establish the
identity of Tigranocerta with Martyropolis. Edward the First
erected many crosses in memory of Queen Eleanor ; and Tigranocerta was not the only city where a church was founded in honour of
the martyrs.

The geographical position of Farkin corresponds closely enough
with Ptolemy's estimate (39° 40') of the latitude of Tigranocerta,[5]
and perhaps also with the measurements given in the *Table* of
Peutinger,[6] according to which ' Triganocarten ' was 47 Roman miles
from Sardebar (Kal' at–Zarzawa). But, as I have already remarked,
no reliance can be placed upon Ptolemy's calculation ; and the *Table*
is equally untrustworthy.[7]

Lehmann-Haupt[8] points out that Farkin answers to the words of
Pliny ; for while it is below the ridge of the Hazru-Daghlary, the
plateau on which it stands dominates the lower slopes, and could
therefore be truly described as *in excelso*. He admits, indeed, that
the Farkin-Su, which flows below the town, is not more than 3 or
4 metres broad ;[9] but this little difficulty he waves aside. Mommsen,
he remarks, has shown that the statement of Tacitus referred not so
much to the breadth of the river as to the volume of water which it
contained. Besides, the Batman-Su, of which the Farkin-Su is an
affluent, ' is a stream of considerable breadth, and if Tacitus somewhat loosely included the Farkin-Su in its system, his statement was
generally true, though not precisely for the part which surrounds
the walls.' Now when Mommsen asserted that Tacitus, although he
characterized the Nicephorius as a river ' of no mean width ', did
not mean width but depth,[10] he came near to talking nonsense ;
I doubt whether he would have so committed himself if he had not
known that the stream near Tell Abad (which he originally identified
with Tigranocerta) was a little brook ; and even then he might have

[1] *Briefe über Zustände . . . in d. Türkei*³, 1887, p. 285.
[2] *Klio*, 1908, pp. 519–20.   [3] v, 27. Cf. *Klio*, 1908, p. 214
[4] *Journ. Roy. Geogr. Soc.*, 1865, p. 24. ' It is undoubtedly of far more ancient
date [than the early Christian period], and the numerous isolated heaps and
long low mounds probably cover ruins much older than any at present visible
above ground.'
[5] *Geogr.*, v, 13, 22.   [6] Segm. x.
[7] See Sir W. M. Ramsay's *Hist. Geogr. of Asia Minor*, 1890, pp. 62–7.
[8] *Armenien einst und jetzt*, p. 390. Cf. *Zeitschr. f. Ethnologie*, 1899, p. 270.
[9] *Armenien einst und jetzt*, p. 392.   [10] *Hermes*, 1875, p. 133, n. 2.

hesitated if he had known that the brook was not more than one foot deep. Tacitus may have been mistaken, but he meant what he said ; and that he would have knowingly described a streamlet 3 or 4 metres wide as a river ' of no mean width ' is not credible. The suggestion that when he named one river he meant two—the Farkin-Su and the Batman-Su—does not call for refutation. Kiepert, who had originally accepted von Moltke's view, found himself obliged to discard it, not only because Farkin was in Sophene whereas Tigranocerta (according to Eutropius and Faustus) was in Arzanene, but also because the Farkin-Su, when Taylor visited it in October—that is, at the time of year when the battle of Tigranocerta was fought—was an insignificant and shallow stream.[1]

As for the statement that Tigranocerta was 37 miles from Nisibis, Eckhardt hastily dismisses it, remarking that Kiepert has proved that the text of Tacitus is corrupt and that for *septem et triginta* we should substitute *centum et triginta*.[2] Now Kiepert merely asserted that a line of 37 miles drawn from Nisibis, either along the road leading to Amida or northward across the Masian range, reaches no point where a great city could have lain.[3] Mommsen [4] condemned Kiepert's emendation because the statement of Tacitus plainly shows that the troops in Nisibis and Tigranocerta were in touch with one another ; and, as we have seen, the distance given by Tacitus corresponds approximately with the position of Tell Ermen. Moreover, Kiepert himself by finally accepting the identification of Tell Ermen with Tigranocerta withdrew both his emendation and the objection from which it arose.

Lehmann-Haupt endeavours to explain away another difficulty. While he insists that Tigranocerta, according to Eutropius [5] and Faustus, was in Arzanene, he is confronted by the facts that, according to Procopius,[6] Martyropolis was in Sophene, and the river Nymphius, or Batman-Su, which is east of Martyropolis, was, after A. D. 364, if not before, the western boundary of Arzanene. But, he assures us, the difficulty is only apparent : ' People do not reflect

[1] *Monatsberichte*, &c., pp. 183–4. ' Two small streams of little depth ', wrote Taylor (*Journ. Roy. Geogr. Soc.*, 1865, pp. 23–4), ' that have their rise in copious springs close to the town walls, wash them on either side '. Von Moltke, who visited Farkin in July, says that ' an abundant stream ' (*ein reicher Fluss*) issues from the high ground on which the town stands. R. Kiepert's *Karte von Kleinasien* (C. VI) shows the Farkin-Su as a single stream flowing past the western side of Farkin ; but Lehmann-Haupt (*Armenien einst und jetzt*, p. 391) says that a branch of the Farkin-Su flows round a part of the northern as well as round the western and the southern wall, and elsewhere (*Zeitschr. f. Ethnologie*, 1899, p. 605) he tells us that the Farkin-Su rises from springs NW. and W. of the town, which is enclosed by its various arms.
[2] *Klio*, ix, 1909, pp. 406–7.
[3] *Monatsberichte*, &c., pp. 195–6.   [4] *Hermes*, 1875, p. 131, n. 2.
[5] Sachau (*Abhandlungen*, &c., p. 50) argues that Eutropius merely inferred from the computations of Ptolemy that Tigranocerta was in Arzanene, which Ptolemy does not mention. Lehmann-Haupt (*Armenien einst und jetzt*, p. 518) justly ridicules this theory.
[6] *Bell. Pers.*, i, 8, 21–2 ; 21, 6 ; *Aed.*, iii, 2, 2. Cf Amm. Marc., xxv, 7, 9, who reckons Arzanene among the regions beyond, that is, north of the Tigris.

that territorial designations are not to be understood in a purely geographical sense, but that administrative districts are commonly designated by the existing geographical names.'[1] Besides, although Martyropolis was the capital of Sophene in the sixth century, when Procopius wrote, we are not told that it was by any earlier writer, and we do not know when it became the capital. But we do know that when Epiphanius founded his church in Tigranocerta, Tigranocerta, which was soon to become Martyropolis (observe how Lehmann-Haupt begs the question!), was not in Sophene but in Arzanene. The inevitable conclusion is that under Tigranes also Tigranocerta was in Arzanene, and that the western frontier of the province was not at that time the Nymphius.

No, No! The conclusion is not inevitable—unless Tigranocerta and Martyropolis were one; and if they were, the conclusion is superfluous. In the time of Tigranes Arzanene *may* have extended westward of the Nymphius and have included Tigranocerta; that it must have done so is a mere assertion.[2]

And what about Strabo? Lehmann-Haupt evidently fears that his statements may prevent some obstinate scholars from accepting the identification of Farkin with Tigranocerta; but he makes an effort which is almost heroic, to demonstrate that Strabo is really on his side. Strabo's testimony, he pleads, acquires an entirely different aspect when one reflects that 'Mesopotamia' may have denoted a province in the kingdom of Tigranes which did not necessarily coincide with the Mesopotamia of geography[3]—which, in other words, was partly on the left bank of the Tigris. I will not dispute about what may have been; but my readers will perceive that in order to establish his theory, Lehmann-Haupt must prove that the Masian range extended on the left bank of the Tigris as well as on the right. In order to enable them to judge whether such proof is possible,[4] I need only refer to the passages in Strabo— xi, 5, 6; 12, 4; 14, 2; xvi, 1, 23—which throw light upon the geographical position of those hills.[5] But even if Lehmann-Haupt had proved his case, it would avail him nothing; for Strabo says that Tigranocerta was in the country of the Mygdones, on the southern side of the Masian range.[6]

Much has been made by Lehmann-Haupt[7] and Eckhardt[8] of the

---

[1] *Armenien einst und jetzt*, pp. 501–2.
[2] Cf. the remarks of H. Hübschmann (*Indo-german. Forschungen*, 1904, p. 475). K. Miller (*Itin. Rom.*, 1916, col. 744) also rejects Farkin because it was not in Arzanene, and decides for Arzen.
[3] *Armenien einst und jetzt*, p. 384. Cf. pp. 390, 502, &c.
[4] Lehmann-Haupt's arguments are to be found in *Armenien einst und jetzt*, pp. 504–5, 509–11. *I* have written a refutation; but to print it would be superfluous.
[5] *I* have collected and translated the passages in *Class. Quart.*, vii, 134.
[6] Kiepert, who, like Lehmann-Haupt, endeavoured to show that Strabo included in Mesopotamia Sophene, Arzanene, and Gordyene, also ignored the stubborn fact that Strabo placed Tigranocerta in Mygdonia (*Monatsberichte*, &c., p. 169; *Hermes*, 1875, pp. 139, 141), but ended by doing the same himself.
[7] *Armenien einst und jetzt*, p. 385.
[8] *Klio*, 1909, p. 406

opinion of von Moltke, and if there were reason to believe that he formed it after studying the original authorities, it would of course command the most respectful attention, but of this there is no evidence : he merely wrote, 'Towards morning we reached Meiafarkin, the ancient Tigranocerta' (*Gegen Morgen erreichten wir Meja-Farkin, das alte Tigranocerta*).

The point, however, upon which the champions of Farkin lay the greatest stress is that it alone corresponds, and that it corresponds absolutely, with Plutarch's description of the battle and of the operations that preceded it. We know that Lucullus crossed the Euphrates opposite Tomisa.[1] Thence, says Eckhardt, he moved along the ancient road to Arghana, crossed the Tigris about 12 miles above Amida, and advanced eastward to Tigranocerta. Tigranes moved northward, assembled his army in the plain of Musch, and, returning to relieve Tigranocerta, marched over the undulating country east of the Batman-Su and encamped about 19 miles south-east of the beleaguered city on the plateau which slopes gently south-westward towards that river below its confluence with the Farkin-Su. On the 5th of October Lucullus, leaving Murena to prosecute the siege, marched 12 miles down the right bank of the Farkin-Su and encamped in the plain westward of the stream and just below its confluence with the Batman-Su. Next morning he moved on about 5 miles along the right bank, and forded the river where it made a bend towards the west. The Armenian army was arrayed on the south-western slope of the plateau, its right flank being covered by the steep banks, while in front of the right wing was posted the heavy cavalry. Lucullus commanded his Thracian and Galatian horse to attack the heavy cavalry in flank, which Tigranes had left exposed ; for at the point where the heavy cavalry stood the bank was flat. Immediately after fording the river and while his infantry were deploying in front of the enemy, Lucullus led two cohorts unobserved up a gently sloping hill beneath which the heavy cavalry stood, and then charged into their rear. Threatened simultaneously by the Thracian and Galatian cavalry in flank and confronted by the Roman infantry, they were forced to rush pell mell into the ranks of their own infantry, and then followed utter rout.[2]

Now it may be readily admitted that the battle-field which Eckhardt indicates corresponds with the narrative of Plutarch. But two questions arise. First, why did Tigranes, though his object was to relieve Tigranocerta, march past it and leave it a day's march in his rear ? Must not the answer be substantially the same as that with which Eckhardt taunted Sachau : because close to Farkin, where one would naturally look for the battlefield, it is impossible to find a site which will satisfy the requirements of Plutarch ? Eckhardt tells us that Tigranes intended ' to cross the Batman-Su . . . and then to march along the valley of the Farkin-Su direct to

[1] Strabo, xii, 2, 1. Cf. Tac., *Ann.*, xv, 26–7.
[2] *Klio*, 1910, pp. 82, 86, 93–6, 101–5. Cf. *Zeitschr. f. Ethnologie*, 1899, pp 271–4.

Tigranocerta.'[1] But what was to be gained by making this détour ? Why did not Tigranes march direct from the bridge on the Batman-Su, which Eckhardt marks on his plan, along the road shown in Richard Kiepert's *Karte von Kleinasien*,[2] due west to Farkin ?

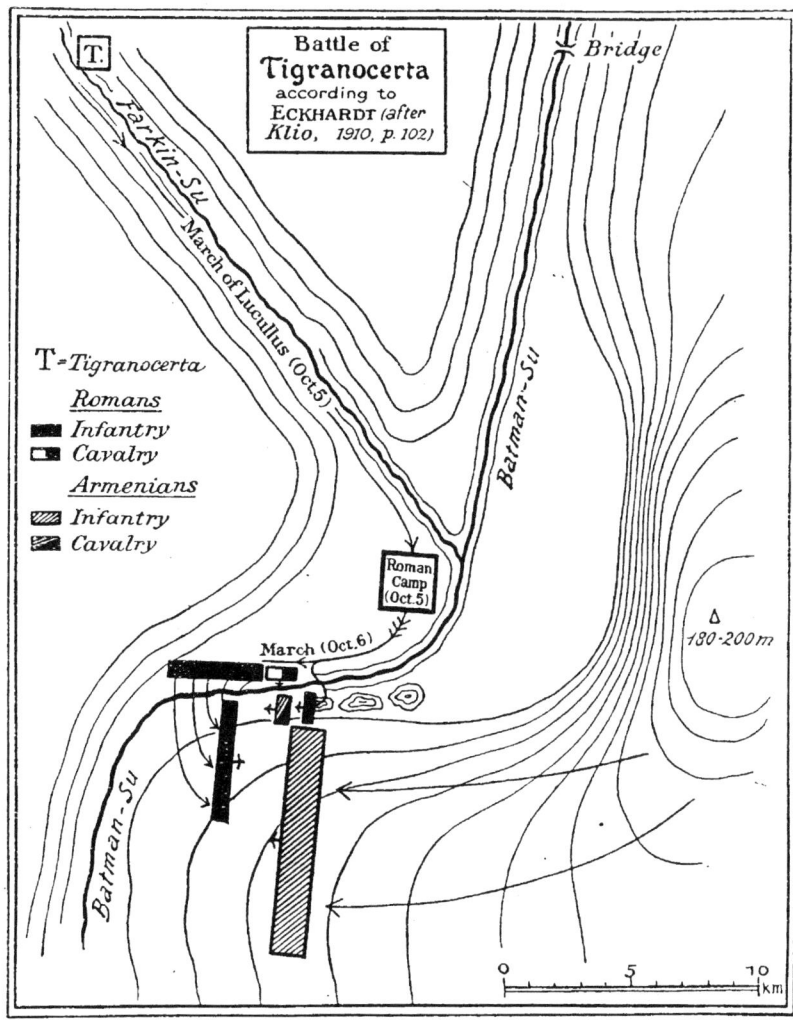

Secondly, Plutarch says that Tigranes on his march saw the Roman army besieging Tigranocerta, and that the garrison of Tigranocerta saw the army of Tigranes ; Appian says that the commander of the garrison saw the Armenian defeat. Lehmann-Haupt[3] and Belck[4]

[1] *Klio*, 1910, p. 94.   [2] C. VI.
[3] *Zeitschr. f. Ethnologie*, 1899, pp. 604-5.   [4] *Ib.*, pp. 273-4.

insist on all these facts. According to Lehmann-Haupt's map, the army of Tigranes on the march was never less than 14 miles from Tigranocerta, and the battlefield was still more remote. Were Tigranes, Mancæus, and the garrison equipped with telescopes? 'Good eyesight', said Lord Wolseley,[1] 'can distinguish bodies of troops at 2,000 yards; at that distance a man or horse appears like a dot.' What do they appear like at 24,000 yards? I am not sure that it would be possible, even with a telescope, to see from Farkin an army moving on the further bank of the Batman-Su, for, if Lehmann-Haupt's map is accurate, the line of vision would seem to be obstructed; and Lehmann-Haupt himself was uneasy on this point.[2] Still, I will suggest two considerations by which these objections might conceivably be removed. It may be—our imperfect maps do not permit one to say more—that the country between the Batman-Su and the Farkin-Su presented difficulties which forbade Tigranes to take the direct route; and, if it was possible to see from Farkin the uplands on which he is supposed to have marched, a cloud of dust may have been visible, which would have indicated the presence of a moving column. But would Tigranes have been able, at a distance of fourteen miles, to discern the stationary army of Lucullus?

Our choice is apparently restricted to three sites,—Arzen and Farkin on the left, Tell Ermen on the right bank of the Tigris. Arzen has been ruled out, on grounds which have not perhaps been quite sufficiently explained. If the objections to which Farkin is open can be answered, they certainly cannot be ignored.[3] The pretensions of Tell Ermen have been assailed from every side, but not, so far as I can judge, destroyed; for we have not yet got sufficient information to decide whether the topography is irreconcilable with Plutarch's description of the battle.

The contradiction between the statements of Strabo and Tacitus on one side and of Pliny, Eutropius, and Faustus on the other has never been explained. It is not easy to believe that Strabo made a huge mistake, and several times repeated it, when he placed Tigranocerta in Mygdonia below the Masian range, and Tacitus when he, like Strabo, coupled Tigranocerta with Nisibis: one can perhaps conceive that Eutropius, or even his ultimate authority, made a slip when he placed Tigranocerta in Arzanene, but that Faustus was guilty of the same blunder seems all but inconceivable. May the explanation be that the contradiction is only apparent? May I suggest that just as one Nicopolis is represented by Niboli and another by Purkh, just as Tash Keupri arose out of one Pompeiopolis and Mezetli out of another, so the Tigranocerta which Lucullus and

---

[1] *The Soldier's Pocket-Book* [5], 1886, p. 491.
[2] 'Zudem', he says (*Zeitschr. f. Ethnologie*, 1899, p. 604), 'erschien es unter den Voraussetzungen, die ich mir auf Grund dieser Ermittelungen [a map which a Turkish engineer sent him] zu bilden hatte, unmöglich, das Heranziehen des Tigranes von Farkin aus zu bemerken.' See, however, pp. 273–4.
[3] In any case the champions of Farkin must discard the testimony of Tacitus and Strabo.

THIRD MITHRADATIC WAR 425

afterwards Corbulo captured may have stood upon the site of Tell Ermen, and the Tigranocerta in which St. Epiphanius founded his church upon that of Arzen or of Meiafarkin?

The date of the siege of Nisibis.—Both Plutarch[1] and Dio[2] relate that Lucullus set out on his expedition against Artaxata in the middle of summer: when Dio[3] says that he began the siege of Nisibis, which followed the failure of the expedition, ἐν τῷ θέρει he is evidently using θέρος in the sense in which Caesar uses *aestas*,— the season for campaigning; and when Plutarch[4] says that about the time of the autumnal equinox 'heavy storms set in' (χειμῶνες ἐπέπεσον βαρεῖς), after which the expedition was abandoned, it is evident that χειμών does not mean winter. As Eckhardt observes, ' we must date the beginning of the siege ... in October when in this region great heat still prevails '.[5]

The campaigns of Mithradates against Fabius and Triarius and the ultimate failure of Lucullus.—The original accounts[6] of the campaigns in which Mithradates defeated the lieutenants of Lucullus have been explained by Mr. J. A. R. Munro.[7] After giving the interpretation which I have quoted in a former article[8] of the operations of Lucullus and Mithradates between Amisus and Cabira, he says, ' It was near the same point that Mithradates resumed the contest on his return to Pontus three years later. He entered his old kingdom perhaps by the valley of the Lycus, and blockaded ... Fabius ... in Cabira. Triarius opportunely arrived from Asia and raised the siege. Mithradates withdrew up the pass to Comana, and held the line of the upper Iris. Both took up winter-quarters, Mithradates at Zela,[9] Triarius confronting him at Gazioura (now Turkhal). Triarius had only to cover Amasia and wait for Lucullus, who was falling back through Cappadocia, followed by Tigranes. The main object of Mithradates was to prevent their junction and deal with each separately. By a demonstration against Dadasa[10] he provoked the legate to attack him, and inflicted on him a crushing defeat. Then he turned to face Lucullus. But so strong was the position which he occupied on the heights above Talaura that the Roman general declined to attempt to dislodge him, and Mithradates did not repeat the error of Triarius by taking the offensive.

The general strategic situation is clear. Mithradates was threatening and Triarius defending the road from Zela to Amasia and Amisus. Lucullus was coming up from Nisibis, doubtless by the road from Melitene to Sebasteia (Sivas). Where then is Talaura? It ... is mentioned three times in literature. ... (1) Appian, *Mithr.*, 115 ... without indication of position. (2) Plutarch, *Luc.*, 19. Lucullus pursues Mithradates as far as Talaura on his flight from Cabira to

---

[1] *Luc.*, 31, 1. [2] xxxvi, 4, 2. [3] *Ib.*, 6, 3.
[4] *Luc.*, 32, 1. [5] *Klio*, x, 1910, p. 217.
[6] Plut., *Luc.*, 35; App., *Mithr.*, 88–90; Dio, xxxvi, 9–15, 17.
[7] *Journ. Hell. Soc.*, xxi, 1901, pp. 58–9.
[8] See pp. 406–8.
[9] *Bell. Alex.*, 72, 2. Cf. App., *Mithr.*, 120, and Dio, xlii, 48, 2.
[10] Mr Munro asks, ' Can Dadasa be Dazya near Turkhal?'

Tigranes. The King had first escaped to Comana (Appian, *Mithr.*, 82), so Talaura must lie on the road from Comana to the Euphrates. (3) Dio Cassius, xxxvi, 16, the passage here in question. The two latter passages point in the direction of Sivas. The earliest name of Sivas is unknown. From Strabo[1] we gather that it was Pompey's Megalopolis before it was Sebasteia, but it evidently existed before Pompey's colony. Talaura, which disappears with Mithradates, would fit the position well enough.[2] Mithradates would naturally await Lucullus on the hills north of Sivas near the parting of the roads to Zela and Comana ', &c.

POMPEY IN THE EAST

Did Pompey and his army winter in Cilicia before he marched against Mithradates?—According to Appian,[3] Pompey was still in Cilicia when he was appointed to command against Mithradates ; but, says Long,[4] ' Cicero,[5] who must have known, informs us that he was in ... the province Asia.... Cicero also says that his legions were there in winter quarters at the time when he was delivering his speech for the bill of Manilius, and that ... letters daily reported how well they were conducting themselves towards the people.[6] It is absurd to suppose that Pompeius would spend the winter in Cilicia, where he could not have fed his men.... Besides, if he had penetrated into the continent from Cilicia, he must have crossed the ... Taurus, and given his army a useless and laborious march '. The mere fact, Long adds,[7] that when Pompey in his campaign against Mithradates occupied Anaitis [or Acilisene in the valley of the Euphrates], he was joined by the army of Marcius Rex from Cilicia ' proves ' that he ' was not in Cilicia when he received his new commission '. Nevertheless Théodore Reinach[8] holds that he was, and that in the spring of 66 B. C., after the Manilian law was passed, he marched into Galatia, leaving Marcius Rex to cover Cilicia and Cappadocia.

What Long says about Marcius Rex needs no refutation : Pompey could feed his army in Cilicia just as well as Marcius Rex, who certainly fed his own three legions ; for even if there was not enough corn in the province for both, Pompey had command of the sea ; and Long might have ascertained by looking at his map, that if Pompey had transported his troops from Cilicia to the province Asia, they would have had twice as far to march before they encountered Mithradates as if they had marched from Tarsus across

[1] xii, 3, 37.
[2] Groebe (W. Drumann's *Gesch. Roms*, iv², 1908, p. 153, n. 6) says that Kiessling [the editor of Asconius ?] has informed him by letter that it was near the modern Aghwanis, south of the river Lycus and between Nicopolis (Purkh) and Dracones. But he gives no reasons.   [3] *Mithr.*, 97.
[4] *Decline of the Roman Republic*, iii, 1869, p. 144.
[5] *De imp. Cn. Pomp.*, 15, 45.   [6] *Ib.*, 13, 39.   [7] p. 148.
[8] *Mithr. Eupator*, 1890, pp. 381-2.

the Taurus by the great road that passed through Mazaca. This road led into the country of the Trocmi, where Pompey met Lucullus.[1] To take the army round the coast to Ephesus or any other port, and then to impose upon it a really 'useless' march, would have been an act of lunacy : yet this was what Long attributed to an experienced commander.

Are we then to reject the testimony of Cicero, who, as Long says, must have known ? Not altogether. Some foundation for what he said there must have been ; but, considering that he wrote his speeches some time after he delivered them [2] and that his historical statements are notoriously loose, we need not take it literally. May we not suppose that Pompey went on business from Cilicia to Asia, accompanied by a bodyguard, which the rhetoric of Cicero magnified into an army, and that his legions marched from Tarsus to Danala in the country of the Trocmi, where he met Lucullus ?

The strength of Pompey's army in 66 B.C.—Attempts have been made to estimate the strength of the army with which Pompey took the field against Mithradates from the amount of money paid to the surviving officers and men at the end of the war ; but, as we do not know what proportion the survivors bore to the whole force or what reinforcements, if any, Pompey received during the war, this information, though it shows that his force was much larger than that of Lucullus, is not sufficient. According to Appian,[3] the sum distributed was 16,000 talents (384,000,000 sesterces) ; each private received 1,500 drachmas (6,000 sesterces), centurions and tribunes proportionately; Pliny[4] says that the share of the *legati* and quaestors amounted to 100,000,000 sesterces : therefore 284,000,000 remained for the military tribunes, centurions, rank and file.[5] In each legion there were 6 tribunes and 60 centurions ; but the number of the legions is unknown.

When Tigranes made a present to Pompey's army (see page 207), he gave every legionary 50 drachmas,[6] every centurion 1,000,[6] and every tribune 10,000 [7] or, according to Strabo [8] and Plutarch,[8] a talent (6,000). Groebe [9] assumes that Pompey followed the same proportion. Perhaps ; but the pay of a centurion in the time of Polybius was only twice that of a private. Groebe assumes, further, that the average strength of the legions had been reduced from 6,000 (an estimate which is certainly too high) to 4,000 men, and thus arrives at the conclusion that the recipients, exclusive of *legati* and quaestors, numbered 48 tribunes, 480 centurions,

---

[1] Strabo, xii, 15, 2.
[2] Prof. Reid (*Hermathena*, xii, 1903, p. 142) calls attention to 'the freedom, or rather license, with which speeches were in ancient times recast before publication'.
[3] *Mithr.*, 116.   [4] *Nat. Hist.*, xxxvii, 2 (6), 16.
[5] Presumably the veterans who settled at Nicopolis (see p. 211) received their share.
[6] Strabo, xi, 14, 10 ; Plut., *Pomp.*, 33. 4 ; App., *Mithr.*, 104.
[7] App., *l. c.*   [8] *l. c.*
[9] W. Drumann's *Gesch. Roms*, iv², 1910, p. 486, n. 5.

32,000 rank and file. Kromayer[1] calculates that if we take the [much more probable] proportion adopted by Caesar at his triumph, when centurions received twice, tribunes four times as much as privates,[2] we may estimate the number at about 45,000.

Pompey's campaign against Mithradates.—The historian of the Peninsular War, writing to his brother Captain Henry Napier about Dr. Arnold's *History of Rome*, ended his letter with the words, ' Tell the Doctor to beware of falling into the error about Pompey being a bad general—he was a very great one '.[3] Unfortunately the materials for judging Pompey's generalship in the years when he was making his reputation are as bad as any from which military history has ever been composed. It is not till we come to study the last eighteen months of his life that we have the guidance of a real authority. The work that he did for Sulla can only be appraised by its results. He defeated Lepidus, who was confessedly an amateur; but the battle is merely registered; and since Pompey failed to prevent the beaten army from embarking and leaving Italy, the victory was not complete. The one detailed description, written by a military expert,[4] of Pompey's tactics in the Sertorian War, shows that in the first campaign he had not yet learned his trade : at Lauro he was utterly out-generalled. After five years' fighting he and his colleague got the better of their enemy ; but while we know that Metellus, whom nobody has ever called a great commander, performed his share, we have not the means of adequately estimating the strategy or the tactics of either. The fame of Pompey was not increased by the part which luck enabled him to play in hunting down the fugitives who survived the overthrow of Spartacus. The operations which he directed against the pirates were well planned and ably executed; but his movements were absolutely free : he was, so to speak, prime minister, chief of the general staff, and commander-in-chief in one ; and the force at his disposal was irresistible. The conquest of the East remains. When Pompey took over the command, the power of Mithradates was broken, and the army with which Pompey set out to crush him was twice as great as that with which Lucullus had vanquished, first him and then the King of Kings when their power was at the height. But in the records of the conquests which dazzled the contemporaries of Pompey there is only one that enables us to get even a glimmering of the manœuvres by which he conquered [5]—the one that describes the short campaign which ended with the flight of Mithradates ; and even that has to be pieced together out of materials which are so imperfect that again I feel bound to exhibit them to the reader and enable him to see whether I have told the truth. If any student

[1] *Neue Jahrb. f. d. klass. Altertum*, xxxiii, 1914, p. 160, n. 5.
[2] App., *B. C.*, ii, 102, 422.
[3] H. A. Bruce's *Life of Gen. Sir W. Napier*, ii, 1864, p. 54.
[4] Frontin., *Strat.*, ii, 5, 31.
[5] Except perhaps the account, given by Frontinus (ii, 3, 14), of a stratagem which Pompey practised in Albania. Cf. Plut., *Pomp.*, 35, 1 ; App., *Mithr.*, 103 ; Dio, xxxvii, 4.

of the art of war shall read these articles, he will conclude that before he can assent to or dissent from Napier's estimate he must wait until he can take the *Commentaries* of Caesar, supplemented by the letters of Pompey that survive, for his guide. For my part, having followed the career of this consummate soldier from first to last, I am reminded, when I compare him with Lucullus, of a remark which Sir Henry Havelock-Allan made to me a few months before he died : ' Lord Roberts is the most fortunate man that ever lived ; and Wolseley is a genius.' [1]

PLUTARCH	APPIAN	DIO
Pomp., 32, 1. Pompey marches against Mithradates, who has 30,000 foot and 2,000 horse : Mithradates does not venture to fight. § 2. Pompey occupies a hill which Mithradates has abandoned, and (§ 3) makes a contravallation round the army of Mithradates,[2] who, after having been blockaded for 45 days, secretly escapes with his best troops.[3] Pompey pursues him, encamps opposite him near the Euphrates, and, fearing that he may cross that river and escape, marches against him soon after midnight, (§ 4) but, seeing that he is prepared to resist, wishes to postpone fighting till dawn : the senior centurions, however, urge him to attack at once, as the moon gives sufficient light. § 5. In the ensuing battle the Romans have the moon behind them ; Mithradates is defeated, losing more than 10,000 men, and his camp is taken.[4] § 6. At the outset of the battle he cuts his way through the Romans with 800	*Mithr.*, 98. Pompey posts some of his cavalry in ambush and sends the rest to attack the outposts of Mithradates and then to retreat before them : the outposts are lured into the ambuscade and routed,[5] but Mithradates by displaying his infantry prevents the pursuers from rushing his camp. 99. Pressed for supplies, he retreats and suffers Pompey to invade his kingdom, hoping that he will there suffer from lack of food ; but Pompey, ordering supplies to be brought up from the rear, advances and surrounds the army of Mithradates, who is on his eastern side, with a contravallation 150 stades [18¾ Roman miles] in extent. Before the 50th day of the blockade Mithradates silently escapes by night. Pompey, following in the morning, harasses the rear of the fugitives. Mithradates halts at nightfall in a dense forest. On the next day Mithradates occupies a strong position surrounded by rocks, guarding the	xxxvi, 46, 2. Pompey marches against Mithradates, (47, 1) who, being inferior in numbers, retreats and devastates the country, hoping to starve the Pompeian army. As Pompey enters [the Lesser] Armenia in order to get supplies, (§ 2) Mithradates does likewise and occupies a hill near Pompey, hoping to exhaust him by famine. His cavalry harass the Romans by desultory attacks. Many of the Pompeians desert, and (§ 3) Pompey moves to a safer position, surrounded by forest : (§ 4) by a stratagem he entices the Mithradatic cavalry into an ambuscade and slays many of them. 48, 1. Mithradates, learning that Pompey has got supplies, that he has occupied the district of Anaitis [or Acilisene [6]] in Armenia, and (§ 2) that he has been reinforced by Marcius Rex, escapes by night and moves by nocturnal marches towards that part of Armenia which belongs to the Tigranes : (§ 3) Pompey

[1] An officer to whom *I* mentioned Havelock-Allan's remark, said, ' That 's what we all think ', and others without exception have confirmed it.
[2] Cf. Oros., vi, 4, 3.
[3] The stratagem by which Mithradates escaped is described by Frontinus (i, 1, 7).
[4] Cf. Livy, *Epit.*, 101 ; Frontin., ii, 1, 12 ; Flor., i, 40, 23 ; Eutrop., vi, 12 ; Oros., vi, 4, 4.
[5] Cf. Livy, *Epit.*, 100. Pompey's stratagem is described minutely by Frontinus (ii, 5, 33).
[6] See Strabo, xi, 14, 16.

430 POMPEY IN THE EAST

PLUTARCH	APPIAN	DIO
horse, nearly all of whom disperse, and ultimately escapes with three men to the fort[1] of Sinora, (§ 7) whence he flees into Armenia, intending to join Tigranes: but, as an asylum is refused to him and a price is put upon his head, he passes by the upper waters of the Euphrates and escapes through Colchis.	only approach with four cohorts:[2] Pompey posts troops opposite to cut off his escape. 100. At dawn a skirmish ensues between the outposts: some Mithradatic troopers hurry on foot to help their comrades, but, being attacked by the Roman cavalry, retreat to their camp, intending to mount their horses and renew the fight: their comrades above, fancying that they are trying to escape, throw away their own weapons and flee, but, as there is no free exit, become confused and rush down the rocky slopes. About 10,000 perish, and camp and equipage are captured. 101. Mithradates, escaping with his bodyguard alone, meets some horsemen and about 3,000 foot in the course of his flight, and with them goes to the fort of Sinora, thence to the upper waters of the Euphrates, which he crosses on the fourth day, and finally to Dioscurias in Colchis.	follows him in the hope of bringing him to action, but Mithradates remains in his camp by day, and Pompey shrinks from attacking by night in an unknown country. § 4. At length, however, fearing that Mithradates will escape, he determines to risk attacking by night. Accordingly he marches at mid-day unperceived by the enemy, who are resting, and occupies some heights enclosing a hollow through which they will have to pass. § 5. They enter the hollow unsuspiciously, and Pompey attacks them in the dark. 49. Assailed first by missiles from the heights and then with the sword, the troops of Mithradates with their camels, horses, and wagons are thrown into confusion, and when the moon rises they are dazzled by its light; many are slain, many are taken prisoners, many including Mithradates flee. 50. Mithradates, anxious to join Tigranes, sends envoys to plead his cause; but Tigranes, suspecting that his son has been incited by Mithradates to rebel, imprisons them. Mithradates therefore flees to Colchis.

Before we examine discrepancies in the evidence let us try to determine the geography. We are not told where Mithradates was when his retreat began; but he was evidently somewhere west of the Lesser Armenia, and the general direction of his march was towards the Euphrates. Strabo[3] says that the hill on which he was blockaded was Dasteira in Acilisene, and that it was not far from the Euphrates, which separates Acilisene from the Lesser Armenia. It would appear from the narratives of Appian and Dio that the scene of Pompey's decisive victory was a day's march or more further eastward; but,

[1] Cf. Oros., vi, 4, 6.
[2] F. and E. Cumont (*Studia Pontica*, 1906, p. 313) identify this position with the height, just east of Purkh (Nicopolis), on which the village of Eski Sheir (or Sheher) stands.
[3] xii, 3, 28.

according to Plutarch and Appian, Mithradates had not crossed the river when he was attacked. Pompey afterwards founded a city, which he called Nicopolis ('the city of victory') in the Lesser Armenia [1]—according to Appian on the site of the battle; but this statement must evidently be taken in an extended sense, for Nicopolis stood upon the site of Purkh,[2] on the great road south of the river Lycus and about 50 miles in a straight line from the nearest point of the Euphrates.

Drumann [3] and Mommsen,[4] relying upon Strabo, hold that Dasteira was on the left or eastern bank of the Euphrates, and that Mithradates, having crossed the river and occupied that stronghold, recrossed it and moved to the neighbourhood of Nicopolis, where the decisive battle was fought. Any one who will take the trouble to compare Mommsen's narrative with the original authorities will see that it is hopelessly confused: consistent with the statements of Strabo, it is consistent with nothing else—not even with itself. Pompey, he says, 'marched to the upper Euphrates, crossed it, and entered the eastern provinces of the Pontic empire . . . Mithradates followed along the left bank of the Euphrates, and when he had reached the Anaitic or Acilisenian province, intercepted the route of the Romans at the stronghold of Dasteira'.—Parenthetically I may remind the reader that Dio does not say that Mithradates entered Acilisene at all: he says that Mithradates learned that Pompey had occupied it.—Pompey, Mommsen continues, blockaded Mithradates, who at the end of 45 days escaped, and moved 'towards the east'. 'Cautiously Pompey followed', and when he saw that Mithradates 'intended . . . to draw the enemy after him into the remote and boundless East', he took up a position 'at the point where Nicopolis was afterwards built'. There the decisive battle was fought. Thus, according to Mommsen, Mithradates, who, ever since he left Acilisene, had been pushing further and further eastward, was finally defeated 50 miles NW. by W. of that part of the Euphrates, on the further bank of which, according to Mommsen, Acilisene lay! Drumann avoids this absurdity, but contrives to commit his own. After relating that the Romans invaded Armenia, followed by Mithradates, who, however, was soon forced to return to Pontus, he remarks in a footnote that Dio 'alone mentions this movement of the two armies, which therefore later recrossed from the left or eastern bank of the Euphrates to the right, moved westward, and when the King again tried to approach the river, engaged in a decisive battle'.[5] Now Dio, as the reader will remember, does not say that 'the two armies' entered Acilisene; he only says that Mithradates learned that Pompey had taken possession

---

[1] *Bell. Alex.*, 36, 3; Strabo, xii, 3, 28: App., *Mithr.*, 105, 115; Dio, xxxvi, 50, 3; Oros., vi, 4, 7.
[2] *C. I. G.*, iii, No. 4189; P. Le Bas and W. H. Waddington, *Inscr. grecques*, &c., iii, 1870, No. 1814 *d*.
[3] *Gesch. Roms*, iv², 1910, pp. 443–4.
[4] *Röm. Gesch.*, iii⁸, 1889, p. 127 (Eng. tr., iv, 1908, pp. 408–9)
[5] *Op. cit.*, p. 444, n. 1.

of it: he neither says nor implies that the two armies, or even one, 'recrossed from the left or eastern bank of the Euphrates to the right', or that they 'moved westward'. On the contrary, he says that Mithradates, when he escaped [from Dasteira], moved 'towards the Armenia which belonged to Tigranes' (ἐς τὴν τοῦ Τιγράνου Ἀρμενίαν), that is towards the east. It is therefore clear that if, as Strabo seems to mean, Dasteira was on the left bank of the Euphrates, so also was the battle-field. But, I repeat, Nicopolis, which was built to commemorate the victory, was in the Lesser Armenia and stood upon the site of Purkh; and, as every one admits, the battle-field was also on the right bank of the Euphrates. How, then, are we to reconcile Strabo with Plutarch and Dio? If Strabo meant his statement to be taken literally, he made a great mistake; for since the battle-field was on the western bank, so also *a fortiori* was Dasteira.[1] But may we not suppose that Acilisene was partly on the right bank, where Kiepert and Mr. J. G. C. Anderson[2] locate it, and that Strabo's statement was misleading? What he says elsewhere about the river Saône[3] is equally uncertain.[4]

Théodore Reinach[5] offers a different explanation. He identifies Dasteira with Nicopolis, and therefore in the passage in which Strabo, if the MSS. are right, says that Dasteira was in Acilisene he boldly 'suppresses' the words καὶ τῆς Ἀκιλισηνῆς.[6] But he accepts Strabo's other statement, that Acilisene was separated from the Lesser Armenia by the Euphrates; and since, more clear-sighted than Drumann and Mommsen, he sees that Pompey remained on the right bank throughout, he interprets Dio as meaning that Pompey sent a detachment across the river to occupy Acilisene, from which he drew supplies. This explanation is ingenious, and doubtless Pompey did send a detachment to seize Acilisene and prevent Mithradates from escaping by that way; but would he have sent troops to the further side of a great river more than 50 miles away? And does a theory recommend itself which depends upon the mutilation of a text?

I am glad to find that I am supported by Mr. J. A. R. Munro, whose explorations have illuminated Pontic history. 'The narratives ... of this campaign', he writes, 'are too vague to identify the localities with any precision. Probably the preliminary skirmishes and manœuvres took place in the hilly country traversed by the Lycus between Nicopolis and Cabira [Niksar]. Mithridates' last stand [on the hill where he was blockaded] must be put somewhere near Nicopolis, and the crowning catastrophe two nights' march farther east. Dasteira ought, on the analogy of Dasmanda and Dastarkon, to be a fortress on a rock. Either Koilu Hissar

[1] Orosius (vi, 4, 3) says that Dastracus (= Dasteira) was in the Lesser Armenia, that is, on the right bank of the Euphrates.
[2] *Asia Minor* (Murray's Handy Classical Maps).
[3] iv, 1, 11; 3, 2.
[4] *Caesar's Conquest of Gaul* [2], pp. 352–3.
[5] *Mithr. Eupator*, 1890, pp. 384–5.
[6] *Ib.*, p. 384, n. 4 ('supprimer les mots καὶ τῆς Ἀκιλισηνῆς').

POMPEY IN THE EAST

or Shabkan Kara Hissar might be suggested. At all events the whole campaign moved on the great trunk road up the Lycus '.[1]

It will be noticed that Plutarch omits to mention the combat of cavalry which the epitomizer of Livy and Frontinus as well as Appian and Dio record; that this combat, according to Appian, occurred before, according to Dio, during the blockade; that Dio, although he evidently has the blockade in mind,[2] does not expressly mention it; that the stratagem by which Mithradates extricated his army from blockade is noticed by Frontinus alone; that Appian transforms the nocturnal battle, which is attested by overwhelming authority, into one fought by day; and that his description of this battle and of the locality differs radically from that of Dio. As Long plaintively remarks, 'It is painful work to construct a narrative out of such materials':[3] but one must either make a choice or else leave a gap in history. On the whole, I think that Dio's narrative is the most probable. The notorious carelessness of Appian becomes so glaring in the last phase of the Mithradatic War that when he differs from other writers he is never to be trusted. We may, I think, rest assured that the combat of cavalry took place during the blockade; that Mithradates broke the blockade after it had lasted six or seven weeks by a stratagem; and that the decisive battle was fought by night.[4]

Pompey's winter quarters in 65-64 B. C.—According to Dio,[5] Pompey spent the winter of 65-64 B.C. in 'Aspis' (Πομπήιος δὲ ἐν τῇ Ἀσπίδι καὶ τότε ἐχείμασε); and Niese remarks[6] that the words καὶ τότε prove that he wintered in the same country as in the preceding year, when he had a camp in Armenia on the upper Kur.[7] Mommsen[8] concludes that his quarters were near the Caspian Sea. Plutarch,[9] however, relates that after he had subdued the Albanians he returned to the Lesser Armenia; and since Dio[10] says that in the winter of 66-65 he encamped in Anaitis, Théodore Reinach[11] infers that the camp was in Acilisene, another name of Anaitis. Reinach also remarks that Aspis is otherwise unknown,[12] but, as Dio's subsequent

[1] *Journ. Hell. Studies*, xxi, 1901, p. 59.   [2] 47, 2; 48, 2.
[3] *Decline of the Roman Republic*, iii, 149, n. 1.
[4] W. Fabricius (*Theophanes von Mytilene*, &c., 1888, pp. 94–115), who thinks that the original report of the campaign can be reconstructed by combination of the authorities, fails to allow for the blundering of such chroniclers as Appian and overlooks palpable inconsistencies. To take two instances: he does not notice that the surprise by which Pompey disposed of the Pontic cavalry was put by Appian before, by Dio after the armies entered the Lesser Armenia; and the blind faith with which he accepts the statements of every authority compels him to assume that the combat which Appian describes in *Mithr.*, 100, was not the decisive battle, and therefore that Appian did not mention the decisive battle at all! It does not require much acumen to perceive that the combat which Appian described in his hundredth chapter—the combat in which Mithradates is said to have lost 10,000 men and from which he is said to have escaped into Colchis—*was* the decisive battle, and that his description, which is unique, is incorrect.
[5] xxxvii, 7, 5.   [6] *Hermes*, xiii, 1878, p. 38.   [7] Dio, xxxvi, 53, 5.
[8] *Röm. Gesch.*, iii⁸, 1889, p. 144, note (Eng. tr., iv, 1908, p. 429, n. 1).
[9] *Pomp.*, 36, 1.   [10] xxxvi, 53, 5.   [11] *Mithr. Eupator*, p. 399 and n. 3.
[12] Long (*Decline of the Roman Republic*, iii, 178), who wrongly supposes that

narrative shows, must have been in the Lesser Armenia. By Dio's subsequent narrative Reinach evidently means the statement that Pompey received from Stratonice, one of the wives of Mithradates, the fort of Symphorium. Niese [1] argues that Συμφόριον is a corruption of Σινορία, which, according to Strabo,[2] was in the Lesser Armenia. There is no inconsistency in the statements of Dio, nor does he really differ from Plutarch, for he says that in the winter of 66–65 Pompey divided his army into three parts, which he cantoned in Anaitis *and* on the river Kur. Mommsen's remark is therefore misleading; we may accept Reinach's view and conclude that Pompey spent the winter of 65–64 in that part of Acilisene which was on the right bank of the Euphrates.[3]

The date of the award made by Pompey to Deiotarus.—B. Niese [4] argues that Deiotarus received his reward in 63 B.C., after Pompey returned from Syria, because Strabo [5] says that Galatia was divided into three parts, of which Deiotarus subsequently became the sole ruler, ' in our time ' (καθ' ἡμᾶς), and Niese claims to have proved that Strabo was born in 63. Strabo, however, mentions the reward which I have described in my narrative (pp. 210–1) in another passage,[6] and I doubt whether he would have intended to convey that an event happened in his lifetime when *ex hypothesi* he was less than a year old: it is surely more probable that he meant ' within the memory of living men '. I therefore agree with Théodore Reinach [7] that the award in question, being connected with the settlement of Pontus, was made in 64.

The 'eleven cities' of Pontus.—The cities to which Pompey assigned territories in that part of the Pontic kingdom which he annexed to Bithynia [8] have not all been identified with certainty. It is agreed that they included Pompeiopolis [9] (Tash Keupri), Neapolis [10] (Vezir Keupri), Zela,[11] Megalopolis [12] (Sivas), Diospolis [13] (formerly Cabira), Magnopolis [14] (formerly Eupatoria), Amisus, Sinope, and Amastris. The other two, according to Théodore Reinach,[15] were Amasia and Nicopolis; according to B. Niese,[16] Heraclea and Tieum; according to Mr. J. A. R. Munro,[17] Nicopolis (or Amasia or Tieum) and Heraclea. Mr. J. G. C. Anderson, Franz Cumont, and H. Grégoire [18] include Amasia. Reinach finds fault with Niese's choice, on the ground that Heraclea was 'in ruins and that Tieum belonged to Bithynia. The latter statement is inaccurate;[19] the former, which, if Appian [20] may be trusted, would

Dio was referring to the winter of 64–63 B.C., concludes that Aspis was in Syria!   [1] *Op. cit.*, p. 39.   [2] xii, 3, 28.   [3] See p. 432.
[4] *Rhein. Mus.*, xxxviii, 1883, p. 584.
[5] xii, 5, 1.   [6] xii, 3, 13.   [7] *Mithr. Eupator*, p. 400.
[8] Strabo, xii, 3, 1.   [9] *Ib.*, § 40.
[10] Formerly Phazimon (Strabo, xii, 3, 38).   [11] *Ib.*, xi, 8, 4 ; xii, 3, 37.
[12] Afterwards called Sebasteia. See Strabo, xii, 3, 37, and cf. *Royal Geogr. Soc. Suppl. Papers*, iii, 1893, p. 719.
[13] Strabo, xii, 3, 31.   [14] *Ib.*, § 30.
[15] *Mithr. Eupator*, pp. 400–1, n. 7.   [16] *Rhein. Mus.*, xxxviii, 1883, p. 597.
[17] *Journ. Hell. Studies*, xxi, 1901, p. 61, n. 1.   [18] *Studia Pontica*, iii, 109.
[19] See Strabo, xii, 3, 2.   [20] *Mithr.*, 115.

POMPEY IN THE EAST

apply equally to Magnopolis (Eupatoria), is probably an exaggeration; and Mr. Munro, observing that Reinach was mistaken when he said that Heraclea was not restored before the time of Caesar,[1] holds, rightly in my opinion, that, as one of the four great coast towns—Heraclea, Amastris, Amisus, and Sinope—it was 'certainly included'. He adds that 'if Nicopolis must be surrendered to Deiotarus', he would substitute for it Amasia or Tieum. I can see no reason for supposing that Pompey ceded to Deiotarus the city which he had founded to commemorate his own decisive victory; for Nicopolis was in the Lesser Armenia, and Strabo[2] expressly states that the territory assigned to Deiotarus extended as far as ($\mu\acute{\epsilon}\chi\rho\iota$)—and therefore did not include—that region: on the other hand, Nicopolis was founded primarily for the sake of war-worn veterans who wished to settle in the East; and it seems to me probable that Amasia, the inland capital of Pontus, which stood upon the great north road—not Tieum, which appears to have been less important—would have better served the purpose that Pompey had in mind. My list therefore comprises Pompeiopolis, Neapolis, Zela, Megalopolis, Diospolis, Magnopolis, Amisus, Sinope, Amastris, Heraclea, and Amasia.

Some incredible statements in the original authorities.—Appian[3] says that Pompey, after he restored Cappadocia to Ariobarzanes, and before he captured Jerusalem, attacked Antiochus of Commagene, defeated Darius, the King of Media,[4] and attacked Aretas, King of the Nabataean Arabs. According to Dio,[5] Pompey subdued Aretas after settling Syria and Phoenicia, but before he captured Jerusalem. Orosius[6] relates that, having settled the affairs of Syria, he advanced from Pontus (!) against Parthia and reached Ecbatana; that after he heard of the death of Mithradates he invaded Coele Syria and Phoenicia, subdued the Ituraeans and Arabs and captured their stronghold, Petra; and that he then besieged Jerusalem. Plutarch, on the other hand, who knows nothing of the invasion of Parthia or the defeat of Darius, after describing the conquest of Judaea,[7] says that Pompey made an expedition against Petra,[8] but that when he was not far from that stronghold he heard of the death of Mithradates[9] and thereupon returned to Pontus.[10]

Now, as Mommsen remarks,[11] the alleged subjection of Aretas and the alleged capture of Petra are 'sufficiently accounted for by the fact that it was Pompey [or rather Pompey's lieutenant Scaurus] who occasioned his [Aretas's] withdrawal from Jerusalem'.[12] As to the invasion of Parthia, the defeat of Darius, and the expedition to Ecbatana, whether or not the historians were misled, as

[1] Cf. Memnon, 60.   [2] xii, 3, 13.   [3] *Mithr.*, 106, 117.
[4] Cf. Vell. Pat., ii, 40, 1.   [5] xxxvii, 15.   [6] vi, 4, 9; 6, 1-4.
[7] *Pomp.*, 39, 2.   [8] *Ib.*, 41, 1.   [9] *Ib.*, §§ 4-5.   [10] *Ib.*, 42, 1.
[11] *Röm. Gesch.*, iii[8], 1889, p. 147, note (Eng. tr., iv, 1908, p. 432, n. 1).
[12] See p. 213. It is safer to accept the statement of Josephus, the one tolerably trustworthy authority for the conquest of Judaea, as to the time when Pompey heard of the death of Mithradates than that of Plutarch.

Mommsen conjectured,[1] by 'the grandiloquent and designedly ambiguous bulletins of Pompey', they may safely be dismissed as mythical; for it is impossible to determine any period in 63 B.C. in which Pompey could have marched several hundred miles eastward from his line of advance through Syria.

WAS CAESAR BORN IN 100 OR IN 102 B.C.?

The view, originally advocated by Mommsen,[2] that Caesar was born in 102 B.C., was controverted by A. W. Zumpt[3] and C. Nipperdey,[4] and has recently been examined by Professor Monroe E. Deutsch,[5] who comes to the following conclusion,—'that Caesar secured a dispensation during 67 B.C. or early in 66 B.C., allowing him to hold the various offices two years before the legal age, seems the simplest solution of the problem'.
The direct evidence is well known. Caesar was born in July.[6] According to Velleius,[7] he was about 18 when Sulla became supreme, that is, in 82 B.C. Plutarch[8] says that he died 'at the age of fifty-six years all told' (τὰ μὲν πάντα γεγονὼς ἔτη πεντήκοντα καὶ ἕξ). Suetonius[9] and Appian[10] agree that he died in his fifty-sixth

[1] Op. cit., p. 149, note (Eng. tr., iv, 434, n. 1).
[2] Röm. Gesch., iii⁸, 1889, p. 16, note (Eng. tr., v, 1894, p. 278, n. 1).
[3] De dict. Caes. die et anno natali, 1874, pp. 10–23.
[4] See pp. 440–2, infra.
[5] Trans. Amer. Philol. Assn., 1914, pp. 17–28.
[6] According to Macrobius (Sat., i, 12, 34), Caesar's birthday was the 12th of July; and this statement is supported by the Fasti Amiterni (C. I. L., i, p. 324), in which we read that on July 12 ludi feriae were held ' because Gaius Caesar was born˙on that day', and by the Fasti Antiates (ib., p. 328). Dio, however (xlvii, 18, 6), says that as the games in honour of Apollo were commonly held on Caesar's birthday, and as a passage in the Sibylline Books forbade that that day should be sacred to any god except Apollo, the triumvirs in 42 B.C. ordained that the preceding day should be observed as Caesar's birthday. These games were at that time celebrated on eight successive days, July 6–13; and accordingly some scholars have explained Dio's statement as meaning that Caesar's birthday was to be kept on July 5 (C. I. L., i, p. 396. Cf. W. Warde Fowler, The Roman Festivals, &c., 1899, p. 174). If so, it would follow that, according to Dio, he was born on the 6th. But Dio, who did not refer to the eight days on which the games were held, but to one only, and that the most important, was of course thinking of July 13, on which day alone the ludi Apollinares were originally held (see Warde Fowler, op. cit., p. 180). His statement cannot be explained away, and it therefore seems to me probable that the compilers of the calendars were misled into supposing that Caesar was born on the 12th of July, on which his birthday was kept, whereas his birthday was really the 13th, and that Macrobius followed them. [I find that A. W. Zumpt (op. cit., pp. 8–9), who argues, as I have done, that the day which Dio had in mind was July 13, supposes that those who compiled the calendars were aware, but did not think it necessary to explain, that Caesar was really born on that day. W. Christ (Sitzungsber. d. phil.-philol. . . . Classe d. K. b. Akad. d. Wiss. zu München, i, 1876, pp. 194–5) points out, as a further reason for regarding July 13 as the day of the ludi Apollinares, that on it the games took place in the Circus (see C. I. L., i, pp. 324, 328).]
[7] ii, 41, 2. [8] Caes., 69, 1. [9] Div. Iul., 88. [10] B. C., ii, 149, 620.

year. Eutropius[1] remarks that at the time of the battle of Munda (March 17,[2] 45 B. C.)—just a year before his death—he was 56. Thus four of our authorities assign his birth to 100 B. C., one only —Eutropius—to 102; and, says Professor Deutsch,[3] Eutropius 'clearly employed for the life of Caesar not Suetonius, but an author who had used his work'.

The gist of Mommsen's argument is this:—The view that Caesar was born in 100 B. C. 'is absolutely inconsistent with the facts that Caesar held the aedileship in 689 [65 B. C.], the praetorship in 692 [62], and the consulship in 695 [59], and that these offices could ... be held at the earliest in the 37th, 40th, and 43rd years respectively of a man's life. ... One cannot conceive why Caesar should have held all the curule offices two years before the legal time, still less why there should be no mention anywhere of his having done so ... the case of Pompey [who became consul in 70 B. C., when he was only 35, and who had never served as quaestor or praetor] was totally different ... but ... it is several times expressly stated that the Senate released him from the laws as to age.[4] That this should have been done for Pompey, who stood for the consulship as a commander-in-chief, crowned with victory and honoured with a triumph, at the head of an army, and after his coalition with Crassus, who himself represented a powerful party, one can fully understand. But it would be in the highest degree astonishing if the same thing had been done for Caesar in his candidature for the minor magistracies, when he was of little more importance than other political beginners.' Furthermore, remarking that, according to Velleius,[5] Caesar was appointed a priest of Jupiter by Marius and Cinna [in January, 86] when he was 'almost a boy' (*paene puer*), Mommsen points out that if he was born in 100, he was 'not "almost" ... but actually still a boy, and for this very reason hardly capable of holding such a priesthood'; and he maintains that the number L II on certain coins of Caesar, which, he says, were probably struck early in 49 B. C., indicates his age. As for the authorities who imply that the date of Caesar's birth was 100, their statements 'may very well be traceable to a common source; nor can they claim any very high credibility, seeing that for the earlier period before the commencement [in 59 B. C.] of the *acta diurna* [official gazette] the statements as to the natal years of even the best known and most prominent Romans—for instance, as to that of Pompey[6] —vary in the most surprising way'.

In reply to this last argument Deutsch has nothing to say; but

---

[1] vi, 24.   [2] *Bell. Hisp.*, 31, 8.   [3] *Op. cit.*, p. 18.
[4] Cic., *De imp. Cn. Pomp.*, 21, 62; App., iii, 88, 361.
[5] ii, 43, 1.
[6] Cf. Livy, *Epit.*, 89, with Licinianus (ed. Flemisch), p. 31, ll. 1-3, Ps. Victor (*De vir. ill.*, 77), and Eutropius, v, 9. See also Plut., *Pomp.*, 46. 1, 79. 2, and App., i, 121, 560. The former wrongly says that Pompey was not quite 40 when he celebrated his third triumph [in 61 B. C.], and that he died at the age of 59; the latter that when he stood in 71 B. C. for the consulship he was in his 34th year!

he urges [1] that '*pueritia* might have been loosely taken to end at an age less than fourteen years', and that Velleius himself,[2] ' speaking of the young Ptolemy in 48 B.C. when he was thirteen years old ', says that he was then ' nearer boyhood than youth ' (*qui tum puero quam iuveni propior regnabat Alexandriae*). Now allowance must be made for the vaguely rhetorical language of Velleius ; nevertheless Deutsch's retort is fair, and Mommsen's case would not have been weakened if he had omitted to press this point.

Deutsch [3] then proceeds to collect references to Caesar's age which seem to him to harmonize with the traditional date. Tacitus,[4] speaking of men who achieved oratorical fame while they were still young, remarks that Caesar prosecuted Dolabella 'in his twenty-first year'. ' That age ', says Deutsch, ' cannot possibly be correct [Caesar prosecuted Dolabella in 77 B.C.] ... but the point that he [Tacitus] is stressing is the youth of these orators, and a Caesar in his twenty-fifth year would have been quite outside of the group just mentioned ; but if in his twenty-third year he would easily belong to it.' Surely this is splitting hairs ; but anyhow the argument only tends to show that Tacitus, like other writers, believed that Caesar was born in 100 B.C. ; and the question is, Were they not mistaken ? Again, when Deutsch points out that Sallust [5] called the Caesar of 63 B.C. an *adulescentulus*, he has to admit that he was comparing him with the elderly Catulus ; and he forgets that Cicero spoke of himself as having been an *adulescens* when he was 43.[6] Lastly, Deutsch notes that there are ' numerous passages referring to Pompey as aged, in marked contrast . . . to Caesar ', and that, on the other hand, Sallust [7] observes that Cato, who was born in 95 B.C., was of almost the same age as Caesar. ' Once more ', he concludes, ' the year 100 B.C. is the more appropriate.' It would seem, then, that the age of the ' aged ' Pompey, who was born in 106 B.C., was ' in marked contrast ' with that of Caesar, who was born *ex hypothesi* in 100 ; but that the age of Caesar was almost the same as that of Cato, who was born five years later. So one year transforms ' marked contrast ' into virtual identity ! When Professor Deutsch affirms that ' the indefinite statements as to Caesar's age . . . point clearly to his birth ' in 100 B.C., I must demur. As to the definite statements, why does the professor assume that that of Eutropius was based upon a mistake made by ' an author who had used ' Suetonius ? That author, whoever he may have been, was not necessarily the only authority whom Eutropius employed.

Professor Deutsch relegates the numismatic evidence to a footnote [8] :—' it is by no means conclusively proved that LII appears on these coins, and . . . even if LII be accepted as the interpretation of the letters . . . the evidence is extremely slight for concluding that this indicates Caesar's age at the time '. Now both the inter-

[1] *Op. cit.*, pp. 19-20. [2] ii, 53, 1. [3] *Op. cit.*, pp. 20-3.
[4] *Dial.*, 34, 8. [5] *Cat.*, 49, 2. [6] *Phil.*, ii, 46, 118.
[7] *Cat.*, 54, 1. [8] *Op. cit.*, p. 19, n. 10.

pretation and the evidence have been accepted not only by Mommsen, but also by other numismatists,—the Comte de Salis, Babelon (with some reserve), Dr. George Macdonald,[1] and Mr. G. F. Hill.[2] ' On voit de même ', says Babelon, ' sur les pièces de Marc Antoine le chiffre XL et XLI indiquant l'âge du futur triumvir.'[3] The letters on the relevant coins of Caesar are ⊥II, or TII, or IIT. ⊥ is another form of L[4] (50) : TII is obviously meaningless : Eckhel[5] suggested that IIT signified *Imperator ITerum*, which would fix the date in 54 B.C.[6] Mr. Hill, like the Comte de Salis, explains that the reason for stating Caesar's age ' would be to remind the Romans that in the next year he would constitutionally be entitled to hold the consulship for the second time ', and in common with the Comte de Salis and Dr. Macdonald he believes that the coins belonged to a series minted at Rome after Caesar plundered the treasury in April, 49 B.C. The Comte de Salis,[7] giving technical reasons, which all numismatists accept, for believing that they came from Rome, argues that it is infinitely more probable that they were put into circulation while Caesar was present than in his absence. It would follow that they were not struck in 48–47, because Caesar left Rome in January of the former year and did not return till September, 47 [when, on the theory that he was born in 100, he was 53]. The choice would therefore lie between Caesar's stay at Rome in April, 49, and that which he made in the late autumn of the same year before he set out for Greece. The former alternative is by far the more probable ; for Caesar must have desired to reward his troops as soon as possible [after he ransacked the treasury]. The objection occurred to me that the moneyers would not have been able to prepare the dies and complete the issue in the very short interval —not more than 3 or 4 days—between the plundering of the treasury and Caesar's departure for Massilia ;[8] and though Mr. Hill assures me that the dies could have been made and the production of coins begun before he started, it is evident that the vast number required for the payment of 13 legions[9] could not have been got ready until a later time. Reviewing the evidence, one must, I think, admit that the date of the coins is hardly certain ; so let us consider that question which Mommsen and Deutsch alike regard as vital.

Deutsch of course admits that if any exception was made in Caesar's favour, permitting him to stand for the consulship before the legal

[1] *Coin Types*, 1905, p. 179.
[2] *Hist. Roman Coins*, 1909, pp. 101–3.
[3] *Descr.* . . . *des monn. de la république rom.*, ii, 1886, pp. 18–9.
[4] See R. Cagnat, *Cours d'épigr. lat.*², 1890, p. 31.
[5] *Doctrina numorum veterum*, vi, 1795, p. 16.
[6] Caesar was saluted as *imperator* in Spain (Plut., *Caes.*, 12, 2) and again in Gaul (Cic., *Fam.*, vii, 5). The coins bear on the reverse a portrait, intended, according to Babelon, to represent Vercingetorix, whom Caesar encountered for the first time in 52 ; but the attribution is doubtful. Cf. C. Jullian, *Vercingétorix*², 1902, p. 356, n. 3.
[7] *Rev. arch.*, xiv, 1866, p. 21.
[8] Cf. Caes., *B. C.*, i, 32–3, with Cic., *Att.*, ix, 17, 1 ; x, 8, 6 ; and x, 8 B.
[9] *B. G.*, viii, 54, 3–4 ; *B. C.*, i, 25, 1. *I* include the legion called *Alaudae*.

440 WAS CAESAR BORN IN 100 OR IN 102 B. C. ?

age, it must have been made at least six years in advance, before he stood for the aedileship. The Comte de Salis denied that there was any evidence that such a dispensation had ever been granted to any one : Deutsch [1] replies that 'in Cicero's *Fifth Philippic* [2] there is an example and a very striking one'. There we read that a quaestor, Lucius Egnatuleius, was privileged by the Senate, as a reward for distinguished service, to stand for a magistracy three years before the legal time. ' That Caesar', says Deutsch, ' should have received the same kind of exemption seems the most likely solution. It would involve but one dispensation instead of three, and of course the failure to mention one is far more easily accounted for than the failure to mention three ... most important of all, such an exemption so early in his career ... would have been more readily passed over in silence on the part of the historians than would have been the case when he reached the higher offices.' Deutsch goes on to argue [3] that Caesar's position in public life was sufficiently high to justify such a dispensation : for ' his conduct of the quaestorship was evidently conspicuously able ' ; he ' had already allied himself with both Pompey and Crassus ' ; he ' had been reckoned among Rome's leading advocates from 77 B. C.' ; and ' his greatest asset throughout this period (70–66 B. C.) was the favour of the commons '. No doubt ; but for this particular object was not a more desirable asset the favour of the Senate ? Which of these alternatives is the more probable—that the four writers who date Caesar's birth in 100 B. C., and of whom two grossly miscalculate the age of Pompey, were wrong, or that the dispensation which he must have received if they were right passed without remark ? I cannot conceive that Cicero would never have alluded in his correspondence to a measure without which the coalition of Caesar, Pompey, and Crassus in 60 B. C. would have been impossible, and which he must have regarded as fraught with disaster to his own party and to the stability of the Republic.

It is surprising that Professor Deutsch omits to notice the arguments by which Nipperdey [4] endeavoured to demolish Mommsen's theory. Nipperdey begins by attempting to show that the passage in which Suetonius [5] relates that Caesar, when he went to Spain as quaestor and saw at Gades a statue of Alexander the Great, lamented that at the age at which Alexander had conquered the world he had himself done nothing memorable, proves that he died in his 56th year. For a passage in the next chapter of Suetonius—' On his departure [from Spain] . . . he approached the Latin colonies [of Transpadane Gaul], which were agitating for the [Roman] citizenship, and would have incited them to attempt some *coup* if the consuls had not for that very reason detained for a time the legions that had been raised for service in Cilicia ' (*Decedens* [ab Hispania]

[1] *Op. cit.*, p. 25.   [2] 19, 52.   [3] *Op. cit.*, pp. 26–8.
[4] *Abhandl. d. philol.-hist. Classe d. Königl. sächs. Gesellsch. d. Wiss.*, 1870, pp. 3–62. See especially pp. 3–4, 37, 53–62.
[5] *Div. Iul.*, 7, 1.

WAS CAESAR BORN IN 100 OR IN 102 B.C.?

... *colonias Latinas de petenda civitate agitantes adiit, et ad audendum aliquid concitasset, nisi consules conscriptas in Ciliciam legiones paulisper ob id ipsum retinuissent*)—shows that Caesar was quaestor between December 5, 69, and December 4, 68 B.C.;[1] Alexander died in his 33rd year; and if Caesar was born in 100 B.C., his 33rd year began on July 13, 68. Now, for aught that Nipperdey could tell, Caesar may have made his remark about Alexander in the early part of 68, when, according to Nipperdey, he was in his 32nd, according to Mommsen in his 34th year. In the former case he would have been a year younger, in the latter a year older than Alexander. Such a minute difference matters nothing; and, as Mommsen[2] observed, Suetonius's anecdote cannot reasonably be regarded as a basis for chronological research. Nipperdey, who maintains, as I have done, that it is out of the question that Caesar could have received a dispensation which none of his contemporaries noticed, devotes the rest of his article to an elaborate attempt to demonstrate that a man could legally become consul at the age of 38; but the whole question turns upon two passages of Cicero, the plain meaning of which he struggles to explain away. In the second speech which Cicero delivered against the proposed law of Rullus he boasted that whereas others had obtained the consulship 'somewhat later than the legal age' (*aliquanto serius quam per aetatem ac per leges liceret*), he, alone of all the 'new men' whom he could remember, 'stood for the consulship at the earliest date permissible, and was elected consul at the first time of asking' (*me esse unum ex omnibus novis hominibus de quibus meminisse possimus, qui consulatum petierim cum primum licitum sit, consul factus sim cum primum potuerim*).[3] Everybody knows that Cicero became consul in his 43rd year. Again, in his *Fifth Philippic*[4] he reminded his hearers that Alexander the Great, who died in his 33rd year, was then 10 years below the minimum age fixed by law for candidates for the consulship (*Macedo Alexander . . . nonne tertio et tricesimo anno mortem obiit? quae est aetas nostris legibus decem annis minor quam consularis*). Nipperdey[5] admits that the former passage would be conclusive 'if we had to do with a trustworthy historian; but', he insists, 'we have an orator before us, who desired to put his official career in the most favourable light possible'. Accordingly he claims that 'a sound canon of interpretation' justifies him in assuming that Cicero deliberately chose an ambiguous expression, in order to let the ignorant suppose that he had attained the consulship at the earliest age recognized by the law, while he could maintain, in reply to experts, that he simply meant that he became consul at an age which was not abnormally late; for if a man became quaestor at the age of 30—the earliest age permitted by the law—and served all the offices—quaestorship, tribuneship, aedileship, praetorship,

---

[1] The legions of which Suetonius speaks were raised by Marcius Rex, who was consul in 68 B.C.
[2] *Röm. Staatsr.*, i³, 1887, p. 570, n. 1.
[3] *De lege agr.*, ii, 2, 3.   [4] 17, 48.   [5] *Op. cit.*, p. 52.

and consulship—leaving clear intervals of two years, he would become consul in his 43rd year. As for the passage in the *Fifth Philippic*, Nipperdey gives us a choice between two explanations.[1] First, since the view that Cicero meant that the earliest legal age for the consulship was a man's 43rd year clashes with our knowledge that Caesar obtained it in his 41st (!), it is more probable that the number [*decem*] was altered by a careless copyist than that Suetonius, Plutarch, and Appian should have taken their statements of Caesar's age from one erroneous authority. We need only change X into V to remove all contradictions. However, says Nipperdey, we need not, after all, change Cicero's words, but only interpret them differently. One is not surprised to find that the interpretation is the same as that which Nipperdey proposed for the passage in the speech on the law of Rullus; and whoever cares to read Mommsen's comments [2] on his countryman's 'sound canon of interpretation' will find them caustic enough.

I conclude that if we cannot fix the date of Caesar's birth with mathematical certainty, it is in the highest degree probable that he was born in 102 B.C.[3]

EARLY EVENTS IN THE LIFE OF CAESAR

We read in Plutarch [4] that Caesar presented himself as a candidate for a priesthood after Sulla's final victory, that is, in 82 or 81 B.C.; but Plutarch stultifies his own statement by adding that Caesar was ' hardly more than a child ' (οὔπω πάνυ μειράκιον ὤν), though in 82 he was at least eighteen and most probably twenty.[5] He was appointed (*creatus*) [6] a priest of Jupiter (Flamen Dialis) by Marius and Cinna in January, 86 B.C.[7] Plutarch goes on to say that Caesar fled from Rome because Sulla, when he was urged to spare him on account of his youth, remarked that ' in the boy there were many Mariuses '. According to Velleius,[8] his motive was to

---

[1] *Op. cit.*, pp. 57–8.
[2] *Röm. Staatsr.*, i³, 1887, pp. 568 n. 2, 569 n. 2.
[3] After writing this article I find that Prof. E. Meyer (*Caesars Monarchie²*, 1919, p. 59, n. 2) has come to the same conclusion.
[4] *Caes.*, 1, 1.   [5] See pp. 436–42.
[6] Does *creatus* here mean 'nominated to fill the next vacancy'? See the next foot-note.
[7] Vell. Pat., ii, 43, 1. Suetonius (*Div. Iul.*, 1, 1) says that Caesar 'in his sixteenth year lost his father,' and that 'under the consuls of the following year, having been appointed Flamen Dialis . . . he married Cornelia ', &c. (*Annum agens sextum decimum patrem amisit; sequentibusque consulibus flamen Dialis destinatus . . . Corneliam Cinnae quater consulis filiam duxit uxorem*). This seems to mean that Caesar was appointed Flamen Dialis ' under the consuls of the following year ', that is, in the fourth consulship of Cinna and the second of Papirius Carbo (84 B.C.); but probably Suetonius did not intend to connect *flamen Dialis destinatus* with *sequentibus consulibus*. A. W. Zumpt, however (*De dict. . . . die . . . natali*, 1874, p. 15), distinguishes *destinatus* from *creatus*, and supposes that Caesar was co-opted as Flamen in 84.
[8] ii, 41, 2.

EARLY EVENTS IN THE LIFE OF CAESAR 443

avoid being killed by Sulla's myrmidons; and Suetonius,[1] after relating how he was obliged to hide from his pursuers, and how he bribed them to spare him, says that he was afterwards pardoned [by Sulla] through the intercession of the Vestal virgins and others, and that it was well known that when men of high standing pleaded for him with Sulla, who remained for some time obdurate, Sulla at last gave way and made the remark which I have already quoted from Plutarch. Long,[2] referring to the statement of Suetonius, says, ' if Caesar was hunted and saved himself by bribing his captors, there is an inconsistency in saying that his friends asked for his pardon after he had made his escape. It seems then that the true order of events is this : that Caesar was at one time in Sulla's power, that the tyrant deprived him of his wife's portion, and perhaps of his property, but for the time he proceeded no farther, either because Caesar had powerful friends to speak for him, or for other reasons ; but the murderers would let him have no rest, and he escaped from Rome and made his way to Asia.' I cannot see the alleged inconsistency, and I can conceive that Caesar, after he was pardoned, was allowed to go to Asia. The narrative of Suetonius seems to me the most trustworthy.

Maurenbrecher[3] asserts that the praetorship of Marcus Lucullus, before whom C. Antonius, whom Caesar prosecuted, was tried, occurred in 77 B.C.: Drumann[4] and his editor, Groebe,[4] refer it to 76. Nipperdey,[5] quoting a fragment from Caesar's speech *pro Bithynis—Vel pro hospitio regis Nicomedis . . . defugere hoc munus, M. vince, non potui*[6]—argues that for the corrupt *vince* we should read *Iunce*, for we learn from Plutarch[7] that when Caesar was captured by pirates, Juncus ('Ιουγκος) was Governor of the province of Asia. Velleius,[8] if the MSS. are right, calls the same Governor Junius. The question is whether Velleius should be corrected by Plutarch, or Plutarch by Velleius. Nipperdey insists that the text of Plutarch must be preferred, because the corruption would have been more difficult in Greek than in Latin. Moreover, citing the text of Velleius—*perrexit* [Caesar] *ad proconsulem Iunium cum idem enim Asiam eam quam obtinebat petens, ut auctor fieret*, &c.—he argues that the nonsensical *cum* was obviously inserted by a copyist who could not decide whether the name in his copy was *Iunium* or *Iuncum*.[9] Juncus was Governor of Asia in 74 ; [10] and as Caesar travelled to Rhodes immediately after he prosecuted Dolabella,[11] Nipperdey assigns the prosecution to 75.

[1] 1, 2–3. Cf. 74, 1.   [2] *Decline of the Roman Republic*, ii, 1866, p. 379.
[3] *C. Sall. Crispi hist. rel.*, fasc. i, 1891, p. 77.
[4] *Gesch Roms*, iii², 1906, p. 130·and n. 3.   [5] *Philol.*, vi, 1851, pp. 377–8.
[6] Gell., v, 13, 6.   [7] *Caes.*, 2, 2.   [8] ii, 42, 3.
[9] Accordingly the passage in Velleius has been restored as follows : *perrexit ad proconsulem Iuncum* (*is enim cum Asia eam* [sc. Bithyniam] *quoque obtinebat*) *petens*, &c.
[10] Junius was Governor of Asia from May 76 to May 75 (Pliny, *Nat. Hist.*, ii, 35, 100).
[11] Suet., 4, 1. According to Velleius (ii, 42, 3) and Plutarch (*Caes.*, 1, 2 ; 4, 1), before he prosecuted Dolabella. Both were mistaken (see Long, *op. cit.*, p. 448).

CICERO'S TUSCULAN VILLA

Otto Eduard Schmidt has written two interesting articles [1] on Cicero's country houses; but the exact site of the famous *Tusculanum* remains unknown. Schmidt clung to what he candidly called 'the now discredited view' that it was behind the modern Villa Rufinella, which overlooks Frascati.[2] All the necessary information will be found in Dr. Ashby's treatise on the Campagna (*Papers of the British School at Rome*, v, 1910, pages 232–8; cf. Map II in vol. iv) and in a lucid article by R. Cagnat (*Journal des Savants*, 1911, pages 145–52). The villa was supplied with water by an aqueduct from a source called Aqua Crabra,[3] which has been identified with the springs now called Angelosa and Canalicchio in the valley of Ladroni. The course of the aqueduct is said to have been traced thence north-westward across the road that leads from Marino to Frascati, along the Colle delle Ginestre, and past the Villa Cavaletti to Frascati.[4] Somewhere near this line Cicero's house must gave been. Ashby [5] and Cagnat [6] think that the Colle delle Ginestre is the most probable site and exclude the vicinity of the Villa Rufinella, which, owing to the contour of the ground, could not have been supplied from the Aqua Crabra.

[1] *Neue Jahrb. f. d. klass. Altertum*, iii, 1899, pp. 328–55, 466–97.
[2] *Ib.*, pp. 466, 469. Schmidt observes (p. 469) that a scholiast, commenting on the words of Horace—*Neque ut superni villa candens Tusculi* (*Epod.*, i, 28), says that Cicero's Tusculan villa was on the higher flanks of a hill (*hoc est in monte siti ad cuius latera superiora Cicero suam villam habebat Tusculanam*); but this does not prove that it was near the Villa Rufinella. Schmidt also reminds us that a tile with the inscription *M.TVLI* was found at the ancient villa near the Rufinella; but he evidently forgot the warning of Mommsen, who pointed out (*C. I. L.*, xv, No. 2277) that in the Ciceronian age the double consonant in *Tulli* could not have been denoted by a single letter; and, moreover, tiles never bore the name of the owner of the house in which they were used. Finally, says Schmidt, Cicero remarked in December, 50 B. C., that he did not intend to go to his Tusculan villa because 'it is out of the way for people coming to meet me' (*Devium est τοῖς ἀπαντῶσιν* [*Att.*, vii, 5, 3]). This passage alone, he triumphantly concludes, proves that it was not on the Colle delle Ginestre, where Lanciani located it, for that hill is hard by the Via Latina. Even if it did prove that, it would not prove that it was close to the Villa Rufinella; but Dr. Ashby (*Papers Brit. School at Rome*, 1910, p. 237) explains that it 'does not mean that the villa was a mile or half a mile, more or less, from the Via Latina . . . but that the Via Latina was not one of the main highways of Italy, like the Via Appia, on which are situated all the places he names in his letter, and along which he himself was travelling from Brundisium . . . Tyrrell and Purser rightly translate "it is out of the way for chance rencontres" (with travellers of his acquaintance who would convey his letters)'.
[3] Cic., *De lege agr.*, iii, 2, 9.
[4] Cagnat, *op. cit.*, p. 148. 'Il semble', he says, 'que l'on ait déterminé d'une façon très sûre . . . le cours de l'aqueduc', &c. Dr. Ashby, on the other hand, whom he repeatedly cites with approval, affirms that 'we do not know . . . what was the actual course of the ancient aqueduct'. Whether he means that its general direction is unknown *I* am not sure.
[5] *Op. cit.*, pp. 232–3, 235.   [6] *Op. cit.*, pp. 150, 152.

CATILINE'S INTENDED CANDIDATURE FOR THE CONSULSHIP IN 688 (66 B.C.)

According to Asconius,[1] Catiline, on returning from Africa [in 66 B.C.] to stand for the consulship, received notice of prosecution for extortion, and L. Volcacius, one of the consuls, decided, after consulting the Senate, that in view of the impending trial, he should not be allowed to stand, whereupon he withdrew his candidature. The trial took place in 65.[2] Sallust,[3] after stating that [in 66] the consuls designate, P. Autronius and P. Sulla, were convicted of bribery [in consequence of which their election was annulled], adds that 'soon afterwards' (*post paulo*) Catiline, being under notice of prosecution for extortion, was prevented from standing for the consulship, 'because he was unable to announce his candidature within the time fixed by law'. Dio,[4] immediately after relating the conviction of Autronius and Sulla and the plot which they formed against Cotta and Torquatus, who had been elected in their stead,[5] remarks that Catiline, who joined the plot, had himself 'sought the office' ($\mathring{\eta}\tau\acute{\eta}\kappa\epsilon\iota$ δὲ καὶ αὐτὸς τὴν ἀρχήν) and had been exasperated by his failure, which means that he had intended to stand—whether at the first or the second election is not clear—but had been prevented.[6] Cicero in his speech for P. Sulla [7] affirms that the prosecutor (a son of Torquatus) had said that Sulla, in order to carry the election of Catiline, had raised a force to act against Torquatus (*dixisti hunc* [Sullam], *ut Catilinam consulem efficeret, contra patrem tuum manum comparasse*). From this passage it might be inferred that the candidature of Catiline had been rejected at the first election, but that he did stand at the second. But before the attempted execution of the plot which I shall presently discuss he would hardly have ventured to disregard the prohibition of Volcacius, and the question arises whether Cicero can be trusted. John in his famous dissertation on the conspiracy of Catiline argued that Cicero distorted the words of the prosecutor in order to discredit him in the eyes of the jury.[8] The prosecutor, he holds, had intended to convey that Sulla had assisted Catiline to collect the armed men who were to murder Cotta and Torquatus: Cicero affected to believe that he meant that Sulla had raised them in order to carry the election of Catiline. John remarks further—I have often thought the same—that the conclusive proof that it was not Catiline who intended to seize the consulship in conjunction with Autronius

---

[1] Ed. Clark, p. 85, ll. 10–12; p. 89, ll. 9–12 (ed. Stangl, pp. 66, 69). In the former passage, as we may infer from the latter, the comma which Clark and Stangl place after *coss.* should follow *Africa*.
[2] Ascon., p. 85; Cic., *Pro Cael.*, 4, 10. Tyrrell (*The Correspondence of Cicero*, i², 1885, p. 147) incorrectly says that the trial occurred in 66.
[3] *Cat.*, 18, 2–3.   [4] xxxvi, 44, 4.   [5] See p. 234.
[6] G. Long (*Decline of the Roman Republic*, iii, 1869, p. 196) is certainly wrong in suggesting that Dio meant that Catiline had been a candidate 'when Autronius and Sulla were elected'.   [7] 24, 68.
[8] *Jahrb. f. class. Philol.*, viii. Suppl., 1876, pp. 709–11.

is that Cicero in his speech *In toga candida*, while he enumerated every crime, real or imaginary, of which Catiline had been accused,[1] was on this point dumb.

Asconius seems to mean that Catiline was prevented from standing at the first election, whereas Sallust refers his disqualification to the second. Their statements can, however, be reconciled (apart from the reason, not found in any other authority, which Sallust gives [2]) if we may assume that before Catiline left Africa or after he arrived in Rome he learned that the first election was void.[3]

THE SO-CALLED FIRST CONSPIRACY OF CATILINE

According to Sallust,[4] Autronius Paetus, one of the consuls-elect for 65 B.C., having been convicted of bribery and deprived of office, formed a conspiracy with Catiline, who had not been permitted to stand for the vacant consulship, and communicated the design to Gnaeus Calpurnius Piso. The three conspirators planned to murder the consuls on the 1st of January, 65 ; and it was arranged that Autronius and Catiline should then seize the *fasces*—the symbols of consular power—and send Piso with an army to take possession of the provinces of Spain. The conspiracy was discovered ; but the conspirators formed a new plot to massacre the consuls and most of the senators on the 5th of February. This plot also failed, because Catiline gave the signal prematurely : nevertheless Piso was sent by the Senate, who wished to get rid of him, and at the instigation of Crassus, who knew that he was an enemy of Pompey, to the province of Nearer Spain.

The epitomizer of Livy [5] says, 'The conspiracy for murdering the consuls, formed by those [Sulla and Autronius] who had been condemned for bribery in standing for the consulship, was crushed'.

---
[1] See p. 240.
[2] Dr. Hardy discusses it in the *Journal of Roman Studies*, vii, 1917, pp. 157–8.
[3] C. John (*Rhein. Mus.*, xxxi, 1876, p. 413), who, on the ground of the silence of Asconius, rejects the view that Catiline offered himself as a candidate a second time, concludes that Sallust, if he had attended to chronology, would have written not *post paulo* but *ante paulo*. Dr. Hardy (*op. cit.*, p. 157) is evidently unaware that the reading *post paulo* has been questioned.

The theory of Mommsen (*Röm. Staatsr.*, i³, 1887, p. 503, n. 1), that Catiline did not return to Rome in time for either the first or the second election of 66, and that Volcacius intended to prevent him from standing in 65, rests upon a passage in Cicero's speech *Pro Caelio*, 4, 10, in which he says that in his own praetorship (66) Catiline was in Africa. Certainly he was there during the earlier half of the year, but not, at all events, in the autumn. As Dr. Hardy says (*op. cit.*, p. 157, n. 2), Volcacius could not bind the consuls who succeeded him.

Groebe (W. Drumann's *Gesch. Roms*, v, 1912, p. 419, n. 4) thinks that Catiline was unable to stand in 65, for the reason given by Sallust ; but Sallust, as the context shows, certainly meant 66, and if Catiline had attempted to stand in 65, Cicero would probably have said so in *Att.*, i, 1, 2, where he mentioned the candidates for that year.

[4] *Cat.*, 18, 2–8 ; 19, 1.   [5] 101.

Suetonius,[1] quoting as his authorities a history written by Tanusius Geminus, the edicts of Marcus Bibulus (one of the consuls of 59 B. C.), and the orations of the elder Curio, states that in December, 66, Caesar was suspected of having conspired with Crassus, Autronius, and Publius Sulla to massacre certain senators at the beginning of 65. Crassus was then to seize the dictatorship with Caesar as his Master of the Horse, while Autronius and Sulla were to be reinstated as consuls. Suetonius adds that Cicero was apparently referring to the plot when he remarked in one of his letters [which is not extant] that Caesar in his [first] consulship established the dominion which in his aedileship he had planned. According to Tanusius, the plot was abortive because, owing to procrastination on the part of Crassus, Caesar did not give the prearranged signal for the massacre. Curio affirmed that Caesar arranged with Piso that they should each attempt a revolution—Piso in Spain and Caesar in Rome—but that, owing to the death of Piso, this conspiracy also failed.

Dio[2] relates that Paetus and Sulla, on being convicted of bribery, conspired against their accusers, Cotta and Torquatus, who had been appointed consuls in their stead. Others, including Piso and Catiline, joined the conspiracy, which, however, failed because it was revealed prematurely and because a guard was assigned by the Senate to Cotta and Torquatus. The Senate would have passed a resolution against the conspirators if a tribune had not exercised his veto. As Piso continued defiant, the Senate dispatched him, ostensibly to hold some command, to Spain, where he was murdered.

Cicero in his speech *In toga candida*[3] (64 B. C.), addressing Catiline, said, ' I pass over that nefarious attempt of yours . . . when with your associate Gnaeus Piso, not to mention any one else, you purposed to murder the optimates '. Asconius,[4] commenting on this passage, says, ' It was generally believed that Catiline and Gnaeus Piso . . . had conspired to massacre the Senate . . . in the consulship of Cotta and Torquatus and that the massacre did not come off because Catiline gave the signal to the conspirators before they were ready. When this speech was delivered Piso had perished in Spain, whither he had been sent by the Senate, to get him out of the way.[5] There he had been put to death, as some believed by adherents of Pompey and with his approval.' Asconius remarks, further,[6] that Caesar and Crassus were the most determined opponents of Cicero when he was standing for the consulship, and that Cicero stated in 64 B. C. that Crassus had approved the conspiracy which had been formed by Catiline and Piso in the previous year ; and he hints that Caesar may have been one of the conspirators.

[1] *Div. Iul.*, 9.
[2] xxxvi, 44, 3–5.   [3] Ascon., ed. Clark, p. 92, ll. 11–4 (ed. Stangl, p. 71).
[4] *Ib.*, ll. 15–25.
[5] The MS. reading—*ut avus suus ablegaretur*—is obviously corrupt Clark merely obelizes *avus* : Vonck conjectures that what Asconius wrote was (ut) *pravus civis* (ablegaretur).   [6] p. 83, ll. 18–25 (ed. Stangl, p. 65).

In his first Catilinarian oration[1] Cicero said to Catiline, 'You are aware that nobody here is ignorant that on the 29th of December [66 B. C.] in the consulship of Lepidus and Tullus you took your stand in the comitium [that part of the Forum where popular assemblies were held] with a weapon in your hand, and that you had organized a force to massacre the consuls and the leading men of the state.' In his speech *Pro Murena*,[2] delivered towards the end of 63 B. C., he charges Catiline and Piso with having plotted three years before to massacre the Senate. In his speech *Pro Sulla*,[3] delivered in 62 B. C., he says that Torquatus, a son of the ex-consul, affirmed that Sulla was one of the conspirators, but that Hortensius, who knew the facts, denied his guilt; he implies [4] that in a letter about his consulship which he wrote to Pompey he alluded to 'the incredible outrage, planned two years before [66 or 65 B. C.], which had broken out in my consulship', and hints that Piso, Catiline, Vargunteius, and Autronius were in the first conspiracy: in a later passage of the same speech [5] he says that when Catiline was tried in 65 for malversation, the consul, Lucius Torquatus, who assisted him in his defence, testified that he had heard something about the first conspiracy, but did not believe it (*post delatam ad eum primam illam coniurationem, indicavit se audisse aliquid, non credidisse*).

Strachan-Davidson [6] says, 'the story ... contains so many contradictions and improbabilities, that I prefer to pass it over as wholly or almost wholly apocryphal'. Let us see what the contradictions and improbabilities are. All the authorities but one implicate Autronius; all but one Piso; two omit to mention Sulla, and three Catiline; Caesar and Crassus are noticed by Asconius and Suetonius alone; no one except Cicero speaks of Vargunteius. Sallust's unsupported statement that the intended massacre was postponed is inconsistent with his remark that the postponement was due to the discovery of the plot (*Ea re cognita*) unless, as has been suggested, there is a gap in the text before these words.[7] As to the date, Cicero apparently differs from Sallust by one day; but the discrepancy is only apparent, for when Dio says that the plot was prematurely revealed and that the Senate granted Cotta and Torquatus a guard, he is plainly alluding to the display of armed men, which Cicero mentions, on December 29, and means that the guard protected the consuls on the following day, January 1. Suetonius, differing from Sallust, says that Sulla was to be one of the new consuls,[8] and he differs as to the signal from Sallust and Asconius, who agree. The latter contradiction is trivial: as to the former, I have shown in the preceding article that Sulla, not Catiline, was to be one of the new consuls. The implied statement of Sallust that the conspirators were left at large although the con-

[1] 6, 15. [2] 38, 82. [3] 4, 11–12.
[4] 24, 67. [5] 29, 81. [6] *Cicero*, 1894, p. 91.
[7] C. John (*Jahrb. f. class. Philol.*, viii. Suppl., 1876, p. 711, n. 16). Asconius gives the same reason for the failure of the attempt as Sallust does for the alleged failure of Feb. 5, but, like Cicero and the other authorities, only mentions one attempt. [8] Livy implies the same.

spiracy was discovered, may appear incredible; but the reader will, I believe, accept the explanation which I have given in my narrative.[1] 'The strangest part of the story', says Long,[2] 'is that Piso, though the conspiracy failed, obtained what he would have got if it had succeeded.' Nevertheless it is idle to dismiss the story as 'apocryphal'. A plot there certainly was. What was its ulterior aim? Were Caesar and Crassus involved in it? Mommsen[3] admits that 'the testimony of their political opponents cannot be regarded as sufficient evidence'; but, remarking that Crassus 'made preparations to enrol Egypt and Cyprus in the list of Roman domains',[4] and that 'Caesar about the same time got a proposal submitted by some tribunes to the citizens to send him to Egypt', he concludes that 'These machinations suspiciously coincide with the charges made by their antagonists', and that 'there is a great probability that Crassus and Caesar had formed the plan of seizing the military dictatorship during the absence of Pompey; that Egypt was selected as the basis ... and that ... Catiline and Piso had thus been tools in the hands of Crassus and Caesar'.

Now the conclusive evidence of an inscription[5] shows that Piso was sent as propraetor to Spain, and there is reason to accept the statement of Sallust that he was appointed through the influence of Crassus, who knew that he was an enemy of Pompey; for it was the interest of Crassus and of Caesar to counterbalance the power of Pompey, and the interest of Crassus coincided with that of the Senate. But that, as John[6] thinks, they originated the plot, seems to me improbable: is it not more reasonable to suppose that, as men of sense and judgement, they purposed to take advantage of it if it should succeed?

CICERO'S ALLEGED DEFENCE OF CATILINE

Writing to Atticus in July, 65 B. C., Cicero says, 'I am thinking of defending my fellow-candidate Catiline'[7]—against the charge of having committed malversation in his government of Africa. Accord-

---

[1] p. 234.   [2] *Decline of the Roman Republic*, iii, 1869, p. 199.
[3] *Röm. Gesch.*, iii⁸, 1889, pp. 176–8 (Eng. tr., iv, 1908, pp. 467–8).
[4] Cic., *De lege agr.*, ii, 17, 44; Plut., *Cras.*, 13, 2. John (*op. cit.*, pp. 721-3) thinks that the testimony of Suetonius is irrefragable, for, writing long after the event, he could test the evidence impartially; and, whereas he says nothing to show that he was convinced of Caesar's having participated in the conspiracy of 63 B. C., he unmistakably endorsed the statements of the authorities whom he quoted for the first. *I*mpartiality is rather a matter of temperament than of date.
[5] *C. I. L.*, i, No. 598, vi, No. 1276 (= H. Dessau, *Inscr. Lat.* 875).
[6] *Op. cit.*, p. 720. Cf. Dr. Hardy's remarks in *Journ. Rom. Studies*, vii, 1917, pp. 163–4. G. Ferrero (*Grandezza e decadenza di Roma*, ii, 1902, p. 545 [Eng. tr., ii, 333]), from whom Hardy differs, disbelieves the rumour recorded by Suetonius that Crassus intended to be dictator with Caesar as his Master of the Horse; for, he asks, how would the office have availed him 'if he had no army to back him up?' *I* agree.
[7] *Att.*, i, 2, 1. A sentence which *I* have quoted on p. 235 from this letter is susceptible of two interpretations. Referring to the impending trial, Cicero

ing to the historian Fenestella,[1] Cicero carried out his intention; and Long[2] remarks that he never denied the imputation. But how could Long tell that in Cicero's lifetime the imputation was ever made ? Tyrrell makes a point when he says [3] that the following words in the *Oratio in toga candida* ' seem quite inconsistent with the theory of Cicero's defence of Catiline ',—' You wretched creature, can't you see that you were not really acquitted by that trial but reserved for a more serious trial and for heavier punishment ? ' (*O miser qui non sentias illo iudicio te non absolutum, verum ad aliquod severius iudicium ac maius supplicium reservatum*).[4] Asconius [5] questions the statement of Fenestella, because Cicero did not say in the *Oratio in toga candida* that he had defended Catiline when, if he had defended him, he could have charged him with ingratitude in having tried to thwart his own candidature. I agree with E. Schwartz [6] that Fenestella must have made a false inference from Cicero's momentary intention.

THE *COMMENTARIOLUM PETITIONIS*

The authenticity of the famous ' Handbook for Candidates ' (*Commentariolum petitionis*)—a letter, commonly attributed to Quintus Cicero—was denied by Mommsen,[7] and has been impugned by Professor G. L. Hendrickson, but nevertheless reaffirmed by Leo,[8] Tyrrell,[9] and others. ' We find ', says Hendrickson,[10] ' . . . between the style of the Commentariolum and the literary activity and tastes of Quintus, as his brother reports them, a contrast not less striking than the contrast between his character as portrayed to us by other sources and as revealed in this work. But ', he admits, ' such considerations can do nothing more than arouse suspicion ' ; and may they not be explained by the nature of the

wrote, *Spero, si absolutus erit, coniunctiorem illum nobis fore in ratione petitionis : sin aliter acciderit, humaniter feremus*. My translation is, ' If he is acquitted, I hope he will join me more closely in canvassing ; but if it happens otherwise, I shall bear it with resignation.' *I* believe that ' if it happens otherwise ' means ' if he is not acquitted ' ; but it has been suggested that it may mean ' if he does not co-operate with me '. *I* prefer the former interpretation both because it is more pointed and because *sin aliter acciderit* seems to me to correspond to *si absolutus erit*.
[1] Ascon., ed. Clark, p. 85, ll. 13–4 (ed. Stangl, p. 66).
[2] *Decline of the Roman Republic*, iii, 1869, p. 201.
[3] *The Correspondence of Cicero*, i³, 1904, p. 157.
[4] Ascon., ed. Clark, p. 87, ll. 5-8 (ed. Stangl, p. 67).
[5] p. 85, ll. 14–20.
[6] *Hermes*, xxxii, 1897, pp. 602–3. Tyrrell and Purser, remarking that Cicero's letters to Atticus were probably not published before A. D 60 (*Rhein. Mus.*, xxxiv, 1879, pp. 352–4), affirm that Asconius had not seen the letter in question. *I* doubt whether he would have changed his mind if he had.
[7] *Röm. Staatsr.*, iii, 1887, pp. 484 n. 3, 497 n. 3.
[8] *Nachrichten von d. Königl. Gesellsch. d. Wiss. zu Göttingen*, philol.-hist. Klasse, 1895, pp. 448–9.
[9] *The Correspondence of Cicero*, i², 1904, pp. 128*–131*.
[10] *Amer. Journ. of Philol.*, xiii, 1892, p. 203.

theme ? Hendrickson's principal argument is based upon 'the resemblance between the Commentariolum and other works of Roman literature ',[1] especially Cicero's orations *In toga candida* and *Pro Murena*. Strachan-Davidson [2] maintains that 'a forger of later times, when detailing a list of Catiline's enormities, would never have omitted, as this writer does, the so-called First Conspiracy of . . . 66 B. C. . . . If the treatise . . . were really written, as it professes to be, at the end of . . . 65 B. C. or quite early in the next year, the omission may easily . . . be explained by the supposition that at that time the myth had not . . . taken shape '. Is not this argument weakened by the facts that Cicero himself believed and utilized 'the myth', and that the 'First Conspiracy', though Catiline's part in it was subordinate, cannot be explained away ? [3] Still, I see no sufficient reason to doubt that the letter was written by Quintus.

ON CASSIUS DIO, xxxvii, 37, 1

Long [4] remarks that Dio does not say whether the bill, proposed by Labienus, for restoring to the people the election of the priests was proposed before the death of Metellus, Caesar's predecessor in the office of Chief Pontiff, or after ; but, he adds, ' we can hardly suppose that a measure evidently intended to secure the election of the popular favourite [Caesar] was passed after the death of Metellus '. It seems to me that this was just what Dio meant ; for immediately after telling us that the bill proposed by Labienus became law he gives the reason, ' For Caesar, on the death of Metellus Pius, desired to obtain his pontifical office ' (ὁ γὰρ Καῖσαρ, τοῦ Μετέλλου τοῦ Εὐσεβοῦς τελευτήσαντος, τῆς τε ἱερωσύνης αὐτοῦ . . . ἐπεθύμησε). But Cicero in his second speech *de lege agraria* (7, 18), delivered soon after the 1st of January, 63 B. C., said that the second chapter of the proposed agrarian law provided that the election of decemvirs should be made in the same way as the election of the Pontifex Maximus at the Comitia (*eodem modo . . . ut comitiis pontificis maximi*), which method of election had been extended to other priestly offices by the law of Cn. Domitius (*atque hoc idem de ceteris sacerdotiis Cn. Domitius . . . tulit*). The effect of Labienus's bill was, as Dio says, to revive the law of Domitius. May we not conclude that Labienus had proposed his bill between December 10, 64 B. C., when he entered office, and a date early in January of the following year ?

[1] *Ib.*, pp. 204–11. Cf. *Decennial Publications of the University of Chicago*, vi, 1904, pp. 71–94. Hendrickson's arguments were refuted by Sternkopf (*Berl. philol. Woch.*, Feb., 27, 1904, col. 265–72, March 5, col. 296–301).
[2] *Problems of the Rom. Crim. Law*, ii, 1912, p. 89.
[3] See pp. 446–9.
[4] *Decline of the Roman Republic*, iii, 1869, p. 267

THE PROSECUTION OF RABIRIUS

The famous case of Rabirius has occasioned voluminous controversy; but the points in dispute have lately been cleared up. Suetonius,[1] says that Caesar suborned an agent to prosecute Rabirius (who was alleged to have killed Saturninus 37 years before) for treason; that Caesar was himself chosen by lot as one of the judges, and that he showed such animus in pronouncing sentence that when Rabirius appealed to the people the bias of the judge told more than anything in his favour. According to Dio,[2] Labienus, instigated by Caesar and others, created great disturbances in Rome by his prosecution of Rabirius; the object of the tribunes [of whom Labienus was one] was to undermine the authority of the Senate—in other words, as Dio doubtless meant, to deter them from again passing the 'ultimate decree', in pursuance of which Rabirius had acted; violent contentions arose between the two parties [the senatorial and the popular] about the court which was to try the accused, the former desiring to prevent it from being formed; the judges, Gaius and Lucius Caesar, condemned Rabirius although they had not been appointed, as ancient usage required, by the people, but unconstitutionally by the praetor; Rabirius appealed to the people, and would certainly have been convicted (here Dio virtually contradicts Suetonius) if Metellus Celer had not put an end to the proceedings by hoisting the red flag on the Janiculum. The extant speech of Cicero *Pro Rabirio* supplies further evidence, which shall be presently considered.

The questions which we have to settle are, first, Did Caesar aim at preventing the Senate from again passing the ultimate decree? Secondly, how were the two judges, who, as we learn from Cicero,[3] were called *duumviri*, appointed? Thirdly, what did Cicero mean when he said[4] that he had quashed the condemnation of the accused? Fourthly, what was the trial which, according to Dio, was stopped by Metellus Celer, for we learn from Cicero[5] that Rabirius was also tried on a charge for which the penalty was to be a fine? Fifthly, was this latter trial distinct from the one (which, according to some commentators, was never held) of Rabirius's appeal against his condemnation for treason? Lastly, on what occasion was the extant speech of Cicero delivered?

Dr. Hardy, who admits[6] that Caesar desired to prevent the Senate from resorting to the ultimate decree in the year of Cicero's consulship, quotes from the *Bellum civile* the well-known passages[7] in which he afterwards implied that it was legitimate in grave emergencies, and concludes that modern historians are wrong in

---

[1] *Div. Iul.*, 12. Suetonius incorrectly uses a legal phrase—(qui C. Rabirio perduellionis) *diem diceret*—implying that Labienus fixed a day on which Rabirius was to appear before his court.
[2] xxxvii, 26–8.　　　[3] *Pro Rab.*, 4, 12.　　　[4] *Ib.*, 3, 10; 5, 17.
[5] *Ib.*, 3, 8.　　　[6] *Journ. of Philol.*, xxxiv, 1915, p. 14.
[7] *B. C.*, i, 5, 3; 7, 5.

maintaining that his object in instituting this trial was to impugn its validity.[1] Now one may admit that in 50 B. C. Caesar did not question the validity of the decree, and yet without any inconsistency hold that thirteen years earlier he attacked it, whatever his real opinion may have been, for a political purpose. But the modern historians would probably endorse Dr. Hardy's pronouncement that he intended ' so to expose certain illegalities which had been covered by its supposed sanction, as to discredit a procedure capable of such abuses '; for the distinction between this judgement and their own would hardly provoke dispute.

The second question can be easily answered. Dio and the commentators[2] who accept his statements that the constitutional mode of appointing the *duumviri* was popular election and that their nomination by the praetor was illegal, are mistaken; for there is no evidence that such judges had ever been appointed since the period of the kings, and Dio was perhaps misled by the remark of Cicero that Rabirius had been condemned without a mandate from the people (*iniussu vestro*[3]). But though the *duumviri* were not elected by the tribes, their choice must have resulted from a *plébiscite*, proposed by Labienus, which provided for their appointment by the praetor, who presumably nominated certain individuals of whom two were selected by lot.[4]

Strachan-Davidson[5] suggested that Cicero quashed the duumviral condemnation of Rabirius[6] ' by the instrumentality of a tribune '; but Hardy[7] and Eduard Meyer[8] maintain that the Senate acted on Cicero's initiative, and the former, after citing precedents, quotes a passage from Cicero's oration *in Pisonem*[9] which seems to me almost decisive—' when Rabirius was tried for treason, I upheld the authority of the Senate exerted in his favour against a scandalous abuse ' (*ego in Rabirio perduellionis reo interpositam senatus auctoritatem sustinui contra invidiam*, &c.). But what was the effect of the Senate's intervention? Mr. Heitland[10] supposes that the Comitia Tributa (not the Senate) substituted the ordinary capital sentence of outlawry—' interdiction from water and fire ' (*aquae et ignis interdictio*)—which the defendant could only evade by voluntary exile, for the sentence intended, but, as Mr. Heitland believes, not passed, by the *duumviri*,—death on the cross. But the duumviral sentence *was* passed—as Suetonius says, with indecent

---
[1] The latest exponent of this theory is Prof. Eduard Meyer (*Caesars Monarchie*[2], 1919, p. 563).
[2] e. g. W. E. Heitland in his edition of Cicero's *Pro Rabirio*, 1882, p. 113.
[3] *Pro Rab.*, 4, 12. As Dr. Hardy says (*op. cit.*, pp. 30–1), when Cicero, addressing the people, said of Labienus, *hic . . . a IIviris iniussu vestro non iudicari de cive Romano sed indicta caussa civem Romanum capitis condemnari coegit*, he coupled *iniussu vestro* not, as Heitland (p. 57) supposes, with *coegit*, but with *condemnari*.
[4] A. H. J. Greenidge, *Legal Procedure*, &c., 1901, pp. 355–6; Hardy, *op. cit.*, pp. 25–6; Meyer, *op. cit.*, p. 560.
[5] *Problems of the Rom. Crim. Law*, i, 1912, pp. 197–8.
[6] *Pro Rab.*, 3, 10; 5, 17.   [7] *Op. cit.*, p. 30.
[8] *Op. cit.*, pp. 553–4.   [9] 2, 4.   [10] *Op. cit.*, p. 32.

haste;[1] and since Caesar, doubtless in order to impress the popular imagination, had revived the obsolete duumviral procedure, he would surely, with the same object, have passed the grim sentence which it involved or none at all; for, as Hardy says,[2] 'the *duumviri* were only important as having figured in the ancient trial, and if the kernel of that trial was extracted, it was futile to keep the shell': I therefore agree with him that the effect of Cicero's intervention was to render the proceedings of the duumvirs 'null and void'. It follows that the appeal which Rabirius had doubtless made against the sentence lapsed, and that the trial which Dio describes as having been held before the people was not on *that* appeal. Hardy, indeed, is confronted by the fact that Dio, directly after mentioning the appeal, passes to the 'final incident' in the Field of Mars, when the trial was closed by the intervention of Metellus; but he 'cannot regard the considerable gap' in Dio's narrative 'as a serious objection' to his own conclusion.[3] The reader will presently be able to decide. It is certain that at the time of the 'final incident' Rabirius was still being tried for treason: that is made evident by Cicero's speech[4] to all who admit that it was delivered when the 'final incident' occurred. How, it may be asked, could Rabirius have still been tried for treason if the duumviral sentence had lapsed, and likewise his appeal? Dr. Hardy is ready with an answer, which results logically and inevitably from the view that the appeal had lapsed. Cicero in his speech[5] alluded to a 'fine-process' (*multae irrogatio*), that is, a process concerning charges for which the threatened penalty was a fine. Greenidge,[6] who holds that the speech was delivered when Rabirius was appealing from an amended duumviral sentence, suggests that combined with outlawry—one of the penalties, which he supposes to have been fixed thereby—was the confiscation of his property,[7] and that 'it is probably this aspect of the condemnation that is described as *multae irrogatio*'. Hardy[8] insists that that phrase was 'far too technical to be used in any but its strict and literal sense'; in other words, he believes that Labienus had summoned Rabirius to appear before his tribunal in the Forum on a charge distinct from that of *perduellio*. 'But',

---

[1] As Livy's account of the condemnation of Horatius shows, it was not the business of the *duumviri* to try the case, but merely to pass the antiquated sentence prescribed in the bill of Labienus. This, as Hardy remarks (*op. cit.*, p. 26), 'explains, what Suetonius did not understand, the apparent haste of Caesar's condemnation'. Cf. Meyer, p. 558.

[2] *Op. cit.*, p. 29.   [3] *Op. cit.*, p. 31.
[4] *Pro Rab.*, 1, 1–2; 2, 5; 9, 26; 11, 31; 13, 37.
[5] 3, 8.   [6] *Op. cit.*, p. 355 and n. 5.
[7] Meyer (*op. cit.*, p. 554) thinks that a fine alone was imposed, but regards the view of Greenidge (whom, however, he ignores) as possible. Hardy (p. 33) holds that a double sentence would have been illegal: Greenidge (p. 359) understands the well-known passage in Cicero's *De domo*, 17, 45—*ut ne poena capitis cum pecunia coniungatur*—to mean, 'that no one, for one and the same offence, should be accused in a capital process before the centuries and a pecuniary process before the tribes'. *I* doubt whether this translation will commend itself. Cf. Strachan-Davidson, *op. cit.*, i, 198, n. 1.
[8] *Op. cit.*, p. 31.

he adds,[1] citing a precedent described by Livy,[2] 'it was open to a tribune ... to convert ... what had begun as a fine-process into a capital impeachment'. This, he maintains,[3] was actually done. After the duumviral procedure had been quashed, 'Labienus at once received instructions [from Caesar] to convert his prosecution into a normal tribunician impeachment for *perduellio*'; Rabirius was condemned and appealed to the people; and it was on this appeal that Cicero delivered his famous speech.

But, strange as it may appear to those who without bias have read that speech, Mommsen,[4] following B. G. Niebuhr,[5] maintained that it was delivered in a 'fine-process' substituted for the trial for *perduellio*, and that the title *Pro Rabirio perduellionis reo* was added by a later hand.[6] His theory is stultified not only by the proofs, already given, that Cicero was defending Rabirius against the charge of *perduellio* and by the narrative of Dio, but also by excerpts from Cicero's oration *In Pisonem*[7] and his treatise *Orator*.[8] The former, which I have already quoted, Mommsen could only evade by asserting that the decisive words—*ego in C. Rabirio, perduellionis reo ... senatus auctoritatem defendi*—were spurious; in the latter Cicero says, 'The case of Rabirius involved the right of maintaining the dignity of Rome: therefore my language glowed with all rhetorical fervour' (*Ius omne retinendae maiestatis Rabirii causa continebatur; ergo in omni genere amplificationis exarsimus*).[9]

THE CONSPIRACY OF CATILINE

Some disputable statements of Sallust.—Dr. Hardy,[10] like John and other scholars, rejects Sallust's[11] story of a conspiracy formed by Catiline in June, 64 B. C. on the grounds that it is not confirmed by any other evidence; that it is incredible that Catiline, 'having

[1] *Ib.*, p. 32. [2] xxvi, 3, 7. [3] *Op. cit.*, p. 33.
[4] *Röm. Staatsr.*, ii³, 1887, pp. 298 n. 3, 615 n. 2; *Röm. Strafr.*, 1899, p. 588, n. 1.
[5] *M. T. Ciceronis orat. ... pro C. Rab. fragm.*, 1820, pp. 69–70.
[6] Strachan-Davidson (*op. cit.*, p. 200), who was not, like Mommsen, blind to the passages which prove that Rabirius was still being tried for *perduellio*, nevertheless maintained that the speech was delivered in the Forum 'at one of the ... meetings which were to introduce the *multae irrogatio*', and that the meeting of the people on the Field of Mars was dissolved by Metellus 'before Cicero ... opened his lips on the [final] day of trial.' He admits, however (p. 190, n. 7), that the prayer which Cicero (1, 5) addressed to the gods 'May they grant that *this day* has dawned to assure the safety of the defendant and the foundations of the commonwealth' (*ut hodiernum diem et ad huius salutem conservandam et ad rempublicam constituendam inluxisse patiantur*), though (p. 201, n. 1) he struggles to explain it away, 'would be more appropriate if the voting were to follow immediately after the speech'.
[7] 2, 4. [8] 29, 102.
[9] Cf. E. Meyer, *op. cit.*, pp. 550–2. The people were, of course, summoned to hear the final trial by the praetor, acting on behalf of Labienus, who played the double part of president and prosecutor (*Pro Rab.*, 2, 6). Cf. Hardy, pp. 37–8 and Meyer, pp. 555–6.
[10] *Journ. Rom. Studies*, vii, 1917, pp. 169–70. [11] *Cat.*, 17.

made ready to strike in June or July ', ' allowed all his preparations to be held up for more than a year ' ; that the interests of Crassus, who supported Catiline's candidature in 64, ' were diametrically opposed to such a programme ' as Catiline is said to have announced ; and that it is not ' easy to understand how Cassius Longinus, a candidate for the consulship, could have joined a conspiracy avowedly counting on the election of Catiline and Antonius '.

Now I, of course, agree with Hardy that in 64 there was no conspiracy providing for the execution by violence of certain definite plans and like that which was formed in the latter part of the following year ; but I think that he goes too far in rejecting the story of Sallust altogether as a deliberate attempt to antedate the existence of a conspiracy in order ' to exonerate Caesar from all suspicion of complicity with what happened in the second half of 63 '. I lay no stress on the fact that Plutarch [1] supports Sallust, for he may have followed a writer who copied Sallust : I freely admit that Hardy is justified in insisting upon the silence of Quintus Cicero [2] and of Asconius ; and I would add that Dio,[3] apparently referring to the meeting of conspirators which Sallust describes, assigns it not to 64 but to 63. Still I believe that Sallust had some foundation for his story. He does not say one word about Catiline's ' having made ready to strike in June or July ' : on the contrary, he makes Catiline say twice over [4] that he intended to execute his plans *as consul*, in other words by legislation, and in the second passage he makes him say that when he became consul he would *begin* to act (*i n i t i u m agundi facturum*). Cassius, if he were beaten at the polls, might still expect, as a fellow conspirator, to profit by the success of the rival candidates, and Hardy, while he urges that the interests of Crassus were opposed to the alleged programme of Catiline in 64, maintains [5] that in 63 Crassus again supported his candidature although he ' must have realized that it might be necessary to go all lengths '. My own belief is that, although Sallust doubtless embellished his authority, Catiline even before the election of 64 confided to his friends the programme to which he hoped to give effect.[6]

Then comes the question whether Fulvia had really informed Cicero of Catiline's intentions from the beginning of his consulship. Here again Hardy [7] throws Sallust overboard, because ' we have no

---

[1] *Cic.*, 10, 2.
[2] In the *Commentariolum petitionis* (Ep. xii in Tyrrell's *Correspondence of Cicero*, vol. i).
[3] xxxvii, 30, 3.   [4] *Cat.*, 20, 17 ; 21, 3.   [5] *Op. cit.*, p. 177.
[6] Are not these words of Cicero (*Pro Mur.*, 38, 82), spoken in November, 63, significant ?—*Omnia quae p e r h o c t r i e n n i u m agitata sunt, iam ab eo tempore quo a L. Catilina et Cn. Pisone initum consilium senatus interficiendi scitis esse . . . in hoc tempus erumpunt.* It is the fashion to deride the story variously told by Sallust (22, 1), Plutarch (*Cic.*, 10, 2), Florus (ii, 12, 4), Dio (xxxvii, 30, 3), and Minucius Felix (30, 8) as a pure invention ; but it is not inconceivable that there was some foundation for it. Cicero (*In Vat.*, 6, 14) charged Vatinius with a similar atrocity. See Long's note (*Cic. Orat.*, iv, 1858, p. 13)
[7] *Op. cit.*, p 176.

evidence whatever of a definite conspiracy up to' the spring of 63. What does Hardy mean by 'a definite conspiracy'? What I mean the reader knows. Hardy himself implies[1] that Catiline framed 'a revolutionary programme', and though he is 'sure' that in standing for the consulship in 64 he 'made no promise of *novae tabulae*' (abolition of debts)—why 'sure' if, as he believes,[2] some tribune introduced at the end of 64 a bill which made the self-same promise?—he admits[3] that even in the summer of that year there may have been 'some vague and irresponsible talk'. Why should it be deemed incredible that in the earlier months of 63 Catiline talked to Curius about the 'revolutionary programme' which he hoped to carry out? Surely he must have prepared against the contingency of defeat at the election, and Hardy affirms[4] that he tried to win over voters 'by specious and reckless promises'. Again, Hardy says, 'though there is no direct evidence that he was still supported by Caesar or Crassus, I argue that he must have been, unless we suppose that ... they were prepared to leave the elections of this critical year to chance'.[5] Yet immediately afterwards he makes that remark the inconsistency of which with an earlier utterance I have noticed in the previous paragraph—'they must have realized that it might be necessary to go all lengths, or that ... Catiline, if unsuccessful or desperate, might decide to go all lengths in his own way'; and he adds that 'nothing is more likely ... than that his promises went far beyond what Crassus or Caesar would have sanctioned'.[6] Surely a sufficient explanation of their having declined to continue their support.

Cicero's relinquishment of his claim to the province of Macedonia.—Hardy 'can find no evidence whatever' that Cicero renounced his claim to Macedonia in favour of Antonius before he entered on the consulship.[7] How then does he explain the announcement of Cicero, made on the 1st of January, 63, that he did not intend to accept a province?[8] Is it not probable that as he was aware of the sympathies of Antonius, he would have bought off his opposition before he entered office and not waited, as Hardy[9] insists that he did, till the fourth week of October, when Catiline was declared a public enemy. It is true that Cicero[10] relates that Catiline in his canvass said that Antonius had promised to support him, and, according to Dio,[11] Antonius was present at a meeting in which Catiline, after the election, unfolded his plans to the conspirators. But is it not conceivable that Antonius, having com-

[1] p. 172.   [2] p. 174.   [3] p. 172.
[4] p. 178.   [5] p. 177.
[6] pp. 178–9. *I* see no reason to doubt that before the election Catiline was associated with Lentulus, Cethegus, and the rest. Hardy admits (p. 187) that 'he had long had a dangerous *clientèle* of profligate young men' and 'relations more or less questionable with men like Antonius'. *If* he had neglected to make overtures to Lentulus, he was strangely improvident.
[7] p. 184.
[8] *De lege agr.*, i, 8, 26. Cf. Plut., *Cic.*, 12, 2.
[9] *Op. cit.*, p. 185.   [10] *Pro Mur.*, 24, 49.
[11] xxxvii, 30, 3.

mitted himself with Catiline in the previous year, did not openly break with him, but affected to side with him and learned his plans ? Considering Cicero's express statement, I conclude that he had let Antonius know that Macedonia should be his on condition of good behaviour, though the formal transference [1] was not made until Antonius ceased to be dangerous.

The date of the consular election in 63 B.C.—It is now universally admitted that the consular election in 63 B.C. was held not, as Mommsen [2] asserted, on the 28th of October, but considerably earlier.[3] Consuls were normally elected in July : the election of 63, if we may trust Plutarch's words, ' Not long afterwards ' (οὐ πολλῷ δ' ὕστερον)—that is, after the day on which Cicero went to the Field of Mars with a bodyguard [4]—occurred some little time before the 21st of October, the day preceding that on which the Senate passed the ' ultimate decree ' [5] (senatus consultum ultimum). Is it possible to obtain a more precise date ? Lange,[6] remarking that, according to Suetonius,[7] Augustus was born ' in the consulship of Cicero . . . on the ninth day before the Kalends of October ', in other words, ' on the day when the conspiracy of Catiline was debated in the Senate ',[8] supposed that the day originally fixed for the election was September 23. I have proved elsewhere that Suetonius ' was speaking proleptically in terms of the Julian calendar ',[9] and Ludwig Holzapfel, pointing out that Cicero in his second Catilinarian oration (10, 23) on November 9 of the old calendar foretold that the conspirators were about to encounter frost and snow on the Apennines, infers that in that year the old calendar nearly coincided with the new, and proceeds to demonstrate that if, as he maintains, January 1, 709 corresponded with January 2, 45 B.C., September 23, 63 B.C. of the Julian, corre-

---

[1] Cic., Att., ii, 1, 3.
[2] Röm. Gesch., iii⁸, 1889, p. 184 (Eng. tr., iv, 1908, p. 475).
[3] I may refer to my article in the Journal of Roman Studies, viii, 1918, pp. 15-17. The proof, given independently there, had been anticipated by C. John.   [4] See p. 259.
[5] Given the date (Nov. 8), which I shall presently establish, of Cicero's first oration against Catiline, it has always seemed to me evident from a well-known statement of Asconius (ed. Clark, p. 6, ll. 2-8) that the ' ultimate decree ' was passed on Oct. 22 ; but John (Philol., xlvi, 1888, pp. 663-4) fixed that date by an ingenious argument. Heretofore, he remarks, it has been generally believed on the combined evidence of Cicero (In Cat., i, 3, 7), Sallust (Cat., 29, 2), Plutarch (Cic., 15, 3), and Dio (xxxvii, 31, 1-2) that the date was Oct. 21. Cicero, the only one of the four who mentions a date, reminds Catiline of a prophecy and a statement which he himself had made in the Senate on Oct. 21 ; and the commentators jumped to the conclusion that this session of the Senate was that in which the senatus consultum ultimum was passed. But John argues that Dio distinguished between two sessions, in the first of which anonymous letters of warning about the massacre planned by Catiline for Oct. 28 were read and a state of war in Italy was proclaimed, in the second the senatus consultum ultimum was passed ; and he cites Dio, xli, 3, 2 to show that a distinction was drawn between the proclamation of a state of war in Italy (tumultus) and the senatus consultum ultimum.
[6] Röm. Alt., iii, 1871, p. 241.   [7] Aug., 5.   [8] Ib., 94, 5.
[9] Class. Quart., vi, 1912, pp. 73-4. See p. 459, n. 3, infra.

THE CONSPIRACY OF CATILINE 459

sponded with September 24, 691 of the old calendar.[1] As I hold that January 1, 709 corresponded with January 1, 45 B. C.,[2] I would substitute September 25 for September 24. Since, then, Suetonius was evidently alluding to one of the sessions which Cicero records, and certainly not to the sessions of October 21, October 22, November 8, December 3, or December 5, it seems most probable that the one which he had in mind was that which was held on the day originally fixed for the consular election. If, then, Suetonius can be trusted, the election occurred soon after September 25.[3]

Having written so far, I turned to the famous dissertation of John. This scholar maintains that the election was held as usual in July. The gist of his argument is that since, as he claims to have proved, the conspiracy of Catiline did not begin until after the electors had rejected him, he would not have had time to raise and arm recruits and to complete his other preparations before the 21st of October.[4] Besides, he remarks,[5] it is clear from what Cicero stated in his speech for Murena (25, 50–1) that the conspiracy was not discussed by the Senate in the session that was held on the day originally fixed for the election, but only what Catiline had said in the meeting which he had convened on the previous day : the first session in which the conspiracy was discussed was that of the 21st of October ; therefore the day to which Suetonius referred could not have been in September.

These arguments can be easily disposed of. It is not true that, 'according to the unanimous testimony'[6] of our authorities, the conspiracy did not begin until after the election. The epitomizer of Livy,[7] to whom John[8] appeals, merely says that 'Catiline, having twice failed in his candidature for the consulship, conspired with Lentulus ... to massacre the consuls and the Senate'. Granted that he formed this particular plot after the election, no one who remembers that the *Epitome* is no more than a Table of Contents will conclude from this passage that Catiline did not conspire before. Did he not tell Cato a few days before the date originally fixed for the election that 'if a conflagration were kindled against his fortunes, he would quench it not by water, but by ruin' ?[9] Does not Cicero[10] say that before the election the conspiracy was beginning (*coniurationem nascentem*[11]), that Catiline occupied the Field of Mars with armed conspirators (*homines iam tum coniuratos in campum deduci a Catilina sciebam*), and that he had already

---

[1] *Röm. Chronol.*, 1885, p. 333.   [2] See pp. 339–41.
[3] Mr. J. Gilbert Smyly (*Hermathena*, xxxviii, 1912, pp. 150–2, 158), remarking that the date of Augustus's birth 'is given by the Julian calendar, because it is found as the date of a letter written by Augustus (Gell., xv, 7, 9 [read xv, 7, 3]) on his birthday ... after the introduction of the Julian calendar', adds that when he was born September had only 29 days, 'and, as Augustus, like Cicero, would probably have retained the name of his birthday under the reformed calendar, we may take the date to have been September 22'. If so, for September 25 *I* should substitute September 24.
[4] *Jahrb. f. class. Philol.*, viii. Suppl., 1876, pp. 742, 749, 758, 762–3.
[5] *Ib.*, p. 759.   [6] *Ib.*, p. 758.   [7] 102.   [8] *Op. cit.*, p. 756.
[9] *Pro Mur.*, 25, 51.   [10] *Ib.*   [11] *In Cat.*, i, 12, 30.

assembled troops (*Catilinam ... vallatum ... sicariis ... circumfluentem colonorum Arretinorum et Faesulanorum exercitu*[1] &c.) ? Does not Dio say[2] that Catiline collected a band of armed men to murder Cicero during the election and that when his design was rumoured the people were indignant and 'Catiline's fellow-conspirators took alarm and remained quiescent' (οἱ συνομωμοκότες τῷ Κατιλίνᾳ φοβηθέντες αὐτὸν ἡσύχασαν) ? That Catiline hoped, as John insists, to execute his schemes legally as consul goes without saying; but when John admits[3] that before the election Manlius was 'in open revolt' (*in offenem Aufruhr*) and, contradicting his own assertion[4] that 'Catiline then had no thought of fulfilling his promises by other than the legal means of the consular authority', affirms that 'the contingency of revolution, while he was confident of succeeding in the election, was treated by him as an *ultima ratio*', he unwittingly throws up his case. By John's admission Catiline contemplated violence in case of failure : is it conceivable that he took no steps in advance to organize violence ? Is it not proved by Dio and by Cicero that he conspired with this aim ?[5] And since troops had already been raised before the election, what becomes of the argument that if the election had been held in September Catiline would not have had time to prepare ?

The weakness of John's reasoning is particularly conspicuous when he deals with Suetonius. He fails to see that Suetonius, like Dio and Cicero, may well have used the word *coniuratio* of the machinations with which Catiline was busy before the election ; and, having neglected to master the intricacies of Roman chronology, he overlooks one fact which alone demolishes his argument: Suetonius implicitly places the session on September 23 of the Julian, which, as I have shown, corresponded with September 25 of the old calendar ; therefore, John notwithstanding, the 'conspiracy' *was* discussed in that month.

Dr. Hardy,[6] who infers from *Pro Murena*, 26, 52 and Plutarch (*Cicero*, 14, 3) that the election followed 'at once'—I should say 'on the day to which it had been postponed'—after the meeting in which Cicero challenged Catiline to explain, argues, quite fairly, that 'not long afterwards' (οὐ πολλῷ δ' ὕστερον) 'means little in

---

[1] *Pro Mur.*, 24, 49.   [2] xxxvii, 29. 2. 5.   [3] *Op. cit.*, p. 743.
[4] *Ib.*, p. 744.
[5] G. Boissier (*La conjuration de Catilina*, 1905, p. 112 and n. 1) supports my view. 'Tout ce qu'on peut croire', he says, ' c'est qu'à partir de l'échec de Catilina la conjuration dut prendre un caractère particulier de violence.' Everything depends upon the sense in which the word 'conspiracy' is to be understood. That the particular measures planned by Catiline for the last months of the year were not contemplated, or not definitely prearranged until after he was defeated at the polls, is self evident.

Dr. Hardy (*Journ. Rom. Studies*, 1917, p. 178) argues in the same sense as John. Does he believe that Catiline, who must have known that his defeat at the polls was not improbable, had neglected to tell Manlius or Sulla's old soldiers, who were already thronging the streets of Rome, that in the event of his defeat their services would be required ?

[6] *Op. cit.*, pp. 181–2.

Plutarch'. If the elections were originally fixed for July, Dr. Hardy may be right (though in that case the statement of Suetonius, whom he ignores, must be rejected); but it may have been Cicero's interest to fix the elections unusually late.

The dates of the attempt to murder Cicero and of his first oration against Catiline.—The meeting of conspirators at the house of Laeca was held on the night of November 6.[1] In his first oration Cicero asks Catiline, ' What you did last night and the night before, where you were, who were the individuals you assembled, what the plan you formed—do you imagine that any one of us is ignorant ? ' (*Quid proxima, quid superiore nocte egeris, ubi fueris, quos convocaveris, quid consilii ceperis, quem nostrum ignorare arbitraris ?* [2]) Obviously *proxima* (nocte) was the night that preceded the speech ; *superiore* the night before *proxima nox* ; and one or the other, as every one admits, was the night of November 6. In the same speech Cicero says to Catiline, ' Recall with me the last night but one . . . I affirm that on that earlier night you went to Laeca's house ' (*Recognosce mecum noctem illam superiorem. . . . Dico te priore nocte venisse . . . in M. Laecae domum* [3]). If my translation is correct, it solves the problem : let me justify it. Evidently *priore nocte* is synonymous with *noctem illam superiorem* ; and since *prior* means the former of two, *priore nocte*—the night on which Catiline visited Laeca— cannot mean the night that immediately preceded the day on which Cicero spoke, but must mean the last night but one. Therefore *priore nocte*, the night of November 6, is identical with *superiore nocte* in the earlier passage; and it follows that the speech was delivered on November 8.[4]

I doubt whether there ever would have been a question about the day on which the attempt was made to assassinate Cicero if Mommsen had not argued for November 8.[5] Hear the original authorities. ' Catiline ', says Cicero, ' on that night [November 6] you were with Laeca. . . . Two Roman knights were found who promised to . . . murder me in my bed that very night a little before dawn. I learned the whole plot almost before your meeting dispersed ; strengthened and secured my house by additional guards ; and shut out the individuals whom you had sent to pay their respects to me in the morning. The individuals who came were the very same whose arrival at that time I had already foretold to many distinguished men ' (*Fuisti igitur apud Laecam illa nocte, Catilina . . . Reperti sunt duo equites Romani qui . . . sese illa ipsa nocte paulo ante lucem me in meo lectulo interfecturos esse pollicerentur. Haec ego omnia, vixdum etiam coetu vestro dimisso, comperi ; domum meam*

---

[1] Cic., *Pro Sulla*, 18, 52. Perhaps it is unnecessary to remind readers that Sallust (*Cat.*, 27, 3) antedates the meeting.
[2] *In Cat.*, i, 1, 1. [3] *Ib.*, 4, 8.
[4] C. John, *I* find, has elaborately demonstrated (*Philol.*, xlvi, 1888, pp. 650-65) the correctness of the date which *I* have fixed; but it has been recently disputed (see pp. 464-6, *infra*), and in order to make the rest of this article clear, *I* let what I have independently written stand.
[5] *Hermes*, i, 1866, pp. 435-7.

maioribus praesidiis munivi atque firmavi ; exclusi eos quos tu ad me salutatum mane miseras, cum illi ipsi venissent quos ego iam multis ac summis viris ad me id temporis venturos esse praedixeram [1]). On November 9, addressing the populace, Cicero said, 'Yesterday, having narrowly escaped being murdered in my house, I summoned the Senate' (*Hesterno die . . . cum domi meae paene interfectus essem, senatum . . . convocavi* [2]). Sallust [3] says that 'on that night' (*ea nocte*)—the night of November 6—Gaius Cornelius and Lucius Vargunteius determined to murder Cicero 'a little later' (*paulo post*), but that, as he had been warned by Curius and Fulvia, they were prevented from executing their design. Again, in his speech *Pro Sulla* [4] Cicero, after stating that the meeting at Laeca's house was held on the night of November 6 and after detailing the arrangements that were made 'then' (*tum*), ends by saying that 'then' Cornelius undertook to assassinate him *prima luce*,—obviously the dawn of November 7.

Mommsen supposes that the meeting at Laeca's house lasted so long that the assassins were compelled to wait till the morning of the 8th ; and Professor H. C. Nutting [5] has, perhaps independently, reproduced Mommsen's reasoning. He insists that 'The plain and obvious sense' of the words *Hesterno die . . . convocavi* 'is that the attempt on Cicero's life was made on the same day as that on which' the first oration against Catiline 'was delivered', that is on November 8. But Nutting's principal argument is based upon considerations of time. 'If', he says, 'the news [of the intended murder] came through the usual channels (Curius and Fulvia), some considerable time must be allowed for the transmission. After the news arrived . . . additional guards were called in to protect Cicero's house ; and . . . Cicero had interviews with many prominent citizens, telling the names of the would-be murderers and predicting the time of their coming. . . . It really strains the probabilities to bring all these events within a compass that would allow of the conspirators arriving before daylight on the . . . 7th'. Surely everything depends upon the time when the meeting at Laeca's house broke up. 'The probabilities' are not in the least strained by supposing that the conspirators dispersed at, or even before, midnight ; and on November 7 day did not break, even in the strict astronomical sense, till after 5 a.m. Was not the interval sufficient ? Is Nutting's argument strong enough to justify us in accusing Cicero of deliberate misrepresentation ? [6]

But Nutting tries again. 'Further information', he says, 'is afforded by *in Cat.* ii. 6. 13 . . . Cicero is manifestly taking up that

[1] *In Cat.*, i, 4, 9–10.   [2] *Ib.*, ii, 6, 12.   [3] *Cat.*, 28, 1.
[4] 18, 52.   [5] *Proc. Amer. Philol. Assn.*, xxxv, 1904, pp. lxxiii–lxxvi.
[6] Mommsen (*op. cit.*, p. 436) urges that it was characteristic of Cicero to gloze over the interval between the mornings of November 7 and 8. As John acutely remarks (*Jahrb. f. class. Philol.*, viii. Suppl., 1876, p. 778, n. 50), Mommsen forgot that Cicero was addressing an audience many of whom had heard from his own lips when the attempt to murder him was made. This argument is unanswerable except on the assumption that the relevant sentence in Cicero's written version of his speech does not represent what he said.

part of *in Cat.* i. in which 4, 9 falls. Referring back to that passage, it will be seen that after telling what business was·transacted . . . at Laeca's house . . . the very next thing mentioned is the plan . . . to murder Cicero. That this was the plan for the following night (*quid in proximam constituisset*) would be a natural assumption from a comparison of the two passages ; and this assumption grows to conviction when a diligent search throughout the first oration . . . fails to bring to light a reference to any other plan for the night which followed that on which the meeting at Laeca's house took place '. Natural assumptions occasionally mislead ; and 'diligent search', unless it is also vigilant, may fail to discover what is obvious. If Nutting will search once more, he will find in i. 4, 9 that the plan which Catiline had formed ' for the following night ' was to leave Rome and join Manlius. Long before Nutting wrote John [1] called attention to this passage ; and Karl Halm,[2] after he had read John's article, expunged the note in which he had committed himself to the opinion that the words *Hesterno die* . . . *convocavi* were almost decisive in favour of Mommsen's view. What is there to prevent us from taking *Hesterno die* with *convocavi* and not also with *cum paene interfectus essem* ? [3]

Having convinced himself that ' it was on the morning of the 8th that the actual attempt took place ', Nutting boldly asserts that ' Cicero has not made it all clear whether *the original plan* was for that morning or for . . . the 7th '. Then most of us suffer from defective vision. ' Of course ', Nutting adds, ' at first sight i. 4. 9 seems to decide that question definitely in favour of the earlier date '. Yes, and at last, and as often as we look ; and if the decision is wrong, there is no other means of deciding. Those who hold that 'the actual attempt ' was made on November 8 must assume not only that Cicero gratuitously lied, but either that before the meeting at Laeca's house broke up Catiline determined that the would-be murderers had better postpone their plan, for which there is not a particle of evidence, or that they independently resolved to wait, in which case the argument based upon the words *quid in proximam constituisset* breaks down. For my part, since I cannot doubt what action of Catiline Cicero referred to in those words, I prefer his guidance to the guesses of his critics.

The question has, however, been asked, If the attempt to murder Cicero was made on the morning of November 7, why did he allow a whole day and night to pass before summoning the Senate ? Various reasons, of which we are ignorant, may have influenced him : John suggests two. The Senate had not hitherto been disposed to give full credence to Cicero's denunciations of Catiline : he therefore decided to allow time for news of the intended assassina-

---

[1] *Philol.*, 1888, p. 657.
[2] *Ciceros ausgewählte Reden*, iii¹³, 1891, p. 10.
[3] As John observes (*Jahrb. f. class. Philol.*, &c., p. 784, note), the people whom Cicero addressed knew perfectly well when the attempt had been made to murder him, and he therefore could say *Hesterno die* . . . *convocavi* without the least risk of being misunderstood.

tion to make its due impression.[1] Again, Catiline had resolved to leave Rome on the night of the 7th in order to join his lieutenant Manlius in Etruria, and Cicero may have expected that, although the would-be assassins had failed, he would adhere to his resolve and thereby supply evidence which would convince the most sceptical of his guilt.[2]

Since I wrote the foregoing paragraphs I have read a Programm[3] in which R. Wirtz sets himself to prove that the first Catilinarian oration was delivered on the 7th of November, that is, on the evening that followed the attempted murder. He begins by affirming, without any evidence, that two meetings were held in the house of Laeca, the first on the night of November 5–6, the second on the night of November 6–7. Like Professor Nutting, he holds that the words *Hesterno die . . . convocavi* prove that the first oration was delivered on the day on which the attempt was made to murder Cicero, and he adds that Plutarch[4] says the same. What Plutarch says, immediately after describing the attempt, is that 'Cicero proceeded to summon the Senate' (προελθὼν δὲ ὁ Κικέρων ἐκάλει τὴν σύγκλητον). No fair critic would contend that these words are decisive of the date; moreover, Plutarch here mentions the summons only, not the meeting of the Senate. Wirtz goes on to say that Cicero several times speaks of two nights. In his first oration (1, 1) he calls one of the two *proxima*—the night preceding the day on which he spoke. Obviously; but when Wirtz adds that *proxima nocte* was the night on which the attempt was made to murder Cicero, he is merely making an assertion. Continuing his argument, he cites a passage in the second oration (3, 6) in which Cicero spoke of one night only, which he called *superior*: 'They are aware that all their plans formed on the earlier night were reported to me; I revealed them in the Senate yesterday' (*Omnia superioris noctis consilia ad me perlata esse sentiunt; patefeci in senatu hesterno die*). Since, says Wirtz, the second oration was delivered one day after the first, *superioris noctis* clearly denotes the night which in i. 1, 1 is called *proxima*. The reasoning is unsound. The plans which Cicero had revealed in the Senate *hesterno die* were those which Catiline had formed on the night of November 6—the night which in the first oration (1, 1) Cicero called *superiore nocte* and (4, 8) *noctem illam superiorem*. Therefore *superioris noctis* clearly denotes, not the night which in i, 1, 1 is called *proxima*, but the night which is there called *superiore* and in i, 4, 8 *illam superiorem*; and if the expression *superioris noctis* is literally incorrect, it is justifiable, because Cicero, recounting to the people what he had said in the Senate on the previous day, was, as it were, putting himself at the standpoint of that day. Two nights are mentioned again in ii, 6, 13 : 'I asked Catiline whether he had been present in the nocturnal meeting at Laeca's house or not. As he was at first silent, I revealed the rest of the proceedings,—what he had

[1] *Jahrb. f. class. Philol.*, &c., pp. 784–5, note. [2] *Philol.*, 1888, p. 657.
[3] *Beiträge zur cat. Verschwörung*, 1910, pp. 1–4. [4] *Cic.*, 16, 2.

THE CONSPIRACY OF CATILINE

done on that night, what arrangements he had made for the next'
(*quaesivi a Catilina in nocturno conventu apud M. Laecam fuisset
necne. Cum ille primo reticuisset, patefeci cetera; quid ea nocte
egisset, quid in proximam constituisset*). *Ea nocte*, says Wirtz, refers
to the second meeting at Laeca's house : what Catiline determined
then we read in the first oration (4, 9) : he determined, if the attempt
to murder Cicero succeeded, to leave Rome on the following night.
So far Wirtz finds everything clear ; but in i, 4, 8 he sees a difficulty,
which he undertakes to remove. Here, he says, both the nocturnal
meetings are alluded to : again the one emphasized is the second.
Cicero calls the first *superior*, just as he did in 1, 1 : the second,
which he there calls *proxima*, he here calls *prior*. But since *prior*
always means the former of two, of which the latter is *posterior*,
it is clear that the first oration was delivered after sunset, and that
the *posterior nox* was the night on which it was delivered. The
proof which Wirtz offers that it was delivered after dark depends
upon his theory that it was delivered on the same day as that on
which the attempt to murder Cicero was made : there would not
have been time, he says, for the senators to assemble before 2 or
3 o'clock in the afternoon.

Now to every one except Wirtz it is obvious that in i, 4, 8 one
nocturnal meeting only is alluded to, and that *priore nocte* is equivalent to *noctem illam superiorem*. But, apart from that, I would
ask him, first, how he can maintain that the Senate, in violation of
long-established custom,[1] continued to sit after sunset, and, secondly,
what happened between the alleged opening of the session at 2 or
3 p.m. on November 7 and the beginning of Cicero's speech, which
ex hypothesi was delivered after dark. Surely Cicero spoke first.[2]
Again, every unbiased reader will, I am sure, agree with me that
no educated Roman, least of all Cicero, speaking after sunset on
November 7, would have called the night of November 6-7 *prior
nox*: he would only have used that expression of the former of
two nights both of which had preceded the evening on which he
was speaking.[3] Finally, it is to my mind inconceivable that Cicero,
speaking on November 7, would have alluded to the night of
November 6-7 as *illa nocte*. Wirtz asserts that the expression
presents no difficulty : will any Latin scholar deny that the difficulty
which it presents is insurmountable ?

Catiline's pretended intention of going to Massilia.—Hardy [4]
argues, despite the statement of Sallust,[5] that as Catiline's 'plea
of going to Massilia is alluded to in Cicero's first speech ', the letters

---
[1] See P. Willems, *Le sénat*, &c., ii, 1883, pp. 147-8.   [2] Sall., *Cat.*, 31, 6-7.
[3] Dr. Hardy (*Journ. Rom. Studies*, 1916, pp. 56-7), though he of course
assumes that only one meeting, that of Nov. 6, took place in the house of
Laeca, nevertheless maintains, like Wirtz, that Cicero delivered his first
oration on the following day, because, first, it is 'inconceivable that Cicero
would have waited till the 8th', and, secondly, 'in i, 4, 8 ... *superior* is equivalent
to *prior*', the meaning of which is 'incontrovertible'. The first argument
has been answered by anticipation : with the statement on which the second
rests I entirely agree.
[4] *Op. cit.*, pp. 198-9.   [5] *Cat.*, 34, 2.

in which he announced it were probably 'sent round as a blind before the meeting at Laeca's house'. But Cicero's allusion is not in his first, but in his second speech.[1]

The plan of Catiline for conflagration and massacre in Rome.—According to the evidence given on December 3 by the Allobrogian envoys,[2] the conflagration and massacre planned by Catiline were to take place on the Saturnalia (December 17); but Dr. Hardy[3] holds that 'Sallust[4] is no doubt correct in making the date provisional on the advance of the army'. There is no inconsistency between the two statements. Sallust implies that the appointed day was later than December 10, when the tribune Bestia, whose intended invective against Cicero was to precede the massacre, would enter office; and Lentulus was quite credulous enough to believe that by December 17 the army would be at hand.

Sallust, as the commentators have pointed out, is of course wrong (if the MSS. are right) in saying that the massacre was to begin on the night after the army arrived *in agrum Faesulanum*, for Faesulae was much too far from Rome, and Sallust himself[5] repeatedly says that the army was to come quite close; but the attempts which editors have made to amend the text are futile, for Appian,[6] who copied Sallust, repeated his mistake.

Hardy[7] goes on to say, I do not know on what authority, that 'The original scheme had been for Manlius to reach Rome by the end of October, before an army was ready to meet him. ... This plan', he explains, 'was foiled by the revelations made to Cicero in the middle of the month'. Did Hardy forget when he gave this explanation, that he had already[8] given another—that 'the cause of the delay lay no doubt with Manlius, whose numbers increased but slowly'? Whatever the cause may have been, 'the revelations made to Cicero' did not prevent Manlius from reaching Rome by the end of October; for the Senate did not pass the ultimate decree until the 22nd of that month, and to raise an army which could stop him within the next nine days was impossible.

The mission of Metellus Nepos.—Dr. Hardy has attempted to explain Pompey's motive in sending Metellus Nepos to Rome to stand for a tribuneship: 'Metellus was to be the intermediary of a more or less definite understanding between Pompey on the one hand and Caesar and Crassus on the other, which might foreshadow an ultimate coalition.'[9] That 'Pompey had no idea of a *rapprochement* with the senatorial party, is clear', Dr. Hardy adds,[10] 'from the haste with which Cato was put up to oppose him. That Metellus was to have acted alone in Pompey's interest against both *optimates* and popular leaders, it is impossible to believe'. Granted: both propositions are proved by the co-operation of Metellus with Caesar in the early part of 62.[11] Hardy[12] then points to the bill

---
[1] *In Cat.*, ii, 6, 14. [2] Cic., *In Cat.*, iii, 4, 10.
[3] *Journ. Rom. Studies*, 1917, p. 202.
[4] *Cat.*, 43, 1.   [5] *Ib.*, 33, 2; 43, 2; 44, 6.   [6] *B. C.*, ii, 3, 10.
[7] p. 203.   [8] p. 195.   [9] *Journ. Rom. Studies*, 1917, p. 194.
[10] *Ib.*, p. 224.   [11] See pp. 285–6.   [12] *Op. cit.*, p. 225.

which Caesar proposed 'for transferring the honour of completing the Capitoline temple from Lutatius Catulus to Pompey': it seems to him 'an indication of completely changed relations between the two men'. To me it seems unsafe to regard it as more than an indication that Caesar, who had supported Pompey in respect of the Gabinian and the Manilian laws, and had failed in covert attempts to counterbalance his power, desired to stand well with him; for there is no reason to suppose that Pompey had prompted Caesar through Metellus to effect the transference of this honour. Hardy goes on to notice the law, proposed by Metellus and supported by Caesar, for recalling Pompey to Italy. He 'can find no indication in the authorities that the idea of recalling Pompey had ever had any connexion with putting down the conspiracy'[1] of Catiline. Did he forget the passage in which Plutarch[2] expressly stated that Metellus proposed a bill for that very purpose? To Hardy it seems 'unmistakable' that the proposal of Metellus was 'the first formal step towards establishing' a coalition between Pompey, Crassus, and Caesar, and he has no doubt that if it had succeeded, 'there would have been an end to' that supremacy of the Senate which had been confirmed by the suppression of the Catilinarian conspiracy.[3] Finally, he suspects that 'Pompey's resignation [on his return from Asia] of his military command and his retirement into a private position was ... in conformity with previous understandings arrived at with Caesar and Crassus'.[4]

Dr. Hardy must have forgotten that Crassus, in view of Pompey's expected return, left Rome with his family for Asia—probably because he shared the general belief that Pompey would not disband his army.[5] That Pompey desired to coalesce with Crassus, who apparently did nothing to support Metellus, there is not a shred of evidence. Crassus was still at enmity with Pompey in 60 B.C., when Caesar effected a hollow reconciliation between the two. That Pompey instructed Metellus to make overtures to Caesar is likely enough; but while Metellus obviously did not intend to act against 'the popular leaders', or at all events against Caesar, Pompey had reason to believe that he was himself the idol of the populace, and that the knights, to whose support he had largely owed his extraordinary command, were on his side. Long before he returned to Italy the attempts which Metellus and Caesar made to promote his interests had completely failed; there is no evidence that after that failure Caesar acted with or for him until on the eve of his consulship he was in a position to form the triumvirate; and I see no reason for believing that Pompey disbanded his army because he had anything to expect from Caesar.

The senatorial debate on December 5, 63 B. C.—If, as Dr. Hardy thinks, the 'general agreement' of the original authorities who have

---

[1] *Ib.*, n. 3.
[2] *Cato min.*, 26, 2. Cf. *Schol. Bob.* (*Pro Sest.*, § 62), p. 302 Or. (ed. Stangl, p. 134). See also Plut., *Cic.*, 23, 2, and Dio, xxxvii, 43, 1.
[3] *Op. cit.*, p. 226.
[4] *Ib.*, p. 227.
[5] Cic., *Pro Flac.*, 14, 32; Plut., *Pomp.*, 43, 1.

described the debate on the punishment of the Catilinarian conspirators is 'very remarkable', I cannot endorse his opinion that 'the few differences of detail' are 'quite insignificant'.[1] The chief questions to be settled are these :—when did Tiberius Nero propose his amendment ? when did Silanus change his mind ? what were the terms of Caesar's proposal ? To begin with, I must point out that when Cicero remarked in the letter which he wrote to Atticus on March 17, 45 B.C.[2]—seventeen years after the debate—(Brutus) 'imagines that Cato was the first to give an opinion in favour of [capital] punishment, whereas *every one except Caesar had expressed this opinion before him*' (*Catonem primum sententiam putat de animadversione dixisse, quam omnes ante dixerant praeter Caesarem*), he was inaccurate. His statement, not confirmed by any other writer, is implicitly contradicted by Sallust,[3] Velleius,[4] Plutarch,[5] Suetonius,[6] Appian,[7] and Dio.[8] He remembered that every one who spoke before Caesar had pronounced for the extreme penalty; but about those who spoke later his memory, weakened by lapse of time and perhaps biased by the desire of showing that the punishment which he inflicted had been almost unanimously sanctioned even before Cato spoke, played him false.[9]

The part which Tiberius Nero played in the debate is ignored by every authority except Sallust and Appian. Sallust, immediately after relating that Silanus proposed that the prisoners should be put to death, adds that 'afterwards, being greatly impressed by the speech of Gaius Caesar, he said that he intended to vote for the motion of Tiberius Nero',[10] namely (as Sallust explains), that the guards in the city should be reinforced and the discussion adjourned. Cicero, Plutarch,[11] and Dio[12] agree that every one who spoke before Caesar advocated the execution of the conspirators; and if they are right, Nero spoke later. The statement of Sallust is not incon-

---

[1] *Journ. Rom. Studies*, 1917, p. 212.
[2] *Att.*, xii, 21, 1.
[3] *Cat.*, 52, 1.
[4] ii, 35, 4.
[5] *Caes.*, 8, 1; *Cato min.*, 22, 3: *Cic.*, 21, 1.
[6] *Div. Iul.*, 14, 2.
[7] *B. C.*, ii, 6, 21.
[8] xxxvii, 36, 2.
[9] Strachan-Davidson (*Cicero*, 1894, p. 139) holds that Cicero's letter 'is our best guide through the labyrinth of contradiction', and accordingly loses his own way. He says (p. 148, note), 'That Nero's proposal came last of all is proved ... by Cicero's statement ... that all who spoke before Cato, excepting Caesar, had spoken for death'. Evidently he forgot that he had already (p. 142) committed himself to the statement that before Cicero and therefore also before Cato spoke, 'many of the senators ... signified their assent, to the proposal of Caesar'.
[10] *Cat.*, 50, 4. Dr. Hardy (*op. cit.*, p. 216, n. 1) says that the statement of Plutarch (*Cato*, 22, 3) that Silanus explained away his original proposal, remarking that he had not meant to advocate execution, but only imprisonment, 'does not deserve to be set against the statement of Sallust'. *I* cannot see that the two are necessarily inconsistent. Strachan-Davidson (*Cicero*, pp. 142-3, 148) attempted to reconcile or to combine them by assuming that Silanus changed his mind twice—first solely under the influence of Caesar, secondly under that of Nero. *I* doubt whether this guess will be accepted.
[11] *Caes.*, 7, 2; *Cato min.*, 22, 2; *Cic.*, 20, 3
[12] xxxvii, 36, 1.

sistent with this conclusion;[1] but Appian,[2] who describes Nero's amendment more fully than Sallust—that the prisoners should be kept in custody until Catiline was defeated and further evidence obtained—seems to mean that he spoke before Caesar. Cicero in the written version of his speech twice called attention to the original proposal of Silanus,[3] but said nothing about his retractation, apparently implying that he had not yet made it, and also that Nero, whom he did not mention, had not moved his amendment. On the whole, then, it seems probable, considering the notorious inaccuracy of Appian's chronology, that Nero spoke and Silanus retracted after Cicero intervened.[4] Still, it is quite conceivable that, if Silanus was ultimately converted by the influence of Cato to his own original view, Cicero in his written speech chose for artistic reasons to ignore his recantation.[5] According to Sallust,[6] Caesar proposed that the property of the prisoners should be confiscated; that they should be confined in municipal towns; that no one should propose a motion for their release either to the Senate or to the people; and that any one who did so should be declared by the Senate a public enemy.[7] This account is confirmed by Cicero[8] and Dio,[9] and (with the omission of the last two clauses) by Plutarch[10] and Suetonius;[11] but Plutarch and Appian,[12] evidently following the same authority, affirm that Caesar proposed that after the defeat of Catiline the prisoners should be brought to trial. This would imply that their property was only to be sequestrated; and therefore Plutarch, when he says that it was to be confiscated, virtually contradicts himself. But, apart from this question, his account of Caesar's proposal is identical with the account, which he omits, of that of Nero; and it seems not unlikely that he confounded the two.[13] At all events the weight of evidence is in favour of the account of Caesar's proposal given by Sallust, Cicero, Suetonius, and Dio.[14]

[1] Hardy (*op. cit.*, p. 213) says that Sallust asserts 'that, before Caesar's turn came, Tiberius Nero proposed that the question should be postponed'. Unbiased readers will agree with me that Sallust makes no such assertion.
[2] ii, 5, 19–20.   [3] *In Cat.*, iv, 4, 7; 6, 11.
[4] Plutarch (*Cic.*, 21, 1) appears to mean that Silanus recanted at this stage.
[5] Cf. Hardy, *op. cit.*, p. 215, n. 3.   [6] *Cat.*, 51, 43.
[7] We learn from Cicero's speech (4, 8) that Caesar also proposed that any municipality which allowed a prisoner to escape was to be severely punished (*Adiungit gravem poenam municipiis, si quis eorum vincula ruperit*)—as Hardy explains (p. 214 and note), by a heavy fine.   [8] *In Cat.*, iv, 4, 7–8; 5, 10.
[9] xxxvii, 36, 1–2.   [10] *Cic.*, 21, 1.   [11] *Div. Iul.*, 14, 1.   [12] ii, 6, 20.
[13] I find that J. Besser (*De coniuratione Cat.*, 1880, pp. 20–1) has anticipated my suggestion.
[14] Hardy (pp. 214–5) apparently thinks that Sallust's account of Caesar's proposal is consistent with that of Plutarch and Appian; in other words, that, according to Sallust, Caesar proposed that any one who introduced a bill for the release of the prisoners *before they were brought to trial* should be punished. 'Cicero's contention', he observes, 'that Caesar was proposing a sentence of perpetual imprisonment [*In Cat.*, iv, 4, 8; 5, 10] is ridiculous.' Anyhow Cicero's contention was not, as Hardy says, 'affected': his letter to Atticus, in which he emphasizes the severity of Caesar's proposal (*cum ipsius Caesaris* [*sententia*] *tam severa fuerit*), shows that he was sincere. It is not reasonable

The execution of the conspirators.—Sallust[1] relates that immediately after the conspirators were condemned Cicero ordered the *triumviri* [*capitales*] to prepare for their execution, and that the *vindices rerum capitalium* carried it out by strangling : Mommsen,[2] citing Valerius Maximus[3] and Tacitus,[4] maintains that the *vindices* were identical with the *triumviri*, who, he says, executed persons of distinction and women, while the common executioner only had to do with slaves. 'Is it possible', asks Mr. A. M. Cook,[5] 'that these dignified chiefs of the police . . . should have had to sink to be executioners ? . . . The evidence . . . seems somewhat insufficient.' Perhaps that of Valerius Maximus is ; for nobody, except Miss Marie Corelli, interprets the words of St. Matthew[6]—'when he [Pilate] had scourged Jesus ', &c.—literally. But Tacitus clearly means that the *triumviri* had to strangle female criminals, unless they were virgins, with their own hands—*tradunt temporis eius* [Seiani] *auctores, quia triumvirali supplicio adfici virginem inauditum habebatur, a carnifice laqueum iuxta compressam.*[7] Plutarch,[8] indeed, says that Cicero delivered Lentulus to the common executioner (τῷ δημίῳ) ; but no doubt he was imperfectly acquainted with Roman procedure.

The alleged complicity of Caesar and Crassus in the conspiracy.—' That . . . Crassus and Caesar had a hand in the game . . . must be regarded—not from a judicial, but from a historical point of view—as an ascertained fact.' Such is the judgement of Mommsen.[9] Let us examine the evidence.

Sallust[10] says that about the 1st of June, 64 B.C., 'some people believed that M. Licinius Crassus was aware of the plot [formed by Catiline] ; for Pompey, whom he hated, was master of a large army, and he desired that some one should counterbalance his power, being confident that if the conspiracy succeeded, it would be easy for him to dominate the conspirators '.

to read into Sallust's account a meaning which is not there. *If* Caesar did not propose perpetual imprisonment, why did he propose that the property of the prisoners should be confiscated ? Hardy insists that he only desired to ' impound ' it. But the meaning of the word *publicare*, which is used by Suetonius (14, 1) as well as by Sallust and Cicero (4, 8) is unmistakable ; and the words of Dio—τῶν οὐσιῶν ἐστερημένους (xxxvii, 36, 2) and Plutarch—τὰς οὐσίας εἶναι δημοσίας (*Cic.*, 21, 1)—are equally clear. Besides, Hardy's translation of *publicandas* is irreconcilable with Plutarch's statement (§ 2) that when the prisoners were condemned to death Caesar protested against the confiscation of their property (περὶ δημεύσεως χρημάτων) on the ground that it was unfair to reject the milder part of his proposal and yet to adopt the more severe.

[1] *Cat.*, 55, 1. 5.
[2] *Röm. Staatsr.*, ii², 581, n. 5. Cf. *Paulys Real-Ency.*, iii, 1599 and A. H. J. Greenidge, *Legal Procedure*, &c., 1901, p. 343.
[3] v, 4, 7.   [4] *Ann.*, v, 9.   [5] *C. Sall. Crispi bell. Cat.*, 1884, p. 159.
[6] xxvii, 26.   [7] Cf. Suet., *Tib.*, 61, 5.
[8] *Cic.*, 22, 2. Cicero (*Pro Rab.*, 3, 10) calls the executioner who, as he pretended, was to have put Rabirius to death a *carnifex* ; but that word was apparently sometimes loosely applied to a *triumvir*. See Val. Max., ix, 12, 6. Mommsen (*op. cit.*, i³, 1887, p. 381 and n. 1) takes *carnifex* in *Pro Rab.* literally.
[9] *Röm. Gesch.*, iii⁸, 1889, p. 193 (Eng. tr., iv, 1908, p. 486).
[10] *Cat.*, 17, 1. 7.

THE CONSPIRACY OF CATILINE 471

Asconius[1] notes that [in 64 B.C.] when Catiline and Antonius combined to exclude Cicero from the consulship, their strongest supporters were Crassus and Caesar.

Cicero, writing on February 13, 61 B.C., says 'Crassus... rose [in the Senate] and spoke of my consulship in the most enthusiastic terms, going so far as to say that he owed it to me that he was still a senator, a citizen, a free man,—aye, that he was still alive; that he never beheld wife, home, or country without recognizing my beneficent hand'.[2]

Plutarch[3] affirms that Piso and Catulus denounced Cicero for having forborne to seize the opportunity of crushing Caesar when he laid himself open to attack in connexion with the conspiracy;[4] that Cato in his speech on the 5th of December threw suspicion on Caesar;[5] that when Caesar was leaving the House after the debate Cicero's bodyguard were ready to assassinate him, but that Cicero was said to have refrained from giving them the signal, either because he feared the populace or because he thought that the assassination would be unjust. Plutarch then expresses astonishment that, if the story is true, Cicero did not confirm it in his book on his consulship. In his biography of Crassus[6] he relates that Cicero accused both Crassus and Caesar in a speech which was published after both were dead, but that in his treatise on his consulship he admitted that Crassus had given him information about the plot.

Appian[7] states that Caesar was suspected of being privy to the plot, but that Cicero did not point to him as one of the conspirators because he was afraid to inculpate a man who was so popular with the multitude.

According to Suetonius,[8] Caesar was named as a conspirator by Lucius Vettius in the court of the quaestor Novius Niger, and in the Senate by Quintus Curius, who mentioned Catiline as his informant, while Vettius promised to produce a document in Caesar's handwriting, given to him by Catiline. Caesar thereupon invoked the testimony of Cicero, and proved that he had spontaneously given him information about the plot.

Mommsen begins by brushing aside the allegations of Piso and Catulus as worthless. But, he adds, 'a series of other facts is of more weight'. First, 'it was Crassus and Caesar above all who supported the candidature of Catiline for the consulship', and in the same year (64 B.C.), when Caesar 'brought the myrmidons of Sulla before the Commission for Murder, he allowed the most guilty... Catiline to be acquitted while the rest were condemned'.[9] That Caesar supported the candidature of Catiline in 64 B.C. does not seem a sufficient reason for affirming that a year later he supported

---

[1] Ed. Clark, p. 83, ll. 3–4 (ed. Stangl, p. 64).
[2] *Att.*, i, 14, 3.   [3] *Caes.*, 7, 2; 8, 2–3.
[4] Sallust (*Cat.*, 49, 1) says that Catulus and Piso could not induce Cicero to allow Caesar to be falsely accused.
[5] Cf. Plut., *Cic.*, 21, 2.   [6] 13, 4. Cf. *Hermes*, xxxii, 1897, p. 558.
[7] *B. C.*, ii, 6, 20.   [8] *Div. Iul.*, 17.   [9] See Dio, xxxvii, 10, 3.

him in a criminal conspiracy; but on this point as well as on the significance of Catiline's acquittal the reader will be better able to judge later on. Secondly, says Mommsen, 'in later years, when Cicero had no reason to disguise the truth, he expressly named Caesar [and Crassus] among the accomplices'. So Plutarch says; but Mommsen omits to add that Cicero stated that Crassus had given him information about the plot. Does not this suggest that if we could control Plutarch's statement by Cicero's own words we should find that what he meant was that Crassus and Caesar supported Catiline up to a certain point, but withdrew their support when they knew what he really designed? And, unless Cicero sacrificed honesty to vanity, does not the letter which I have quoted suggest that he did not suspect Crassus? Thirdly, on the 3rd of December, 63, two of the five conspirators who had just been arrested were placed 'in the custody of Caesar and Crassus': 'it was manifestly intended', says Mommsen, 'that they should either, if they allowed them to escape, be compromised in public opinion as accessories, or, if they really detained them, be compromised in the view of their fellow-conspirators as renegades'. 'Manifestly intended!' If this is to be 'regarded, from a historical point of view as an ascertained fact', who will escape the condemnation of history? That Caesar and Crassus would allow their charges to escape was out of the question, and what could it matter to them, at that stage, whether their alleged fellow-conspirators, who were doomed men, regarded them as renegades or not? Finally, says Mommsen, 'at a much later period'—in 46 B.C.—Caesar 'was in the closest alliance with the only Catilinarian still surviving, Publius Sittius, and ... he modified the law of debt quite in the sense that the proclamations of Manlius demanded'. The latter statement, referring to the expedient which Caesar devised in his first dictatorship in order to restore financial confidence,[1] is at least misleading; as for Sittius, if the fact of Caesar's having utilized the services of that able *condottiere* in the African campaign is needed to convince us that Caesar was in the conspiracy of Catiline, we can judge what Mommsen meant by 'an ascertained fact'.

Tyrrell[2] undertakes to supplement Mommsen's arguments by 'the following considerations'. 'We have', he says, 'the unequivocal testimony of Suetonius', and when Caesar 'said to his mother ... after lavishing a fortune on his suit for the Pontificate, *domum se nisi pontificem non reversurum* [that he would not return home unless he were Pontiff], he spoke the words of a desperate man'. Perhaps; but when he returned the same evening his despair had presumably vanished. 'The unequivocal testimony of Suetonius' was precisely as unequivocal as the testimony of counsel for *The Times* when he called as one of his witnesses the late Richard Pigott. Mommsen did well to omit it, since it rested partly upon an alleged utterance of Catiline, partly upon the 'promise' of

---

[1] Caes., *B. C.*, iii, 1, 2–3.
[2] *The Correspondence of Cicero*, i³, 1904, pp. 18–9.

THE CONSPIRACY OF CATILINE 473

Vettius,—as notorious a liar as the adventurer who tried to ruin Parnell.[1]

Since evidence which would be admitted in a court of law is wanting, it behoves the historian to consider whether it is likely that Caesar and Crassus would have associated themselves with the crime of Catiline. There is no evidence that they even assisted him in his candidature for the consulship in 63 : [2] that they assisted him after his candidature failed, when he could not gain his object by legal means, no reasonable man will believe. As Long remarked, 'nothing is less likely than that the Pontifex Maximus of Rome, now praetor elect, with the prospect of the consulship . . . a man of ability and good sense, was conspiring with a set of fools. . . .' [3]

But let us hear Mommsen to the end. 'The circumstances', he says, 'were very similar to those of Cinna's time. While in the East Pompey occupied a position almost the same as Sulla did then, Crassus and Caesar attempted to raise a counter-power in Italy like that which Marius and Cinna had possessed. . . . The way thereto lay once more through terrorism and anarchy', &c. And Mommsen believes that Caesar and Crassus intended to tread that way! It would have led them straight to perdition. Who was to be terrorized ? Pompey with his powerful army ? By a couple of legions, of whom three-fourths were armed with sticks ?[4] The circumstances were not very similar to, but, as Strachan-Davidson [5] pointed out, very different from those of Cinna's time. Cinna had three years for preparation, and it was his own fault that he did not use them ; Pompey would return before any adequate preparation could be made. Besides, the only real soldiers whom Catiline commanded were Sullan veterans : were they likely to welcome Caesar, notoriously a Marian, as their chief. 'It is obvious', says Strachan-Davidson,[6] 'that Crassus, however willing he may have been to use Catiline as a tool in his designs against his rival Pompey, can have had no sympathy with his schemes of national bankruptcy, and we may be sure that Caesar was no less averse to a movement which would have united the Senate and Pompey, the constitutional and the military power, once for all firmly together. . . . Both Crassus and Caesar got wind of the plot which was formed inside the ranks of their party. They did their best at first to gain for Catiline an official position which would have enabled him to dispense with actual armed rebellion ; when this failed and it was manifest that the conspirators would proceed with their further designs, Caesar and Crassus both warned Cicero of the danger and gave him such information as they possessed about the plot.'

[1] See pp. 288, 324, 479.
[3] *Decline of the Roman Republic*, iii, 326.
[5] *Cicero*, pp. 118-9.
[2] See pp. 456-7.
[4] Sall., *Cat.*, 56, 3.
[6] *Ib.*, pp. 119-20.

THE CONSULAR PROVINCES ALLOTTED BY THE SENATE BEFORE THE ELECTIONS OF 60 B. C.

Suetonius [1] says (if the MSS. are correct) that it was provided that to the consuls who were about to be elected there should be assigned *provinciae minimi negotii, id est silvae callesque*. This has been understood to mean that they were to administer the forests and pastures of Italy. But no such consular provinces existed: the superintendence of forests and pastures, if it belonged to any magistrate, was perhaps a function of one of the quaestors.[2] P. Willems [3] accordingly regarded the words *id est silvae callesque* as a gloss, added by a scribe who, as Professor Rolfe suggests,[4] 'first misunderstood the meaning of *provinciae* and then confused a quaestor's sphere of duty with a consul's'. The professor, however, thinks it more probable that *silvae callesque* 'is a colloquial term, " mere woods and pastures "', applied to the unknown consular provinces which the Senate assigned. The words *id est* seem to me to tell against this view; but anyhow the provinces in question were outside Italy.

CAESAR'S COALITION WITH POMPEY AND CRASSUS

The conservative party in the Senate, anticipating that Caesar would be elected consul in 60 B. C., resolved that the province which he was to hold after his consulship should be one in which he would be reduced to political inaction.[5] Long [6] remarks that 'this insult, in the opinion of Suetonius, was the immediate cause of Caesar seeking a closer union with Pompeius'. 'Perhaps', he adds, ' we may infer from the words of Suetonius that he supposed the confederation to have been made after Caesar's election, but some authorities tell us that it was made before.' Now the opinion of Suetonius was not authoritative unless he had access to some lost letter of Caesar or derived his information from one of Caesar's friends. Caesar's political action was not determined by wounded *amour propre*. To join Pompey was so manifestly the most advantageous step which he could take that he must have contemplated it before he returned from Spain. As to the question which Long raises, there is no reason to suppose that Suetonius differed from the authorities to whom Long refers. He begins by saying that the

[1] *Div. Iul.*, 19, 2.
[2] Tac., *Ann.*, iv, 27—quaestor, cui provincia vetere ex more calles evenerat.
[3] *Le sénat*, &c., ii, 1883, p. 576, n. 5.
[4] *Amer. Journ. Philol.*, xxxvi, 1915, p. 326. Cf. Th. Mommsen, *Röm. Gesch.*, iii³, 1889, p. 214 (Eng. tr., iv, 1908, p. 512).
[5] See the preceding article.
[6] *Decline of the Roman Republic*, iii, 1869, p. 401.

COALITION OF CAESAR, POMPEY, CRASSUS 475

Conservatives, fearing that Caesar, if he became consul, would go all lengths (*nihil non ausurum*), subscribed money to assist Bibulus in his canvass. Then, after recording the election of Caesar and Bibulus, he goes on to say that 'for the same reason'—the fear that Caesar would stick at nothing—the Conservatives took care that provinces of no importance should be assigned to the future consuls. Finally, he tells us that, stung by this insult, Caesar courted Pompey. It is certain that (unless the Sempronian law was violated [1]) the provinces were assigned before the election. Surely then Suetonius meant that Caesar began to court Pompey before he was elected consul.[2]

According to the *Epitome* of Livy (103), Caesar formed the coalition while he was standing for the consulship. Velleius [3] says that it began in Caesar's consulship; but in his brief and rhetorical narrative he might well say this even if the arrangement had been completed before the election. Plutarch [4] tells us that Caesar, before he was elected, reconciled Pompey and Crassus to each other and secured the friendship of both. Dio,[5] while he agrees with Livy that Caesar gained the support of both Pompey and Crassus during his candidature, does not expressly say that they were reconciled to each other then; and in one passage [6] he seems to mean that the reconciliation came later. From Appian [7] we learn that Pompey, in order to secure the ratification of the arrangements which he had made in the East, obtained the support of Caesar by promising to back his candidature; and that soon afterwards Crassus was reconciled to Pompey. This last statement is confirmed by Cicero, who at the end of 60 B.C., some months after the election, wrote, 'I have had a visit from Cornelius (I mean Balbus, Caesar's intimate friend), who said positively that Caesar ... would do his best to reconcile Crassus with Pompey'(*fuit apud me Cornelius: hunc dico Balbum, Caesaris familiarem. Is adfirmabat illum ... daturum operam ut cum Pompeio Crassum coniungeret* [8]). Shuckburgh,[9] indeed, in a note on this passage, says, 'Cicero was apparently not behind the scenes. The coalition with Pompey certainly, and with Crassus probably, had been already made ... soon after the elections'. Before the elections, as we have just seen, according to every authority except possibly Suetonius and probably also according to him. But what then? Surely it is probable that Pompey and Crassus, for their own purposes, had severally agreed to act in

[1] See vol. i, p. 26.
[2] *I* am therefore unable to agree with Mr. J. D. Duff, who (*Journ. of Philol.*, xxxiii, 1914, pp. 166–7), considering Suetonius's 'rigid adherence to chronological sequence', affirms that 'when we are told first of Caesar's election to the consulship, and then of the Triumvirate Mr. Heitland rightly infers that Suetonius believed the election to have preceded the coalition', &c. So far as *I* know, Mr. Duff is alone in believing that Suetonius adhered rigidly to chronological sequence. His frequent disregard of it will be illustrated in this book.
[3] ii, 44, 1. [4] *Cras.*, 14, 1; *Pomp.*, 47, 1; *Caes.*, 13, 3; 14, 1.
[5] xxxvii, 54, 3; 55, 1. [6] *Ib.*, 56, 1. [7] *B. C.*, ii, 9, 31–3.
[8] *Att.*, ii, 3, 3. [9] *The Letters of Cicero*, i, 1900, p. 69.

conjunction with Caesar, and yet remained privately on bad terms. If they had been really reconciled before Balbus visited Cicero, would not Cicero have heard of it ? Even in the following year their reconciliation was only nominal.[1]

THE FIRST CONSULSHIP OF CAESAR

The agrarian laws.—According to the *Epitome* of Livy (103), Caesar carried more than one agrarian law in his first consulship ; and this statement is confirmed by Cicero [2] as well as Plutarch,[3] who relates that Caesar passed a law for the establishment of colonies and the distribution of lands and another by which the whole of Campania was to be divided among the poor, or, as he says in his biography of Cicero,[4] among the soldiers [who had served under Pompey]. We learn from Appian[5] and Velleius[6] that the Campanian land, from Suetonius[7] that the Campanian land with the district of Stellas[8] was divided among 20,000 citizens ; while Appian and Suetonius add that each of the allottees had three children.[9] Dio[10] informs us that Caesar proposed a law for dividing among the people all the public land of Italy except the Campanian land ; also for distributing lands which were to be purchased from proprietors who were willing to sell ; but when he mentions the enactment of the law he adds that it was further decreed that the Campanian land was to be distributed among those who had three or more children.[11] Thus we must suppose that he meant either that before the bill became law Caesar changed his mind, or that he afterwards enacted a second law. Cicero, the only contemporary authority, acknowledging a letter from Atticus, which he had received on the 29th of April, said, ' it is a consolation to see that the hope of a distribution of land is now all diverted to the Campanian territory. That land, supposing the allotments to be ten *iugera* [about 6¼ acres] apiece, cannot support more than 5,000,' &c. (... *ut me egomet consoler, omnis exspectatio largitionis agrariae in agrum Campanum videtur esse derivata, qui ager, ut dena iugera sint, non amplius hominum quinque milia potest sustinere* [12]). Elsewhere Cicero (or the author of *De domo*) asserts that the money intended for the purchase of land was afterwards assigned by Clodius to Gabinius when the latter was about to depart for his province Syria.[13]

It seems to me that we are justified in concluding from the evidence of the *Epitome*, of Cicero, of Plutarch, and of Dio, notwithstanding

[1] *Att.*, ii, 21, 3-4.   [2] *Ib.*, 18, 2.
[3] *Pomp.*, 47, 3. Cf. *Caes.*, 14, 1 ; *Cato min.*, 31, 3 ; 33, 1.
[4] 26, 3. Cf. Caes., *B. C.*, i, 14, 4.   [5] *B. C.*, ii, 10, 35.   [6] ii, 44, 4.
[7] *Div. Iul.*, 20, 3. Cf. 21 and *Aug.*, 4, 1.
[8] The district of Stellas was in Campania, but expressly distinguished by Cicero (*De lege agr.*, i, 7, 20 ; ii, 31, 85) from the Campanian public land.
[9] Suetonius says ' three or more '.
[10] xxxviii, 1, 2-5.   [11] *Ib.*, 7, 3.   [12] *Ib.*, 16, 1.
[13] Cf. *Att.*, ii, 17, 1 with *De domo*, 9, 23.

THE FIRST CONSULSHIP OF CAESAR 477

the silence of the other authorities, that two agrarian laws were passed. Professor Reid, however, affirms [1] that 'it is clearly shown [by Drumann-Groebe (*Gesch. Roms*, iii [2], 182 f.)] that Caesar passed only one agrarian law'. What Drumann said was that, 'Although Cicero and Livy speak of Julian agrarian laws in the plural, the Roman writers, including Cicero, authorize the belief that there was only one.' Groebe, commenting on this, says, 'The discrepancy originates in the fact that Caesar enacted a general law touching the technical questions belonging to the foundation of colonies, which is to be regarded as identical with the *lex Mamilia Roscia Peducaea Alliena Fabia*, and takes its name from a commission of five, to whom Caesar entrusted the drafting of the said law, with the view of afterwards making it the groundwork of the regulations of the colonies which he was to plant.' Where is the demonstration to which Professor Reid appeals? It would seem that he disagrees with Groebe; for, remarking [2] that Mommsen regarded the *lex Mamilia Roscia Peducaea Alliena Fabia* as a part of Caesar's agrarian law, he stigmatizes this view as 'hazardous in the extreme; [3] Drumann's 'belief' is certainly not authorized by Cicero, and my reasons for believing that Caesar passed two laws dealing with different lands remain unaffected. The 'twenty commissioners' (*vigintiviri*) appointed by Caesar to superintend the distribution of lands were mentioned by Cicero in two letters (*ad Atticum*, ii, 6, 2 and ii, 7, 3), both of which were earlier than the one (ii. 16) in which he mentioned the Campanian land for the first time. Since he had only just heard that it was to be distributed when he wrote this

[1] *Journ. Rom. Studies*, v, 1915, p. 247, n. 1.
[2] *Ib.*, p. 247.
[3] Let us see what Mommsen said. Proving that the *lex Mamilia Roscia Peducaea Alliena Fabia* was identical with the *lex Mamilia* mentioned by Cicero (*De leg.*, i, 21, 55), he argued (*D. Schr. d. röm. Feldmesser*, ii, 1852, p. 224) that it was drafted by a sub-commission of five—*quinqueviri* (Cic., *Att.*, ii, 7, 4)— of the twenty land-commissioners—*vigintiviri* (*ib.*, 6, 2; 7, 3)—appointed by Caesar in 59 B. C., and that it was identical with, or rather a reproduction of, a general agrarian law passed by Caesar in that year. This conjecture, he says, is confirmed by the fact that the second chapter of the *lex Mamilia Roscia Peducaea Alliena Fabia* is substantially repeated in chapter CIIII of the *lex colonia Genetiva* of 44 B. C.; and E. Cuq (Daremberg and Saglio, *Dict. des ant. grecques et rom.*, iii, 1154) finds additional confirmation in the fact that Callistratus, a jurist of the second century (*Dig.*, xlvii, 21, 3 *pr.*) attributes to 'the agrarian law carried by Gaius Caesar' a provision which figures in the second chapter of the *lex Mamilia Roscia Peducaea Alliena Fabia*. P. Willems (*Le sénat*, &c., i, 1878, p. 498, n. 5), differing so far from Mommsen, gives reasons for believing that the *lex Mamilia Roscia Peducaea Alliena Fabia* was not a regulation drafted by a commission of *quinqueviri*, but a law carried by five tribunes in 55 B. C.; at the same time he regards it as supplementary to Caesar's agrarian law. [E. Meyer, who supports my view that Caesar passed two agrarian laws in 59 (*Caesars Monarchie*[2], 1919, p. 63, n. 1), remarking (p. 65, n. 3) that one of the *Vviri* was M. Valerius Messalla, an ex-consul (*C. I. L.*, vi, 3826 = H. Dessau, *Inscr. Lat.*, 46), rightly insists that this fact disproves Mommsen's theory that the *lex Mamilia Roscia Peducaea Alliena Fabia* was drafted by the *Vviri*. It is impossible, he holds, to tell which statements in the writings of the *agrimensores* refer to Caesar's laws of 59, which to those of 46 B. C.]

letter the commissioners must have been appointed to superintend the distribution of other lands as well. Zumpt,[1] whose argument is identical with mine, points out that comparison of ii, 16, 1 with 15, 1 shows that in the former Cicero was speaking of a law just promulgated, whereas the agrarian law (§ 2) which Pompey approved had obviously been promulgated before; in other words, it was the *first* agrarian law.[2] Again, Suetonius,[3] after stating that Caesar promulgated an agrarian law and then dilating upon his differences with Bibulus, mentions, as something new, that he distributed the *campus Stellatis* and the *ager Campanus*.

Other difficulties remain. Long[4] insists that even if we suppose that the inclusion of the Campanian land was an afterthought, ' this supposition will not save Dio's credit, for if the Campanian land was not included in the original bill, it is hard to say what [public] land was included in it ': certainly not that of Volaterrae, which Sulla had confiscated, ' for Cicero (*Ad Fam.* xiii. 4, 2), who must have known the facts, says that Caesar . . . in his first consulship relieved the territory and town of Volaterrae of all fear for the future '. This is true; but, on the other hand, as Mr. Warde Fowler observes,[5] ' Cicero's letters show no anxiety about ' the Campanian land ' until the end of April ', although the agrarian law had been introduced at the beginning of the year. I have therefore no doubt that Dio was right in saying that the Campanian land was originally exempted, and we are reduced to these alternatives : when he said that Caesar originally proposed to distribute all the public land except the Campanian land, either he meant that the public land which Caesar originally intended to distribute was the *campus Stellatis*, as distinct from the *ager Campanus*, or that Caesar had thought of including in his distribution the land of Volaterrae, but afterwards exempted it, or, as seems more probable, he ought to have said that Caesar originally intended to distribute such land only as he could purchase and afterwards added thereto the Campanian land and the *campus Stellatis*.

But what about the land which Caesar bought or intended to buy ? Strachan-Davidson[6] says that Pompey's veterans were provided for ' on lands acquired by purchase ', and that the Campanian land ' was destined for distribution among the poor citizens '; but we may infer from a passage in Caesar's *Civil War* (i. 14, 4) that some, at all events, of Pompey's veterans were settled in Campania.[7] Again, if Clodius really misappropriated the money which Caesar had allocated for the purchase of lands, what became of his scheme ? Even if, as

[1] *Comm. epigr.*, 1850, p. 288.
[2] Note also the words in which Cicero (*Att.*, ii, 16, 2) proceeds to apostrophize Pompey: *Nunc vero, Sampsicerame, quid dices? vectigal te nobis in monte Antilibano constituisse, agri Campani abstulisse?* (Now, Sampsiceramus, what will you say to this ? That you have secured us a revenue from the Antilibanus and *abstracted that from the Campanian land ?*) [3] 20, 3.
[4] *Decline of the Roman Republic*, iii, 1869, pp. 417–8.
[5] *Julius Caesar*, 1892, p. 109. [6] *Cicero*, 1894, p. 260.
[7] Cf. Cic., *Phil.*, ii, 39, 101.

Long supposes, the *De domo* was the work of a Pseudo-Cicero,[1] it is unlikely that the charge which the writer made against Clodius was wholly unfounded; and, on the other hand, it is incredible that Caesar would have allowed Clodius to wreck his scheme. I agree with Professor Reid,[2] who says, ' All that lies behind the exaggerated language ' in *De domo* ' is this, that if Gabinius had got all the money which the measure passed by Clodius professed to give him, the colonists would have gone short.'

One puzzle remains. Besides the twenty commissioners (*vigintiviri*) Cicero, as we have seen (page 477, note 3), mentions five (*quinqueviri*). What were they ? If they were not distinct from the *vigintiviri* (both *quinqueviri* and *vigintiviri* had been appointed before Cicero heard that the Campanian land was to be parcelled out), they were probably either, as Mommsen[3] originally held, one of four sub-commissions, charged with the superintendence of a part of the land that was defined in the agrarian laws or, as he afterwards thought,[4] exercised judicial functions while the rest were occupied solely in assigning lands.[5]

The affair of L. Vettius.—Cicero, writing to Atticus, says, ' Vettius . . . promised Caesar, as far as I can make out, that he would contrive to have young Curio brought under some suspicion of crime ' (*Vettius . . . Caesari, ut perspicimus, pollicitus est sese curaturum ut in aliquam suspicionem facinoris Curio filius adduceretur*). Cicero then gives details. Vettius told Curio that he had resolved to assassinate Pompey. Curio told his father, who informed the Senate. Vettius, examined in the House, contradicted himself and (though Bibulus had himself warned Pompey) charged Bibulus with having sent him a dagger. This statement was of course received with derision. Young Curio, brought before the Senate, answered Vettius, who was shown to have lied ; and the Senate decreed that Vettius should be committed to prison. ' The general impression ', says Cicero, ' is that the whole affair was pre-arranged. Vettius was to be caught in the Forum with a dagger and his slaves also with weapons, and he was then to offer to lay an information : the scheme would have succeeded if the Curios had not informed Pompey before ' (*Res erat in ea opinione ut putarent id esse actum, ut Vettius in foro cum pugione et item servi eius comprehenderentur cum telis, deinde ille se diceret indicaturum, idque ita actum esset, nisi Curiones rem ante ad Pompeium detulissent*). Next day, Cicero continues, Caesar brought Vettius on to the Rostra. Vettius, ' having come there primed and coached, first struck Caepio's [M. Brutus's] name out of his list, though he had named him most emphatically in the Senate, so that it was patent that a nocturnal

---
[1] See p. 482. [2] *Hermathena*, xiii, 1905, p. 384.
[3] *D. Schr. d. röm. Feldmesser*, ii, 224.
[4] *Eph. epigr.*, iii, 1877, p. 3.
[5] Professor Reid formerly supposed (*Hermathena*, 1905, p. 373) that the Vviri were those charged under the second of the two laws with the distribution of the *ager Campanus* and the *campus Stellatis*. But it is doubtful whether Caesar had decided to allot the Campanian land before the Vviri were appointed.

intercession had intervened [in other words, that Servilia, the mother of Brutus, had pleaded with her lover, Caesar] : next he named certain individuals on whom he had not cast even the slightest suspicion in the Senate,—L. Lucullus . . . L. Domitius . . . he did not name me, but he said that an eloquent consular, who lived near the consul [Caesar], had told him that a Servilius Ahala or a Brutus was badly wanted. . . . At present Vettius is on trial for violent crime before Crassus '[1] (*qui illuc factus institutusque venisset, primum Caepionem de oratione sua sustulit, quem in senatu acerrime nominarat, ut appareret . . . nocturnam deprecationem intercessisse ; deinde, quos in senatu ne tenuissima quidem suspicione attigerat, eos nominavit,— L. Lucullum . . . L. Domitium . . . me non nominavit, sed dixit consularem disertum, vicinum consulis, sibi dixisse Ahalam Servilium aliquem aut Brutum opus esse reperiri . . . Nunc reus erat apud Crassum Divitem Vettius de vi,*[2] &c.).

Three years later Cicero affirmed that Vatinius had brought Vettius, ' who had confessed in the Senate that he . . . had intended to assassinate Pompey ', on to the Rostra ; that Vettius had named as his instigators and accomplices Bibulus, Lucullus, the elder Curio, L. Domitius, L. Lentulus, and L. Paullus ; that Vatinius promulgated a law to the effect that an extraordinary commission should be appointed to try those whom Vettius denounced, and that Vettius should be admitted as a witness and rewarded for giving evidence ; and that as this proposal was indignantly rejected, Vatinius had Vettius murdered in prison, ' lest any proof of fabricated evidence should come to light ' (*ne quod indicium corrupti iudicii exstaret*).[3]

Plutarch [4] says that Vettius was produced by certain Pompeians who reported that they had caught him plotting against Pompey. Examined in the Senate, he accused various persons, but when he was brought before the people [on to the Rostra] he affirmed that Lucullus, whom he had not mentioned in the Senate, had commissioned him to kill Pompey. No one believed him, and it was evident that he had been suborned by Pompeians in order to discredit their opponents. A few days later his corpse was found outside the prison in which he had been confined and bearing marks which showed that he had been murdered.

According to Suetonius,[5] it was believed that Caesar had bribed Vettius to say that he had been instigated to kill Pompey, and that, after Vettius had inculpated several individuals without producing any impression, Caesar despaired of the success of his scheme and poisoned him.

Vettius, says Appian,[6] appearing in public with a dagger, said that he had been commissioned by Bibulus, Cicero, and Cato to kill Caesar and Pompey, and that the dagger had been given to him by a lictor who attended Bibulus. Caesar used this opportunity to

---

[1] Not the triumvir, but one of the praetors.   [2] *Att.*, ii, 24, 2–4
[3] *In Vat.*, 10–1. Cf. *Schol. Bob.*, p. 320 Or. (ed. Stangl, p. 148)
[4] *Luc.*, 42, 7–9.   [5] *Div. Iul.*, 17 ; 20, 5
[6] *B. C.*, ii, 12, 44–5.

THE FIRST CONSULSHIP OF CAESAR 481

inflame the passions of the mob. The examination of Bibulus was deferred till the next day; but in the intervening night he was murdered in prison, and Caesar asserted that the murder had been committed by those who dreaded the evidence which he might give.

Dio [1] affirms that Cicero and Lucullus commissioned Vettius to assassinate Pompey, but that Pompey had been warned in time by Bibulus.

The certain facts are that Pompey was warned by Bibulus; that Vettius was suborned; that his statements were worthless; that he was murdered in prison; and that in the belief of Cicero's informants, which at the time he probably shared, Caesar had planned that Vettius was to be arrested, to lay an information against certain persons, and to throw suspicion on Cicero.

Long,[2] pointing out that Cicero in his letter to Atticus accused Caesar of having instigated Vettius, but in his speech accused Vatinius, says, 'Cicero lied either one way or the other. It is probable that in his letter to Atticus he told the truth.' I have no doubt that he told the truth to Atticus, so far as he could ascertain it, and that in his speech he did not dare to attack Caesar. When he wrote the letter he probably did not know what Vatinius had done, or he would have named him : on the other hand, in his speech he would hardly have said that Vatinius brought Vettius on to the Rostra if there had been no foundation for the statement. Probably Vatinius acted as Caesar's tool.

Tyrrell,[3] remarking that 'Merivale [4] thinks there was a real plot against the triumvirs among some of the violent young nobles', goes on to say that 'Merivale holds that if it had been prompted by the triumvirs, Vettius would not have included Brutus in his charge, since his mother, Servilia, was a favourite of Caesar'. 'But', says Tyrrell, 'Merivale's objection overlooks the fact that Caesar had quite sufficient *finesse* to direct Vettius to include Brutus, so as to deceive the public as to the true source of the move. Brutus was afterwards... struck off the list of the accused.' Then what becomes of Caesar's *finesse*? Does not the removal of Brutus's name suggest that Caesar had had no communication with Vettius before his arrest? 'Perhaps', says Tyrrell, 'the truth ... is that a plot was formed against the triumvirs by the young nobles, and when it broke down through the blundering of Vettius, it was at once ascribed to Caesar by the nobles.' This is substantially the view of Merivale; but a few lines further on Tyrrell concludes that 'we shall most safely agree with Cicero that the authors of the plot [or rather, those who invented the story of the plot which Cicero regarded as fictitious] were the triumvirs, who wished to get rid of some of the leading *Optimates*'. Evidently we shall never learn the whole truth; but is it likely that Caesar would have selected such a bungler as Vettius, who, remember, had made a false charge against him four years

---

[1] xxxviii, 9, 2–3.   [2] *Cic. orat.*, iv, 1858, p. 19.
[3] *The Correspondence of ... Cicero*, i², 1904, p. 320.
[4] *Hist. of the Romans under the Empire*, i, 1850. p. 197.

before,[1] as his instrument ? That Vettius was murdered by the order of those who had suborned him is probable : that Caesar ordered the murder there is no sufficient evidence.[2] That Cicero planned to assassinate Pompey was a fiction too absurd to impose upon any one except the malignant calumniator, Dio.

A COMPLAINT OF CICERO AGAINST TORQUATUS

Cicero in his speech *Pro Sulla*[3] complained that the prosecutor accused him of having falsified the evidence recorded on the 3rd of December, 63 B. C., against the Catilinarian conspirators ; and the author of the speech *De domo*[4] says that Clodius stated in the law which he carried against Cicero ' that he had forged a senatorial decree ' (*quod M. Tullius falsum senatus consultum rettulerit*)— evidently the decree passed on the 5th of the same month for their execution. P. Willems[5] concludes that the author made an unwarrantable inference from the passage in *Pro Sulla* ; and it is hardly credible that even Clodius would have ventured to introduce into his bill a statement so transparently false. Though the speech *De domo*, like the three others of the same group, is now generally admitted to be genuine, I cannot believe that Cicero would have committed himself in the Senate to the absurd fiction that in the early months of 58 B. C. Caesar, whose only legions were at Aquileia and in the province of Transalpine Gaul,[6] was ' at the gates [of Rome] with a large army ' (*ad portas cum imperio . . . magnoque exercitu*[7]). Strachan-Davidson[8] actually repeats this rubbish, adding the invention that the legions were ' newly levied ', but omitting to tell us what use Caesar afterwards made of them. As Long[9] points out, Cicero[10] tells the truth about Caesar and his army—' Caesar . . . was at the gates . . . his army [three of the four legions] was in Italy ' (*Caesar . . . erat ad portas . . . erat in Italia eius exercitus*).

CICERO'S JOURNEY INTO EXILE

The letters (*ad Atticum*, iii, 1–6) which Cicero wrote in exile before he reached Brundisium were discussed many years ago by C. L. Smith of Harvard University.[11] The chronological order in which he arranged them is 1, 3, 2, 5, 4, 6. Independently I have done the same ; and so, I believe, would any one who carefully compared them.[12]

---

[1] See vol. i, p. 288.
[2] E. Meyer (*Caesars Monarchie*², 1919, p. 87, n. 1) thinks it very naïve not to assume Caesar's guilt.
[3] 14, 40.   [4] 19, 50.   [5] *Le sénat*, &c., ii, 1883, p. 205, n. 4.
[6] *B. G.*, i, 7, 2 ; 10, 3.   [7] *Cum senatui*, &c., 13, 32.
[8] *Cicero*, 1894, p. 229.   [9] *Cic. orat.*, iii, 1856, p. 321.   [10] *Pro Sest.*, 18 41.
[11] *Harvard Studies in Class. Philol.*, vii, 1896, pp. 65–84.
[12] Smith's arrangement has been generally accepted.

CICERO'S JOURNEY INTO EXILE 483

Let us now consider the law to which Cicero referred in 1, 2, and 4, and an earlier one which he mentioned in a later letter (*ad Atticum*, iii, 15, 5).

According to Velleius,[1] Clodius proposed a law by which any one who had put to death a Roman citizen uncondemned should be 'interdicted from fire and water'—in other words, outlawed;[2] and he adds that although Cicero was not named in the law, it was directed against him alone. Dio[3] says much the same.

The epitomizer of Livy[4] says that Cicero 'was exiled by a law carried by Publius Clodius, on the ground that he had put citizens to death uncondemned' (*lege a P. Clodio . . . lata, quod indemnatos cives necavisset, in exilium missus* ⟨*est*⟩).

Appian[5] relates, incorrectly, that Clodius 'indicted Cicero for having illegally put to death Lentulus and Cethegus without trial' (Κικέρωνα δὲ γράφεται Κλώδιος παρανόμων, ὅτι πρὸ δικαστηρίου τοὺς ἀμφὶ Λέντλον καὶ Κέθηγον ἀνέλοι) and that Cicero 'went into voluntary exile'[6] (ἔφευγεν ἑκούσιον . . . φυγήν).

Plutarch,[7] who states that the law banishing Cicero was carried after he had gone into exile, adds that it forbade any one to shelter him within 500 Roman miles from Italy.

From Dio[8] we learn that after Cicero had gone into voluntary exile Clodius carried a second law, by which his property was confiscated, his house destroyed, he himself forbidden to stay in Sicily and ordered to remain 3,750 stades from Rome.

Cicero himself, writing from Nares Lucanae, explains (in 2), 'My reason for having made this journey is that there was no place where I could long be unmolested except on Sica's estate, especially since the bill has not yet been amended' (*Itineris nostri causa fuit quod non habebam locum ubi pro meo iure diutius esse possem quam in fundo Sicae, praesertim nondum rogatione correcta*), &c. A little later he says, ' A copy of the bill . . . was brought to me ; the correction of which I had been told was to the effect that I might remain anywhere beyond 400 miles. As I was not allowed to go to Sicily,' &c. (*Adlata est . . . nobis rogatio . . . in qua quod correctum esse audieramus erat eius modi, ut mihi ultra quadringenta milia liceret esse.*[9] *Illo* [to Sicily] *cum pervenire mihi non liceret*, &c.). On April 29 he announces his intention of going to Cyzicus in the province of Asia ;[10] and on the same day he writes again that he would have preferred to go to Athens, but fears lest ' they might hold that even that town is not far enough from Italy ' (*veremur ne interpretentur illud quoque oppidum ab Italia non satis abesse*[11]). On August 17 he says, ' the previous law did not touch me' (*prior lex nos nihil laedebat*[12]), evidently meaning the law which did not mention him by name.

It results from the evidence, first, that the second law, naming

[1] ii, 45, 1. [2] Cf. Plut., *Cic.*, 32, 1. [3] xxxviii, 14, 4.
[4] 103. [5] *B. C.*, ii, 15, 54. 57.
[6] Cf. Cic., *Fam.*, xiv, 3, 1 ; Plut., *Cic.*, 31, 4 ; Dio, xxxviii, 17, 4 : &c.
[7] *Cic.*, 32, 1. [8] xxxviii, 17, 6–7. [9] *Att.*, iii, 4.
[10] *Fam.*, xiv, 4, 2 [11] *Att.*, iii, 7, 1. [12] *Ib.*, 15, 5.

Cicero, was amended in respect of the distance beyond which he must remain; secondly, that the amendment is mentioned by Cicero alone; thirdly, that the distance named was, according to Plutarch and Cicero, whose statement is of course conclusive, from Italy; fourthly, that Plutarch and Dio, who reckoned 7½ stades as equivalent to a Roman mile,[1] agree as to the distance; lastly, that, since Cicero says that the amendment fixed the distance at 400 miles, we have to decide (1) whether Plutarch and Dio quoted from the unamended draft, (2) whether they or Cicero made a mistake, and (3) whether there is some error in the manuscripts.

Any one who compares the statement of Plutarch with the letters of Cicero numbered 2 and 4 will see that Plutarch supposed the limit of 500 miles to have been fixed in the original bill which mentioned Cicero by name; but Plutarch is so careless in chronology that it would be unsafe to infer that the amendment reduced 500 to 400. The distance of Athens from Brundisium *in a straight line* was about 385 Roman miles;[2] but of course what the legislator meant was the distance by sea and road. Now the voyage from Hydruntum (Otranto)—the nearest port—to Avlona is about 61 Roman miles; from Avlona to Athens the journey was 411.[3] But the shortest route from Italy to Athens was from Brundisium via Corcyra to Actium (about 200 miles), and thence by road (231 miles[4]). Thus the shorter journey amounted to 431, the longer to 472 miles. The conclusion would seem to be that the limit which, as Cicero feared, would make it dangerous for him to stay at Athens, was not, as the manuscripts make him say, 400, but 500 miles. The question, however, is, not what the actual distances were from port to port, but what were the official estimates of each passage. Now, according to the *Itinerary* of Antonine,[5] the voyage from Hydruntum to Avlona was 1,000 stades, or 125 Roman miles, from Brundisium to Dyrrachium 1,400 stades, or 175 Roman miles. Thus (if the estimates in Cicero's time were the same) the longer journey would have been officially considered equivalent to 536: but Clodius of course contemplated the shorter; and while Cicero could have had no fear of taking up his abode at Athens if the limit had been 400, he might well doubt whether, even if the voyage from Brundisium to Actium was also officially overestimated,[6] Athens would be deemed outside the line of 500 miles. It is therefore certain that the limit prescribed by the amendment was 500 miles, and that Plutarch was wrong in implying that this distance was specified in the original bill; and it follows that, as Sternkopf[7] and others hold, the original bill outlawed

---

[1] Fr. Hultsch, *Griech. u. röm. Metrologie*², 1882, p. 570.
[2] Sternkopf (*Philol.*, lxi, 1902, p. 63) says that Athens was 'about 350 Roman miles' from Italy. Any one who can use a map-measurer may ascertain that his estimate was wrong.
[3] *Itin. Ant.*, ed. Wesseling, pp. 323–6.
[4] *Ib.*, pp. 325–6.
[5] Ed. Wesseling, p. 479.
[6] Strabo (vii, 7, 5) *underestimated* the distance from Brundisium to Corcyra.
[7] *Philol.*, lxi, 61.

Cicero in general terms without prescribing any limit—in other words, made the whole Roman Empire the sphere of his outlawry. Still, the emendation—*quingenta* for *quadringenta*—adopted by Sternkopf [1] in order to reconcile Cicero with Plutarch and Dio, can hardly be deemed certain; and Gurlitt [2] has condemned it on palaeographical grounds. It is incredible, he maintains, that any copyist should have written *CCCC* by mistake for *CCCCC*; for, 500 was denoted not by *CCCCC* but by *D*. Sternkopf [3] replied that a careless scribe might have substituted *CD* for *D*; but Cicero may conceivably have written *CCCC* for *quadringenta* by a slip of the pen just as Gurlitt himself repeatedly wrote *quadraginta* (40) and *quinquaginta* (50) in mistake for *quadringenta* and *quingenta*.

Two peculiar theories remain to be noticed. Ludwig Lange [4] took the words *in qua quod correctum esse audieramus erat eius modi, ut mihi ultra quadringenta milia liceret esse* to mean that in the original bill 400 miles was prescribed as the limit, which was extended to 500 before the bill became law. The interpretation is surely perverse: besides, as Purser says,[5] ' it appears very unlikely [or rather, inconceivable] that Cicero would inform Atticus of the unamended form of the bill, and not the amended form, immediately after having heard of the latter.' Further, we may gather from Cicero's fifth letter [6] that the amendment did not aggravate, but mitigated his penalty. Sternkopf, indeed, argues that it made matters worse by threatening with heavy penalties any one who should harbour him before he reached the limit.[7] He arrives at this conclusion by altering the text: instead of (liceret esse) *Illo* [to Sicily] *cum pervenire mihi non liceret*, &c., he proposes to read (liceret esse) *illuc pervenire non liceret*. His translation of the whole passage would then run, ' the correction of which I had been told was to the effect that I might remain anywhere beyond 500 miles [from Italy], but that I am not allowed to get there.' Purser rightly rejects this explanation. ' No doubt', he says, referring to the passage which I have quoted from Dio,[8] ' some such clause was in the bill . . . but surely such a clause is implied in the very nature of *interdictio* . . . and was probably in the first draft of the law. Such a self-evident and traditionary clause would hardly have been the subject of an elaborate " amendment ",'[9] &c. Nothing could be better, but what puzzles me is that Tyrrell and Purser [10] nevertheless accept with exultant approval the emendation on which Sternkopf's explanation rests.

[1] *Philol.*, lix, 1900, p. 287. [2] *Ib.*, pp. 582–3.
[3] *Ib.*, lxi, 62. [4] *Röm. Alt.*, iii, 1871, p. 296.
[5] *The Correspondence of Cicero*, i³, 1904, p. 431.
[6] *Att.*, iii, 4, quoted above (p. 483). Cf. 2.
[7] *Philol.*, lix, 282–4, 294–5; lxi, 64–9.
[8] xxxviii, 17, 7. [9] *Op. cit.*, p. 434. [10] *Ib.*, p. 433.

ADDENDA

PAGE 117. 'The officers . . . military tribune.' Centurions were sometimes of high social standing. Valerius Flaccus, who served under Pompey at Dyrrachium, was the son of an ex-Governor of the province Asia (Caes., *B. C*, iii, 53, 2).

PAGE 210. 'Pompey, who could . . . monarch,' &c. The monarch, Ariobarzanes II, died in 52 B. C. The interest on the money lent by Pompey, which Cicero collected, as his agent, in 51 (vol. ii, p. 259), was due from Ariobarzanes III; but, as the debt was apparently of long standing, I believe that the loan was originally made to Ariobarzanes II.

PAGES 315. ('It is not certain . . . by purchase'), 476-9. M. Cary (*Journ. of Philol*, xxxv, 1920, pp. 174-90), who endorses the view that Caesar carried two agrarian laws in 59 B. C., points out that Cicero, when he said (*Att.*, ii, 16, 1) that the Campanian territory could not support more than 5,000 colonists, must have meant 'the *ager Campanus* in the narrower sense', that is 'the former municipal domain of Capua', and makes the not improbable conjecture that one reason why Caesar introduced his bill for distributing the Campanian land was that the knights who had speculated in land demanded higher prices for the allotments which he had tried to purchase than he would pay. This, he remarks, would account for the hostile demonstration which the knights made against Caesar in July (pp. 321, 323, n. 2). He holds, further, that the theory (which perhaps derives some support from Dio, xxxviii, 1, 6) that the *Vviri* were 'a managing sub-committee' of the *XXviri* (p. 479) 'is belied by the fact that Caesar offered a place . . . to Cicero [*De prov. cons.*, 17, 41], who was notoriously hostile to the land laws', and accordingly concludes that the *Vviri* 'were an ornamental body'. Finally, Cary gives good reasons for believing that the *lex Mamilia Roscia Peducaea Alliena Fabia* (p. 477, n. 3) was passed by five partisans of Caesar in 49 B. C.; that its object 'was to find land for Caesar's veterans and to regulate the tenure thereof'; and that it 'served as the constitutive act under which Caesar's later colonies were founded'. Cary's article deserves close study.

PAGE 347. Judeich (*Hist. Zeitschr.*, cxi, 1913, p. 483) thinks that Appian ascribed C. Gracchus's colonial law to his second tribunate because he confounded the right, conferred by the law, of founding colonies, with the actual foundation.

CORRIGENDA

PAGE 140, line 4 (margin) from foot. *For* Cordova *read* Cordoba.
PAGE 211, line 12 from foot. *For* Keupru *read* Keupri.
PAGE 218, note 1. *For* 453-6 *read* 435-6.